1855

1855

A HISTORY OF THE BORDEAUX CLASSIFICATION

Dewey Markham, Jr.

JOHN WILEY & SONS, INC.
New York | Chichester | Weinheim | Brisbane | Singapore | Toronto

Published by John Wiley & Sons, Inc.

Library of Congress Cataloging-in-Publication Data

Markham, Dewey, 1953–
1855 : a history of the Bordeaux classification / Dewey Markham, Jr.
p. cm.
Includes bibliographical references and index.
ISBN 13: 978-0-471-19421-7
1. Wine and wine making—France—Bordelais—Classification.
I. Title.
TP553.M335 1997
641.2'2'094471—dc21 97-20015

10 9 8 7 6 5 4 3

This book is dedicated to

DEWEY "PIGMEAT" MARKHAM, MY FATHER

and

BERNICE PENN MARKHAM, MY MOTHER.

They taught me absolutely nothing about wine,
but everything I have needed to know
to live a good and decent life
in which to enjoy wine to the fullest.

CONTENTS

PREFACE

This book has its origins in the time I spent working at two New York City wine shops during 1989 and 1990, probably the finest merchants in town catering to knowledgeable wine drinkers and the carriage trade. Occasionally, there would be customers who would approach the sales counter and ask for "a bottle of Bordeaux," adding, more specifically, "a classed-growth Bordeaux."

My first question was always "how much would you like to spend?" and upon being told the amount I'd bring the customers over to the display presenting the selection of Bordeaux wines. Indicating, say, a Pontet-Canet or a Prieuré-Lichine, I'd present the bottle to the clients, who'd inspect the label, letting their eyes stop at the words "cru classé".

"Okay," they'd say, running their fingers over the words, "this is a classed growth all right." Then, turning to me they would add, "So this is a first growth then, right?"

"Ah, no," I'd explain, "this wine is a fourth growth [or a third, or a fifth, depending on the wine in question]. It's not a first growth but nonetheless it is still an excellent wine and a very good value."

"Um, no, I don't think this is really what I want then," and the bottle would be lowered back to its place in the display rack.

At this point, I would begin to explain that a fifth-classed growth was not the same as a fifth-rate wine, quite the contrary, in fact. Fortunately, reason would usually win out and these customers would leave the store with the wine that they wanted, a classed-growth Bordeaux, and a little more knowledge as part of the bargain (which, after all, was what I was there for). This scene occurred often enough—and not just among the less wine-experienced clientele—that I decided to undertake a little research into the origins of this classification that carried so much weight yet was so little understood, in order to better dispel customers' confusion when the question would inevitably arise in the future.

I made two interesting discoveries.

First, there was more or less widespread agreement among the various sources I consulted as to the "when" and the "why" of the drafting of the Bordeaux classification: 1855, for the Universal Exposition to be held in Paris that year. It was when it came to the "how" that things became significantly less clear. Differences in the accounts of how the classification came to be drafted ranged from minor discrepancies to the outright fantastic: according to a favored explanation, it was the French emperor Napoleon III who ordered that the wines of Bordeaux be displayed at the exposition and that a classification be drawn up by the members of the wine trade; there were some versions in which Napoleon III himself drew up the list in his own hand. It was evident that a certain inexactitude had come to surround the history of this classification.

The second discovery was even more puzzling: practically every book that deals with the wines of the world will certainly have a section on Bordeaux, and in that section there will inevitably be a presentation of the list of classed growths, with anything ranging from a paragraph to several pages dedicated to an account of its background. But no one had ever written an entire book on how the 1855 classification of Bordeaux's wines had come to be created.

Such a lacuna in the literature of wine was more than a little mystifying to me, particularly since the classification is one of the cornerstones of an understanding of Bordeaux; it was as if in the study of American history no one had ever written a book on the Civil War. I could think of only two possible reasons why such a work had never been written before. Perhaps the documents and material pertaining to the classification's origins were no longer in existence. This seemed possible—after all, since 1855 there have been many events in the history of Europe and the Bordeaux wine trade which could have led to a loss of important documents. (For example, during a bombardment of Bordeaux on December 8, 1940, a shell fell directly on the Chamber of Commerce and Industry. Among the damage that occurred was the loss of the archives of the Union of Brokers that were stored in the building's attic, a major source of documentation regarding the 1855 classification.) Fortunately, research in Bordeaux disclosed a wealth of original source material still extant.

This left the other possibility as to why a book on this subject had never been written: it would be an understatement to say that the 1855 classification has always been a somewhat sensitive subject in the Bordeaux wine trade. A review of local newspaper files since the 1950s offers ample evidence of the stormy emotions that this classification has evoked in just the last few decades alone. Added to this is the longstanding reputation of the Bordeaux wine world being a closed society, impenetrable to those outside of its inner circle. The thought occurred to me that other attempts may have been made to write a history of the 1855 classification, but when the wine trade caught wind of the project there was a discreet joining of ranks and a closing of doors, effectively killing any such book in its inception—rather than have anything written that might arouse controversy and emotions, it was preferred that nothing be written at all. Here, too, I was very much mistaken.

As for the reputation of Bordeaux being a hermetic and excluding society, I can only attest to the openness and warmth with which I was met at every level of the wine trade. Brokers, merchants, and château proprietors all received me with a degree of cooperation and an understanding of what this book hoped to achieve, irrespective of their varying opinions regarding the classification. A list of these people follows this preface, together with the names of many others whose advice and aid helped make the writing of this work possible. To all of them I am most grateful for an experience that has made the four years in Bordeaux researching and writing this book among the richest of my life.

When I set out on this project, my aims were clear: to discover what were the circumstances under which the 1855 classification was drafted, who were the people behind it, how they set about their task, and why they made the decisions they made. This is what appears in the pages that follow. This book is not an account of the decades-long campaign which resulted in the 1973 reclassification of the first growths and the promotion of Mouton-Rothschild to the top rank of the Bordeaux hierarchy. Aside from two or three peripheral remarks, there is nothing here about that episode which is worthy of a book of its own. Neither is there a discussion of the various classifications that rank the production of the region's other vineyards. In referring to the 1855 list drawn up by the wine trade's brokers as "the Bordeaux classification," I am making reference to the fact that although only wines from the Médoc, Sauternes, and the Graves appear in this hierarchy, this represents only the tip of what was an all-encompassing system which ranked the entirety of Bordeaux's production. A century after 1855, other Bordeaux regions—the Graves and Saint Emilion—developed classifications of the wines that they produce, and my styling of the earlier list as "the Bordeaux classification" is not meant to deny the importance or the authority of these latter efforts. No denigration of these classifications is intended, and I trust that no offense on the part of these regions will be taken.

I have already mentioned the wealth of material that exists regarding the circumstances surrounding the drafting of the 1855 classification. It was my firm intention from the very beginning to base my research on original documents to the greatest extent possible, in order to avoid what has undoubtedly been responsible for so much of the mythology that surrounds the classification today. Rather than quote what other books had written on the subject (books which, in turn, copied accounts gleaned from yet other secondary sources) and therefore perpetuate and reinforce already well-established misconceptions, I determined to pursue my investigations not only among the archives and libraries of Bordeaux, Paris, New York, and London, but also among the classed growths themselves. Every one of the properties in the Médoc, Graves, and Sauternes that appears on the 1855 classification was visited to learn if it held private archives whose contents could help in the research for this book. Without exception, proprietors, managers, or representatives at each of these châteaux offered me every assistance that they could. At some properties (and not only those known for the size of their archives), documentation was quite extensive, and even where the quantity of material was not voluminous the quality of information was very helpful. At the majority of châteaux, however, it was explained to me that, given the many changes of ownership that had occurred over the preceding century and a half there were virtually no records other than the deed to the property itself. Very frequently, after hearing that the subject of the book was a history of the 1855 classification, a proprietor or manager would reflect for a moment and then explain that there was nothing at the château which either dated from 1855 or which spoke about the classification, and thus nothing that could be of interest for my work.

As I discovered during the course of my research, and as will be evident to the reader in the pages that follow, the subject of the 1855 classification is a complex one, touching on related questions somewhat further afield than the year of its drafting and the document itself. It is quite possible that while reading certain sections of this book, those who believed that they had nothing of pertinence may think "Well, I didn't know he was interested in *that* when he told me he was writing about the classification." Upon reflection, some people (including those that the restrictions of time and circumstance did not permit me to visit) may see that they, in fact, have material that might bring amplification to certain aspects of the text, indeed, may even contradict certain details that appear herein.

This book is based on the information that I have been able to find, and by no means on all the information that probably exists; I would be most interested to know of any material that I have failed to see, in order to arrive ever closer to a correct recounting of the events that are touched on in this work should a second edition ever be undertaken. One of my hopes in writing this book is that from the veritable desert of literature on the subject, where the occasional landmarks have often been mirages, other works will arise to give us all a better understanding of this classification, and a more exact appreciation of its actual significance in the world of Bordeaux wine today.

DEWEY MARKHAM, JR.

ACKNOWLEDGMENTS

The writing of my previous book, *Wine Basics,* was practically a one-man affair, involving the simple transfer to paper of observations that had developed during several years of teaching classes in wine appreciation. This book has been an entirely different experience, involving the contact and cooperation of scores of people to gain access to the information that was indispensable to this work.

Of foremost importance in a book dealing with the 1855 classification was the assistance of the classed growths themselves. Each of the proprietors, managers, and other representatives whose names follow agreed without hesitation to meet with me and listen to my ideas for this book, generously offering their perspectives on the subject, and, where available, access to documents they felt would be useful. Some of these people have since retired or moved to other properties; others, unfortunately, have died. The following list reflects the location of each person at the time of my visit to each château.

In the Médoc and Graves: Christophe Salin, Charles Chevalier, Gilbert Rokvam (Lafite-Rothschild, Duhart-Milon-Rothschild, Rieussec); Paul Pontalier (Margaux); John Kolassa, Colette Haramboure (Latour); Jean-Bernard Delmas, Alain Puginier (Haut-Brion); Philippe Cottin (Mouton-Rothschild, Mouton-d'Armailhac, Clerc-Milon); David Orr, John Kolassa (Rausan-Ségla); Jean-Michel Quié (Rauzan-Gassies, Croizet-Bages); Michel Delon, Jacques Depoizier, Michel Rolland (Léoville-Las-Cases); Didier Cuvelier (Léoville-Poyferré); Anthony Barton, Hervé Vaissié (Léoville-Barton, Langoa-Barton); Lucien Lurton (Durfort-Vivens, Brane-Cantenac, Doisy-Dubroca); Philippe Caumagnac (Gruaud-Larose); René Vanetelle (Lascombes); Henri Lurton (Brane-Cantenac); Jean-Michel Cazes (Pichon-Longueville-Baron, Cantenac Brown, Lynch-Bages, Suduiraut); May-Eliane de Lencquesaing, Gildas d'Ollone (Pichon-Longueville-Comtesse de Lalande); Jean-Eugène Borie (Ducru-Beaucaillou, Haut-Batailley); Bruno Prats, Catherine Di

Costanzo (Cos-d'Estournel); Jean-Louis Charmolüe (Montrose); Jean-Henry Schyler (Kirwan); Lionel Cruse (Issan); Marcel Ducasse, Yukio Kitao (Lagrange); Pierre Tari (Giscours); Roger Zuger (Malescot-Saint-Exupéry); Pierre Guillemet (Boyd-Cantenac, Pouget); Bertrand Bouteiller (Palmer); Mme. Duvivier (La Lagune); Denis Lurton (Desmirail); Philippe Gasqueton (Calon-Ségur, du Tertre); Claire Villars (Ferrière, Haut-Bages-Libéral); Jean-Claude Zuger (Marquis d'Alesme-Becker); Jean-Louis Triaud (Saint-Pierre); Hélène Callen (Talbot); Philippe Dhalluin (Branaire-Ducru); Olivier Dauga, Philippe Achener (La Tour-Carnet); Alfred Tesseron (Lafon-Rochet, Pontet-Canet); Maurice Ruelle (Beychevelle); Sacha Lichine (Prieuré-Lichine); Jean-Pierre Hugon (Marquis de Terme); Emile Castéja (Batailley, Lynch-Moussas); François-Xavier Borie (Grand-Puy-Lacoste) ; Jean-Pierre Angliviel de la Beaumelle (Grand-Puy-Ducasse); André Lurton (Dauzac); Bemard Jugla (Pédesclaux); Jean-Paul Jauffret (Belgrave); Henri Forner (Camensac); Bernard Audoy (Cos-Labory); Philippe Dambrine (Cantemerle).

In the Sauternes region: Aléxandre de Lur-Saluces, Valérie Lailheugue (Yquem); Jean-Pierre Jausserand (La Tour-Blanche); Michel Laporte (Lafaurie-Peyraguey, Sigalas-Rabaud); Jacques Pauly (Haut-Peyraguey); Patrick Eymery (Rayne-Vigneau); Pierre Pascaud (Suduiraut); Philippe Baly (Coutet); Bérénice Lurton (Climens); Xavier Planty (Guiraud); Philippe Dejean (Rabaud-Promis); Xavier de Pontac (de Myrat); Pierre Dubourdieu (Doisy-Daëne); Pierre Castéja (Doisy-Vedrines); Pierre Pierromat (d'Arche); Henri de Vaucelles (Filhot); Didier Laulan (Broustet); Nicole Tari (Nairac); Jean-Bernard Bravo (Caillou); Roger Biarnès (Suau); Nancy de Bournazel (de Malle); André du Hayot (Romer du Hayot); Mme. Jean Despujols, Guy Despujols (Lamothe-Despujols); Philippe Guignard (Lamothe-Guignard).

In addition, the following people were kind enough to facilitate access to resources at, or to furnish me with information about, several of the classed-growth properties: Eric de Rothschild (Lafite-Rothschild); Georges Pauli (Gruaud-Larose, Talbot, Cantemerle, Lafaurie-Peyraguey); Jean-Michel Ducellier (La Lagune); Bertrand Guillot de Suduiraut (Suduiraut); François de Roton (Rayne-Vigneau).

Several of Bordeaux's professional organizations have an especial connection with the history of the 1855 classification. Bruno Prats and Lionel Cruse, former and present Presidents of the Conseil des Grands Crus Classés du Médoc; Xavier de Pontac, President of the Syndicat des Crus Classés de Sauternes; and Max de Lestapis, President of the Syndicat Régional des Courtiers de Vins et Spiritueux de Bordeaux, de la Gironde et du Sud-Ouest, all took a particular interest in the research of this book. Each was instrumental in providing introductions that opened doors to sources of information that were of prime importance to the work. Also indispensable was Anne Marbot, head of documentation at the Conseil Interprofessionnel du Vin de Bordeaux; Anne was the first person I contacted upon my arrival in Bordeaux, and her assistance was invaluable for my getting off on the right foot in the Bordeaux wine world.

Several sources of archival material were vital to the success of this book. Foremost among them was the Bordeaux Chamber of Commerce and Industry. Claude Sanchez, in charge of the archives, was extremely generous with his knowledge of the Chamber's holdings, bringing to my attention material of whose existence I had no knowledge, but which was exactly what I had hoped to find. His assistant, Corinne Weber, was also extremely kind in helping me to fully benefit from the material that the Chamber of Commerce had to offer, and I greatly appreciate the amiability extended to me by them both. Similarly valuable were the records at the brokerage firm of Tastet & Lawton, where Daniel Lawton graciously offered me unrestricted access to the archives located throughout the premises. For several months, I became a fixture in the offices, and I thank the firm's associates Erik Samazeuilh and Bertrand de Lesdain for their patience in supporting the intrusion of my daily presence.

The Archives Municipales de Bordeaux offered many rich resources, not least of which was its chief, Jean-Paul Avisseau, who was a wealth of information and kindly provided introductions to other people for further elucidation of various obscure or elusive details. The Archives Départementales de la Gironde proved to be a key source for biographical material, as well as providing unexpected treasures such as several of the diplomas awarded at the 1855 Universal Exposition. I am particularly grateful to Hélène Avisseau, Hélène Prax, and Christian Dubos for their help in locating material that I suspected was available, but was not quite sure how to find.

At the Bibliothèque de Bordeaux, I am indebted to Hélène de Bellaigue and her staff at the Fonds Patrimoniaux, who for several years supplied me with the majority of the titles that are listed in this book's bibliography. I am also grateful to the staff at the library's Service des Catalogues et Bibliographies; like the Fonds Patrimoniaux, they kindly made available to me a number of works that were not normally distributed to the public.

Other archives and libraries were also consulted in the research and writing of this book, and I appreciate the help offered by the staffs at the Archives Nationales and the Bibliothèque Nationale de France in Paris, the Public Record Office and the British Library in London, and the New York Public Library. My thanks also go to Marie-Christine Lelue and Line Videau at the Musée des Beaux Arts de Bordeaux, the staff at the library of the Musée d'Aquitaine in Bordeaux, and the Archives Départementales of the Côte-d'Or and the Pyrenees-Atlantiques.

A number of individuals kindly offered answers and advice, and supplied me with material that provided a better understanding not only of the classification but of the Bordeaux vineyards and wine trade. For this assistance I am indebted to Simon Berry, Patrice Calvet, Jean-Louis Deyris, Philippe Gajac, Michel Guillard, Claudine Izabelle, Nathaniel Johnston, Nathaniel Lee Johnston, Jean-Marie Johnston, Jean-Paul Kauffmann, Antoine Lebègue, Jean-Bernard Marquette, Jean Miaille, and Gérard Séguin. I am especially grateful for the help and advice that was most generously offered me—both personally and through their writings—by two eminent scholars of the history of Bordeaux wine, René Pijassou and Philippe Roudié.

The writing of this book has spanned two continents, three countries, and four years; it has been a complex undertaking in which I depended at various times and in various ways on the logistical help of Annie Bernhard, Hélène Breitinger, Gerard Crochet, Marc Greenberg and Karen Kluge, Edward Schlich, and Julie O'Haver-Schlich. My heartfelt thanks go out to them all.

Claire Zuckerman, my editor at John Wiley & Sons, was involved with this book since its inception, and the support and encouragement she offered during the long years in which it took shape helped calm the nerves on more than one occasion. I would also like to express my appreciation to Bruno Boidron, Marc-Henry Lemay, and Remi-Marie Dantin at my French publisher Editions Féret, for what started out as an interest and then became a belief in this book.

On a personal level, Bernice Markham, my mother, and Cathy Markham, my sister, helped to tie up the loose ends of my life back home in the United States as I set about the long transition from New York to Bordeaux. This was a transition that became more permanent than originally intended, thanks to the chance meeting of Catherine Goyon during research at Mouton-Rothschild. More valuable than any information gathered as a result of that visit was the association that gradually developed, as Catherine first offered to share in the effort of so many phases of this work, then more importantly, with time, offered to share her future as my wife.

History is the rumor we choose to believe.

—Attributed to Napoleon Bonaparte

INTRODUCTION

It was good to be French in 1855. The three generations of domestic unrest and foreign estrangement that began with the Revolution in 1789 seemed to have reached a conclusion with the ascension of Napoleon III; since his establishment of the Second Empire in 1852, stability and prosperity had returned to a nation feared by many to be on the verge of anarchy.

It had been a tough six decades for France, as much for its successes as for its defeats. The Revolution that promised social reform with the creation of a Republic evolved into the Terror and the reign of the guillotine. Such a state could not continue indefinitely, and with its resolution came the rise of the Corsican general, Napoleon Bonaparte. His Empire fell victim to overreaching ambition with the doomed invasion of Russia in 1812, and Napoleon's hundred-day return from exile in Elba effectively cut short the First Restoration of France's monarchy before giving way to the Second. The nation was internationally isolated after Napoleon's defeat at Waterloo, and domestically hobbled by the return of an aristocracy that, it has been said, had learned nothing and forgot nothing: intent on settling old scores and recovering property lost in the revolution, they did little to help stabilize a country struggling to resolve the problems of its recent, turbulent, past.

In 1848, as revolutions swept through Europe, the monarchy was driven again from France and replaced with a Second Republic. Once more, conflict among contentious factions prevented any effective progress in bringing stability to the nation; it seemed that France's destiny was to hurtle from one insupportable political condition to another. The country was exhausted, emotionally and economically, and the consequence, feared by all, was anarchy.

France did not lack for saviors, but no one during these years felt himself better suited by nature or fortune to restore the nation to its former grandeur than Louis Napoleon, nephew of Napoleon Bonaparte.

Louis Napoleon Bonaparte was born in 1808, four years after the proclamation of the French Empire. Napoleon Bonaparte was not only his uncle, but his godfather as well, further reinforcing the infant's imperial connections. From his earliest years, Louis Napoleon was instilled with an appreciation for the power his family name possessed as well as the destiny that name imposed upon him; although the Bonapartes were forced into exile after the Empire's collapse in 1814, Louis Napoleon never lost his sense of vocation as heir to the Bonaparte legacy. He profoundly believed that his name obligated him to restore France to greatness, and that France could never be great without a Bonaparte to lead the way. Such sentiments would lead him to two abortive attempts at a coup d'état aimed at overturning the monarchist form of government reestablished in the wake of the Empire. As he grew older, his conception of Bonapartism came to encompass an active social consciousness dedicated to achieving the greatest good for the greatest number of French citizens. "I will strive without end to govern in the interest of the masses," he wrote to a relative. "It's the mission attached to the great name we bear." Authorship of a work entitled The Extinction of Pauperism, *a manifesto of social and economic philosophy, further indicated the direction in which his interests lay: "The working class has nothing; it is necessary to give it ownership. Its only wealth is its labor; that labor must be given useful employment for all. . . . [The working class] must be given a place in society and its interests connected to those of the land. Finally, it is without organization and without attachments, without rights and without a future: it must be given rights and a future and self-esteem through partnership, education, discipline."*

As popular dissatisfaction with France's leaders grew in the aftermath of 1848's revolutionary events, it appeared that the long years as guardian of the family legacy were finally going to pay off. The ever-increasing nostalgia for the glory of Bonaparte and the greatness of the French Empire made Louis Napoleon appear as the leader most likely to divide France least, resulting in his election as president of the Second Republic. This positioned him to take matters a step further: on December 2, 1852, Louis Napoleon staged a third—and finally successful—coup d'état. He abolished the Republic and replaced it with a Second Empire, giving himself the imperial powers necessary to ensure the nation's stability while (not coincidentally) fulfilling his own destiny. To underscore the connections with the reign of his uncle, he also assumed the title of Napoleon III. These actions were put to the French in a national plebiscite, and approved by an overwhelming majority. For the first time in decades, national confidence was strong, and France was once again ready to take its place among the world's great nations.

However, while France had been sorting out its domestic life through interminable cycles of civil insurrection, England, its traditional rival, had leapt ahead with a

Napoleon III
(Roger-Viollet)

revolution of its own, in which industrial power was to fuel the creation of an empire that was the envy of nations. Especially France.

For centuries, France had been an agrarian society, but Louis Napoleon was intent on creating a great power with a strong industrial base and colonies to nourish it. Among his priorities were the encouragement of commerce and the development of projects to eliminate underemployment. In an address delivered in Bordeaux shortly before proclaiming the Empire, Louis Napoleon outlined his aims for the future of France: "We have immense uncultivated territories to clear, routes to open, ports to dig, rivers to make navigable, canals to finish, our network of railways to complete." Massive undertakings such as the extension of the nation's inadequate railway system not only served an immediate practical need for effective transportation, but also promoted secondary industries such as foundries, which would reduce the necessity of importing rail from England.

The French welcomed these initiatives, and enthusiastically put the nation's dormant reserves of capital to work. The strong performance of the nation's stock market gave solid testimony to domestic confidence in Louis Napoleon's economic policies.

Internationally, however, the appearance of a second French Empire, especially one with a Bonaparte at its head, brought back disturbing memories. Although Louis Napoleon did not intend to repeat the errors of his uncle's first Empire ("The Empire means peace," declared Louis Napoleon in the Bordeaux address of 1852), it would take time to establish Europe's confidence in a newly powerful France.

Other nations had to become accustomed to the idea of France as the French themselves saw it. What better way than to put France on display and invite the entire world to witness its grandeur? It was time for another exhibition of the glories of French industry and commerce.

The French had been staging what we today would call "world's fairs" since the end of the eighteenth century; indeed, they practically invented the modern industrial exhibition. These commercial displays were descended from the market festivals and trade fairs that had been common throughout Europe for centuries. Occasionally such a festival became an annual event, defined by the major commercial activity of a city. Bordeaux, for example, was accorded a royal patent to stage a wine fair beginning in 1212, and by the century's end the affair had enlarged its scope to encompass other goods produced throughout the region. Gradually, the idea of a multidisciplinary fair on a national scale took hold, and the first of these to be staged on a truly grand scale was planned for the year 1797.

This first French exposition was originally something of a distress sale: the continental blockade by the British navy, in response to Napoleon Bonaparte's conquest of mainland Europe, had contributed to a state of overproduction at the French national workshops. At the Gobelins tapestry works, warehouses were full of unsold goods that threatened prolonged unemployment among the workshop's craftsmen. The story was the same at the Savonneries carpet factory and the Sèvres porcelain works.

The solution devised by the commissioner responsible, the Marquis d'Avèze, was to stage a collective display of the workshops' production in the magnificent and, conveniently, unfurnished Château de Saint-Cloud on the outskirts of Paris. Its rooms were transformed into showcases for the hitherto unseen splendors that had been stockpiled in the warehouses, and it was made clear to all that the goods were most certainly available for purchase. To further stimulate interest in possessing these items, a lottery was organized offering a selection of the displays as prizes. Unfortunately, just as this exhibition was set to open its doors, Napoleon Bonaparte learned of plans for a reactionary uprising, and among his measures to head it off was the expulsion from Paris of all members of the aristocracy—including the Marquis d'Avèze. This effectively ended the exhibition before it ever began, but only temporarily. In a few months' time, the political crisis had passed, and the Marquis could return and begin where he had been forced to abandon his project. Now his plans were for an even grander exhibit, this time in Paris itself. The Hôtel d'Orsay was the site Avèze chose for an expanded display, which now included the products of workshops other than the three that were under his charge. Fine art, timepieces, furniture, and silks were among the items that now joined the list of goods to be displayed.

The exhibition not only met Avèze's hopes of financial success, but it also impressed his superior, François de Neufchâteau. As Minister of the Interior, Neufchâteau was responsible for the nation's police forces and the domestic tranquility they were supposed to guarantee. Public entertainments had been a traditional method of pacification ever since the circuses of the Roman Empire, and such exhibitions of French-made goods might be useful in this regard. In addition, another benefit suggested itself to the minister: a showcase for French industrial production could serve as a domestic complement to Napoleon's military success abroad. Deciding that a series of such displays could be very much in the public interest, he announced a new exhibition for September 1798, this time as an official undertaking of the French government.

The sale of goods was no longer a priority; no arrangements were made for public purchase of the items on display. The purpose of this exhibition was made clear by Neufchâteau in the report he wrote at its conclusion: "This is a first campaign against English industry." The exhibition was intended as the continuation of war by other means, which made it appropriate that the exhibition was held on the military parade grounds of the Champ de Mars. Another innovation was the jury established to award prizes for the finest products. Among its members was Jean-Antoine-Claude Chaptal, a distinguished chemist and member of government, whose experiments in increasing a wine's alcohol content by adding beet sugar to fermenting grape juice would be important in developing the process known as Chaptalization.

Participation in the exhibition was solicited throughout the country, and the 110 exhibitors who met the deadline for entries demonstrated the wide scope of French manufacturing ability: domestic goods such as furniture and ceramics vied for public attention with industrial products from type foundries and armament works. Chemical laboratories and scientific instrument makers also displayed their inventions, testifying to French progress in the physical sciences.

In all, it was an impressive display, and during its three-day existence suggested quite convincingly that French industry could successfully compete abroad with the best that British manufacture could produce. (French manufacturers were more secure in the domestic market, enjoying the protection of high import duties on

British-made goods.) However, displaying the potential to vanquish Britain's commercial power was one thing, actual victory was another. Since the battle on the commercial front was far from over, it was decided that national exhibitions would be annual events, intended not only to present the finest that French manufacturers could produce, but to stimulate the industrial development necessary for the country's prosperity. Unfortunately, political uncertainties again exerted their influence and plans for the next exhibition had to be postponed; three years would pass before another would take place.

The French exhibition of 1801 built upon the experience of 1798, establishing an organizational structure that would serve for the future. The requirements for entry were more exacting than in the past, emphasizing some fundamental advance in the method of production or the benefit to be gained by the object on display. To determine whether these criteria were successfully met, committees were established in each of France's eighty-six administrative divisions, known as departments; their function was to pass initial judgment on the articles produced in their areas. Those items possessing sufficient merit would be sent to the exhibition in Paris, where they would compete for medals awarded by the jury of experts.

So it was that for six days in September 1801, 220 representatives of French industry displayed their goods in the courtyard of the Louvre, in an exposition whose date and duration were determined by Napoleon Bonaparte. The head of state himself had come to recognize the value of these events, establishing the close links that developed between France's rulers and these exhibitions.

National exhibitions continued to take place at irregular intervals, resulting in a total of eleven events through 1849. (For the exhibition of 1806, a Bordeaux resident named Quinton suggested that the Gironde's departmental jury include samples from the region's first-growth wine producers, but this idea was rejected.) This last edition had grown to include 4,785 exhibitors for a six-month run on the Champs Elysées, but although each new version tended to be larger, longer, and more ambitious than its predecessor, the fundamental theme remained the glorification of French industry.

Industrial exhibitions were now imitated in numerous cities throughout Europe with varying degrees of ambition and success, but across the Channel in England such displays were largely ignored. Great Britain was the world's preeminent manufacturing nation, and that was satisfaction enough for most British industrialists. Their general attitude was that these expositions were the sort of affairs that might be perfectly acceptable for the French, but British goods could sell themselves without such trumpery.

Still, the idea was in the air, and it was inevitable that someone would eventually attempt such a display. In 1828, a "National Repository for the Exhibition of New and Improved Productions of the Artisans and Manufacturers of the United Kingdom" was launched, only to be met with general apathy despite the patronage of King George IV. It was not until 1851 that an exhibition succeeded in attracting the attention not only of the British population, but of the entire world.

The Great Exhibition of the Works of Industry of All Nations was a celebration of the Industrial Revolution and the advancements it had made possible. Although clearly modeled on the French example, with juries and awards as incentives to bring forth the best for display, this was but a point of departure. The organizers, principal among whom was Queen Victoria's consort Prince Albert, had the inspired idea to solicit participation not just from industry all over Great Britain, but from every nation across the world. This fundamentally changed the scale of the event from a parochial display of "local" talent, to an opportunity for people from every point on the globe to come together in London to see and compare national standards of production.

The tone for the exhibition was set by Prince Albert in his invocation, which was reprinted in the official catalog:

> *The progress of the human race,*
> *Resulting from the common labour of all men,*
> *Ought to be the final object of the exertion of each individual.*
> *In promoting this end,*
> *We are carrying out the will of the great and blessed God.*

Gone was the belligerent tone of the original French exhibitions and the condescending attitude of previous British efforts. More significant, however, was the size and scope of this first international exhibition.

Housed in a monumental structure of glass and iron, which itself was hailed as chief among the wondrous objects on display, the "Crystal Palace" was erected in Hyde Park as a temporary structure to satisfy opposition to a permanent building, which would detract from one of London's principal green spaces. The materials used and their method of mass production made the hall truly representative of the industrial progress the exhibition was intended to celebrate: 300,000 panes of glass measuring 25 × 125 centimeters, cast-iron girders weighing no more than a ton, and 3,300 hollow iron columns were independently manufactured and transported to the building site where assembly was completed in just seventeen weeks.

The 94,000 square meters of the Crystal Palace could accommodate about 15,000 exhibitors, nearly one-half of whom were from Britain and its dominions; the remainder came from over forty nations across the globe. The structure itself was oriented on an east–west axis, with a high, arched transept intersecting the building at its middle. The western half of the display space was given over to the British exhibitors, the eastern portion to the international visitors. The organization among these latter was arranged according to their geographic location: countries in the warmer latitudes were placed near the center of the building, and those from colder areas were given space toward its ends.

French participation was important to the success of this exhibition. France had actively geared its industries to compete in foreign markets, and was the country most able to present a display to match the British. Prince Albert had hoped that British industrial design would be inspired to greater refinement upon being exposed to the finer example of French production; France's representative in London was invited to serve on the royal commission charged with organizing the exhibition. Still, the timing was less than ideal for the French, coming as it did between two political crises. "If France had been able to choose the moment," explained one of the organizers of its national display, "it would not have selected this time between 1850 and 1852; it would have preferred another time when not weakened by such harsh ordeals which have lessened its confidence in the future." The French, however, took up the challenge of showing the English on their own ground the superiority that France had claimed for so long, and mounted the largest display among the foreign contingents, sending 1,710 items, among which were a variety of mustards from M. Grey of Dijon, examples of preserved food from a company in Bordeaux, and an "apparatus for aerating and clarifying Champagne" from a wine merchant in Rheims. According to French explanations, wine itself was not admitted for display, owing to the fact that it was not a major part of British production. Other reasons were also put forth. "The whole range of alcohols and alcoholic drinks are very poorly represented," explained the *London Illustrated News.* "Regardless of their value in the arts, or as an article of food or medicine, they were not allowed to be exhibited, because they are sometimes turned to a bad purpose. For similar reasons, types might have been prevented, because bad books were sometimes printed; writings, because forgeries were committed; and electrometallurgic specimens, because they might be serviceable to the false coiner." Among the items that came closest to an inclusion of wines at the Exhibition was a display of "six bottles of champagne wine manufactured in England from rhubarb stalk."

The French showed well at this exhibition, earning 1,043 awards, far more than any other foreign country (the German states were next with 493 awards for 1,402 exhibitors). However, this was small consolation for the unavoidable conclusion that the glory of France's national exhibitions had been hijacked by the British in making their event international in scope. The idea of opening up the French 1849 exhibition to foreign competition had been suggested by the minister of agriculture and commerce Louis-Joseph Buffet. However, the idea came up against one of the cornerstones of French trade policy: the unspoken fear that in a direct comparison with British goods French industry would simply be unable to compete. Although never openly acknowledged, this fear found its most eloquent expression in the decades-old prohibitive French tariffs against British goods. Inviting foreign participation in the 1849 exhibition would have meant opening the door to British competition, which ran counter to traditional protectionist philosophy, and therefore the idea was rejected; now the decision was deeply regretted. "I insist on claiming for France the original idea of a Universal Exposition," the president of the next French exposition would write.

> As early as 1849, the suggestion was put to our legislative assembly. If England preceded us in its application, we must attribute this to political circumstances, to certain interests too easily frightened, and also to the difference in the genius of each of our two nations, one more ready to imagine, the other more ready to conceive. But the success of the Universal Exposition in London excited our emulation. Hardly had the doors of the Crystal Palace closed than from all parts came the demand for Paris to mount a comparable competition.

The next French national exhibition was scheduled to open three years later. In England, a correspondent for the *London Illustrated News* proved prescient when he wrote: "The French exhibition of 1854 will, no doubt, be on a grander and more liberal scale than any of its predecessors; and the example of England will, no doubt, lead the authorities of Paris to a different conclusion from that to which they came [in 1849], viz. not to admit the contributions of foreigners."

One

T… RSAL EXPOSITION … F 1855

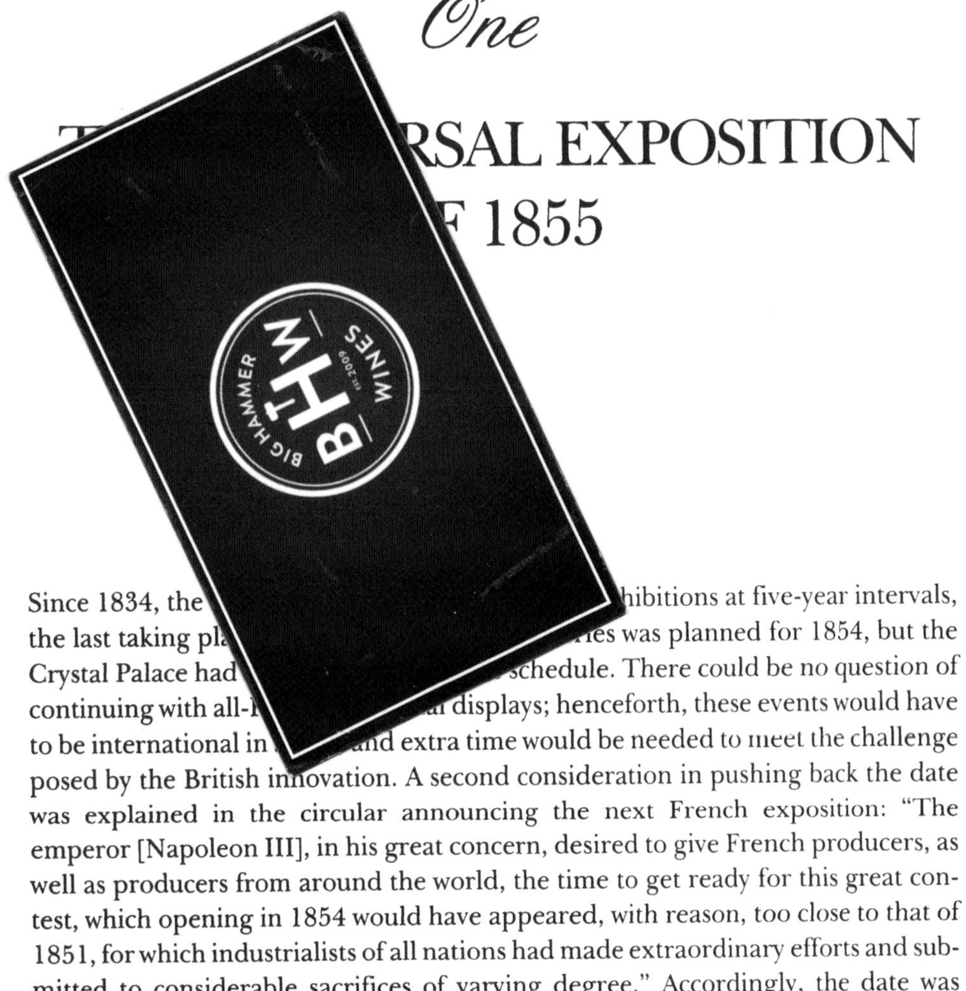

Since 1834, the … hibitions at five-year intervals, the last taking pl… es was planned for 1854, but the Crystal Palace had … schedule. There could be no question of continuing with all-… displays; henceforth, these events would have to be international in … and extra time would be needed to meet the challenge posed by the British innovation. A second consideration in pushing back the date was explained in the circular announcing the next French exposition: "The emperor [Napoleon III], in his great concern, desired to give French producers, as well as producers from around the world, the time to get ready for this great contest, which opening in 1854 would have appeared, with reason, too close to that of 1851, for which industrialists of all nations had made extraordinary efforts and submitted to considerable sacrifices of varying degree." Accordingly, the date was pushed back to 1855, but even with a one-year delay it was unlikely that sufficient technological developments were likely to occur in the short space of four years to give the new French exhibition the degree of novelty hoped for by its organizers. A longer postponement would doubtless have been better, but France was impatient to welcome the world.

On March 8, 1853, barely three months after Louis Napoleon's establishment of the Second Empire and himself as its Emperor, a decree was issued declaring that a six-month Universal Exposition would take place in Paris beginning on May 1, 1855; on March 26, a notice was dispatched to governments around the world soliciting their participation in this new extravaganza. The news was enthusiastically received both in France and abroad: internationally, the London spectacle had been extraordinarily popular and a new opportunity for another such gathering was certainly welcome; at home, the Universal Exposition offered a chance for French manufacturers to consolidate the victory they had scored in 1851.

Organization for this event promised to be much more complex than that for any of the previous national exhibitions. Coordinating communications with authorities around the world and arranging for the arrival of their exhibits would introduce a host of circumstances unique to this edition; for example, France's traditionally high customs duties would have to be adjusted to facilitate the entry of foreign goods for display. In the past, committees from the Ministry of Agriculture and Commerce were sufficient for staging the all-French national exhibitions, but now a special commission was needed. Consequently, on the day before Christmas in 1853, Louis Napoleon issued a decree creating an Imperial Commission for the Universal Exposition of 1855 to coordinate its preparation and execution. In the key post of Commission President, the Emperor appointed his cousin, Napoleon Jerome.

Thirteen years the Emperor's junior, Napoleon Jerome was the one other member of the Bonaparte clan possessed by the same sense of mission that Louis Napoleon attached to the family name. This common bond was at the heart of their lifelong association, begun in 1835 when Napoleon Jerome was just thirteen; the strength of this bond enabled the cousins to surmount the conflicts that all too often arose between them, for in almost every way they were polar opposites, in appearance, thought, and character.

For all his identification with the Bonaparte cause, Napoleon Jerome never knew the French Empire or its founder. Born September 9, 1822, in Trieste, this nephew of the Emperor inherited the legacy of exile that was the family's fortune in the decades after 1814. The youngest of three children, Napoleon Jerome was his mother's particular favorite, not least because of a physical resemblance to his illustrious uncle, which was evident from infancy. Although he was gifted with a precocious intellect, an inclination to laziness took the upper hand, and his mother's doting attentions compounded matters to bring forth a petulant side of his character at an early age. "For a long time I set myself to throwing his cap to the ground whenever he would forget or neglect to remove it in greeting," reminisced his sister of their childhood years together.

In adolescence, Napoleon Jerome's innately quick intellect was subjected to a rigorous program of tutoring, which transformed his natural indolence to an active and wide-ranging pursuit of knowledge, although his equally natural insolence still refused to come under control. Learning came easily for him, as did impatience when he felt that the pace of instruction lagged behind his abilities. Discouragement and disinterest were his standard responses when faced with some problem not readily resolved.

Napoleon Jerome
(Roger-Viollet)

Napoleon Jerome's increasing resemblance to his uncle Napoleon Bonaparte struck one observer upon seeing him as a thirteen-year-old: "I believe that it is impossible to find a more striking resemblance to the great Emperor than his." This impression became even more pronounced with time, and at twenty-five years of age he was said to have "the same Roman-medal profile, but taller, shorter in the neck and also more stout." This youthful stoutness was one consequence of Napoleon Jerome's indisposition to physical activity, aggravating his tendency to put on weight with age. One pastime he eventually came to enjoy was hunting, preferring small groups rather than large social affairs complete with hounds. However, it was noted that "he had a 'hot finger,' which is to say that he pulled readily on the trigger, without overly concerning himself about the calves or the eyes of those around him."

In the 1840s, the monarchy began to relax its restrictions against the Bonapartes, allowing the young exile to finally enter France in the spring of 1845. In the aftermath of the revolution in 1848, when barely twenty-six years old, Napoleon Jerome presented his candidature for the nation's new Assembly and became its youngest elected member. This official entry into France's political life offered him the opportunity to give full expression to his republican views: from his seat on the chamber's left wing, he soon became one of that body's principal orators, actively championing the working class with proposals for reductions in the taxes on salt and other basic necessities and demanding the underwriting of workers' associations. Such liberal—indeed, radical—positions and the force with which they were put forth eventually earned Napoleon Jerome the nickname "the Red Prince."

As Napoleon Jerome's political prominence grew, the contrast with his cousin became ever more apparent. It had often been noted that Louis Napoleon bore little resemblance to the great Emperor he took for his model. Awkward by nature and halting in public speech, his voice and phrasing betrayed the unmistakably German influence of a childhood spent in Swiss exile. Like Napoleon Jerome, he, too, was elected to the Assembly in 1848, but Louis Napoleon's speeches were so poorly delivered that a motion aimed at barring him from becoming a candidate for President was contemptuously withdrawn after his clumsily stated opposition to the measure convinced listeners, incorrectly, that such a person could never be taken seriously. Lacking the gift of quick, decisive thought, which characterized the family legend, he seemed much less of a Bonaparte than Napoleon Jerome, whose very appearance was more obviously reminiscent of the Corsican patriarch. "The Emperor," Napoleon Jerome is said to have chided his cousin in challenging his role as keeper of the Bonaparte flame, "why, you have nothing of him." "I have his family," was Louis Napoleon's short and sufficient response.

This conflict was a constant undercurrent running through their lives: Napoleon Jerome possessed the characteristic flair and dynamic presence to be a credible successor for the Bonaparte dynasty, but found his ambitions blocked by the candidature of his older, more ambitious cousin. His interpretation of Bonapartism, as with so much else, tended to go beyond the bounds of political practicality established by Louis Napoleon. Although they were both fervent supporters of the laboring class, their solutions to its problems were fundamentally different in scope: Louis Napoleon saw the Empire as the form of government best able to ensure workers' well-being, whereas Napoleon Jerome was a fervent supporter of the Republic, which the Emperor had overturned. To make matters more difficult, there was the question of Napoleon Jerome's character.

Where Louis Napoleon was patient and perseverant, devoting decades to carefully setting in place the foundations that would bring him the power he considered his birthright, Napoleon Jerome was still too often impetuous and impatient for results: he would avidly demand new tasks and responsibilities, then invariably shift his attention to some new undertaking and lose interest in the project at hand. In the spring of 1849, Louis Napoleon appointed his cousin as French ambassador to Spain, but finding the Spanish court not at all to his liking, Napoleon Jerome simply returned to Paris without notice, giving his cousin little choice but to interpret his action as a resignation. Five years later, upon declaration of the Crimean War, Napoleon Jerome insisted upon taking part in his capacity of division general, a title conferred upon him by the Emperor shortly after coming to power. He actually acquitted himself quite well in the battle of Alma, displaying his quickness of mind and spirit to their best advantage. When he was well on his way to establishing a sterling and well-earned military reputation, in the winter of 1854, Napoleon Jerome suffered from a mild bout of fever and diarrhea, which left him in a weakened state. Although it was far less severe than the cholera that ravaged the French forces, it was enough to make him decide to quit the war. In a letter to Constantinople, where Napoleon Jerome was recuperating, the Emperor counseled his cousin to resist his weaker nature:

> *I have learned with great sorrow that you have become ill following the rigors of the campaign. I can understand, up to a point, your return to Constantinople to recover, but I beseech you, as soon as you are able, to return to the army. Your conduct until now has won the hearts of all. The news from the Orient has done you infinite good and yet (if the truth be told), should you return now, leaving the army in a precarious situation with the aims of the expedition not yet achieved, you would lose in a moment all the fruits of your labors. And finally you would lose the benefit of public opinion, on that point there is no question. Your return to Constantinople has already aroused unpleasant rumors. Still, if you are ill, stay there until you are better, but* make it clear that you are going to return *and do return to the army as soon as you are able.*

Having tired of the war Napoleon Jerome ignored his cousin's sensible advice, and nine months after departing for the Orient he embarked from Constantinople to return to France.

This inability to reflect upon the consequences of his actions eventually brought forth a rebuke from the Emperor which cataloged the long list of indiscretions Napoleon Jerome had managed to accumulate:

> *From the day following my election as President of the Republic, you have never ceased to be, by your words and your actions, hostile to my policies. . . . How have I revenged myself for your conduct? By seeking every occasion to advance you, to create a position worthy of your rank and to open an arena for your brilliant qualities. Your command in the Crimea, your marriage, your endowment, your ministry in Algeria, your army regiment in Italy, your entry in the Senate and the State Council are evident proof of my feelings for you. Need I remind you of how you responded! In the Orient, your discouragement lost you the fruits of a campaign well begun. . . . Your endowment? One would rightly be amazed that you have never opened your doors [to entertain], and your name appears on no list of charities. . . . As for your statements in the Senate, they have never been anything but a serious source of embarrassment for my government, and you complain of my conduct towards you! One wonders that I have tolerated for so long from a member of my family an opposition which alarms and sows doubt among my supporters. In speaking of you not too long ago, the* Times *said that if an English prince had followed the same line of conduct in England as you have done here, he would have been written off by public opinion. . . .*

This rebuke characterized the man who would oversee the organization of the Universal Exposition of 1855 and through whom all decisions concerning it would eventually pass.

In defining the structure of the Paris exposition, the Imperial Commission consciously strove to improve upon the London example. Perhaps its major innovation was the organization of an allied exhibition of fine arts; this would constitute a parallel exposition with its own administration, its own judges, and its own display space separate from the products of industry. This focus on the arts was as natural for the French as it was unimaginable for the British, who had difficulty in even incorporating the idea of fine art in the basically utilitarian design of their manufactured goods.

Another difference reflecting the cultural philosophies that separated the two nations' approaches to these exhibitions was the decision to include the prices of objects on display. Whereas the British had a repugnance for the commercial aspect of these events and could only be convinced to create an industrial exhibition—much less participate in one—with the high-minded ideal of international peace through commerce, the more practical French tradition brought the mercantile aspect to the fore. The display of an object's price had been a part of the last National Exposition in 1849, and the Imperial Commission believed that the price of an object was of definite importance in assessing its quality, for if a plow could be sold for 100 francs while an identical one cost 125 this clearly spoke in favor of the former: its lower price reflected a more efficient method of manufacture, enabling it to be produced and offered at a lesser cost, and the encouragement of methods to bring more goods within the reach of the average person was a principal aim of the Bonaparte philosophy.

Because of the Emperor's concern for the professional development of France's workers, a major effort was made to encourage their attendance at the exposition in order that they themselves might become more efficient and innovative through exposure to the new ideas they would discover there. Furthermore, in the awarding of medals, consideration would be given for "the services rendered to industry by the heads of enterprises, foremen, workers or day-laborers." It was all well and good to salute the big industrialists, but this time the common worker would receive due recognition, too.

However, for all these changes, the Universal Exposition's charge remained basically unchanged: to showcase the latest developments in manufactured goods. It was therefore to its workshops and factories that France once again directed its search for entries, not to the country's vineyards. Wine was "made," not "manufactured"—a subtle but key distinction, which defined the thinking of Exposition organizers and wine producers alike. In past exhibitions, were viniculture to be represented at all, it might be by the display of some innovation such as a cask with a newly developed vacuum spigot rather than through the inclusion of any wines themselves; spirits and *eaux-de-vie* were more likely candidates for display, since their production relied more on the technology of distillation than the less mechanical (and poorly understood) process of fermentation. Thus, for the Universal Exposition of 1855, it was not unnatural to think in terms of displaying an imitation Chartreuse liqueur "invented" by a special process rather than a genuinely fine wine which was the result of generations of patient observation and experimentation. Although the Imperial Commission would establish a system of organizing exhibits allowing for the admission of wine to the Exposition, no particular efforts would be made to officially encourage winemakers to submit their products for display; it was simply not one of the goods that came to mind for inclusion at a celebration of industry.

While the Imperial Commission set about establishing the Universal Exposition's basic structure, Napoleon Jerome began coordinating the participation of France's manufacturers. On March 15, he had a circular sent to the prefects in charge of each of the country's eighty-six departments, ordering the creation of regional committees to stimulate the enthusiasm of local industry and to screen the items submitted for display. Two hundred eight committees were established (many departments establishing more than one), and for the first time in the country's history of exhibitions, every department without exception would be represented. Just as the Imperial Commission sought to present French industry at its best and claim for France the majority of the awards to be won, so was each Departmental Committee impelled to promote its own superiority over the country's other regions. With the greater challenges posed by this new Universal Exposition, these Departmental Committees would be held to higher standards than had been required of local judges for previous national exhibitions. Each prefect was therefore directed to consult with the various commercial, industrial, and agricultural organizations in his department for advice on how their regional selection could best meet the challenge presented by this international exposition.

In the Gironde, the task of establishing the Departmental Committee for the Universal Exposition of 1855 was the responsibility of Pierre de Mentque, a career administrator whose previous posts as prefect and underprefect at nine other locations throughout France had well prepared him to administer the country's largest department. Born to a noble family with generations of government experience and possessed of a comfortable private fortune, he was well positioned to use his political authority and personal standing to draw upon the full range of talent available in the Gironde.

On the same day he received Napoleon Jerome's circular, de Mentque wrote to several of the Gironde's Chambers of Agriculture, including those at Bazas, Blaye, and La Réole, districts that were all important wine-producing areas.

In their responses to de Mentque's request for advice, these agricultural bodies offered over sixty names for his consideration in assembling the official Departmental Committee of ten members. These rosters of candidates offered by the Chambers of Agriculture drew heavily from each district's locally prominent citizens: judges, mayors, and major landowners invariably formed the core of each group's list. If the owners of major wine-producing properties were proposed as candidates, it was not with the idea that their winemaking abilities would be useful in judging items to send to Paris; their qualification was listed merely as "proprietor," signifying a particular economic and social standing as a landowner, regardless of what was produced on that land. In the list submitted from Bazas, the nominees included "the Marquis de Lur-Saluces at Sauternes," with no mention that he was the owner of Châteaux d'Yquem, Coutet, and Filhot, which produced some of the finest wines that the district had to offer.

The thinking regarding the suitability of wine as an exemplar of French advances in manufacture can be summed up by the response of the Blaye Chamber of Agriculture: "The Chamber, after having examined with the greatest attention . . . the spirit of the prefect's letter calling for local committees wherever industry, the arts, and agriculture have made great developments, also recognizes that this importance is considerably diminished in the absence of workshops or marked developments in agriculture. As a result, the district of Blaye which finds itself in this latter condition, believes itself unsuited to organize a committee here. . . ." All that Blaye had to offer was a concentration of vineyards and wine producers relying more on tradition than technology, and which therefore could not possibly be of interest to the organizers of the Universal Exposition at Paris.

In addition to these various agricultural bodies, de Mentque also wrote to the Bordeaux Chamber of Commerce. Although the circular from the Imperial Commission did not stress the importance of any particular source of advice over another, the Chamber's authority gave its opinions precedence over those of all others.

The Bordeaux Chamber of Commerce was undoubtedly the most influential commercial organization in the Gironde, representing directly and indirectly the economic interests of the entire department. A century and a half of existence had established the Chamber as a primary force in the political and social life of Bordeaux since its founding in 1705, with an influence extending far beyond the city's borders. Exercising a controlling influence on the city's port, the leading maritime gateway for goods leaving and entering France, the Chamber was in a position to affect trade not only domestically but internationally. If this represented great power, it was also a major responsibility, one which its members clearly understood.

Composed of Bordeaux's leading citizens, the Chamber was actively involved in much of the city's social and charitable activity, evidence of a civic awareness which is today reflected in the numerous local streets and avenues that bear its members' names.

If the Chamber of Commerce had a guiding principle, it was that what was good for international trade was good for France. Its philosophy was one in support of reduced tariffs and free trade, which would increase shipping, increase the activity of Bordeaux's port, and increase the city's wealth. This was clearly in opposition to the protectionist principles of traditional French commerce, but completely in line with the region's commercial history, a history shaped at first by wine, then expanded to include a major interest in other goods—in the nineteenth century, for instance, Bordeaux was the major port of entry for France's chocolate and coffee imports. Unlike most of France, whose economy was based on selling to domestic markets, Bordeaux's wealth was founded on international commerce, particularly through its wine trade with England and northern Europe. When economic conditions in the rest of the country demanded a greater emphasis on protecting domestic production through the establishment of ever-more restrictive trade policies, the measures instituted were invariably at odds with Bordeaux's particular interests. Given the exceptional needs of the city's commerce, the Bordeaux Chamber of Commerce developed into an organization particularly effective in exerting its influence whenever and wherever necessary. It was not unusual for the Chamber to be represented on various committees and deliberating bodies whose outcomes were likely to have commercial consequences; when possible, it was preferable that this representation be decisive. On a question of major importance regarding navigation in the port of Bordeaux, negotiations between the Chamber and the naval authorities had reached a standstill when it was decided to form a commission to deliberate on the matter. "As to the ongoing question regarding mixed-use navigation," the Chamber reported to its representative dealing with the question in Paris, "the chief naval administrator in Bordeaux has created a commission which it seems is to be composed of seven members; three from the naval administration, two members from the Chamber, and two directors of transport companies, chosen by us. Thus, you see, we have the majority." It therefore was natural for de Mentque to give particular weight to the opinions of the Bordeaux Chamber of Commerce regarding the composition of the Gironde's Committee for the Universal Exposition of 1855.

In response to de Mentque's request, the Chamber suggested a roster of twenty-five names from which they believed a good selection might be made. Again, wine-making was not high on the list of qualifications: among those proposed were two science professors, a cabinetmaker, two architects, two shipbuilders, a carriage maker, a lawyer, several politicians, a sculptor, a paper maker, and two members of the Chamber of Commerce itself. In the final composition of the Departmental

Committee, de Mentque would draw eight of its ten names from this proposed list, including the two suggested members of the Chamber of Commerce.

The Committee was presided over by the mayor of Bordeaux, Antoine Gautier; he was seconded by a member of the General Council for the Gironde and the Bordeaux Advisory Chamber of Agriculture, Charles Legrix de Lassalle, who acted as Committee secretary. Jean-Charles Alphand, a member of the Bordeaux city council and the director of the local division of France's Department of Civil Engineers, served as spokesman. The other members were Joseph-Benoit Abria, a professor of physics and dean of the faculty of sciences, as well as a member of the Bordeaux Academy of Science, Literature, and Art; Jean-Paul Alaux, director of the school of design and painting, and a member of the Society of Friends of the Arts; Jean-Lucien Arman, shipbuilder; Stéphan Bertin, vice-president of the Chamber of Commerce; Pierre Beaufils, cabinetmaker; Gabriel-Charles Jaquemet, a manufacturer; and Nathaniel Johnston, the second member of the Chamber of Commerce. Of these ten men, only Johnston had a direct connection with the wine trade.

Nathaniel Johnston was born in 1804, and was the fourth generation to head the family merchant business. Under his stewardship beginning in the 1820s, the firm, Nathaniel Johnston and Son, became one of the greatest in Bordeaux. Licensed to deal in goods as varied as lumber and foodstuffs, the buying and selling of wine constituted the foundation of the company's fortunes.

As a young man, Johnston was initiated into the intricacies of the Bordeaux wine trade, eventually becoming owner of several châteaux in the Médoc. By 1854, he was a major buyer of every type of wine made throughout the Gironde, which afforded him a substantial appreciation of the importance and high quality of this aspect of the region's production. Still, it was never suggested that his experience in this regard be put to use in steering the Departmental Committee to include wine as part of the Gironde's contribution to the Universal Exposition, and he himself did not propose it in any of the Committee's meetings. Rather, it was his prominence as one of Bordeaux's leading businessmen, his civic activity as a member of the department's General Council and the Bordeaux Chamber of Commerce, and his rank as Chevalier of the Legion of Honor that was of greater importance in his selection for the Committee.

The Committee first met on May 1, 1854 in the presence of all ten members, to fulfill its mandate to find the best of the Gironde to represent the department at the Universal Exposition. Accordingly, Committee members considered ways of encouraging a greater participation among the department's industrialists, and whether the region's renowned rope makers would be suitable exhibitors since a display of their products, despite the acknowledged excellent quality, would still be just rope and might not excite the imaginations of the public. Alaux was delegated the task of stimulating interest in the Universal Exposition among the region's artists. The subject of wine was never mentioned that day, and in six months of meetings the question of whether the produce of the region's vineyards was worthy of inclusion among the goods to display in Paris never occurred to anyone. When the subject finally was proposed, no one seemed to know exactly what to do about it.

At the Committee's fourth meeting on November 7, the secretary, Legrix de Lassalle, read a letter which had arrived from the president of the Chamber of Commerce in Dijon, who was writing in his capacity as a member of the Departmental Committee for the Côte-d'Or. The letter informed the Gironde Committee that Burgundy and Champagne were planning to send a selection of their wines to Paris; did Bordeaux wish to include its wine in this joint display, too? Taken unawares by this unexpected offer, Legrix de Lassalle had sent a provisional, noncommittal response to Dijon, and now presented the question before the Committee. What *did* it intend to do?

Lacking a representative of the region's wine trade that day (Nathaniel Johnston was absent; in fact, after the first Committee meeting in May, Johnston had been unable to attend any of the organization's subsequent sessions), none of the Committee members present was sure quite how wine would fit in with what was, after all, supposed to be a display of industrial production, or what was involved in doing for Bordeaux what was being done for Burgundy and Champagne. After a long discussion of the matter, it was decided that the best thing to do was to do nothing at all, at least until the Committee had an opportunity to find out how the vineyard owners themselves felt about the idea of sending their wines to Paris. Accordingly, it arranged for the local newspapers to run a notice inviting all the region's winemakers to the next Committee meeting on Tuesday, November 21. On November 9 and 10, the following notice appeared in the Bordeaux press:

> The Committee responsible for assuring the Gironde's participation at the Universal Exposition of 1855, invites vineyard owners intending to display their products to meet at the prefecture on Tuesday, November 22 at noon.
>
> Common wines as well as fine wines are eligible for admission to the Exposition. The Committee needs to know the position of the exhibitors before making a final list

Unfortunately, neither Legrix de Lassalle, the editors of the various newspapers, the typesetters who printed them, nor anyone else for that matter, noticed that Legrix de Lassalle had inserted the wrong date—the penultimate Tuesday in November 1854 was the *21st* not the *22nd.* Now the question in the minds of all who read the notice was, did they mean *Tuesday* the 21st or Wednesday the *22nd*? Apparently, the majority of vineyard owners took it to mean the latter, for when the 21st arrived, only a handful of people turned up at the prefecture. Only then was the Committee aware of the mistake that had occurred. Further compounding the situation, the Committee had intended to send personal invitations to many of the leading wine producers but had not found the time to do so, contributing to the disappointingly low turnout. Since it was impossible to reach any decision based on so small a response, it was decided to give it another try and reschedule the meeting for the following week, November 28.

This time, "a great number" of vineyard owners turned out for the meeting, and the Committee members heard much indeed. First the Committee president, Gautier, read the letter from the Côte-d'Or Committee stating Burgundy and Champagne's intention to take part in the Universal Exposition; then he asked for the opinions of those assembled.

It was unanimously agreed that the wines of the Gironde must be present in Paris, given the benefits such exposure could bring. Everyone also agreed that the region should prepare a separate, collective display of the Gironde's production, as complete and representative as possible. So far, so good. Then things became a little less unanimous: how was the display to be organized? Who would arrange it? Several of those present suggested that a subcommission of vineyard owners be created to advise the Departmental Committee on this question.

At this point, Gautier decided that the Committee had heard enough to know that it should proceed with the idea of including the region's wine among the products from the Gironde it would be sending to Paris. The question now was how to organize it?

Not only had the vineyard owners come to the meeting, but this time Nathaniel Johnston was present, too. For over half a year since the initial meeting, Johnston had been unable to attend the Committee's previous five sessions, but learning that a presentation of the region's wines was under discussion, his presence at the November 28 meeting became imperative. Johnston had spent a lifetime developing the experience necessary to understand the complex relationship that existed among the vineyard owners, merchants, and all the other links in the commercialization of Bordeaux's wine. And now, having heard the direction in which the Committee had allowed the proceedings to take, it was not unlikely that Johnston saw the danger in allowing the winemakers—with their own particular interests—the responsibility of organizing a display of their wines, a danger that would not be evident to the other Committee members whose activities as professors and painters and cabinetmakers constituted a minimal involvement with the wine trade.

There was nothing in the Committee's mandate necessitating that this question be referred to another body, nothing specifying that the Chamber of Commerce would be more competent than any other organization in offering advice. Nevertheless, it is not unreasonable to believe that in attending his first meeting in six months, Nathaniel Johnston may have been instrumental in steering this question from the Departmental Committee to another organization of which he was a member, an organization capable of ensuring that any presentation of the region's wines did nothing to disrupt the delicate operation of the Bordeaux wine trade.

Consequently, it was decided to contact the Bordeaux Chamber of Commerce for advice on how best to proceed from here, and directly after the meeting a letter was dispatched to the Chamber:

> Before giving a definitive answer to the request addressed to us [by the Côte-d'Or], the Committee thought it should bring this situation to the attention of the Bordeaux Chamber of Commerce for your consideration, that you might formulate an opinion for which this Committee attaches great importance, and to indicate the practical means you believe to be useful in achieving the desired result. . . .

The Chamber of Commerce would be happy to offer the Departmental Committee the benefit of its opinion. Eventually, it ended up doing much, much more.

Two

THE BORDEAUX CHAMBER OF COMMERCE STEPS IN

On November 29, 1854, the Bordeaux Chamber of Commerce met for its weekly Wednesday meeting. Pierre de Mentque was there, exercising the prefect's right to preside as he frequently did whenever departmental matters of particular interest were before the Chamber.

As usual, the agenda was varied, reflecting the diverse nature of the Chamber's activities. A letter from the Chamber of Commerce at Le Havre requested its Bordeaux counterpart's participation in petitioning for a reduction of the tax on foreign sugar, rum, tafia, raisins, and French molasses (the Chamber of Commerce gave its assent); two letters were read from the Chamber's Paris representative relating his ongoing efforts toward achieving this same end—cheap imported raw sugar was of prime importance for Bordeaux's shippers and sugar refineries, both major commercial activities since the early nineteenth century; a letter from the Minister of Agriculture, Commerce, and Public Works was read concerning a reduction of taxation on soda nitrates and potash (the Chamber was opposed); a letter from the local Director of Customs and Taxes expressed his regret that his recent promotion would prevent a continued collaboration with the Chamber of Commerce (the Chamber expressed the sentiment that the regret was mutual); there was a letter from the General Commissioner of Naval Operations in Bordeaux concerning the loss of three fishing boats with all twelve crew members and requesting a contribution to the widows and orphans fund (the Chamber donated 500 francs, a generous amount at the time); a letter from a Mr. Ménard sought the Chamber's support for a new steamship service between Dunkirk and Bordeaux which hoped to use the facilities available to other shipping companies (the Chamber agreed to help); there was a letter from the prefect himself explaining why he had not acted on a request from the Chamber regarding the establishment of docking facilities in Bordeaux—he suggested that the mayor, Antoine Gautier, bring the matter up before the City Council. Finally, the last bit of business under the heading of correspondence was a letter from the Departmental Committee for the Universal Exposition:

> Sirs,
>
> The Committee charged with assuring the Gironde's participation at the Universal Exposition of 1855 has received a letter from the president of the Chamber of Commerce of Dijon in his capacity as a member of the Committee for the Côte-d'Or, in which he makes known the decision taken by the proprietors of Champagne and Burgundy to present their wines at the Great Exposition of 1855.
>
> . . . The committee for the Gironde, fully aware of the importance of its mission, held two meetings with vineyard owners; a certain number have responded to this call, and today expressed the unanimous opinion that a display of their wines would be useful and advantageous, and that such a display of small samples be collective in nature, and be comprised as much as possible of wines of both great price as well as common consumption.
>
> Before giving a definitive answer to the request addressed to us, the Committee thought it should bring this situation to the attention of the Bordeaux Chamber of Commerce for your consideration, that you might formulate an opinion for which this Committee attaches great importance, and to indicate the practical means you believe to be useful in achieving the desired result. . . .

It was recognized by the Chamber that this was not a simple case of merely assenting to an idea already formed by the Departmental Committee. Unlike that body, the Chamber of Commerce possessed members who had a more immediate connection with the Bordeaux wine trade, and who understood that, for all its innocuousness, there were aspects of this question that necessitated careful thought before embarking on a course of action.

After some initial deliberation, the majority of the members concluded that it was indeed indispensable that the wines of the Gironde be represented at the Universal Exposition; less clear, however, was how this might best be accomplished. Accordingly, the Chamber decided to establish a commission of its own to consider the matter, composed of four of its best qualified members: Blondeau; André Ferrière, a broker licensed to handle transactions in German and Dutch; Nathaniel Johnston; and the president of the Bordeaux Chamber of Commerce, Duffour-Dubergier.

Born December 10, 1797, to a family whose commercial prominence in the city dated back to the seventeenth century, Lodi-Martin Duffour-Dubergier was the very model of Bordeaux's civic and social life during the middle decades of the nineteenth century.

As patriarch of the family merchant firm, Duffour-Dubergier's father was fiercely proud of his profession, and was determined that his daughter and three sons follow his example: "I'm impatient to see you all in the business, some of you out on the road, others here at the tiller with me." Duffour-Dubergier was the eldest child and thus heir to the reins of the family firm, but although his father believed in Lodi's intelligence and ability, the rest of the family felt that the youngster possessed neither the makings of a merchant nor a head for business. Despite these misgivings, Duffour-Dubergier's father persisted in his intentions, and set out a program which he hoped would prepare Lodi to effectively manage a large merchant firm.

Thus, in 1814, at the age of seventeen, Duffour-Dubergier was sent to England with his thirteen-year-old brother Antoine-Simon, for an apprenticeship in a commercial house in order to learn the language, develop a head for figures, and perfect his handwriting by copying correspondence. The father wrote often to the young apprentice, offering counsel and direction to help Duffour-Dubergier get the most from this period of training; his theme was constant, his advice both simple and comprehensive: "Engage yourself in all aspects of business and put yourself in a position to do honor to this profession."

Four years later, in the next phase of training, the two brothers were dispatched to Germany, this time with their younger brother Jules, aged ten. Unfortunately, Duffour-Dubergier had shown himself more inclined toward leisure rather than commerce, confirming the family's misgivings regarding his aptitude for business. Preferring to perfect his riding, shooting, and fencing skills, Duffour-Dubergier's disregard for his commercial education was his father's despair: after all his years of training and life abroad, the young man still proved incapable of mastering the intricacies of foreign exchange.

Despite patient and sound advice which continued to arrive by post from Bordeaux, and occasionally more directly during visits from the father himself, Duffour-Dubergier's shortcomings persisted; in addition to his taste for the easy life, he seemed unable to summon the concentration necessary to reach the heart of a question, or to adopt the moderate temperament of a successful merchant. "My problem," he wrote, "comes from the fact that I am affected too deeply by circumstances; it's either yes or no, with no middle ground: this is my character, the key to my conduct."

After a brief return to the family's Bordeaux offices, where his father could more closely monitor his wayward son, in 1821 Duffour-Dubergier was sent once again to Germany, with the Netherlands thrown in for good measure. This time things were different: seven years of frustration and resistance had finally given way to an acceptance of the merchant's life, and at last Duffour-Dubergier decided to settle down and apply

Duffour-Dubergier
(Musée des Beaux Arts, Bordeaux)

himself seriously to his work. This newfound dedication inspired a more productive use of Duffour-Dubergier's dormant talents, and his progress was significant enough for him to be summoned back to Bordeaux, where he began to play a more active part in managing the merchant firm.

As his role in increasing the family fortune grew, Duffour-Dubergier's commercial prominence drew him into a greater involvement with the affairs of his native town. In 1831, he accepted a position on the Bordeaux City Council where his first essays into politics were far from promising. The cost of repairs to Bordeaux's Grand Theater was considered during one council meeting in September 1832, and, in commenting on Duffour-Dubergier's remarks on the subject, Antoine Gautier noted that "he was right, he is almost always right, but he is a terrible speaker and the main idea is always afloat in an ocean of useless verbiage, which makes one hardly able to understand it." Although

Duffour-Dubergier had developed his aptitude for business, he had not yet mastered the ability to focus on the key points of a situation.

Still, Duffour-Dubergier's commercial acumen and his management of the family enterprise brought increasing prosperity and attention to both the company and himself. By the time of his father's death in 1842, the once-wayward son had become mayor of Bordeaux, and three years later assumed the added responsibility of sitting on the General Council for the Gironde, becoming president of that body in 1846. Although Duffour-Dubergier left the post of mayor in the revolutionary year of 1848, other duties continued to fill his time including an ongoing involvement in an association promoting free trade (which he founded in 1846); he was a founding member of the Society of Friends of the Arts; president of the Society of Horticulture; one of the founders of the Academy of Six, a gastronomic society; and president of the Philharmonic Circle from 1848 to 1849, to cite just a few of the activities undertaken during his lifetime. However, for all the variety of his many interests, the constant thread running through Duffour-Dubergier's life was the deep affection he felt for Bordeaux. "My ambition," he once remarked, "has never extended itself beyond the limits of my city."

Wine was behind much of the family fortune, and Duffour-Dubergier's involvement went beyond just its purchase and sale as one of Bordeaux's major merchants; he was also the proprietor of Château Smith-Haut-Lafitte in the Graves commune of Martillac and Château Gironville at Macau in the Médoc. Although possessed of an owner's natural pride in his wines, Duffour-Dubergier's basic integrity acknowledged the justice of Gironville's contemporary commercial reputation as being of average quality, not of the first rank. Consequently, a guest at his table would more likely be served a wine from a superior property, even though it was not made by the host himself. This sign of Duffour-Dubergier's delicate sense of hospitality was noted by one visitor to Gironville:

> *We face no danger here from the heir of Giron,*
> *No boastful producer or false Amphitryon,*
> *Of the prospect of drinking throughout a whole meal,*
> *Only wines from his vines due to unfounded zeal.*
> *We may dine here not feeling we're put on the spot,*
> *He is proud of his wine, but he offers it not.*

The vineyard of Smith-Haut-Lafitte was of much higher quality, yet Duffour-Dubergier was equally accepting of the trade's conservative commercial judgment: "A distinguished new growth has just been created in the Graves by M. [Duffour-Dubergier] at Smith, on one of the most advantageously situated sites in Martillac. The quality of its soil, composed only of gravel, the finest grape varieties which alone have been planted, the well-known care shown by the proprietor, should all come together to earn an elevated rank for this vineyard's wine. The trade, however, has not yet wished to acknowledge this rank. . . ." As one of the most important members of that trade, Duffour-Dubergier was well placed to exercise a considerable influence on his vineyard's behalf if he wished, but there is no evidence that this was the case. Smith-Haut-Lafitte remained at the level set by commerce; it would be for a later generation of owners to bring the vineyard's rank in line with its quality.

Renowned as one of the finest wine tasters in Bordeaux, Duffour-Dubergier's personal cellar contained over 4,100 bottles from the finest regions of France and abroad. Still, his deepest appreciation was reserved for the wines of his native city. "For me," he once proclaimed, "the touchstone of civilization is the wine of Bordeaux!"

The wealth and influence enjoyed by both Duffour-Dubergier and Nathaniel Johnston reflected a comprehensive understanding of the Bordeaux wine trade. Not only were they major buyers through their merchant operations; as vineyard owners they were sellers, earning additional revenue and something equally valuable: a deeper appreciation of how the Bordeaux wine market operated.

As in any market, sellers attempted to obtain the maximum return for their product, and, not unnaturally, buyers did their best to secure a seller's goods at the cheapest possible price. The end result of this commercial tension, according to the fundamental laws of economics, was the establishment of a just price for the goods in question. However, unlike an anonymous product such as, say, refined sugar, wine was intricately connected with the personality of its producer, which added an extra consideration in determining its price.

This close association between owner and wine was reflected in the common trade practice during the early nineteenth century for a property's wine to bear the name of its current proprietor. In his 1824 book *Traité sur les vins du Médoc,* which cataloged the major wine-producing properties throughout the region, William Franck listed the wines not under the name of the property, but under the heading "Proprietor's Name," which more or less amounted to the same thing. Should a property undergo several changes of ownership, the identity of its wine might change from vintage to vintage in accord with the name of the owner of the moment, even if all the other personnel and conditions of production remained the same. Simply put, the owner paid the bills, the owner named the wine. In 1838, the vineyard of Gorce (which itself had earlier been known as Guy) was changed to Branne, at the express and published wish of its new owner, the Baron de Branne; in a ten-year period, the property of Rauzan-Gassies was variously known in the trade as Pelier, Chabrier, and Rauzan-Gassies itself. An even more extreme manifestation of this identification between proprietor and property was the practice in which an owner of a renowned vineyard altered the family name to bask in the reflected glory of its wine; this is seen in the case of Nicolas-Edme Guillot, who, in 1817, added "de Suduiraut" to his name in light of his recent ownership of the eponymous property in the Sauternes region. According to a document in the archives at Château Suduiraut, "This method of proceeding was common at this time, where numerous proprietors attached their name to that of their property."

This question of ego added an extra dimension to the classic tension between buyers (merchants) and sellers (proprietors): not only was the asking price of a wine based on its own intrinsic quality, the proprietors' estimations of their own worth were factored into the equation as well. For the merchants, the proprietors' elevated opinions of the quality of their wines was frequently a galling obstacle to what they considered to be the smooth operation of commerce. Instead of simply putting their wine up for sale and accepting a fair price (as the merchants' saw it), proprietors would invariably make demands in excess of what the market would bear, and then might refuse to sell their wine until they got the price they wanted. The standard refrain of the frustrated merchant is summed up in the notes of one buyers' representative for the wines of 1833: ". . . The proprietors' pretensions are raised in several quarters; it would be unfortunate if they prevented the execution of sales which could be made, pushing purchases back to the spring. This delay would be harmful to the interests of the proprietors, as well as those of the trade."

Of course, things looked different from the proprietor's point of view. The Bordeaux wine trade during the first half of the nineteenth century was most definitely a buyer's market, and proprietors frequently felt themselves, not unjustly, to be at the merchants' mercy. Many merchants of this period were, as we have seen, among the most influential and wealthy of Bordeaux's citizens, while financial obligations and economic conditions weighed heavily on producers during this time; most of the grand chateaux which characterize the vineyards of the Médoc were only constructed toward the middle of the nineteenth century, when economic conditions in the Second Empire brought a change in proprietors' fortunes. Traditionally, the relationship between merchants and proprietors was one of grudging cooperation at best, veiled hostility at worst. In the opinion of one winemaker, merchants "profited from my distress as well as that of every proprietor in the Médoc."

This mutual disdain for the business practices of both sides in the Bordeaux wine trade operated as a system of checks and balances, with each party's interests countering those of the other. This was a delicate situation, based as much on personal temperament as on sound fiscal practice, a system on whose equilibrium the smooth functioning of the Bordeaux wine trade had come to depend: gradually, with time and experience, the relative value of each proprietor's wine had become fairly well established based on its quality and the price that quality would bring in the marketplace. Within reasonably well-defined limits, both merchants and proprietors knew the value of a particular wine, which created a point of departure from which negotiations to arrive at a final selling price could be conducted. This was not to say that a proprietor's wine was eternally locked into a particular level of the price scale: if an owner was willing to invest the money and effort into improving conditions in the vineyard and winery, eventually such improvements would be reflected in the quality of the finished product, this improved quality would occasion its increased popularity among wine drinkers, and if all went according to the laws of economics, this increased popularity for a proprietor's wine would result in a higher selling price for a product whose supply became increasingly inadequate in the face of rising demand. Thus could a conscientious proprietor raise the standing of a wine (and, inversely, an irresponsible proprietor lower the standing of a wine as well).

The danger to this carefully established system was that one side or another, proprietors or merchants, would attempt to alter it by means which had nothing to do with the intrinsic quality of the wine itself. In the words of one former merchant, "Leave it to the proprietors to revise the law, and be assured that each will vote for his own wine. There will be but one vote for each, . . . [and] in the end, they will all be in the first rank."

The potential for such alteration and its consequent disruption of the Bordeaux wine trade was immediately recognized by the members of the Chamber of Commerce. They saw how a display of the region's wines at the Universal Exposition in Paris, *in an exhibit arranged by the proprietors themselves,* could serve as a pretext for adjusting the system of established relative values, and one can imagine the anxiety of those whose fortunes were closely connected with the wine trade's smooth and steady operation.

Thus, when the Chamber of Commerce met on December 13, Duffour-Dubergier's committee report on how the wines of the region might benefit from participation in the Universal Exposition in Paris focused closely on this aspect of the question. But this was not all: other aspects posed potential problems for merchants and proprietors alike, indeed, for everyone for whom the reputation of Bordeaux's wines were a matter of pride and commercial consequence. The observations made by Duffour-Dubergier's committee were compelling enough to be adopted by the entire Chamber of Commerce, and formed the basis for the letter that was sent to the Departmental Committee on the following day:

> Sirs,
>
> In your letter of November 28 last you paid us the honor of consulting us on the practical means to employ in order that the riches of France's vineyards be represented at the Universal Exposition of 1855.
>
> Just as with the Departmental Committee, the Chamber of Commerce believes that this solemn occasion should not be missed to remind our compatriots, and especially foreigners, that in the production of wine, France, and the Gironde in particular, is one of the most favored regions in the world. But, we hasten to add, it is only in the general and national interest that the presence of French wines [at the Exposition] appears to us to be useful. If, however, it serves to favor particular interests, or if, no less grave, the proprietors of a particular region seek to profit from

> the Exposition to mount a fight among themselves with the aim of destroying a classification based on the experience of long years, we would not hesitate to declare that it would be better, in our view, that none of our wines appear in the Exposition.

There could be no question of allowing anything as ephemeral as a trade fair in Paris to disrupt the foundations on which an entire industry was based; the members of the Chamber would doubtless have considered themselves derelict in their responsibilities toward the commercial interests of Bordeaux had they allowed the status quo of the city's wine trade to crumble under an assault from what they termed "particular interests." However, this question was not the only problem presented by the Exposition. The Chamber's letter went on to examine another potential pitfall:

> A competition, properly called, cannot take place among wines without a tasting. Now, to whom is this delicate operation to be entrusted? We are the first to acknowledge the profound abilities and varied knowledge possessed by the members of the Exposition's jury, but who imagines that their opinion regarding the quality of a wine is authoritative? In the trade, tastings are conducted by specialists possessed of great experience, who assure that these events are undertaken with the greatest of precautions; even so, it occurs that they occasionally err. These mistakes are regrettable, without doubt, but how much more harmful would the consequences be were they to come from a jury called to deliver its verdict before the entire world?
>
> A tasting, therefore, seems fraught with danger, and we would like to believe that you share our opinion in this regard.
>
> Thus, given this situation, and after much deliberation, it appears to the Bordeaux Chamber of Commerce that [as regards a tasting of] the wines from our department, an abstention would be best.
>
> They should be exhibited out of competition, first because they share no similarity with any others; next, because (as with most other wines) they draw their principal qualities from the soil which has produced them. Without forgetting that our wines owe much to the manner in which the grapes are grown and the care they receive once harvested, one cannot help acknowledging that it is nature alone which is almost completely responsible for the result. Thus, what right has the proprietor to a reward, to an honor? None, we think.
>
> Given this, it would be best to request that the mayor of each town in our department send the Committee a certain number of bottles of wine to represent that locality's production at the Exposition, but in light of what we said at the beginning, these bottles should carry only the name of the town from which the wine has come, and, if considered useful, the vintage year—but not any designation of property or proprietor.
>
> As for our classed growths, reds or whites, they would appear at the Exposition under their own names, to which could be added that of the town in which the grapes were harvested; the proprietor's name should not appear, in order to avoid any individual competition and all conflicts of self-esteem.

> Above the location where the wines are to be displayed would appear a chart on which the information inscribed on the bottles would be reproduced. A second chart would present the classification and the approximate price of the wines with a brief summary concerning the growing conditions, production and marketing of Bordeaux's wines, edited by the city's union of brokers.
>
> If our ideas were to be adopted, it would be important that all our classed growths, up to the fifths included, be represented; the absence of even one of these would present serious problems; as much as possible, one should be able to take in at a glance the collective production of the Gironde's vineyards. That, in our opinion, would be the main advantage to be gained for our wines from the forthcoming Exposition.
>
> What we have just said, as you can appreciate, Sirs, applies particularly to red wines; but there is nothing to prevent measures similar to these being taken concerning white wines, although the division in five classes is not as well established as that for red wines.
>
> As the quantities of wine sent would be too small for each proprietor to secure its return, we think that after the close of the Exposition a gift could be made of them all to the General Hospital of Paris.

This was what the Departmental Committee had needed from the start: a detailed plan of action from an authoritative source for effectively including the region's wines among the goods representing the Gironde. Everything was here, from the method by which the wines should be collected and displayed, to a charitable means of disposing of what was left. Unfortunately, despite its comprehensiveness, the Departmental Committee still did not get it.

On December 14, the day the Chamber of Commerce returned its opinion, all ten members of the Departmental Committee met and heard the Chamber's suggestions read by Legrix de Lassalle. Then the floor was opened for discussion.

One Member (in keeping with the anonymity-enhancing style favored by recording secretaries of the period) found it unacceptable to exhibit wines without a tasting; since a satisfactory judging (i.e., one without risk) was both impossible and impractical, any display that the Committee might mount would be little more than a collection of bottles, not wine. Under such circumstances, he concluded, it would be better were the Committee to refrain from sending any of the region's wines to Paris.

Another Member, seeing a danger in abstention, argued (incorrectly) that officially the Committee was only an intermediary whose duty was not to reject anything in its entirety; by failing to organize a comprehensive display of the region's wines, it risked having individual producers mount a partial exhibition of their own. (This Member was wrong on both counts: the Committee's primary duty was to judge the quality of potential exhibits and only accept those of superior merit; and, according to the regulations of the Imperial Commission, the Departmental Committee alone was authorized to submit items for display in the Universal Exposition.)

Someone Else found it unacceptable that foreign visitors to the Exposition would find wines from Champagne and Burgundy but none from Bordeaux. A display must be mounted, This Member argued, one that was collective in nature, and which, above all, avoided the individual identification of any particular producer's wine.

So if a display were to be organized, Another Member added returning to an earlier point, it would have to feature something to attract the eye; which meant that despite the shortcomings of exhibiting bottles without a tasting the containers were definitely necessary, since any exhibit consisting of only the proposed charts would be much less distinctive than the bottles themselves.

The general opinion seemed to conclude that the only practical solution was a collective display, similar to the one organized for the 1851 Crystal Palace Exhibition by the Lyon Chamber of Commerce which represented the talents of that city's silk manufacturers. However, enough confusion still surrounded the question for A Member to propose what was becoming the standard approach to Departmental Committee decision making: delay responding to the Chamber of Commerce until it had written to the Imperial Commission in Paris. In effect, the Imperial Commission would be asked for its opinion regarding the opinion of the Chamber of Commerce, whose opinion had been requested in order to arrive at an answer to give to the Departmental Committee from the Côte-d'Or. And it was a comprehensive opinion that the Imperial Commission would be asked to give: the admissibility of a collective exhibition for the wines of the Gironde, how such an exhibition should be organized, whether the tasting of wines was mandatory, and the whole question regarding the system of classification to be used—in other words, to comment on, and possibly alter the delicate balance whose preservation was the Chamber of Commerce's primary concern.

It was bad enough that questions important to the Bordeaux wine trade had found themselves in the hands of locals who had no idea of their consequence; now it was being proposed to send the matter off to Paris, beyond the influence of those who had an understanding of its importance. The risk was just too great: Another Member (quite possibly Nathaniel Johnston, who was one of the four people on the Chamber of Commerce whose report formed the basis of the letter sent to the Departmental Committee), stated that he believed he could assure the Committee of the Chamber of Commerce's willingness to place itself at their disposition in organizing the exhibition of the department's wines.

The Chamber of Commerce would likely have preferred it had the Departmental Committee been in contact immediately upon receiving the inquiry from the Côte-d'Or, in order to have had a free hand in arranging the exhibition of Bordeaux's wines according to the outline proposed in its letter, without involving the proprietors in the task of organizing a display of their wines; now it would be inheriting a process that was badly begun. This was clearly an inconvenience, but not insurmountable. The important thing was to prevent any further close calls of such dire commercial consequence. One way or another, it would be best if from now on the Chamber of Commerce arranged this part of the exhibition of products from the Gironde.

On December 28, two weeks after sending its letter of advice to the Departmental Committee, the Chamber of Commerce received a response, and on January 10, 1855, in the first meeting of the new year, the Chamber addressed itself to this latest correspondence as the seventh order of business on that day's agenda.

The Departmental Committee's letter bore no traces of the confusion or hesitation that marked its deliberations on December 14. Its tone was authoritative, the actions it proposed were clearly marked out; in fact, the proposals sounded just like those in the Chamber of Commerce's December 13 opinion.

The Committee announced that, in light of the Chamber's advice, it had reached several definitive decisions regarding the exhibition of the region's wines: first, the wines of Bordeaux would definitely be sent to the Universal Exposition; the wines would be displayed in as complete a collection as possible; and that it was clearly understood that in no way should this exhibition disturb the commercially established order of quality—all trademarks, labels, or any indications that would contribute to competition among the various wines and a consequent disruption of the trade's long-established classification were to be rejected.

To achieve this result, the letter continued, the Departmental Committee looked to the assistance of an organization that legitimately represented the interests of Bordeaux's wine trade through its activity as intelligent and indispensable mediators between producer and consumer: namely, the Bordeaux Chamber of Commerce. The Chamber would be responsible for collecting samples of the various wines produced throughout the Gironde, for numbering them uniformly with labels bearing the Chamber of Commerce's name, and for creating a chart corresponding with the number on each bottle to indicate the various types of wines. Should a tasting be necessary, any awards would be bestowed upon the region's production in general, and not upon individual wines. To assure that the importance of this was well understood, a person representing the collection of wines could be placed at the jury's disposition. Furthermore, the Departmental Committee wholeheartedly agreed with the idea of donating all excess wines at the end of the Exposition.

The Departmental Committee's letter finished with the following thought:

> Please take into account, Sirs, that this event has attracted the attention of a great number of proprietors, several of whom have raised hopes which can in no way be satisfied; a strong and impartial stand must be taken in the face of these pretensions; it is our endeavor to uphold the interests of this vast trade, which you so admirably represent.

> The Committee hopes that for all of these reasons, you will decide to lend us your full and efficient assistance.

The Departmental Committee had completely and officially delegated the organization of the region's wines to the Chamber of Commerce, having acceded to each and every one of its proposals, down to the donation of the leftover wine to the Paris General Hospital. (This philanthropic gesture would lead one observer to quip that "among drunkards and gourmets, accommodations at the hospital will be at a premium that day.") More importantly, the Chamber was specifically instructed to safeguard the system of classification, which had inadvertently been placed in jeopardy. The Chamber's minutes for this meeting noted that it "allies itself completely with the views expressed in this letter," and well might it have done so: the Departmental Committee's letter could not have been more satisfactory to the Chamber of Commerce had it been written by the Chamber of Commerce itself.

Months later, when the Departmental Committee had finished its work of evaluating the products that would constitute the Gironde's participation in the Universal Exposition, Legrix de Lassalle prepared the Committee's report for the Prefect. It offered the official version of how the wines of the Gironde had come to be represented in Paris:

> A new and very important question for our department presented itself. Was it appropriate, in the midst of this universal competition of the world's riches, to forget the principal and the most important of our productions?
>
> While Champagne, Burgundy and many other regions prepared the most exquisite of their products, could the Gironde rest indifferent and rest in peace on its secular renown? The Committee did not think so. A great number of proprietors, called together by our efforts, shared this view and offered us their cooperation. However, in entering into the details of execution, [the Committee] was not long in recognizing the inconveniences presented by an exposition without unity and offering but several samples of the department's products. It was especially necessary to carefully ensure that this event not become the occasion for any disturbance of the classification of our wines, that personal interest not be substituted for the general interest, and that the advantage that belonged to everyone not turn to the profit of several individuals. . . .
>
> The Committee [believed that a collective exhibit] would be perfect for the wines of the Gironde, and to put it in practice we addressed ourselves to the direct and legal representatives of the trade, intelligent and obliging intermediaries between production and consumption; we solicited the cooperation of the Bordeaux Chamber of Commerce.

This flexibility with events was not of great importance; what mattered most was that the Chamber of Commerce now had the authority for organizing the wines to be sent to Paris. Now things could proceed in a quick and orderly manner. Everything was under control.

Three

THE CLASSIFICATIONS BEFORE "THE CLASSIFICATION"

In its letter to the Departmental Committee, the Chamber of Commerce made clear its distress at the prospect of the Committee's work "destroying a classification based on the experience of long years." What exactly was this classification that was the object of so careful a defense?

It is human nature to try to fashion order out of chaos by establishing a system of results based on a series of causes. Commerce, like all human endeavors, imposes its own order on events to explain its past actions and simplify its future undertakings; the classification of the Gironde's wines was the result of just such a process, evolving with the region's trade as it developed over time.

From Bordeaux's early role during the first century B.C. as an expediter of wines in transit from Mediterranean vineyards, the city's importance grew with the planting of its own vines and an increased exportation of locally made wines. By the thirteenth century, these wines were contributing to a thriving local commerce whose influence went far beyond the city's boundaries and would help establish Bordeaux as the region's capital city.

This region, known today as the Gironde, was a principal part of the duchy of Aquitaine, which came under England's rule for 300 years beginning in 1154. As the foremost French port controlled by the English, Bordeaux was ideally situated to supply the wine needs of the British home territories: its position near the mouth of the Gironde estuary gave direct access to the Atlantic Ocean and from there north to the English Channel.

Bordeaux's location gave it a domestic advantage as well: the city's site on the Garonne River effectively required vineyards planted further inland to sell their wines on the Bordeaux marketplace if they were to reach the Atlantic and the export markets beyond. There was, however, a catch: a series of ever-more lucrative privileges granted to Bordeaux's own vineyard owners prevented upriver wines from entering the marketplace until well after the locally available product had been sold to the English. In a similar manner, the downriver territory of the Médoc was prohibited from shipping wines directly to the sea, which had the secondary result of hampering the development of that region's vineyards for several centuries. Having restricted the availability of competing wines and thus practically guaranteeing the sale of their entire annual production at the most profitable terms possible, the Bordeaux landowners sought to further capitalize on the situation by steadily extending their vineyard plantings to the limits of the city's jurisdiction; this encompassed the Graves and Sauternes regions to the south, as well as Bourg, Blaye, and the Entre-deux-Mers to the east—in all, an area roughly corresponding to the administrative department of the Gironde today. The region's other main river, the Dordogne, also offered direct access to the sea, which allowed vineyards planted in its vicinity to bypass Bordeaux and its attendant restrictions; this circumstance would eventually lead to the development of Libourne as a secondary commercial center endowed with similar commercial privileges to handle the sale of wines from neighboring communes such as Saint-Emilion and Pomerol.

The wines particularly favored in the British market were the "clarets" it was Bordeaux's vocation to produce. These were light red in color and simple in character, intended for current consumption since the methods that enabled a wine to age were still practically unknown. At the height of its reign in the fourteenth century, England had a virtual monopoly on the wines that passed through Bordeaux's port, but this commercial predominance ended when Aquitaine returned to French control in 1453. An ensuing trade war between Britain and France and a concomitant series of tariffs against imports of French wine did little to help Bordeaux's commerce with its traditional best client. With the loss of its principal foreign market, the region's exports fell dramatically, but during the next 100 years Bordeaux's fortunes would rise again as the vacuum in trade left by the English eventually came to be filled by the Dutch.

Although longtime clients of Bordeaux wine, Dutch purchases were relatively small given the English domination of the marketplace. However, as European history ran its course, England's departure from France happened to be followed by the Netherlands' "Golden Century," a period beginning in the 1500s which saw that country become the major commercial power in Europe (and hence, the world) through the creation of a navy and merchant fleet without rival among nations. This enabled the Dutch to establish new markets throughout the world and to supply those markets with goods bought and resold from all over the globe—goods such as wine from the Bordeaux region. Acceding to the role of Bordeaux's new principal client, the Netherlands' volume of purchases (and its influence in both

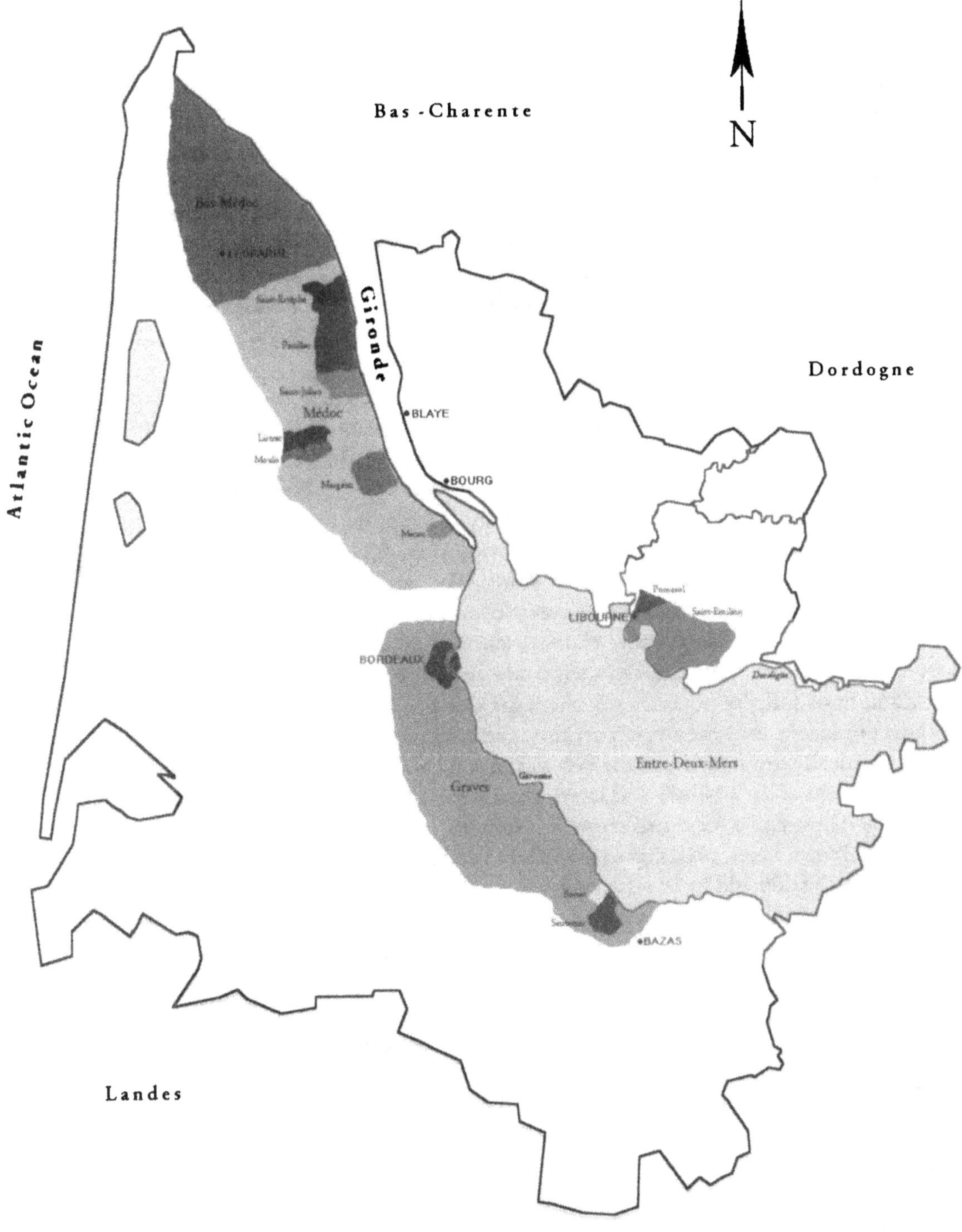

The Vineyards of Bordeaux

marketplace and vineyard) was much greater than that ever realized by England. It was all a question of scale: when the English were the region's major buyers, they were mostly buying for their home market; when the Dutch were buying wine, they were buying for the world.

The domestic Dutch market (as well as that of neighboring countries in northern Europe that were supplied by Dutch shipping) was characterized by a preference for white wines, often dry but usually semisweet; to satisfy this demand, Dutch merchants used their considerable influence as the region's major buyers to persuade proprietors who had traditionally made light-red "clarets" in areas such as Barsac and Sauternes to turn their production over to sweeter white wines.

Deep red wines, known as "black wines" because of their intense color and richness, were also of interest to Dutch merchants, not for consumption by their compatriots back home, but for export to colonies and markets across the globe. These wines (rather disparagingly referred to as "cargo" wines in the Bordeaux trade, owing to a primary concern with their "shipability" as opposed to their "drinkability") became a mainstay of the region's production. One leading merchant explained their traditional utility in these terms: "For cargo or for ocean shipping choose wines as full-colored and firm as possible, capable of standing up to the long voyage and the heat of the burning climates where they are transported. For this sort of employ good Palus and côtes wines are almost always used, because their color and basic fullness perfectly suit them for this purpose." When cargo wines became popular in the seventeenth century, the land best suited to produce their characteristically dense style was the rich fluvial soil known as the "Palus," located along the banks of the Gironde and Dordogne rivers. The fertile nature of this terrain made it best suited for cereal crops, but spurred on by the growing market for robust, full-blown wines, plantings in the Palus were converted from grains to vines. So great was the demand by Dutch merchants for Palus wines, that they were often the region's most expensive.

The English commercial influence, while greatly reduced, was by no means absent at this time and the traditional preference for the lighter, claret style of wine continued to define the primary scope of their purchases. Although considered superior in quality by the Bordeaux wine trade, these clarets were still slightly less expensive than the more sought after Palus wines. It was the Graves region that was renowned for the quality of its claret, as was, to a lesser extent, the gravelly outcrops in the still underexploited vineyards of the Médoc. These regions, whose purpose as producers of finer-quality wines remained fairly constant, retained the bulk of what was left of the British market, while other vineyard areas sought to meet the qualitatively different, but nonetheless lucrative, needs of the Dutch.

Each region's wines, being fundamentally different in character, and selling to fundamentally different markets, sold for prices that were, naturally enough, fundamentally different from each other. A price structure thus evolved based on the classic commercial tension between buyers and sellers, in this case defined by the amount particular nationalities were willing or able to pay for their wines according to their needs, and the amount for which the winemakers were willing to sell according to the expense of their production. These prices were fairly standardized throughout a region, and although an area's better winemakers could command more (and winemakers of poorer quality might receive less), a benchmark figure was able to be established which gave buyers and sellers a point from which their negotiations for a final selling price might proceed.

In the fall of 1647,

> the scarcity of wine was general; there was less than half of what was available the previous year. In Holland, Flanders, Scotland, Ireland, England, all along the coast of Germany and in all of the countries of the North there was a dearth of wheat, and, in consequence, of beer. Wine and even *eaux de vie,* were spoilt to the point where they were not fit to drink; cider was equally lacking, due to the caterpillars having eaten away at all the fruit trees throughout almost all of France. All of this brought to the port and harbor [of Bordeaux] a flotilla of foreign vessels excessively large in comparison with other years, all come to load up with wine.

This exceptional situation, chronicled by a contemporary Bordeaux municipal official, was a boon to the region's winemakers.

Unlike the conditions that beset farms and orchards in the northern parts of Europe, the vineyards of southwestern France enjoyed a different growing season in 1647: winemakers throughout the Bordeaux region produced "a prodigious quantity" that year, six thousand tuns recorded in Preignac and Barsac alone. There was, however, one problem: although the foreign buyers were present in Bordeaux, as was the wine that they eagerly wanted, no sales could be made because prices had yet to be set. According to regulations enacted in 1635, prices for each year's new wine were to be determined at an annual assembly held at the city hall, an event that had to take place by St. Michael's Day, September 29. That year St. Michael's Day had come and gone with neither this assembly having taken place nor prices having been established for the region's wines.

Although the situation was an inconvenience for the foreign buyers, this delay presented Bordeaux's winemakers with more serious consequences: each passing day brought them closer to November 11, the date when the upriver wines that local producers had managed to exclude from the market through their system of privileges would have the right to enter the city. This would put these wines in direct competition with local production and, by increasing the quantities available, inevitably drive prices down.

In order to stave off this unwelcome eventuality, on October 21 the Bordeaux Jurade—a sort of municipal council endowed with executive powers, whose authority extended throughout the city's wide-ranging jurisdiction—summoned mayors, councilors, judges, and prominent producers from throughout the district to appear at a special session of the Jurade to take place four days later at the Bordeaux City Hall. On October 25 the assembled officials were told that the meeting was to be delayed for one day so that the provincial governor who had just returned from a voyage could attend. The following day saw no appearance by the governor, and the chief jurat assured the increasingly restive assembly that with or without the governor, the matter would be determined the following day.

Accordingly, on October 27, with the provincial governor still absent and after a brief delay caused by a dispute between the judges from the Entre-Deux-Mers and Blaye as to which of the two had precedence, the "first jurat very eloquently explained the necessity of fixing the price of the jurisdiction's wines . . . basing his reasons on the wine brokers' regulations requiring each member of the assembly to state the appropriate price to place on the wines from each quarter of the jurisdiction. Thereupon, each of those convoked, one after the other, gave his opinion, after which the jurats ordered and fixed the prices of the wines of 1647. . . ."

These deliberations resulted in a decree establishing minimum and maximum prices for that year's production. (For this classification and all others mentioned throughout this chapter, see Appendix I.) The Jurade's intent was not to establish a qualitative classification of the region's wines, nor did it fabricate prices. The Jurade simply used its authority to expedite a commercial practice first begun three decades earlier. Similar price lists were probably drawn up in the years prior to 1647—the fact that the annual assembly to establish prices was late in being convened meant that the results of that year's deliberations were recorded in the Jurade's records, which survive today. Thus, although the Jurade did not intend to establish a qualitative classification, their decree is generally acknowledged as the first attempt at classifying the wines of the Gironde and, as such, established the general patterns that would characterize later efforts.

The Jurade's system of classification is rather simple, using entire regions as the basis for differentiation among wines. Individual producers had not yet established distinct commercial identities that informed the purchases of the average wine drinker (although this was shortly to change). Although some members of the British wine trade had begun to make distinctions based on particular proprietors as early as the latter part of the fifteenth century, this specialized information was generally the province of merchants on the spot in Bordeaux; in the mid-seventeenth century, knowledgeable consumers (and most of the merchants who catered to them) were still likely to limit their demands to a wine that conformed to a regional style, since common trade practice involved blending various producers' wines to achieve a standard, uniform character. The Jurade's deliberation reflected this commercial state of affairs in the degree of detail contained in its classification.

The higher prices paid for the Palus wines reflected the insufficiency of supply in light of the great demand by Dutch merchants, not necessarily the qualitative merits of these areas' production. The prices for the white wines of Langon,

Bommes, and Sauternes, as well as Barsac, Preignac, Pujols, and Fargues (all in the Sauternes region), were a function of not only the great Dutch demand for these semidry and sweet white wines, but their quality as well: these were the wines that the Dutch and their northern neighbors themselves preferred and drank, not the cargo wines that were bought only to be shipped off to some distant colonial market where the consumers were happy with anything potable they could get.

The British influence on the Bordeaux marketplace is reflected in two categories in which prices are quoted in pounds. No longer the region's principal customer, Britain's interest in quality focused its commercial activity on the vineyard areas that had demonstrated a propensity for producing wines with the characteristic finesse favored by the British middle class. For red wines this was the Graves and Médoc, while Britain's white wine purchases centered on Barsac, Preignac, Pujols, and Fargues. In these two categories of the Jurade's list, the high-end prices were quoted in pounds, reflecting the British demand for the top-quality wines they produced. Wines of lesser quality from these communes and regions were quoted in ecus, as was the case for all the production in the rest of Bordeaux's vineyards. Unlike the Dutch, British merchants sought quality over quantity, a fact acknowledged in a report by the French Commercial Council:

> No nation in the universe trades more nobly. It is a generally recognized truth that in all the places where the British land they make a great many purchases, raising the price of goods and merchandise and seeking out those which are the most expensive and most perfect. This method is in contrast to that of the Dutch, who spend frugally, are accustomed to great savings, and are less attentive to the quality of what they buy than to its low price.

Competition among British merchants for wines of the finest quality could be quite active, a state of affairs reflected on by the physician, philosopher, and wine connoisseur John Locke during his visit to Bordeaux in 1677: "A tun of the best wine at Bourdeaux, which is that of Médoc or Pontac, is worth . . . 80 or even 100 crowns. For this the English may thank their own folly for, whereas some years since the same wine was sold for 50 or 60 crowns per tun, the fashionable sending over orders to have the best wine sent them at any rate, they have, by striving who should get it, brought it up to that price." In short, "the English love to raise the market on themselves."

In latter-seventeenth-century England, as indicated by Locke, two wines enjoyed commercial prominence: Médoc and Pontac. The Médoc was just consolidating its young reputation for quality with a growing number of vineyards planted on gravelly outcrops similar to those found in the benchmark region for fine wine, the Graves; "Pontac" referred to a property in the Graves district itself, owned by Arnaud de Pontac, president of the Bordeaux parliament and one of the region's wealthiest individuals. The vineyard, today known as Château Haut-Brion, benefited greatly from its proprietor's financial resources: the funds made available for ever better vineyard conditions and winemaking techniques contributed to a constant improvement in the quality of its wines. This improvement did not go unnoticed among England's wine drinkers: a 1663 reference to the wine in the diaries of Samuel Pepys indicates that it had established an identity for itself among London's connoisseurs. Pontac himself intervened to help his wine become more renowned in the English capital by establishing a tavern called "The Pontac's Head" shortly after the great fire of 1666; it soon became one of the city's more fashionable public houses and succeeded greatly in furthering Haut-Brion's popularity.

As the "locomotive" that pulled a certain segment of Bordeaux's production along with it, Haut-Brion in particular and Graves wines in general came to define for the English the characteristics that a wine of quality was expected to possess. The commercial success of Pontac's initiative led to several developments in both England and Bordeaux: English wine drinkers became more appreciative of the qualities inherent in a particular proprietor's efforts, the areas defining quality wine production became more specific, and the idea of *terroir,* or terrain (that combination of influences including—but not limited to—soil composition, climate, and topography), began to develop a greater importance among wine drinkers and producers alike. As it became better understood that the gravelly topsoil typical to the region south of Bordeaux contributed to a wine's quality, other areas exhibiting a similar terrain were sought after for development.

To the north, the Médoc proved sufficiently attractive in this regard to encourage the creation of new vineyards during an eighteenth-century "furor of planting" which saw the veritable birth of this region as a major wine-producing area. With the gravelly outcrops of the Médoc valued because of their similarity to the best Graves terrain, it was evident that the proprietors of these new vineyards would follow the older region's lead and attempt to produce wines comparable in character to those most favored by the English. Similar grape varieties and winemaking methods were employed, but because of the unique characteristics of the Médoc's terrain, its wines, while sharing a familial resemblance to those from the Graves, were individual enough to establish their own reputation for quality on the English market. So although Graves wines did not decrease in quality, the increasingly superior prices obtained by producers in the Médoc simply reflected the greater commercial favor these new wines enjoyed. This development did not go unnoticed in the Graves: "The Médoc is a canton in favor: the wine which is gathered there is very much in fashion and to the English taste. The Proprietors in our Graves have looked on with jealousy at the favor the Médoc wines have enjoyed during the last thirty or forty years."

Other regions throughout the Gironde were also capable of producing claret-style wines, but, owing to the influence of their terrain, their character was different—not necessarily inferior; as a result, these wines enjoyed neither the same fashion nor favor in England, nor could they command the same high prices. Thus the production of vineyards in other areas, such as the territory around the town of Libourne (Saint-Emilion and Pomerol in particular) and the *côtes* of Bourg and Blaye, was usually shunted to the (qualitatively) secondary Dutch market. The producers in these regions came to embrace the cargo style of winemaking, with the apparently sound reasoning that it was better to give the Dutch the type of product they wanted and obtain prices near the high end of that market, rather than to sell a better wine to a less-satisfied English clientele and be remunerated on the lower end of their price scale. By the early years of the nineteenth century, this situation had become institutionalized; as noted by one respected member of the Bordeaux wine trade who specialized in wines from the left bank of the Gironde:

> St. Emilion has several growths which show a marked preference over other communes' basic wines, but in a comparison with those of our Graves these St. Emilion first growths can only compete with [relatively minor properties]. By this I mean to say that there is no wine in St. Emilion as distinguished as. . . La Mission in the Graves. In general, it is the merchants in Libourne who buy these wines. As regards their price, in those years where our own wines are expensive [1,000 to 2,400 francs for first growths], first quality wines from over there sell for only 500 & 550 francs.

The commercial policy adopted by the Libournais winemakers in the 1600s would haunt the Saint-Emilion and Pomerol vineyards for centuries to come.

With the evolution of commercial tastes and the shifting fortunes of the region's vineyards came a change in the prices merchants were willing to pay for the different wines offered in the Bordeaux marketplace, and new classifications arose which took into account these evolving conditions. In the 1740s, a document drawn up by the Bordeaux Chamber of Commerce for the Intendant of Guyenne (as the Gironde was known at this time) classified the region's wines in a manner that showed how far circumstances had come since the Jurade's deliberations one century earlier. Entitled "State of the parishes from which are made the wines of the district of Bordeaux and their differences in price," the document's purpose was to furnish the Intendant with sufficient information to ascertain the economic state of the communes under his jurisdiction. Once again, there was no intent to establish a classification among wines based on relative quality; the prices obtained by each commune's production were of prime importance, not the excellence that those prices reflected. As such, the hierarchy established here was relatively free from the influences of self-promotion that were likely to result in an overestimation of the value of a particular producer's wine. Indeed, it would probably have been in the producers' interest for the standing of their area to be *underestimated,* since this sort of survey was often undertaken by Intendants to ascertain how much taxation a commune could afford to sustain. Nevertheless, the document's inadvertent value as a classification of the Gironde's wines is significant in several respects.

The number of communes listed as wine-producing entities is much greater and more detailed than was the case in 1647. Instead of a global listing of simply "Graves and Médoc," there were now twenty communal subdivisions for the former and nineteen for the latter. Many of these areas (particularly in the Graves) were planted with vines at the time of the Jurade's deliberations in 1647, but the distinctive character possessed by each of their wines was not recognized to the same degree, if at all; the intervening years saw the evolution of a more finely tuned assessment of the qualities particular to specific types of terrain.

The human element was also a factor, as differences in communal winemaking standards contributed in setting the price a locality obtained for its production. The prices commanded by flagship properties such as Haut-Brion in Pessac or Lafite in Pauillac might well trickle down and influence purchases on a communal level; but since the majority of an area's winemakers were small landowners, the quality of their practices also influenced the overall appreciation (and prices) that a commune enjoyed in the trade. This is reflected in one merchant's contemporary observations: "The peasant's wine must be bought pretty early, to never let to lie long on their hands after the purchase, as they will be apt to *ullage* with Beverage or other bad Wine; some of the better peasants in Cantenac & Margaux will not be so apt to ullage with bad wines as many in low Médoc." The knowledge that *ullage*, or the topping off of a cask as its contents evaporated during storage, was less likely to be done with inferior wine did no harm to the reputations of Cantenac and Margaux, the price of their wines, and their consequent standing in communal classifications.

Another development to be found in the Intendant's document is the use of the term *cru* as a categorical division to group together the expanding number of wine-producing entities. If it was no longer sufficient to simply state that Graves wines sold in a certain range of prices, a method for comparing their more finely tuned distinctions had to be devised. Thus, wines from communes selling for a similar price were now grouped together in the same cru, or growth.

This "classification" of the Gironde's wines was sufficiently detailed to meet the governmental needs for which it was commissioned, but the requirements of the wine trade were becoming more exacting. Arnaud de Pontac's initiatives in the 1660s made clear to both merchants and consumers alike that a wine's quality was directly linked to a proprietor's particular efforts. To properly trace the effects of this relationship, a more detailed classification was necessary.

Two documents suggest that during the next three decades the classification did evolve to meet the wine trade's needs. The first item, a list entitled "Price of wines in good years from 1745 and after" was broadly organized by commune, as were the lists from the Jurade and the Intendant; however, this was not the criterion by which prices were assigned. This classification was based on a more detailed assessment, and the notion of cru was applied not to entire communes, but to particular properties. Still, although more specific than the two earlier classifications, this ranking by individual property was intracommunal, with each locality possessing its own first, second, third, and even fourth growths. Depending on the sales price of a commune's best wine, the others that followed were assigned their relative standing. Thus, in Margaux and Cantenac, where a wine selling for 1,000 to 1,300 francs per tun was only a second growth because of the higher price commanded by the Château (Margaux), this price would have earned it a first-growth status in almost every other communal classification. (Several models of such intracommunal rankings exist, usually as a base for establishing local taxation—a 1795 list for Cantenac is one such example—and vestiges of this intracommunal system of classification continued to exist well into the twentieth century: as late as the 1940s, it was not unusual to find a wine from Pomerol, for instance—an area that has never established an official classification for its wines—styling itself a first growth on its label.)

The second document suggesting the same development of a classification by individual properties instead of by commune bears the title "First known classification of the wines of Guienne, executed in 1776 according to the prices they had then, [drawn up] on the order of Mr. Dupré de St. Maur, Intendant at this epoch." Here, like the document "from 1745 and after" (whose dating suggests an advance of thirty years on this "first known classification"), individual properties are named, arranged in order of the sales price of their wines, and grouped by commune.

Both of these documents suggest the classification's passage through a transitional stage in its development from a comparison of communes to a global comparison of properties throughout the Gironde, but, unfortunately, not much more of an exact nature can be reliably drawn from them, at least as regards the relative standing of the properties they list. The reason is that neither document is contemporary with the period about which it reports. The first, although drawing on information from as early as 1745, was written at least seven decades later. Evidence of this comes in several of the property names: for example, Degasq Palmer (at the end of the third growths for Margaux and Cantenac) refers to the property originally called Degasq which was bought by Major General Charles Palmer and served as the anchor for subsequent purchases which eventually came to constitute his eponymous vineyard. However, Degasq was purchased in June 1814, and there is no trace of any important property bearing the name Palmer in eighteenth-century Cantenac. Similarly, the listing "Barbos, Palmer" among the fourth growths refers to a later acquisition made by the General sometime after 1816.

The other work, the "First known classification of the wines of Guienne, executed in 1776," presents several problems of its own, the greatest being that it is a second-hand transcription written more than one-half century after the original document on which it is based. A preface gives an explanation of the origins for the classification that it introduces: "immediately after" being installed as Intendant of Guyenne in August 1776, Dupré de St. Maur began compiling information for

"Turgot, then Minister of Finance... to establish a *single tax,* based on the [region's] agricultural products.... From this enterprise was naturally born a classification...."

The classification in question comprises nineteen pages which list the names of proprietors for the major properties in the Médoc, Graves, and Palus. Here, as with the "1745 and after" classification, the overall arrangement is by commune, with properties ranked within each according to the sales price of their wines. In addition to merely copying the original document, the editor attempted an addition to Dupré de St. Maur's work: "... I will transcribe the work that was done and I shall make known, to the extent possible, the names of the current proprietors who have succeeded those who were the owners at that period." Unfortunately, several errors and glosses introduced into the document (perhaps due to the fact that it was written some sixty-five years after the state of the commerce to which it refers) make its use as an authoritative classification somewhat unreliable. For instance, one property in Saint-Laurent—the future fifth-growth Camensac—is listed as being owned by Popp in 1776, even though the document's editor states in an accompanying note that "This property was formed since the Revolution...," an event that would not arrive for another thirteen years. What is important, however, is that the original listing presented the properties in an intracommunal format, whereas by the nineteenth century intercommunal classifications had become the style. Thus, although certain weaknesses in the "1745" and "1776" documents make it risky to depend on them as authoritative classifications on which the relative quality of individual properties can be reliably based, their common format strongly suggests that intracommunal rankings were a phase in the classification's development by the second half of the eighteenth century. Evidence of the classification's final major development, a global comparison of crus that went beyond communal boundaries, would come from two sources, both contemporary to the period they chronicle and both foreign.

In 1786, William Eden was appointed by George III of Great Britain to negotiate a comprehensive trade treaty with the French court of Louis XVI. The aim was to open both nations' markets to a greater variety of goods and establish appropriate tariffs. Among the French products to be included in the treaty was wine—which for the British market meant Bordeaux. As an aid in his negotiations, Eden made use of an analysis giving production figures for those wines regularly sold in London. This was an unsigned document, written in English, which displayed a considerable familiarity with the Bordeaux wine trade, and featured a transcription of the classification currently in use. Beginning with a list of "The 1st growths," yields were offered for Château Margaux, Lafite, Latour, and Haut-Brion, in that order; of these, it was estimated that "at least 2/3ds goes for England." This was followed by a listing of "The Second and Third growths fitt for the London Market," a simple two-column presentation of thirty-seven names which contained neither dividing point between the two classes nor any exact indication of a relative standing for the properties included. The lack of such details, in contrast to the precision regarding price and commercial practice evident elsewhere in the document, suggests that the strict distinction between second and third growths may not have been as well defined as it was to become several decades later. Nonetheless, corroboration for this classification's accuracy appears the following year in the diary of a visitor to Bordeaux.

In the spring of 1787, Thomas Jefferson, then ambassador to France for the newly established United States of America, embarked on a tour which brought him through the southwestern portion of the country. He made a point of visiting Bordeaux, where his catholic interests, combined with an appreciation of the finer aspects of French gastronomy, led him to investigate the region's vineyards and attempt to understand the reasons for the superior character of its wines.

During his stay, Jefferson met Bordeaux's leading merchants and brokers, people whose familiarity with the region's wines was of long date and well founded. They were able to arrange for him to see some of the principal Graves and Médoc vineyards, and his notes of those visits furnish the basis for the classification presented in Appendix I. Although Jefferson's appraisal has been considered authoritative based on his reputation as a connoisseur of fine wines, it is highly unlikely that a visit of less than one week would have given him a sufficient familiarity with the entire region's production to create a detailed and exact classification, which is usually the result of many years' experience. It is much more probable that Jefferson's classification is but the transcription of information imparted to him by the professionals who acted as his hosts. (This is not to say that Jefferson's own observations are without value: from the mass of information that was undoubtedly presented to him, his astute choice of what was important and what was mere tourism gives his three pages of notes on the wines of Bordeaux their especial richness and importance.) On an evidential level, however, Jefferson's comments are of particular interest in establishing a more exact understanding of the degree to which Bordeaux's wines were classified; combined with the document drawn up for William Eden one year earlier, it becomes possible to understand how the classification's structure was a result of the Bordeaux wine trade's needs at this time.

The primary function of the classification that evolved toward the end of the eighteenth century was to facilitate the establishment of opening sales prices for each year's new wines. Rather than attempt to determine a just price on an individual basis for each of the hundreds of properties dealt with by brokers and merchants, it became much more efficient to set the parameters for a vintage's value based on the wines at the high end of the quality scale. These properties provided benchmark indications that helped establish the trade's appraisal of the overall success or failure for a given year's wine; they were sure values, whose demand indicated the degree of commercial interest for the totality of the region's production.

Four properties had obtained this status on the Bordeaux marketplace: Haut-Brion in Pessac, Château Margaux in the commune of Margaux, and Latour and Lafite in Pauillac. In the document dated 1745, these four alone are listed as first growths, sharing an identical sales price unmatched in the Bordeaux marketplace. By the end of the century, their unrivaled status was an established fact, among themselves as well as in the marketplace. Although each constantly strove to produce and sell the finest wine possible, intragrowth rivalry was not yet the consuming preoccupation it would occasionally become; on the contrary, their position as undisputed leaders in the trade led the firsts to adopt a spirit of cooperation remarkable in its transparency. It was not at all unusual in 1820 for Latour's manager, Pierre Lamothe, to write to the winemaker at Lafite: "Today I have begun harvesting at Latour, my dear Eymeric, and as I am not possessed of an innate knowledge, I appeal to your experience for guidance in a chemical operation you have witnessed and that your good judgment has surely grasped in all its detail. Accordingly, I write to ask for a little instruction regarding a test that I would like to make to strengthen the wine, considered rarely firm enough by our buyers. These are the details. . . ." Such cooperation would become increasingly rare in light of growing market pressures on the classification as the nineteenth century progressed.

Once the price for the four first growths was established, it was then possible to extrapolate figures for the rest of the year's production based on a property's standing in the hierarchy. As explained by one prominent Bordeaux merchant, the system worked like this: "Starting with a price of 2400 francs for the first growths, those of the 1st second growths are ordinarily 2100 francs, those of several other second growths a little less than 1900 to 2000 francs, those of 1st third growths from 16 to 1700 francs, those of fourth growths known as Bourgeois Supérieurs from 12 to 1500 francs." Although the price commanded by the first growths would always be markedly superior to the rest, that price was not eternal. The figures cited previously were for years of better quality, but lesser vintages sold for lesser amounts and entailed a proportionate adjustment of that year's overall price structure. Thus, for instance, in 1816 (a vintage one brokerage firm frankly termed "detestable"), first growths sold for 500 francs, while seconds began selling at 450, third growths at the bottom of that class went for 400, and fourth and fifth growths were selling for 380 francs and up.

However, it was not unusual for a first growth to delay setting a price for its wines while it waited to see what the mood of the market would be; in such circumstances, the proportions between growths would work from the bottom up. Shortly after one year's harvest, the manager at Lafite received a preliminary visit from a broker offering 1,000 francs, "telling me that it was the proportion according to the prices that had already been paid. But. . . shortly before this broker came to see me again I learned that one of the proprietors at Léoville (Mr. de Poyferré) had just sold for 800 francs. Thus, when [the broker] returned I asked for 1200 francs." To the manager of the first-growth Lafite, this appeared to be a more just proportion in light of the price attained by the second-growth Léoville, and eventually a price of 1,100 francs was agreed upon.

With such a system in place, everyone in Bordeaux's commercial chain—proprietors, brokers, and merchants—knew more or less where a particular property was positioned in the marketplace, and could thereby establish more reasonable expectations for the outcome of their negotiations. Given the particular circumstances at each property (abundance of the harvest and quantity of wine available, general state of the vines compared with other properties in the same class, a particular proprietor's talents as a negotiator, etc.), the price of a wine might be higher or lower in its particular level of the classification.

Thus, the structure of the Bordeaux classification in the late eighteenth and early nineteenth century had the singular characteristic of being constructed from the top down. The capstone of this hierarchical pyramid was solid and well defined: there were four first growths and they floated immutably above all the others. The framework became less well defined as the distance increased toward its base. In the 1780s when William Eden and Thomas Jefferson were concerned with the structure of the Bordeaux marketplace, the wine trade's classification consisted of three levels; during the early decades of the nineteenth century, there is evidence of five, at which point the indistinctiveness of the second and third growths evident in William Eden's document was transferred to the fourth and fifth growths instead. Volatility was greatest at the lower echelons as well, with properties included or omitted depending on the source for a particular list. (Indeed, for decades there was not even a consensus as to whether or not there was a fifth-growth level—some lists stopped at four classes, others contained five, while a further option was the designation of "first-fourth" and "second-fourth" categories.) Among third growths, there were properties generally acknowledged to have a definite claim to classed-growth status, but not without question as to exactly where they placed—these might appear on some lists as an upper fourth, on others as a middle or lower third, shifting from year to year according to the fortunes of each vintage.

Listings among the second growths were generally more stable; the greatest change in evidence at this level was a slight shuffling of the relative position among the wines habitually found here. This did not, however, preclude the introduction of a new property should the quality of its wine merit it. In the first decades of the nineteenth century, Louis-Joseph-Gaspard d'Estournel, the proprietor of then-fourth-growth Cos-d'Estournel in Saint-Estèphe, embarked upon a concerted (and eventually successful) effort to raise his property to the level of a second. One of Bordeaux's leading brokers noted this intention in his journal with the following comment: "As for Cos. . . [Mr.] Destournel would make a second growth of it—which is not prohibited. . . ." Second growths could sustain a certain variety in their composition, since the overall functioning of the pyramid's price structure was not based on this level of properties. It was the first growths upon which everything depended, and thus the first growths that were the most sacrosanct of classes. Given this basic understanding of the classification's function and the presence of all the components that would figure in the 1855 classification, we can begin to see the outline of a structure that would become more definite with time.

The classification offered by Thomas Jefferson is composed of three levels, as is the one used by William Eden; although Eden's reference contains more than twice as many properties, Jefferson's observations are more specific in assigning a class for those in the second and third levels. Jefferson mentions sixteen wines by name—four first growths, five seconds, and seven thirds. The first growths appear (with variations in spelling and relative position) as they would be listed sixty-seven years later. "Red wines of the 2d quality," according to Jefferson's notes, "are Rozan, belonging to Madame de Rozan, Dabbadie ou Lionville, la Rose, Quirouen, Durfort. . . which sell at 1,000 new." ("Rozan" is today known as Château Rausan-Ségla in Margaux; "Dabbadie ou Lionville" refers to Léoville, a property owned at the time by Monsieur d'Abadie and today divided among Léoville-Las-Cases, Léoville-Poyferré, and Léoville-Barton in Saint-Julien; "la Rose" is Château Gruaud-Larose, also in Saint-Julien; "Quirouen" is a phonetic spelling of Kirwan in the commune of Cantenac; and "Durfort" is a direct reference to Durfort-Vivens in Margaux.) Of the five listed here as second growths, all but one (Kirwan) would maintain that status in 1855.

Jefferson continues: "The 3d class are Calons, Mouton, Gassie, Arboete, Pontette, de Terme, Candale. . . [all selling] at 8 or 900." (Here "Calons" is Calon-Ségur in Saint-Estèphe; "Mouton" is Mouton-Rothschild in Pauillac; "Gassie" makes reference to Rauzan-Gassies in Margaux; "Arboete" was a property spelled Arbouet in contemporary accounts, located in Saint-Julien and today known as Château Lagrange; "Pontette," also in Saint-Julien, was soon after known as "Pontet-Langlois" and eventually as Château Langoa-Barton; "de Terme" more directly identifies Château Marquis de Terme in Margaux; and "Candale" was a property owned by Foix-Candale and today known as Château d'Issan.) These seven properties listed as third growths by Jefferson would be somewhat differently arranged in 1855, with some appearing as seconds (Mouton and Gassies), one as a fourth growth (Marquis de Terme), and the remaining four producers (Calon-Ségur, Lagrange, Langoa-Barton, and d'Issan) unchanged as thirds.

Although not presented in a strict classification, Jefferson mentions several white wines as well; not being as important in the British market as Bordeaux's reds, these are completely absent from William Eden's document. Among those whites considered worthy of note, the production of three communes is of particular interest:

> 1. Sauterne. The best crop belongs to M. Diquem at Bordeaux, or to M. de Salus his son in law, 150 tonneaux at 300 new and 600 old. The next best crop is M. de Fillotte's 100 tonneaux sold at the same price. 2. Prignac. The best is the President du Roy's at Bordeaux. He makes 175 tonneaux, which sell at 300 new & 600 old. . . . 3. Barsac. The best belongs to the President Pichard, who makes 150 tonneaux at 280 new and 600 old. . . . There are other good crops made in the same paroisses of Sauterne, Prignac, & Barsac; but none as good as these.

Once again, the opinions of Jefferson's sources in the trade were to be borne out in 1855: all of these properties would be classed among the first growths, with "Diquem," or d'Yquem as subsequent orthography would have it, ranked first-growth superior. (As for the other properties mentioned, "Fillotte" refers to Château Filhot; "President du Roy's" wine would be known as Suduiraut; and "Pichard" makes reference to Coutet, which had been owned by the family of that name since the late seventeenth century.)

Compared with the much more extensive number of winemakers compiled in 1745—and the document consulted by William Eden just the year before—Jefferson's list of sixteen reds is extremely limited in scope. An analysis of contemporary sales prices has shown that a number of other properties were selling their wines for amounts on a par with those ranked here as second and third growths, and therefore could have made this list. Among those qualifying for inclusion among the seconds would have been Lascombes and Brane-Cantenac (known at this time as Château de Gorse). Candidates for third-growth status might have included Pichon-Longueville, Beychevelle, Branaire-Ducru, Talbot, and Saint-Pierre in Saint-Julien; Malescot-Saint-Exupéry and Desmirail in Margaux; La Tour-Carnet in Saint-Laurent; du Tertre in Arsac; and Giscours in Labarde. These properties all figure in the classification drawn up for William Eden.

Had Jefferson's intention been to transcribe the classification of Bordeaux's wines as it was in effect among the trade in 1787, there is no doubt that his observations would have been much more comprehensive, more similar to the source used by William Eden, so it is inappropriate to fault him for a lack of detail or extensiveness. Although of great value for being among the first to present the hierarchy of Bordeaux's wines in its final format, the "Jefferson classification" was but a second-hand rendering of the commercial state of the trade as it was communicated to him by its initiates. A more authoritative listing would have to come from one of their number. This would be Guillaume Lawton.

The Bordeaux wine trade has traditionally been an affair of fathers and sons, with the paternal–filial chain often extending intact over a half-dozen generations and more. Everything has its beginnings, however, and in the Lawton family of wine brokers the patriarch was Abraham Lawton, who came to Bordeaux from his native Cork in 1739 at the age of twenty-three. Born to a family of Irish wine merchants, it was natural that Lawton would be drawn to a life in this trade; but as the fourth child (and, what is more important, the second son), it was likely that the fortunes in the family business shone most brightly on his elder brother Hugh, Abraham's senior by four and a half years. Given such circumstances, a young man seeking to fully realize his ambitions would have had to do so outside the family sphere.

By the early years of the eighteenth century, Ireland had established a flourishing trade with Bordeaux by flouting England's restrictive import laws (an activity otherwise known as smuggling), and the Lawton family doubtless found it advantageous to have a representative in place to facilitate their affairs in the wine country. This was the role played by Abraham Lawton during his first two years in France as he arranged for the shipment of wines back home to Cork. Ultimately, this initial period served as an "apprenticeship" that furnished Lawton with an in-depth understanding of the city's wine business and resulted in his becoming a licensed broker, a more lucrative activity and a position of greater authority in the Bordeaux trade.

Together with the proprietors who made the wine and the merchants who bought it, the brokers were the third driving force in Bordeaux's commercial troika. Given the tensions that defined relations between proprietors and merchants, a mediator was needed to ensure that business was transacted in an equitable and impartial manner; this was the original role of the broker, whose appearance on the commercial scene coincided with the beginnings of the wine trade itself in the thirteenth century.

As the go-between in the proprietor–merchant relationship, it was the broker's responsibility to possess an awareness of the Bordeaux marketplace much more comprehensive than that of either proprietor or merchant:

> *The quantity [of Bordeaux wine] harvested is so considerable, and the nuances which distinguish those of each type are so varied, that the most experienced merchant could not arrive at an appreciation of them all, especially when he buys new wines which must undergo several metamorphoses before reaching their highest degree of quality, and which according to the soil, its exposure, the age of the vine, the variety with which it is planted, the cares given to the growing and vinification, would become perfect or deteriorate after more or less time. In a vineyard of such size and in which the quality of its produce varies infinitely, the knowledge of all these circumstances cannot be acquired by one man. This is why the Bordeaux merchants rarely make important purchases without the assistance of their brokers. . . who compare among themselves the wines of each growth, from the moment of their fabrication through to their extreme old age.*

Such was one assessment of the broker's role in the nineteenth century.

Thus, a merchant seeking to buy a given quantity of wine of a particular quality for a specific price might require weeks of searching throughout numerous communes before arranging a suitable purchase. It was the broker's responsibility to know what wines were available at any given time throughout the Bordeaux region. To this end, a broker would

Guillaume Lawton

visit the vineyards on a regular basis, meet with the proprietors to taste their wines, and exchange information and opinions with his confreres.

Similarly, a proprietor who wished to sell a quantity of wine at a given price might make the rounds of merchants on the Bordeaux marketplace, going from one to the next over a period of days before coming across the one whose needs matched what the proprietor had on offer. The broker's job was to be familiar with merchants' needs based on their individual preferences and the particular niche they filled in the wine marketplace. With the knowledge of what the proprietors had to sell and what the merchants sought to buy, the broker was able to efficiently match the two, and smooth out the questions of price that were invariably part of the commercial process. This was the role Abraham Lawton was henceforth to play in Bordeaux.

During the previous half-century, a sizable Irish expatriate population had established itself in the city's Chartrons district, the commercial hub for Bordeaux wine. With the connections available to the son of a home-country merchant, Abraham Lawton soon made a place for himself in this community, and shortly after his arrival married Charlotte Selves, a young woman born and raised in Bordeaux. Lawton's family grew with his business, and, in October 1740, a daughter was born, to be followed by eleven other children over the next twenty years. However, infant mortality was high in the eighteenth century, and by the time Abraham Lawton himself died in 1776, he had already buried seven of his offspring, four of whom had lived less than a year. Thus it was that the eleventh child, Guillaume Lawton, aged seventeen, came to lead the firm established by his father in 1742.

During the course of thirty-four vintages, Abraham Lawton had become one of Bordeaux's leading wine brokers, in certain years handling the sales for a full 20 percent of the Médoc's total production. Young Guillaume Lawton's ascension to the head of this enterprise may have found him lacking in age but not necessarily in training. By law, brokerage licenses were passed from father to son so that "the knowledge acquired by long and laborious experience should not be lost to the trade." It was therefore likely that the observations and understanding amassed by Abraham Lawton during more than one-third of a century served as a solid foundation on which Guillaume was able to build his own store of experience.

If professional reputation is anything to judge by, Guillaume Lawton soon became one of the most redoubtable brokers in Bordeaux: in the words of the manager at Château Latour he was "inexorable," and his influence was such as "to make the sun rise and set." In the decades following his father's death, Guillaume Lawton had amassed a body of knowledge and experience to earn him the confidence of Bordeaux's major merchants and the grudging respect of the region's proprietors.

Evidence justifying Lawton's authority is both ample and eloquent. In June 1815, he set down his perceptions on the region's wines in a notebook entitled "General Observations." These notes were never intended for publication, but rather as a professional memoir written for the benefit of his successors—by 1815, Guillaume had a daughter and three sons, thus the continuation of the family firm into the next generation was assured. Having entered the family business as a young man, he was well aware of how beneficial his father's experience had been, and this book of observations may have been meant to serve the same purpose for his children in a more tangible and permanent way. (Guillaume Lawton's example was taken to heart: for almost 200 years, succeeding generations have continued compiling a rich collection of observations touching on every aspect of the region's viti- and vinological activity; these notebooks, together with the other documents that have been preserved in the archives of the Tastet & Lawton brokerage firm constitute the veritable memory of the Bordeaux wine trade.)

At the start of his "Observations," Guillaume Lawton set out the principles on which Bordeaux's commercial activity was based: "In each parish are numerous proprietors. Each makes a wine which differs more or less in quality. Experience has taught us to classify them. Each year, among those which we place in a similar category, we find that now some, now others have succeeded best. However, it is rare that this difference is very marked; in general, it is merely a matter of assigning a preference, and for this a great familiarity is necessary."

It is this "great familiarity" that Lawton then went on to display in over 120 pages of finely noted commentary that is nothing short of remarkable for the comprehensiveness of its detail and judgment. The professional integrity that informed his opinion is demonstrated in the section on Arsac, where the Lawtons were themselves proprietors: "Our Property is now the only bourgeois other than du Tertre [a future fifth growth] and is the inferior in quality." Although the family might have drawn a certain income as winemakers, there could be no question of allowing personal interest to influence or conflict with the judgment of the Bordeaux trade.

Commune by commune, Guillaume Lawton introduced each area and the characteristics of its wines; from these observations it becomes possible to reconstruct the classification in use by Bordeaux's wine trade in 1815 and to understand the commercial logic that assigned each property its respective position—a logic that was mastered by few as well as Guillaume Lawton.

Several aspects of this classification are especially worthy of note, particularly the number and identity of the properties included. Sixty-five were named as classed growths, a figure large enough to be comprehensively representative of Bordeaux's premium wine producers while avoiding an all-inclusiveness that would have rendered the classification little more than a directory of everyone with grapevines. (This is not to suggest that Lawton was aware of only the classed growths—his notebooks include detailed listings for hundreds of properties throughout the Médoc peninsula; nevertheless, only sixty-five were considered *crus classés*.) The criteria by which the trade established its rankings were remarkably constant: practically all the wines that would figure in the 1855 classification four decades later are present here. The four first growths are all in place, and every property listed by Lawton as a second would maintain that status in forty years' time.

It is interesting to consider the differences between the two classifications among the third, fourth, and fifth growths. Pichon-Longueville, a future second, is a third growth here (another second growth, Ducru-Beaucaillou, appears among the fourths); 1855 thirds such as Marquis d'Alesme-Becker and Malescot-Saint-Exupéry are fourths in 1815. With very few exceptions, when there was a change in position the overall tendency was for a property to rise in its classification. The science of winemaking was continually being refined, and as more became known about the practices that resulted in a better wine, those proprietors with the interest and financial ability to implement changes and thereby realize the full potential of their vineyards would see their efforts rewarded accordingly.

However, for all the similarities between this classification and that of 1855, there is one aspect that sets Lawton's apart: his detailed commentary that fixed the position of a property not just as, say, a third or fourth growth, but in more precise relation to the other wines within its class. A definite comparison was made among wines, which was careful to take into account the inherent differences resulting from the characteristics typical to Margaux, Pauillac, and each of the other wine-producing communes. Lawton's comments indicate that it was not a question of comparing apples and oranges, but rather appreciating each wine for what it was, and appraising its quality based on "a great familiarity" with the vineyards, the winemakers, and, of course, the wines themselves. What Lawton offered was more than just a classification: it was a guided tour of each of the crus classés that showed just what qualities made one a second growth and another a third.

Others in the wine trade during this time had their own transcriptions of the Bordeaux classification: a memorandum dated February 22, 1813, written by the merchant William Johnston (Nathaniel's father), includes a ranking of fifty named properties that is almost as comprehensive as Guillaume Lawton's. Accompanied by several paragraphs that describe the general characteristics of the wines included on his list, Johnston offers a good, clear account of the qualities that merchants found in their classified growths. Still, there is an evident difference in the tone of two lists—whereas Johnston is descriptive in his commentary and ranking, explaining the state of the wine trade of the day, Lawton takes a more prescriptive approach, actively judging the properties he classifies. This was perhaps based on the fundamentally different roles of merchants and brokers in the Bordeaux wine trade; one observer explained it in these terms: "a competent and respected magistrature is needed to direct [the merchants] in the choices they must make. The members of this magistrature are the brokers; it is to them that has devolved the delicate mission of the tasting and the classification of the wines."

Accordingly, it is Guillaume Lawton's classification that is finally the fullest expression of the methodology that began in 1647 and continued through to 1855. Here everything comes together: relative price comparisons based on individual properties, accompanied by detailed and informed reasoning for the position of each property classified. Unlike the classifications considered so far, in which their function as classifications has been almost coincidental to some other official or informal purpose, this one is a wholly dedicated effort and, as such, provides eminently reliable testimony to the contemporary quality of each property's wine.

During this period, the classification was still in the domain of the wine trade, neither known nor appreciated by the average wine drinker. It was a commercial tool, albeit quite powerful, and in an age before wine books and magazines for the general public, it was not thought that such a rating system could be of interest to anyone outside the profession. When the classification would appear in print, it was invariably as an aide-mémoire for those in the trade, a résumé of the current prices for wines on the Bordeaux market. A sixteen-page pamphlet published in 1816 entitled *Tableau général des qualités et du prix des vins qui se font aux environs de Bordeaux* (*A General Table of the Quality and Price of Wines Made in the Bordeaux Region*) offered descriptions for each of the wine-producing communes in a style similar to Lawton's "General Observations," but without the depth of perception that could be considered proprietary to that brokerage firm. Similarly, the classification that appears opposite the title page offered but a skeleton version in which the four first growths (naturally) and only five second growths are listed by name; the rest are dealt with by an all-encompassing "etc., etc." Names for third and fourth growths do not appear at all. Purchasers of this trade publication were assumed to be already familiar with where each property belonged in the hierarchy, and its main function was simply to list the most recent market prices for the various qualities of wine.

The first book generally acknowledged to offer the public some semblance of the classification was published the year after Guillaume Lawton set down his observations in writing. In 1816, a book entitled *Topographie de tous les vignobles connus* (*Topography of All the Known Vineyards*) was published in Paris; it was written by André Jullien, described on the book's title page as "author of *The Sommelier's Manual,* and the inventor of aerating channels and other devices for decanting and filtering liquids." Not being a member of the Bordeaux trade and writing a book dealing with more than just the wines of that region, Jullien had the freedom (and the necessity) of developing criteria for his classification that had little in common with those used by the professionals in Bordeaux:

> I have considered the wines in general as forming five classes; the first of each type includes fine wines of superior quality, coming from a small number of privileged growths and which are rarely found on the market; the second contains all those of excellent quality, which, being more abundant than the preceding, are also more generally known as first quality wines; the third are all the fine and *demi-fine* wines which, without having the qualities of the preceding, are nevertheless considered as wines of the table, taken between the dishes before the dessert. The fourth class are composed of ordinary wines known as *first quality;* and finally the fifth are those of second and third quality, as well as common wines.

Jullien's purpose was to create a system whereby not just the upper level of a region's wines could be classified, but virtually all of its production would be included. Thus, drawing on information furnished by correspondents throughout France and abroad, Jullien's classification was a hybrid of the methods that had been used in Bordeaux during the previous century and a half. For the first two levels, he indicated individual properties by name, beginning with the by-now standard four first growths, followed by seven wines in the second class; his list of thirds presented no properties by name but instead designated nine communes whose overall production he considered to be a cut below the second-growth properties, and his two fourth growths comprised not just communes but entire regions even broader in their geographic dimensions. His classification finished with one fifth growth, which was made up of the entire Bas-Médoc area. Descending the five levels of this system is, in effect, a voyage backwards through the classification's evolutionary development, from specific properties to ever more widely designated areas. If the trade's classification had achieved a high degree of refinement, those created for the general public would, in turn, have to undergo their own process of development. (Indeed, it would not be until the *Topographie*'s third edition in 1832 that the necessary adjustments would be made to the Jullien classification of the Gironde's wines to bring it in closer accord with the established Bordeaux standard.)

Eight years later, another work attempted to classify Bordeaux's wines for the general reader: *The History of Ancient and Modern Wines* by Dr. Alexander Henderson, published in London in 1824. Although this book, like Jullien's, was written by an outsider to the Bordeaux trade, Henderson had the advantage of being an Englishman whose personal familiarity with the region's finest wines, those which constituted the upper levels of the classification, was more thorough. (The relative rarity of these wines in the French market was attested to by one broker in a discussion of Pauillac's classed growths: "The English, who are great lovers of them, buy almost all the wines produced in this parish." Indeed, Jullien himself stated that "all which sells in Paris under the name of fine Bordeaux wine comes from but third and even fourth class vineyards; rarely from those of the second, and almost never those of the first.") In discussing the merits of the wines of Lafite, for instance, Jullien's comments were rather general in nature: "Lafitte. . . offers wines that are light, very fine, very silky, full of body and bouquet." Henderson's observations, while identifying the same basic characteristics, were nevertheless more detailed, suggesting a more extensive personal experience with the wines themselves: "[Lafite] is the most choice and delicate, and is characterized by its silky softness on the palate, and its charming perfume, which partakes of the nature of the violet and the raspberry."

Henderson's text dealing with the wines of the Gironde mentioned only about a dozen properties by name, constituting but a limited list of wines in a rather informal order; however, in the book's appendix, a table entitled "Wines of the Bordelais. Prices at Bordeaux in 1815, 1818, and 1822," offered a more detailed classification. This table listed almost two dozen properties, with the distinction of being clearly based on their sales prices in the Bordeaux marketplace over a period of years.

Published the same year as Henderson's work, the *Traité sur les vins du Médoc et les autres vins rouges du département de la Gironde* (*Treatise on the Wines of the Médoc and the Other Red Wines from the Gironde Department*) written by William Franck was more focused in its approach, concentrating on only the wines from the Bordeaux region. In addition, this book enjoyed an advantage shared by neither Jullien's nor

Henderson's: Franck had been a merchant in the Bordeaux wine market, and was thus able to draw on more authoritative sources in compiling his text and the classification that accompanied it.

As a member of the Bordeaux trade, Franck was also familiar with the classification's deeper significance and how controversial it could be. While a proprietor may have found it personally satisfying having a wine ranked among the top levels of the commercial hierarchy, of greater importance were the financial consequences of that ranking: a classed growth commanded a higher price than an unclassed one, and the higher the classification, the higher the price. Any judgment that threatened to lower a wine's standing (or eliminate it altogether) risked condemning it to a lower selling price, resulting in a very real loss of revenue. It was not enough for a proprietor to have worked hard and invested heavily to make a property a classed growth—it was constantly necessary to protect that standing, and, if possible, to raise it.

Thus, in publishing his version of the classification, Franck was well aware of the controversy he might arouse. "It is not without mistrust," he explained,

> that I undertook such an enterprise. It was impossible for me to shield myself from the difficulties I would have to overcome, and the delicate nature of such a task. Besides the obligation to be just and speak my mind, I saw there were interests to be treated with tact, claims to be abandoned, biases to be swept aside, and especially certain time-honored opinions that nevertheless I had to defy.

Assisted by the major brokers of the time (doubtless including Guillaume Lawton), but relying on his own winetasting experience as well, Franck assembled his classification "in a manner best designed to give a correct and precise idea of each of the growths common to our wine regions."

Franck's classification was more extensive than Henderson's, acknowledging thirty-three properties as classed growths; still, this was about half the number recognized by the trade according to Guillaume Lawton in 1815. Inevitably there were proprietors who took exception to the position (or absence) of their properties in this new list, and future editions of the *Traité* introduced the classification with a rather defensive paragraph beginning "We now arrive at the most delicate part of our work. . . ." (Beginning with the second edition, responsibility for the *Traité* passed to its publisher, P. Chaumas, who explained that "Mr. Franck, who is in Germany, has with the greatest grace given me his consent and his cooperation in order that his work be once more offered to the public.")

The second edition published in 1845 was prefaced with a note from the publisher defending the accuracy of the opinions presented throughout the book, particularly in the all-important, highly sensitive classification:

> Perhaps the attempt at classifying the wines of the Médoc will arouse some reproof; this is an area which has shown itself to be full of ambitious pretensions which the

> trade no longer heeds. We do not claim that our attempt has the force of law, but we will state that it was reviewed by several well-informed persons, and it obtained their approval.

Perhaps even more effective in reducing the controversy for future editions was the expansion of their classifications to a size more in line with the dimensions established by the trade: the 1845 second edition contained a full seventy-two wines—sixty-four of them as first through fifth growths, and an additional eight *bons bourgeois* for good measure; the third edition in 1853 cut back the number slightly, with sixty-two growths in five classes, and seven *bons bourgeois*.

Despite the controversy that may have greeted Franck's initial classification, it was authoritative enough to become the de facto standard throughout the next decade, appearing with only slight modifications reflecting the change in a property's name owing to its purchase by a new owner. Even when a work was not specifically dedicated to the subject of wine, such as the 1825 tourist guide to Bordeaux entitled *Le guide de l'étranger* (*The Foreigner's Guide*), if it contained a classification, that classification was Franck's.

In 1827, Jean-Alexandre Cavoleau, a member of the Royal Society of Agriculture in Paris, wrote *Œnologie française, ou statistique de tous les vignobles et de toutes les boissons vineuses et spiritueuses de la France, suivie de considérations générales sur la culture de la vigne* (*French Winemaking, or a Survey of All the Vineyards and All the Wines and Spirits of France, Followed by General Observations on Grape Growing*). Here only passing reference was made to the position in the hierarchy held by just a few properties; nonetheless, the classification was acknowledged as being of prime importance in the Bordeaux wine trade:

> These classes have been established by the brokers, and it is they who still decide, perhaps a little arbitrarily, to which [class] the wine of each individual should belong. The proprietors make every effort in order to place their wines in a superior class, and they are right to do so because the prices of their wines are less regulated by their intrinsic merit than by the number that they occupy in the classification's scale. Occasionally it costs them sacrifices to realize this: for example, keeping their wines for several years instead of selling them in the first, as is the custom. It is by such tenacity that in the commune of Saint-Laurent, Mr. Pichon-Longueville has come to have his wine placed in the third class, instead of the fourth, which it had long occupied.

It may have been Cavoleau's distance from Bordeaux and an unfamiliarity with the operation of its wine trade, or perhaps a reliance on proprietors as his primary informants (the book is about winemaking, which suggests that his main source of information was at the production end of the Bordeaux commercial chain), but the explanation of the classification's role confuses cause and effect by attributing a wine's price to its ranking when it was the inverse that was actually the case. Nevertheless, although no classification is given in *Œnologie française,* Cavoleau does acknowledge Franck's *Traité sur les vins du Médoc* for "many details" on the Gironde's vineyards.

Franck turned up again the following year: in 1828 appeared the *Classification and Description of the Wines of Bordeaux,* by a wine broker named Paguierre. Published first in England with a French edition appearing in 1829, the book's very title indicated its primary occupation with the classification—indeed, it offered not just one but two of them. In the appendix was an unacknowledged adaptation from Franck's *Traité* published five years earlier; several extended passages of text appear to have been lifted verbatim from the same source as well. Of greater interest, however, is a second classification drawn from the text in which Paguierre described in detail particular aspects of Bordeaux's vineyards. These comments were more clearly the result of his own professional observations, and testified to developing quality in a number of wines as evidenced by their advancement in the classification. Consider, for example, his description of a property that had been ranked a third growth by both Lawton and Franck: "There is also in this parish [Saint-Lambert] the growth of Pichon-Longueville, which, for some years, has been classed with the second great growths of the Médoc, owing to the care bestowed on its production." Carnet (La Tour-Carnet), Giscours, and La Lagune were also among the beneficiaries of a promotion in rank.

Why the two contradictory classifications? Although the "quotations" from Franck were unacknowledged, unlike the credit offered by Cavoleau in his *Œnologie française,* the text nonetheless offers several clues to an answer. In a foreword entitled "Advertisement," it was explained that "a friend of the Editor being in Bordeaux, during a part of the year 1825 and 1826, happened to see, in the hands of M. Paguierre, a retired Wine-Broker, a well digested set of memoranda, on the subject of the Wine Trade. It appeared to him, that this was a sort of information much required in this country, and he therefore suggested to M. Paguierre, to add to the memoranda in his Carnet a preliminary chapter on the culture, the preparation, and the management of Bordeaux wines, and to send the whole to this country for publication." Furthermore, "an Appendix has been added, containing information which has been obtained from other sources." Evidently, in this "age of Franck," it was apparently inconceivable that a book dealing with the wines of Bordeaux could appear without his now-requisite classification tacked on in an appendix "obtained from other sources," even if the main text itself was sufficiently equipped in this regard.

In 1833, *A History and Description of Modern Wines* by Cyrus Redding was published in London, and it too presented a classification of Bordeaux's wines. Unlike most of the other books touching on the subject during this time, Redding managed to avoid reproducing Franck's 1824 classification, which would have been admirable had he not decided to fall back on the now completely outdated 1816 version from Jullien. It would take another English effort made in 1833 (and published in 1835) to present a more authoritative account of the standing of Bordeaux's wines during this period.

In the 1830s, as the memory of its continental blockade against Napoleon Bonaparte receded into history, Great Britain undertook a reassessment of its trade with France, seeking to establish tariffs that would more effectively serve the nation's best interests. To better fulfill this task, Parliament commissioned detailed inquiries into selected French industries whose products would be a prominent part of any new commercial treaty. The *Second Report on the Commercial Relations between France and Great Britain; Silks & Wine*, compiled by John Bowring in 1835, was an in-depth study concerning two French commodities that were traditional British imports, and the section on wine dealt with virtually every aspect of the subject that might have some bearing on Parliament's deliberations. As might be expected, Bordeaux was prominently featured.

To determine what might be the most equitable manner for imposing a fair duty on imported wines, Bowring approached—naturally enough—the Bordeaux Chamber of Commerce for its opinion. Among the details that concerned the Chamber regarding this question, one point was clear: since the price of wines differed, it would be unjust to levy a uniform tariff across the board. This was the policy Britain had followed throughout most of the eighteenth century, which resulted in closing that all-important market to any but the finest wines whose quality made it worth paying the tariff imposed on them. As the representative of the Bordeaux wine trade, it was clearly in the Chamber of Commerce's interest to advise Parliament against adopting any policy that would restrict imports into Britain. How best to establish a progressive scale of duty? Obviously, it was a question of classifying the wines, but how was this to be done? Rather than risk having the British reinvent an imperfect wheel, the Chamber (not for the last time) steered its inquirers toward the effective, ready-made solution.

"According to the statement of one of the most distinguished members of the Chamber of Commerce of Bordeaux," Bowring wrote, "the difficulties of classification by district or by quality would, in the judgment of this authority, be invincible; but he thinks a classification by value would be by no means impracticable. . . ." This was precisely how the Bordeaux wine trade saw the utility of its classification: not as a measure of quality, which was a purely subjective matter far too volatile for commerce to be based on, but as a representation of value in the guise of sales prices, hard cash amounts which had a definite, measurable identity. As stated by the Chamber's "distinguished member":

> They could not be classified by communes, for the same commune frequently produces very inferior wines and very superior wines; neither could they be classed according to quality, for this varies infinitely amongst wines of different growths, and even in wines of the same growth, according to the diversity of the seasons. A

growth of Médoc, for instance, may in one year be worth fr. 1,500 per tun, and the following year only fr. 500 per tun. The price varies even more than the quality, for besides the difference of the vintage, it is influenced by its greater or less productiveness, as well as the state of demand for it.

All idea of a positive classification with reference to quality must be abandoned, and an arbitrary one adopted.

It might, therefore, be settled:—

That all white and red wines, value under fr. 1,000 should pay such and such duty.

That all white and red wines, value from fr. 1,000 to 2,000 should pay such and such duty.

That all white and red wines, value from fr. 2,000 to 3,000 should pay such and such duty.

That all white and red wines, value from fr. 3,000 and upwards, should pay such and such duty.

In short, it was just a suggestion, but one that distilled down to its simplest, most basic form, was, in fact, the structure of the Bordeaux classification.

The classification itself formed part of Bowring's report, in an appendix compiled by J. Exshaw and dated March 27, 1833, entitled "Classification of the Wines of the Gironde Department, with Average Prices at which, since the Peace, they have been sold by the Growers when new." Its originality and perspicacity are attested to by the inclusion of two young properties each less than twenty years old—Montrose, a future second growth introduced here among the fourths, and Palmer, which was emerging from almost two decades of vineyard consolidation and beginning to hit its stride as a producer of top-quality wine. Another major difference that sets this classification apart was the scope of its listings: not limited to just the Médoc's reds, of which fifty-three are listed, it touched briefly on red Graves, Saint-Emilion, and Palus wines before turning, in some detail, to the white wines of the Gironde.

With a listing of twenty-nine properties in three divisions, this classification was one of the most extensive to date in an area that had been too often neglected when discussing Bordeaux's production. As one contemporary writer commented, "who would believe it, twenty authors have written about the Gironde's vineyards, and none have cared to venture upon a fitting description of our white vines." On those occasions when they were accorded recognition, white-wine producers generally were not "classed in order of merit" but merely presented as the best to be found in particular communes that were themselves the object of classification; this was the method Jullien adopted when he increased the number of properties named in the 1832 third edition of the *Topographie de tous les vignobles connus*.

Such a presentation provided no basis for a direct comparison of wines, which (as Guillaume Lawton demonstrated) was at the heart of the classification of the Médoc's reds. Most works that took this indirect approach limited their remarks to a basic selection of named properties: in general, Yquem, Filhot, Coutet, Climens, and Suduiraut among the sweet white wines, and Carbonnieux, St. Bris, and Pontac (also known as Dulamon) among the dry. These wines, as well as others that were either subsumed under an all-encompassing "etc." or else amalgamated within the reputations of their respective communes, were recognized as being of fine quality, occasionally exceptional in their class. The problem was with the class as a whole.

Bordeaux's identity as a quality wine-producing region was now based on its reds from the Médoc (and, to a lesser extent, the Graves), and while the whites were by no means negligible, they nevertheless formed a market apart. Since their area of production was predominantly to the south of Bordeaux, the white wines were geographically distant from the center of activity in the Médoc, and the brokers (like Guillaume Lawton and his successors) who specialized in those vineyards to the north did not have the same expertise with what was a quite different wine. Given the legal and traditional divisions among brokers, there were those who "bought only little-quality white wines, others those of the Côtes and Palus fit for the Colonies, others those of Bourg and Blaye which make very ordinary wines and finally others who buy only the fine wines of the Graves and the Médoc."

When a broker specializing in the Médoc handled a merchant's order that included a portion of white wines, it was customary for these brokers to subcontract this part of the transaction to colleagues closer to this end of the market. Since these white-wine brokers were generally registered and domiciled in communes south of the Bordeaux city limits, they, like the wines they specialized in, were physically removed from the heart of affairs as well. All of this contributed to a marginalization of the region's white wines, both sweet and dry, but most decisive in their diminished position was the incontrovertible fact that the sales price for the best of these did not meet the level of their red-wine homologues. Thus, for all their excellence, circumstances in the Bordeaux marketplace had not encouraged the establishment of a classification for white wines as detailed or extensive as that of the reds. Nonetheless, there were signs that this may have been changing.

White wines figured prominently in an 1834 classification that formed part of the *Statistique Œnologique du département de la Gironde* (*Winemaking Statistics of the Gironde*). Written by "An Agronomist" and published in Bordeaux, the work presented an encyclopedic survey, according to the book's subtitle, of "the process of grape growing; the quantity of hectares dedicated to this culture; the names of the grape varieties; the average price of the wines, by tun and by class of the most renowned growths; the average quantities harvested, the expenses of cultivation, etc." Of greatest interest here is "the average price of the wines, by tun and by class of the most renowned growths," represented by two tables of classificatory information: the first was a price list for seven vintages from 1825 to 1833, which named the same properties as Jullien among the first and second growths, but offered greater detail in the thirds and fourths before trailing off into the catch-all "etc." which was still too often a part of published classifications.

Fortunately, the gaps represented by the "etcs." are more than amply filled in by the second table entitled "Names and Expanse of Vineyards Producing the Best Quality Wine." Here in four classes appear the names of thirty red-wine producers in the Médoc, the heart of the by-now traditional classification, with additional lists of properties making red wine in the Graves and Côtes, as well as white wines both sweet and dry—over fifty properties in all. This table suggests a fairly close understanding of the classification as it existed among the Bordeaux wine trade, and is certainly among the most comprehensive appearing in French to date. Excepting the complete absence from the list of Lascombes and Montrose, as well as the third-growth status of Cos-d'Estournel and Ducru-Beaucaillou (not yet having completed their ascension), the second growths are presented in virtually the exact order they would assume two decades later. From the top down, the classification was beginning to take on its final form: of the thirty Médoc properties listed, only one (Tronquoy Lalande, here a fourth growth) would not be included in 1855. As for the more than two dozen omissions in this 1834 version, over half of them are among the future fifth growths; had the Agronomist extended this list to include a fifth class, the correspondence between the two lists would doubtless have been more exact.

Since the early years of the nineteenth century, the classification had developed a double existence: there was that of the trade, whose extensiveness and detail was exemplified by Guillaume Lawton's exhaustively annotated comments; and there was its less specific reflection, cluttered with district names and all-encompassing "etcs.," which was the classification's public identity. That it had developed a public identity at all was altogether significant—no longer a tool exclusive to Bordeaux's brokers and merchants, its existence was becoming better known and more readily adapted to the varying needs of an ever-widening audience. It was becoming rarer to find works touching on Bordeaux's wines, be it traveler's guidebooks or government reports, which did not include some sort of classification as a guide to understanding the quality of the region's production.

The inexactitude common to these public classifications had been continually drawing closer to the comprehensiveness that characterized the trade's, and with a growing number of versions being published that distance was shrinking rapidly. No longer in the thrall of Jullien and Franck's traditional authority, new renditions now appeared with increasing regularity—even the guidebook *Le guide de l'étranger*, which had simply reproduced Franck's 1824 classification in its first two editions, came up with a new list of over seventy properties for its third in 1834, virtually doubling its previous size. This twofold increase in ten years' time illustrates how the classification was evolving: as it became more specific, with fewer "etcs." dotting its landscape, the number of properties establishing a public identity as a classed growth grew.

However, despite the growing concordance between the trade and public classifications, in the end it was still the professional version that mattered in the Bordeaux marketplace. The importance of a property's classification had always been important, but during the 1830s the difference for a proprietor between an assignment to one class by the brokers and being ranked a level higher (where most proprietors believed they rightly belonged) was of greater financial consequence than ever before. In 1825, the Bordeaux wine market entered a severe depression, a period of financial difficulty that would not recede until the 1850s. Properties that had formerly enjoyed prosperity now found themselves struggling for survival. If a proprietor could obtain a promotion in the trade's classification, it would increase the value of the property's wine and bring much needed additional revenue. The only thing standing in the way of this promotion, as many proprietors saw it, was the obstinacy and prejudice of the classification's arbiters, the brokers.

"Except for the small number placed in the first rank, all the others protest and curse the classification," commented one observer of long experience on the proprietor's commonly shared sentiment. "It's a universal chorus against the injustice and the arbitrariness of the brokers and against the legislators of the classification. The proprietor is born with the sentiment that the broker is the natural enemy of his caste; he always believes that he leans to the side of the merchant, with whom he is in much closer contact." For those proprietors, generally in the third class and below, whose position in the hierarchy was not absolutely established, each newly published classification placing them in a next-higher class was welcome ammunition in the proprietor's argument for a promotion in grade. Thus, a proprietor classed by the brokers among the fourth growths could claim that "the wines rival the best thirds, because the classifications of 1775, 1834, 1844, 1854, and 1865 have always ranked it as a third growth."

Proprietors who felt themselves at the mercy of brokers and merchants were to find a champion in *Le Producteur,* a monthly journal that its publisher and editor, Lecoultre de Beauvais, promised "will defend the interests of the Gironde's vineyards." In the editor's opinion, the Gironde's proprietors were beset by a menace that threatened the very existence of the vineyards themselves. "From where comes this evil?" *Le Producteur* asked. "It is the tyranny of the industry and its lack of good faith that is the cause." The editor did not hesitate to suggest conspiracies among the brokers, to accuse the merchants of questionable practices that compromised proprietors' efforts to produce wines of quality, or to claim reluctance among the trade in more accurately appraising the qualities of various properties.

Inevitably, *Le Producteur* saw the classification as a principal source of the injustice inflicted upon the region's proprietors. "The wine classifications. . . seem to us to be limited to a far too few number of properties. These are the ones acknowledged by the trade, which imposes its law where it has no business; it is not its place to come and dictate what the merchandise of others is worth, but rather for the owner of the merchandise to set his price, and for the buyer to take it or leave it." For *Le Producteur* the classification, as it was currently established, was little more than the means by which the Bordeaux wine trade conspired to stifle the free market forces of supply and demand. Priding itself on the justice of its cause and its independent point of view, the journal set about to rectify the classification's artificially induced flaws. To this end, *Le Producteur* proposed such modifications as the elevation of Mouton to the first-growth status of Lafite, and put forward the proposition that Pichon-Longueville was the equivalent in quality of Latour—by extension, a suggestion that Pichon be elevated to a first growth as well. The editor was confident enough in the legitimacy of his position to state that "The trade will doubtless appreciate our candor and our impartiality once convinced that in defending the properties' interests, we never retreat before the truth. For their part, the rich proprietors in question will, we hope, do justice to our efforts, which have no other end but that of keeping the scales in balance as much as possible, to show consideration for that part of the trade that shows good faith and to put aside immoderate pretensions."

Not everyone, however, agreed with *Le Producteur*'s methodology. After reading the first issue, a subscriber calling himself "The Old Proprietor" wrote to counsel prudence in the journal's approach:

> The established classification is without question a custom, a sort of law, which despite rivalries, complaints and recriminations of interested parties, persists nonetheless. It necessarily follows that this classification is neither a chimera, an illusion, nor a simple fantasy; I would go further and say that even if this were its character it would still be necessary to respect it, since for centuries it has assured the prosperity of our region, it has contributed to the reputation of our wines, it is the very foundation of its commerce. But far from being an illusion, this classification is necessarily based on the taste, the experience, and the time that has established its consecration.

Not to be dissuaded from its mission, *Le Producteur* pushed on, each month focusing on a different commune and proposing classifications for the properties it surveyed. A preview of the journal's advocacy could be seen in an appendix to the first issue of January 1838: a table quoting prices for the Médoc's red wines. According to the table (based on sales for 1837), first growths sold from 2,400 to 3,000 francs per tun, seconds from 1,800 to 2,000 francs, thirds from 1,400 to 1,600, wines classed as fourth growths sold for 900 to 1,000 francs, and fifth growths went for 550 to 650 francs. Based on these figures, *Le Producteur* found a full 186 properties worthy of classification. There was complete accord with the accepted opinion of Latour, Margaux, and Lafite as first growths. (Although not listed on this table dedicated to Médoc wines, Haut-Brion was acknowledged a first growth in the issue dealing with the Graves district.) With the exception of Ducru-Beaucaillou—here still listed among the thirds—second growths included the same properties that would earn this status in 1855. Third growths, however, contained thirty properties, sixteen more than would have this rank in 1855; the majority of these were promotions from fourth- and even fifth-growth wines. *Le Producteur*'s fourth growths numbered fifty-one, and the fifths filled out the list with ninety-two wines—over 50 percent greater than *all* the properties that would be accorded classed-growth status in 1855. This wholesale generosity shown by the journal's editors would be further enhanced in the months to come as proprietors came forward with their claims for reclassification.

It was true that these properties all earned the prices quoted in the table for 1837, but this was not sufficient for the trade to accord them the rankings that *Le Producteur* awarded in its classification. A wine's standing in the classification was not based on the sales of a single vintage. As the Chamber of Commerce indicated to the British Parliament, "price varies even more than the quality, for besides the difference of the vintage, it is influenced by its greater or less productiveness, as well as the state of demand for it."

The trade had established its classification based on the reputation a property had created for itself over a period of time sufficient to absorb the effects of year-to-year fluctuations in price. (See Appendix III.) Had the classification functioned as posited by *Le Producteur*, its utility would have been practically eradicated since it could no longer be cited as a stable, authoritative guide to opening sales prices. (There would also be the constant risk that a property could fall victim to a year in which its wine sold for an unusually low price, as happened here with Ducru-Beaucaillou: according to the current sales prices considered by *Le Producteur*, the property appears in this classification as a third growth, although the commentary on the wines of Saint-Julien acknowledges its standing in the trade as a second, the class it would have in 1855.)

Le Producteur proved to be unique in its maverick approach, and although its influence would resurface before the decade was over, its disappearance after the December 1841 issue saw a return to more traditional versions of the classification. In 1842 appeared a slim volume of pieces titled *Les Vins*, which had comprised the final section of a work written for maîtres d'hôtel and domestic cooks on how to conserve fruits, vegetables, and meats. Even though the work was not intended for members of the trade, the classification had become so well known among the wine-drinking public at this time that the publisher found it advantageous to include the subtitle "Classification des Grands Vins de Bordeaux" as a feature of the work's contents. The piece containing the classification was titled *Etude sur les vins français et étrangers* (*A Study of French and Foreign Wines*) by Louis Leclerc, and given his intention to cover a subject so extensive in scope, Leclerc naturally found it necessary to depend on (and credit) additional sources as references for his text. Relying on second-hand information and attempting to discuss more than just the wines of a single region, the classification he presented was characterized by many of the same limitations and inexactitudes as beset Jullien's over twenty-five years before.

Although quite detailed in its naming of individual properties for the first and second growths, ambiguity begins to surface with a reference to "several *clos* of Cantenac and Margaux" among the thirds, and the entire commune of Saint-Julien listed as a fourth growth. Having divided the fourth-growth category into first-fourths and second-fourths (the latter composed of "the large properties of Pauillac and Saint-Estèphe, and several others from Labarde and Margaux"), Leclerc summed up with a catch-all fifth class "in which are ordered many wines still worthy of esteem from Pauillac, Saint-Estèphe, Saint-Julien, Soussans, Labarde, Ludon, Macau, Cantenac." In total, Leclerc presented only twenty-seven wines by name (twenty-eight, if one includes La Lagune, which was not part of the classification but identified later in the text as a fourth growth), a figure much less extensive than the English *Report on Commercial Relations* of a decade earlier. Still, for all its limitations, Leclerc's effort offered evidence that once again the classification was continuing to consolidate: not only were each of the first and second growths listed here to maintain this status in 1855; now all but two of the thirds would as well (Montrose would rise to a second while Pouget would be placed among the fourths), evincing a greater accuracy in this regard than was the case in either the *Statistique Œnologique* or the *Commercial Relations* classifications.

It becomes clear at this stage that for a classification to be authoritatively "in the tradition," that is, recognizably in the same thread that ran from Guillaume Lawton in 1815 to the apotheosis of 1855 itself, two criteria had to be met: it was imperative that the authors limit themselves solely to a rating of Bordeaux's wines, and it was necessary to be on the scene in the region to gather the relevant information in person. This was most decidedly demonstrated by P. Batilliat in his 1846 book *Traité sur les vins de la France, des phénomènes qui se passent dans les vins, et des moyens d'en accélérer ou d'en retarder la marche (Treatise on the Wines of France, the Phenomena That Occur in Wines, and the Means of Accelerating or Retarding Their Progress).* In keeping with the publishing style of the age, the title page was a veritable author's curriculum vitae:

> Pharmacist in Mâcon; former pharmacist-major to the armed forces; member of the Society of Agriculture, Sciences, Arts and Letters of Mâcon; correspondent of the Royal Society of Agriculture, Natural History and Useful Arts of Lyon; correspondent of the Society of Pharmacology of the same city; correspondent of the Society of Physical Sciences, Chemistry, and Agricultural Arts and Industries of France; correspondent of the Society of Medical Chemistry, Pharmacology and Toxicology of Paris; assayer of gold and silver; member of the medical jury and central health council of the department of Saône-et-Loire; patent-holder of inventions, etc., etc."

Besides his scientific qualifications, Batilliat also owned vines "more advantageously situated than many others" on which he performed numerous experiments, and his *Traité*'s purpose was to make their results known. It was his hope that this work would lead winemaking along "a new path, on which chemists will soon be taking giant steps." Believing his discoveries applicable to all of France's vineyards, Batilliat included a statistical description for each one as an annex to the main text; upon reaching the Gironde—thirty-second on his alphabetical list of departments—it was practically obligatory that he attempt a classification of its wines. Acknowledging that his list doubtless contained omissions and even errors due to insufficient information, Batilliat's classification mentioned only the four first growths by name and grouped the rest of the region's production communally, topped off with "etcs." and the equally unspecific designation of "a host of others." Although hampered in his research by advanced age and failing health, Batilliat's view of the whole process of classification might have been shaded by the altogether reasonable belief that although wines could be categorized by the geographic location of their vineyards, "their classification by order of merit as a beverage would be impossible, since as a rule each person prefers the wine to which he is accustomed."

Another book, less ambitious but more authoritative, also appeared in 1846, whose primary purpose was not to classify the wines of Bordeaux but rather to serve as a guide to the city and its surrounding vineyards. Charles Cocks, a language professor in the Royal Colleges of France (as well as "Translator of 'Priests, Women, and Families,' 'The People,' 'Antonio Perez and Philip II,' etc., etc."), had developed a familiarity with the city and its resources that enabled him "to consult all the most authentic documents relating to Bordeaux and its famous wines." The result was published in London as *Bordeaux: Its Wines, and the Claret Country*. This "little volume" of 215 pages was not unlike *Le guide de l'étranger à Bordeaux* or the *Nouveau conducteur de l'étranger à Bordeaux*, two French guidebooks that enjoyed numerous printings throughout the middle of the nineteenth century; indeed, the entire first half of Cocks' work was dedicated to introducing the English-speaking visitor to such diverse aspects of the city's life as its "Public Instruction" and the "Superstition of the People." It is not until page 130 that Cocks turned his attention wholly to the subject of Bordeaux's wines, quoting extensively from various books, including the *Traité sur les vins du Médoc* by Franck. Initially dependent on these works for technical details concerning soil types and vine varieties, Cocks spoke in his own voice when describing the actual winemaking process, apparently confident in the value of his personal observations made since his arrival in Bordeaux in the early 1840s. These sections were followed by a commune-by-commune tour of the region's various wine-producing districts, leading the reader to the text's penultimate chapter entitled "Classification of the Médoc or Best Claret Wines."

Cocks introduced this section by quoting at length, again, from Franck's *Traité*, in effect acknowledging the basic truths of the earlier writer's opinions on the classification. Although Cocks the language teacher may have deferred to Franck's experience as a merchant in borrowing character descriptions of the Médoc's wines, his own observations of the wine scene suggested a somewhat different order of merit for their classification. "In forming, therefore, the following lists," Cocks wrote, "I have not only had recourse to whatever has already been written on this subject, but have availed myself of the various information afforded me by those whom I have considered the most competent judges; price having appeared to me the best test of the quality supposed to exist in each wine."

The personal experience and "competent judges" that led Cocks to establish his own classification of forty-seven properties may well have convinced him of the futility of attempting to give definition to the gray areas that resulted from the struggles between buyers and sellers in the Bordeaux trade. Accordingly, the straightforward listing of the less controversially placed first and second growths gave way to a more ambiguous approach for the rest: "As I have already stated, it is absolutely impossible to determine the particular merit of each wine, or to assign with precision the rank which each should occupy in the following enumeration." With this disclaimer Cocks proceeded to present thirty-six properties in one large, undivided category of "Third, Fourth, and Second-Fourth Growths" and attempted to finesse the prickly question of exactly where in the passionately contested hierarchy each of them belonged. (Even the authoritative Franck classification succumbed to a similar sensibility in the face of contemporary controversy, listing properties in alphabetical order within each class—excepting the first—for the second edition of the *Traité* published the previous year, 1845.) White wines were also classified by Cocks, in an arrangement that subdivided the sweet wines from Sauternes, Bommes, Preignac, Fargues, and Barsac into communal first, second, and third growths.

Four years later, in 1850, the first French edition appeared, published in Bordeaux itself by Féret Fils. This entailed not just a simple translation of the English edition into French, but an enlargement of the book's second half in size and scope. In addition, with a local publisher's appreciation for what would sell copies, the title was changed to *Bordeaux, ses environs et ses vins classés par ordre de mérite* (*Bordeaux, its environs and its wines classed in order of merit*).

In a preface outlining the work's methodology, Cocks explained that

> to give this part a practical and positive use we have tried, in spite of the difficulties that presented themselves and the demands that will arise from this innovation, to create lists of all the *classed* wines, both red and white, *by order of merit* and not *by alphabetical order* as has been done by our predecessors; in addition, and more delicate yet, we have made a similar effort for the *non-classed* properties in the most important communes. . . .

This last point was, in fact, an imitation of a similar change that had been made in Franck's second edition of 1845, but its adoption here by Cocks and Féret reinforced for the wine-drinking public a basic truth vital to understanding the professional conception of the classification: quality in Bordeaux's wines did not stop after the last of the fifth growths. Brokers and merchants did not limit their critical judgment of a commune's wines to just the classed growths, leaving the rest in an indiscriminate (and evenly priced) mass.

Fifth growths were followed by bourgeois supérieur, bons bourgeois, and bourgeois wines, for just as the trade had become ever more specific in the formulation of its classification beginning with the first growths, commercial logic dictated a continuation of the process down to the least of a commune's producers, and this was reflected in Cocks' French edition of 1850. Not only did Cocks and Féret classify the red wines at the top of the Bordeaux hierarchy (this time in five distinct levels containing sixty-three properties), not only were white wines classified (with Yquem already acknowledged as being in a class superior to the rest of the first growths), but in a work destined for the greater wine-drinking public, major producers in each commune were arranged in order of relative value to a depth similar to that used by Guillaume Lawton and his confreres. Although in no way meant to challenge the authority of the established five-level classification by inflating the ranks of top-quality wines, it did give active acknowledgment for what was becoming a standard qualification: the idea that "one would fall into the greatest mistake in considering that all the wines that are not included in the lists of the best growths are inferior and without quality." The second edition of Franck's *Traité* had made this distinction in 1845, and now it was Cocks' turn. This was an idea whose time had come, and it might be tempting to see this as an example of how the new edition of the *Traité* was wielding an influence similar to that of its predecessor, but this is not necessarily so. In looking for the source of this development, it is not insignificant to note that among the works Cocks cited as reference material for his French edition was "a journal titled *Le Producteur*."

During the four years between Cocks' English and French editions, two rather different documents, while not classifications themselves, offered unconventional testimony regarding the ranking of the various properties that comprised them.

On January 3, 1849, mayors throughout the department received a letter from Georges Haussmann, acting-prefect of the Gironde (and future prefect for the Seine department, in which post he would oversee the reshaping of Paris for Napoleon III). He was passing along a request from the Minister of Agriculture and Commerce for information regarding the state of the nation's vineyards during 1847 and 1848; a general economic depression beginning in 1846 had been a principal factor leading to the 1848 revolution which deposed the Citizen-King Louis-Philippe, and the newly installed government was seeking to ensure its own longevity by compiling information that would help relieve the crisis that was afflicting French vineyards, one of the chief sectors of the nation's economy. To aid the mayors in their task, a model form was furnished to help standardize their presentations. Entitled "Vine Growing, Evaluation of the Produce for 1847 and 1848," the form was composed of columns requesting specific facts: vineyard size; average yield; whether the harvests in 1847 and 1848 were greater, equal, or less than average; and an overall appreciation of those harvests' quality. The first column was entitled "Vineyard Designation," and this was filled out by the mayors in a variety of different ways.

Several reports, like that from Bruges, offered information on planting methods, such as whether a property's vines were trained high ("*vignes hautes*") or low ("*vignes basses*"); others, like Podensac's, simply grouped the commune's production into basic "red" and "white"; responses from Bègles and Macau specified whether vines were planted on gravelly soil or on Palus loam. The mayors in several of the principal wine-producing communes, including Margaux, Pauillac, Saint-Estèphe, Saint-Julien, and Saint-Laurent, saw fit to include in their responses the rankings held by the classed properties in their jurisdictions. (Unfortunately, no response from Cantenac, with its eight classed growths, is extant.)

The compiled list of classed growths that was drafted by the underprefect at Lesparre is interesting not least because its sources—the commune's mayors—were largely external to the commerce affected by these rankings, and its destination—the Minister of Agriculture and Commerce—had no concern with influencing any change in the status quo; thus, these standings might be considered relatively free from the polemics that were raging around the classification at this time. The rankings in this list were intercommunal: each property's standing was based on the overall classification of the Gironde's wines, not just those of its commune (in the Saint-Julien list, for example, Léoville was ranked a second growth, but had the rating been based on its standing within the commune, it would have been a first—of Saint-Julien); however, the fact that each mayor compiled an individual list prevents an intercommunal comparison within each class—there is no way to tell if Lascombes in Margaux was a higher or lower second growth than Pichon-Longueville in Pauillac. Even without this feature, it is interesting to see the degree to which there was a correspondence with the classification to come six years later. In Margaux, Macau, and Ludon in the Médoc, and in Bommes, and Preignac in the Sauternes region, the correspondence was exact (although the Margaux list presented just its first and second growths by name); Pauillac, Saint-Julien, and Saint-Laurent showed slight variations.

It was in Saint-Estèphe where the greatest differences occurred, with twenty-five properties identified as classed growths instead of the four that would eventually make the cut—evidently here the mayor did use the communal classification as the basis for the rankings on his list, which allowed Pomys and Tronquoy-Lalande (ranked among the bourgeois growths in the overall Gironde classification) to appear as Saint-Estèphe thirds. By this standard, the high prices for the wines from Cos-d'Estournel and Montrose, unmatched by any other property in Saint-

Estèphe, should have qualified them as communal first growths, but on the list they appeared as communal seconds: the first growth for Saint-Estèphe was not a property, but a vineyard *parcel* owned by a property in neighboring Pauillac: "Caillava, belonging to Château Lafite." Although Lafite itself was contiguously situated in a different commune, its vineyard in Saint-Estèphe produced wine that commanded first-growth prices, skewing the communal classification accordingly. (A similar situation involving multicommunal vineyards appeared in the list for Saint-Laurent, where "several vines belonging to Mr. Duluc" were ranked among the fourth growths; the bulk of Duluc's property—the future Branaire-Ducru—was duly listed among the fourths in the neighboring commune of Saint-Julien. In the days before the laws controlling appellation boundaries, it was much more common for properties to possess vineyard parcels in more than one commune—as is the case today with the vines in Saint-Julien whose grapes go into the Pauillac wine of Pichon-Longueville, Comtesse de Lalande.)

Although phonetic spelling and illegible handwriting make accurate decryption of property names a challenge (in 1844, Honoré de Balzac observed that "As for the mere mayors of communes you would be shocked by the number who cannot read or write and by the way in which the civil registers are kept"), the compiled list—excepting the entries from Saint-Estèphe—reinforces the sense of consolidation in the classification as 1855 approached.

Later in 1849, there appeared a second curiosity: a poem entitled *Les grands vins de Bordeaux* by Pierre Biarnez. A native of the Gironde, Biarnez was born in Podensac in 1798, and although biographical sketches also bestow upon him the title of poet, his main occupation was as an associate in the firm of Duffour-Debarte, the influential merchant house owned by Duffour-Dubergier. As a principal employee of one of Bordeaux's leading wine buyers (eventually he would acquire the business entirely), Biarnez was well acquainted with the region's great wines. His fame as a poet rested largely on *Les grands vins*, and even if this achievement was unlikely to qualify its author for the Academie Française, the poem was sufficiently appreciated in the treatment of its subject to serve as a reference in the literature of Bordeaux's wines.

Like Guillaume Lawton in his "Observations," Biarnez did not lay out a classification per se, but indicated the standings of the classed growths in the lines of his text. Unlike Lawton, Biarnez did not make extensive cross references when mentioning the rank of most properties, so his ratings provide little means of comparing the standing of a wine with others in its class. However, this deficiency is compensated by details inserted here and there, owing to a gossipy quality that did not fail to express itself whenever Biarnez felt that a property's ranking differed with his own estimation—generally because he felt the acknowledged ranking was too low. It may be that as a merchant Biarnez recognized the commercial necessity of keeping the classification's authority intact: despite differences that his own preferences may have suggested, he did not embark upon wholesale adjustments to make the hierarchy conform with his opinion, but instead indicated a property's accepted ranking to which he added his own remarks. The poem's value as contemporary commentary is thus twofold: not only are we offered the classification as it existed, but we also have evidence, in one merchant's opinion, of which properties were the ones to watch—and why.

Biarnez offered difference of opinion: second-growth Léoville ("I can not understand by what test ill-defined/Experts rank Léoville as a second class wine") and Mouton ("Who'd believe that Mouton, wine both modest and great/Can come after Lafite, and is but second rate?"); evidence of recent promotion: Lagrange ("A fourth growth at first sight, to raise its condition,/A wealthy new owner has changed its tradition.") and Prieuré ("In a merited rise to the fourth rank reclassed/Its wine glimmers today thanks to its brilliant past"); and the possibility of promotions to come: Montrose ("And Montrose, today, with its delicate flavor,/Almost like a second in finesse and savor;/If '34's standard were met every year/It could challenge those higher with nothing to fear"). A close reading of the poem shows how the classification was continuing to evolve, identifying the properties likely to rise in the hierarchy and those that had arrived at their just position.

It has been suggested that Biarnez's opinions were shaped by the quality of the hospitality he received during his visits throughout the Médoc, and the impartiality of his opinion was certainly compromised by the inordinate amount of space he devoted to a glowing account of Gironville and its proprietor: "Although this wine is not classed among our great growths, we have had to stop at this charming domain where the proprietor Mr. D. D. . . . , exercises a most generous hospitality." (In truth, Biarnez did more than just briefly stop; he devoted more than five pages to the only unclassed property mentioned in the poem—which just happened to be owned by his boss, "Mr. D. D." being Duffour-Dubergier.) However, although his comments could be catty and his opinions predominate over precedent, they were nonetheless the informed opinions of an experienced member of the trade, and, as such, are a reliable picture of the state of the classed growths in the mid-nineteenth century.

It should not be thought that the classification was the exclusive concern of only the French and the English. By the mid-nineteenth century, Belgium had become an important market for Bordeaux, and its classification had accordingly become an object of interest—in 1852, a version was reprinted in Brussels as part of a guide for Belgian wine drinkers. As Bordeaux wine continued to find favor in new markets around the world, the classification followed in its wake, becoming an international reference for the appreciation of its wines. From its origins as a discreet, albeit powerful, commercial tool, the classification had evolved into a universally recognized standard. It had triumphed over attempts to subvert its authority; it had woven disparate strands of professional, semiprofessional, and amateur opinion into a single, strong cable in which first and second growths were stable, recognized values, and thirds through fifths gave promise of following suit. Bordeaux was the world's largest wine marketplace, and the classification was the system that made it work.

By 1855, the classification was in danger of total collapse.

Between 1852 and 1855, Bordeaux experienced unprecedented circumstances that would forever alter the way the wine trade did business. Some of these situations had origins dating back to the 1840s; other events were more immediate. The depression that had afflicted Bordeaux since 1825 continued to exert financial pressure on the region's proprietors, and after two decades of difficult economics, even the first growths were feeling financially constrained. Thousands of barrels filled with wines from poor vintages lay unsold in proprietors' cellars: in June 1844, the owners of Latour could gaze with anxiety at wine from 1838, 1839, 1842, and 1843 that remained in their cellars having found few takers. Their spirits could hardly be consoled by the fact that when the wine did sell, it was often in quantities of several barrels at a time, a pattern of small sales that could extend over almost a decade. With a less-than-pleasant recent past behind them and an uncertain future ahead, the proprietors of Latour and Margaux, two of the three Médoc first growths, made the decision in 1844 to sell their wines by "subscription," Margaux for a period of nine years, Latour for ten. Good year, poor year, until 1852 Margaux sold its complete production to a consortium of merchants at 2,100 francs per tun, while Latour remained under contract through 1853 to the firm of Barton and Guestier at 1,750 francs. It was designed to be a win–win situation: the properties calculated their average operating expenses for the contract period to establish a price sufficient to maintain the quality of the wines (and the comfort of the proprietors); the merchants had sure supplies of the best Bordeaux wines without having to outbid competitors for what they hoped would be a series of good vintages. It was a gamble for both sides, but in the end it was the merchants who came away the winners, there being more good vintages than poor during the contract period.

Lafite remained free of any contractual obligations during this time, while Haut-Brion, the Graves first growth, was experiencing difficulties owing to the economic climate—considerable financial investment was required to produce a grand cru wine, and first growths required the greatest investment of all. The result of the crisis on Haut-Brion was that it found itself caught in an ever-descending spiral: it was unable to make the best wine its terrain was capable of producing because of insufficient income available for investment in the property, and the wine was unable to provide the necessary income because its quality could not command a sufficiently high price. One observer noted that the proprietor, Eugène Larrieu, was faced with "harvests piled up in his cellars, and he runs the risk of keeping them all and perhaps condemning himself to drinking them with his friends. . . ." For a time beginning in 1846, price quotations on the Bordeaux marketplace put Haut-

Brion in a category apart, where it hovered just below the other first growths, although well above the seconds.

With three of the four first growths no longer in a position to establish benchmark opening prices, the effect was a wobbling of the classification pyramid: as has been seen, it was during this period that the composition of the second growths became more well defined as they came to fulfill the traditional role of the firsts. One analysis of the situation among the first growths concluded that "The result of all this is that no longer do the first growths establish the price proportions for the various classes; today, this is based on the seconds: the fifths, which used to sell for half the price of the firsts, no longer sell but at about half the price of the seconds."

Still, by incorporating modifications that compensated for the prevailing commercial situation, the classification continued to work. It was not until the Latour and Margaux contracts were reaching the end of their terms that events truly began to shake the classification to its very foundations.

In March 1851, the manager of Brane-Mouton (the future Mouton-Rothschild) wrote in response to a classification-related query by Isaac Thuret, son of the property's owner, "Mouton, being the first of the second growths, must keep its rank. I know that there exists an established classification and that if Lafite sells for a given price, Mouton is worth a given proportion." The manager, Lestapis, was also a merchant and thus well aware of the classification's sacrosanct role in the Bordeaux marketplace. The following year, however, Lestapis was succeeded by Theodore Galos, and the ambitions among Mouton's proprietors to challenge the classification and raise their property to a first growth found a willing, and able, ally. Working in tandem, and taking advantage of the situation created by the Latour and Margaux subscriptions that created an increased demand for Mouton in the Bordeaux marketplace, Mouton's owners and manager pursued their efforts with discretion, anticipating the resistance their initiative would arouse among the city's merchants; Galos wisely counseled his employers "to maintain an absolute silence on your intention to stage a declassification."

The 1851 harvest was a good one, and in June 1852, Mouton's owners met the merchants initial offers of 1,700 francs per tun with a higher one of their own—2,000 francs; this was closing the gap that traditionally existed between Mouton and the first growths, but still shy of the 3,000 francs set by Lafite, the only first growth currently capable of demanding top-level prices. This first series of purchases was followed four months later by the sale of a further three tuns at an even higher price, 2,400 francs. "Now that experience has taught us that Mouton continues to sell well by waiting a little, it must never again be sacrificed," wrote L. Fould, another member of the proprietor's family and one of the main forces behind the attempt at reclassification. "I am every day more convinced of the enormous difference between Brane-Mouton and the second growths." A third offering in the beginning of 1853 did indeed bring 3,000 francs per tun and the coveted parity with first-growth Lafite, and this impetus carried the remaining 1851 to a sales price of 3,800 francs. In 1853, the Thurets sold Mouton, and in 1854, under the direction of its new owner, Baron Nathaniel de Rothschild, Mouton succeeded in obtaining an opening price of 5,000 francs per tun—the same as Lafite. It was the first time that a second growth had dared to achieve parity with the firsts, and the exploit not only further weakened the ordered price structure represented by the classification, but gave credence to the arguments that had been made by *Le Producteur*, Biarnez, and others that perhaps the four first growths should now be five.

While this drama was unfolding, which was limited to the properties at the top of the Bordeaux hierarchy, another development was beginning to sunder the relative values of classed and unclassed properties alike. In 1852, grapevines were showing the unmistakable signs of a new disease that had arrived in the Gironde: powdery mildew. Originally identified in Margate, England, in 1845 by a botanist named Edward Tucker, it spread throughout Britain, crossed the English Channel to Belgium, and reached northern France in 1848. Its effects were well documented: "a white powder first appears on the leaves or the ripening grapes; the leaves then shrivel, turning up at the edges, and little by little wither away without dying completely; at the same time, the wood deteriorates, the bark on the branches blackens, either completely or in small sooty patches; the branches attain only a part of their natural thickness and length; the wood does not reach maturity, the ends of the branches remain herbaceous, the pith swells in volume; the interior of the wood is dry and brittle." Reports continued to be heard of the disease's spread south, and it was in Podensac that the first signs were seen in the vineyards of the Gironde, toward the end of the 1851 growing season.

The following year powdery mildew was widespread throughout the Médoc, the Graves, and the Sauternes region. Harvests were cut in half and the quality of the wines suffered, but, depending on a variety of factors, including soil, grape variety, and the type of remedy a particular proprietor had chosen to combat the disease, the effect on a wine was more or less pronounced. Suddenly (and it was literally suddenly: from an average of around 3,800 tuns per year in 1852, 1853's production among classed growths fell to 1,800—and continued to drop), proprietors had to discover means not only to preserve the health of their vineyards, but also how best to produce wines that measured up to their traditional quality; suddenly there were no longer any "sure values." The Bordeaux wine market was in crisis and the classification could no longer serve as the stable rock upon which commerce could safely rest.

The result of all this was to be seen in two books that were written about the Médoc's vineyards, both published in 1855. In each, the classification is still prominently presented, but accompanied by commentary that threw into doubt the standings of wines at every level, from first down through fifth.

La culture des vignes, la vinification et les vins dans le Médoc; avec un état des vignobles d'après leur réputation (*Grape Growing, Winemaking, and the Wines of the Médoc; with an Estimation of the Vineyards According to Their Reputation*) by Armand d'Armailhacq was a major work close to 600 pages in length written not by a former merchant or broker, but by a currently active proprietor. His property, Mouton-d'Armailhacq, was classed "among the fifth great growths; but it cannot be long in meriting a promotion given the continued application of the excellent doctrines professed by its proprietor." It was those doctrines based on his experience of the terrain, practices, and wines of his fellow winemakers that comprised the body of this prescriptive book, and which its author believed could show proprietors throughout the Médoc how to produce a better wine more efficiently and economically. Armailhacq also included a survey of the Médoc's classed growths to give his readers an idea of the range of prevailing methodology and conditions, identifying sixty-four properties as crus classés and indicating the standing held by each in the classification. (Although included in this section profiling the Médoc's classed properties, Pauillac's Ducasse and Moussas—the future fifth-growth Grand-Puy-Ducasse and Lynch-Moussas—were not identified as belonging to a particular class; Haut-Brion did not appear, being located in the Graves region and thus outside the scope of the book.)

Although Armailhacq's classification, particularly among the first and second growths, is similar in size and composition to those which had recently appeared, it is his comments regarding the properties' rankings that are of particular interest. Well aware of what had been previously published (reference was often made to Franck's classification), Armailhacq did not limit his observations to whether a property was deserving of its rank, but also to recent promotions and demotions by the trade. The resulting commentary drew a portrait of a classification in full turbulence.

Among the second growths, Armailhacq stated that Beaucaillou should be placed among the seconds, and that Franck wrongly classed it as a third; Montrose was here a third, the trade having refused to maintain it as a second; Trentaudon (today Larose-Trentaudon, and a cru bourgeois) was not a fifth or a fourth, but a third—as it was in the 1849 prefect's survey—although Armailhacq mentioned that several merchants rated it no higher than a fourth and that its class had not yet been exactly determined; La Tour-Carnet was also a third, although Franck placed it among the fourths; Calon-Ségur was here a fourth, with the comment that it had formerly been at the head of the thirds and would make a comeback; Langoa-Barton was a fourth growth, although, again, Franck placed it among the thirds. Interesting details crop up here and there: in Cantenac, two gentlemen, one named Verrière who was the mayor of Margaux, and the other named Arquié, bought vines from the third-growth property Brown (Cantenac-Brown). According to Armailhacq, their wines were classed among the fourths, but he argued that since the vines were formerly producing third-growth wine, they should have kept that ranking with the trade; this was an issue that the classification would be faced with repeatedly in the future.

All of this might be considered an aberration, the cranky opinion of a dissatisfied proprietor who had a bone to pick with the classification (Armailhacq ranked his own property among the "second-fourth" growths, instead of with the fifths as others had placed it), and might be easily dismissed were it not for the similar tone in another book published in 1855, *Le vin de Bordeaux; promenade en Médoc* (*The wines of Bordeaux; a promenade through the Médoc*) by a former merchant named Charles Pierre de Saint-Amant.

Saint-Amant was familiar with Armailhacq's book, and even quoted approvingly from it in support of promoting second-growth Mouton to a first. However, the classification in *Le vin de Bordeaux* was not just a copy of the earlier work's opinions. (For starters, Saint-Amant only ranked Armailhacq's property a fifth growth, albeit with the comment that it should soon be a fourth as Armailhacq himself had classed it.) It, too, found the trade's estimation to be faulty, but for different reasons: here "the two Rausans," that is, Ségla and Gassies, "are equal to the Château"—Château Margaux; Lagrange, having risen to a third growth, is the object of speculation whether it would become a second in the future; among the fourth growths, Palmer is considered a likely candidate for promotion to a third, while Beychevelle, Saint-Pierre, and Duluc (Branaire-Ducru) are said to be often better than many third-growth wines.

Some of the judgments made by Armailhacq and Saint-Amant would indeed find confirmation in the very near future; others would remain hypothetical. Despite the differences of opinion expressed by each of their classifications, both nevertheless evidenced an overall consistency—the wine trade's version was still the nominal authority that served as the point of departure, but it was an authority that was now subject to open debate. Unlike the decade-long "age of Franck" when the classification could be adequately represented in a single public manifestation, in 1855 everyone seemed to have his own opinion. No longer a touchstone for assessing the quality of Bordeaux's wines, it had become a lightning rod for criticism. There were doubtless other opinions, other rankings made that year that were registered in merchants' offices, written in proprietors' diaries, or kept in other forms that have not survived. In the end, there would be only one that would have any lasting importance.

Toward the end of his book, Saint-Amant mentioned in passing that "we have been present at the departure of Bordeaux's best wines which have been summoned to take part in the Universal Exposition. . . . It is presumed that the classification about which we have spoken at length, and which serves as the starting point, perhaps too often for Bordeaux's brokers, will weigh heavily on the decision of the grand jury." This would remain to be seen.

Four

THE CLASSIFICATION OF 1855

Everything was under control.

Upon hearing on January 10 that the Departmental Committee had ceded it the authority for organizing the Gironde's wines at the Universal Exposition, the Chamber of Commerce immediately set to work. Its initial concerns were to obtain the wines needed for shipment to Paris and to ensure that they would be well cared for once there. As the businessmen responsible for the business of Bordeaux, the Chamber was at the hub of a network interweaving the political and commercial lives of the region. This gave it a clear idea of who possessed the talents or connections appropriate for practically any given situation, and it was to these contacts that the Chamber now turned.

On January 11, the day after officially assuming control of the project, the Chamber of Commerce wrote to Jean-Charles Alphand of the national Department of Civil Engineers. Recently transferred to Paris, Alphand had literally left his mark on Bordeaux during the fifteen years he was assigned there, overseeing such major projects as the waterfront constructions that enabled the port to accommodate ships larger than had been previously possible. No mere functionary, Alphand's professional and social achievements were acknowledged in 1852 when he was awarded the rank of Chevalier of the Legion of Honor. Georges Haussmann, during his tenure as prefect of the Gironde, had ample opportunity to appreciate Alphand's abilities; when Haussmann was called to Paris to undertake the rebuilding of the capital, he in turn summoned Alphand at the end of 1854 to be Administrator and Chief Engineer for Promenades and Parks.

Alphand had been a member of the Departmental Committee for the Universal Exposition until December 18, departing for Paris before the arrangement with the Chamber of Commerce had been made. The Chamber's letter brought him up to date on the steps it planned to take for the wines' display. "The aim we have set for ourselves," explained the Chamber, "is to offer as complete a collection of the Gironde's production as possible, in a manner both accurate and advantageous; this collection will be realized by means of a vast assemblage of carefully chosen samples." The Chamber planned to invite the mayors of the department's wine-producing communes to furnish examples of their local production; the proprietors of the classed growths would be individually contacted, although their exact count was not yet fixed ("they are from 60 to 70 in number"). It was estimated that this would result in 2,500 to 3,000 bottles for shipment to Paris.

The actual purpose of the Chamber's letter was to request Alphand's assistance in his capacity as a senior civil engineer with access to the administrators of the Palace of Industry and the complex of exhibition halls nearing completion on the Champs Elysées:

> We have reason to believe that in the Exposition buildings a little decorated cellar could be placed beside or below the wines. This cellar would have to be set out with taste and simplicity; all these arrangements should come together to give the multitude of French and foreign visitors converging on the Champs Elysées a favorable idea of our wine industry.
>
> You will add a new service to those that you have already rendered to our city if you would undertake to gather the information that we need to make final arrangements based on the ideas we have outlined for you. What space will we have available? When will our wines have to be delivered to Paris? Is it necessary to contact the general commission for the Exposition in advance?

In a fortnight, the Chamber had its reply. On January 26, Alphand wrote:

> I have had the honor of conversing with His Excellency the Minister of State and General Morin, the president of the executive commission for the Exposition [in the absence of Napoleon Jerome, who was still in Constantinople recovering from his adventure in the Crimean War], regarding the requests contained in your letter of January 11, 1855 relative to the exposition of the wines from the Gironde.
>
> His Excellency and the General see no difficulty in admitting the Gironde's wines to the exposition under the conditions that you indicate.

Alphand went on to explain that although the display's specific location had not yet been determined, the Chamber of Commerce could be assured that once the wines arrived in Paris they would be safely stored in one of the Palace of Industry's existing cellars.

This was an example of how the Chamber of Commerce preferred to work—at the uppermost levels of authority where a hearing of its concerns was most likely to result in a satisfactory resolution. The answer to all of its questions and the arrangements that it sought might have been obtained through the Departmental Committee, but although nominally subordinate to that body, the Chamber of Commerce preferred to rely on its own intermediaries whom it knew could effectively present its case to those in charge in Paris. Indeed, from the moment that the Departmental Committee delegated responsibility for organizing the display of the Gironde's wines to it, the Chamber effectively closed the Committee out of any further participation in this process as much as possible. Of course, the Chamber was happy to refer other matters to the Committee, as was the case with a request from the head of Harald Bay & Company who wrote to the Chamber of Commerce requesting that it include his company's product in the collection of wines to be sent to Paris:

> Dear Sir,
> The Chamber has read the letter (undated) that you have addressed to us, in which you speak of the work you are engaged in extracting alcohol form Jerusalem artichokes.
>
> We have read with interest the details that you set forth concerning an enterprise deserving of favor; we will be happy to learn that your efforts have been crowned with the success that they so richly deserve.
>
> As for your request for us to include a case of alcohol issuing from your factory with the wines that we are sending to appear in the Universal Exposition in Paris, the Chamber regrets that the specialty to which it has been necessary to restrict our shipment forbids us from admitting any product other than the wines of the Gironde. You will have doubtless addressed yourself to the Committee charged to oversee the participation of our department in the Exposition; it is they alone who are competent to make a decision concerning such matters, and we do not doubt that you will find them most benevolent in their support.

Meanwhile, on January 13, the Chamber of Commerce sent out a circular letter to the mayors of the department's wine-producing communes. In an appeal that blended national patriotism and local pride, the letter made it known that "the principal winemaking regions of France and abroad take it as a great honor to be part of this exposition; Burgundy, Champagne, Spain, the provinces of the Rhine will all be represented; the Gironde cannot stand aside."

The Chamber's request was simple:

> We ask that you send us a small case with 6 bottles of the best wines from your commune; choose from good years and take that which is capable of giving the most favorable and exact impression of your commune's production. This is a matter concerning the general good and not particular interests; the names of proprietors will not be known, so you will not have an awkward situation in choosing the samples that we ask of you; the wines should adhere to the overall purpose of offering a complete and advantageous image of winemaking in the Gironde, and avoid anything that would by nature stir up individual competition or contribute to rivalries of which there can be no question in these circumstances.
>
> The bottles should bear neither labels nor distinguishing marks; the Chamber will affix labels to them in Paris. . . .

A similar notice was individually addressed to the proprietors of each classed growth.

On January 15, the Chamber wrote to the director of the municipal warehouse instructing him to clear a space for the 400 to 500 six-bottle cases of wine that were expected to arrive by the February 15 deadline indicated in the letters sent to the mayors and proprietors. In addition, each week a note was to be sent to the Chamber's secretary informing him of the number and origin of the cases as they arrived.

And, finally, the Chamber wrote to its representative in Paris, Henri Galos.

With the change in regime brought about by the events of 1848, the ideological differences between Louis-Philippe's deposed monarchy and the republic that replaced it forced a personal choice upon many who had served in the former government. Among the first to resolve this dilemma and submit his resignation was Henri Galos, the Administrator of the French Colonial Office attached to the Minister of the Marine. Galos' political career had been marked by acts of moral choice, imposed by circumstance rather than freely decided upon according to plan.

Henri Galos was born in Bordeaux on 9 Brumaire, Year 13, according to the revolutionary calendar still in official use on October 30, 1804. His father, Jacques François Galos, was a leading merchant whose commercial success led to prominent local positions as Municipal Councilor, officer in the State Council, and Regent of the Bank of Bordeaux. In October 1830, the elder Galos was imported to the nearby town of La Réole as a candidate for a seat made vacant in the National Assembly when the royalist deputy Ferdinand de Lur-Saluces refused to swear allegiance to the government of Louis-Philippe, newly installed in the wake of the revolution that had just deposed the reactionary Charles X from France's throne. Jacques Galos' campaign was successful, but he nonetheless failed to enter the Assembly, dying in Paris at the end of December on the eve of his investiture.

Five months earlier, as Jacques Galos unknowingly approached the final phase of his public (and private) life, Henri Galos made his unexpected debut. As tensions spread from Paris to the rest of France during the month which gave the July Revolution its name, the evening of the 30th saw a mob in Bordeaux march on the Prefecture, the local representation of the hated Charles X. Dragging the prefect, Viscount François de Curzay, from his residence, they demanded that he accompany them to the parade ground at the Place de Quinconces and renounce the repressive measures that had brought France once more to the brink of anarchy. Along the way, Curzay briefly escaped his captors, wounding one of their number. The mob, now enraged, retook its prisoner with the intention of hanging him from a tree once they reached Quinconces, when Henri Galos and a friend happened upon the scene. Galos was twenty-five years old, and like his father a merchant. Outspoken in the expression of his liberal views, he too was opposed to the current threat to constitutional liberty that had originally motivated the crowd, but not at all partial to their methods in this instance. Convincing the mob that the prefect would meet a more suitable end by drowning in the Garonne River, he led them toward the waterfront by a route which

Henri Galos
(Archives Municipales de Bordeaux)

happened to pass his father's house. Upon reaching the building, Galos pushed the prefect into the entry and locked the gate behind them; after a rapid change of clothes they passed through another door to a neighboring house from which the prefect escaped Bordeaux. Having made a futile attempt to recapture their prisoner, the crowd contented itself with returning to the Prefecture and ransacking the building before being turned away by a troop of gendarmes.

This impulsive (and highly public) act helped launch Henri Galos on the local political scene in a career that broadly followed in his father's footsteps. He first served as a district councilor, from which post he succeeded in establishing a local reputation as an orator and a specialist in political economy. In 1837, he, like his father before him, was imported as a candidate for the National Assembly, in Henri's case to the nearby town of Bazas. Winning election but escaping his father's destiny, Galos took his seat among the conservatives on the right of the Assembly chamber, entering national politics with a strong belief in Louis-Philippe's "citizen-king" approach to French rule as the model for a successful coexistence between liberty and monarchy. The young deputy would become one of the regime's most ardent supporters, despite several areas of government policy to which he found himself opposed. Perhaps most significant of these was the question of free trade. Coming from a region whose income depended on exports of its wine—as well as imports of raw materials from France's colonies and foreign markets—opposition to France's restrictive tariffs was practically a matter of faith for Galos. This advocacy of free trade not only helped ensure his popularity among constituents at home, but also put him in opposition to most of his colleagues in the Assembly. In debate, however, Galos tended to avoid the heated tone common to much legislative discourse and to rely on his oratorical skills instead. Within three months of entering the Chamber of Deputies, Galos was building upon his reputation as a speaker with the delivery of long and detailed addresses that earned the young deputy a growing public profile in both Paris and Bordeaux. When the heir to the throne, the Duc d'Orléans, and his entourage paid a royal visit to Château Margaux in the summer of 1839, it was in the company of Henri Galos; four years later Galos would deliver the eulogy at the funeral of the property's owner, Alexandre Aguado, Marquis de las Marismas. In the capital, the young deputy from the Gironde enjoyed a growing social prominence as well, and in 1840 he made a fortunate marriage to the daughter of one of Napoleon Bonaparte's generals, Marshal Foy.

In the National Assembly, Galos' political career continued its ascendance as he focused his energies on budgetary questions concerning the departments of finance and the marine in particular, leading him to rise in defense of the government's ministers on more than one occasion. These actions did not go unnoticed by a government seeking to promote the careers of its most promising junior deputies, and Galos' reward came in March 1842, when he was named Administrator of the Colonial Office. Since France's colonies were attached to the nation by its ships, the colonial office was attached to the Minister of the Marine—who, as it happened, Galos had supported so often in debate. Among the questions that occupied Galos in this office was the abolition of slavery in France's possessions around the globe, the arrangements for which he was in the midst of resolving when the revolution of 1848 brought Louis-Philippe's fall from power, and with it, Galos' resignation from the government. By this time, he had become a consummate insider in the capital's political world. "Enemies he never had," observed one of his Bazas constituents, "and his political adversaries, like his friends, always found in him a warm supporter, an enlightened advisor. Who, having recourse to him, ever received less than full and complete satisfaction?"

Ironically, although Henri Galos avoided making enemies while in government, it was in retirement that he found himself in greatest jeopardy from the political opposition. On November 30, 1851, the Bordeaux newspaper Courrier de la Gironde *published an article written by Galos that was highly critical of the dismissal of several prefects throughout France that had just been announced by the President of the Republic, Louis Napoleon Bonaparte. Galos was particularly opposed to the replacement of Alexandre Neveux, the Gironde's prefect since 1848, by Georges Haussmann. Haussmann had already served as an assistant prefect in Blaye so he was very well suited for his new post, but his main qualification for promotion was an unconditional dedication to Louis*

Napoleon—the change in prefects was part of the groundwork for the coup d'état that would be staged by the President two days later, and Haussmann's mission was to quell any opposition to the event that might arise in the Gironde. Although Henri Galos maintained a discreet silence in the aftermath of the coup, the damage had been done, and several weeks later Haussmann struck: at 7:30 on the morning of February 13, a police commissioner and three officers arrived at the Galos family residence in Bordeaux with orders signed by the new prefect to search the premises. Finding nothing incriminating, Haussmann telegraphed Paris with an order for a further search of Henri Galos' home in the capital. One way or another Haussmann was determined to get his man, and in March he set his name to an order for Henri Galos' exile from France, one of more than 26,000 arrests and warrants for deportation that were issued nationwide against those who might present a danger to the new government. Considering the charges brought against him as an attack on his honor, Galos refused to contest the order for exile; his deportation was avoided only by the intervention of his uncle, General Baraguey-d'Hilliers, who was among those enjoying the confidence of Louis Napoleon.

This brush with exile had placed in jeopardy a position Henri Galos had assumed shortly after his departure from government: in September 1848 he had become the Parisian representative of the Bordeaux Chamber of Commerce. Galos' defense of free trade (a matter dear to Duffour-Dubergier), his familiarity with the city of Bordeaux and the department of the Gironde, and his well-placed influence in the government all made him a natural choice to represent the Chamber's interests in the capital. There was also a further connection between Henri Galos and the Chamber: his older brother Emile, a merchant prominent in Bordeaux's commercial and political affairs, had been a member of the Chamber during the 1830s, whose entry into municipal politics coincided exactly with Duffour-Dubergier's.

As his man in Paris, Duffour-Dubergier employed Henri Galos in a variety of ways beyond his duties as the voice of Bordeaux's business interests in the political world of the capital. When the Chamber of Commerce voted to present a medal to Jean-Charles Alphand for his services to the city in directing the renovation of Bordeaux's waterfront, Galos was directed to go to the mint in Paris to arrange for the medal's impression. When the Chamber decided that it needed a globe of the world for its offices in Bordeaux, Galos was given the task of making the rounds of shops and finding a suitable model. Now, with the approach of the Universal Exposition, Duffour-Dubergier intended to make the Chamber's representative useful once more by having Galos ensure that the Gironde's wines were safely stored upon their arrival in Paris, and by finding suitable help for the person who would be sent from Bordeaux to set up the Chamber's display. Galos' role in this affair was to be minimal, and his responsibility would end when the representative from Bordeaux arrived in Paris with the wines; until then his function was to act as a go-between for the Chamber with the Exposition's organizers. As stated in a letter from the Chamber to Galos:

> *We were asked to designate a representative in Paris, naturally we were led to choose you.*
> *Therefore, we ask you to promptly get in contact with the Exposition's Directors to assure that the reception of our samples is handled responsibly and that they are put in a safe place. . . . As for the opening of the cases, the affixing of the labels to the bottles, and their arrangement, we anticipate sending an intelligent individual to Paris who will have our instructions concerning this subject and who will be charged with this work. Tell us at what period he should be sent to Paris. . . .*

In the weeks following the Chamber's call for samples, it received letters from the mayors of Moulis, Fronsac, Virelade, and other communes throughout the Gironde requesting clarification of minor details before they submitted their wines. The manager at Giscours wrote to inquire if it was a problem that their corks were branded with the property's name; the Chamber assured him that it was fine. The Chamber wrote to the widow Lafon de Camarsac at Rochet in Saint-Estèphe (Château Lafon-Rochet today) to thank her for the six bottles that had been duly received. Pierre-François Guestier received acknowledgment for the four six-bottle cases representing wines from Léoville, Langoa, Beychevelle, and Batailley; the first two properties were owned by Guestier's partners in their merchant business, Nathaniel and Bertram Barton, the last two belonged to Guestier himself. By January 25, the Chamber's President, Duffour-Dubergier, could write to the Departmental Committee that all was moving ahead according to plan and that the response to the Chamber's circular had been well received, quoting again the 2,500- to 3,000-bottle estimate for shipment to Paris.

One month later, however, the picture had become somewhat less promising. At the Chamber of Commerce's meeting on February 28, "a member announced that the samples requested from the proprietors of the classed growths and the mayors of wine-producing communes have not brought results as complete as was hoped for; the grand crus, especially, have left much to be desired in this regard." It was decided to push back the deadline for submissions and publish a new appeal in the local newspapers. Accordingly, the March 1 edition of the *Courrier de la Gironde* included the following notice:

> The Chamber of Commerce informs the proprietors of the classed growths and the mayors of the department's wine-producing communes that the samples destined to take part in the Universal Exposition of 1855 may be addressed to Mr. Lafon, director of the municipal warehouse at the Place Laîne until March 10. This date is final. A new appeal is being made to the goodwill of those who have not yet sent the samples requested by the Chamber in its circular of January 13. It would be regrettable if the grand crus were not present on this august occasion and the Gironde's wines were not represented as completely as possible.

It may be that the proprietors were too preoccupied by their struggles against powdery mildew and the other concerns that beset the Gironde's vineyards, or that they shared the lack of understanding originally shown by the Departmental Committee in not appreciating how their wines could fit into a "trade fair" for industrial products. Politics may have entered the picture, too. There was still much resentment and suspicion among many French citizens against Napoleon III, whose coup d'état had overthrown the Republic he had sworn to uphold when elected President; such sentiments could have led some proprietors to forego participation in any project such as this Universal Exposition that was likely to lend support to his reign as Emperor. (Nonetheless, this did not prevent Count Duchatel, a former minister under Louis-Philippe the Citizen-King whom Louis Napoleon had twice attempted to overthrow, from sending a case of six bottles from his Saint-Julien property Lagrange for display in Paris.) For whatever reason, it was becoming clear to the Chamber of Commerce that its projection of 400 to 500 cases was not likely to be met.

The second call for wine samples did not arouse much additional interest among proprietors or mayors, and discussion at the Chamber's meeting on March 7 acknowledged that the renewed appeal had not met with success:

> Despite the repeated request addressed to the proprietors of the classed growths and the mayors in the wine-producing communes, significant gaps exist in the collection of wines that have been sent to the warehouse, and this collection must be completed, especially as concerns the [wines of] superior quality. The President will take it upon himself to have a broker approach the grand cru proprietors personally to ask them to send the requested samples, and if these steps remain fruitless the broker will be authorized to purchase the necessary wines so that the Chamber's shipment will be suitable in all respects.

The Chamber of Commerce had assured the Departmental Committee of its ability to effectively organize the Gironde's winemakers; as early as January 25, it had informed the Committee that "a large enough number of proprietors and mayors of various communes have answered the call addressed to them," and, on February 16, had reiterated that "a large enough number of cases of wine samples have already been deposited at the warehouse, in accordance with the request that the Chamber had addressed." The Chamber was obliged to produce a respectable turnout, even if it meant having to buy the wines from the classed growths to fill out its shipment. As it turns out, however, this step was never taken and it was an incomplete representation that was eventually put on display in Paris.

Among the properties considered classed growths, only twenty-three red- and ten white-wine samples were submitted (see Appendix IV); this represented far fewer than the sixty to seventy properties the Chamber of Commerce had originally estimated to be worthy of this status. Because the Chamber had no definitive list of classed growths, it developed that some wines solicited and sent off to Paris as crus classés were endowed with a status that would not last out the year; this was the case with Haut-Pessac and Haut-Talence, two red wines in the Graves produced by a Mr.

Pomez, as well as Château Carbonnieux, the dry white wine that had long been recognized as the finest of its type.

The Chamber of Commerce had not specified particular vintages to be submitted, only that they be "from good years." In the majority of cases the vintages of the wines received at the municipal warehouse were either not recorded or simply not indicated by the proprietors themselves. It was noted, however, that Batailley sent six bottles of its 1844 (a year most wines were considered to be of "ordinary" quality according to contemporary records kept by Tastet & Lawton) and Langoa sent its 1846 (a generally "full-bodied, good" vintage throughout the Médoc). Léoville was divided into three distinct properties at this time, as attested to by contemporary sales records; however, the fact that the only bottles received from Léoville were sent in by Pierre-François Guestier along with the samples from the other classed properties owned by him and the Bartons suggests that it was wine from the Barton vineyards that carried the Léoville standard to the Universal Exposition with its 1847 vintage (overall, an "exquisite, not very full-bodied" year according to the Tastet & Lawton vintage notes for the Médoc). Château Lafite submitted two wines, three bottles each of its 1846 and its 1848 (the latter vintage considered to have produced "exquisite, full bodied" wines). If these can be taken as an indication of the overall choices made by the other proprietors, wines that were six to ten years old were generally considered to best represent a property's quality during this period.

When the revised deadline of March 10 had come and gone, only 110 cases from classed growths and wine-producing communes combined had been gathered in the municipal warehouse—one-third to one-fourth of the total originally anticipated. On March 31, these were packaged into thirty-six lots and sent to Paris with the first delivery of the Gironde's exhibits for the Universal Exposition; the Departmental Committee made two subsequent shipments of goods on April 7 and 12, but there is no indication that wines formed any part of them. (The manuscript of the Departmental Committee's report to the prefect later claimed a more creditable 148 cases of wine were sent; in a subsequent published version, the figure became 145.)

During this time, the Chamber had continued to occupy itself with arrangements for the wines once in Paris. On February 16, it wrote to the Departmental Committee requesting details of how these wines were to be presented at the Universal Exposition. To give a sense of unity to the Exposition, the Imperial Commission had established specific dimensions for the display cases that would contain the products submitted by the Departmental Committees. Three types were permitted: glass-fronted cases, from ½ to 1 meter long, designed to rest horizontally on 1-meter-high tables; similar cases 1 to 1½ meters high, which would stand vertically on tables backed by a wall or partition for support; and freestanding showcases 3 or 4 meters tall. As the authority empowered to distribute the 140 linear meters of display space that had been allotted to the Gironde by the Imperial Commission in Paris, the Departmental Committee had selected the largest option available for the Chamber of Commerce's collection: a showcase 4 meters high, 1 meter deep, and 3 meters long.

If collecting the wines in Bordeaux had become a problem for the Chamber of Commerce, its display in Paris presented a complication of its own, one that was recognized when the project was first proposed to the Departmental Committee the previous autumn. Unlike the products traditionally presented at this type of exposition, where the difference between two similar tapestries or two similar jeweled necklaces was evident to the eyes of all who viewed the displays, mere visual comparison offered no basis for understanding the relative value that made one bottle of wine unlike another. In the end, this could only be done by taste. Since there was just enough wine being sent to Paris to allow for the exhibit and a tasting by a limited panel of judges, how were the different qualities among the wines on display to be communicated to the public at large? Back in December 1854, a member of the Departmental Committee remarked that any submission of wines would be little more than an exhibition of bottles. The same concern was voiced by another commentator when questioning what the public might derive from such a display: "What could they see, what could they appreciate? In this sort of exposition, they will have to content themselves with a view of the *container* and its *label*. And if it is true that nothing resembles an honest man so much as a rogue, one could more pertinently observe that enclosed within its bottle nothing so resembles a good wine as a poor one." How could the Chamber of Commerce give its display a visual focus that would explain the differences in quality fundamental to Bordeaux's wines and attract the eye of the exposition's visitors? Duffour-Dubergier thought he had the answer.

During the Chamber's meeting on March 7, Duffour-Dubergier produced a sketch for a map of the Gironde's wine regions to accompany the display in Paris. The members' response was positive: "This large-scale map is judged to be capable of offering great interest, and the President should see to its production." This map would be Duffour-Dubergier's project, his personal contribution to the Universal Exposition of 1855. Not only would it lend visual interest to what would otherwise be just an armoire full of bottles, but it would serve an informative purpose as well. In an age before the commonplace use of wall cards to describe the function or significance of an exhibit, Duffour-Dubergier intended this map to explain the differences between individual wines inside identical bottles. Other methods might have achieved a similar result, but a map had certain advantages: in the mid-nineteenth century, when the vocabulary of winetasting was even less understood than it is today, an organoleptic description of each wine would have been too cumbersome; there was also the risk that such an appraisal of the wines on display might influence the jury during the tasting that would take place at the Exposition.

Duffour-Dubergier believed that a map showing how individual wines came from different locations throughout the Gironde would be the most effective means to communicate the idea that each of those on display possessed a unique character; the vineyards' locations could be indicated by dots placed in the different communes to illustrate clearly the wines' varying origins. More than this, the relative quality of the individual wines could be indicated by an annotation on the map, an annotation based on the wine trade's classification. It was certain that the other wine regions sending exhibits to the Universal Exposition would be facing similar problems of how to present their wines. For the Chamber of Commerce this map would be "the part of our exhibit most likely to attract the public's attention."

Duffour-Dubergier entrusted its production to Jean-Maurille Unal-Serres, one of Bordeaux's premier mapmakers. He had just published a large-scale map of the city the previous year, and had worked for Duffour-Dubergier during the latter's term as mayor of Bordeaux. Originally a professor of mathematics in the Bordeaux schools, Unal-Serres went to work at the city hall as a draftsman in 1840, earning a promotion to surveyor in 1843, a year after Duffour-Dubergier became mayor. This vinicultural map of the Gironde, one of the highlights of Unal-Serres' career, would be drafted in two versions: a large-scale rendition for display at the Universal Exposition and a subsequent edition for public sale that would be slightly reduced in size. This smaller version, 820 cm by 960 cm, would be printed by Chaumas-Gayet, whose firm had become one of Bordeaux's chief publishers through books such as Armailhacq's *Culture des vignes,* Franck's *Traité sur les Vins du Médoc,* and the guidebook *Le nouveau conducteur de l'étranger à Bordeaux.* Chaumas had proven to be a publisher of talent in the printing of large-scale maps with the production of a *Road Map of the Gironde Department* similar to the one proposed by Duffour-Dubergier and Unal-Serres. Their vinicultural map would show the Gironde and the principal roads and railways passing through the department's chief vineyard regions. Engravings of several of the châteaux that were becoming increasingly typical of the Médoc countryside contributed to the image of grandeur that the Chamber hoped to convey for the Gironde's production. A booklet accompanying the public edition of the map explained the method behind its presentation:

> No one is unaware that the department of the Gironde is France's premier vineyard area; here the vine occupies 104,000 hectares, and, in average years, its production reaches 2,050,000 hectoliters.
>
> This great quantity offers wines in every price range; there could be no question of indicating those of an ordinary quality on our Map: this would have required an atlas composed of numerous pages in the largest size; we have had to limit ourselves to the superior wines, to those known as *classed growths,* which ancient usage divides into five categories. They are grouped in several communes of the Médoc, such as Pauillac, Saint-Julien, Cantenac, etc.

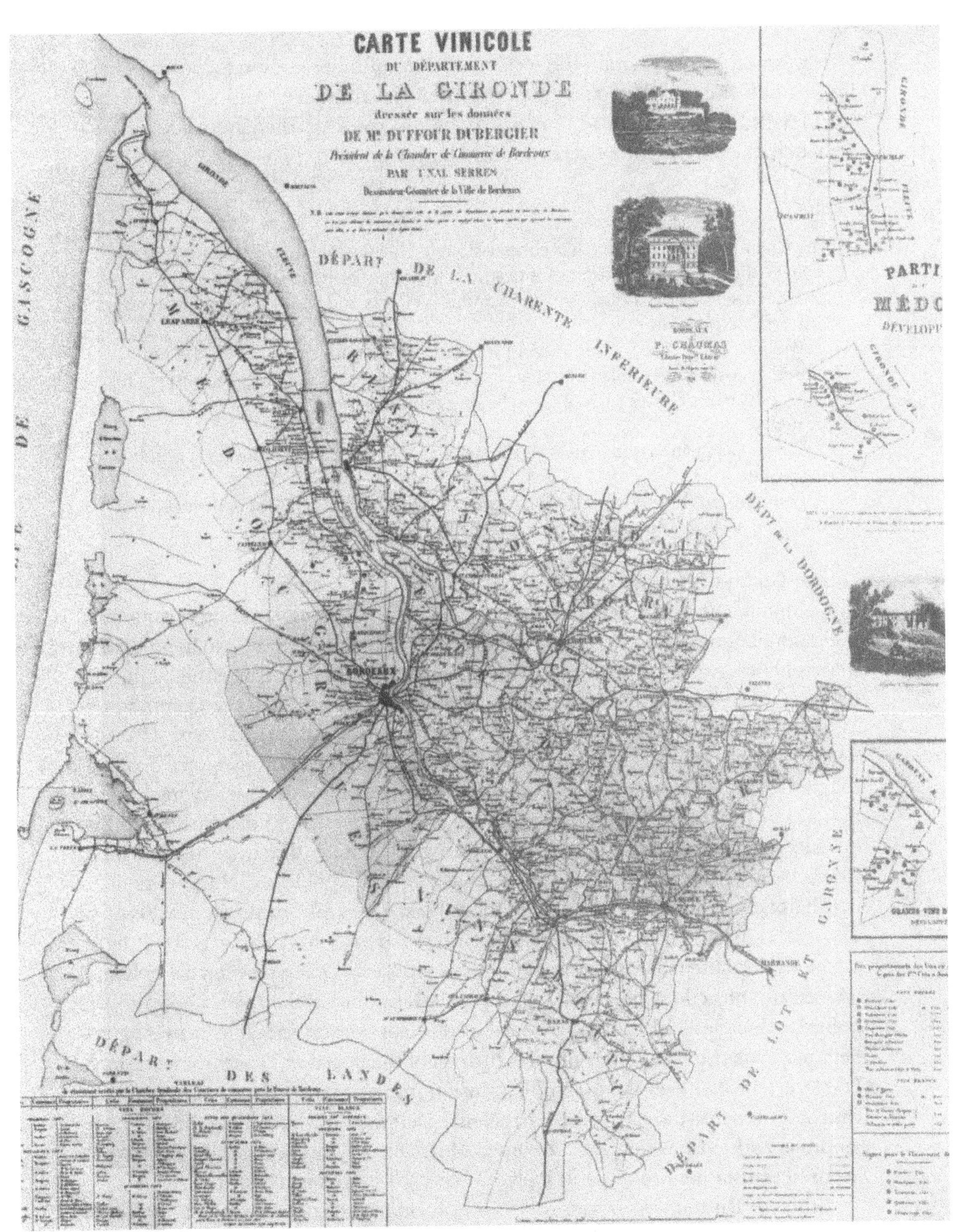

Duffour-Dubergier's Wine Map of the Gironde

(Bibliothèque Nationale de France)

It was necessary to obtain the exact identities of these classed growths; general figures like "60 to 70" would not do in this circumstance. And so, on April 5, Duffour-Dubergier wrote to the board of directors of the Union of Brokers Attached to the Bordeaux Commodities Market.

> Sirs,
>
> The Chamber of Commerce has commissioned a large-scale map detailing the wine regions of the Gironde; this map is destined to accompany the wine samples that have been sent to Paris through the Chamber's efforts and which are to figure in the Universal Exposition.
>
> We have come to ask if you might please furnish us with the list of all the red classed growths in the department, as exact and complete as possible, specifying to which of the five classes each of them belongs and in which commune they are located.
>
> We also ask you to oblige us with the details relative to the classification of the great white wines.
>
> Our map must soon leave for Paris; we ask you, Gentlemen, to send us this information as soon as you possibly can, and thank you in advance.

The Union of Brokers Attached to the Bordeaux Commodities Market was the professional body that regulated the activities of the brokers handling various business transactions in the city; other brokers' associations also existed to handle trade in neighboring districts such as Libourne, Blaye, and Barsac. Since the beginning of the century, an average of seventy brokers were accredited to the Commodities Market, each licensed by the government to transact a particular type of trade. There were brokers for insurance and brokers for translation; some were qualified to handle wines, while others dealt in different types of goods. Just as wine brokers had to satisfy certain criteria of knowledge and experience, so did each discipline have its specialized qualifications. What brought them all together was the Union, which assured that standards of professionalism were upheld and the laws regulating their activity were obeyed. One of those laws, dated 29 Germinal, Year 9 (April 18, 1801), specified that "Brokers will gather together and name among themselves, by absolute majority, a syndic and six deputies to exercise internal policing, investigate infractions of the laws and regulations, and make them known to the public authorities." In 1855, this board of directors was presided over by Auguste Perrin, a broker dealing in insurance; the rest of the board was composed of André Ferrière, a broker licensed to handle translations and transactions in German and Dutch; P. Libéral-Cazeaux and Barthélemy Deleyre, Sr., both licensed in "commodities and various articles"; Georges Merman, a wine broker; B. Tournay, a licensed translating broker; and Pierre Tessié, Jr., a broker in spirits.

Although Duffour-Dubergier's letter was formally addressed to the board, only one of its members was qualified to satisfy the request. Georges Merman (his full name was Charles-Henri-Georges) was the head of a brokerage firm whose origins reached back over several generations. Records for 1808 show a broker named Pierre Merman licensed to transact sales of wine, and upon his retirement in 1816 his son Antoine Merman was registered in his place; when Antoine died in 1843, Georges Merman succeeded him in turn. Merman's firm was one of the principal brokerage houses in Bordeaux: among the comments accompanying the record of transactions in the Tastet & Lawton notebooks, the Merman name often appears as the agent handling the sale of classed-growth wines. Georges Merman was one of the most respected wine brokers in the trade, having established a sufficiency of connections among his confreres to be elected to the Union's board of directors. It was certain to be Merman and not the other board members who handled Duffour-Dubergier's request, and in taking on this task he was undoubtedly able to benefit from the judgment and counsel of his fellow wine brokers in supplementing his own considerable knowledge.

A wine broker's expertise was based on experience and the written records that constituted the heart of a brokerage firm. Although very few of the brokerage houses that were in business in 1855 still exist today, the records in the firm of Tastet & Lawton can provide an indication of the type of information that was instrumental in responding to Duffour-Dubergier's inquiry. Among the details in the Tastet & Lawton notebooks referred to in the previous chapter was an annual recapitulation of the opening sales for hundreds of properties throughout the Médoc peninsula. (The tables in Appendix III represent a compilation of these transactions, rearranged by property instead of by year and commune as originally recorded.) Not only were those sales negotiated by the firm of Tastet & Lawton registered, but the transactions of other brokers were noted as well. For instance, in the table for Brane-Cantenac, observations for the 1839 wine indicate that it was Merman's firm that arranged the sale of twenty-eight tuns at 1,200 francs apiece in February 1840. In the case of Tastet & Lawton, such records extend back to 1775, eighty years before the request for a list of classed growths by Duffour-Dubergier. Had Georges Merman needed details of this sort to supplement the similar material he undoubtedly possessed, not only could he have requested such information from Tastet & Lawton, but also from the half-dozen other brokers whose professional activity predated Merman's (by as much as thirty-three years in the case of François Labory, licensed in 1811).

It has often been remarked that the two-week period between the formulation of the request for "a list as exact and complete as possible" and its receipt was a remarkably short period to have achieved a classification with claims to authority or thoroughness. As has been seen, the classification of the Gironde's wines had been well documented for decades before 1855, so it was hardly a matter of inventing one from scratch. Indeed, the fact that there was such a delay suggests that consultation did take place among those brokers licensed in the transaction of wine,

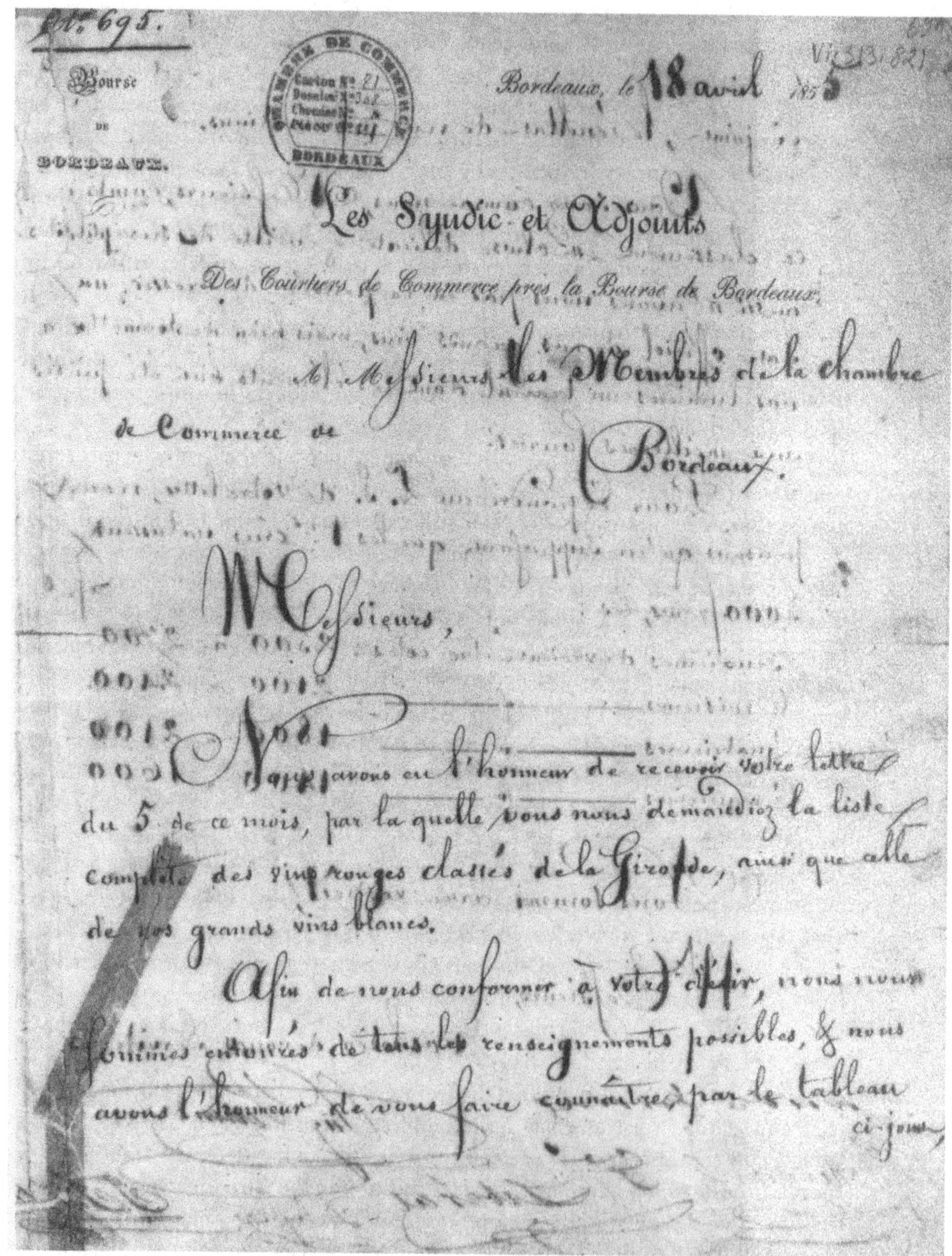

N° 695.

Bourse de Bordeaux.

Bordeaux, le 18 avril 1855

Les Syndic et Adjoints

Des Courtiers de Commerce près la Bourse de Bordeaux,

A Messieurs les Membres de la chambre de Commerce de Bordeaux.

Messieurs,

Nous avons eu l'honneur de recevoir votre lettre du 5 de ce mois, par laquelle vous nous demandiez la liste complète des vins rouges classés de la Gironde, ainsi que celle de nos grands vins blancs.

Afin de nous conformer à votre désir, nous nous sommes entourés de tous les renseignements possibles, & nous avons l'honneur de vous faire connaître par le tableau ci-joint,

The 1855 Classification—page 1

18 avril

ci-joint, le résultat de nos informations.

Vous savez comme nous, Messieurs, combien ce classement est chose délicate & éveille des susceptibilités; aussi n'avons nous pas eu la pensée de dresser un état officiel de nos grands vins, mais bien de soumettre à vos lumières un travail dont les éléments ont été puisés aux meilleures sources.

Pour répondre au P. S. de votre lettre, nous pensons qu'en supposant que les 1ers crus valussent 3,000 francs, les:

	Fs	
Deuxièmes devraient être cotés:	2500	à 2700.
Troisièmes ———	2100	„ 2400.
Quatrièmes ———	1800	„ 2100
Cinquièmes ———	1400	„ 1600

Nous sommes avec respect,

Messieurs,

vos bien dévoués Serviteurs.

The 1855 Classification—page 2

Vins rouges classés du Départ de la Gironde

Crûs	Communes	Propriétaires
Premiers crûs		
Chateau Lafite	Pauillac	Sir Samuel Scott Baronet
Chateau Margaux	Margaux	Aguado
Chateau Latour	Pauillac	de Beaumont de Courtivron de Flers
Haut Brion	Pessac (Graves)	Eugène Larrieu
Seconds crûs		
Mouton	Pauillac	Bon N. de Rothschild
Rauzan Ségla	Margaux	Comtesse de Castelpers
Rauzan Gassies		Viguerie
Léoville	St Julien	Marquis de las Cases Baron de Poyféré Barton
Vivens Durfort	Margaux	de Puységur
Gruau Laroze	St Julien	de Bethman Baron Sarget de Boisgerard
Lascombe	Margaux	Mademoiselle Hue
Brane	Cantenac	Baron de Brane
Pichon Longueville	Pauillac	Baron de Pichon Longueville
Ducru Beau Caillou	St Julien	Ducru — Ravez
Cos Destournel	St Estèphe	Martyns
Montrose	—	Dumoulin

The 1855 Classification—page 3

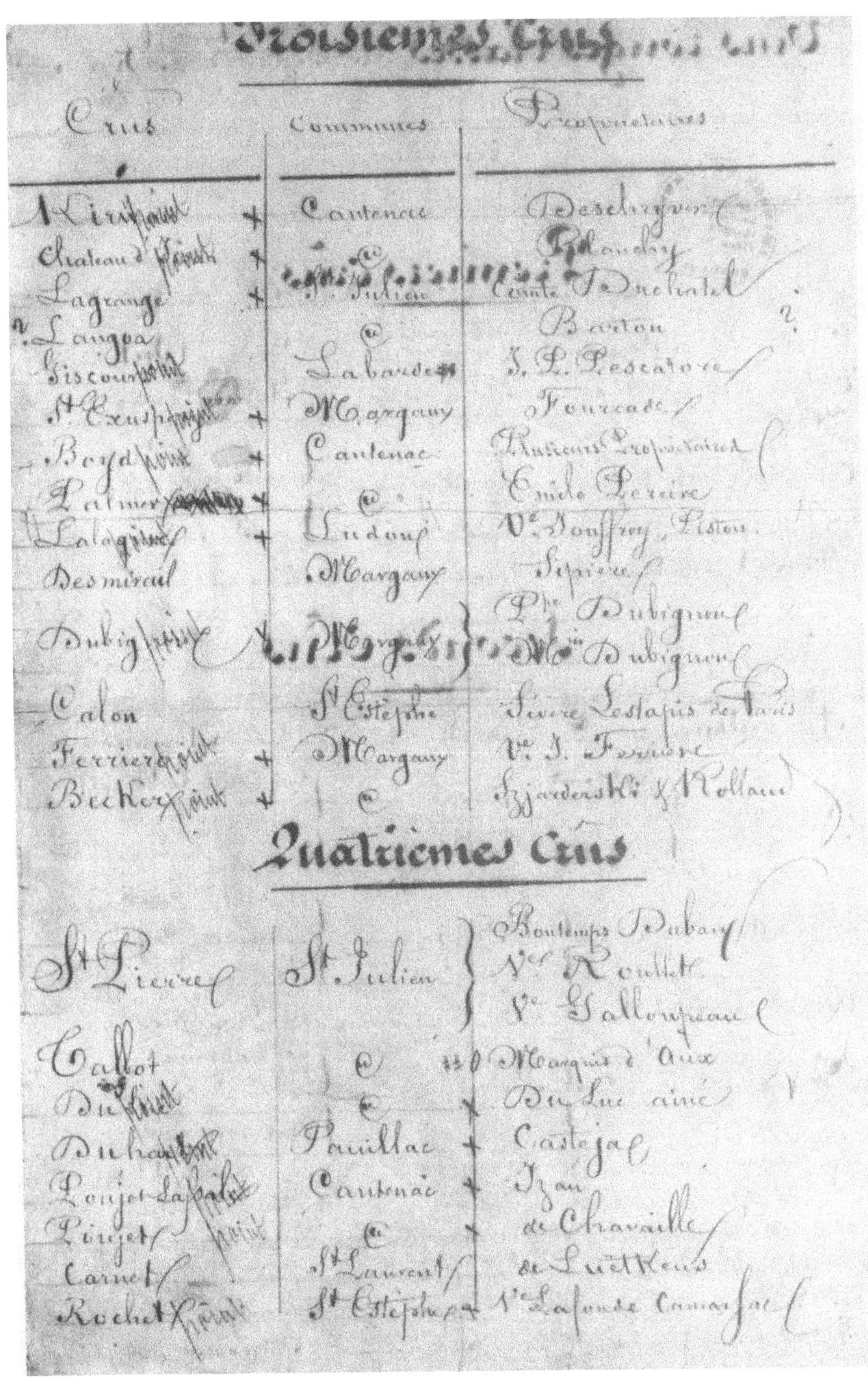

Troisièmes Crus

Crus	Communes	Propriétaires
Kirwan	Cantenac	Deschryver
Château d'Issan	id.	Blandy
Lagrange	St Julien	Comte Duchâtel
Langoa	id.	Barton
Giscours	Labarde	J. L. Pescatore
St Exupéry	Margaux	Fourcade
Boyd	Cantenac	Plusieurs Propriétaires
Palmer	id.	Emile Pereire
Lalagune	Ludon	Ve Jouffroy Piston
Desmirail	Margaux	Sipière
Dubignon	Margaux	Pre Dubignon Mis Dubignon
Calon	St Estèphe	Sieur Lestapis de Paris
Ferrière	Margaux	Ve J. Ferrière
Becker	id.	Izjardowski & Rolland

Quatrièmes Crus

Crus	Communes	Propriétaires
St Pierre	St Julien	Bontemps Dubarry Ve Roullet Ve Galloupeau
Talbot	id.	Marquis d'Aux
Duluc	id.	Duluc aîné
Duhart	Pauillac	Castéja
Pouget Lassalle	Cantenac	Izan
Pouget	id.	de Chavaille
Carnet	St Laurent	de Luetkens
Rochet	St Estèphe	Ve Lafon de Camarsac

The 1855 Classification—page 4

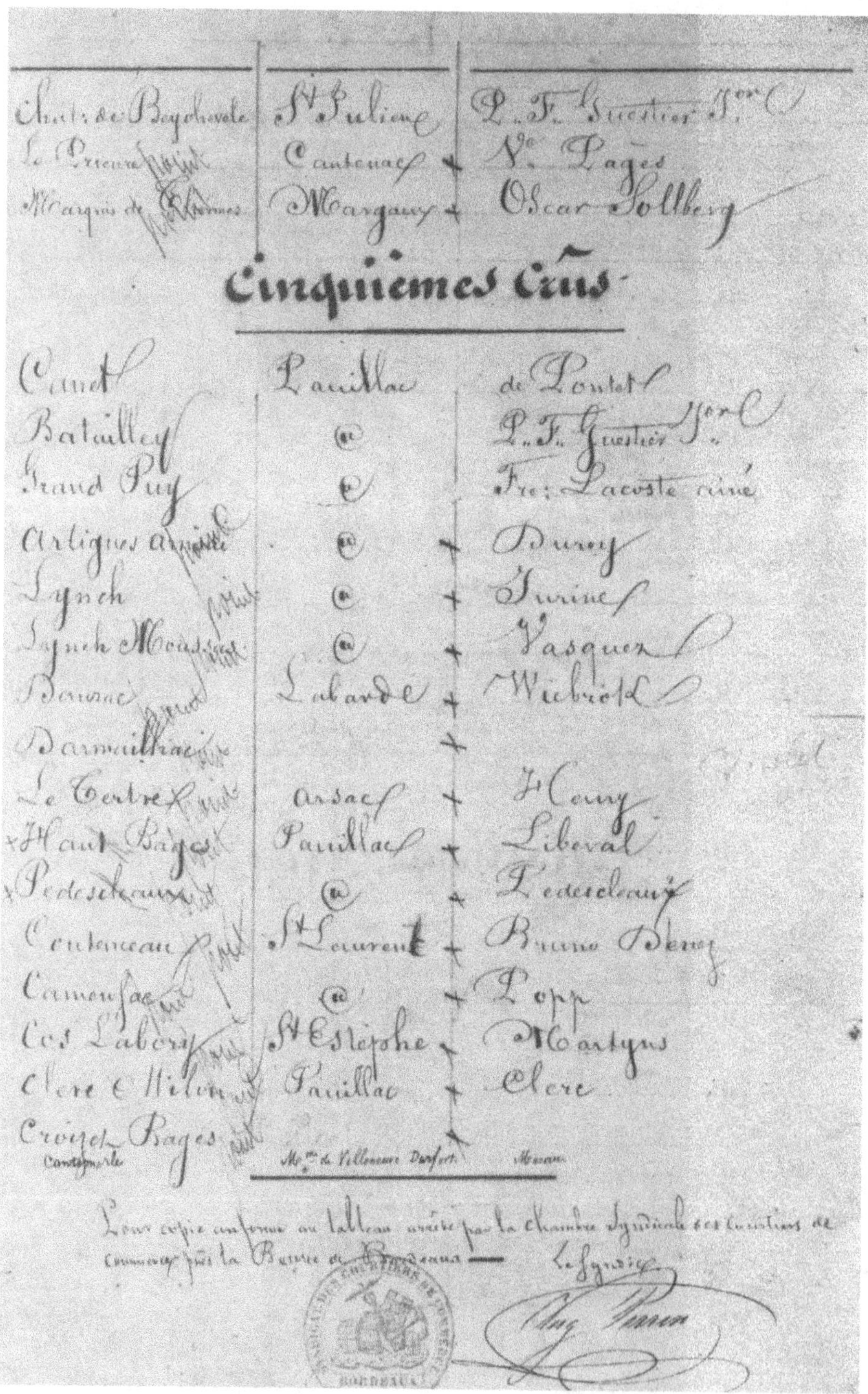

Château de Beychevelle	St Julien	P. F. Guestier Jeune
Le Prieuré	Cantenac	Ve Pagès
Marquis de Terme	Margaux	Oscar Sollberg

Cinquièmes Crûs

Canet	Pauillac	de Pontet
Batailley	do	P. F. Guestier Jeune
Grand Puy	do	Fre Lacoste ainé
Artigues Arnaud	do	Duroy
Lynch	do	Jurine
Lynch Moussas	do	Vasquez
Dauzac	Labarde	Wiebrock
Darmailhac		
Le Tertre	Arsac	H Coury
Haut Bages	Pauillac	Liberal
Pedesclaux	do	Pedesclaux
Coutenceau	St Laurent	Bruno Devez
Camensac	do	Popp
Cos Labory	St Estèphe	Martyns
Clerc Milon	Pauillac	Clerc
Croizet Bages		

Pour copie conforme au tableau arrêté par la Chambre Syndicale des Courtiers de commerce près la Bourse de Bordeaux — Le Syndic

The 1855 Classification—page 5

Vins blancs classés de la Gironde

Crus	Communes	Propriétaires
1er Cru Supérieur		
Yquem	Sauternes	de Lur-Saluces (Bertrand)
Premiers Crus		
Latour Blanche	Bommes	Focke
Peyraguey	id	Lafaurie aîné
Vigneau	id	Vve de Reyne
Suduiraut	Preignac	Guillot Frères
Coutet	Barsac	de Lur Saluces (Bertrand)
Climens	id	Lacoste
Bayle	Sauternes	Dépons & Co
Rieussec	id	Mayé
Rabeaud	Bommes	Deyme
Deuxièmes Crus		
Mirat	Barsac	Moller
Doisy	id	Deane
Peixoto	Bommes	Vve Lacoste
D'arche	Sauternes	Lafaurie Jne & Co
Filhot	id	de Lur Saluces (Bertrand)
Broustet Nérac	Barsac	Capdeville
Caillou	id	Sarraute
Suau	id	Pédesclaux
Malle	Preignac	de Lur Saluces (Henry)
Romer	id	de Lamyre Mony
Lamothe	Sauternes	Ve Baptiste

Pour copie

The 1855 Classification—page 6

otherwise Georges Merman (if the task was undertaken by him alone) or any other single broker could have easily consulted his records at hand and produced a classification in a matter of days, not weeks. The probability of such a collaboration is corroborated by the Tastet & Lawton notebook for April 1855, which contains a transcription of the classification dated April 16, two days *before* the list was sent to the Chamber of Commerce. Given the evidence available and the history of how the brokerage trade functioned, it is very likely that the classification dated April 18, 1855, was a consultative, if not collaborative, effort involving several of Bordeaux's wine brokers. There were no château visits, no requests for samples, no tastings involved in the establishment of the rankings, nor was there any need for them. The 1855 classification was based on the readily available information that was used by the brokers in their daily transaction of business.

The letter that accompanied the classification showed a definite awareness of the delicate nature of the task presented to the brokers:

> Sirs,
>
> We were honored to receive your letter of the 5th of this month requesting of us the complete list of classed red wines of the Gironde, as well as that for our great white wines.
>
> In order to satisfy your wishes, we surrounded ourselves with all possible information, & we have the honor to make known to you by the attached table the result of our investigations.
>
> You know as we do, Sirs, how much this classification is a delicate thing & likely to arouse sensitivities; also it was not our thought to draw up an official state of our great wines, but only to submit for your consideration a work whose elements have been drawn from the best sources.
>
> To answer the P.S. in your letter, we consider that in supposing the 1st crus are worth 1,000 francs, the:

Seconds should be priced:		2,500	to	2,700 frs.
Thirds	"	2,100	"	2,400
Fourths	"	1,800	"	2,100
Fifths	"	1,400	"	1,600

> We are, with respect, your most devoted servants.

This document was signed (counterclockwise from the top) Aug. Perrin, André Ferrière, G. Merman, Cazeaux-Libéral, Deleyre aîné, P. Tessié fils. These were the members of the board of directors for the Union of Brokers Attached to the Bordeaux Commodities Market, the administrators to whom Duffour-Dubergier originally addressed his request (the remaining board member, B. Tournay, was not a signatory); these were not necessarily the classification's authors—their names would be François Labory, licensed wine broker since 1811; Auguste Liberal, licensed since 1814; Miailhe Perrins, wine broker since 1818; Edouard Lawton, licensed in 1826; Ed. Pedesclaux, fils, broker since 1840; Amédée Tastet, licensed as a wine broker in 1842; Stanislas Dubosq, wine broker since 1848; Louis-Gabriel-P. Ferrière, licensed in 1854, and, of course, Georges Merman.

The letter was followed by two sets of tables listing the Gironde's classed growths. The red wines, as requested, were organized in five divisions numbering fifty-seven growths from Château Lafite to Croizet Bages; the list of white wines filled one page and was divided into three levels—"1st Growth Superior" for Yquem alone, nine "First Growths," and eleven "Second Growths."

The brokers' cover letter was intended to stave off what they expected would be the inevitable objections by explaining that they drew their information from "the best sources." As it turned out, however, this classification appeared to have been considered of relatively little significance, even among the brokers themselves. In the Tastet & Lawton notebooks that recorded practically every event in the Bordeaux wine world both great and small, there was no indication of any controversy or discussion; the only reference to the classification at all is the April 16 transcription, simply entered without comment, headed "Note presented by the Union for the *shipment of wines to the Exposition*." It was merely regarded as the latest in a long line of such efforts, and there would doubtless be other classifications to follow it.

On April 18, the same day it was written, the classification was sent off to the Chamber of Commerce. By this time, the Chamber had already collected its wines and sent them off to Paris, all of this done without any involvement by the brokers; thus, there was no connection between whether a property had submitted samples and its appearance in the classification. A property's inclusion in the list was based solely on its merits as reflected in the sales prices registered in the wine brokers' records.

As for the actual document itself, it found a secondary use as a tally sheet to determine which of the classed growths on the brokers' list had responded to the Chamber of Commerce's request for samples. Those properties that had not sent wines were noted by the word "point" ("none") written across their names. [There appears to have been some confusion during this operation, for several classed growths were incorrectly marked "point" although they had actually submitted samples. This happened not only with fifth growths like "Mr. Darmailhac" and "Mr. Jurine" (Lynch-Bages), where their status as crus classés may possibly have been in doubt before the April 18 document, but also with more highly ranked properties such as "Mr. de Pichon de Longueville," "Mme Veuve ("widow") Ferrière," "Mr. Dubignon," and "Mr. Lafon de Camarsac" (Lafon-Rochet). It turns out that before the wines were shipped from Bordeaux, the Chamber of Commerce had drawn up two lists to be used in composing the labels that would be affixed to the bottles in Paris; one list contained the names of the classed-growth wines that had been received at the municipal warehouse, the other listed the unclassed, communal wines. (See Appendix IV.) Composed before the brokers had submitted their work, these label lists erroneously relegated a number of classed growths to the communal listing, and the person checking the brokers' classification against the Chamber of Commerce's label list had neglected to search for their names on the second roster.]

Duffour-Dubergier now had his lists and could proceed with his map. The wines were finally in Paris ready for the opening of the Universal Exposition on May 1. However, the Chamber of Commerce's involvement in the matter was by no means finished—a small detail had arisen and taken on immoderate proportions, resulting in a completely unexpected development that threatened to overshadow the very wines themselves.

Five

MONPLAISIR GOUDAL STEPS IN

On March 8, a letter arrived at the Chamber of Commerce from Monplaisir Goudal, the manager at Château Lafite in Pauillac. He had received the Chamber's letter regarding the display of the Gironde's wines at the Universal Exposition and was planning to send not one, but two vintages for inclusion. There was, however, one point that he wished to have cleared up first.

Would it be possible for the wines from Lafite to be displayed bearing the property's own label?

Monplaisir Goudal was born to be manager of Château Lafite. Just as it was common practice among wine brokers for sons to succeed their fathers, so was it common practice among those responsible for the operation of great Bordeaux wine estates. Monplaisir's father was Joseph Goudal, manager at Lafite since 1797. Prior to assuming this position, Joseph was the capable proprietor of a small wine-producing property in the vicinity of Haut-Brion and a principal in the merchant firm of Goudal, Laforcade & Company. Members of the Goudal family had been active, if minor, participants in the mercantile life of Bordeaux throughout the 1700s; as the century drew to a close, Joseph had managed to establish a niche for himself handling consignments of cotton, prunes, lumber, and other commodities passing through the city's port on behalf of shippers in North and Baltic seacoast cities such as Hamburg, Bremen, and Amsterdam. Although not among the major traders dealing in classed-growth wines to the English market, Joseph Goudal did have solid contacts throughout northern Europe, and these may well have been of capital importance when a Dutch citizen named Jan de Witt sought someone with local vinicultural and commercial experience to oversee affairs at Lafite after buying it at auction from the French Republic in September 1797; the government had sequestered the property (and guillotined its owner) three years earlier, and a new manager was needed to return production to its former state. Up to this time, Goudal's commerce in wine had been relatively slight, mostly limited to warehousing casks in transit from Languedoc, Cahors, and Alicante, along with some transactions for several vineyards in Issan and Blanquefort belonging to a couple of Dutch and German nationals. It was only upon Joseph Goudal's accession to the management of one of the Médoc's premier vineyards that other proprietors and buyers began to look to the firm now known as Goudal, Weis, & Curtius for the handling of their wine transactions, and these soon accounted for the great majority of the company's business. By 1800, however, the firm's activities were focused almost exclusively on Lafite.

At first, given Goudal's traditional contacts and the property's new Dutch ownership, much of Lafite's commercial strategy focused on distributing its production through northern European channels, supplying this market with both red and white wines (the 1798 Lafite white was particularly well esteemed in Amsterdam). Before long, however, Goudal was pursuing a higher goal: it was not enough just to sell his wines for a decent price in whatever market was convenient—Lafite must be recognized as the preeminent wine in the Bordeaux hierarchy. Even though these wines were not part of his prior commercial dealings, Goudal was an experienced merchant in the heart of the Chartrons district with a perfect understanding of how the marketplace worked. He knew that to reach his goal he had to focus on the more-lucrative English market and the merchants who catered to it. And there was one other detail: Lafite's wine had to command a price higher than any of the other first growths. This was the policy that henceforth defined his dealings with Bordeaux's leading brokers and merchants. "Never had the highest price exceeded 2400 francs," Goudal would later boast. "I sold the 1801 vintage for 2500 francs—the other grand crus sold for only 2400. In 1803, I set the price at 2500 francs for all the grand crus, and in 1814 I sold at 3000. The other grand crus, Latour and Château Margaux, sold for only 2600 francs in 1818; it was I who set the price at 3350. In 1825, I sold at 3500 francs and first growth Latour sold at only 3350."

By 1826, when Monplaisir Goudal had joined his father's firm, traveling almost daily between Lafite and the business office in Bordeaux, this singular commitment to maintaining the property's commercial preeminence determined every aspect of operations both in Pauillac and at the Quai des Chartrons. Monplaisir could see how vineyard conditions were maintained at the highest possible standard in order to produce wines that justified his father's demands when negotiations for the new vintage began each autumn. It was around this time that young Goudal learned another basic principle central to the management of Lafite: as important as the quality of the wine itself was the reputation *for quality that the property had established with the public who ultimately fueled its demand.*

In the winter of 1827, a wine salesman named Lemarié appeared in the city of Amiens bearing false papers supporting his claim of being "Mr. Lafite of Bordeaux." Calling upon a number of the city's prominent residents who were in the habit of purchasing entire casks of Bordeaux's finer wines, he presented himself as the proprietor of

Château Lafite offering his own wine at a price 1,000 francs below that being asked by the regular Bordeaux merchants. The opportunity of buying such a prestigious wine at so attractive a price, and from Mr. Lafite himself to boot, proved irresistible to many of Lemarié's contacts who promptly signed orders with the salesman. The wine delivered months later by Lemarié's employers, Audinez and Breslay (a company already subject to legal proceedings for a similar scheme in Normandy), was an inferior product falsely labeled Lafite. Apparently, any disappointment that may have been experienced with the wine was not ascribed to fraud but rather to production at Lafite, and Lemarié remained above suspicion. Indeed, so lucrative had the salesman found Amiens to be that the following winter he returned to the city, installing himself in an apartment for several months while conducting a new round of visits to clients who now included a member of the local prefect's administration. It was only when Lemarié presented himself before someone familiar enough with the Médoc to recognize the imposture that word of these dealings got back to Bordeaux. Joseph Goudal was incensed upon learning of this deception which traded on the reputation he had so painstakingly created for Lafite. He had already established the practice of labeling wine bottled at the property "Ch. Lafite; Mr. Goudal, Manager" as a guarantee of authenticity, but the wine sold to merchants in cask was routinely subject to a variety of manipulations and the very name Lafite was liable to counterfeit. These commercial practices, ranging from unfortunate to unscrupulous, served to reinforce Joseph Goudal's adversarial position toward Bordeaux's wine merchants.

This jealous protection of Lafite's good name and a deep-seated suspicion of the Bordeaux merchants were two basic tenets inherited by Monplaisir Goudal when he became the manager in 1834. His own initiatives building on his father's efforts to preserve the quality and reputation of Lafite's wine were frequently met with resistance by the trade: one measure he instituted—branding the vintage date on the corks for wines bottled at Lafite—was termed "vicious" by a prominent Bordeaux merchant. Nevertheless, the desire to more closely control the wine between Lafite's cellar door and the customer who would ultimately drink it led to a shift in policy circumventing traditional channels of distribution. As a result of Joseph Goudal's demands on the Bordeaux merchants, Lafite regularly equaled or surpassed the other first growths in price; Monplaisir now sought to expand on that base by actively working to sell his wine directly from the property. The importance of these sales in Goudal's commercial strategy is indicated by the reprimand he once delivered to the business manager in Pauillac upon learning that there was no one available to present the wines to potential customers: "I must tell you that I am more than annoyed *by what happened yesterday; at a domain like Lafite (excepting Sundays—and including Sundays, if at all possible) there must always be* someone ready to offer *the wines for tasting to the regular buyers or strangers who arrive. . . ." Goudal himself embarked upon numerous voyages to Paris to directly sell to restaurants and hotels, as well as negotiate with wine merchants outside Bordeaux's sphere.*

The manager's insistence on a measure of independence from the traditional channels of distribution was a particularly bold position to take during the decades of stagnant sales for the region's wines during the first half of the nineteenth century. Bordeaux's financial crisis was most deeply felt among the producers, and the first growths were no exception. Goudal, however, through a combination of sound financial management and an acuity in avoiding long-term contracts with the merchants during the 1840s, was in a position to demand—and get—prices for Lafite's wines well above those set for the contract-bound Latour and Margaux. So well had Goudal managed the sale of the property's wines during a period when economics had established the merchants as the dominant force in the Bordeaux wine trade that, at the beginning of the 1850s, Lafite was established more firmly than ever at the head of the Bordeaux hierarchy, selling at an average price of over 2,500 francs per tun, while Margaux was locked into a contract paying 2,100 francs and Latour had committed itself to 1,750. Such managerial astuteness could only contribute to the wine's public image: by 1855, one writer attested "Commercially, Lafite [is] placed the first wine of the Médoc and the only one which, for ten years, had the incentive to improve its quality, since its sales depended on it. . . . By estimation, one may judge the price of the other wines." Just as the first growths had traditionally established the prices of the seconds (and, by extension, every other wine regardless of its rank), so had Lafite ascended to the role of arbiter for the other first growths.

Monplaisir Goudal enjoyed a fairly wide scope for his initiatives, benefiting from the absentee ownership characteristic at Lafite throughout the early nineteenth century. It was not unusual during this period for the owners of the Médoc's classed growths to rarely visit their vineyards. Even if a proprietor was not based in distant Paris but lived in nearby Bordeaux, it was still a considerable undertaking to travel up the Médoc by horse over kilometers of poor roads, or to make the voyage by boat along the Gironde River. From the final years of the eighteenth century, after Lafite's confiscation and subsequent sale to the Dutchman Jan de Witt, the vineyard had been in the possession of a succession of absentee owners. Beginning in 1818, Lafite became the property of a wealthy Parisian businessman named Ignace-Joseph Vanlerberghe and, in one guise or another, various members of his family. A passionate aversion to creditors and death duties led to a number of elaborate changes in the ostensible ownership of Lafite, but ultimately Vanlerberghe or his family were always in ownership, if never quite in evidence. It was under such circumstances that, in 1821, title to Lafite passed to a London banker named Sir Samuel Scott in a "sale" of the property for one million francs. In reality, Scott acted as financial manager of Lafite for the Vanlerberghe family, and this arrangement was assumed by his son, also named Samuel, upon the elder Scott's death in 1849; it was under the younger Scott's name as owner that the brokers listed Lafite in the classification they delivered to the Chamber of Commerce.

Throughout all these decades of complicated legal maneuvering, there was one consistent thread that ran through the organization of Lafite: the operation of the property and sale of its wine was managed on a daily basis by the family Goudal, first father, then son (and, eventually, grandson: Monplaisir Goudal's own child, Emile, succeeded him upon his death in December 1863, and held the post for a further two decades). The convoluted situation involving the Vanlerberghes in Paris and the Scotts directing business affairs by correspondence in London served to reinforce the local authority of Monplaisir Goudal. Through a constant stream of correspondence to the business manager at Lafite, he oversaw the quality of the wine and the day-to-day commercial decisions of the property; these letters were regularly punctuated with announcements of his arrivals at Pauillac or filled with detailed instructions when he was at Bordeaux. Goudal's tenacious pursuit of quality in every aspect of Lafite's operation kept the property, in Samuel Scott's words, "at the top of the tree."

By the 1850s, Monplaisir Goudal was *Lafite in the minds of many of those in the trade, as attested to by the property's letterhead during this period whose upper-left corner bore the inscription "Château Lafite, near Pauillac (Gironde)," and just below, in letters larger than that for Lafite itself, "M^{ir} Goudal, Manager." For Monplaisir Goudal, his identification with Lafite was total.*

On November 28, 1854, Monplaisir Goudal was among those in attendance at the prefecture for the meeting of proprietors called by the Departmental Committee to present the idea of displaying the Gironde's wines at the upcoming Universal Exposition. A fortnight later, Samuel Scott received a letter dated December 10 in which Goudal informed him of the request he had received "asking if you would be interested in sending several bottles of your famous wine from Lafite to the Exposition of 1855; a similar invitation has been made to all the proprietors. I believe, Sir, although your wines are well known throughout Europe, that it would be good for an example of the most distinguished wine from the Gironde to be seen at the Exposition; I suppose that several bottles will suffice." Goudal saw this as an ideal opportunity to showcase the Lafite 1846 and 1848, vintages still lying in the property's cellars largely unsold; these were wines that no amount of negotiation could convince the Bordeaux merchants to buy at a price Goudal considered to be fair. From the beginning, he felt that Lafite had succeeded in making very good wines in those years, despite the merchants' dismissal of the vintages as being of but mediocre quality; *he* saw no reason to accept a mediocre price for them, regardless of how difficult the merchants claimed they would be to sell. So sure was Goudal of the potential for the 1846 to become even better with time, that he went to the lengths of sending two cases containing fifty bottles each to India and back in order to subject the wine to the accelerated aging that such sea voyages provoked and prove the justice of his opinion.

Several weeks later, Goudal received the letter making a similar request for wines from the Chamber of Commerce. He was still prepared to send along his 1846 and 1848, and his response on March 8 stated that Lafite would be sending a case containing three bottles of each vintage to the municipal warehouse under separate cover. But would it be possible for those bottles to bear the property's own label listing the names of Sir Samuel Scott as owner and Monplaisir Goudal as manager?

On the surface, this appeared to be a rather simple request having nothing to do with the stability of the classification, the primary concern that had led the Chamber of Commerce to undertake the task of organizing the wines for the Exposition. Indeed, with Lafite ensconced at its summit there would have been nothing for the property to gain by an assault on the classification's authority. For Duffour-Dubergier, however, the question appeared to have the potential of completely upsetting the structure laid out for the Gironde's wine display. He and the Chamber had carefully established a framework within which the wines would be presented at Paris, a framework which would avoid any possible attempt at competition among the various proprietors and communes participating in the exhibit. The extreme caution informing their deliberations on the subject led them to consider any deviation from their original program as laid out in the December 14 letter to the Departmental Committee as a threat to the whole structure, leading inevitably to a complete collapse of the classification which was at the heart of the entire enterprise. It was clear to the Chamber that a display of the proprietors' own labels on the bottles could offer any number of ways of suggesting to the Exposition's visitors the idea that one owner's wine was superior to the others. Although Monplaisir Goudal's particular request to include his name and that of Sir Samuel Scott was not intended to produce such a result (Lafite having no need to make claims which its price in the Bordeaux market had long since established), it was still considered a question that could not be entertained without completely endangering the Chamber of Commerce's display.

Thus, on March 10, Duffour-Dubergier replied to Monplaisir Goudal:

> Sir,
>
> I have received your letter of the 8th of this month.
>
> I can only refer you to the circular that the Chamber addressed on January 13 to the grand cru proprietors of our department, concerning the labels to be applied to the wine samples that the Chamber will be sending to the Exposition and to the wines' disposition once the Exposition is finished.
>
> These conditions, whose utility has been generally acknowledged, cannot be subject to individual exceptions. I believe that you too will recognize their fairness, and this being the case, the Chamber will be pleased to receive the wine samples from Lafite you will be so kind as to send.

In effect, Duffour-Dubergier was saying that, according to the rules under which the display was organized, his hands were tied and the Chamber could not accede to his request any more than if Goudal had asked to include a sample of spirits distilled from Jerusalem artichokes.

However, Monplaisir Goudal was not the proprietor of an artichoke distillery who could be turned away with a reference to the Departmental Committee; he was the manager of Château Lafite, and was not prepared to take a refusal by Duffour-Dubergier—who, as one of Bordeaux's leading merchants, belonged to that faction of the trade Goudal considered to be his implacable adversary—as the final word in the matter. From the manager's point of view, the refusal by the Chamber of Commerce was not tied to any overriding concern with an orderly presentation of the Gironde's wines designed to prevent an assault on the classification, a question that Goudal was neither aware of nor interested in. Just as the adversarial relationship between proprietors and merchants led Duffour-Dubergier to assume that Goudal's request might harbor a veiled challenge to the classification, so did it contribute to Goudal's perspective on the Chamber's position in this matter. As Goudal stated in a letter to Scott:

> The Chamber of Commerce (composed of merchants) [has been] delegated to send your wines to Paris, but without any label on the bottles, saying that they have taken it upon themselves, once the bottles are in Paris, to place on each the name of the wine but not the name of the proprietor. You will easily understand, Sir, why these gentlemen are opposed to our including, after the name of the wine, the name of the owner and that of his representative who could be contacted to obtain the wines directly from the property. They fear that clients will approach the proprietor rather than the merchant.

It may be difficult to understand today, when the names and faces of vineyard owners can be as well known as the very wines themselves, that in the middle of the nineteenth century a wine's origins were not identified with the proprietor so much as the merchant through whose hands it had passed. Once a barrel of wine left a property for a merchant's cellar, it was routinely subjected to various manipulations and alterations to render it more salable according to the tastes of a particular market. Such "making up" could involve adding Hermitage from the Rhone or Benicarlo from Spain, for example, to add body to the more delicate wines of Bordeaux; this was a common (and even publicized) practice, and, depending on the quality of these manipulations, one merchant's wine might be preferred over another's—even if both had originally come from the same property.

As one leading merchant counseled his son regarding this aspect of the profession, "One thing that must not be lost sight of in making up the wines is that they will come into competition with those of other houses. We must not depend on our name, but on the superior quality of our wine." The reference to "our wine" was entirely accurate. Although the property name was still a wine's primary identification, things had changed in the two centuries since Arnaud de Pontac offered his wine from Haut-Brion directly to the London public: the merchants' intercession in the chain of distribution had now largely eclipsed the owner from the public's view. New proprietors might still alter the name of their wine to reflect a change in ownership, but this practice was becoming limited to the cru bourgeois; among the classed growths whose names were becoming established "brands" in the market, such ego gratification was now increasingly rare. For Monplaisir Goudal, the name Lafite offered no publicly recognizable connection with Samuel Scott; this would only be possible by including his name on the label, and the merchants in the Chamber of Commerce were not going to prevent this rightful acknowledgment of the owner—nor of the manager, for that matter.

Like the Chamber of Commerce, Monplaisir Goudal preferred to seek satisfaction for a problem at the highest level of authority. He had planned a voyage to Paris in April with the object of interesting that city's buyers in several of Lafite's unsold vintages, hoping to capitalize on the increase in tourism anticipated for the Universal Exposition. He would use the occasion to demand an audience with Napoleon Jerome, President of the Imperial Commission for the Universal Exposition.

Few people in Paris could have been as busy as Napoleon Jerome in the final weeks before the Exposition's opening. To the inevitable last-minute pressures of overseeing such a complex enterprise, Napoleon Jerome had added additional complications for himself: less than four months after being appointed as the head of the Imperial Commission for the Exposition, he had decided to take part in the recently declared war against Russia and headed off to the Crimea as a general in command of a French army division. Eight months later, with winter approaching, he excused himself from further participation in the war and was now back in Paris supervising the Exposition's organization with the added burden of having to deal with the changes and developments that had occurred while he was away. "He found the regulations adopted by his colleagues in his absence faulty in many respects," according to one reporter who characterized the Imperial Commission as subject to a "wild spirit of thoughtless activity—continually erecting only to destroy—commanding only to countermand." Consequently, upon resuming the duties of Commission President, "the plans of the Commissioners were reconsidered and many alterations were made." However, despite all the claims on Napoleon Jerome's attentions, Monplaisir Goudal, as the manager of a property that the Emperor himself had been rumored especially desirous of seeing during his 1852 visit to Bordeaux, had the necessary influence to gain his ear. "This audience was accorded me right away," Goudal wrote to Scott, "and the Prince [Napoleon Jerome] told me that each proprietor should be able to put on their bottles their name with that of the wine, and that the Chamber of Commerce had nothing to say about the matter."

Such a quick and definitive decision, while characteristic of Napoleon Jerome's temperament, was particularly forceful in this case: the situation as presented by

Monplaisir Goudal had touched a nerve. Just as Goudal had responded to Duffour-Dubergier's position regarding the labels based on his particular perspective as manager of Lafite, so did Napoleon Jerome respond to Goudal's complaint based on concerns beyond those immediately relating to this question.

As a leading proponent of Bonapartism, Napoleon Jerome saw the Universal Exposition as a means of giving practical application to one of the main principles this political philosophy had come to assume under Napoleon III: an improvement in the condition of the working class. This was a concern dear to Napoleon Jerome since adolescence, and he embraced this principle with a characteristic vigor which surpassed even that of the Emperor himself. As President of the Imperial Commission, Napoleon Jerome intended the Exposition to offer workers every opportunity to benefit, from organizing state-subsidized visits for artisans in each of the nation's departments, to a greater recognition of the role played by the workers in the production of the items on display. This latter aspect was particularly present in Napoleon Jerome's thoughts during the spring of 1855: shortly before the Exposition's opening, he issued a directive instructing the juries to accord workers a recognition equal to that traditionally given the owners of factories and workshops in the awarding of prizes. As he later wrote when explaining his reasons for instituting this measure, "By an innovation based, I believe, on justice and testifying to our concern for the working class, the decree placed foremen and workers on the same level as exhibitors in recognizing their services rendered to industry, or their participation in the production of objects on display and judged worthy of recompense." The intention was to raise workers to a new level of authority, to create "in industry a new status, that of *collaborator*." Thus, a major purpose of the Exposition was to give workers the recognition they were due, and here was a situation (as presented by Goudal) in which merchants and go-betweens were conspiring to deny that very aim. For Napoleon Jerome, there was no question about it: Goudal and Samuel Scott's names had every right to appear on the label with Lafite's.

For all his single-mindedness, Napoleon Jerome was recognized as possessing a flexibility of spirit capable of considering all aspects of an argument. In the words of one contemporary, "he was a born dialectician—a logician—but rare in a dialectician, he could put up with an opposing point of view." It was possible that there was a second side to this question regarding the labeling of the Gironde's wines, and ordinarily Napoleon Jerome may have been disposed to consider it. However, this case was different: it was a question of a trespass against the rights of workers, encouraging Napoleon Jerome to fall back on his habitual volatility. "In doubtful circumstances," he later explained, "I gave preference to the most liberal interpretation, with the agreement and informed advice of the Imperial Commission." Thus, rather than being solicited for its position in the matter, the Chamber of Commerce found itself presented with an ukase. On April 15, Napoleon Jerome wrote to the Chamber:

> As for the collective display under the name of the Bordeaux Chamber of Commerce, I see no objection. But this does not consequently follow that the names of the wines and of the proprietors should not be fixed to the products, this being contrary to the principle given and stated by the Imperial Commission, that the producer has the right to be compensated before the merchant. In this case, the title and the right of the producer are so clear as to be beyond doubt.
>
> This question has not proved to be a problem among the other French vineyards proposing collective regional displays.
>
> Consequently, I am informing you that the wines of the Gironde will be accepted in the collective name of the Bordeaux Chamber of Commerce, in the display galleries as well as in the cellars reserved for this purpose, but that the proprietors will have the right to indicate on their samples the name of the wine with their own.

Napoleon Jerome's letter was read during the April 18 meeting of the Chamber of Commerce and the ensuing discussion occupied almost the entire session. This question of labels had now become more of a problem than originally anticipated when Duffour-Dubergier addressed his summary reply to Monplaisir Goudal. Officials in Paris were now involving themselves in the arrangements for the Bordeaux display based on an incomplete understanding of the underlying commercial circumstances; this was practically as bad as having the wines subject to a tasting in the capital by judges insufficiently experienced to appreciate the particular qualities of the region's production. With representatives from the individual properties going over the heads of the local authorities to gain a favorable hearing of their complaints in Paris, the Chamber feared that such a precedent could ultimately lead to the complete disintegration of the Chamber's unified display at the Exposition. Taking the long view, the Chamber worried that owners petitioning the Imperial Commission would be allowed to directly submit their wines for display, ultimately resulting in the assault on the classification which the Chamber sought to avoid in the first place. As Duffour-Dubergier wrote to Henri Galos,

> You know very well that the Parisians have a poor understanding [of this matter]; they are unaware of what the classification of the Médoc's wines signifies, they do not see, as we do, all the ambitious pretensions which would sow discord in this classification so important to conserve; the classed-growth proprietors want to place themselves on a rank superior to that which they are assigned; others not classed want to be fifth growths at least. If these demands were heeded, absolute anarchy would shatter a wisely established order.

The Chamber of Commerce had to convince Napoleon Jerome that it was not trying to deny anyone legitimate recognition by organizing the display as it did; that its work was serious and based on more than just the circumstances surrounding this Universal Exposition; that it was not only the Chamber of Commerce, but the needs of an entire winemaking industry that insisted on these precautions.

On April 19, Duffour-Dubergier sent a letter to Napoleon Jerome that was an adroit combination of obsequiousness, backtracking, and shifting of responsibilities:

> Your Highness,
>
> I have received the letter Your Imperial Highness did me the honor of writing on April 15. The Bordeaux Chamber of Commerce read it during its meeting yesterday, which was presided over by the Prefect; it demands a response which I hasten to address to Your Highness.
>
> I fear that the Imperial Commission for the Universal Exposition has been mislead regarding the position of the Bordeaux Chamber of Commerce.
>
> Would Your Highness permit me to briefly recount the circumstances behind the shipment of wine samples made by the Chamber for the Exposition; I must also explain the principle which has guided the Chamber in this matter; it will not fail, I hope, to gain Your Highness' approval.
>
> The Departmental Committee charged to assure the participation of our department addressed itself to the Chamber for the organization of the shipment of wines; it judged that we had, in this respect, the means and an authority not to be found elsewhere.
>
> The Chamber understood that in this august circumstance there could be no question but that of the general good, namely the Gironde's wine making industry as a whole; rivalries, contradictory pretensions of numerous proprietors, views based on personal interests all had to be put aside as a whole.
>
> A circular. . . was thus addressed to the proprietors of those growths whose superiority is attested to by an authentic classification. This classification has been sanctioned by an experience which goes back over a century, and in the proprietor's own interests it would be extremely dangerous to attempt any modifications.
>
> A similar circular was sent to the mayors of the vine-growing communes throughout the Gironde.
>
> The Chamber expressly specified that it would reject individual labels and special markings other than those which it would affix on the bottles itself. Close to two-hundred shipments were received; the people who sent us their wines had thus accepted the conditions that we set; we refused to give in to requests which sought to modify these conditions.
>
> Your Highness does me the honor of pointing out that the proprietors have the right of indicating their names together with that of their wines on their samples.
>
> The Chamber, Mr. President, does not reject the indication of the names of the wines and their proprietors; it had always been our intention to inscribe the two names on each bottle of the wines we have sent, when it concerned the properties whose products are of superior merit; the name of the commune will suffice when it is a question of wines of ordinary rank.
>
> We thought that this information should be written by a person gifted with a special understanding, sent by us to Paris for this purpose; this person would be supplied with labels bearing the Chamber's name, and on which has been left the space necessary to inscribe the growth's designation and the name of the proprietors.
>
> The Chamber would have to contend with very serious inconvenience which would follow from an authorization given to proprietors to individually send samples without our authorization, where nothing would guarantee their authenticity. It suffices to indicate the deplorable circumstances which would arise from such a state

> of affairs; the Departmental Committee was struck by this, and this is what determined them, after considering another method of action, to ally themselves with the Chamber and to give its approval to the system we have adopted.
>
> Our work has been undertaken without any thought of personal gain. The classification that we have followed has been drawn up by the Union of Brokers Attached to the Bordeaux Market; it is thus, to a certain extent, official in character, and it is reproduced on a wine map of the Gironde, a map we have had printed on a large scale, that is being made at this moment, and which is to accompany our shipment of samples.
>
> I flatter myself, Mr. President, that these explanations will suffice to resolve any difficulties. I repeat that the Chamber is well disposed to inscribe on the samples the names of the classed growths and their proprietors, but that it formally refuses all individual labels and announcements dictated by personal speculation. Our work is serious and genuine in nature, and we can only accept responsibility for it so long as no outside intervention comes to alter it in its entirety or change it in its details.

Duffour-Dubergier was being less than frank in his explanation of the Chamber of Commerce's intentions. In its December 14 letter to the Departmental Committee, the Chamber had clearly intended that the proprietors' names—even for the classed growths—*not* appear on the labels. ("As for our classed growths, reds or whites, they would appear at the Exposition under their own names, to which could be added that of the town in which the grapes were harvested; the proprietor's name should not appear, in order to avoid any individual competition and all conflicts of self-esteem.") Now, in the interests of limiting the damage being done to its grand design, the Chamber was being forced to admit this change, even claiming that it had intended this course of action all along. The names of the proprietors for the classed growths *only* would now be inscribed on the labels. However, if the Chamber of Commerce was willing to concede this point, it was determined to go no further; altering its plans to put the classed-growth proprietors' names on the labels was, at best, an annoyance, but any additional changes would inevitably lead to unacceptable consequences touching directly on the classification.

Ordinarily, the weight of the Chamber's authority might have been sufficient to secure a reversal of Napoleon Jerome's position, but this had become a question touching on the principle of workers' rights, a subject on which his sympathies were well known. Additional documentation was needed to support the Chamber's argument. It so happened that, on the same day the Chamber met and read Napoleon Jerome's letter, the brokers delivered the classification intended to accompany Duffour-Dubergier's map of the Gironde's winemaking regions. It could not have arrived at a better moment: the brokers' classification offered an authoritative document drawn up by agents duly licensed by the government as proof of the degree to which the Chamber had gone to organize its display in a manner as serious and thoughtful as possible. Had Duffour-Dubergier's map been ready, he would undoubtedly have been proud to send it to Napoleon Jerome, convinced that it would clearly support his argument here just as surely as it would support his display at the Exposition. However, it would not be finished for another month, and he could only content himself with a mention of the great map in his letter. Instead, Duffour-Dubergier called the brokers' just-delivered classification into duty to give documentary weight to his argument that the Chamber's display went beyond mere questions of names on the label, and he included a copy of the list as an annex to his letter. Thus it was that Napoleon Jerome came to receive a copy of the brokers' classification, unsolicited by him and, ultimately, unheeded.

For on April 27, the Chamber received a response from Napoleon Jerome indicating his satisfaction that the labels for the classed growths would be bearing the owners' names, but also insisting on the inclusion of the proprietors' names for the communal wines as well. "I hope," the letter concluded, "that you will be able to easily find the means of reconciling the interests represented by the Bordeaux Chamber of Commerce at the Exposition with the principles of order and justice adopted by the Imperial Commission."

In its tone and its content, Napoleon Jerome's letter suggested that he had reached the limits of his patience regarding this question of wine labels, and the Chamber decided to let the matter rest before the situation deteriorated any further. "We won't answer this letter for fear of adding to the misunderstanding besetting the members of a commission who are not at all possessed of a correct idea of our department's wine production," wrote Duffour-Dubergier to Henri Galos. After conceding to labels that included the names of the classed-growth proprietors, the Chamber was now being pressed to extend this arrangement to *all* the wines in its display. This was impossible to arrange for the nonclassed growths, since the mayors who submitted samples from their communes had not indicated the names of the proprietors whose wines had been selected. The difference between classed and nonclassed growths was beginning to lose its definition, and any further pursuit of the label question was likely to blur the distinction even more. The important thing now was to ensure that other proprietors did not try to enlarge upon Monplaisir Goudal's precedent and go around the Chamber of Commerce in an attempt to present their wines at the Exposition outside of the official display. This posed a far more serious threat to the classification's integrity than the sideshow question of labels.

On his end in Paris, Henri Galos had been actively working toward this goal on the Chamber's behalf. Seeking another avenue of approach among his contacts in the capital, Galos hoped to gain a more favorable hearing for the Chamber's cause from François-Barthélemy Arlès-Dufour, a Lyon silk merchant and member of that city's Chamber of Commerce, whose free-trade views and active belief in Napoleon III's social agenda had led to his appointment as General Secretary for the Universal Exposition. If Galos thought that the similarity of Arlès-Dufour's background with Duffour-Dubergier's would put him in a mind to sympathize with the President of the Bordeaux Chamber of Commerce, he was very much mistaken. As Galos wrote in a letter to Duffour-Dubergier:

> I explained your position as best I could that it was in the grand cru proprietors' interest that the classification of our vineyards not be disturbed in the eyes of the European public who will flock to the Exposition; I tried to demonstrate the danger there would be in opening the door to individual demands concerning a product whose quality can be judged neither by sight nor touch. . . .The General Secretary, for whom this language was brand new, answered with phrases of a general vagueness in no way applicable to the technicalities of the question under discussion. He told me that the intention of His Imperial Highness was entirely democratic; that he wanted the Exposition to be principally an occasion for the little producer and the little industrialist to surmount their obscurity, to flaunt themselves openly and to compete with the big proprietor or big manufacturer for the confidence and preference of the public. It's this principle that they want to apply to the wines. . . .Nonetheless, it is established here and now that the Exposition will not accept any wine samples which have not been submitted by the Chamber, since, for this product, it is the substitute of the Departmental Committee of the Gironde.

The Chamber, if not triumphant, was satisfied. With this guarantee that it alone was authorized to display the wines from the Gironde in Paris, "we have obtained in large part what we have wanted. . . .[The proprietors'] names are inscribed; they have nothing else to ask for; and no doubt Mr. Arlès-Dufour will understand so simple a thing, thanks to the further explanations you will make to him, should the need arise." Henri Galos was reminded that no proprietor was permitted to affix any label to the bottles "*that we have sent*."

Monplaisir Goudal had won his point, but only in the very narrowest of terms: the bottles from Lafite would bear Samuel Scott's name on the label, but that label would still be the one created by the Chamber of Commerce. Whether Goudal would accept this remained to be seen, but, as far as Duffour-Dubergier was concerned, things were now arranged in such a manner that he had no choice.

Six

"... A SOURCE OF EMBARRASSMENT AND A REGRETTABLE WASTE OF TIME...."

Spring came late to Paris in 1855. The city was chilly and gray, with the sun only occasionally breaking through the low-lying overcast covering the skies for most of every day. "Never has our Spring been so slow in arriving," was a complaint reflecting the mood of many Parisians grown tired of waiting for the long winter to end. "Despite the frigid temperatures one yearns for outdoor amusements. With Spring making itself more and more rare, one finishes by forgetting it and doing without." Toward the end of April, however, the weather broke and the capital enjoyed a full week of clear blue skies with temperatures rising into the 70s. It augured well for the coming celebrations, and after initial morning cloudiness the afternoon of May 1 shone clear and brisk. The few remaining clouds in evidence scudded across the sky with the light breeze which lifted flags from their poles; Parisians profited from this break in the weather to promenade along the city's streets and avenues. It was a perfect day for the opening of the Universal Exposition.

Unfortunately, it had been decided to push the inauguration back two weeks to May 15. As the scheduled opening on May 1 drew ever closer, it became clear to Napoleon Jerome and the Imperial Commission that construction on the exhibition halls and installation of the displays was not going to be completed on time. The original plan was to house the event in the Palace of Industry, a permanent structure on the Champs Elysées containing 45,000 square meters of space already under construction when the Universal Exposition was announced. This building was designed to house the next in the ongoing series of French National Exhibitions which had been scheduled for 1854, and it might well have been sufficient for that purpose; but with the decision to make this Exposition international in scope, the Palace of Industry had immediately become inadequate in size. If France's Universal Exposition of 1855 were to rival England's 1851 presentation—whose Crystal Palace enclosed 94,000 square meters—more than double the space of the Palace of Industry would have to be made available.

In February 1854, the Imperial Commission proposed the construction of additional buildings to bring the total display area to around 100,000 square meters, a decision that was seconded by Emperor Napoleon III. However, the following month, France joined England in a declaration of war on Russia, and this financial burden became a major obstacle to additional governmental expenditure for an exhibition hall intended to be "a temple of peace, bringing all nations together in concord." As explained by one of the Exposition's organizers, "Ideas very different from those expressed by the Commission predominated, and. . . instead of a splendid display, richer than London's, we were faced with the prospect of realizing nothing more than an abridged exhibition, influenced by the circumstances of the war."

The Crimean War had a further impact on the organization of the Exposition: in March 1854, Napoleon Jerome excused himself from his responsibilities as President of the Imperial Commission assumed less than four months earlier and on April 10 went off to the Crimea as a divisional commander of the French army; January 1855 saw him back in Paris, resuming his duties overseeing preparations for the Universal Exposition. This eight-month absence had deprived the Imperial Commission of its most influential asset in its quest for a larger venue—a persuasive personality with the influence to effectively champion the Exposition's cause. "This question of buildings was truly deplorable," recalled Napoleon Jerome later. "Upon my return from the Crimea and presiding once more over the Commission, my first concern was to take a stand on this question."

Consequently, it was not until late in June 1854, less than ten months before the Exposition's scheduled opening, that authorization was given for the construction of an Annex composed of two long halls totaling 1,200 meters in length along the nearby banks of the Seine. Although this certainly helped matters, more space was still needed: the Annex added only 30,000 square meters to the Palace of Industry's 45,000, and further negotiations were necessary for the construction of additional galleries, which eventually brought the total to 117,000. In addition to the Palace of Industry and the Annex, the Panorama, a preexisting rotunda in the gardens of the Champs Elysées, was fitted with circular galleries to display the finest products of French industry such as a silver table service for 100 ordered by the Emperor from Christofle, tapestries from Gobelins, and the imperial crown jewels. Various other corridors and passages were built and equipped with showcases to serve as links between the Palace of Industry and the Annex in an effort to give a sense of unity to

The Palace of Industry, the Panorama, and the Annex, site of the Universal Exposition of 1855; the wines from Bordeaux were displayed in the foreground section of the Annex along the river.
(Bibliothèque Nationale de France)

the Exposition's disparate elements. Unfortunately, by the time these additions were finally decided upon opening day was only months away, and try as they might it was impossible for the Imperial Commission to have all construction finished in time.

Although construction problems were a major factor, administrative questions also contributed to delays. At one moment during the organization and classification of the displays, the Commission considered placing together all products of a similar type to facilitate a direct comparison of variations in style and quality, but this turned out to be unworkable. For such a system to succeed it would have been necessary to have a detailed knowledge of the nature of each nation's and department's exhibitors early enough to arrange an exact distribution of display space, but the Commission anticipated that the inevitable delays in obtaining this information would throw the organization of the exhibits into hopeless chaos. (The

Commission was proved correct: the final bulletins from the French Departmental Committees specifying the number and size of their exhibits were scheduled to be received by November 30, 1854, but this stage of the organization was not finished until four months later.) Thus, display space was arranged by country and department, but vestiges of the original idea were nonetheless retained: according to the general nature of their products, national and departmental exhibits were distributed in subgroupings throughout the various areas of the Exposition.

The Palace of Industry was reserved for manufactured products, whose fabrication resulted in items with a graceful and stylish aspect which would best profit from the setting of the main building and contribute to the splendor of the Exposition. At the two long halls of the Annex along the river, the westernmost one stretching from the Pont d'Alma to the Pont des Invalides was dedicated to an exhibition of working steam engines and other machinery; the spectacle presented by the movement and sound of these huge mechanisms would be among the event's chief attractions. The Annex's eastern half, which began at the Pont des Invalides and reached to the Place de la Concorde, was devoted to displays of natural products; this was a section that could boast of neither the elegance nor the dynamism which characterized the rest of the Exposition. "It is only in the aggregate of the riches they represent that these products, fairly ordinary in themselves, can offer a striking spectacle," was how one guidebook summed up the interest offered by the exhibits here. In the Exposition's system of classification, wine was considered a natural product, categorized under "preparation and conservation of alimentary substances" in the official catalog. Thus was the Chamber of Commerce's exhibit consigned to the Annex's alcove 48, among displays of wood, metal, and fabric samples, refined sugar, and other similar goods from the Gironde. Nearby, the Austrian wine display, a collection of bottles arranged in a tall column, was positioned among samples of corn, grain, and wood. Wines from Australia, Spain, and other nations were also displayed in the Annex with the various natural products that constituted those countries' exhibits.

The fine points involved in classifying the displays would continue for some time, and it was not until April 20, 1855, ten days before the scheduled inauguration, that a definitive system for organizing the placement of exhibits was finally adopted. On April 22, a notice was issued declaring that no further admissions of displays would be considered, but weeks later new requests were still being accepted, further impeding completion of the Exposition's preparations. Supposedly final arrangements were filled with last-minute changes reflecting Napoleon Jerome's volatile temperament, similar to his handling of Monplaisir Goudal's request earlier in the month. The practical result of all this on the eve of the opening was to render the Exposition a veritable construction site, filled with carpenters, masons, and other workers hurrying to complete their tasks while the setting up of displays was also due to take place. "The installation of glass panels [in the roof of the Palace of Industry] entailed major inconveniences for the installation of products," according to one account, "due to numerous pieces of glass which were falling at each instant." Faced with such conditions, many exhibitors feared for the safety of their more delicate items and preferred to leave goods packed in their shipping crates until the more hazardous aspects of construction were finished. Members of the public who were among the first to visit the Exposition were greeted with a view more akin to a common warehouse than a glittering showcase of the world's finest products. "It cost us ten francs," said a woman to her husband who had just offered her a visit to the Palace of Industry, "but we did get to see some beautiful crates being opened." It would not be until June 29 that the last of the display areas would be finished and a completed Universal Exposition could be presented to the public, but in April it was still believed that the Exposition would open as scheduled. "To see the activity which prevails over the Palace and its annexes, one could hope that all will be ready by opening day," wrote a visitor inspecting the exhibition halls toward the end of that month, but such hopes were soon to be disappointed. On April 27, a decree was issued pushing back the opening two weeks to May 15.

Henri Galos was a frequent visitor to the halls of the Universal Exposition in the weeks leading to the inauguration. Beginning in late March, he had become more actively involved in the arrangements for the Gironde's wine display, serving as Duffour-Dubergier's on-site eyes and ears. His initial instructions were to report back to Bordeaux not only on the progress of the Chamber of Commerce's exhibit but also on how it was shaping up in comparison with the displays from France's other wine regions and those from the rest of the world. On March 30, as the Chamber was fretting about the Departmental Committee's slowness in arranging for the delivery of its wines to Paris, Galos was told to assure that all would be ready on his end once the shipment was underway:

> We ask that you get in touch at once with the Exposition's directors in order that the reception of our samples takes place in an orderly fashion and that they are deposited in a safe place. Also, go see the location which has been assigned to us. As concerns the opening of the cases, the affixing of the labels and their arrangement, we plan on sending to Paris an intelligent individual who will have our instructions regarding this subject and who will be responsible for this work. Tell us when he should be sent to Paris. . . .Would you also tell us if it is true, as we have heard, that the other wine displays have already completed their installations.

Duffour-Dubergier's precautions were well founded, given the chaos that reigned at the Exposition site: crates would arrive and be stacked in their designated location of display, only to be moved when the organization of the exhibits was changed or that particular area of the Palace of Industry underwent some aspect of construction which necessitated clearing away the items awaiting unpacking. As a result, it was not unusual for exhibits to become lost behind stacks of other goods in some distant corner of the exhibition halls, or to be shifted to outdoor holding areas where they would be exposed to the vagaries of the Parisian spring weather. While such treatment was not recommended for any of the Exposition's displays, this would have been particularly unfortunate for wines which were to undergo the rigors of a jury tasting. Owing to the foresight of Duffour-Dubergier and the presence of Henri Galos, the Gironde's wines were safely sheltered in the cellars of the Palace of Industry.

Galos anticipated spending relatively little time at the Exposition himself. The nature of his duties as the Bordeaux Chamber of Commerce's Paris representative generally involved lobbying ministers and commissioners who were often acquaintances of long standing from his years in government. Given Bordeaux's status as France's principal Atlantic coast port, much of Galos' activity was centered on the Ministry of Maritime Trade to which he was attached when he served as administrator of France's colonies. He knew the people in government, they knew him, and a successful hearing for the Chamber of Commerce's position was usually just a matter of course. When the complications with Monplaisir Goudal arose, Galos went to see Arlès-Dufour, "whom I have known for a long time," and secured recognition of the Chamber as the sole authorized agent for the submission of wines from the Gironde to the Exposition. This is how he was habitually of use to the Chamber of Commerce and how he foresaw his utility in the present circumstances. The actual work related to setting up the Gironde's wine display was to be the responsibility of the delegate who would be arriving from Bordeaux; apart from being available to offer advice should the need arise, Galos foresaw little that would disrupt his habitual travels through the governmental halls of power.

After the postponement of the Universal Exposition's opening and the assignment of the Bordeaux wines to the Annex, which was even further from completion than the Palace of Industry, it was clear that it would be some time before the Gironde's wine display would be ready for viewing by the public. In the wake of this delay arose second thoughts in Bordeaux concerning arrangements in Paris, and, on May 11, the Chamber of Commerce sent Henri Galos a letter informing him of its latest decision:

> After reflecting on the matter, we do not believe the occasion requires the dispatch of the agent we had first considered sending to Paris. His presence does not seem to be necessary enough for us to engage an expense which would be quite large, and our financial situation imposes upon us the responsibility, regarding disbursements, to observe a great caution. We thus ask you to hire some active and intelligent worker to open our crates and to arrange the samples. . . .We also believe that it would be necessary that the space assigned to us be given some sort of decoration in harmony with the nature of our shipment; we would wish it to be simple and in good taste; a well-executed painting of vine stocks, branches, a sort of trellis all

> around and above our display case, would doubtless be most fitting. You'll have no trouble finding some artist who will be able to undertake this work; we want it to be well done but without incurring too great an expense. You will be able to reconcile all of this after an examination of the manner in which the other wine displays have been organized.

The Chamber also thought it important to advise Galos to expect delivery of "the wine map of the Gironde; it is very large in size and it must be properly placed, because it is the part of our display which will most attract the public's attention."

Henri Galos now found himself faced with having his habitual activity, his standard responsibilities, his ordered existence thrown into disarray. The Chamber's decision to economize meant that he would now be at the Universal Exposition on an almost daily basis, overseeing the affixing of labels, the arrangement of wine bottles, the decoration of the display space, and the positioning of the all-important map, in addition to the numerous other responsibilities that would doubtless arise given the confused state of affairs at the Exhibition halls. This was not the sort of thing that he had been in the habit of doing in Paris, and he did not look forward to doing it now. On May 14, Galos wrote to the Chamber of Commerce trying to convince them of the complex nature of the arrangements, of how beneficial a full-time representative for the wines would be, of how subjective a thing was the whole issue of the display's decoration, in short, of how ill equipped he was to undertake such a task. A letter from Duffour-Dubergier on May 18 reiterated the Chamber's position.

> We do not think that it is necessary to send an agent to Paris; if it is only a matter of procedure [that concerns you], you will quickly find out what is necessary; if it is a question of a man with a certain social position, it would be expensive and his presence seems superfluous for the six months that the Palace of Industry will be open.
>
> The installation is a simple thing; don't exaggerate the difficulties for yourself. There is no need to arrange the wines in an order rigorously in accordance with the Bordeaux wine trade's classification. The great growths, the celebrated communes, Lafite, Château Margaux, Latour, Mouton, and other great vineyards of Margaux and Saint-Julien in the first row with the great white wines; all which is inferior and little known, behind; the unclassed communes without a proprietor's name in the back or [left] in the cellar.
>
> . . . See if the other wine displays have any ornaments, and if so we would want you to make some similar decoration. If they have passed on this, we won't have any either.
>
> The little details of the installation must be left to your discretion; the shape, the expanse of the area assigned to us will inspire you in what is necessary for the particularities that our distance prevents us from seizing upon.

And again, Duffour-Dubergier's pride and joy, the wine map: "This last object, the most interesting of our display, will have to be placed with care and be as visible as possible. Once you receive it you'll be able to judge how to use it to its best advantage." Detailed instructions were also given on how to open the cases and affix the labels to the bottles in such a way as to avoid any misidentification of the wines; this could certainly not be left to just any worker, regardless of how active or intelligent, and would require Galos' personal supervision.

The Annex on the Quai de Billy containing the exhibits of heavy machinery and natural products opened its doors toward the end of June, but the Chamber of Commerce's display was not yet ready. Nathaniel Johnston had traveled to Paris in the middle of May, at which time he brought with him the completed labels for the bottles; the wine map of the Gironde was sent from Bordeaux on May 25. Nevertheless, the display space for the Gironde's wines remained vacant. In early June, Henri Galos made a final attempt to free himself from involvement with the Universal Exposition and to convince the Chamber of Commerce to send someone with a specialized knowledge to attend to the display. Like his previous attempts, this latest request was rebuffed:

> We do not think that there is reason to send a special agent to remain beside our display and provide explanations. It would be difficult to find a man suitable for so delicate a mission; an individual well familiar with the Médoc would not be familiar with the white wines; besides, it would be a cause of considerable expense; for a suitable representative it would be necessary to devote several thousand francs, and as we've already told you, our financial situation forces us to be extremely prudent regarding new expenses.

A more direct cause for the delay and of greater concern to the Chamber of Commerce than Henri Galos' procrastination while attempting to escape the burden of arranging the Gironde's display was the matter of how to preserve the wines at their best for the upcoming jury tasting. The idea of setting up a little decorated cellar in which the jury would judge the Gironde's wines had to be abandoned when the decision was made to place the Bordeaux display in the Annex, an area designed as a temporary structure and thus lacking the cellars that existed beneath the Palace of Industry. Storing the cases on site now meant exposing the wines to the high temperatures that plagued the Exposition's halls. The glass roof over the exhibition spaces had been designed to freely allow sunlight in to illuminate the items on display; unfortunately, it also admitted the heat of the summer sun as well. Temperatures inside the halls became so uncomfortable that a further adjustment to their design was necessary and muslin screens were hung just beneath the roof to reduce the intensity of the sun's rays. This was an improvement for the visitors, but temperatures still remained well above what was necessary for the storage of fine wines. There was little doubt that they would suffer from the heat, and the concern to present the wines at their best led the Chamber and Galos in search of a solution. There was a momentary return to the idea that, in the absence of a tasting for the general public, nothing really existed to distinguish a showcase full of wines from a mere display of bottles, and a suggestion was made to substitute tinted water in Bordeaux-shaped bottles bearing the Chamber of Commerce's labels; this would enable the actual wines to be maintained under optimum conditions for the tasting jury, which was the truly important public for the display. The Chamber stated its views on the subject in a letter to Henri Galos:

> The idea of substituting red-colored water in the bottles on display in order to conserve the classed wines in a state fit for tasting appears to us, as to you, to pose certain problems; it would be difficult to make the Exposition Commission correctly appreciate this measure; the thing would end up becoming known and would have a very bad effect. It is thus no use even thinking about it. Instead, a more suitable solution seems to us to expose just one bottle of each of the classed wines, in such a manner that their labels are in evidence and to conserve the five other bottles for the tasting.

As for the storage of the other five bottles, the Chamber envisaged digging a hole beneath the display area into which the cases could be placed. "This excavation. . .does not need to be of large dimension since it is a matter of placing there only the *classed* wines, red and white, and you have 30 to 40 little cases of those. As concerns the non-classed wines, they will have to be placed at the back of the showcase, and if they are altered by the heat it will be a small inevitable misfortune." Once again, the Chamber of Commerce's primary concern was the classed growths; it was these wines on which they saw the region's reputation for quality resting and for which the jury would be most likely to reward the Chamber's display. The communal wines were the ballast that had to be carried to provide the semblance of a comprehensive display and calm the sensibilities of winemakers back home who might otherwise have attempted to overturn the wine trade's classification.

At last, on June 24, Henri Galos went to the Universal Exposition and made his way to the Annex, prepared to spend the better part of his Sunday engaged in affixing the Chamber of Commerce's labels and arranging the bottles in the display case. He had hardly begun when he was accosted by Amédée Rouget de Lisle, a civil engineer by training and the inventor of numerous devices for preserving foods and for carbonating water and alcoholic beverages. His varied interests had led him to undertake the writing of a book on Bordeaux's classed-growth wines, and it was in preparation of this work that Rouget de Lisle had made the acquaintance of Monplaisir Goudal during the latter's visit to Paris that spring. During the course of that meeting, the subject of the manager's grievance against the Chamber of Commerce came up, and Rouget de Lisle had volunteered his assistance in support of Lafite's cause. (Ten years later, Amédée Rouget de Lisle's sense of justice would be roused once again, in a vigorous defense of his uncle Claude-Joseph's recognition as author of the French national anthem *La Marseillaise.*)

Although Napoleon Jerome's decision regarding the labeling of the Chamber of Commerce's bottles had won the right for Samuel Scott's name to appear on Lafite's wines in the display, this still fell short of what the manager sought. Goudal wanted his own name included as well as Scott's, in keeping with his father's decades-old practice of placing the manager's name on the label; this would also enable the bottles to serve as advertisements indicating to whom one should address inquiries in order to obtain Lafite's wines, particularly the 1846s and 1848s which were on display. Accordingly, after his meeting with Napoleon Jerome in April and before leaving Paris to return to Bordeaux, he had given copies of Lafite's labels to Rouget de Lisle with instructions to look for the wines he had sent to the Chamber of Commerce and place his own labels on those bottles.

Rouget de Lisle approached Henri Galos and stated that his purpose was to affix Monplaisir Goudal's labels on Lafite's bottles in place of the labels from the Chamber of Commerce. This was in direct conflict with the very specific instructions issued by Duffour-Dubergier and Galos informed the journalist of this. He flatly refused any intervention in his work, stating that the labels from Bordeaux were the only ones authorized to be placed on the bottles in the Chamber of Commerce's display. Rouget de Lisle pursued his point with increasing vigor, leading to a "very unpleasant" exchange between the two men. Faced with Galos' staunch refusal to allow any interference in his work or alterations in his instructions, Rouget de Lisle went off in search of a member of the Imperial Commission in order to request permission for an independent display of Lafite's wines apart from those in the Chamber of Commerce's showcase.

Upon hearing of this newest development from Henri Galos, the Chamber reacted strongly. On June 29, a letter was sent to Napoleon Jerome informing him of this latest problem concerning Monplaisir Goudal and the wine labels:

> Mr. Henri Galos, the Chamber's representative in Paris, informs us that Mr. Rouget de Lisle asks in the name of the manager at Château Lafite that the name of Mr. Goudal be inscribed on the samples from this property.
>
> We cannot accede to such a request; the labels that we have sent to Paris bear exactly, following the name of Château Lafite, that of its owner, Sir Samuel Scott; but Mr. Goudal, a simple manager of a property which does not belong to him, has no right to place himself beside the owner.

The Chamber was incensed. After giving in to the Imperial Commission by altering the labels for the classed growths, it still had to contend with Monplaisir Goudal. Its insistence in the matter was further spurred on by a piece of news that Rouget de Lisle had imparted to Henri Galos during their confrontation: a couple of other managers had also made demands similar to Monplaisir Goudal's. (One of these was the manager at Cos-d'Estournel, a property that adjoined Lafite to the north and between which existed family connections in the management of the two properties.) Things were now threatening to disintegrate into a wholesale assault on the Bordeaux wine display, and in defense the Chamber's argument fell back on the authority invested in it according to the regulations of the Imperial Commission itself:

> ... [T]he Commission whose work Your Imperial Highness directs has established a very sensible principle as an absolute barrier to the anarchy which would overwhelm the Exposition. No object coming from the provinces is to be admitted if it has not received the sanction of the Departmental Committee. The samples that we have sent have been approved and shipped by the Committee for the Gironde. . . .To maintain order and remain in the right, it was believed that the Bordeaux Chamber of Commerce alone was called upon to organize the representation of the Gironde's wine production.

The Chamber believed that the strength of this argument, based on the absolutely unambiguous regulations of the Imperial Commission itself, could only carry the day and the pretensions of Monplaisir Goudal would be swept away once and for all. It was wrong.

On May 15, the postponed inauguration of the Universal Exposition was set for 1 P.M., the hour at which Napoleon III was scheduled to arrive at the Palace of Industry from the Tuileries. The streets along the route which the Emperor and his entourage would travel had been lined with crowds for hours, despite the chill rain which had been falling since the early morning. Inside the exhibition hall everything had been arranged to minimize the chaos of the unfinished installation and present a fittingly splendid impression for the capital's political and social elite. Members of the French government and foreign representatives were seated on the main floor of the Palace of Industry's long rectangular exhibition space. Upon entering the building through its imposing main portal and emerging onto the transept's central area, these guests found themselves directly before a platform draped in tapestries on which were set the imperial thrones of Napoleon III and the Empress Eugénie, overhung by a red velvet canopy bearing the insignia of the imperial crown. From either side of this focal point, rows of crimson benches stretched toward each of the building's ends: members of the foreign diplomatic corps and France's legislature, army, and judiciary were seated on the right, while the left was occupied by the officers of the Crown and the sizable imperial household. "From 10 till 12 o'clock the space reserved on the ground floor in front of the throne was gradually filled," reported the correspondent from the London *Times*, "and the eye soon became dazzled with the brilliancy of the costumes, French and foreign, covered with embroidery and *insignia* of orders belonging to every Government in Europe." To one side an orchestra of 150 musicians filled the air with "Partant pour la Syrie," the theme from "Queen Hortense," and other well-known melodies of the time.

Over 4,000 exhibitors and invited guests whose stature did not merit places at throne level were seated in the mezzanine, which ran the length of the Palace of Industry. Here sartorial color was supplied by "the outfits of the ladies pleasantly interrupting and brightening the monotone background formed by the black suits of the men." More elaborate decoration was offered by the flags that draped the mezzanine railings representing the nations whose products were on display, while the supporting pillars bore plaques on which were inscribed the names of these countries' principal cities. These pillars marked off the alcoves assigned to the various national displays, the principal countries located nearer the transept's center, the lesser ones toward the ends. The general effect was one of pomp and splendor fully befitting the showcase that France intended the Universal Exposition to be.

Still, when Napoleon III finally entered the Palace of Industry at twenty minutes past one, it was unlikely he failed to notice what had attracted the attention of others on that day: the central alcove before which the imperial thrones had been placed, officially allocated for the display of the United States' exhibits, was conspicuously absent of any displays. The vacant American alcove was the most visible sign of a problem that had caught the Exposition's organizers unprepared—after months of concern about not having enough display space, they were now faced with having too much.

As the host nation, France was the principal exhibitor, its displays occupying half of the Palace of Industry's ground floor and a major proportion of the Annex; England was accorded the second-largest area for its displays, reciprocating the courtesy shown to the French in the Crystal Palace exhibition. Other nations allotted major emplacements were Prussia and the Confederation of German States, Austria, Belgium, Switzerland, and the United States. In dividing the exhibition areas throughout the Palace and the Annex, the Imperial Commission had to establish an equitable allotment between France and the rest of the world; a similar balance had to be struck among the French departments. Throughout the Commission's deliberations and the process of distributing display space, it was always a main concern that there would not be enough square meters available to satisfy the international and domestic demand. Most of the lists that the Commission received from the French departmental committees contained a surfeit of exhibits requiring a space in excess of what the committees knew had been allotted to them. The department of the Seine, whose main contingent was the city of Paris, submitted a bulletin containing exhibits necessitating 7,000 square meters, a full 2,000 more than it had been assigned. Although these efforts at slipping in extra displays were routinely refused by the Imperial Commission, they greatly contributed to an anxiety that led to the construction of additional display corridors, which threw the Exposition's completion even further behind schedule. In the end, however, a number of nations and departmental committees failed to use all of the space that they had at their disposal. This was the case with the United States. As the correspondent from the *Illustrated London News* sharply criticized, "There is America—with its hundred exhibitors. . . —still unrepresented, occupying, to make the case more deplorable, space immediately opposite the principal entrances!" For various reasons, although allotted 1,619 square meters and an alcove in place of honor at the center of the Palace of Industry, the American contingent finally comprised only sixty-seven exhibitors. Much of the space in the American alcove was filled by bales of cotton, various articles of vulcanized rubber from Charles Goodyear, and several of the latest-model repeating pistols from Samuel Colt, but this was largely insufficient to fill the area and the consequent impression of emptiness led to a disappointment which was noted by more than one visitor to the Exposition.

Displays from French departmental committees also came up short of their original estimates of space, and the Exposition's organizers were faced with gaping empty areas which were decidedly out of place at an event in which every space was intended to fill the eye with sights of pomp and progress. "What can the imperial Commissioners do to remedy shortcomings like these?" wondered a journalist in his reporting of this embarrassing situation. By the end of June, as the Universal Exposition was finally finishing the installation of its last uncompleted areas, a solution had been decided upon. On June 27, exhibitors received the following notice from the Imperial Commission's General Secretary, Arlès-Dufour:

> In light of exhibitors' continued persistence, despite repeated requests, in not occupying the display space which they have been assigned, the Administration having exhausted all means of persuasion and desiring to satisfy the demands of those exhibitors already installed as well as the just impatience of the public, will assign from today, without further notice, the best positions on a first-come, first-served basis to those presenting their products.

Accordingly, the sparse and conspicuous United States alcove was eventually filled out with pieces of furniture and musical instruments of French manufacture. The shipment from the Gironde was scheduled to comprise ninety-nine exhibitors requiring just over 137 square meters of display space distributed throughout the various areas of the Exposition. As it turned out, thirteen of them were unable to prepare their exhibits for shipment to Paris and had to cede their places. Among these cancellations, six had withdrawn too late to surrender their display cases to other products from the department, and so were left empty. For Rouget de Lisle, the need to fill these vacant exhibition spaces was a stroke of luck which introduced a measure of flexibility in Article 8 of the Universal Exposition's General Regulations: "No product will be admitted to the Exposition if it has not been sent with the authorization and seal of the Departmental or Foreign Committees." When the journalist appealed to the Imperial Commission for the opportunity to independently present Lafite's wine bearing Monplaisir Goudal's labels, there were four vacant showcases available in the Gironde's Annex-based exhibition whose size was appropriate for the display of a couple of wine bottles. On July 12, a satisfied Monplaisir Goudal was able to inform Samuel Scott that "I have received word from Paris that we are definitively installed in the Palace of Industry at no. 48 (in the Annex). We are just beside the exhibition from the Bordeaux Chamber of Commerce which did not wish to allow us to place our labels on our bottles; they were forced to see things otherwise. But," Goudal sniffed, "this exhibition of the principal wines from Bordeaux makes little effect, having been done without taste."

During its meeting on July 4, the Chamber of Commerce learned about the success of Monplaisir Goudal's challenge, leading it to immediately dispatch a formal complaint to Henri Galos with instructions for its further communication to the Imperial Commission. Additional complaints followed in the succeeding weeks as Galos was instructed by the Chamber to continue pressing its protest:

> It is less a matter of preventing Mr. Goudal from putting his name on the bottles of wine belonging to Sir Samuel Scott, but rather an observation of the principle that there should be no exposition of wines from the Gironde outside of the exhibit of samples sent by the Chamber with the cooperation and sanction of the Departmental Committee. If this principle is not respected, others besides Mr. Goudal can also ask to exhibit their wines, to obtain what he has obtained, and all the inconveniences of anarchy and complaint that it was the object of the Chamber to prevent will freely produce themselves.

The Chamber was prescient in its concern: in the end, it was not only Lafite that decided to stage an independent display—the Baron Pichon-Longueville as well as Eugène Larrieu of Haut-Brion also decided to present their wines apart from those assembled by the Chamber of Commerce, making use of the other empty display cases that were available. "It goes without saying that we would not have gotten ourselves involved in this business which has brought us unpleasant problems, and is a source of embarrassment and a regrettable waste of time. . . ." Nonetheless, in the interest of staging as complete an exhibit as possible, the Chamber of Commerce would still include in its presentation the samples originally received from Lafite, even if differently labeled bottles were to be on display nearby. Circumstances had facilitated another bending of the Imperial Commission's rules and the Chamber of Commerce had lost another piece in the carefully constructed organization of its display of the Gironde's wines at the Universal Exposition. It was determined, however, to lose no others.

Seven

"...A QUESTION OF JUSTICE, OF GOOD FAITH, AND OF APPEARANCES..."

At 7 P.M. on July 28, twenty-one people sat down to dinner at 20, rue Barbet de Jouy in Paris. "You must come," a reluctant guest was implored by his host. "The dinner to which I am inviting you is special in character; its composition, its form, its manner of preparation are unique: there will not be another occasion for me to offer you, or for you to accept, such a gastronomic experience. Everything down to the guests in attendance is singular in nature." The meal in question was being offered by Edmond-François Fouché-Lepelletier, who often entertained at home in his capacities as a member of the Legislature and owner of the Javel chemical works, one of the nation's leading industrial laboratories. ("Javel water," Fouché-Lepelletier's flagship product, is the name by which chlorine bleach is still commonly known in France.) This dinner, however, was occasioned by one of his more recent activities: since June 25, he had been serving as a juror and the secretary for the group judging the XI class of exhibits at the Universal Exposition. These were the items classified under the heading "Preparation and Conservation of Alimentary Substances," and everything to be served at the dinner that evening (excepting the bread) would be based entirely on the products the jury was in the process of judging.

Among the twenty-one guests at the table that evening were the nine members of the jury for the XI class. Beyond its basic function as a social event, the dinner was intended to supplement in a more agreeable manner the rather sterile daily judging sessions at the Palace of Industry, during which the nine jurors would wend their way across the length and breadth of the display areas in search of the products they were to evaluate. This dinner was a bonus unique to this jury; neither "Mining and Metallurgy Arts," "Industries Involving the Economic Use of Heat," nor any of the other classes of exhibits could offer their judges a similarly pleasant opportunity for extramural investigation. The "alimentary substances" comprising the XI class included a wide range of products: flours and other starches such as pastas and rice; sugars and confectionery; vinegars and oils; conserved foods, such as dried fruits and smoked fish; and coffees, teas, and chocolates. The XI class was also the province of "Fermented Drinks," the category under which wines at the Universal Exposition were to be judged.

Given the nature of the dinner's ingredients, most of its preparation was a matter of opening packages, applying heat to already prepared foods, and artfully arranging the result on serving platters for presentation. Nonetheless, a chef, three cooks, a maître d'hôtel, and ten servers were employed in the preparation of a menu composed of 188 items organized according to the finest traditions of French cuisine: five soups, four *relevés*, twelve opening courses, seven roasts, six vegetable dishes, *hors-d'oeuvre*, and thirty-two items under the heading of desserts. Also presented for inspection was a selection of oils, condiments, coffees, tea, and milk. The wine service consisted of forty-six bottles selected from the Universal Exposition's international offering; Bordeaux was represented by Château Margaux, Mouton, Latour, and the 1848 Lafite. Judgments were made and recorded on the various foods served that evening. Crayfish from the Rhine "left something to be desired"; a chicken processed and preserved in 1831 was found to be "very good for [a bird that has undergone] 25 years of conservation," although the final verdict considered it more of a curiosity than a truly commercial product; truffles presented a problem, since no reliable process for conserving them had yet been perfected—all ten examples served that evening had fermented and were deemed "terrible"; but the deer in pepper sauce was unanimously judged "exquisite." As for the wines served at the dinner, no remarks were recorded.

The jury's silence regarding the quality of the wines was indicative of a circumstance fundamental to the organization of the XI class. Among these exhibits, as was the case elsewhere from armaments to textiles, the Exposition's focus was on the technological advancements that had made possible the exhibits on display. This was clearly indicated in the very title for the XI class: it was the *preparation and conservation* of alimentary substances that was being judged, not the alimentary substances (otherwise known as food) themselves. Although the taste of the product was not inconsequential, the jury was mainly concerned with how well the processing of raw ingredients—wheat, sugar beets, poultry, milk—had been handled to preserve their nutritional qualities while enabling the finished products—flour, sugar, twenty-five-year-old salsifis of chicken, cheese—to be made available to the greatest number at the least cost. The taste of the foods was little more than an indicator suggesting the success or failure of the processing.

Like the members of the Departmental Committees who selected the local products for shipment to Paris, the jurors at the Universal Exposition were chosen based largely on their past experience as either judges or exhibitors in this type of venue and on how well they could appreciate the technology represented by the products on display. The president of the XI class jury, Richard Owen, was Britain's foremost anatomist and paleontologist, a corresponding member of the French Institute, and a former jury president at the 1851 Crystal Palace exhibition; the vice-president, Anselme Payen, was an eminent food scientist who had served as a judge at the 1849 French National Exhibition and again at London in 1851. Their fellow jurors were no less qualified to sit in judgment, their stature confirmed by memberships in various legislatures, learned bodies, and chambers of commerce across Europe. In addition to Payen and Fouché-Lepelletier there were two other chemists, Charles Balling, professor at the Polytechnic School of Prague, and Doctor Weidenbusch, a manufacturer in Wurtemberg; Numa Grar and Guillaume Joest were sugar refiners, the former French, the latter Prussian; Aimé-Stanislas Darblay had made his fortune in the French grain market, and was the inventor of a revolutionary method for the fabrication of flours; Florent Robert was an Austrian manufacturer. All were leading names in the science and industry of alimentary substances; none were chefs with a practical appreciation for the gastronomic qualities of food.

Culinarians did exist with the industrial expertise necessary to serve as judges for the XI class: there was Alexis Soyer, for instance, the French-born chef whose great renown in mid-nineteenth century England anticipated the celebrity accorded his successors today. His inventiveness was not limited to the creation of recipes for the one thousand members of London's elite while overseeing the kitchens at the exclusive Reform Club throughout the 1840s; Soyer helped design the kitchens themselves, using technology and principles of efficiency that were still effective in the same facility over 100 years later. Turning his attention beyond his own kitchen, he designed cooking implements for domestic use, made widely used improvements on gas ovens and field stoves, and developed a line of popular patent sauces manufactured by Crosse and Blackwell. However, he was not called to serve at either the Crystal Palace or the Palace of Industry, and, in 1855, Soyer instead went off to the Crimea, where he put his culinary and industrial genius to use in improving the nourishment of the British army.

Just as there were no chefs present to judge the gastronomic aspects of the foods on display, there were no winemakers on the jury with a competence to judge the quality of the wines. Faced with no fewer than 1,294 wine samples from 456 exhibitors evenly divided between France and the rest of the world, the jurors recognized that their industrial and academic credentials were inadequate to the task, and so a special panel of tasters was assembled to assist them during two months of "tiresome work" judging the wines, alcohols, beers, vinegars, and ciders on display. This panel was composed of Castera, chief taster at the prefecture of police; Jacques-Auguste Ancelin and Hemmet, a pair of wine brokers; Duluart, who directed the union of Parisian wine tasters; Jean-Claude Landre and Hippolyte Rousseau, merchants. All were from the capital, and as was only natural in a city not itself a major producer but rather a magnet for wines from all over France, these professionals' expertise, albeit considerable, was general in nature.

In their discussion of the wines published after the official tastings, the XI class jury made clear that it was "the fabrication of wine which is the essential object of this report." Where they had to deal directly with the wines themselves, their comments were marked by a notable lack of precision. Since the final decade of the previous century, an extensive vocabulary had gradually developed to effectively communicate the characteristics of a wine's taste; this vocabulary was commonly understood by professionals and amateurs alike, but was entirely absent from the report's discussion of Bordeaux's wines. Even with their advisory panel of Parisian experts, the jury's commentary failed to rise above the ambiguous simplicity of folklore: "The wines of Bordeaux give tone to the stomach, while leaving the mouth fresh and the head clear. 'More than one invalid abandoned by the doctors has been seen to drink the good old wine of Bordeaux and return to health.'"

Not far behind its initial concerns of defending the Bordeaux classification was the Chamber of Commerce's anxiety regarding how the wines might fare in the jury tasting, which would determine the honors, or lack of any, to be awarded at the Universal Exposition. The Chamber feared that judges unfamiliar with Bordeaux's wines might lack the experience to properly appreciate them, resulting in an unfavorable comparison with others they were more used to drinking—indeed, could Bordeaux's wines even be compared with those from elsewhere, given the unique character of each region's production? The Bordeaux Chamber was well aware that a wine's success in the market was based on its reputation as much as its quality, so the economic consequences of an insufficient appreciation by the Exposition's judges were simply too great to subject the Gironde's most important industry to such a risk. As the Chamber of Commerce originally explained to the Departmental Committee, its preference was for the wines to be presented out of competition.

On May 10, five days before the postponed inauguration, the regulations governing the Exposition's juries were issued. Four types of awards would be given to exhibitors judged worthy of recognition: medals of gold, silver, and bronze, followed by honorable mentions. (In light of the great number of gold medals the various juries would award, the system would later be modified to allay fears of a diminution of the top award's value owing to the judges' largess. The gold-medal category would be divided into two parts, "Grand Medals of Honor" and "Medals of Honor," with the silver and bronze medals renamed "First Class" and "Second

Class"; honorable mentions remained unchanged.) More important, however, was the official adoption of the system by which exhibits at the Universal Exposition were to be judged on intrinsic worth and not comparative value. There were not a limited number of awards to be won, with those exhibitors not making the grade in comparison with others of the same type losing out; conceivably, if a dozen exhibitors were entered in a particular class and all twelve were found to be of excellent quality, the jury had the option of awarding each a gold medal. Bordeaux's wines would therefore not be judged against any other region's production, but would be considered on their own merits. Under these circumstances, the Chamber of Commerce's fears evidently were allayed and the Gironde's wines were made available for examination by the jury.

The judging was scheduled for Friday, July 20. On the eve of the tasting, Duffour-Dubergier wrote to Henri Galos with his reflections concerning a question that had come to occupy their thoughts. "We think, like you, that in the case of a medal being awarded to the Chamber it would be best [for the jury] to add that this distinction is accorded us in recognition of the collection of wines. . . in which the jury honors the samples of superior quality coming from diverse growths of distinguished merit belonging to various people whose names will be indicated [separately]." Winning a medal for itself was never part of the Chamber of Commerce's purpose in organizing the Gironde's wines for display; its intention was to present the region's production in a manner as complete and organized as possible without jeopardizing any constituent part. Presenting itself as the intermediary between the proprietors and the Exposition had proved a thankless task fraught with misunderstanding of the Chamber's motivation, and it had no need now of anything that would add to the idea that Duffour-Dubergier and his colleagues were usurping the rightful recognition of those actually responsible for the quality of the wines being honored by a medal. However, there was another reason behind the Chamber's preference for individual acknowledgment in what was officially a collective award, one which at that moment was more important than the sensibilities of Bordeaux's proprietors: "We will thus avoid for Lafite the individual distinction that Mr. Goudal seems to seek."

Monplaisir Goudal, having secured the right to exhibit Lafite's wines apart from the Chamber of Commerce's collective display, intended to participate in the tasting on an independent basis as well. There was never any question in Goudal's mind that Lafite would not take part; he had none of the doubts regarding competition that occupied the Bordeaux Chamber of Commerce. Given his belief in Lafite's greatness, he could well reason that the finest wine in the Gironde had little to fear in a comparison with those from any other producer, French or foreign. Accordingly, during a visit to Paris in the spring, Monplaisir Goudal had taken the same precaution as the Chamber of Commerce and set aside in the Palace of Industry's cellars one bottle each of Lafite's 1846 and 1848 for the jury tasting. Any connection with the Chamber of Commerce's display on any level had become anathema, and the possibility that Lafite's wine might be judged and awarded a prize under the Chamber's banner was not any more appealing. The idea that it would be the Chamber and not Lafite which would profit from an award earned by Goudal's efforts could only have been considered absolutely unacceptable, reinforcing the manager's determination to have Lafite judged apart.

Now, if it turned out that the Chamber of Commerce's display were to be marked for distinction by the jury, Duffour-Dubergier sought a change in the precedent established at the Crystal Palace: individual classed growths should receive acknowledgment, thus preventing the singular recognition of Lafite earned by flouting the rules whereby the Chamber of Commerce was solely empowered to present the Gironde's wines at the Exposition. These were but preliminary thoughts; depending on the results of the tasting there would be more to discuss regarding this matter. In the meantime, Henri Galos was instructed to attend the jury tasting in order to assure "that all takes place in the most favorable manner for Bordeaux's interests." With Monplaisir Goudal 600 kilometers away in Bordeaux, Rouget de Lisle once again assumed the role of defender for Lafite, making sure that it was the wine set aside by Goudal which the jury would taste. In addition, Haut-Brion and Pichon-Longueville, which like Lafite had mounted individual displays, would be judged independently as well.

Richard Owen was a frequent letter writer, and during his sojourn in Paris he filled pages of correspondence with accounts of his various activities and social engagements during the Universal Exposition. In one letter, written on July 27, he offered this description of the manner in which the tastings by the XI class jury were performed:

> The morning occupations of our jury are curious and various, each one well adapted to its end, but performed amidst a scene of gesticulation and action and a Babel of seeming altercation which renders the result, when we come afterwards coolly to sum up the notes, surprising to me. Take the following as an example: Time, 7 A.M.; subject, Wines of Austria; scene, Grande Exposition, in a small whitewashed chamber with a skylight; a table with green cloth, and books, papers, writing materials; another with rows of bottles of wine, corkscrews, &c. Hampers of wine on one side of the room. President and two or three members of the jury in green velvet *fauteuils*; three experts seated in a corner of the room with a tin pail before them, each with a silver chalice like a Highland quaigh, and a small napkin. The Austrian Commissioner and the representatives of the several wine-growers; a man in green and silver uniform to uncork; a grinning negro to serve the wine to the tasters; a worthy 'blouse' to hand and take back the sample-bottles. Commissioner calls out the number and vintage year of the sample. A juryman enters it in a ruled book, the uncorker uncorks the bottle; the grinning negro pours a little into the pail, then fills the chalice. Each taster agitates the wine, carries it to his nose, draws it slowly into his mouth, rinces and spurts it out into the pail; then the three interchange knowing remarks in a low tone, their heads together, and bawl out a number, 3, 6, 10, as the

> case may be, indicative of their verdict as to quality. The same entered by secretary of jury and vouched by president. After each trial the expert wipes his chalice and recommences. After five or six trials water is served to each, with which he rinces out his mouth and chalice, then wipes his tongue with his napkin. The trial recommences: Number and vintage of bottle called; clack goes the cork; black Hebe bottles up the sparkling ruby or gold-colored wine in the silver chalices; sniffing, rincing, smacking of lips, and all goes into the pail. Two of our experts are *décorés*, and their jovial fellow is bearded like the pard. Strange and outlandish are the shapes of the bottles, and quaint their labels, from Hungary and Bohemia. As the tasting progresses, the din of discussion waxes louder and fiercer. Any peculiarly fine wines are submitted in *petits verres* to the jury; the progress is from the ordinary to the *recherchés*; most delicate and *aromés* were some, and more especially the concluding sample entitled "Tokay-Essence, du Cru de Monak, du Comte George Andrassy." It was grievous to see the amber-coloured, sparkling Tokays liberally added to the now almost brimming pailful of the mixture of all the choicest wines of the Austrian Empire.

Hours after the tasting, Henri Galos wrote a report to the Chamber of Commerce which was read at its next meeting on July 25. The judging had taken place as scheduled and the jury had been very favorably impressed with the Chamber's display. The wines would be awarded a medal, of this there was no doubt; the only question was the manner of its attribution. This would be determined by a "special commission" of the jury, which would draft the report on the XI class of products. On July 26, a response was sent to Galos which clearly stated the results sought by the Chamber of Commerce:

> Sir, we are answering your letter of the 20th of this month, which was read during our meeting yesterday.
>
> Here is our opinion on the subject of the medal about which you have written us.
>
> If a medal were accorded to the wines of Lafite, in consequence of the display that Mr. Goudal was authorized to make and against which we rightly protested, this growth would be placed in a more favorable position than the others. You understand how this would be disagreeable for the proprietors of the same rank who conformed to the formal rules of the Commission.
>
> Thus, if Lafite has a medal, it must be insisted upon that the one awarded to us stipulate that it is accorded for *the collection of wines that the Chamber has sent, and in which figures, in the first line, the wines of Château Margaux, Lafite, and Latour.*
>
> We insist that Château Margaux be named before Lafite, in order that all the honors not fall upon the latter. Besides, these three first growths are arranged *ex aequo*, and if Lafite seeks superiority, this is a claim that can not be permitted.
>
> There must be no mention of *Haut-Brion; the proprietor of this growth did not wish to furnish us with any samples.*

Clearly, the Chamber of Commerce's instructions were motivated by what had now become practically a personal test of will between Duffour-Dubergier and Monplaisir Goudal; however, it was no less true that the continued viability of the wine trade's classification was of equal importance at this moment. The Chamber's thoughts focused on the Médoc's first growths, still the ostensible foundation of the red-wine classification. In Monplaisir Goudal's actions, which threatened a singular recognition for Lafite, there was the danger of creating a "super-first" growth in a class apart from the others, based not on price but on a perception of quality given tacit acknowledgment by the awarding of an individual medal at the Universal Exposition. However, this was not the only threat to stability among the first growths and, by extension, the classification in its entirety. A bid for change had also arisen from within the Chamber of Commerce's camp itself.

Henri Galos was one of five siblings, with two sisters and two brothers; these latter were both in the wine trade. The eldest of the three brothers was Emile, who had become prominent in Bordeaux city politics beginning in the 1830s and was a merchant like their father Jacques. The younger brother was Theodore Galos, whose professional activity was at the production end of the Bordeaux commercial chain: he was the manager for several properties, including the Saint-Julien third-growth Lagrange, and, in Pauillac, Mouton, at the head of the seconds.

Upon assuming management of Mouton in 1852, Theodore Galos at once dedicated himself to satisfying the owners' ambitions to raise the property to a first growth. In 1854, he succeeded in establishing an opening price for his wine equal to Lafite's 5,000 francs per tun, in effect bringing Mouton to commercial parity with the firsts. Now all that was necessary was consecration of this status in the classification, and here Theodore Galos enjoyed a great stroke of luck: his brother Henri was currently in a position of influence in a matter that touched on this very subject.

Once the jury tasting had taken place, Henri Galos evidently thought the moment ripe to suggest Mouton's elevation to first-growth status, and he included this thought in his letter of July 20. The Chamber of Commerce would have none of it. Having issued its instructions on how Lafite was to be handled, its letter then went on to address this new point:

> *Neither must Mouton figure beside Château Margaux and Latour,* as you indicate. *Mouton is only a second growth* and must not place itself with the firsts.
>
> We attach a *great importance to maintaining intact the classification of wines as established for so long a time in the Bordeaux marketplace.* The proprietors' ambitious claims continually aim at disturbing this classification that is so essential to respect under pain of falling into an inextricable confusion and a disastrous state of affairs.
>
> *If Lafite receives no medal* (but this does not seem probable) *there is no need to designate by name the first growths for the* [medal] *which will be awarded to the Chamber.*
>
> So much for the medal. *As for the report, it will be necessary that it designate all the classed wines sent by the Chamber, with the names of the proprietors.*
>
> *It is very important that the list of these wines conform to what may be considered the official list which was sent to us by the union of brokers.*
>
> We have sent you a copy of this list and it also figures on our large map.
>
> In the event of any demands and complaints, the responsibility for the. . . classification, will thus fall on the brokers; the Chamber is shielded from criticism.

> As for the classed growths which figure on the union's list but for which no samples were sent because, in spite of our appeal, the proprietors did not wish to send us any, it goes without saying that there should be no question of including them in the report concerning our shipment.
>
> You well understand all our thoughts on this affair; do all that you can so that the Commission acts in accordance with our desires, which are, after all, only just and reasonable.

Curiously, it was not the members of the XI class jury that the Chamber of Commerce instructed its representative to see; it was they, after all, who were directly involved with the question at hand. Perhaps the Chamber had by now established a fixation on the Imperial Commission (there was to be renewed—and futile—correspondence with the Commission on the subject of the wine labels); it may be that it was simply following the practice of addressing itself to the highest level of authority; in any event, obeying the instructions received from Bordeaux, Henri Galos set about trying to convince the Imperial Commission to see things the Chamber of Commerce's way. An almost daily series of letters kept Duffour-Dubergier and the other members continually informed of his efforts, which, in a repeat of previous appeals to the Commission, were met with resistance at numerous points. As in the past, there were misunderstandings on both sides. Since Lafite's wines were exhibited apart from the Chamber of Commerce's display, the Commission insisted on considering them as a separate entity, and thus eligible for an award of their own; this was also its position regarding Haut-Brion. Upon learning from Galos that this latter property was to be given an award, Duffour-Dubergier protested strongly. This objection was based on his ignorance of the fact that Haut-Brion had arranged a separate display; he thus could not understand how an honor was to be accorded a wine which (as far as he knew) was not even present at the Exposition:

> Mr. Larrieu, the owner of this growth, did not wish to give us any samples. One or two proprietors at Pessac (notably Mr. Pommez) gave us theirs and it is possible that they had designated their wines as Haut-Brion, a name that is readily assumed by several vineyard owners in Pessac, but [these are] not *Château Haut Brion*. These wines, as you are aware, are placed a rank well below that given to Mr. Larrieu's growth. Unless surreptitiously included in our collection (which is not at all probable), we have no wines from the *Château* which are ranked with the three first growths. It would thus be absurd to indicate the presence of wines in our display which are not there.

(Pichon-Longueville, which had also presented itself independently, did not occupy the Chamber's thoughts to the same degree, not being a first growth.)

However, the main targets of Duffour-Dubergier's complaints continued to be Monplaisir Goudal and Lafite:

> We continue to insist that Château Margaux and Latour have an individual medal if one is accorded to Lafite. . . .Make it understood that the samples of Lafite 1846 and 1848 are included in our shipment. Château Margaux, Latour and it are thus,

> in this context, in the same position. Lafite, after the fact, wished to obtain a special situation for itself in raising a claim for admission outside of the action of the Departmental Committee, but it would be very unpleasant were it to obtain, in reward for such maneuvers, a distinction that is refused Château Margaux and Latour. [These properties] well merit it and. . . their proprietors would be punished for not having attempted to circumvent the formal injunctions of the Commission.
>
> This Commission would thus reward the flaunting of its authority to the detriment of those who have respected and obeyed it.
>
> There is here a question of justice, of good faith, and of appearances; we like to believe that the Commission will give itself over to your observations on the subject.

For Duffour-Dubergier, it was all a matter of respect for the rules set down by the duly empowered authorities, in the first instance the Bordeaux Chamber of Commerce, and in the second the Imperial Commission for the Universal Exposition. Recent history had vividly demonstrated the consequences of abandoning the respect for order which gave institutions their authority and society its stability; memories of the 1848 revolution whose violence shook the nation and toppled the monarchy just seven years before were still fresh in the minds of all. For Duffour-Dubergier and the other members of the Chamber of Commerce, whose lives, both personal and commercial, were built on the foundation of law, the disregard for established authority shown in this episode with Monplaisir Goudal (and the willingness of the Imperial Commission to abdicate its own control) could only have filled their imaginations with horror. It was less with a sense of resignation and more with a sense of despair that Duffour-Dubergier acknowledged the difficulties of Henri Galos' task as he instructed the Chamber's representative to continue to press for acceptance of its position: "We are really sorry for all the difficulties that you are caused by this eternal affair. We hope, for you as for us, that this will soon be over."

As mid-August approached, the Chamber of Commerce grew ever more pessimistic in its efforts with the Imperial Commission to arrange the distribution of awards. On August 9, the members wrote to Henri Galos that "we thank you for all the efforts you have made regarding our disputes with the Exposition's Commission; we are persuaded that you have done your best to obtain the justice that we seek; it is neither your fault nor ours if the Commission persists in refusing to listen to the perfectly-founded observations that we present. . . .Do your best regarding the medals and the report. Obtain what you can; we have nothing more to tell you in this regard. . . ."

It was at this time that Duffour-Dubergier went to Paris. As reported by Rouget de Lisle to Monplaisir Goudal, the purpose of this trip was to personally argue the Chamber of Commerce's case before the Imperial Commission. "His request is illegal," wrote Goudal to Samuel Scott, "but with scheming it is possible that he could come out on top." In fact, that body remained impervious to the Chamber's arguments; it was from another quarter that progress would finally be achieved. After weeks spent in vain trying to sway the Imperial Commission, Henri Galos departed from the Chamber's tactic of appealing to the highest authority and sought redress at a lower level: the "special commission" of the XI class which was directly responsible for the report on the wines and the distribution of their medals. Here he found an audience more disposed toward the Chamber of Commerce's arguments, and, on August 14, Galos could at last write to Bordeaux with good news. "Finally, after a good many difficulties and by dint of perseverance, I have succeeded in obtaining a hearing by the Exposition's special commission charged with the report on the wines. I can only congratulate myself on my persistence, since as you will see, I have won acceptance of the solutions which most closely follow your views." The news was as heartening as it was unexpected: "This success has somewhat surprised the Chamber," wrote its secretary, Jules Fauché, to the still-absent Duffour-Dubergier, "which was far from flattering itself of success."

Under the terms secured by Henri Galos, a Grand Medal of Honor would be awarded to the Chamber of Commerce "for its precious collection of wines from the Gironde." Lafite's wines would be considered part of the Chamber's exhibit, and the order of the first growths in the Exposition's official report would be Château Margaux, Lafite, and Latour. "I took care to note that Château Margaux should be placed at the head of its peers," explained Galos, referring to his argument before the special commission, "since in the tasting it had obtained a score of 20 [out of 20], while Lafite had only 19. They were in agreement with me." With inconsistent reasoning, the other classed growths in the Chamber's exhibit would not be listed in the order of their results in the tasting, which Galos went on to characterize as "a completely accidental occurrence"; instead, these wines would appear in the jury's report as they did in the brokers' classification. As to any hopes Theodore Galos may have harbored for Mouton's promotion to a first growth owing to his brother's advocacy, these were hopes that would remain unfulfilled: "Mouton returns to its place at the head of the second growths, as you have wished," continued Henri Galos in his letter to the Chamber. (And that, at least for the next 118 years, was that, until Mouton-Rothschild finally succeeded in its efforts for promotion to a first growth in 1973.)

By now very much aware of the areas of real importance for certain members of the Chamber of Commerce, Galos even arranged for the commission to acknowledge the wine map of the Gironde as evidence of the care shown by the Chamber in the organization of its exhibit. In short, the Chamber was assured of practically all that it had requested, and with this successful completion of his assignment, Galos took the liberty of giving voice to the sentiment he had harbored since finding himself drawn into involvement with the Gironde's wine display: "These are, Sirs, the results that I have obtained; I now hope that the general commission [that is, the Imperial Commission] will accept the propositions of its special commission. I heartily desire to be finished with this long and difficult affair, which has given me no little annoyance!"

The Chamber responded with praise for Galos' perseverance and dedication throughout the preceding months, emphasizing the significance of what had been achieved: "The success was very important, because the declassification of the growths would have been a most regrettable occurrence, introducing anarchy to an order of things necessary to maintain in the interest of the proprietors and the trade; the great domains would have found their worth appreciably affected." There was also a note of caution amid the Chamber's congratulations: "Is it not to be feared that Lafite's manager, unhappy at the decisions of the special commission, will either seek to make it reverse itself as concerns his part in this, or take his complaint to the general commission? We advise you to keep an eye open for these moves."

The caution was well founded. One week later, on August 30, Monplaisir Goudal was at Lafite when he received word from Rouget de Lisle that the Chamber of Commerce had set about influencing the jury's report. Although lacking details of the agreement reached by Henri Galos, the manager feared the worst: that Lafite's wines would be judged as part of the Chamber's display which would receive sole recognition by the jury. "As they cannot give two awards, if Mr. Duffour[-Dubergier] obtains what he asks, we will be completely pushed aside," wrote Goudal that day to Samuel Scott. "This is why I am firmly committed to go to Paris and present myself as I have already done before Prince Napoléon [Jerome] and demand justice. This is a very important affair for us, being placed in the first rank of Bordeaux wines; it would count for much among the foreigners who never cease saying that Château Margaux, even Mouton, are the equals of Lafite—several of them even believe it." The manager planned to leave for Paris at once, spending a week at the capital and returning before September 15 in time for the harvest. Once again, Monplaisir Goudal intended to have his say.

There was yet another change in the organization of the Universal Exposition after opening day. Thomas Twining, a member of the British delegation, had observed that at previous exhibitions, in both Paris and London, the emphasis had been on objects of great cost and artistry. As a member of the London Society of Arts, the group that had organized the Crystal Palace exhibition of 1851 and was now in charge of coordinating Britain's participation at the Palace of Industry, Twining had proposed assembling a collection of everyday products designed for the housing, furnishing, and feeding of workers. In June 1854, a report on the subject was submitted to Napoleon III, who, as the author of *The Extinction of Pauperism*, naturally welcomed the idea and ordered that the means for its implementation be studied. At the same time, the London Society of Arts inquired of the Imperial Commission if space in the Palace of Industry could be found to house such a collection. The request was badly timed: the Commission was in the thick of its building crisis and was struggling to find a way to include all of the standard exhibits focusing on technology and luxe that were anticipated; the prospect of squeezing in an additional collection of "workers' goods" was an unwelcome complication of its task. Two members of the Commission were assigned to look into the matter, with which action the project was left to languish and die. In the meantime, the idea of a special exhibit had gained a wider exposure, and an international group of charities and benefactors had independently formed to see how such a collection of goods could be included as part of the Universal Exposition. Upon Napoleon Jerome's return from the Crimean War, representatives of this group furnished him with a study demonstrating the merits of Thomas Twining's proposal, and the idea was suddenly resuscitated within the Imperial Commission. Responding with habitual dispatch when presented with an idea especially close to his interests, Napoleon Jerome at once arranged for the construction of a 500-square-meter building to house what would officially be known as the Gallery of Domestic Economy.

The problem, however, was how to stock it. The Imperial Commission had not foreseen the existence of such an exhibit in its original announcement to the French and international selection committees, and soliciting goods from them now at so late a date was out of the question. Once the Gallery was finally completed, the only practical solution was to cull appropriate items already on display throughout the Exposition. A new division was created, the XXXI class, as an official entity for the Domestic Economy products, and, on August 24, exhibitors received notice that a special commission had been formed with the purpose of seeking out "objects whose low price and good quality make them particularly useful for the simplest of domestic life." Part of the items selected would be transferred to the Gallery; others would be left in their original place and simply be reclassified and judged by a XXXI class jury. The exhibits selected were divided into three groups: clothing, furniture (including household goods), and foods.

Because of the powdery mildew blight that had swept though Europe's vineyards during the previous ten years, wine production had fallen dramatically, and what had been one of the staples of the common diet, a beverage considered healthy and beneficial, had become expensive and increasingly out of the reach of the average person. "Whatever a wine's price relative to its quality and its rarity," stated the report on the Domestic Economy class of products, "it is impossible not to place it among the most useful of nutriments for people in good health, and, more often, for invalids and convalescents. . . ." As pernicious as the rise in the price of wine were the concoctions created to fill the gap in the market created by the scarcity of the genuine article; made from inferior ingredients, these "wines" provided few of the benefits offered by the real thing. "The jury dismissed from competition all of these fabrications, whose utility, healthfulness, and nutritional qualities have not appeared to be sufficiently certifiable," explained the report. Bordeaux's production, with its attention to quality, provided a positive example which offered hope for the beleaguered international industry and for the average wine drinker who depended on the beverage as a source of daily nourishment. While the classed growths with their elevated prices were obviously not the sort of wines that would constitute the regular fare of the common consumer, the communal wines collected by the Chamber of Commerce perfectly met the criteria of good quality and low price, and this part of the Chamber's shipment was reclassified to the Domestic Economy division.

On October 2, a jury for the XXXI class was created. This group comprised seventeen judges, with over half brought in from the other established juries. (Fouché-Lepelletier was called from the XI class jury to serve as a judge for the "alimentary substances"; Thomas Twining was also a juror for these products.) Their judging and deliberations took place during the final weeks of the Universal Exposition. Representing no danger to the Bordeaux classification, perhaps exhausted by their recently concluded experience with the classed growths, Henri Galos and the Chamber of Commerce did not concern themselves with this group of wines with the vigor they had devoted to the XI class exhibit; no mention of the Domestic Economy jury's judging and deliberation was made in Galos' ongoing correspondence with the Chamber.

Closing ceremonies were originally scheduled for November 1, but, in light of the inauguration's two-week delay in May, the decision was made to postpone the finale an equivalent two weeks to November 15, extending the Exposition's run to a full 200 days; in addition, owing to disappointing attendance, it was decided to keep the Exposition open beyond the closing ceremonies through to the end of the month. The official explanation was that several foreign dignitaries who were unable to attend during the scheduled summer months were being extended the courtesy of having the displays maintained in place for their perusal; of course, the paying public would be able to come and see the Exposition, too.

To add to the splendor of the closing ceremonies, several displays were selected to be moved from the locations they had held throughout the Exposition and placed in more prominent places of honor in the Palace of Industry's main hall; in late October, the Chamber of Commerce was notified that its display of classed wines was solicited for this recognition. On October 27 the Chamber wrote to Henri Galos to see about satisfying this request, instructing him also to attend to other questions regarding its classed-growth display: "Please look into what has to be done. We are sure that you have not lost sight of the Grand Medal that we have been promised, and in the interest of the [Gironde] and the trade it is thus greatly desired that we obtain a resounding distinction." The following week, Galos received further instructions from Bordeaux:

> After our meeting last Wednesday, the secretary has been charged to write and tell you that you are authorized to incur the expenses necessary for the installation of our wines which will take part in the Exposition's closing ceremonies.
>
> We advise you once again to do your best in order that a Grand Medal be awarded to us. It is essential for the department's interests and for the Bordeaux wine trade.

After months of experience with the authorities in Paris, the Chamber of Commerce could not allow itself to take anything for granted now that the end was so near.

The Universal Exposition's closing ceremonies put the best face on what had never been less than a difficult undertaking. Highlighted by the premiere of the *Impériale* cantata for two orchestras and two choirs by Hector Berlioz, with the composer conducting 1,250 musicians and singers before an audience of 40,000, the overall effect was as splendid as the Exposition itself had been. Once again, however, the schedule of events had to be changed. It was originally planned for the Emperor to personally present each of the medals and diplomas awarded by the juries, but their number had grown to 12,000, making such an undertaking far too long to be practical. Thus it was that although the recipients of the various awards were made known on November 15, it was not until months later that the actual prizes were conferred upon the majority of their winners in smaller local ceremonies in each department.

In the list of awards for the Gironde's wines, the fruits of Henri Galos' efforts were visible throughout. All the classed growths displayed in the Chamber of Commerce's exhibit received recognition, with the distribution of prizes reflecting the broker's classification—already showing signs of becoming the official reference for purposes other than the wine trade's pricing. First-growth wines from Château Margaux, Lafite, and Latour received first-class medals (in that order). The Médoc second growths were duly awarded second-class medals. The classed growths of Sauternes and its neighboring communes, however, did not similarly benefit from their ranking in the classification. These first and second growths were grouped with the rest of the Médoc's classed wines and the nonclassed growths judged worthy of recognition, and given honorable mentions. Haut-Brion, which had decided to strike out on its own, although a first growth, was limited to an honorable mention. If all of this was part of the arrangement reached by Henri Galos, Monplaisir Goudal's efforts did not go unrewarded either. Lafite's manager had the satisfaction of seeing the property individually acknowledged and rewarded with the other first growths. Furthermore, as the sole employee presented to the XI class jury from the entire Bordeaux wine industry (albeit by his own efforts), Monplaisir Goudal was given an honorable mention in accordance with Napoleon Jerome's desire for workers to receive recognition for the contribution of their labor. In addition, his tenacity in securing for Lafite the right to display its wine with the

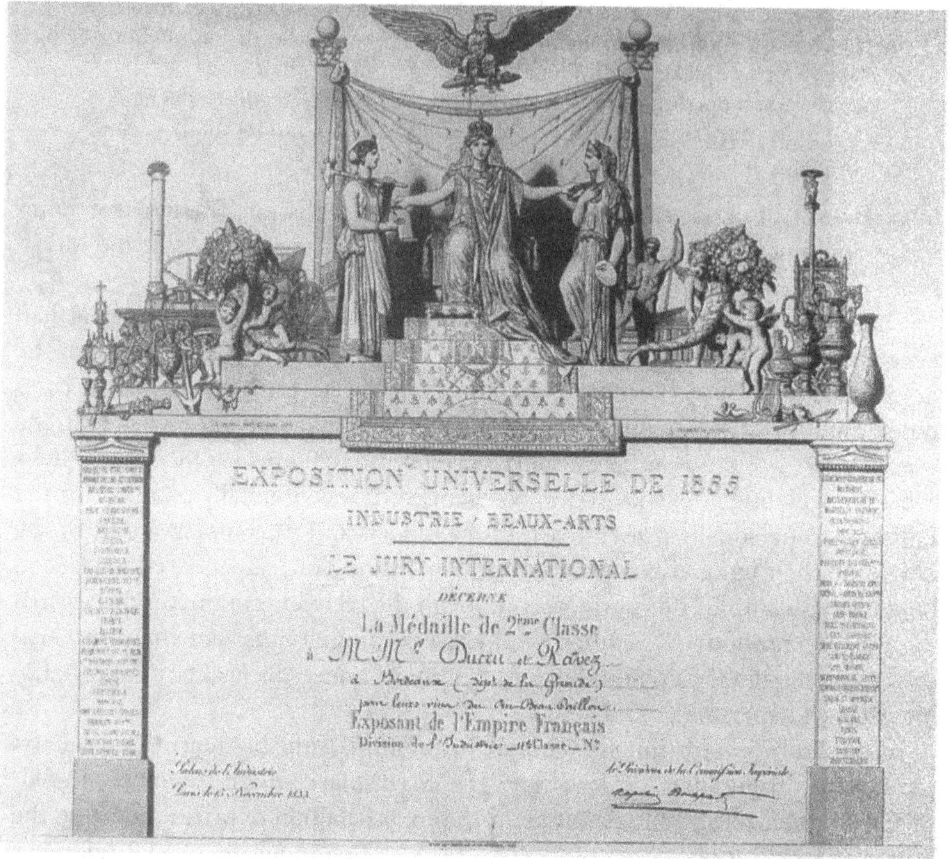

The Diploma awarded to Ducru-Beaucaillou
(Archives Départmentales de la Gironde)

property's own label bearing his name together with Sir Samuel Scott's earned Monplaisir Goudal a *second* honorable mention as an exhibitor.

The Chamber of Commerce, for all its trouble in organizing the participation of the Gironde's wines, for having to deal with the increasing complications of what had originally been seen as a relatively simple matter of collecting six-bottle cases and shipping them off to Paris, and in the process commissioning the transcription by the brokers of the classification that was currently in effect among the trade, for all of this the Chamber of Commerce was awarded a first-class medal, exactly like that bestowed upon the first growth wines it had sent to Paris. However, it was not from the XI class jury, in recognition of the quality represented by the finest of the Gironde's wines—the now "officially" classed growths—that the Chamber received its prize. Its medal was awarded for the collection of wines which were incorporated into the XXXI division, the Domestic Economy display. In the end, it was the collection of anonymous communal wines, sent along to the Universal Exposition with no particular care for their storage or display, for which the Bordeaux Chamber of Commerce was recognized.

Eight

1856, 1857, 1858...

With the Chamber of Commerce's request for samples in the early months of 1855, the presence of the Gironde's wines at the Universal Exposition had been widely publicized throughout the department; however, it was not until after the Exposition's close that the majority of people in Bordeaux learned of Duffour-Dubergier's wine map and the classification's public display. On December 13, the Bordeaux daily newspaper *La Gironde* published an article by its editor André Lavertujon, who was given access to the Chamber of Commerce's files and made privy to its members' intentions concerning the organization of its exhibit in Paris. Prominently featured on the newspaper's first page, the article was entitled "Wines of the Chamber of Commerce," and began with a brief review of the efforts involved in staging the display at the Universal Exposition, whose doors had definitively closed just thirteen days before. The heart of the article, however, began in the second paragraph: "Before proceeding further, we must enter upon several technical details which are hardly known but to those in the trade, who we hope will not be troubled to find them [printed] here." This was the introduction to a presentation of the classification drawn up by the Brokers' Union eight months earlier.

The existence of a classification was a well-known fact of commercial life among the three main parties in Bordeaux's wine trade, and this latest version contained no radical departures from what currently guided the brokers and merchants. Inevitably, however, there were some proprietors who were taken by surprise at the rankings as newly presented here. On January 3, a letter arrived at the Chamber of Commerce from Messrs. Bernet and Ducasse, two gentlemen who had recently become the proprietors at Liversan in the commune of Saint-Sauveur, just west of Pauillac.

Sirs,

We have just become aware of the new classification of the Médoc wines, drawn up at your request last April by the Union of Brokers Attached to the Bordeaux Commodities Market, and which has only recently been published.

We note with regret that Liversan, the growth which we have come to own, does not figure among the fifth growths, the class to which it belongs according to the former classifications.

We are unaware of the reason for this. It might be through inadvertence, or perhaps because of some legitimately recorded grounds not known to us.

This property, which had been divided among a great number of legatees foreign to the department, has had no one to defend its rights.

Today, it is in the hands of proprietors, we dare to say, who are making great sacrifices for its improvement, sacrifices which their precursors had never made, and which will certainly maintain this wine at the level of its ancient reputation.

It is with confidence that we therefore address you, Sirs, in order to ask that you please present our request to the Brokers' Union, certain that they will recognize its justice, and that with their benevolent assistance you will return to our growth the place it is due.

This letter echoed one received six days earlier by Duffour-Dubergier from Louis de Chavaille, the owner of the Cantenac fourth-growth Pouget. Citing classifications dating from 1755 as justification for placing his property among the thirds, Chavaille also thought it fit to note that

all the parcels of my vineyard are situated on Cantenac's southern slope, facing the vineyards of Rausan [Ségla], Rauzan [Gassies], Kirwan, Château d'Issan, Palmer, Brown (some of whose vines I have purchased), Philippe Dubignon, and Marcellin Dubignon (from whom I have also bought vines), having sold all my vines situated in the commune of Arsac as being inferior to [those] in Cantenac.

If in some difficult years I sometimes had been obliged to sell my harvest before the prices were fixed, this could not change the nature of the soil of my beautiful vineyard, for which I have always made the greatest sacrifices in order to improve its [wines].

Chavaille also touched on family history, explaining that it had been necessary to divide the original property in two and suggesting that it was through confusion with the vineyard known as Pouget-Lassale (which, according to Chavaille, was less carefully tended) that Pouget had been classed as a fourth growth. "I therefore demand in the name of justice," concluded the proprietor, "that the brokers who signed the classification printed on [December] thirteenth in *La Gironde* declare... that it is by error that they confused my domain of Château Pouget with the property of [Lassale], which is farmed out to Monsieur Izan."

These requests for adjustments in the brokers' classification resulted in practically identical letters being addressed to Chavaille on January 1, and to Bernet and Ducasse on January 7:

> You will easily understand, Sir, that it was not the Chamber's place to make a list of the classed wines; we were obligated to rely on another official body whose competence is evidently obvious, that is to say, the Brokers' Union, and we were equally obligated to reproduce without modification the work which they sent us.
>
> Thus we're afraid that we cannot be called upon to give an opinion on the merit of the observations which you have communicated to us. It is before the Brokers' Union itself that you must bring them if you think it necessary; I have no doubt that [your observations] will be the object of careful examination.

On January 12, it was the Brokers' Union who was, in turn, the recipient of a letter from the Chamber of Commerce:

> We attach to this correspondence a letter addressed to us by Messrs. M. Bernet and F. Ducasse, current owners at Liversan. These gentlemen complain that their growth does not figure in the table of classed wines that you addressed to us in your letter of last April 18, the table which was reproduced on the wine map at the Exposition.
>
> We will be sending you, Sirs, [all] demands of this type, considering that the classification of wines is not at all within our competence, but entirely within yours.

The Chamber of Commerce was well aware, as previous classifiers such as William Franck had come to learn, that the ranking of Bordeaux's wines was invariably a controversial undertaking, one in which the Chamber had no desire to become involved. Having commissioned the drafting of the classification, the Chamber now washed its hands of the inevitable protests from proprietors either not classed or not classed highly enough. With habitual prescience, the Chamber foresaw this course of action when it wrote to Henri Galos the previous summer, "In the event of any demands and complaints, the responsibility for the. . . classification, will thus fall on the brokers; the Chamber is shielded from criticism."

It was left to the brokers to deal with the consequences, and the fact that their classification remained unchanged after the *Gironde*'s dissemination of its existence shows that they dismissed these and all subsequent claims. However, there was one prior claim they *had* accepted.

At the Chamber of Commerce's weekly session on September 19, 1855, a letter was read from the Brokers' Union, signed by Auguste Perrin, the head of the Union's board of directors. Word of its classification's display at the Universal Exposition had gotten back to certain parties in Bordeaux, and harbingers of the complaints that would later arise had begun circulating. It appears that some proprietors were upset upon learning that their position in the classification was more or less distant from the head of their respective class. Not every property could be a first growth, but most could claim to be at the head of their division; after all, since the five ranks were based on the sales price of the wines to the trade, at one time or another and with more or less frequency many of the properties had achieved parity with the highest price of their class. The classification on public display in

Paris, however, threatened this fancy held by many proprietors. Hoping to forestall what the brokers saw as immense future complications, Perrin had written to the Chamber of Commerce on September 16 that the Union's intention in drafting the list of classed growths was not to assign a degree of superiority to the properties within each of the five divisions; in future presentations of this classification, intra-class listings should henceforth be presented in alphabetical order.

And there was a second request in Auguste Perrin's letter. According to the minutes of the Chamber's meeting that day, "The Union of brokers has written [us a letter dated] September 16 in order to make known that the wine of Cantemerle (commune of Macau) belonging to Mme. de Villeneuve Durfort, should be added to the list of fifth growths."

The original document drafted by the brokers and sent to the Chamber of Commerce on April 18, 1855, was written in a large, regular, easily readable hand. The list of red-wine producers filled three pages, beginning with Château Lafite at the head of the first growths and finishing with Croizet-Bages at the end of the fifths. Immediately after Croizet-Bages a 7½-centimeter line was drawn, 7½ centimeters which have ever since served to seal the fate of Bordeaux's red-wine producers into the classed and the nonclassed. However . . . in a different hand, smaller and squeezed in above the fatal line is written "Cantemerle, Mme. de Villeneuve Durfort, Macau." It was obviously written in sometime after April 18, by someone other than the drafter of the original list; in the wine map that was created in May and placed on display at the Universal Exposition, Cantemerle did not appear.

The commune of Macau, like its neighbor Ludon, had traditionally been a major supplier of wines to the less-esteemed Dutch market. In this regard, Cantemerle had stood out as the commune's finest producer; as Guillaume Lawton wrote in 1815, "The wines of Macau sell perfectly in the North, & even two or three of its proprietors—Messrs. de Villeneuve, La Lande, and Duffour [this latter refers to the property of Gironville, purchased by Duffour-Dubergier's grandfather in 1776]—take advantage of their proximity to Ludon to export to Holland, where they succeed. The first especially."

By the first half of the nineteenth century, Cantemerle could boast a long and noble history: owned by the Villeneuve family since 1579, the length of this association exceeded even that of the Ségur-Beaumont ownership of Latour. At this time, Cantemerle was the possession of Jean de Villeneuve-Durfort; born in 1758, he was the latest in the line of Barons de Villeneuve who were the property's hereditary owners. Captain of an army regiment in Languedoc before the Revolution, the years after 1789 saw Villeneuve-Durfort back in Bordeaux, serving as the mayor of Macau and managing the affairs of the family property. The commercial policy he followed for the sale of his wine reflected Cantemerle's longstanding trade with the Netherlands: the totality of his production was sold directly to Dutch buyers, bypassing the brokers and merchants on the Bordeaux marketplace. Guillaume Lawton noted this practice of direct exportation in a notation dated 1816, remarking that "[Villeneuve is in the] 1st rank of this commune. His wines do very well in Holland & he sends them there." As a result of this policy, details of the transactions between Villeneuve-Durfort and the Dutch—particularly the price fetched by the wine—were largely unknown to the brokers. Still, the property was one of Macau's principal producers, and even though they were not involved in its sale, Bordeaux's brokers attempted to track Cantemerle as best they could given the relatively little information available to them. In the usually closely detailed records maintained by Guillaume Lawton and his successors, comments on this property were mostly limited to recording the number of tuns produced, frequently settling for the sole notation "Holland" in years where any further information was lacking. Occasionally, a sales price would be entered, but, in general, this aspect of Cantemerle's listings was distinguished by an atypical lack of continuity—over the eighty-year period between 1775 and 1854 only six prices were recorded.

On December 13, 1834, Jean de Villeneuve-Durfort died, leaving Cantemerle to his son, Pierre Jules. The new Baron de Villeneuve, however, had not yet reached his majority, so responsibility for the property passed to Pierre Jules' mother, Caroline. Born Caroline Joséphine Françoise Josephe de Lalande, she was not the only member of her family to bear the title of baroness through marriage: her sister had wed one of the Médoc's other noble proprietors, the Baron Joseph de Pichon-Longueville. In a combination of prudence and foresight that would characterize her management of Cantemerle, the widow Villeneuve-Durfort summoned the family notary six days after her husband's death to draw up papers naming her sister, the Baroness Pichon-Longueville, legal procurer for Cantemerle should she (Caroline) die before Pierre Jules came of age. This amounted to little more than an administrative detail, since it was only a matter of several months before her son would assume legal ownership, but it was this sort of detail to which Caroline de Villeneuve-Durfort paid strict attention in her management of Cantemerle's affairs. In the end, the procuration was never evoked, and in due course her son took up residence at the property in Macau where he could oversee operations on a daily basis. Then, in August 1844, Pierre Jules de Villeneuve-Durfort unexpectedly died, just nine years after coming into possession of Cantemerle. He was twenty-nine years old, and, lacking his mother's prudence, died intestate; ownership reverted to his mother and his sister, Jeanne Armande. The latter was married to a landowner whose property was in the foothills of the Pyrenees, and although legally involved with Cantemerle, Jeanne Armande's distance made her participation in its affairs little more than a formal technicality. It was Caroline de Villeneuve-Durfort who once again directed operations at Cantemerle, ever dedicated to the quality of the property's wines and very active in her defense against any challenge to its reputation.

Such a defense led the widow Villeneuve-Durfort to embark upon legal proceedings in 1845, proceedings which, over two decades later, were still described as "a trial which has remained famous in the Gironde." That year Pierre Chadeuil, the new proprietor of a neighboring wine-producing property called Priban, had begun labeling his wines "Chadeuil Cantemerle Château Priban." His claim was that the name "Cantemerle" had long since become associated not only with the Villeneuve's individual estate, but with the surrounding area as well; he was thus justified in incorporating "Cantemerle" into the name of his wine since this specified its district of origin. (Of course, the fact that this might engender confusion with a wine whose reputation for quality had allowed it to command prices far above those earned by the majority of others in the commune was just coincidental, at least according to Chadeuil.) Mme. Villeneuve-Durfort, however, was having none of it. Producing documents dating back to the Villeneuve family's acquisition of Cantemerle in the 1570s, she was able to prove that there was no basis in fact for Chadeuil's argument. Her documentary evidence was conclusive enough to have Chadeuil's wine stripped of any mention of Cantemerle, and to have the tribunal require his payment of punitive damages and all court costs.

With the 1854 vintage, Caroline de Villeneuve-Durfort made a commercial decision that marked a significant break with the past: henceforth, Cantemerle's wine would be sold in the Bordeaux marketplace, passing through the traditional network of brokers and merchants. That year, for the first time in three decades, Tastet & Lawton were able to enter a sales price for the property in their records: 2,100 francs per tun. This is 100 francs more than Croizet-Bages, the property with which the brokers originally closed off their 1855 classification on April 18; the next earliest price for Cantemerle in the Tastet & Lawton records was made in 1825, when the per-tun price was 1,500 francs, the same as for Croizet-Bages. In 1819, Cantemerle sold for 850 francs, 100 francs more than Croizet. The previous year, Croizet was clearly ahead with 1,000 francs to Cantemerle's 710, but, in 1815, the difference was much closer with 900 francs for Croizet-Bages and 850 for Cantemerle. And in 1775, the prices listed by Guillaume Lawton were 300 to 330 francs for Cantemerle, and 270 to 300 for Croizet-Bages. Evidently, the property's wine had regularly achieved fifth-growth prices for decades before 1855, but details of the transactions between Villeneuve-Durfort and the Dutch merchants were not consistently communicated to the brokers. It is likely that but for the particularity of Jean de Villeneuve-Durfort's commercial strategy, the parity achieved by Cantemerle's prices (even when sold in the traditionally parsimonious Dutch market) would have established the property as a fifth growth well before 1855. Unfortunately for Cantemerle, by entering the Bordeaux marketplace at fifth-growth prices for only the first time in 1854 (and at the top end of the class, at that: prices among the fifths that year ranged from 1,200 to 2,100 francs), it lacked the track record among the brokers that would have brought it to mind when thinking of fifth-growth wines. Given the urgency of the Chamber of Commerce's demand and the two-week period in which the brokers drafted and delivered their list, their main task was to assure the accuracy of the classification they were to deliver, not to go in search of properties for inclusion.

The timing of Caroline de Villeneuve-Durfort's decision to bring Cantemerle onto the Bordeaux marketplace was remarkably fortuitous: it allowed her to mount a convincing argument for the incorporation of her property in the brokers' classification of 1855. Upon learning of Cantemerle's omission from the list on display in Paris, she immediately acted to protect her property's standing in the trade and demand its inclusion among the fifth growths, not with an appeal to the Chamber of Commerce as others were to do months later, but directly to the classification's source—the Brokers' Union. Undoubtedly in possession of a more complete record of Cantemerle's sales prices than that held by the brokers, the case she presented before their official body was apparently irreproachable, and, in September 1855, while the Universal Exposition was still welcoming visitors and well before there was any reason to believe that this newest incarnation of the wine trade's classification would have a greater importance or longevity than any of its many predecessors, Cantemerle was added to the fifth growths, in what was actually the first change to the 1855 classification in its history. (Mouton-Rothschild's 1973 promotion to a first growth is, in fact, the classification's *second* adjustment.) The Brokers' Union had shown itself willing to entertain requests for changes in its classification, and, if the evidence was sufficiently authoritative, to act accordingly. Cantemerle was inadvertently excluded owing to oversight and circumstance; succeeding claims by other proprietors to the Union for inclusion or promotion of their properties evidently lacked the justification for additional adjustments. Any further changes would have to wait until the next time the brokers undertook—or, rather, were asked to undertake—another such classification.

On Sunday afternoon, January 6, 1856, Pierre de Mentque, Prefect of the Gironde, officiated at the departmental ceremony for the bestowal of awards earned at the Universal Exposition, scheduled to take place in the concert hall of Bordeaux's Grand Theater. Designed by Victor Louis and inaugurated in 1773, the building was the city's architectural pride; in 1787, an English visitor found the theater to be "by far the most magnificent in France. I have seen nothing that approaches it." Nevertheless, by 1856, the Grand Theater was showing the effects of age and neglect. Writing for *La Gironde*, André Lavertujon noted with disapproval:

> the state of ruin and virtual filth in which these magnificent premises find themselves. In several places the ceiling is collapsed and the plaster work threatens to fall; the floorboards stave in beneath one's feet, and the glass in the windows, covered with a thick layer of dust, allow but only a sad and unwholesome light to enter.

> . . .One thing contributed not a little in depriving the celebration of all brilliance: we refer to those rows of horrid chairs in white wood whose ugliness and discomfort are no longer acceptable since they have begun manufacturing so inexpensively such elegant seats and gracious stools in iron mesh. In Paris, in the Bois de Boulogne and all along the Champs-Elysées, the chairs made of straw have been removed and replaced by iron mesh seats. It is true that some spirits of a political bent have chosen to see police intent behind this reform made in the name of elegance and comfort. Indeed, it has not been forgotten the use that was made [during the revolution] in February 1848 of the chairs of the Champs-Elysées.

In an effort to lend a festive air to the event, numerous decorations were installed. The tricolor was hung everywhere and shields bearing the initials of Emperor Napoleon III and the Empress Eugénie were displayed throughout the theater. Banners inscribed with the words "Industry," "Commerce," "Agriculture," "Science," and "Fine Arts" were raised; music was provided by a newly reorganized Bordeaux firemen's band, which played a varied selection of melodies and fanfares.

At one o'clock, Pierre de Mentque rose and delivered his address, congratulating the laureates on the glory they had earned for the Gironde. In a survey of the exhibitors to be presented with awards, the Prefect drew attention to the display of the department's wines:

> Bordeaux's wines, which enjoy so great and just a renown throughout the world, had to figure with honor at the Universal Exposition.
>
> Thanks to the efforts of the Chamber of Commerce, samples of various growths were sent to the Palace of Industry, and the jury appreciated them with the distinction they merited. A first-class medal was awarded to the Chamber of Commerce. The producers obtained four first-class medals, ten of second class, and ten honorable mentions.
>
> The department and the city owe a profound thanks to the Chamber of Commerce, who, once again, have shown such care for the interests which are confided to it, and which it directs with such great intelligence.

After these remarks came the distribution of the awards. Duffour-Dubergier mounted the stage on behalf of the Chamber of Commerce, and Monplaisir Goudal was present to represent Lafite. The manager briefly related his impressions of the event in a letter to Samuel Scott: "The day before yesterday I received from the hands of the Prefect your first-class medal from the Exposition. . . .I received two honorable mentions. The ceremony was not very impressive." Applause accompanied all of the prize winners as they were handed their awards, the firemen's band playing on in the background. After the last medals were distributed, the crowd of spectators surged forward to congratulate the winners. Having embraced and shaken hands, the group gradually dispersed, filing out of the Grand Theater into the darkening winter afternoon. And with that, it was over.

The brokers' classification of April 1855 was but one more presentation of an ever-evolving commercial tool, albeit more authoritative than most of the versions that had preceded it. The wine trade would continue to base its operation on updated rankings, but the classification's public identity gradually came to settle on the 1855 model, although there was nothing at first which suggested that the brokers' list carried greater weight than any other. In the years immediately following 1855, classifications continued to make their now-standard appearance in books about Bordeaux and its wines, and these rankings continued to be compiled by their authors using the traditional method of personal inquiry among members of the trade. The results reflected the ongoing shifts in the commercial fortunes of Bordeaux's wine producers.

In the case of the 1856 edition of the *guide de l'étranger à Bordeaux Nouveau* by Léonce Lamothe, the tourist guidebook first published decades earlier, its classification of red wines simply updated that of the fourth edition of 1851—which was itself a revision of lists from the 1840s. The few changes that appeared in this new version took account of the wine trade's evolution during the previous five years: Montrose was promoted one grade to a second growth and a similar elevation raised Palmer and Dubignon to thirds; Talbot's addition to the list and a redistribution of rankings among the third growths account for most of the remaining differences. The following year another guidebook, the *Guide-poche de l'étranger à Bordeaux* (*The Visitor's Pocket Guide to Bordeaux*) written by Raoul de Lamorillière, included the same list, but here incorporating the Graves wines of La Mission (La Mission Haut-Brion), Pape-Clément, and Château Talence within the structure of the main Médoc ranking instead of presenting them as an appendage.

More significant was the classification in Cyrus Redding's book *French Wines and Vineyards*, published in 1860, for here one can more closely see a development from the 1855 brokers' list, as opposed to a revision of a pre-1850s' effort. Being a completely new attempt at describing this aspect of Bordeaux's commerce—in a book whose main subject was wine, not tourism—Redding's classification was more closely based on the then-current state of the wine trade. This is most evident in his inclusion of a fifth-growth level, an element lacking in the guidebook rankings; this difference alone brings Redding's count to sixty-two properties, a figure well in line with the brokers' classification and other lists of the 1850s. By contrast, the guidebook classifications stop with the fourth growths and thus contain only forty-four named properties, a total in the tradition of lists from the 1840s.

In keeping with the classification's traditional evolution from the top down, the names in Redding's first and second growths were in complete agreement with the brokers' 1855 listing, while his thirds and fourths showed the intermingling typical of the classes whose identities had yet to achieve the stability of the top two tiers. While the majority of the 1855 fifth growths appeared on Redding's list, he also included six Médoc properties which did not make the brokers' grade, providing evidence that the classification was continuing to evolve as it always had done: with new names appearing to fill out the base of the pyramid, the fifth-growth level now assumed the volatility that had been characteristic of the thirds and then the fourths when those grades formed the hierarchy's foundation earlier in the nineteenth century. Redding noted this when he wrote that the fifth-growth "class is numerous, and there are differences in the excellence of the wines; therefore the price borne, must not be judged too nicely as the means of exactly determining their merit." (He also mentioned that "These [fifth growths] are composed of the great proprietorships of Pauillac and St. Estèphe, to which may be assimilated some others of Labarde and Margaux." This inclusion of Labarde is almost certainly an acknowledgment of Dauzac, the sole property from that commune to have been classified among the fifth growths by the brokers five years earlier. As for the reference to Margaux, it is interesting to note that no wines from that commune were included among the fifth growths in 1855, suggesting that with time yet more properties from Margaux and Cantenac may well have earned promotion to classed-growth status. As to the identities of the likely candidates, however, Redding offered no specifics.) In all, Redding's list may be taken as an indication of the direction the Bordeaux classification might have assumed in the absence of the increasing authority gained by the brokers' list during the 1860s.

Indeed, there is no reason to believe that the classification would have stopped at the relatively new formation of a fifth-growth level. The tendency for continued expansion through the creation of new levels at its base is suggested by a paragraph in the third volume of Edouard Guillon's *Les châteaux historiques et vinicoles de la Gironde* (*The Historic and Winemaking Châteaux of the Gironde*) which appeared in 1868:

> The *sixth growths* or *Bourgeois Supérieurs* designated by the oenologists are those of Citran, Monbrison, Siran, Séguineau [this property today forms part of Marsac Séguineau], Labégorce, Lynch-Pontac [the name is now Pontac-Lynch], Belair [today Bel Air-Marquis d'Aligre], Paveil [now Paveil de Luze], Poujeaux, Chasse-Spleen, Angludet, Roullet [now Fourcas-Dupré], Fonréaud, Mauvezin, Duplessis [divided between Duplessis Fabre and Duplessis Hauchecorne], Lanessan, Ducluzeau, Labaut, and doubtless others, this classification being in no way official. . . .

This manner of creating new levels of growths through the assimilation of bourgeois supérieurs was an established part of the classification's history: in 1813, merchants made reference to "1st, 2nd, and 3rd growths, and the 4th growths or principal Bourgeois supérieurs"; included in this last class were such properties as Beychevelle, Saint-Pierre, Pouget, and Duluc (today Branaire-Ducru).

In 1869, a work titled *Notice sur les vignobles et les vins du département de la Gironde* (*Notes on the Vineyards and Wines of the Gironde Department*) by a merchant named Auguste Laumond also suggested the emerging existence of a sixth-growth level. In a brief discussion of the Bordeaux system of classification, Laumond offered a list based on the 1855 brokers' version giving the number (not the names) of properties in each class, finishing not with the fifths but "finally, the most remarkable of the bourgeois growths... from 12 to 15 in number." Thus, in the dozen years following 1855, updated versions of the Bordeaux hierarchy reflecting the latest information in use by the wine trade continued to make their public appearance. The brokers' list was still just one of several presentations that were current at this time.

The 1855 classification had nonetheless begun making ever-more regular appearances in print, owing to a certain utility it offered authors writing about Bordeaux wine. Among its earliest consecrations was its inclusion by the publisher Chaumas in the fourth edition of William Franck's *Traité sur les vins du Médoc* published in 1860—the first post-1855 version of the work. After thirty-six years of struggling with the task characterized as "the most delicate part of our work," it is not surprising that the brokers' classification was seized upon as a solution to the prickly matter of ranking Bordeaux's wines: "To bring some clarity to these often difficult questions we can do no better than to reproduce the classification table drawn up by the Union of Brokers Attached to the Bordeaux Commodities Market on the occasion of the Chamber of Commerce's shipment of the Gironde's wine samples to the Exposition of 1855." By reproducing the brokers' list, responsibility for the assignment of rank among proprietors could be avoided, if only partially; it was not a complete solution because the 1855 classification was not yet endowed with a patina of unchallengeable authority. Furthermore, the closed nature of the brokers' list presented its own special drawbacks, and long experience regarding proprietors' sensibilities to their place in the hierarchy led the publisher to seek some means of mitigating the inevitable unhappiness of those who had not been included in 1855. Chaumas fell upon the happy idea of appending the list of bons bourgeois growths from the previous edition of 1845, although this resulted in the double appearance of Pedesclaux as a fifth growth in the 1855 brokers' list and a bon bourgeois from 1845. This was little more than a typographical error, however—there would be more significant complications to come from the publisher's efforts at reconciling the 1855 classification with the demands of Bordeaux's proprietors.

The next edition of the *Traité*, published in 1864, saw an attempt to satisfy Bernet and Ducasse, the proprietors at Liversan in Saint-Sauveur. Having failed in their request to the Chamber of Commerce and the Brokers' Union to have their property recognized as a fifth growth, the two owners continued to pursue their claim elsewhere, and the publisher of Franck's *Traité* was evidently contacted after the fourth edition's reproduction of the offending 1855 classification. Chaumas could hardly usurp the brokers' authority and change their 1855 listing, so it was again reprinted unaltered; however, in the section elsewhere in the volume concerning Saint-Sauveur, the publisher could more easily accede to Bernet and Ducasse's demands. Here, in contradiction to the hierarchy presented in the brokers' classification, Liversan was labeled a fifth growth. In order that this designation not stand out too greatly, however, the commune's other properties were also labeled according to their standing as bon bourgeois, premier bourgeois, bon paysan, and so on. Unfortunately, what probably seemed an elegant way of finessing the 1855 classification created complications of its own.

Arnaud Roux was the new proprietor at Peyrabon, a bourgeois growth in Saint-Sauveur. In the short time since acquiring the property, he had succeeded in obtaining classed-growth prices for his wine through direct sales to foreign customers, although brokers and merchants on the Bordeaux marketplace remained unchanged in their pricing and estimation of Peyrabon as a bourgeois growth. Nonetheless, on the basis of its recent sales prices Roux—on his own authority—had begun attributing classed-growth status to Peyrabon, a claim that was jeopardized by its designation as a *bon bourgeois* in the fifth edition of Franck's *Traité*. Roux made his dissatisfaction known to Chaumas, and in yet another accession to the sentiments of a proprietor, the 1868 sixth edition of the *Traité sur les vins du Médoc* carried the following footnote for the section dealing with Saint-Sauveur: "A proprietor at Saint-Sauveur complained of the qualification, in all respects very conscientiously made, which had been given to his growth in our edition of 1864; in the future, this growth will carry no designation in our work, at least until an official document positions it among the classed wines." While Chaumas may have found this sufficient to satisfy Roux, the proprietor did not agree; his feelings were probably not assuaged by the designation of Peyrabon as a *bourgeois ordinaire* in another of Chaumas' titles, the third edition of Armand d'Armailhacq's *Culture des vignes*, published the previous year in 1867.

This led Roux to take an exceptional step: in what was probably the first instance of a proprietor bringing legal action based on a property's standing in the classification, Roux took his complaint to the Bordeaux law courts. In the case of Franck's *Traité*, Roux brought suit against the publisher, Chaumas, who had been responsible for the book's contents since its second edition in 1845. By contrast, Armand d'Armailhacq had personally overseen the preparation of the third edition of his book, but had died in 1868 shortly after its publication; here Roux sued every member of Armailhacq's family he could find, including one of the author's brothers who was not even living in France owing to the obligations of his calling as a priest.

On January 13, 1869, the Bordeaux court hearing the cases handed down two identical decisions finding against Arnaud Roux. The factual basis of both Franck's and Armailhacq's books—including the 1855 classification—had provided ample justification for both works' denial of classed-growth status to Peyrabon. Furthermore, nothing in the documents the proprietor had produced showed that his commerce parallel to the Bordeaux marketplace had suffered since the books' appearance—despite the property's continued designation as a bourgeois growth, its wines still continued to obtain classed-growth prices from its customers. Although Roux's suit was rejected and he was ordered to pay all court costs, the decision nonetheless held out hope for the future:

> Given the observation that Peyrabon is not included in the five classes which constitute the finest growths of the Médoc, and that it is considered to be a bourgeois growth (a claim that is inarguably correct), there is nothing which prevents Peyrabon from obtaining a higher classification in the future if, as its proprietor contends, the quality of its wines has considerably improved and if the public can be made to share this view.
>
> There is nothing official about the classification of the Médoc's wines, nor is it definitive and irrevocable; it changes according to the opinions of the wines' relative quality as formed by the brokers, those who sell the wine, and those who consume it; [the classification] always leaves open the hope for all proprietors of a new and higher standing for their wines.

This opinion reflected the prevailing view in the Bordeaux wine trade: the classification was bound to be revised one day, and in the interim proprietors could still entertain hopes of promotion. Such were the thoughts of Gustave Roy, the new proprietor of third-growth Issan, who contemplated the elevation of his property to a second growth in light of the commercial esteem his wines were enjoying during this period. "Perhaps it will come to pass," was one contemporary comment on Roy's ambitions, echoing Guillaume Lawton's sentiment expressed a half-century earlier when Louis-Joseph-Gaspard d'Estournel embarked upon the same goal.

Several authors had already anticipated the Bordeaux court's opinion regarding both the authoritativeness of the 1855 classification and the ephemeral nature of the list's authority. For example, as expressed in an 1866 work entitled *Notice sur le Médoc* (*Notes on the Médoc*) by C. Bigeat, "the current classification is only transitory, as I see it. Because it is a human effort it is, by consequence, perfectible. . . . Now, there's nothing to prevent the same Brokers' Union that drew up the current classification from enlarging its scope, all the while respecting the positions already established; as for me, I see no possible inconvenience in this measure, neither for the proprietors of the currently classed growths, nor for the trade." Bigeat was a retired notary turned proprietor, and as the owner of a property on the lower rungs of the commercial hierarchy, he was openly critical of the classification and the entire system it represented. He expressed incredulity at the fact that "*one* tun of Latour from 1863 or 1864 is worth. . . as much as almost *two* tuns of its remarkable neighbor Léoville from the same years, and *eleven* tuns, still from the same years, of a *cru paysan* from Cussac, for example, which touches Saint-Julien." (The citation of a "*cru paysan* from Cussac, for example," was probably not as offhand as might appear—Bigeat was the proprietor of the *cru paysan* Romefort in Cussac.) Nonetheless, for all his reservations he found it convenient to use the brokers' classification in his presentation of the Médoc's wines as "an official base which shelters me from any suspicion of partiality." In 1868, Charles de Lorbach would echo Bigeat in his introduction to a survey of the classed growths in *Les richesses gastronomiques de la France* (*The Gastronomic Riches of France*): "In touching on the holy ark, in treading on the burning terrain of self-esteem and rival interests, I have but one means of sheltering myself from all suspicion of partiality, and that is to adopt, in its entirety and without alteration, the *classification* of the Gironde's wines as it was established by the Union of Brokers and the Bordeaux Chamber of Commerce." As had been the case with the 1860 edition of Franck's *Traité sur les vins du Médoc*, the 1855 classification offered the convenience of falling back upon a ready-made list, thus avoiding all responsibility for the inclusion of properties and their order of presentation; it was a solution that would be adopted with increasing frequency by authors in the years to come.

It was a different reasoning that led to the 1855 classification's inclusion in the second French edition of Cocks and Féret's work, now titled *Bordeaux et ses vins*. Beginning with this edition published in 1868, the book became the complete undertaking of Edouard Féret and his successors, Charles Cocks having died in his adopted Bordeaux in June 1854 at the age of forty-one. (Cocks' name, however, continued to appear on the title page of each new version in the series until the work's thirteenth edition in 1982.)

The second edition of *Bordeaux et ses vins* had already begun to assume the format and the air of authority that it would come to possess throughout the nineteenth and twentieth centuries. In the first French edition, Edouard Féret had transformed what was originally a guidebook for Bordeaux's English-speaking visitors into a handbook focusing on the region's principal product by enlarging Charles Cocks' text on wine to comprise the full latter half of the volume. In this second edition, described on its title page as being "entirely recast," Féret completed the transformation by reducing the touristic overview to just the first five pages of this work, having spun off the rest into a separate guidebook published in 1865 under the title *Guide de l'étranger à Bordeaux* (*Visitor's Guide to Bordeaux*). (Here the information dedicated to wine appeared on only the last eight pages, including truncated versions of the red- and white-wine classifications, the former listing properties in just the first and second ranks, the latter offering only six of the Sauternes region's first-growth wines.) The remaining 466 pages of what would henceforth be called *Bordeaux et ses vins* was now a comprehensive treatise wholly dedicated to all aspects of Bordeaux's viti- and viniculture, from soil and grape varieties to customs duties imposed on French wine by sixty-seven countries and territories around the world. Unlike Chaumas' revisions to William Franck's *Traité*, Féret did not simply paste updated information into decades-old text. To ensure the exactitude of the material presented, the reader was assured that "Mr. Edouard Féret neglected no information, knocked on every door, and especially had recourse to the practical science of the brokers." Just as other writers since 1855 had made their

Edouard Féret
(Editions Féret)

own inquiries into the current state of the Bordeaux classification, so had Edouard Féret. Yet, in the section entitled "Classification of the Médoc's Wines," Féret prefaced his presentation of the Bordeaux hierarchy with the explanation that "we have followed the text of the last official document established by the Union of Brokers in 1855." Given the extensive research undertaken to ensure that only the most recent information appeared throughout the rest of the book, what could have happened to establish a thirteen-year-old classification as the model to be followed in so authoritative a work?

In his comments, Féret mentions the "official" character of the classification. The brokers' list was "official" insofar as it was drafted by a body whose members were licensed by the government as a means of ensuring that their professional activity was beyond reproach, but there was not much else that could support the claim. (Indeed, in a matter of months, a Bordeaux law court would unequivocally declare that the classification was *not* official.) While it was entirely true that the

Bordeaux wine brokers were the people best placed to establish an authentic and authoritative hierarchy, their classification was neither solicited nor actively sanctioned by the French government; the brokers' participation in the process which led to the drafting of their document in April 1855 was a coincidental circumstance occasioned by that year's Universal Exposition in Paris. Obviously, none of this places in question either the soundness of the classification's conclusions or the importance of the brokers who drafted it. The question lies elsewhere: if the Universal Exposition was the pretext for the drafting of one "official" classification, why had subsequent expositions—1862 in London, or 1867 in Paris—failed to inspire similar efforts from the Brokers' Union?

On July 17, 1861, the Bordeaux Chamber of Commerce met for its weekly Wednesday meeting. On the agenda that day was a discussion regarding the Gironde's participation in the new Universal Exhibition which had been announced for the following year in London. Once again, French prefects had been instructed to organize Departmental Committees, and all the apparatus that had been developed for the Paris exhibition in 1855 was being called back into service. As before, the Bordeaux Chamber of Commerce had been invited to take part in organizing the presence of the Gironde's wines at the event.

Duffour-Dubergier no longer sat in the president's chair; he had died in April 1860, having guided the fortunes of the Chamber of Commerce for twelve years. His successor was Henri Basse, the Chamber's vice-president at the time of Duffour-Dubergier's death. Basse had not been part of the Chamber in 1855 but half of its fourteen members were, and the six intervening years were unlikely to have greatly dimmed their memories of the struggles with the Imperial Commission and Monplaisir Goudal. Accordingly, the Chamber of Commerce met this invitation to repeat the experience with caution, having no desire to become entangled in another long and unpleasant altercation unexpectedly arising out of a relatively simple matter. Unable to entirely refuse the prefect's request, the Chamber sent Alfred Léon, a veteran of the 1855 controversy, to represent it at the organizational meeting of the Departmental Committee. It was with relief that the Chamber of Commerce's members heard Léon explain at their July 17 meeting that "in this circumstance, the Chamber has nothing other to do than to address an appeal to the Gironde's industrialists and agriculturists in order to make them aware of the importance [of the London Universal Exhibition]." A suitable notice was duly drafted and inserted in the Bordeaux newspapers. Having fulfilled this obligation, the Chamber of Commerce expected no further demands to be made on it, and Basse actively sought to avoid all attempts at drawing the Chamber more deeply into the event.

In April 1862, with the opening of the London Exhibition imminent, an appeal from the International Jury was addressed to the Chamber to furnish one-third of the costs, set at "115,000 francs necessary to underwrite the general expenses of the industrial and agricultural exposition, particularly the collective exposition of the wines of the Gironde." The Chamber's cool response to this appeal was evident in the fact that only 5,000 francs were forthcoming, together with an apology that circumstances forced the Chamber to limit itself to this amount. Two months later, with the exhibition well underway, a further communication regarding the Gironde's wines was addressed to the Chamber by a Mr. Léon Riaut about the "state of abandon into which the products sent by the Gironde to the London Exposition have fallen"; the Chamber of Commerce took no action other than to simply forward the letter to the Gironde's Departmental Committee.

A final attempt at drawing the Chamber of Commerce into concerning itself with the Gironde's wines was made after the Exhibition's close, when the Chamber received a letter from a Mr. Glass in London regarding the disposition by sale of the wines that had been on display. Henri Basse forwarded this correspondence to the prefect with a cover letter dated December 9, 1862:

> Mr. Prefect, I have the honor of sending you a letter written to me from London by a person who is a complete stranger, regarding the exhibition of the Gironde's wines. This is not the first time I am forwarding to you. . . communications relative to this exhibition about which the Chamber has no authority, its role being limited to the allocation of 2,000 [sic] francs.

With the Bordeaux Chamber of Commerce absolutely refusing to repeat its pivotal role as the locomotive driving the organization of the Gironde's wines at the London Exhibition of 1862, the drafting of a new classification reflecting the changed circumstances of the Bordeaux wine trade became difficult to arrange. (Here, in the absence of archives from the Brokers' Union, it must be surmised that a similar reticence was at work among that body, in light of the demands from proprietors such as Chavaille at Pouget and Bernet and Ducasse at Liversan in the aftermath of the brokers' previous attempt at a public classification. Having once been drawn into making public a ranking of the region's wines, they, too, might well have been leery at a repetition of the experience, even if directly approached by the Departmental Committee.)

Under such circumstances, the Gironde's Departmental Committee—designated a "jury" under the terms of the London exhibition—was left with little to fall back on in formulating its display but the 1855 brokers' list drawn up for the Paris Exposition. A pamphlet entitled *Note du jury de la Gironde sur les vins de Bordeaux envoyés à l'Exposition universelle de Londres en 1862* (*Notice from the Gironde Jury on the Wines of Bordeaux Sent to the 1862 London Universal Exposition*) written by the secretaries of the Gironde committee—W.B.G. Scott, the British consul at Bordeaux and an acknowledged connoisseur of the region's finer wines, and Georges Merman, the Bordeaux wine broker who was instrumental in drafting the classification in 1855—presented the Gironde's wines using the hierarchy established for the previous exposition, unaltered to reflect the commercial changes of the intervening years.

In 1867, another Universal Exposition was held in Paris, and again, neither the Bordeaux Chamber of Commerce nor the Brokers' Union undertook the production of a new classification. In another pamphlet accompanying the new display of Bordeaux's wines—written once more by Georges Merman, this time in collaboration with Gustave Brunet, the administrative secretary and librarian for the Bordeaux Chamber of Commerce—it was the 1855 classification which again was referred to as the authority upon which the rankings of the Bordeaux wine trade were based, although, in fact, this was no longer the case at all.

In 1856—as with every new vintage—the launch of negotiations among producers, brokers, and merchants resulted in the establishment of new prices for the wines. Although these were based on the 1855 sales figures, they were by no means bound by them—wines that merited a higher price in 1856 had obtained them, regardless of how much they had brought the year before. The dynamics driving the Bordeaux trade had never been constrained by its classification; although important as an *indicator* of relative quality as reflected by price, the classification never acted as a *dictator* of the prices themselves, neither in the years before 1855 nor in the years after.

The basic idea presented to the public at the London Universal Exposition in 1862, and again five years later in Paris, was sound—the 1855 classification indeed remained a dependable indicator of relative quality for consumers of Bordeaux wine; the weakness, not with the classification itself but rather with its presentation at those venues, was to suggest to the exhibitions' spectators that it was still the model by which the Bordeaux wine trade continued to operate. Nonetheless, these displays of an "official" classification (which became more "official" with each presentation at the two Universal Expositions) began to reinforce its public image as not just *a* classification, but rather *the* classification, and in the year following its Paris display, Edouard Féret felt justified in following "the text of the last official document established by the Union of Brokers in 1855" in his new edition of *Bordeaux et ses vins*.

This was no pretext for "seeking shelter from any suspicion of partiality," however; on the contrary, Féret understood the problem in the burgeoning public perception of the 1855 classification and how this misconception of its role prevented a true assessment of its practical importance. In prefacing his presentation of the brokers' list, Féret noted:

> This classification serves as the basis for most of the purchases made in the Médoc's better communes. It was not the result of the personal appreciation of a collection of brokers in 1855; it was the fruit of long observation and the calculation of the average price obtained by the principal growths during a very long period of years.
>
> What's more, the classification of the Médoc's wine dates back to the 18th century, and the latest version is based on its predecessors, which have been modified according to the improvements or the decline experienced by the classed vineyards.
>
> Like all human institutions, this one is subject to the laws of time, and must certainly, in certain periods, be updated, brought to the level of progress. . . .[I]t was necessary, in 1855, to modify the ancient classifications.

Rather than being a commentary on the undependability of the 1855 classification, Féret's remarks might better be understood as a reflection on the inertia that was beginning to make that document *the* public reference for the relative quality of Bordeaux's wines, whereas the wine trade itself had since moved on. It was his expectation that sometime soon a more current version would be established by the same methods that led to the 1855 draft. This same sentiment had been expressed by both Bigeat and Lorbach, but unlike those authors, Edouard Féret did not leave it at that—the eighteen-year-old brokers' list was, in effect, a point of departure for the main part of his book in which he promised the reader "we will visit each individual commune, where the properties will be classed by order of merit." Here is where Féret applied the fruit of all his investigation among the wine trade and "the practical science of the brokers." By slightly shifting the order of the properties' presentation, a more current image of the wine trade's classification might be placed before the public, not a rejection of the version from 1855 but rather its acknowledgment by adapting the brokers' ranking just as the brokers themselves had adapted the previous versions used by the trade. As was the case with Franck, Armailhacq, Redding, and the others who had presented a hierarchy of Bordeaux's wines, Edouard Féret was not offering a personal choice but rather a reflection of the current state of affairs in the trade, one that might serve until the brokers got around to drawing up another "official" classification.

Interestingly enough, in 1867 a broker did produce a new classification with an eye to updating the 1855 list. On March 27 of that year Philippe Daney, one of three brokers based in the town of Langon, the commercial hub of the nearby Sauternes region, drafted a new classification of the white wines of Bordeaux. These had been his specialty since becoming a broker in 1821, and Daney's forty-six years of familiarity with these wines led Edouard Féret to note that "This work, [was] produced by one of the most experienced and honorable brokers in the department," an appraisal of the classification's author seconded by the prominent merchant and owner of the classed growths Beychevelle and Batailley, Pierre-François Guestier, in referring to Daney as "the Lawton of white wines."

Daney's classification showed clear ties to the 1855 version, with Yquem set apart as a superior first growth, and the same nine properties named as firsts by the brokers maintaining their rank in this new list, albeit in a somewhat different order. (Of note is the replacement of the name "Bayle" by the more standard designation of "Guiraud.") It was among the second growths where twelve years' difference was most evident: in place of the eleven properties identified as seconds in 1855, Daney set their number at thirty-five, a threefold increase. This is striking inflation, unmatched by anything since *Le Producteur*'s adversarial attempt at classification in the 1840s. The expansion here might be equally suspect and personal interest might reasonably be assumed were the classification's source not so unimpeachable. Clearly, there were other influences at work.

Although prices for Bordeaux's sweet white wines were on a par with those for red Graves and Médoc in the 1647 Jurade deliberations, the trade's evolution during the eighteenth and nineteenth centuries proved to be harder on the properties in the Sauternes region than on their counterparts to the north. With the passing of the Netherlands' Golden Century, principal demand for these wines shifted to Russia and the Germanic states. These were important markets, but less broad based than the Dutch had been—here the appreciation of these fine wines was concentrated among the nobility; a significantly large and prosperous middle-class clientele did not exist which could keep demand for sweet white wines high enough to maintain price parity with the reds. By 1845, Franck's *Traité sur les vins du Médoc* could report that prices for wines from the commune of Sauternes ranged from "450 up to 1,200 fr. *en primeur* for the first growths. Second growths [sell] from 350 to 600 fr." In the Médoc, by contrast, "first growths occasionally sell for 1,800 fr., more often 2,400; in good years they have sold for 3,500 fr. and sometimes more. . . . Seconds sell at 2,100 to 2,050 fr."

The foundation for change was laid in 1847 when the Sauternes region enjoyed a spectacularly good growing season. Conscientious producers such as some classified growths applied more exacting standards to practices that were already well known, although infrequently or imperfectly employed (for example, later harvesting and multiple passes through the vineyards by the pickers to select only grapes touched by "noble rot"). This resulted in richer and more concentrated wines than the moderately sweet ones that had heretofore been the style. The 1847 foundation was finally built upon twelve years later when Grand Duke Constantine, brother to Russia's Czar Nicholas I, purchased a single 900-liter tun of the 1847 Yquem for the extraordinary price of 20,000 gold francs. With one leap, this property had brought its wine several hundred francs above the average price for first-growth Médoc, and, true to its role as the region's "locomotive," Yquem carried along other local producers who saw prices for their wines rise if they followed the same techniques to create wines of a similarly rich character.

While this trickle-down effect arrived too late to be reflected in the 1855 classification, by 1867 it had become so pervasive and permanent that Daney was able to look at records of almost a decade's worth of sales and could confidently broaden the white-wine classification's base. (Of course, Yquem had established itself as an exceptional wine well before the 1847 vintage—as early as 1843, public price quotations show that it was commanding prices two to three times higher than those from the better properties in the Sauternes region. See Appendix II.) Of the eleven 1855 second growths, the majority take their place at the head of Daney's list for this rank; it is not until the eighth position that a property appears that had not been classified by the brokers twelve years earlier. Perhaps, had more than two basic levels existed in the traditional white-wine rankings, most of these new second growths might formerly have been ranked as thirds, and their promotion to seconds would not have had the effect of suddenly swelling the classification but instead have been merely a redistribution of positions; however, with the recent impulsion of prices in the Sauternes region, these unclassed properties had now closed the gap and were more or less on a par with the second growths.

In the same year Daney presented his revised white-wine classification, a very similar effort appeared in the third edition of Armand d'Armailhacq's *Culture des vignes*. In his original edition of 1855 (and in the 1858 second edition, as well), Armailhacq limited his observations to the vineyard area he knew best, the Médoc. However, in the 1867 edition, two brief appendices were added, the first on the wines of Saint-Emilion and the second on the Sauternes region. The latter included a white-wine classification which appears to be a close adaptation of Daney's ranking, since, apart from minor differences in the names of several properties and Armailhacq's addition of an extra producer in the penultimate spot on his chart, both lists are practically identical. Still, one major difference between the two stands out: whereas Daney had remained faithful to the classic division of first and second growths, Armailhacq created a third tier in the hierarchy after the first score of second growths. Although Daney was willing to flex the limits of the white-wine classification, his broker's conservatism stopped short of the more radical establishment of a third-growth category. Armailhacq's initiative was an established part of the red-wine tradition by which the expansion and evolution of that classification occurred not only through an augmentation in the quantity of classed growths, but in the number of ranks as well. Just as the white-wine classification with its two levels instead of five was a sort of concentrated version of the red-wine hierarchy, so was its proposed growth a concentrated, practically revolutionary, version of the Médoc's slower, evolutionary development.

Following the example set by Daney and Armailhacq, Edouard Féret exercised a certain flexibility with the 1855 white-wine classification in his third edition of *Bordeaux et ses vins* published in 1874. Citing "important modifications. . . in the vinification of the products of these favored slopes over the past twenty years," and the fact that "a crowd of well-situated smaller proprietors have imitated the great growths in their winemaking, and have more or less raised themselves to their level," Féret felt justified in exercising a greater liberty in dealing with the Sauternes region than he employed with the Médoc. Whereas the presentation of classed-growth red wines adhered closely to the 1855 list, with changes in position being limited to shifts among properties in the same class (for instance, the fifth growths of Pauillac might appear in a different order than that given by the brokers' list of 1855, but a bourgeois growth would never pop up among them), the lines were less rigidly drawn among the second growths of the Sauternes region.

For example, the communal listings for Sauternes and for Preignac in the category unambiguously titled "2nd growths" each contain properties not classed in 1855. Similar assimilation occurs in the listings for Barsac where the category was titled "2nd growths and bourgeois supérieurs" with no dividing line or distinguishing feature to indicate where the seconds ended and the bourgeois growths began. In theory, there being no indication to the contrary, even the last producer on the list could claim to be rated among the seconds—just as the first could be considered a bourgeois superior; in practice, the former was more likely to be claimed than the latter. In a footnote to the Barsac second-growth listing, Féret explained that "For several years the new style of winemaking among the grand crus has changed all the rules of the classification, and in Barsac as in Sauternes, several unclassed growths now obtain the same price as the classed growths."

Succeeding editions of *Bordeaux et ses vins* tracked the changing fortunes and abilities of the winemakers in the Sauternes region, enlarging, contracting, and redistributing positions on the lists of second/bourgeois growths for Preignac, Bommes, Barsac, and Sauternes—the four communes whose wines figured in the 1855 classification. (First growths never experienced the promotion of seconds among their number—it was always and only the second growths which showed this sort of evolution. As was traditionally the case with the top tier of the red-wine classification, the first-growth whites were immune from intrusion.) For the 1874 third edition, Féret listed thirty-two properties in Barsac as "seconds/bourgeois supérieurs," with a four-commune total of fifty-nine classed and bourgeois growths. For the next seventy-five years, there would never be fewer than twenty-five properties in Barsac qualifying for this category—more than appeared on the entire 1855 white-wine classification—the number most often staying well into the thirties.

Similarly, the combined total of classed and bourgeois growths also fluctuated, expanding to 101 properties overall in Féret's ninth edition of 1922. The swelling among the second growths could be attributed, in part, to the more restrictive structure of the white-wine classification as fixed in 1855, with only two levels for first and second growths. Armailhacq's initiative of creating a third-growth division had found no sequel, and Féret had chosen to work within the traditional framework. Undoubtedly, most of the properties that found their way into the second-

and perhaps even a fourth-growth level had the white-wine classification continued to evolve, but it was the authority of the 1855 classification which increased instead, freezing the ranking's structure even as sales prices for wines, classed and non-classed, continued to change.

By the 1870s, new rankings had ceased making regular appearances in books on Bordeaux wine, but there was still no general acknowledgment by the classed-growth proprietors that the 1855 classification possessed any particular practical value; their attentions remained largely focused on the continually evolving trade classification, as it was the merchants' and brokers' judgments on each new vintage that resulted in very real financial consequences. The term "first growth" remained a free-floating designation, tied to no particular standard; well into the twentieth century, proprietors of bourgeois growths continued to use the phrase to identify their standing at the head of a particular commune's ranking, as opposed to the global classification represented by the 1855 list. Although the owners of properties named in the red-wine classification banded together in August 1901 to form the Union of Classed Growths of the Médoc and the classed-growth white-wine proprietors later formed the Union of Classed Growths of Sauternes-Barsac, neither group had any legal claim to the title "classed growth." It would not be until September 30, 1949, that legislation would finally be enacted regulating the use of the term *cru classé,* linking it once and for all to the 1855 classification. Prior to this period, however, the status conferred by the 1855 classification did not seem to particularly matter.

For the greater part of the century after 1855, most classed growths made little effort to capitalize on the status conferred on them by the classification. Labels bearing the legend *grand cru classé* or *cru classé en 1855,* which today so frequently proclaim a property's standing to the wine-drinking public, were until recently quite rare. Although the classed growths experienced periods of great variation in sales, their clientele had remained relatively stable during the hundred years following 1855—perhaps the greatest change among the traditional markets came with the fall of the 300-year-old Romanov dynasty and the entire social system it represented in the 1917 Russian Revolution: at a stroke, this major market for the sweet wines of the Sauternes region was gone. However, the clientele for the classed red growths remained, as it had been for centuries, the British. Here, the appreciation of fine wines was practically hereditary, passed from generation to generation like the stately homes whose cellars sheltered bottles from so many of Bordeaux's great vintages. A knowledge of which properties were classed growths and at what level of the hierarchy they ranked was commonplace in this market. There was little need for a wine to adorn its label with the term *cru classé*; its status was a fact already well known. (Manifestations of this particularity in the British market continue today: for instance the catalog at Berry Bros. & Rudd, one of London's premier wine merchants and certainly its most traditional, lists a wine's color, vintage, and commune of origin, but makes no mention of its standing in the 1855 classification.)

In the early years of the twentieth century, virtually none of the classed growths bothered to identify this status on the wines they themselves bottled at the property. Merchants, however, being closer to the final customer in the chain of distribution, had recognized the promotional value of the 1855 classification much earlier, and the labels they had printed for the wines they bottled showed this: for example, a label from an 1858 merchant-bottled Duhart Milon included the words "cru classé" prominently displayed; H. & O. Beyerman & Co. placed the term "1er Grand Cru" on its bottling of the 1865 Latour. An 1888 Palmer bottled by the firm of Cruse Fils & Frères carried the term "grand cru classé" in red letters at the top of the label, although even today Palmer itself shuns any mention of its 1855 classification.

It was usually when a classed growth changed hands or passed through one of the twentieth century's all too frequent periods of financial crisis that properties would begin including the words "cru classé" on the labels they affixed to their wines. As newer markets became ever more important when sales in traditional ones lagged, proprietors increasingly came to recognize the 1855 classification as a commercial advantage that set them apart from their competitors among new customers seeking an assurance of quality in Bordeaux wine. So it was for first-growth Margaux, which added the term "cru classé" to its label with the 1917 vintage, released after four years of war which rocked the market for Bordeaux wines. After André Gibert's purchase of Haut-Brion in 1925, the mention "cru classé" regularly appeared on the label, beginning with the first vintage he released in 1926. Although third-growth Malescot-Saint-Exupéry included sporadic mentions of its classed-growth status as early as 1912, it was not until 1922—in the midst of Bordeaux's postwar slump—that it became a regular part of the label.

Once the classification began appearing on labels, there was often no hesitancy about identifying one's specific level in the hierarchy. A second growth in the classification did not signify a second-rate wine, and even in Bordeaux's new markets in the early twentieth century, the community of wine drinkers was still predominantly sophisticated enough to appreciate the difference. In vintages from the 1920s, estate-bottled Saint-Pierre was labeled "4th Grand Cru," and the owners of Château d'Issan saw no inconvenience in identifying their property as a "troisième cru classé" on the labels of their château-bottled wine in the 1930s; similarly, the 1926 Lagrange bore the legend "3e Grand Cru," and labels on succeeding vintages continued to do so until the mid-1940s. The timing of Lagrange's decision to drop the specific third-growth identification was not a matter of chance.

After World War II, things significantly began to change in the commercial wine world and in the importance of the public perception of the 1855 classification. In 1945, the Bordeaux wine trade emerged from half a century of severe economic

Label from Château d'Issan

Label from Château Lagrange

depression marked by two world wars, an international financial crisis, and the American experiment of Prohibition. The traditional market for Bordeaux wine had changed. The English were still avid in their appreciation and purchase of the classed growths, but they were now joined by new groups of wine drinkers whose numbers would steadily grow in the decades to come. One side effect of World War II was to introduce Bordeaux to entire classes and nationalities that had never been major consumers of the wine. "We should remember the extraordinary number of soldiers from every nation who traveled up and down France until 1946," wrote one journalist, "and who all, regardless of their various ranks, discovered our wines and generally found them to their taste." For many of the men and women who served overseas in the armed forces during the war it was their first experience with a world different from that they had known back home—and wine was no little part of that world. This experience played its part in shaping postwar attitudes about wine: a 1946 survey of American service personnel stationed in England found that 85 percent would declare themselves opposed to a renewal of Prohibition should the question arise again.

It was these Americans that Edouard Kressmann, the prominent Bordeaux merchant, targeted as the most promising market for the region's wines. Returning to France after a tour through the United States where he observed the buying and drinking trends in that country, he advised the Bordeaux wine trade of the great opportunity this territory presented: "The American is, without doubt, the newest consumer we possess, but also the most rich in new possibilities. . . . Americans have become more 'wine-conscious,' as they say, than they were before the war. There are more consumers; in addition, the millions of soldiers and officers who came to Europe had the opportunity to acquire a taste for our wines and will want (if only for the memories) to drink our wines back home. . . ." Kressmann was right.

Returning home after their European experience, they brought with them the memory not only of the events they witnessed and the sights they saw, but also of the foods they ate and the wines they drank. A new interest was sparked in French gastronomy—magazines like the appropriately French-titled *Gourmet*, saw their postwar circulations grow ever higher as increasing numbers of American hostesses sought help in imparting a European flair to their cooking. Food was only part of the experience: wine was the other half of the gastronomic equation, and here, too, Americans were in need of guidance. Benefiting from the world's strongest economy, these budding wine drinkers could largely afford the finest of what was available, but they lacked the lengthy wine experience of the British as to what that might be. Signposts were needed, and the 1855 classification served that function admirably. Here was a ready-made list with a century's authority that straightforwardly identified the best from one of the world's major wine regions. Of course, even with this list there was still some confusion, particularly regarding the numerical significance of the five levels of growths—second, third, fourth, and fifth growths were regularly interpreted as signifying second-, third-, fourth-, and fifth-rate wines. Properties that had formerly stated these levels on their labels soon removed the indications, settling for the more ambiguous but less dangerous term *cru classé* instead.

The first wave of new American wine drinkers was soon swelled by travelers from other countries, as advances in transportation technology increased world travel and the distances one could easily cover. The burgeoning availability of automobiles allowed entire families throughout Europe to discover France, while jet airplanes cut travel times significantly, bringing greater numbers of tourists from lands as distant as Japan and Australia. They, too, would receive their baptism in Bordeaux wine, and they, too, would come to depend on the 1855 classification as the reference that would guide their purchases and determine their drinking preferences.

By 1960, the utility of the brokers' list was clearly recognizable and readily acknowledged by the classed growths themselves—"The classification is: An Instrument of Notoriety," more specifically, "an instrument destined to make known to the public, clearly and without mistake, the distinctions established among a limited and chosen number of high quality products due to their subtle differences." The classification of Bordeaux's wines, originally a tool whose use was the exclusive province of the trade centered on Bordeaux's Quai des Chartrons, had evolved into a publicity device whose importance was completely divorced from its original purpose. Today, having become the public standard for quality in Bordeaux wine, the classification has also become the wine trade's double-edged sword: although establishing a unique image based on high standards that works to the benefit of all its wine whether classed or not, the 1855 classification has also become the focus of controversy, requiring its frequent defense against critics both from without and within the hierarchy of which it is the symbol, and necessitating continual justification for its 140-year existence.

Nine

CONCLUSIONS

I was not at all sure, when beginning this book, what my position regarding the continued viability of the 1855 classification would be. Although the focus of this book's research and writing has been mainly limited to the classification's origins and early history—how it came to be drafted, by whom, and why those individuals acted as they did— nonetheless, the question of whether a ranking almost a century and a half old could still be useful today was a constant presence. As the facts emerged which led to an understanding of the details of how, by whom, and why, they inevitably led to conclusions as well. Those conclusions have been reserved for this last chapter.

Within a few years after the brokers sent their list to the Bordeaux Chamber of Commerce, authors and others had begun to anticipate its revision. One of the most famous examples of this view was Edouard Féret's 1868 commentary in the second edition of *Bordeaux et ses vins*:

> Like all human institutions [the classification] is subject to the laws of time, and every so often it must certainly be revised, brought up to the level of progress. With a change of ownership a property can often be modified. A growth neglected by a careless or financially-pressed proprietor can fall into the hands of a wealthy, active, and intelligent man, and thus end up producing better wines. The contrary can also happen, which is why in 1855 it was necessary to modify the ancient classifications.

For 100 years, this passage appeared in *Bordeaux et ses vins*; it was not until the twelfth edition published in 1969 in the thick of Philippe de Rothschild's controversial campaign to bring about a change in the classification, as Edouard Féret had prescribed one century earlier, that the paragraph disappeared from view. However, the reasons Féret offered for the necessity of updating the 1855 classification have remained as the classic arguments of those who would seek its revision: changes in proprietors, changes in the grape varieties planted in the classed-growth vineyards, indeed, changes in the vineyards themselves—one of the particularities of the brokers' classification is that rankings were not assigned to proprietors, vineyard parcels, or even the château building itself. (In the Médoc, for instance, the edifice that is today the château for Marquis d'Alesme-Becker was originally the château for Desmirail: the change occurred in 1938 when Paul Zuger purchased Alesme-Becker and found that it lacked a house, the original château having been previously acquired by Lascombes for use as a secondary residence. In Sauternes, the château and cellars at Romer were razed when the authorities planning the highway from Bordeaux to the south in the 1960s traced a path which passed directly through the buildings—fortunately, the vineyard was left undisturbed and the wine itself survives; similarly, the vines of second-growth Suau in Barsac have been separated from their original château building since 1961, when the property's longtime owners decided to sell the vineyards while retaining the house for their personal use.) In theory, there is nothing to prevent a classed growth that consisted of, say, 25 hectares in 1855 from acquiring 100 hectares of neighboring vineyards that were classed lower in the hierarchy—or, for that matter, not classed at all. A property could thus quadruple its original surface area, with the result that the majority of its vines are now planted in terrain that in 1855 was not producing wine of the same high caliber; one would expect that the quality of this resulting wine would therefore not be up to the standards represented by the property's position in the classification, yet its 1855 standing remains unchanged.

These arguments cry out for an updating of the classification to rectify such possible abuses in so outmoded a hierarchy. There is also the question of the inequity incorporated into the rankings, owing to a rigid conservatism surrounding the classification's drafting as well. Such conservatism was at the heart of why Mouton, a property that enjoyed an outstanding contemporary reputation, was denied a berth among the first growths that it almost universally was said to have deserved. To have tampered with the capstone of the classification could have shaken the pyramid down to its base, destroying the structure on which the Bordeaux wine trade depended and creating that much-dreaded "anarchy"—the word runs repeatedly through the correspondence of the Chamber of Commerce and the Departmental Committee, a sort of hobgoblin for all the commercial, social, and political threats that were ever present in the minds of those involved in the caretaking of the classification. (The idea that such potential dangers could so deeply preoccupy business and community leaders cannot easily be dismissed, when just the mere sight of wicker chairs in Bordeaux's Grand Theater could evoke reflections on the riots in the Champs Elysées during the 1848 revolution eight years earlier.) Such seemingly inexplicable unfairness did not do much for the classification's reputation among its contemporaries, and, as time passed, endowing an air of permanence upon what was originally intended as a temporary construct, the sense of inequity grew as properties whose improvements in the years since 1855 were not rewarded with promotion or inclusion in the hierarchy. Today, the 1855 classification, for all of its exalted reputation, is the legatee of over 140 years of perceived injustice that seriously undermines any authority that it may still claim.

And yet . . .

Although the arguments raised in protest against the 1855 classification's continued existence are certainly compelling, do they really make the best possible case for an "official" updating of the rankings? The Bordeaux classification has always trailed financial consequence in its wake, but since 1855 other considerations have come to play a role in the calls for revision. The question is whether the satisfaction of those considerations is worth placing at risk a standard that is unique in the world of wine.

A classification like the Bordeaux hierarchy depends on the conjunction of three conditions for its development. First, the wine-producing region itself must have a reputation for quality that is exceptional, universally acknowledged, and of uninterrupted long standing. In France, there are only three areas that can meet this criterion: Champagne, Burgundy, and Bordeaux. It is true that Alsace produces wines of great quality, but, in general, they are very much underappreciated. Whatever system has been developed by the region's brokers and merchants to rank the quality of the wines in which they deal has remained within the trade, since the public perception of Alsacian wine has not warranted reference to a classification when buying it. Similarly, although the Loire Valley also produces some of the world's finest wines, its current public identity as a region of quality is relatively recent. The Rhone Valley's reputation for fine wine is of longer date, but although selected appellations such as Chateauneuf-du-Pape and Hermitage have long served as the region's standard bearers for quality, the overall public perception of Rhone wines has suffered from their closer association with the more nondescript production from the Côtes-du-Rhone. (In fact, producers in the Rhone had been classified by members of the wine trade as early as the first decades of the nineteenth century—Guillaume Lawton's notebooks contain a list ranking the finest Hermitage into first, second, and third classes. However, this was not a classification that judged these producers' wines based on quality in their own right, but rather on their aptitude for use as a raw material in the process known as "Hermitaging," in which they were added to Bordeaux in need of fortification. Thus, this classification remained a tool of the wine trade, never entered the public domain, and was abandoned when this practice of blending wines gradually fell out of use.)

The second requirement necessary for the development of an 1855-type classification is that the wines from a region of recognized quality must be readily identifiable with their individual producers at every step of production, from planting the vines to making the wines. In the absence of such identification, it becomes impossible for a classification to fulfill one of its major functions, namely the attribution of responsibility in the assessment of a wine's reputation. A classification such as the brokers' 1855 list reflects the commercial judgment on the entity responsible for the quality that has earned the wine its reputation. Of the three French regions, only Burgundy and Bordeaux meet this qualification, since Champagne is a relatively anonymous wine, assembled from grapes that have come from numerous vineyards that are not strictly tied to a particular producer. Although there are exceptions, such as Krug's "Clos de Mesnil" which is made from grapes grown in a delimited vineyard owned by the Champagne house itself, most of the region's wine is made from grapes bought from independent growers under contracts which can change over a period of years. The fact that Champagne producers arrive at a consistency in style and character given such circumstances is eloquent testimony to the winemakers' art, but it is contrary to the development of a classification ranking a hierarchy of producers. There is an element of terrain (or as the French call it, *terroir*) that plays a role in the development of a classification, an importance given to the fact that the grapes used in classed-growth wines were grown on land belonging to the proprietors themselves. This is absent in Champagne.

The third condition necessary for the development of an 1855-style classification is continuity of a producer's identity over an extended period of time. Traditionally, in Bordeaux the producing entity—the name presented to the public on the wine bottle's label—has been the property itself, today almost universally identified by the title "château." In Burgundy—not discounting the commercial importance of merchant producers such as Drouhin or Leroy—the producing entity is the individual winemaker. This highly personal aspect of Burgundian production allows for the creation of excellent wines, but has left the vineyards vulnerable to the inheritance clauses of the Napoleonic Code and their successors in French civil legislation. From generation to generation, a parcel of land can be divided among two or more inheritors, and although this is not necessarily detrimental to the quality of the wine an exceptional vineyard can produce, the commercial identity of a Burgundian wine—the name of the winemaker on the label—can change. Burgundy and Bordeaux are similar in that over time the sizes of producers' vineyards have changed—in Burgundy primarily through inheritance, in Bordeaux through purchases or sales of vines—but in Bordeaux the production entity (the château) remained a commercial constant whose quality could be tracked and classified over a century or more by the wine trade and its customers. This has not been possible in Burgundy.

(It must be emphasized that the presence or absence of these conditions does not necessarily reflect on the quality of a region's wine, only on the development of a classification similar to that in existence in Bordeaux. The preceding discussion is offered to explain the uniqueness of Bordeaux's classification, not to suggest any superiority of its wine over those from Burgundy, Champagne, Alsace, or any other region.)

Each of the three conditions necessary for the development of a Bordeaux-style classification is ever-more subtle in its degree of significance. Having established itself as a producer of quality wine by the fifteenth century, the Bordeaux region passed through a stage in which that quality was identified according to a wine's geographical origin. This is reflected in the classifications of the seventeenth and eighteenth centuries, where first entire areas were ranked (the 1647 Jurade deliberation), then more finely delimited communal units became the basis for judgment (the Intendant's classification from the 1740s). In Burgundy, the system of classification remained fixed at this level of development in which a wine's quality is strictly linked with the terrain that has produced it, with further refinement producing the geographically based hierarchy of grand cru, premier cru, communal, and regional levels that exists today. It is a logical approach reflecting the nature of a region where the identity of a great wine can change from the singular to the plural in the space of a generation, the only characteristics common to each of the newly created properties being the family name of the owners—and the terrain that each has inherited. In Bordeaux, the classification continued its evolution throughout the eighteenth and nineteenth centuries to arrive at a system which acknowledged that the influence of the producing entity was as important as the terrain—if not more so. In effect, the Bordeaux classification suggests that although terrain plays an important role in the quality of a wine, it is not the predominant one. Changes in a classed growth's vineyard did not determine a property's position in the classification; rather, it was the quality of the wine that a proprietor made and the higher or lower price that the wine brought on the market that established a property's standing. As important as their terrain was, it was not the determining factor for including these properties in the classification, but only one element in the overall quality of their wines which made possible their high prices—and it was price that directly established the rankings. A classed growth could alter its vineyard composition, adding and subtracting parcels of subtly different terrain through purchases and sales; as long as the quality of its wine remained the same (or improved), its position in the classification was never questioned. Proprietors were free to alter their vineyards' dimensions as was seen fit, or as conditions made necessary; it was up to the winemakers' vinicultural skills to manage to continue producing wines that were up to the property's acknowledged standard—if not to surpass it.

The wine trade that developed the Bordeaux classification understood that a property's ranking could not be tied solely to the maintenance of a status quo in vineyard dimension. The operation of a Bordeaux wine property simply did not work like that. A proprietor's function at the head of an estate consisted of two main duties: (1) to make the finest wine possible and (2) to ensure the financial viability that facilitated the production of the finest wine possible. One of the primary means available to the proprietor in achieving this end was the effective management of the real estate portfolio that was the vineyard and its dependencies (château, winery, cellars, arable land, etc.). A good part of a proprietor's time might be involved in the purchase, sale, and exchange of land to optimize the operation of the property. This could involve buying land for the construction of a road enabling easier access to the vineyards by workers and equipment, or the exchange of a distant parcel of vines for one contiguous with the main vineyard to allow the property to be more easily worked. (This last point became increasingly important in the twentieth century as tractors gradually replaced manual labor in vineyard maintenance, making smaller, disperse parcels less practical to work than larger, unified plots.) Such purchases and exchanges of vines were common practice in the years before 1855, as attested to by the archives at Château Latour, which contain numerous records of real estate activity between the first growth and its neighbors. Between 1841 and 1850, fifteen transactions occurred, several with the neighboring Pichon-Longuevilles and Lalandes, but most with less-exalted families whose own wines have since disappeared and whose names exist only as designations for vineyard parcels scattered throughout Pauillac. With such activity commonly occurring before 1855, it would be unrealistic to criticize classed growths for not refraining from all real estate transactions in the years since. Wine-producing properties are living entities that, by nature, are subject to change in their composition and dimensions; they are not vine museums whose purpose is to preserve the aspect of a nineteenth-century vineyard.

One reason such shifts in composition are so common in Bordeaux vineyards is because it is the exception rather than the rule to find a property's vines grouped together in one undivided piece, and, in the nineteenth century, the tendency to small parcels of vines was even more extensive than it is today. For example, in 1853, the vineyards at Malescot-Saint-Exupéry consisted of 111 parcels totaling almost 25 hectares "situated in the commune of Margaux, and by extension in the communes of Cantenac, Soussans and Avensan" according to the notice of sale published at the time; Cos-d'Estournel's 55⅓ hectares of vines were distributed over 120 parcels in 1868. Although these individual groups of vines tended to form larger contiguous blocks, this parceling did lead to situations where "so-called bourgeois or peasant wines are intermingled with the most illustrious of vineyards." Through circumstances of family history, for instance, it could happen that a commune's butcher, baker, or candlestick maker might own a parcel of vines in the very midst of a classed-growth vineyard. This plot would be worked on weekends or afternoons when the owner's primary occupation was done; the grapes would be harvested when time permitted and vinified in small-scale family conditions to produce a simple beverage suitable for domestic consumption throughout the year.

One observer of the Médoc's vineyards in 1858 commented at length on this circumstance and the consequences it had for the wine:

> What is the cause of these differences [between classed growths and bourgeois and peasant wines]? We cannot find it in either the soil, or the grape variety, or the exposition, or in the cultivation, because very often these so-called bourgeois or peasant wines are intermingled with the most illustrious of vineyards. It is to the winemaking processes that we must look.
>
> First, at the châteaux a great number of harvesters are employed, which permits a vat to be filled in one day, while the small proprietors looking to economize, carry out their harvests within the family, and call on the smallest number of outsiders possible. The result of this method of proceeding is that these harvests go on for far too long a time, and that once fermentation begins it is subject to several halts before the vat is filled. This is a great inconvenience, because nothing is more important for a good vinification than an uninterrupted fermentation. Second, the small proprietors have only small vats, and experience has shown that vinification occurs better in large vats and produces superior results. A large vat once underway is less likely to be affected by variations in temperature, which slow or over stimulate the fermentation process. These are the most appreciable circumstances for which one can attribute the differences among châteaux, bourgeois and peasant wines.

A similar analysis of the Gironde's vineyards led another contemporary commentator to the conclusion that "the broker is right [in his classification of properties]: the peasant growths the better communes, and the bourgeois growths even more so, would quickly rise in the wine hierarchy if the proprietors dedicated themselves above all to quality. The peasant growths would soon obtain their titles of bourgeois, and the bourgeois could stand as equals with their powerful neighbors, titled and noble. There would no longer be, strictly speaking, commoners among the great growths . . . ." It was therefore of little importance that the baker's vines were planted in terrain capable of producing a wine of exceptional quality; because of the treatment and facilities that were available for those vines and their grapes, the resultant wine could never realize all that the terrain had to offer. Since these parcels of land held the potential for producing a quality wine, it would have been negligent on the part of classed-growth proprietors not to buy them as they became available for purchase and thus augment the production and revenue of their properties without sacrifice to the quality of their classed-growth wines.

The idea that by 1855 all of the terrain with a propensity for producing classed-growth wine was already under vines—and that those vines were owned by the classed growths—is an illusion of history. In the second decade of the nineteenth century, an entire classed growth, Montrose in Saint-Estèphe, was created out of uncultivated land when the owner, Etienne Théodore Dumoulin, observed that the gravelly nature of his soil was similar to that producing wine of fine quality elsewhere in the Médoc; twenty-five years before the drafting of the 1855 classification,

Charles Palmer was still purchasing vineyards in Cantenac to build the third growth that bears his name today; and, as late as 1848, the indefatigable Louis-Joseph-Gaspard d'Estournel was staving off creditors and bankruptcy while continuing to buy and exchange vineyard parcels in his effort to perfect the composition of his second-growth Cos-d'Estournel—beginning in 1820, over eighty such transactions are on record, some involving areas as small as "a patch of land four meters large." There is no event, no decree, which can claim to signal a definitive closure on the exploitation of vineyard land in the Médoc. To attribute such a significance to the year 1855 is to impose an artificial double duty on the date: the year of the brokers' classification and the precise moment when, as symbolized by the Oklahoma land rush in the American west, the frontier had ceased to exist. It is entirely possible that in the years after 1855 unplanted land of great potential and classed-growth quality vineyards belonging to smaller proprietors were still available for purchase and exploitation by the classified properties.

Equally important is the opposite situation, namely that not every vine belonging to a classed growth is planted in equally exceptional terrain; this was not the case in 1855 and is not the case today. This is an extremely subtle point, and highly relative, too—terrain that is deemed to lack the qualities necessary to produce a wine worthy of one property's reputation may be perfectly acceptable to another. To deal with these discrepencies in the varied quality of their terrain, proprietors engage in a practice that makes it extremely risky to draw simple conclusions about the quality of classed-growth wines based on an increase in a property's size between 1855 and today: the production of a second wine. Not all of the grapes planted on a property's land necessarily goes into the making of the *grand vin*. Young vines whose immaturity prevents them from from producing fruit of sufficient quality and vines planted in terrain whose characteristics are not up to producing grapes that meet the standards of a property's reputation are "declassified"—their grapes are used instead to produce a wine bearing the property's second label. Although this practice has variously come in and out of favor among Bordeaux properties, it has a history that is centuries old: by the 1760s, to cite just one example, Rauzan in Margaux (long before the property was split into Ségla and Gassies) had already made the production of a second wine a standard part of its operations.

Consider this more recent example at Château Latour: a comparison of its dimensions clearly indicates that Latour's vineyards have increased by some 23 hectares since 1855, but what such a comparison will not show is that the grapes from the majority of the added land in question (comprising three vineyards called "Comtesse de Lalande," "Petit Batailley," and "Saint Anne") are destined for the second wine, "Les Forts de Latour," and not the *grand vin*. (The 10 hectares of Petit Batailley were brought into production in the early 1960s specifically to provide grapes for the second wine created in 1966.) Vineyard land, even if not of the highest quality, is nonetheless a highly valuable asset, and inferior parcels obtained by a classed growth as part of a transaction whose main purpose is the acquisition of first-class terrain might well be retained and its vines dedicated to the production of a second wine (or even undergo a further declassification for use in a generic appellation wine bearing the name "Pauillac" or "Bordeaux," for instance). Thus, an increase in the size of a classed growth's vineyard and the resultant change in the nature of its terrain since 1855 does not inevitably mean that the property is no longer worthy of its rank in the classification. Such simple conclusions fail to take into account associated factors such as the production of a second label, which can earn revenue for a property without sacrificing the quality of the wine on which its classification is based; it is a much more complex equation than is generally acknowledged.

Of course, the influence of terrain on a wine cannot be discounted: a great terrain might not necessarily be producing a great wine, but a great wine can never be produced on anything less than a terrain of the finest quality. The key is in the conjunction of an exceptional terrain with the conditions and circumstances necessary for the full exploitation of its potential. Thus, although terrain has an intrinsic *quality*, with certain soil types being more apt to produce a fine wine than others, its *value* as a factor in the classification of a property is relative, not absolute. Throughout the classification's history, the Bordeaux wine trade has faithfully observed this distinction, not only as it relates to the acquisition of vineyard land by a classed growth but in the opposite circumstance as well.

When a classed growth has been forced to reduce its size through the sale of some of its vines, an expedient commonly resorted to during periods of economic distress, the Bordeaux wine trade has been consistent in the distance it accords the relationship between terrain and the classification. During the extended commercial crisis that hit the Bordeaux region throughout the first half of the twentieth century, vines from many classed growths passed into the hands of other proprietors, classed and unclassed alike. However, although the new owners may have acquired terrain that had shown itself capable of producing, say, first-growth wines, it was well understood that the classification was not linked to the terrain itself, and no one reasonably expected to see a property promoted to the top of the hierarchy because it now possessed vines that had formerly contributed to wines of the highest rank. Even during previous centuries, in the absence of any official body to oversee the classification's integrity, vines that were separated from the main body of a classed growth did not necessarily retain their classed-growth status with the trade.

This was the case in the 1840s when financial constraints forced John Lewis Brown to sell his classed growth in the commune of Cantenac. Fifty-eight hectares, including the château and production buildings, which constituted the majority of Cantenac Brown, were acquired by Messrs. Fruitier and Gromard, and this portion retained the third-growth status that the property had earned by this time; a much smaller portion of the vineyard—around 8 hectares—was purchased by Jean Verrière, a municipal counselor and future mayor of Margaux. In writing about the latter's property, Armand d'Armailhacq noted that Verrière "has equally bought vines from Mr. Brown, and should conserve the class of that wine; but [the trade] only acknowledge it as a fourth." It may have been this same reasoning that led the brokers to discount Louis de Chavaille's demand for an elevation of Pouget's position from the classification's fourth tier, despite the claim he raised in defense of his request that he had acquired vines from Brown and Dubignon, both third growths. Here again, it was not the land itself—much less proximity to the terrain of a classed growth—that was acknowledged as the determining factor in a property's position in the classification, it was the quality of the property's wine.

Thus, if a discussion of terrain has been virtually absent from the preceding chapters, it is because of this fundamental condition of Bordeaux's commercial tradition—terrain has a direct importance in the making of a fine wine, but only an indirect importance in the position (or omission) of a wine in the 1855 classification.

It is an undeniable fact that the great growths of Bordeaux are planted in terrain of exceptional quality, gravelly outcrops whose propensity for producing fine wine was earliest recognized and exploited by the first growths. It was no coincidence that when Bordeaux was making its modern reputation as a producer of quality wine in the seventeenth and eighteenth centuries, these properties were owned by the city's most wealthy and well-placed citizens: Haut-Brion by the Pontacs, Margaux by the Aulèdes, Lafite and Latour (as well as Mouton and Calon) by the Ségurs; other prominent families were equally busy at this time creating domains that would take their place in the upper tiers of the classification, such as the Rauzans whose vineyards eventually included what are today the properties of Ségla/Gassies, Desmirail, Marquis de Terme, and the two Pichon-Longuevilles (Baron and Comtesse).

In many cases, these illustrious families were not the first proprietors to dedicate these lands to vines, but as the quality of the wines that these favored gravelly outcrops produced (and the prices they brought) came to rise above the average, the value of such land, all sharing the same general characteristics of terrain, increased to the point where only the most wealthy of citizens could afford to own them. This endowed these vineyards with a second shared characteristic: owners who considered the wines that issued from these investments in real estate as personal reflections on their own prominent social reputations, and, more importantly, who were possessed of the financial resources to promote the quality inherent in the terrain.

There is a fundamental truth common to all winemaking: it takes money to make a wine, and it takes great amounts of money to make a great wine. This addresses the point raised by Edouard Féret regarding a proprietor's primary importance for a classed-growth property—a source of capital (and the will to spend it) to ensure the conditions necessary for the production of a wine worthy of its rank in the classification. As a rule, the arrival of a new proprietor will signal the *improvement* of a wine and not a decline in its quality, for when a classed-growth changes hands it is invariably because of one overriding circumstance: the current owner is no longer able—or willing—to continue providing the money necessary to produce a wine commensurate with the property's standing. When Charles Palmer sold his property in 1843, it was because he could no longer place at its disposition the money such a domain required; a more recent case is Prieuré-Lichine, which as Château Le Prieuré was in a state of virtual ruin when bought by Alexis Lichine in 1951, decades of financial stress having bled the previous owners dry.

No one buys a vineyard of whatever stature with the idea of losing money, and whatever sums are spent on a property after its acquisition are considered an investment, not money spent just for the sake of it. Often the return on that investment is small, or nonexistent; such was the case in most years during the first half of the twentieth century, and it is the proprietor's responsibility to continue to support the property financially when commercial circumstances prevent the wine from doing so itself. When such periods persist or changes in a proprietor's fortunes result in a steady diminution of financial input, the quality of the wine will suffer, its reputation will decrease, and the price it commands among the public will drop. This exacerbates the financial pressures that weigh on a proprietor, creating an economic whirlpool from which it is practically impossible to escape. Partners may be taken in and other measures may be employed, but usually matters end in one result: the property changes hands, either through sale or through seizure by creditors, and a new proprietor comes in. During this period of difficulty, which can last for a decade or more, the quality of the wine produced by a classed growth can be so disappointing as to give rise to calls for an official declassification of the property, demoting it from, say, a second to a fifth growth—or even a cru bourgeois.

The fact that no downgrading has ever occurred invariably gives support to the idea that the 1855 classification is a fossilized construct lacking the flexibility to reflect the changing circumstances affecting the properties it contains. Such calls for altering the 1855 list are largely rooted in a misunderstanding of the classification's origins, a belief that the brokers based their rankings on the properties' commercial performance in 1854 alone, or for the five or even ten years previous to 1855. This gives rise to a further distortion in appraising the classification's accuracy: if, by chance, a property was fortunate enough to produce an exceptionally good wine in 1854, or enjoyed a string of five or ten fine vintages, then it won a ranking as a classed growth, even if its previous—and subsequent—history was not up to its performance during the crucial period considered by the brokers. In reality, as attested to by the continuity of the records at Tastet & Lawton, the 1855 classification was the result of a much longer period of assessment by the brokers, almost half a century, if Guillaume Lawton's 1815 classification is taken as an authoritative point of departure. (And, of course, that classification did not spring full blown into being but was itself the result of many years' prior observation and experience among Bordeaux's wine brokers—"an experience which goes back over a century," according to the Chamber of Commerce's letter to Napoleon Jerome.)

Thus, to demand a property's demotion in the hierarchy after even a decade of producing disappointing wines is unjust, when it may have taken at least five times as long for it to have reached its given level of the classification. Let a property produce poor wines for fifty years or more and then one might begin to be justified in considering if perhaps the brokers were mistaken in 1855.

A recent example illustrates this quite well. In 1934, Château Margaux came under the administration of the Ginestet family, who were among Bordeaux's leading wine merchants. Fernand Ginestet, doyen of the family firm, was one of the leading figures in the Bordeaux wine world during the first half of the twentieth century; in addition to founding the company that still bears the family name, he began acquiring some of the Gironde's finest wine-producing properties, putting into practice his belief that merchants and producers could successfully work together while avoiding the confrontations that traditionally had characterized their relations in the past. Fernand Ginestet further built upon this idea by actively working to create the Union of Property and Commerce just after World War I, the first organization whose aim was to foster cooperation between the two ends of the Bordeaux wine trade. By the 1930s, Fernand was succeded by his son, Pierre, whose faith in these ideas was as strong as his father's: after the Union of Property and Commerce had ceased to exist, it was Pierre Ginestet who was a major force behind the creation of its successor in the years just following World War II—the Interprofessional Council of Bordeaux Wine, which today oversees the standards and commercialization for all of the Gironde's production. Another aspect in which Pierre followed in his father's footsteps was in the acquisition and successful management of wine-producing properties. During the course of their long and accomplished lives, the Ginestets were the owners and administrators of numerous properties throughout the region such as Clos Fortet in Saint-Emilion, Petit-Village in Pomerol, Cos-d'Estournel in Saint-Estèphe, Boyd-Cantenac in Cantenac, Durfort-Vivens in Margaux, and Rabaud-Promis in the Sauternes region, to name but a very few.

Practically unequaled in depth or breadth, such experience furnished the Ginestets with the requisite knowledge and capital to give full expression to the quality that Château Margaux had to offer, and during their ownership the property continued to produce wines justly deserving of its first-growth classification. However, toward the end of the 1960s and in the early years of the 1970s, difficulties arose in the Ginestet family and in their merchant business—difficulties completely independent from their operation of Château Margaux; the effect of all this on their first growth was that it became increasingly difficult to invest the money necessary to continue producing wine worthy of its classification. However, with its acquisition in 1977 by the Mentzelopoulos family and the infusion of money that had long been needed, Château Margaux produced what many observers considered to be the wine of the year in the second vintage produced under the new ownership. "By general opinion, the Margaux 1978 was 'number 1' among the first growths. This sudden return to the head of the class made quite an effect," recalled oenologist Emile Peynaud. Nonetheless, "the team of workers was the same"; it was the massive investment made by André Mentzelopoulos that brought out Margaux's unchanged potential to its best advantage. To have declassified the property from a first growth after even a decade of disappointing wines would have been extremely premature, a short-term solution with long-term consequences.

Emile Peynaud's observation regarding the personnel at Margaux touches on a commonly held idea, namely that when referring to the importance of individuals in the quality of a wine one is automatically speaking of the proprietor as the sole determining personality responsible for its success or failure. This is not entirely accurate. While the proprietor of a classed growth is undoubtedly the principal actor in the making of a fine wine, it must be kept in mind that there is a whole supporting cast involved as well. The production of a classed growth is not an individual endeavor. This was well understood by the owners at Latour in 1869, when in their annual report on the state of the property they noted that "the fortune of Latour's proprietors is in the hands of several winemakers and depends on the choice of a manager." With only four exceptions—Mouton-Rothschild, Léoville-Barton, Langoa-Barton, and Yquem—all of the classed growths have changed proprietors since 1855, but it would be a mistake to believe that these changes have necessarily been detrimental to the quality of the wine these properties have produced. The arrival of a new owner is certainly a major event in the life of a property, contributing to its improvement by bringing an infusion of badly-needed capital to maintain or improve conditions in the vineyard and winery, for example. However, although the person at the head of the property's hierarchy has changed, there usually remains much of the same team that has been responsible for the production of the wine; few proprietors would disagree that it is these workers' long experience that provides the continuity that can keep a classed growth great.

Even when a proprietor takes some drastic action that places a property's classed-growth status in question, in the end the invisible hand of the market has always been the enforcer behind the accuracy of the Bordeaux classification's authority, sooner or later forcing producers to change their ways—or sell—in order to restore their wines to the classification's assessment of them. Such was the case at Durfort-Vivens in the first half of the nineteenth century when the Count de Puységur came into possession of the property by marriage and undertook a policy of planting inferior vines to increase the vineyards' quantity at the expense of their quality. By the 1840s, the property's long-standing reputation as a second growth had suffered so badly that market pressure soon led Puységur to see the error of his ways, forcing him to replant the property with superior quality vines; by 1855, the vineyards' reconstitution was complete enough for Saint-Amant to remark that "*Durfort-Puységur* cedes nothing to its two neighbors *Rauzan*."

As the example of Durfort-Vivens shows, drastic departures from standards of quality in the choice of grape varieties planted will produce a definite reaction among the wine-drinking public that no property's reputation, regardless of how high its classification, can deflect. (Indeed, the more highly regarded a property is, the greater the reaction should be since the effect produced by a wine made from inferior grapes will be even more in contrast with the expectations that its reputation raises.) However, such detrimental changes in varietal planting must not be confused with the constant evolution that has always occurred in vineyards throughout the Gironde. Both before 1855 and in the years since, this evolution has led to shifts among the percentages of grape varieties planted by classed and nonclassed growths alike, as winemakers have sought ever more successful organoleptic results in response to changing winemaking techniques and the evolution of public taste. As the Bordeaux classification developed during the eighteenth and nineteenth centuries, the composition of the Gironde's vineyards was in a continual, if subtle, state of flux. Cabernet Sauvignon, now the Médoc's predominant grape variety, began its ascendancy around 1815, by which time Guillaume Lawton had already drafted his classification of the region's wines; even without the influence of Cabernet Sauvignon, Lawton's estimation of their relative quality was remarkably similar to the brokers findings forty years later. Other similar changes occurred in the Gironde's vineyards during the decades before 1855, yet the evolution of the wine trade's classification continued in a steady, consistent manner.

After 1855, changes in properties' varietal composition continued, if for no other reason than the wholesale replanting made necessary first by the attack of powdery mildew in the middle of the nineteenth century, then in the wake of the phylloxera infestation during the century's final decades. These were circumstances that touched all properties, classed and nonclassed alike; while some may have simply replanted their vineyards with the same varieties that had been destroyed by the various afflictions, most took the opportunity to alter their plantings with those that were proving more resistant and profitable. In short, the classic objection to the continued validity of a 140-year-old classification based on the change in grape varieties is negligible, since one would be hard pressed to find any property that has not altered its vineyard composition in any way during the last century and a half. The argument concerning changes in grape varieties is a tide that floats all boats.

In the years following 1855, the Bordeaux wine trade continued its traditional system of classifying properties based on long-term sales prices of their wines; judgments were continually refined as the brokers entered the commercial results of each new vintage into their ledgers and the merchants noted changing customer demand for their wines. A measure of the continuing evolution of the Bordeaux hierarchy is shown by the homologation of the Gironde's wines drafted by France's Vichy government in 1943.

In an effort to establish effective rates of new taxation, and to combat the black-marketeering that touched so many sectors of French production as a result of World War II rationing, a table of authorized prices was published to provide a measure of stability in the market for the country's better wines. As demonstrated by the table's figures, wines in regions such as Saint-Emilion and Pomerol had succeeded in attaining classed-growth prices even without the benefit of inclusion in the 1855 classification, a reflection of a finer appreciation and an increased demand that raised their prices to a level commensurate with their quality.

However, such shifts in the wine trade's rankings have been most clearly understood within the trade, and outside of the profession this method of tracking properties has been found wanting for various reasons. As a result, the past 140 years have seen the frequent proposal of numerous alternatives intended to produce a more authoritative classification of Bordeaux's wines.

In 1857, a doctor in Pauillac named Jean Ferrier offered his thoughts "On the Utility of a Congress of Wine Tasters in the Gironde": "[S]ince the period when the growths of the Médoc were [first] classified, which already goes back to the distant past, there has existed a sort of rivalry among the proprietors which would be simple to end by once again submitting the wines of the Gironde in general, and especially those of the Médoc in particular, to an evaluation free from preconceived ideas and beyond any influence."

Ferrier's idea was simple:

> A congress to taste the red and white wines from the Gironde department, with admission to this competition also open to the great wines from [Burgundy and the Rhone], will take place in Bordeaux, in the month of . . . 185 . . . by subscription.
>
> All of the guests, French or foreign, attending the tasting banquet will automatically be entitled to be part of the tasting jury.
>
> *Ordinary* wines will be excluded from the competition because the purpose is to present wines whose quality classes them in the category of exceptional wines; the *great red wines alone* will be admitted to compete among themselves, and the white wines will be appreciated in a session devoted to their particular evaluation.
>
> All wines participating in the competition will be decanted in advance, by the proprietors, into ordinary bottles offering no sign that can indicate their origin; they will bear neither seal nor capsule, and the cork shall carry no mark. A single label attached to the bottle will indicate the year in which the wine was harvested in order to facilitate the order in which they should be served; but these labels will be replaced, in the very presence of the proprietors if they wish it, by others bearing a printed number in order that no one be able to identify either the products in advance of the tasting or the judgment made on them afterwards. Each bottle will

> have attached to its neck, in a manner impossible to remove, a piece of white paper sealed with red wax and bearing no other exterior sign, containing a statement indicating the names of the proprietor, the growth, and the age of the wine. Before the competition numbers will be placed on each bottle to aid the jury members in making their notes. It is in this academic manner that the wines shall be sent to and received at the competition.
>
> Each guest arriving at the tasting banquet, armed with the doubting frame of mind prescribed by Descartes for seeking out the truth, will be supplied with a piece of paper to record the impressions received from each of the wines tasted during the meal; this will be done in a suitable manner—by points alone if so wished—in order that at the end of the meal [each guest] may, with full knowledge of the facts, pronounce upon the merits of each competitor; this precaution is useful to compensate for lapses in the taste memory, which in the course of a long tasting can easily become unreliable.
>
> Following the competition, each guest will be called upon to give an opinion on the quality of the different wines tasted, and the notes that will have been taken or the points that will have been awarded to each number will more easily enable the guest to indicate the preference accorded to one wine over another.
>
> The statements on those bottles whose numbers have obtained the most votes will then be unsealed in order to learn the identity of those which have earned prizes, certificates of merit, and honorable mentions. To this end, minutes of the meeting will be compiled, signed by all the guests, and will include the votes obtained by each of the wines presented at the competition.
>
> In this manner, at the very least, one will arrive at an opinion founded on the superiority of some wines over others, and this type of classification will have the advantage of faithfully assigning to each the place that it should occupy in the category of the great wines of our department.
>
> Unless he wishes to admit himself beaten in advance, and to declare by abstaining that his wine is markedly inferior, there is not a single proprietor who would refuse to submit to the test of a competition in which at least he could be certain of the judges' complete impartiality, simply because under the circumstances it would be impossible to know the origin of the wine in advance of its being judged.

Almost every element of the method described in Ferrier's proposal has been adopted at one time or another by various tastings and competitions in the past 140 years, and each event in which the wines of the Gironde have been comparatively judged has been heralded as resulting in a more exact estimation of the relative quality of Bordeaux's wine producers than is provided by the 1855 classification. Nevertheless, the tastings continue to follow one another in a never-ending series, each comparison "more definitive" than the last. The idea that a single tasting could arrive at a judgment on which an authoritative classification of the Gironde's wines could be based is frankly unrealistic. In Ferrier's case, his belief in the efficacy of the method he propounded was based on a nineteenth-century faith in the reliability of academic methodology in the attainment of an ultimate truth; in more recent tastings, such a belief stems from the widespread idea that a tasting was how the 1855 classification was created. Both beliefs are false.

A tasting of wines from one or two vintages can indeed be used to assess the relative quality of the wines being judged, but the results are valid only for those years being sampled, and are heavily influenced by the more or less temporary conditions in effect during the making of those particular vintages. Several circumstances can affect the results of such a tasting: a property may be going through a rough patch during the years being sampled (as has happened at one time or another in the life of every growth, be it classed or nonclassed), or a property may not yet be in step with changing public preferences, having remained true to its traditional standards of quality while popular tastes have shifted. In both of these cases, a wine may show unfavorably, giving rise to the inevitable calls for a property's demotion from its 1855 classification, even though the market may have already taken into account the wine's disappointing quality by discounting its price relative to other growths in the same class. Ten years later, a new set of circumstances will undoubtedly arise that will render the judgment that was reached on a narrow selection of vintages obsolete and open the way for yet another "updating" of the 1855 classification.

In light of such weaknesses inherent to this method of classifying Bordeaux's wines, two main points speak to the strength of the brokers' judgment: first, that it was based on a sampling of information that was decades deep; and, second, that it was not the result of a personal estimation arising from a tasting of the wines, but rather based on the historical performance of the property in the rather less erratic arena of the Bordeaux wine trade. Both factors impart more than just a formidable authority to the 1855 classification; they have also provided a foundation for its rankings that has absorbed the transient occurrences that can skew a hierarchy based on smaller samplings. At best, a comparative tasting of the wines from one or two years can only result in an estimation of the quality of the *wines* from those particular vintages, not a classification fixing the relative quality of the *properties* themselves, something that can only be ascertained over a much longer period of consideration.

A belief in the 1855 classification's superiority in comparison with more recent efforts at judging relative quality should not be seen as implying that the brokers' judgment of 140 years ago is unalterably valid today; such a position verges on the fantastic. According to a more moderate opinion, the classification is "a snapshot," a judgment rendered on the Gironde's vineyards at one moment in time, but this is only partially true. While the 1855 classification is an accurate representation of the mid-nineteenth-century Bordeaux wine world, it also expresses some rather less temporal circumstances of the region's wine scene. The undeniable truth of the 1855 classification is that the sixty-one red-wine and twenty-six white-wine properties that appear on the list today are inarguably capable of producing the finest wines that Bordeaux has to offer. There can be no question about whether any of the classed growths are deserving of the title when they are producing wine at their best. If there is one major problem with the 1855 classification it is that properties that were just a notch below the fifth tier in the mid-nineteenth century whose quality now matches that of the classified growths are denied the chance to put the magic words "cru classé" on their labels. The term is viewed by many winemakers (generally those whose properties are not on the list) as the closest thing in the world of wine to a license for printing money, and the unchanging nature of the 1855 classification, which prevents them from assuming a distinction their wines have justly earned, is the reason most commonly cited as to why the classification must be updated. Although it probably only assuages without completely satisfying the frustration felt by these bourgeois growths at being denied the title "cru classé," the fact remains that since 1855 there have effectively been two classifications: the "official" one of the brokers' list, and the other one that really counts, arising from the wine trade's continual readjustment of sales prices with each new vintage. It is here that a somewhat truer reflection of a wine's value is to be found, where a bourgeois growth can achieve parity with the crus classés. On the negative side (for the winemaker), although a property without the benefit of the "cru classé" label can command prices equal to those of the classed growths, it is much harder to achieve. On the positive side (for the wine drinker), for a property to achieve the reputation of a classed growth, the winemakers have had to work terribly hard—perhaps even harder than some crus classés—in order to be esteemed worthy of consideration as "a candidate for classification should the 1855 list ever be revised"; the result is greater quantities of better wine for buyers of Bordeaux everywhere. The idea that proprietors of bourgeois growths have simply stopped trying to make the best wine possible because they will not be rewarded with an eventual promotion to the list of classed growths does no justice to these winemakers' dedication.

However, it cannot be denied that the 1855 classification has been the source of some very real disadvantages for the bourgeois growths. For decades, conscientious winemakers sparing no expense to create wines of classed-growth quality through sufficiently long aging in their cellars could justly complain of the unfair financial burden they had to carry, owing to the manner in which the taxable value of their inventory was assessed. Properties included in the 1855 classification enjoyed a higher tax credit on these potential assets than did bourgeois growths (in 1979, this credit was set at 8,000 francs per tun for the classed growths, but only 5,000 francs per tun for the bourgeois), and, consequently, bourgeois producers who undertook to give their wines the aging they required were effectively placed at a financial disadvantage compared to their classed-growth colleagues. This situation has been adjusted somewhat in recent years with a reevaluation of the manner in which this tax credit is calculated, although probably not enough to completely satisfy most bourgeois proprietors who might well cite other inequities based on the classification that have been institutionalized over the past 140 years. It should be noted, however, that these problems are not inherent to the 1855 classification itself, but rather a result of the administrative uses to which it has been put.

Perhaps the truest benefit of the 1855 classification's longevity and the one that speaks most strongly against any future official revision is the uniquely exceptional status it has conferred upon the properties it contains. There are only eighty-seven wines in the world today that can claim the title of "cru classé en 1855." Like Will Rogers' observation on the increasing value of land because "they ain't makin' any more of it," each of the properties producing these red and white wines has a value that can never be matched by a neighboring estate, regardless of the composition of its terrain or the price its wine manages to bring. It is this feature conferred upon the classed growths by the classification itself that is the closest thing to a guarantee that exists ensuring the continued high quality of these rare properties. (Indeed, it might be seen as a sign of the integrity of the Bordeaux wine trade that it has resisted the temptation to alter the 1855 classification and create more classed growths at a time when there are never enough wines bearing this distinction to go around—not, of course, that efforts have not been made toward this end.)

In theory, anyone can purchase a classed-growth property (in the case of the firsts, only as long as you are French, but that is another matter . . .); all that is necessary are two conditions: (1) that it be up for sale, and (2) that the buyer have sufficient money. A potential proprietor need not have any prior winemaking experience; the examples of James de Rothschild at Lafite and Nathaniel de Rothschild at Mouton, to name just two cases, bear this out.

A person seeking to become the owner of a vineyard might have a choice between a classed and a nonclassed growth. However, given a similarity in their sizes and yields, the price of the classed property will be more than that asked for the nonclassed one, probably significantly more. The difference will likely give pause to anyone not seriously interested in producing a fine wine equal to a property's standing in the classification; if it is simply the life of a *châtelain* that a buyer seeks, this style of living is much more reasonably available by purchasing a property with a less impressive pedigree. Should a buyer decide to make the more significant investment that a classed growth represents, it will require a deeper commitment to the wine's quality than the purchase of a nonclassed property might, if only because of the heavier initial investment that has to be protected and recouped. (This should in no way be interpreted as saying that the proprietors of nonclassed growths are any less committed to producing the finest wine possible than are their confreres among the classed growths, only that the outlay of the greater sum necessary in the latter circumstance will tend to concentrate the mind of what might otherwise be a dilettante proprietor and more likely effect a change into a conscientious owner.)

Perhaps more important than any question of increased financial risk that ownership of a classed growth entails is the idea that such a property is more than just a producer of wine. Owing to the unchanging nature of the 1855 classification, the purchase of a classed growth is not akin to buying just any property with grapevines; in effect, one is buying a heritage, not simply belonging to France but to the greater world of wine, and with that comes the responsibility to protect it, to be worthy of owning it. Anyone doubting that such a spirit becomes instilled in a classed-growth owner is invited to consider the case of Count Xavier de Pontac and Château de Myrat in Barsac.

Count Maximilien de Pontac (a descendant of the Pontacs who owned Haut-Brion in the eighteenth century) purchased Château de Myrat in 1938, a property whose ranking at the head of the second growths in the 1855 classification of white wines made it the homologue of Mouton-Rothschild among the reds. Although well regarded among amateurs of the sweet wines of Sauternes and Barsac, Myrat nonetheless could not escape the persistent declining sales and ever-mounting expenses that beset so many of the region's classed growths throughout the 1960s and 1970s, a time in which sweet wines had fallen out of favor with the public. Even an excellent vintage like the 1975 found Pontac unable to sell his wine at a price commensurate with its quality, eventually being forced to accept 3,000 francs per tun. (Today, the trade value of the 1975 Myrat has increased fifteen-fold from this original market price.) There would be no 1976 Myrat: having experienced such difficulties with so beautiful a vintage, what could he expect in lesser years when his expenses and efforts would only be greater? So it was that, in 1976, Count de Pontac decided to cut his losses and halt production at Myrat. However, having made the decision to retire the vineyard, Pontac could not simply abandon the vines, as they would have become subject to diseases that could have affected neighboring properties; all 22 hectares had to be uprooted. For twelve years, Count de Pontac looked out on a terrain denuded of vines, consoling himself that no longer would he have to suffer the frustrations, anxieties, and almost inevitable disappointments that are a part of the life of a proprietor in general and a winemaker in the Sauternes region in particular.

In the spring of 1988, Maximilien de Pontac died, and among the numerous details surrounding the property's succession, the family received notification that Château de Myrat was about to lose its right to produce wine as a Barsac second cru classé: a property could remain unproductive for only so long before its right to its status became forfeit, and the deadline for Myrat was imminent. Jacques and Xavier de Pontac, Maximilien's two sons, acted without hesitation—to save Myrat, they replanted the property's 22 hectares with 150,000 vines within the several weeks left to them by the regulations. Xavier de Pontac permanently returned to Barsac from Paris to personally oversee production at the property, but there could be no Château Myrat in 1988, 1989, or 1990, the three exceptional vintages in which the properties of Sauternes and Barsac reestablished their financial viability after so many years of uncertainty. The property's vines were too young; Myrat would have to wait to declare its first vintage in 1991. Unfortunately, the region was touched by frost in the winter of that year and the vines never fully recovered in the growing season that followed, producing only a small harvest; 1992, 1993, and 1994 were all marked by various problems that prevented the region's properties from recreating the excellent quality and quantity of the previous decade's last three vintages. Although tough for all the properties throughout the area, this was particularly dire in Myrat's case, as it lacked reserves of either revenues or prior vintages to allow it to ride out these four difficult years. Nonetheless, throughout the years of plantation and care of the young vines, throughout the years of waiting for the complex combination of weather conditions to occur without which a fine sweet white wine cannot be produced, throughout the years of being frustrated time and again, Xavier de Pontac continued to nurture Myrat, in practically the same circumstances that led his father to uproot the vineyard in 1976. However, Maximilien de Pontac was not faced with the prospect that a classed growth would be lost forever when he made his decision to halt production; but his son is very much aware of such a possibility, and this awareness has helped him persevere against all financial logic. In the end, Xavier de Pontac's struggle eloquently illustrates the importance of leaving the 1855 classification free from official revision and attests to its continuing value today: the uniqueness conferred upon the classed growths by so long a consecration imposes a duty upon their proprietors to keep alive these very special properties and to continue making wines that are worthy of their reputations.

The 1855 classification is often referred to as a "historical monument," but this does not do it justice. A monument is essentially dead, more important in the past that it commemorates than the present in which it continues to exist. The 1855 classification is very much a vital part of the current Bordeaux wine world in bearing testimony to the high level of quality of which its vineyards are capable. For the proprietors of the growths whose names appear on its lists, the classification presents a perpetual challenge to create the finest wines possible, regardless of the conditions that have made the vintage what it is. If attaining this end means eliminating a significant part of its production, either by removing superfluous bunches of grapes in years of overabundance (a practice known as "green harvesting," since the grapes are removed from the vine while they are still immature to allow the plant to concentrate its energies on improving quality in the bunches that remain), or by making a more severe selection of wine from among the numerous vats that were produced (despite each one having incurred the same great expense whether selected for the *grand vin* or declassified for use as a second wine), these choices entail reductions in potential profits that the proprietor must assume. These decisions, and all the others that go into the making of a great wine, involve sacrifices that can render a classed growth less profitable, hectare for hectare, than a cru bourgeois. Nonetheless, the sacrifices are made because it is the responsibility imposed upon classed-growth proprietors resulting from the status conferred upon their properties by the 1855 classification (and, less altruistically, by the market that would inexorably bring its influence to bear in the form of lower prices for a wine that failed to live up to its expectations as a cru classé). In turn, the quality achieved by the classed growths sets the standards by which the reputation of a vintage is established, and properties that do not figure in the 1855 classification are drawn up in its wake, driven to produce the finest wines of which they are able.

This, at least, is how things should work. In reality, a classed growth may produce wines that are below the level of quality represented by its presence in the classification, or fail to keep up with the advances made by the other properties with which it shares its rank; in reality, properties at the cru bourgeois level or below may produce wines that are disappointing because they are not bound by the same constraints that drive the classed growths since the spotlight of popular expectation shines less brightly upon them. Any number of reasons can be advanced for why, despite the assurances of quality that the 1855 classification is supposed to provide, disappointing wines continue to be made among classed and nonclassed properties alike—and always will be. However, official changes to the 1855 classification will not produce remedies to this; an official update will not make classed growths more conscientious, or non-classed growths more motivated than they already are. It is the nature of ownership of a classed growth to consistently strive to produce the finest wines possible—the numerous antecedents to the 1855 classification show that almost invariably changes in a property's ranking resulted in promotion not demotion; furthermore, the present-day emergence of a corps of wine writers who are both diverse in their tastes and highly opinionated virtually ensures that a property's failure to meet the standards expected of it will result in consequences that are immediate and severe.

Nonetheless, it is practically inevitable that someday there will be an official revision of the 1855 classification, if for no other reason than the pure and simple fact that it can be done. There is no law against it, and—theoretically, at least—it is in the process of being revised right now: when Mouton-Rothschild finally succeeded in ascending to the upper tier of the Bordeaux hierarchy, the promotion was achieved within the framework of a global change in the classification, class by class. In 1973, the program began with the first growths, and their number grew from four to five; the stage was then set for the next part of the process, a reclassification of the seconds. The technical mechanism is all in place, the only thing needed is the agreement of each of the fourteen second growths to set the process in motion; after the seconds are reclassified, it is the third growths' turn to reach unanimous agreement to begin a reevaluation of their class, then the fourths, and finally the fifths. At least in theory. It is commonly believed that this will never come to pass, that the process will stay frozen with the second growths forever because there is no compelling interest in their changing the classification. Well, "forever" is a very long time, and a lot of things can happen before "never" arrives . . . .

Until the day when an official revision occurs, however, unofficial classifications will continue to make their inevitable, periodic appearances. When attempting to develop a new ranking of Bordeaux's wines with the hopes of attaining the authority of the brokers' list, it is important to remember this: practically none of the previous classifications, including that drawn up in 1855, actually attempted to create a ranking or assign a degree of quality to Bordeaux's wines. Rather, they were all merely more or less accurate recordings of the state of the market at the time they were made. (The 1846 classification by Charles Cocks is perhaps the most notable exception.) By contrast, modern reassessments of the 1855 classification, such as Alexis Lichine's admirable attempt in 1959 and all the other reclassifications of varying authority since, are based on a conscious decision to establish a hierarchy according to criteria of quality particular to the person or group behind the effort. Fundamentally different in intent from the work undertaken by the Bordeaux brokers in 1855, these classifications are necessarily less objective, and therefore more open to objection, dooming them to only a transient authority at best, regardless of how sound or well considered they may be.

Still, unofficial reevaluations of the relative qualities of Bordeaux's wines will—and should—continue to be made. They allow connoisseurs, amateurs, and novice wine drinkers the opportunity to express their opinions on the success or failure of winemakers' efforts. These reevaluations can be interesting, and occasionally useful, in revealing tendencies that would eventually, inevitably, be reflected in the market price of a wine. However, to use such periodic reevaluations to create an "official updating" of the 1855 classification would invariably erode the reference that, for good or bad, has made the properties on the list readily identifiable standards of quality in the Gironde and throughout the greater world of wine beyond Bordeaux.

Appendix I

THE BORDEAUX CLASSIFICATIONS BEFORE AND AFTER 1855

The classification of Bordeaux's producers was a well-established fact of life for the wine trade throughout the first half of the nineteenth century. In spite of this, most literature dealing with the classification usually cites about only a half-dozen examples prior to 1855 (Jefferson, Franck, Paguierre, and Jullien are the most commonly mentioned sources), which tends to give the impression that such rankings were the result of special, periodic undertakings rather than fairly common descriptions of the evolving Bordeaux wine market. As the following tables show, well over two-dozen classifications can be found that predate the brokers' list of 1855, and this is by no means an exhaustive collection—other classifications not included here undoubtedly exist. Nonetheless, the sampling offered by this appendix is sufficiently large to demonstrate the process of regular and systematic development of which the 1855 brokers' classification was a part.

Where specific properties are named in these classifications, an attempt has been made to give their current identities. However, several of the more extensive listings, such as those of Jullien from 1832 or Le Producteur *from 1838, contain well over 100 properties, the majority of which were not included in the 1855 brokers' classification. Many of these unclassed growths have since changed their names, have been incorporated into other properties, or have ceased to exist altogether. Unless it was possible to ascertain with certainty that a property's vineyard is not extant in any form, the space in the column titled "Name Today" has been left blank, as opposed to bearing the more categorical "No longer exists." Although great care was taken in the attribution of current names where possible, complete accuracy in the identification of the scores of non-classed producers was simply beyond the scope of this work.*

Classification 1: Bordeaux Jurade (October 27, 1647)

1. Graves and Médoc	26 écus to 100 pounds
2. Entre Deux Mers	20 to 25
3. Cotes	24 to 28
4. Palus	30 to 35
5. Libourne, Fronsadais, Guitras, and Coutras	18 to 22
6. Bourg	22 to 26
7. Blaye	18 to 24
8. St Macaire and its jurisdiction	24 to 30
9. Langon, Beaumes, Sauternes	28 to 35
10. Barsac, Preignac, Pujol, and Fargesse (Fargues)	28 écus to 100 pounds
11. Cerons & Podensac	24 to 30 écus
12. Castres and Portets	20 to 25
13. St Emilion	22 to 26
14. Castillon	20 to 22
15. Riom (Rions) and Cadillac	24 to 28
16. St Croix du Mont	24 to 30
17. Benanget (Benauge)	18 to 20

Classification 2: Bordeaux Intendant (Early 1740s)

State of parishes from which come the [wines of the] Bordeaux Seneschalsy and of their different [prices].

1st Growths ("Crus")	*Price*	*2nd Growths ("Crus")*	*Price*	*3rd Growths ("Crus")*	*Price*
		GRAVES WINES			
Pessac where the growths of Pontac are	15–1800#	Talance Loignan	3–400#	Poudensac Virelade Portets Castres Arbanats Bautiran Martillac Aiguemortes Ayran Cadaujac Canejan Eysmer	150#
Other growths from the same parish	8–1200	Grandignan Caudeyran	2–300		
Merignac	6–800	Begle	200		
		MÉDOC WINES			
Pauillac Margaux	15–1800#	Soussan Labarde	600#		
St Mambert Cerntenan St Seurin de Cadourne St Julien	8–1200	Egassac	4–500		
		Arsac Arsins	400		
		Listrac Moulis St Laurens St Estèphe Lepian Macau Ludon Taillan	3–400		
		PALUS WINES			
Queyrier	3–400#	The second growths all sell from 150# to 200#			
Monferrand Lassoüir Ambez	2–300				
		WHITE WINES			
Barsac Preignac Langon Ste Croix du Mont Sauternes Céron Bommes Pujols Blanquefort	300#	Twenty Parishes whose wines sell from 120 to 150# and 36 Parishes whose wines are converted into eaux de vie *Note:* These are the wines called Entre-Deux Mers			
Gradignan	250–300				
Podensac	150–200				

Classification 3: Anonymous (1745)

Price of Wines in Good Years, from 1745 & After.

	Price	Name Today
Margaux & Cantenac		
1st Growth		
the Château	1500 to 1800^{fr} the Tun	Margaux
2nd Growths		
Rauzan aîné	From 1000 to 1300^{fr}	Rausan-Ségla
Rauzan officier		Rauzan-Gassies
Madame Gassié		Rauzan-Gassies
Durfort		Durfort-Vivens
Lascombe		Lascombes
Candalle		d'Issan
Dessenard		
Gorce		Brane-Cantenac
3rd Growths		
Mercier Dubignon	From 600 to 1000^{fr}	no longer exists
Malescot Roborel		Malescot-Saint-Exupéry
Darche Becker		Marquis d'Alesme-Becker
Joyeun		
Bretonneau Loyac		Became part of Malescot-Saint-Exupéry
Lacolonie		Became part of Malescot-Saint-Exupéry
Massant Séguineur		
Bernard		
Prieur Durand		Prieuré-Lichine
Ledoux Monbrun		Montbrun
Ducasse		
Degasq Palmer		Palmer
4th Growths		
Mercadié Weltner	from 400 to 600^{fr}	Labegorce
Latour Dumon		
Barbos, Palmer		Palmer
Carne		
Dangludet		Angludet
Roux Binet		
Arnbody		
Desmirail		Desmirail
Benoit		
Labarde		
1st Growth		
Giscoux	400 to 600	Giscours
2nd Growth		
Dubosq	300 to 400	Siran
3rd Growths		
Drouillard	200 to 300^{fr}	
Saget		
Galibert		
Desplat		
Luguins		
Renac		
Bellegarde		Became part of Siran

Macau		
1st Growth Villeneuve Cambon	300fr the Tun	Cantemerle Cambon la Pelouse
Malescot* Lalanne Laronde, Dugravieu Lassux Guitard Roquette†	150 to 250fr	
Saint Julien		
1st Growth Leoville	800 to 1000fr	Léoville-Las-Cases/Léoville-Poyferré/ Léoville-Barton
2nd Growths Gruau frères Bergeron Ducru Brassier Comte	400 to 600fr	Gruaud-Larose Ducru-Beaucaillou Beychevelle
3rd Growths Pontet Delag Delage Daux Clauzange } St Pierre Tenac } Duluc	300 to 400	Langoa-Barton Talbot Saint-Pierre Branaire-Ducru
Saint Lambert‡		
Lafitte Branne Mouton the others following	1500 to 1800 400 to 600 200 to 300	Lafite-Rothschild Mouton-Rothschild
Saint Estèphe		
Calon Segur	800 to 1000	Calon Ségur
2nd Growths Tronquoy Joffret Père, Tarteyron Lacoste Phélan Feuillants Meyney Daste Lafon Basterot Segur	300 to 500fr	Tronquoy-Lalande de Pez Phélan-Ségur Meyney Lafon-Rochet
3rd Growths Mercier Coudoc Lagrave Meuriot Superville Borny Ducasse Moulinie Lafon Caseau Capdeville Laborie	200 to 300fr	Capbern-Gasqueton Fonpetite (second label of Phélan-Ségur)
St Seurin and Cadvurne		
Bardis Charmail Adema Labat The other growths from	300 to 500fr 300 to 350	

GRAVES		
Pessac		
1st Growth Haut-Brion	from 15 to 1800 the tun 1600	Haut-Brion
2nd Growth Missionnaires Savignau Madame Sabourin Giac Blansac Chollet Guilleragne & a	from 12 to 1300 f the tun 8 to 1200 f the tun 5 to 800 f the tun 6 to 700 f the tun	La Mission-Haut-Brion
Merignac		
1st Growth Bourran	5 to 800 f	
2nd Growths Chollet, Imbert, Labranche Lemoine aîné Id. jeune Clarck L'abbe Pellet	5 to 650 f 6 to 700 f	
Cauderan		
1st Growth Roulleau, Jurat, Monsejour	5 to 600 f	
2nd Growth Rauesec Ve Claris	3 to 350 f 3 to 350 f	
Communal wines	2 to 225	
Taillan		
Full ordinary wines Blanquefort	2 to 350 f 2 to 350 f	
Gradignan		
Small wines of clean taste	2 to 300 f	
Loignan		
Wines medium and sweet Gueyries, Monferant and Palus	3 to 400 f 2 to 350 f	
WHITE WINES		
Preignac, Barsac, Baummes Sauterne, St Pes Langon	2 to 300 f	

Note: A version of this classification appears in Franck, 2nd edition (1849), pages 241–243; here, the prices quoted are the same numbers, but in pounds, not francs.

*This property is not in Franck.

†Two properties follow in the Franck reprint: Guilhem and Bastares

‡In Franck this part of this list appears as follows:

Saint Lambert	
Latour	1500 to 1800 pnd.
Pichon-Longueville	400 to 500 pnd.
Pauillac	
Laffitte	1500 to 1800 pnd.
Branne-Mouton	400 to 600 pnd.
The others	200 to 300 pnd.

Classification 4: Dupré de St. Maur, 1776

First known classification of the wines of Guienne, executed in 1776 according to the prices they had then, [drawn up] on the order of Mr. Dupré de St. Maur, Intendant at this epoch—March 5, 1842.

MÉDOC PARISHES ALONG THE RIVER		
Blanquefort		
Morian	280–300	
Dulamon		
Dillon		Dillon
Dutasta		
Cholet		
Aquart		
Policar		
Dupaty	260–280	
Magnol		Magnol
Pennet		
Martignac		
Ve Marian		
Lartigau		
Robrig		
Dumas		
Riballes		
Paysans		
Ludon		
La Lagune	500–550	La Lagune
Le Moine		
[here follow another 19 properties whose names appear in columns headed "1811" and "1823" and thus, presumably, are not part of a 1776 classification]		
Macau		
Cambon	300–350	Cambon la Pelouse
Villeneuve		Cantemerle
Abiet		
Dufour		Gironville
Lespiau		
Lassure		
Bieni		
Malescot	270–290	
Lalanne		
Guitard		
Guillem		
Guillautin		
Larrieu		
Roborel & Climens		
Felonneau	200–250	
Labarde		
de Peyraud	600–650	
Pary de Bellegarde	400–425	Became part of Siran
Lynch	350–380	Dauzac
Duboscq	320–350	Siran
Faget	350–380	
Bourgade	320–350	
Risleau	300–320	
Abiet	300–320	
Deyrem	280–300	
Abiet	280–300	

Cantenac		
Gorse	850–900	Brane-Cantenac
Kirwan	750–800	Kirwan
aux Candalles		d'Issan
Pouget	600–625	Pouget
Mar^{q} de Therme		Marquis de Therme
Boyd		Boyd-Cantenac
Desmirail		Desmirail
aux Chanoines de Vertheuil		Prieuré-Lichine
Melle Lynch		Pontac-Lynch
De Gascq		Became part of Palmer
Caussade		Martinens
Changeur		Cantenac Brown
Le Roy		
Roux		Became part of Palmer
Abiet		Became part of Palmer
Margaux		
au Comte de Fumel	1200–1500	Margaux
Rauzan	1000	Rausan-Ségla/Rauzan-Gassies
Montbrisson	900	Durfort-Vivens
Lascombes	750	Lascombes
Mercier Dubignon	600–625	No longer exists
Dunogués		Became part of Malescot-Saint-Exupéry
De Loyac		Became part of Malescot-Saint-Exupéry
La Colonie		Became part of Malescot-Saint-Exupéry
d'Alesme		Marquis d'Alesme-Becker
Presid^{t} Berthomau	This is a mistake. This property is located in Soussans.	
Seguineau		Marsac-Séguineau
Bernard		
Boneaud		
Cazeau		Became part of Palmer
Lapeyruche		Marquis de Terme
Copmartin		Became part of Durfort-Vivens and Ferrière
Capsec		
Segonar		
Lavierre		
Anglade		
Prévaut Lacroix		
Descourt		Became part of Malescot-Saint-Exupéry
Soussans		
Le Pres^{t} Berthomau	350–400	Paveil de Luze
Segondat	320–325	
Mercier Belair		Bel Air-Marquis d'Aligre
Mercadie-Weltener		Labegorce
L'abbé Gorce		Labegorce
Presid^{t} Barbot		Labegorce-Zédé
Deyrem Juge		Haut-Breton-Larigaudière
Deyrem Secrétaire	260–270	Deyrem-Valentin
Plassan Seguinau		Marsac-Séguineau
Richet		
Toujague		
Loustat		
Ve Deyrem	210–230	
Deyrem procureur		
Loustat		
Candeau		
Briolle		
Toujague		

Arsins		
Garat	270–300	
Dubedat	240–270	Arnauld
Arnaud		Arnauld
Larcheveque	200–210	d'Arcins
Ch^{ers} de Malte		
Lamarque		
Bergeron	240–270	
Pignegny		Lamarque
Le château Bracier		
Blanchard		
Eyraud Lafon		
Van der Kunt		
Cussac		
Bergeron	300–350	Lamothe-Bergeron
Bermones		Bermones
Camarsac	270–300	
Ponicaud		
Jeanty		
Ste Geme		
Lachenay	400	Lachesnaye
Lanessan	350	Lanessan
Dumaine	220–240	
St Julien		
Léoville	1000	Léoville-Las-Cases/Léoville-Poyferré/ Léoville Barton
Gruau	600	Gruaud-Larose
Branes Arbouet	600	Lagrange
Pontet Langlois	500	Langoa Barton
Bergeron	500	Ducru-Beaucaillou
Duluc	500	Branaire-Ducru
Beychevelle		Beychevelle
St Pierre	400	Saint-Pierre
Duboscq		
Merian		
Buhé	270–300	
Cadillon		
St Lambert		
Latour	1200–1300	Latour
Pichon Longueville	650–750	Pichon-Longueville (Baron and Comtesse de Lalande)
Malescot	280–300	
Degout	300–320	
Lamestrie		
Desse		
Ferchau	220–230	

Pauliac		
Lafite	1200–1300	Lafite-Rothschild
Mouton	800	Mouton-Rothschild
Pontet Canet	500–550	Pontet-Canet
Casteja		
Lynch		Lynch-Bages
Dinac	370–400	Grand-Puy-Lacoste
Ducasse		Grand-Puy-Ducasse
Darmaillac		Mouton-d'Armailhac
Mandavy		Duhart-Milon-Rothschild
Dame St Martin	270–300	
Martin Notaire		
Croizet		Croizet-Bages
Ducler		
Mondeguerre		
Martin de Bas	250–270	
Ve Petit		
Ve Croizet		
St Estèphe		
Calon	500–600	Calon-Ségur
Mercier Terrefort	350–380	
Morin		Morin
Fumel		de Pez
Tronquoi		Tronquoy-Lalande
Bastirat	300–320	
Les Feuilans		Phélan-Ségur
Lafon Rochet		Lafon-Rochet
Ponicaud		
Destournel		Cos-d'Estournel
Arbouet		
Cazeaux		
Les frères Lagrave		
Superville		Capbern-Gasqueton
Mercier Dubourg		
L'abbé Forton		
Dumoulin Masperé		
Ve Meric	240–250	
Les frères Fatin		
Lussac		
Superville cadet		
Pasteureau		
Delle Commare		
Gaston, Cos		
Malter		
Lafon		
St Seurin & Cadourne		
Ademar	400	
Ve Tutelle	230–240	
Culleller ainé		
Brannes	270–280	Pointoise-Cabarrus
Lamothe		
Ducasse		
de Saujean		
Chevalier		

St Seurin & Cadourne (cont.)		
Lemonnier	240–280	
Cadusseau		
Roudey		
Verthamon		Coufrean
Bonnet Degrange		
Basterot, Amédée		
Ferussac		
BAS MÉDOC ALONG THE RIVER		
St Christoly		
de Saignant	210–220	
Comoden		
Lussac		
Delmau		
Begadan		
Les 3 de^{lles} Daux	200–220	
Civrac		
Fred^{c} Daujeand	180–200	
Brassan		
Rosa	120–125	
INLAND IN BAS MÉDOC		
Verteuilh		
Constant	230–260	
[The names of nine proprietors that follow are illegible]		
MÉDOC PARISHES INLAND FROM THOSE ALONG THE RIVER		
Taillan		
Le Presid^{t} Lavie	280–300	Taillan
Les nombreuse Thomson		
Ve Brasser		
Marat		
Gelin		
Curisol		
Muler	260–270	
Duronsset		
Guy		
L'abbé Gros		
Le Pian		
Dalem	300–320	
Baour		Sénéjac
Lamoreux	270–280	
Basterot		
Dalheol		
Laporte		

Arsac		
Chau de Ségur	350–400	d'Arsac
Guyon Letertre		du Terte
Chauvin	300–325	Became part of Desmirail
Copmartin		Monbrison
Monpontet	200–300	
Avensan		
Chau Citran	360–380	Citran
Moulis-Pujaux		
Budos	300–330	
Gressier		Gressier Grand Poujeaux/Chasse-Spleen
Duplessy	225–240	Duplessis-Fabre/Duplessis-Hauchecorne
Biston		Biston-Brillette
Listrac		
Mauvezin	350–400	
Momane	270–280	
Hostain		Fourcas-Hosten
Jansaud	240–250	
Roullet		
Duranteau		
Clarck		Clarke
Desseraud		
Pech Labarthe		
St Laurent		
Lutkins Carnet	350–380	La Tour-Carnet
Perganson	330–350	Larose-Trintaudon
Molinie	280–300	
Hostain		
Bichon		
Ve Bichon	210–220	
Marain		
Ve Gravere		
Ve Duroy		
Popp	330–350	Camensac
Deverle		
St Sauveur		
Varré	270	Peyrabon
Lesage Martineau	240	
Baumon	200	
de Warré		
Anglade		
Cissac		
Baron Dubreuil	290–300	du Breuil
Lariveaux		Lariveaux Vicontesse de Carheil
Abiet		Became part of Cissac
Deschyler		
Damas	210–220	
Courejolles		
Le Brieux		

Verteuil		
de Camiran	320–330	
Charmois	300–320	
de Roly		
Granda		
Héritiers Constant	230–260	
Lassalle		
Labbaye		
Bernard		
Ve Lacoste		
Depaty	180–195	
Anore		
Roux		
Jeanmarie		
Dezes		
BAS MÉDOC INLAND FROM THE RIVER		
St Germain		
Verthamon	250–300	
Castéra	200–220	Castéra
Potensac		
Daux	220–230	
Henri Daux		
Brana La Cardoune		
Blagnan		
Taffard	200–210	Blaignan
Vermengoly		
de Romfort		Ramafort
Lesparre		
Basterot	200–210	
St Paul		
Dumare		
Daux Laberrede		
Lamothe		
Les Cordeliers		
Monteigne		
St Tertory or Trélody		
Pres^t Basterot	210–220	
Vendrié	180–190	
Daux		
Bontems		
Causan		
Pinaud		
Busch or Besch		
Moutardié	160–170	
Le Prieur		
GRAVES DE BORDEAUX		
Villenave d'Ornon		
Première qualité	240–250	
Deuxième	200–210	
Paysans	135–150	
St Brix—but only the white wines	330–350	

Gradignan & Léognan		
Carbonnieux aux Bénédictins white wines, Boucherau	about 800	
First-quality red wines	250–220	
Seconds	200–220	
Peasants	150–155	
Palus dites Queyries		
The ones of the first quality that are indispensable for arranging the lesser Médocs & sell for	350–370	
Palus de Montferrand		
Which sell just after the Queyries for the same use	270–300	
Ambès		
Fit for drinking	200–215	
La Souïs	220–230	
Latrène & Guinsac	180–200	
The other palus of Blaye, Bourg and lesser côtes, drunk in Brittany and are worth	150–160	

Classification No. 5: Classification According to Document Used by William Eden (1786)

		Property	1855 Position	Name Today
1	1.1	Château Margaux	First	Margaux
2	1.2	Lafitte	First	Lafite-Rothschild
3	1.3	Latour	First	Latour
4	1.4	Pontac haut-brion	First	Haut-Brion
5	2/3.1	Rausan	Second	Rausan-Ségla/Rauzan-Gassies
6	2/3.2	Leoville	Second	Léoville-Las-Cases/Léoville-Poyferré/Léoville-Barton
7	2/3.3	Roulier		
8	2/3.4	Arbouet	Third	Lagrange
9	2/3.5	Château d'Issan	Third	d'Issan
10	2/3.6	Bergeron	Second	Ducru-Beaucaillou
11	2/3.7	Collingwood	Third	Kirwan
12	2/3.8	Brassier	Fourth	Beychevelle
13	2/3.9	Boyd	Third	Boyd-Cantenac
14	2/3.10	Pontet	Third	Langoa-Barton
15	2/3.11	Gorse	Second	Brane-Cantenac
16	2/3.12	Carnet	Fourth	La Tour-Carnet
17	2/3.13	Mercier	Third	Dubignon (no longer exists)
18	2/3.14	Dulucq	Fourth	Branaire-Ducru
19	2/3.15	Mallescot	Third	Malescot-Saint-Exupéry
20	2/3.16	Canet	Fifth	Pontet-Canet
21	2/3.17	Dutermes	Fourth	Marquis de Terme
22	2/3.18	Mouton	Second	Mouton-Rothschild
23	2/3.19	Bretonneau	Third as part of	Malescot-Saint-Exupéry
24	2/3.20	Pichon Longueville	Second	Pichon-Longueville (Baron and Comtesse de Lalande)
25	2/3.21	Desmirail	Third	Desmirail
26	2/3.22	Lynch		Lynch-Bages or Lynch-Moussas or Dauzac or Pontac-Lynch
27	2/3.23	Gescours	Third	Giscours
28	2/3.24	Decasse	Fifth	Grand-Puy-Ducasse
29	2/3.25	Lavaud		
30	2/3.26	Geoffret		

31	2/3.27	Duford	Second	Durfort-Vivens
32	2/3.28	Darte		
33	2/3.29	Lascombe	Second	Lascombes
34	2/3.30	Pez	Not classed	de Pez
35	2/3.31	Callon	Third	Calon-Ségur
36	2/3.32	Tronquoy	Not classed	Tronquoy-Lalande
37	2/3.33	La Colonie	Third as part of	Malescot-Saint-Exupéry
38	2/3.34	Segur	Fifth	du Tertre
39	2/3.35	Dalem	Third	Marquis d'Alesme-Becker
40	2/3.36	Labat		
41	2/3.37	Adhemar		

No. 6: Classification According to Notes Compiled by Thomas Jefferson (1787)

		Property	1855 Position	Name Today
1	1.1	Château Margaux	First	Margaux
2	1.2	La Tour de Ségur	First	Latour
3	1.3	Haut-Brion	First	Haut-Brion
4	1.4	Château de la Fite	First	Lafite-Rothschild
5	2.1	Rozan	Second	Rausan-Ségla
6	2.2	Dabbadie or Lionville	Second	Léoville-Las-Cases/Léoville-Poyferré/Léoville-Barton
7	2.3	La Rose	Second	Gruaud-Larose
8	2.4	Quirouen	Third	Kirwan
9	2.5	Durfort	Second	Durfort-Vivens
10	3.1	Calons	Third	Calon-Ségur
11	3.2	Mouton	Second	Mouton-Rothschild
12	3.3	Gassie	Second	Rauzan-Gassies
13	3.4	Arboète	Third	Lagrange
14	3.5	Pontette	Third	Langoa-Barton
15	3.6	de Terme	Fourth	Marquis de Terme
16	3.7	Candale	Third	d'Issan

No. 7: Classification of Cantenac and Margaux According to Communal Taxation (1795)

	Property	Price	1855 Position	Name Today
1	Les sieurs Dargicourt	900 livres	First	Margaux
2	Montbrizon	700 livres	Second	Durfort-Vivens
3	Rauzan	700 livres	Second	Rausan-Ségla/Rauzan-Gassies
4	Gorce	600 livres	Second	Brane-Cantenac
5	Kirwan	600 livres	Third	Kirwan
6	Boyd	550 livres	Third	Boyd-Cantenac
7	Candale	500 livres	Third	d'Issan
8	Castelnau	500 livres	Third	d'Issan
9	Dubignon at Margaux	500 livres	Third	No longer exists
10	La Veuve Poujet	500 livres	Fourth	Pouget
11	Guyonnet	450 livres		
12	Desmirail	400 livres	Third	Desmirail
13	Massac	400 livres	Third	Cantenac Brown
14	Marcou	400 livres	Not classed	Martinens
15	Cazeau	400 livres	Third as part of	Palmer
16	Thibault	380 livres		
17	Abiet	380 livres	Third as part of	Palmer
18	Roux	380 livres	Third as part of	Palmer
19	Degasq	380 livres	Third as part of	Palmer
20	Goudal	380 livres		
21	Jouneau, curé	380 livres	Fourth	Prieuré-Lichine
22	La Veuve Lynch	350 livres	Not classed	Pontac-Lynch
23	Vincent	350 livres	Not classed	Vincent
24	Dubignon	350 livres	Fourth	No longer exists
25	Legras	350 livres	Not classed	Angludet
26	Dalesme	350 livres	Third	Marquis-d'Alesme-Becker
27	Ferrière	350 livres	Third	Ferrière
28	Berliquet	320 livres		
29	Segonnes	300 livres		
30	Laroze	300 livres		
31	Poveret	270 livres		
32	Jadouin	270 livres	Not classed	Montbrun

Here follows the paysan category, divided into three classes:
5 proprietors at 270 livres
28 proprietors at 255 livres
The rest of the commune's proprietors at 240 livres

No. 8: Classification According to William Johnston (1813)

		Property	Price	1855 Position	Name Today
1	1.1	Château Margaux	1500–1600	First	Margaux
2	1.2	Latour		First	Latour
3	1.3	Lafitte		First	Lafite-Rothschild
4	2^1.1	Rausan	1200–1300	Second	Rausan-Ségla
5	2^1.2	Durfort		Second	Durfort-Vivens
6	2^1.3	Chevalier Gassies		Second	Rauzan-Gassies
7	2^1.4	Lascombes		Second	Lascombes
8	2^1.5	Dabbadie Léoville		Second	Léoville-Poyferré
9	2.1	Gorce	1100–1200	Second	Brane-Cantenac
10	2.2	Larose		Second	Gruaud-Larose
11	2.3	Branne Mouton		Second	Mouton-Rothschild
12	3^1.1	Château d'Issan	900–1000	Third	d'Issan
13	3^1.2	Kirwan		Third	Kirwan
14	3^1.3	Pichon Longueville		Second	Pichon-Longueville (Baron and Comtesse de Lalande)
15	3^1.4	Bergeron Ducru		Second	Ducru-Beaucaillou
16	3.1	L'abbé Malescot	800–900	Third	Malescot-Saint-Exupéry
17	3.2	Cabarrus		Third	Lagrange
18	3.3	Calon		Third	Calon-Ségur
19	4.1	Château de Beychevelle	700–800	Fourth	Beychevelle
20	4.2	Pontet		Third	Langoa-Barton
21	4.3	St Pierre		Fourth	Saint-Pierre
22	4.4	Duluc		Fourth	Branaire-Ducru
23	4.5	Pouget		Fourth	Pouget
24	4.6	Boyd		Third	Boyd-Cantenac
25	4.7	Dalesme		Third	Marquis-d'Alesme-Becker
26	4.8	Loyac		Third as part of	Malescot-Saint-Exupéry
27	4.9	Dubignon		Third	No longer exists
28	4.10	Lacolonie		Third as part of	Malescot-Saint-Exupéry
29	4.11	Giscours		Third	Giscours
30	Bon Bourg.1	St Guirons	600–700	Fifth	Grand-Puy-Lacoste
31	Bon Bourg.2	Pontet Canet		Fifth	Pontet-Canet
32	Bon Bourg.3	Ducasse		Fifth	Grand-Puy-Ducasse

33	Bon Bourg.1	Tronquoy	500–600	Not classed	Tronquoy-Lalande
34	Bon Bourg.2	Le Boscq		Not classed	Le Boscq
35	Bon Bourg.3	Morin		Not classed	Morin
36	Bon Bourg.4	Destournel		Second	Cos-d'Estournel
37	Bon Bourg.5	Lafon Rochet		Fourth	Lafon-Rochet
38	Bon Bourg.1	Faget	400–500		
39	Bon Bourg.2	Lynch			Lynch-Bages or Lynch-Moussas or Dauzac or Pontac-Lynch
40	Bon Bourg.3	Bourgade			
41	Bon Bourg.4	Larrieu			
42	Bon Bourg.5	La Lagune		Third	La Lagune
43	Bon Bourg.6	Lemoine			
44	Bon Bourg.7	Darche			
45	Bon Bourg.8	Bacalan			
46	Bon Bourg.9	Pommiers			
47	Bon Cru.1	Adhémar	350–400		
48	Bon Cru.2	Saujean			
49	Bon Cru.3	Brochon			
50	Bon Cru.4	Charmail			
Average Bourgeois from Pauillac and Saint-Estephe 400–500					
Bourgeois from parishes of average quality such as Macau, Soussans, Arcins, Lamarque, Cussac, Listrac, Moulis, Cissac, Verteuil, Saint-Laurent, Saint-Christoly and others 300–350 or 400					
Paysans from Saint-Estèphe and Pauillac 250–300					
Paysans supérieurs from Saint-Julien, Cantenac and Margaux 300–350 or 400					

No. 9: Classification According to Notes Compiled by Guillaume Lawton (1815)

		Property	Commune	Comments	Price	In 1855	Name Today
1	1.1	Château Margaux	Margaux	"The first growth [in Margaux] is the Château. The other first growths of the Médoc are Latour at St Mambert & Lafitte at Pauillac."	1000–2400	First	Margaux
2	1.2	Latour	St Mambert		1000–2400	First	Latour
3	1.3	Lafitte	Pauillac		1000–2400	First	Lafite-Rothschild
4	1.4	Hautbrion	Pessac	"It is in Pessac that is found Château Hautbrion, whose wines have been classed the equal of those of the three first growths of the Médoc."	1000–2400	First	Haut-Brion
5	2.1	Branne-Mouton	Pauillac	"The second growth Branne Mouton has a nature ordinarily more fine and delicate than Rauzan in Margaux and Lascaze at Léoville. Depending on the year, sometimes we put one, sometimes another in first place. . . ."	650–2100	Second	Mouton-Rothschild
6	2.2	Rauzan	Margaux		650–2100	Second	Rausan-Ségla
7	2.3	Leoville-Lascaze	St Julien		650–2100	Second	Léoville-Las-Cases
8	2.4	Chevalier	Margaux	"The second growths are Rauzan, Chevalier, Lascombe, Montalambert & Montbrison."	650–2100	Second	Rauzan-Gassies
9	2.5	Lascombe	Margaux		650–2100	Second	Lascombes
10	2.6	Montalambert	Margaux		650–2100	Second	Durfort-Vivens
11	2.7	Montbrison	Margaux		650–2100	Second	Durfort-Vivens
12	2.8	Larose	St Julien	"I have designated Larose, Chevalier, & Monbalon because their inferiority **[sic]** is frequent—they contest primacy every year. . . ."	650–2100	Second	Gruaud-Larose
13	2.9	Leoville-Chevalier	St Julien		650–2100	Second	Léoville-Barton
14	2.10	Leoville-Monbalon	St Julien		650–2100	Second	Léoville-Barton
15	2.11	Leoville-D'Abadie	St Julien	"The second growths are those of Leoville, subdivided into Lascaze, d'Abadie, Chevalier & Monbalon; and that of Laroze."	650–2100	Second	Léoville-Poyferré
16	3.1	Pichon de Longueville	St Mambert	"Pichon de Longueville I have classed as a 3rd growth of the Médoc."	750–1700	Second	Pichon-Longueville (Baron and Comtesse de Lalande)

17	3.2	Gorce	Cantenac	"I would put Pichon in first place, followed by Gorce, Kirwan, then Brown & Castelnau . . . next Candale . . . & finally Calon. . . ."	550–1750	Second	Brane-Cantenac
18	3.3	Kirwan	Cantenac		550–1750	Third	Kirwan
19	3.4	Brown	Cantenac		550–1750	Third	Boyd-Cantenac/ Cantenac Brown
20	3.5	Castelnau	Cantenac		550–1750	Third as	d'Issan
21	3.6	Candale	Cantenac		550–1750	Third as	d'Issan
22	3.7	Calon	St Estèphe	"St Estèphe contains the growth of Calon which is classed as a third growth of the Médoc...."	550–1700	Third	Calon-Ségur
23	4.1	Roborel	Margaux	"Margaux contains no third growths; but the following five, namely: Roborel, Loyac, Lacolonie, Dalème & Ferrière form a class superior to all the rest [in the commune]. Of these five, Roborel generally has a marked preference."	500–1500	Third	Malescot-Saint-Exupéry
24	4.2	Dalème	Margaux	"Dalème & Lacolonie almost always go first [ahead of Ferrière]."	500–1500	Third	Marquis d'Alesme Becker
25	4.3	Lacolonie	Margaux		500–1500	Third as part of	Malescot-Saint-Exupéry
26	4.4	Loyac	Margaux		500–1500	Third as part of	Malescot-Saint-Exupéry
27	4.5	Ferrière	Margaux	"Ferrière always comes after these three [Dalème, Lacolonie, & Loyac] . . ."	500–1500	Third	Ferrière
28	4.6	Cabarrus	St Julien	"I think that [Cabarrus] is not at all out of place grouped with Dalème, Lacolonie, & Loyac."	500–1500	Third	Lagrange
29	4.7	Ducru	St Julien	"Cabarrus & Ducru of St Julien are very good wines, nonetheless in all justice the five 3rd growths from Cantenac mentioned above have the edge over them."	500–1500	Second	Ducru-Beaucaillou
30	4.8	Carnet	St Laurent	"We place [Carnet] between the class of Cabarrus & Ducru & that of Pontet [and] St Pierre . . . not being equal to Dalème [and] Lacolonie..."	550–1500	Fourth	La Tour-Carnet

31	4.9	Pontet père	St Julien	"After these two growths [Cabarrus and Ducru], we single out the four following, namely: Pontet père, Conte Beichevelle, St Pierre and Duluc. . . . Among them Pontet indubitably goes first. . . . This class is worth more than that of Canet."	450–1200	Third	Langoa-Barton
32	4.10	Conte Beichevelle	St Julien		450–1200	Fourth	Beychevelle
33	4.11	St Pierre	St Julien		450–1200	Fourth	Saint-Pierre
34	4.12	Duluc	St Julien		450–1200	Fourth	Branaire-Ducru
35	4.13	Canet	Pauillac	"After these two great growths [Lafite & Branne-Mouton] the following four distinguished Pauillacs form a class apart, namely: Canet, St Guiron, Ducasse & Lynch. . . . Not equal to Pontet père, St Pierre [and others of this class] at St Julien, but preferable to Daux and others like it. Naturally, these wines are below Poujet, Massac [in Cantenac] but preferable, I believe, to Tronquoy St Estèphe which is placed as their equal."	450–1100	Fifth	Pontet-Canet
36	4.14	St Guiron	Pauillac		450–1100	Fifth	Grand-Puy-Lacoste
37	4.15	Ducasse	Pauillac		450–1100	Fifth	Grand-Puy-Ducasse
38	4.16	Lynch	Pauillac		450–1100	Fifth	Lynch-Bages or Lynch-Moussas
39	4.17	Giscours, or Jacob	Labarde	"This last [Giscours] is classed 4th growth of Médoc....I prefer the 4th growth of Giscours to that of La Lagune at Ludon. . . . If we put Cabarrus St Julien a 4th growth, I believe that there is a great difference in its favor (Cabarrus). For me, Pontet père has a more satisfying finish. . . ."	400–1200 "and even more"	Third	Giscours
40	4.18	Pouget	Cantenac	"Pouget, Desmirail, Massac...are good wines of a completely different nature from those of Pontet St Julien, but which go in this class."	400–1100	Fourth	Pouget
41	4.19	Desmirail	Cantenac		400–1100	Third	Desmirail
42	4.20	Solberg	Cantenac		400–1100	Fourth	Marquis de Terme
43	4.21	Massac	Cantenac	"After the 3rd growths [of Cantenac] those of Pouget, Desmirail, Solberg & Massac distinguish themselves."	400–1100	Third	Cantenac Brown
44	4.22	Tronquoy	St Estèphe	"Tronquoy, Morin & Delavau have been ranked the equals of Canet and this class at Pauillac. . . . I do not hesitate to give preference to the general class of Canet. . . . These wines should be superior to Daux and similar ones from St Julien."	400–1000	Not classed	Tronquoy-Lalande
45	4.23	Morin	St Estèphe		400–1000	Not classed	Morin
46	4.24	Delaveau or le Bosc	St Estèphe		400–1000	Not classed	Le Boscq
47	4.25	Cos	St Estèphe	"As for Cos . . . we believe we're doing it justice in putting it below Pontet père in St Julien."	400–1100	Second	Cos-d'Estournel

48	4.26	Daux	St Julien	"... next [after Pontet, Beychevelle, St Pierre & Duluc] is generally classed Daux, Dubourg, Deyrem, Poppe & Coutanceau. . . . But I think that St Guiron, Canet . . . are better wines."	400–1100	Fourth	Talbot
49	4.27	Dubourg	St Julien		400–1100		
50	4.28	Deyrem	St Julien		400–1100		
51	4.29	Poppe	St Julien		400–1100	Fifth	Camensac
52	4.30	Coutanceau	St Julien		400–1100	Fifth	Belgrave
53	4.31	Seguineau or Dumas Laroque or La Lagune	Ludon	"The growth named Seguineau or Dumas Laroque or La Lagune is the best in the parish. . . . [But] Dauze even seems preferable to me."	400–1000	Third	La Lagune
54	4.32	du Tertre	Arsac	"As it is, du Tertre is no less preferable than those of Leroy, Legras & similar growths at Cantenac & generally sells at a higher price. . . . Comparing du Tertre & La Lagune . . . when both succeed I believe La Lagune to make the preferable wine."	400–1000	Fifth	du Tertre
55	5.1	Leroy	Cantenac	"After the 3rd classed growths [of Cantenac] those of Pouget, Desmirail, Solberg & Massac distinguish themselves—then come Leroy, Montbrun, Legras. . . .Leroy in general maintaining a slight superiority."	350–900		
56	5.2	Montbrun	Cantenac		350–900	Not classed	Montbrun
57	5.3	Legras	Cantenac		350–900	Not classed	Angludet
58	5.4	Durand	Cantenac	"Leroy, Durand, Montbrun, Legras . . . are not, in my opinion, equal to Daux."	350–900	Fourth	Prieuré-Lichine
59	5.5	D'Armailhac	Pauillac	"D'Armailhac, Vve Croiset–Bage, Malecot, Bedou, & Mandavid au Bourg offer wines that always have something better than [the basic wines of the commune]. . . . This class of wines is superior to the communal wines of Margaux, and consequently of those from St Estèphe, but in this latter parish Tronquoy, Morin & Delavau are greater wines."	350–800	Fifth	Mouton-d'Armailhac
60	5.6	Vve Croiset at Bage	Pauillac		350–800	Fifth	Croizet-Bages
61	5.7	Malecot	Pauillac		350–800		
62	5.8	Bedou	Pauillac		350–800	Fifth	Batailley/ Haut-Batailley
63	5.9	Mandavid au Bourg	Pauillac		350–800	Fourth	Duhart-Milon-Rothschild
64	5.10	Bernard	Margaux	"The rest of Margaux's wines are just about equal in quality, nevertheless putting Bernard and the Dubignons at the head."	350–700		
65	5.11	Dubignon	Margaux		350–700	Third	No longer exists

Communal growths: 300–700 francs

Peasant wines: 600 francs

No. 10A: Classification According to Jullien (1816)

		Property	1855 Position	Name Today
1	1.1	Clos Lafitte	First	Lafite-Rothschild
2	1.2	Clos Latour	First	Latour
3	1.3	Château Margaux	First	Margaux
4	1.4	Château Haut-Brion	First	Haut-Brion
5	2.1	Rauzan	Second	Rausan-Ségla/Rauzan-Gassies
6	2.2	Gorce	Second	Brane-Cantenac
7	2.3	Clos Léoville	Second	Léoville-Las-Cases/Léoville-Poyferré/Léoville-Barton
8	2.4	Clos Larose	Second	Gruaud-Larose
9	2.5	Clos Brane-Mouton	Second	Mouton-Rothschild
10	2.6	Clos Pichon-Longueville	Second	Pichon-Longueville (Baron and Comtesse de Lalande)
11	2.7	Calon	Third	Calon-Ségur
For the third class, Jullien does not name specific properties, but instead lists parishes and communes: Pauillac, Margaux, Cantenac, Saint-Julien, Saint Estèphe (Médoc); Pessac, Talence, Mérignac (Graves); Côte de Canon (Fronsadais)				
For the fourth class, specific properties are not named; instead, Jullien comments on the production of two regions: Haut-Médoc, Saint-Emilion				
For the fifth class, again, Jullien only comments on one overall region: Bas-Médoc				

No. 10B: Classification According to Jullien, Second Edition (1822)

		Property	1855 Position	Name Today
1	1.1	Clos Lafitte	First	Lafite-Rothschild
2	1.2	Clos Latour	First	Latour
3	1.3	Château Margaux	First	Margaux
4	1.4	Château Haut-Brion	First	Haut-Brion
5	2.1	Rozan	Second	Rausan-Ségla/Rauzan-Gassies
6	2.2	Gorce	Second	Brane-Cantenac
7	2.3	Clos Léoville	Second	Léoville-Las-Cases/Léoville-Poyferré/Léoville-Barton
8	2.4	Clos Larose	Second	Gruaud-Larose
9	2.5	Clos Brane-Mouton	Second	Mouton-Rothschild
10	2.6	Clos Pichon-Longueville	Second	Pichon-Longueville (Baron and Comtesse de Lalande)
11	2.7	Calon	Third	Calon-Ségur

For the third class, Jullien does not name specific properties, but instead lists parishes and communes:
Pauillac, Margaux, Pessac, Saint-Julien-de Régnac, Saint Estèphe
Castelnau-de-Médoc, Cantenac, Talence, Mérignac, Canon

For the fourth class, specific properties are not named; instead, Jullien comments on the production of several communes and regions:
Labarde, Cussac (Castelnau-de-Médoc); Blanquefort, Macau (Bordeaux);
Saint-Surin-de-Cadourne (Lesparre); Saint-Emilion; Laujac (Bégadan/Bas-Médoc);
Queyries, Montferrant, Bassens (Carbon-Blanc)

For the fifth class, again, Jullien only comments on communes and regions:
Ambes, Lassouys, Bouliac, Bacalan, Gilet, Saint-Gervais, Asque, Latresne, Quinsac, Saint-Loubez, Valenton, Macau, Boutiran, Izou, Cadaujac, Baurech (Palus); Bourg, le Tourne, Langoiran (Cadillac); Saint-Macaire (la Réole); île Saint-Georges, petit Palus sur la Dordogne, de Libourne, d'Arveyres, de Blaye, de Fronsac

Classification 10C: Classification According to Jullien, Third Edition (1832)

		Property	Commune	1855 Position	Name Today
			RED WINES		
			First Class		
1	$1^{1}.1$	Château Margaux	Margaux	First	Margaux
2	$1^{1}.2$	Château Lafitte	Pauillac	First	Lafite-Rothschild
3	$1^{1}.3$	Château Latour	Pauillac	First	Latour
4	$1^{1}.4$	Château Haut-Brion	Pessac	First	Haut-Brion
5	$1^{2}.1$	Rauzan	Margaux	Second	Rausan-Ségla/Rauzan-Gassies
6	$1^{2}.2$	Durfort	Margaux	Second	Durfort-Vivens
7	$1^{2}.3$	Lascombe	Margaux	Second	Lascombes
8	$1^{2}.4$	Léoville or Labadie	Saint-Julien	Second	Léoville-Las-Cases/Léoville-Poyferré/Léoville-Barton
9	$1^{2}.5$	Larose-Balguerie	Saint-Julien	Second	Gruaud-Larose
10	$1^{2}.6$	Gorse	Cantenac	Second	Brane-Cantenac
11	$1^{2}.7$	Branne-Mouton	Cantenac	Second	Mouton-Rothschild
12	$1^{2}.8$	Pichon-Longueville	Pauillac	Second	Pichon-Longueville (Baron and Comtesse de Lalande)
			Second Class		
13	2.1	Kirwan	Cantenac	Third	Kirwan
14	2.2	Château d'Issan	Cantenac	Third	d'Issan
15	2.3	Pouget-Ganet	Cantenac	Fourth	Became part of Kirwan
16	2.4	Desmirail	Cantenac	Third	Desmirail
17	2.5	de Therme	Cantenac	Fourth	Marquis de Terme
18	2.6	Malescot	Margaux	Third	Malescot-Saint-Exupéry
19	2.7	Loyac	Margaux	Third as part of	Malescot-Saint-Exupéry
20	2.8	d'Alème-Bekker	Margaux	Third	Marquis d'Alesme-Becker
21	2.9	Dubuisson-Talbot	Margaux	Third	No longer exists
22	2.10	Ferrière	Margaux	Third	Ferrière
23	2.11	Lacolonie	Margaux	Third as part of	Malescot-Saint-Exupéry
24	2.12	Bergeron-Ducru	Saint-Julien	Second	Ducru-Beaucaillou
25	2.13	Cabarrus	Saint-Julien	Third	Lagrange
26	2.14	Saint-Pierre	Saint-Julien	Fourth	Saint-Pierre
27	2.15	Duluc	Saint-Julien	Fourth	Branaire-Ducru
28	2.16	Dauch	Saint-Julien	Fourth	Talbot
29	2.17	Château de Béchevelle	Saint-Julien	Fourth	Beychevelle
30	2.18	Carnet	Saint-Laurent	Fourth	La Tour-Carnet
31	2.19	Popp	Saint-Laurent	Fifth	Camensac
32	2.20	Coutanceau	Saint-Laurent	Fifth	Belgrave
33	2.21	Lachenay	Sainte-Gemme	Not classed	Lachesnaye
34	2.22	Delbos	Sainte-Gemme	Not classed	Lanessan

35	2.23	Legalant	Sainte-Gemme		
36	2.24	Pontet-Canet	Pauillac	Fifth	Pontet-Canet
37	2.25	Saint-Guirons-Granpuy	Pauillac	Fifth	Grand-Puy-Lacoste
38	2.26	Ducasse	Pauillac	Fifth	Grand-Puy-Ducasse
39	2.27	Linch	Pauillac	Fifth	Lynch-Bages or Lynch-Moussas
40	2.28	Croizet	Pauillac	Fifth	Croizet-Bages
41	2.29	Calon	Saint-Estèphe	Third	Calon-Ségur
42	2.30	Destournel-Cos	Saint-Estèphe	Second	Cos-d'Estournel
43	2.31	Tronquoy	Saint-Estèphe	Not classed	Tronquoy-Lalande
44	2.32	Merman	Saint-Estèphe	Not classed	Le Crock
45	2.33	Meney	Saint-Estèphe	Not classed	Meyney
46	2.34	Lafond-Rochet	Saint-Estèphe	Fourth	Lafon-Rochet
47	2.35	Labory	Saint-Estèphe	Fifth	Cos-Labory
48	2.36	Morin	Saint-Estèphe	Not classed	Morin
49	2.37	Lebosc-Delaveau	Saint-Estèphe	Not classed	Le Boscq
50	2.38	La Mission	Pessac	Not classed	La Mission-Haut-Brion
51	2.39	Pape-Clément	Pessac	Not classed	Pape-Clément
52	2.40	Canteaut	Pessac		
53	2.41	Cholet	Pessac		
			Third Class		
54	3.1	Château de la Lagune	Ludon	Third	La Lagune
55	3.2	Baricou	Ludon		
56	3.3	Pommier	Ludon	Not classed	d'Agassac
57	3.4	Giscours	Labarde	Third	Giscours
58	3.5	Linch	Labarde	Fifth	Dauzac
59	3.6	Bourgade	Labarde		
60	3.7	Cantemerle	Macau	Fifth	Cantemerle
61	3.8	Trois-Moulins	Macau		
62	3.9	Lachennay	Cussac	Not classed	Lachesnaye
63	3.10	Bergeron-Lamotte	Cussac	Not classed	Lamothe-Bergeron
64	3.11	Château la Marque	Lamarque	Not classed	Lamarque
65	3.12	Girard	Lamarque		
66	3.13	Bergeron	Lamarque	Not classed	Cap de Haut
67	3.14	Pigneguy	Lamarque		
68	3.15	Von-Hemert	Lamarque		
69	3.16	Lapareil	Soussans		
70	3.17	Deyrem	Soussans	Not classed	Deyrem-Valentin
71	3.18	Guichon	Soussans	Not classed	Bel Air-Marquis d'Aligre
72	3.19	Sécondat	Soussans		
73	3.20	Gressier	Arcins		
74	3.21	Couput-Pressac	Arcins		

75	3.22	Subercaseaux	Arcins		
76	3.23	Duperiez	Arcins		
77	3.24	Château-de-Budos	Arcins		
78	3.25	Leblanc	Listrac		
79	3.26	Monraisin	Listrac		
80	3.27	Petit-Labarthe	Listrac		
81	3.28	Von-Hemert	Listrac	Not classed	Fonréaud
82	3.29	Hosten	Listrac	Not classed	Fourcas-Hosten
83	3.30	Damas	Listrac		
84	3.31	Lestage	Listrac	Not classed	Lestage
85	3.32	Château Poujeaux	Poujeaux	Not classed	Poujeaux
86	3.33	Gressier	Poujeaux	Not classed	Gressier Grand Poujeaux
87	3.34	Liversan	Saint-Saveur	Not classed	Liversan
88	3.35	Cavaignac	Saint-Saveur		
89	3.36	Ducasse	Saint-Saveur	Not classed	Hourtin Ducasse
90	3.37	Linch	Saint-Saveur	Not classed	Haut-Madrac
91	3.38	Badimore	Saint-Saveur	Not classed	Peyrabon
92	3.39	Danglade	Saint-Saveur		
93	3.40	Josset-de-Pommiers	Cissac	Not classed	Breuil
94	3.41	de Paroy	Cissac	Not classed	Larrivaux Vicomtesse de Carheil
95	3.42	Dumousseau	Cissac		
96	3.43	Martiny	Cissac	Not classed	Cissac
97	3.44	Bonfils	Verteuil		
98	3.45	de Camiran	Verteuil		
99	3.46	Plaignard	Verteuil		
100	3.47	Lafon	Verteuil		
101	3.48	Skiner	Verteuil		
102	3.49	Luetkens	Saint-Laurent	Fourth	La Tour-Carnet
103	3.50	de la Rose	Saint-Laurent	Not classed	Larose-Trintaudon
104	3.51	Piek	Saint-Laurent	Not classed	Cach
105	3.52	Van-Dœhrem	Saint-Laurent		
106	3.53	Charmaille	Saint-Seurin	Not classed	Charmail
107	3.54	Bacon	Saint-Saurin		
108	3.55	Château-de-Thouars	Talence		
109	3.56	Lafitte-Haut-Talence	Talence		
110	3.57	Luchey	Merignac		
111	3.58	Pique-Cailleau	Merignac	Not classed	Picque Caillou
112	3.59	de Canolle	Léognan		
113	3.60	Literic	Léognan		
114	3.61	Mareilhac	Léognan	Not classed	La Louvière

		Fourth Class			
115	4.1	Sylvestre	Queyries		
116	4.2	Floguergue	Queyries		
117	4.3	Tropeau	Queyries		
118	4.4	Deboucan	Queyries		
119	4.5	Lachèze	Queyries		
120	4.6	Archebold	Queyries		
121	4.7	Brant	Queyries		
122	4.8	Royé	Queyries		
123	4.9	Gondable	Queyries		
124	4.10	Château-du-bel-Air	Saint-Emilion	Not classed	Belair
125	4.11	Canolle	Saint-Emilion		
126	4.12	Berliquet	Saint-Emilion	Not classed	Berliquet
127	4.13	Meynot	Saint-Emilion		
128	4.14	Boyer	Canon		
129	4.15	Saint-Julien	Canon		
130	4.16	Bary-Bertomieux	Fronsac	Not classed	du Gazin
131	4.17	Gombaut	Fronsac		
132	4.18	Lavalade	Fronsac		
133	4.19	Duperrier-Château-Livron	Saint-Germain	Not classed	Livran
134	4.20	Château-de-Langeac	Valeyrac		
135	4.21	Blagnan	Civrac		
136	4.22	Saint-Bonnet	Saint-Cristoly		
		Fifth Class			
137	5^1.1	Château Rousset	Samonac		
138	5^1.2	Tajac	Bâyon		
139	5^1.3	Château-de-Fallax	Bâyon		
140	5^1.4	Château-du-Bosquet	Bourg	Not classed	du Bosquet
141	5^1.5	de Calvimon	Bâyon		
142	5^1.6	Dupouil	Bâyon		
143	5^1.7	Lagrave	Saint-Seurin-de-Bourg		
144	5^1.8	de Bellote	Saint-Seurin-de-Bourg	Not classed	Laurensanne
145	5^1.9	Sou	Libarde		
146	5^1.10	Berniard	Libarde		
147	5^1.11	Gellibert	Camillac		
148	5^1.12	Peychaud	Camillac		
149	5^1.13	Castagnes	Tauriac		
150	5^1.14	Peychaud	Bourg		
151	5^1.15	Charlus	Bourg	Not classed	Croûte-Charlus
152	5^2.1	Saugeron	Blaye		
153	5^2.2	Charron	Blaye		

154	$5^{2}.3$	Cap-de-Haut	Blaye		
155	$5^{2}.4$	Labarre-Présaugeron	Blaye		
156	$5^{2}.5$	Lamare	Blaye		
157	$5^{2}.6$	la Baleingue	Blaye		
158	$5^{2}.7$	Gontaud	Blaye		
159	$5^{2}.8$	Jeanty	Blaye		
160	$5^{2}.9$	Pardaillan	Cars	Not classed	Pardaillan
161	$5^{2}.10$	Dupouy	Cars		
162	$5^{2}.11$	Binaud	Cars		
163	$5^{2}.12$	Armand-de-Fours	Cars		
164	$5^{2}.13$	Lelièvre	Sainte-Luce		
165	$5^{2}.14$	Raymond	Sainte-Luce		
166	$5^{2}.15$	Debaissan	Saint-Paul		
167	$5^{2}.16$	Binaud	Saint-Paul		
			WHITE WINES		
			First Class		
168	$1^{1}.1$	Coutet	Barsac	First	Coutet
169	$1^{1}.2$	Clément	Barsac	First	Climens
170	$1^{1}.3$	Doisy	Barsac	Second	Doisy-Daëne/Doisy-Dubroca/ Doisy-Védrines
171	$1^{1}.4$	Caillau	Barsac	First	Caillou
172	$1^{1}.5$	Pernaud	Barsac	Not classed	Pernaud
173	$1^{1}.6$	Mirat	Barsac	Second	de Myrat
174	$1^{1}.7$	Dubose	Barsac		
175	$1^{1}.8$	Château de Suiduirault	Preignac	First	Suduiraut
176	$1^{1}.9$	Pugnau	Preignac	Not classed	Arche Pugneau
177	$1^{1}.10$	Yquem	Sauternes	First-superior	Yquem
178	$1^{1}.11$	Guiraut	Sauternes	First	Guiraud
179	$1^{1}.12$	Deyne	Bommes	First	Rabaud-Promis
180	$1^{1}.13$	Lafaurie	Bommes	First	Lafaurie-Peyraguey
181	$1^{1}.14$	Dert	Bommes		
182	$1^{1}.15$	Saint-Brie	Villenave		
183	$1^{1}.16$	Carbonnieux	Villenave	Not classed	Carbonnieux
184	$1^{1}.17$	Pontac-Dulamon	Blanquefort		
185	$1^{2}.1$	Focke	Barsac		
186	$1^{2}.2$	Labarde	Barsac		
187	$1^{2}.3$	Dudon	Barsac	Not classed	Dudon
188	$1^{2}.4$	Hertzog	Barsac		
			Second Class		
189	2.1	Capdeville	Barsac	Second	Broustet/Nairac
190	2.2	Neirac	Barsac	Second	Nairac

191	2.3	Cave	Barsac		
192	2.4	Tauzin	Barsac		
193	2.5	Lacoste	Barsac		
194	2.6	Barastre	Barsac		
195	2.7	Alexandre de Saluces	Preignac	Second	de Malle
196	2.8	Montarlier	Preignac		
197	2.9	Guilhon aîné	Preignac		
198	2.10	Mareilhac	Preignac		
199	2.11	Filhol	Sauternes	Second	Filhot
200	2.12	Baptiste	Sauternes	Second	Lamothe/Lamothe-Guignard
201	2.13	Focke	Bommes	First	La Tour-Blanche
202	2.14	Lacoste	Bommes		Became part of Rabaud-Promis
203	2.15	Emérignon	Bommes	Not classed	Mauras
204	2.16	Mareilhac	Villenave		
205	2.17	Tarteyron	Villenave		
206	2.18	Ouvray	Villenave		
207	2.19	de Brias	Blanquefort		
208	2.20	Hesse	Blanquefort		
209	2.21	Cousard	Cérons		
210	2.22	de Calvimont	Cérons		
211	2.23	Olivier	Cérons		
212	2.24	Salvanet	Cérons		
213	2.25	Deloustat	Cérons		
214	2.26	Champion	Cérons		
215	2.27	Bearnes	Podensac		
216	2.28	Ferbos	Podensac		
217	2.29	Jon	Podensac		
218	2.30	Tonnens	Podensac		
219	2.31	Darlaud	Podensac		
220	2.32	G. Cazades	Podensac		
221	2.33	Château	Langon		
222	2.34	Dupuy	Langon		
223	2.35	Testard	Toulenne		
224	2.36	Rivière	Toulenne		
225	2.37	de Rayne	Saint-Pey-Langon		
226	2.38	de Baritault	Saint-Pey-Langon		
227	2.39	Colas	Saint-Pey-Langon		
228	2.40	Saint-Blancart	Saint-Pey-Langon		
229	2.41	Lacoste	Fargues		
230	2.42	Lacombe	Pujols		
231	2.43	Cherché	Pujols	Not classed	Cherchy-Desqueyroux

232	2.44	Duperrier	Sainte-Croix-du-Mont
233	2.45	Mazet	Sainte-Croix-du-Mont
234	2.46	Gensonné	Sainte-Croix-du-Mont
235	2.47	Marbotin	Sainte-Croix-du-Mont
236	2.48	Rolland	Sainte-Croix-du-Mont
237	2.49	Castels	Sainte-Croix-du-Mont
238	2.50	Turman	Sainte-Croix-du-Mont
239	2.51	Chaumette	Sainte-Croix-du-Mont
240	2.52	Marcellus	Loupiac
241	2.53	de la Chassagne	Loupiac
242	2.54	Bidot	Loupiac
243	2.55	Courrege	Loupiac
			Third Class
244	3.1	Dufort	Virelade
245	3.2	Linch	Virelade
246	3.3	Ducasse	Arbants
247	3.4	Daguzan	Arbants
248	3.5	Belso	Langoiran
249	3.6	Palanque	Langoiran
250	3.7	Pollet	Langoiran
251	3.8	Campan	Cadillac
252	3.9	Alard	Cadillac
253	3.10	Dalon	Monprinblanc
			Fourth Class
254	4.1	Larieux	Baurech
255	4.2	Duperieux	Baurech
256	4.3	Roujole	Tabanac
257	4.4	Leblanc	Tabanac
258	4.5	Bertrand	Tourne
259	4.6	Maude	Tourne
260	4.7	Lescours	Tourne
261	4.8	Maudis	Paillet
262	4.9	Vassan	Paillet
263	4.10	Bourbon	Paillet
264	4.11	Faux	Haux
265	4.12	Parouty	Begney
266	4.13	Simon	Begney
			FIFTH CLASS
			[No properties cited by name, only communes.]

Note: Jullien divided his classification into *classes,* within which structure he then arrainged the Bordeaux *crus;* this accounts for the divisions that appear within several of the classes.

Properties appear grouped by commune, thus no conclusion should be drawn as to their relative quality based on their placement compared to others within that class.

No. 11: Classification According to Table in Henderson (1824)

		Property	1855 Position	Name Today
1	1.1	Lafitte	First	Lafite-Rothschild
2	1.2	Chateau Margaux	First	Margaux
3	1.3	Latour	First	Latour
4	1.4	Haut-Brion*	First	Haut-Brion
5	2.1	Rauzan	Second	Rausan-Ségla/Rauzan-Gassies
6	2.2	Durfort	Second	Durfort-Vivens
7	2.3	Lascombe	Second	Lascombes
8	2.4	Léoville	Second	Léoville-Las-Cases/Léoville-Poyferré/Léoville-Barton
9	2.5	Larose	Second	Gruaud-Larose
10	2.6	Branne-Mouton	Second	Mouton-Rothschild
11	3.1	Gorce	Second	Brane-Cantenac
12	3.2	Castelnau	Third	d'Issan
13	3.3	Malescot	Third	Malescot-Saint-Exupéry
14	3.4	Cabarrus	Third	Lagrange
15	3.5	Pichon Longueville	Second	Pichon-Longueville (Baron and Comtesse de Lalande)
16	4.1	Gircors	Third	Giscours
17	4.2	Poujet	Fourth	Pouget
18	4.3	Laujac [Loyac]	Third as part of	Malescot-Saint-Exupéry
19	4.4	Pontet	Third	Langoa-Barton
20	4.5	Becheville	Fourth	Beychevelle
21	4.6	St. Pierre	Fourth	Saint-Pierre
22	5.1	Pontet Cannet	Fifth	Pontet-Canet
23	5.2	St. Guiron	Fifth	Grand-Puy-Lacoste

* Although Haut-Brion does not figure in the table given in the appendix, which is specifically for Médoc wines, in the text this property is discussed as being on a par with the three Médoc first growths.

Note: Although the table does not mention any white wines by name, simply grouping the regions of "Sauterne, Barsac, Preignac", the text mentions "Clos-Yquem" as furnishing the best wine, and in Barsac, "Clos-Coustet, belonging to Mad. De Saluce, gives the first of what are called the High Barsac wines."

No. 12A: Classification According to Franck (1824)

		Property	Commune	1855 Position	Name Today
1	1.1	Château-Margaux	Margaux	First	Margaux
2	1.2	Château-Lafitte	Pauillac	First	Lafite-Rothschild
3	1.3	Château-Latour	Saint-Lambert	First	Latour
4	2.1	Brane-Mouton	Pauillac	Second	Mouton-Rothschild
5	2.2	Rauzan	Margaux	Second	Rausan-Ségla/Rauzan-Gassies
6	2.3	Léoville	Saint-Julien	Second	Léoville-Las-Cases/Léoville-Poyferré/ Léoville-Barton
7	2.4	Gruau, or la Rose	Idem.	Second	Gruaud-Larose
8	3.1	Gorce	Cantenac	Second	Brane-Cantenac
9	3.2	Pichon-Longueville	Saint-Lambert	Second	Pichon-Longueville (Baron and Comtesse de Lalande)
10	3.3	Cos-Destournel	Saint-Estèphe	Second	Cos-d'Estournel
11	3.4	Calon	Idem.	Third	Calon-Ségur
12	3.5	Lascombe	Margaux	Second	Lascombes
13	3.6	Bergeron	Saint-Julien	Second	Ducru-Beaucaillou
14	3.7	Branes-Arbouet	Idem.	Third	Lagrange
15	3.8	Pontet-Langlois	Idem.	Third	Langoa-Barton
16	4.1	Kirwan	Cantenac	Third	Kirwan
17	4.2	Le Château de Candale	Idem.	Third	d'Issan
18	4.3	Giscours	la Barde	Third	Giscours
19	4.4	Saint-Pierre	Saint-Julien	Fourth	Saint-Pierre
20	4.5	Duluc	Saint-Julien	Fourth	Branaire-Ducru
21	4.6	Durefort	Margaux	Second	Durfort-Vivens
22	4.7	Malescot	Idem.	Third	Malescot-Saint-Exupéry
23	4.8	Loyac	Idem.	Third as part of	Malescot-Saint-Exupéry
24	4.9	Mandavit-Milon	Pauillac	Fourth	Duhart-Milon-Rothschild
25	4.10	Canet	Idem.	Fourth	Pontet-Canet
26	4.11	Dinac, Saint-Guirons	Idem.	Fifth	Grand-Puy-Lacoste
27	4.12	Lacolonie	Margaux	Third as part of	Malescot-Saint-Exupéry
28	4.13	Ferrière	Idem.	Third	Ferrière
29	4.14	Tronquoy	Saint-Estèphe	Not classed	Tronquoy-Lalande
30	4.15	Ducasse	Pauillac	Fifth	Grand-Puy-Ducasse
31	4.16	Poujet	Cantenac	Fourth	Pouget
32	4.17	Determe	Idem.	Fourth	de Terme
33	4.18	Boyd	Idem.	Third	Boyd-Cantenac

No. 12B: Classification According to Franck, Second Edition (1845)

		Property	Commune	1855 Position	Name Today
1	1.1	Château-Margaux	Margaux	First	Margaux
2	1.2	Château Lafite	Pauillac	First	Lafite-Rothschild
3	1.3	Latour	*Id.*	First	Latour
4	1.4	Haut-Brion, Larrieu	Pessac	First	Haut-Brion
5	2.1	Brannes (de) formerly Gorsse	Cantenac	Second	Brane-Cantenac
6	2.2	Cos, Destournel	Saint-Estèphe	Second	Cos-d'Estournel
7	2.3	Durefort, de Vivens	Margaux	Second	Durfort-Vivens
8	2.4	Gruaud, formerly Larose, divided among MM. Sarget and the heirs of Balguerie	Saint-Julien	Second	Gruaud-Larose
9	2.5	Lascombes (L.A. Hue; formerly Fabre)	Margaux	Second	Lascombes
10	2.6	Léoville, divided in three Le m[is] de Lascases Bon Poyferé de Cerès Barton	 Saint-Julien *Id.* *Id.*	Second	Léoville-Las-Cases/ Léoville-Poyferré/ Léoville-Barton
11	2.7	Mouton Thuret	Pauillac	Second	Mouton-Rothschild
12	2.8	Pichon de Longueville	Saint-Lambert	Second	Pichon-Longueville (Baron and Comtesse de Lalande)
13	2.9	Rauzan (div. between MM. Castelpert and Gassies, Puilboreau)	Margaux	Second	Rausan-Ségla/Rauzan-Gassies
14	3.1	Desmirail	Margaux	Third	Desmirail
15	3.2	Dubignon (Philippe), formerly Talbot	*Id.*	Third	No longer exists
16	3.3	Ducru at Maucaillou (formerly Bergeron)	Saint-Julien	Second	Ducru-Beaucaillou
17	3.4	Duluc, Château d'Issan	Cantenac	Third	d'Issan
18	3.5	Fruitier, formerly Brown	*Id.*	Third	Boyd-Cantenac/Cantenac Brown
19	3.6	Ganet (vicomte de Lasalle)	Cantenac	Fourth	Became part of Kirwan
20	3.7	Giscours, Promis	Labarde	Third	Giscours
21	3.8	Kirwan (de Scryver junior)	Cantenac	Third	Kirwan
22	3.9	Lagrange, Duchâtel (formerly Brown)	Saint-Julien	Third	Lagrange
23	3.10	Langoa, Barton (formerly Pontet)	*Id.*	Third	Langoa-Barton
24	3.11	Lanoire	Margaux	Not classed	La Gurgue
25	3.12	Montrose, Dumoulin	Saint-Estèphe	Second	Montrose
26	3.13	Pougets, de Chavaille	Cantenac	Fourth	Pouget
27	3.14	St-Exupéry (comtesse de) formerly Malescot	Margaux	Third	Malescot-Saint-Exupéry

28	4.1	Aux (M. le marquis d')	Saint-Julien (at Talbot, growth of Delage)	Fourth	Talbot
29	4.2	Bekker	Margaux	Third	Marquis d'Alesme-Becker
30	4.3	Beychevelle (Guestier junior)	Saint-Julien	Fourth	Beychevelle
31	4.4	Calon Lestapis (was Ségur)	Saint-Estèphe	Third	Calon-Ségur
32	4.5	Carnet (heirs of Luetkens)	Saint-Laurent	Fourth	La Tour-Carnet
33	4.6	Castéja (formerly veuve Duhard, Milon)	Pauillac	Fourth	Duhart-Milon-Rothschild
34	4.7	Dubignon (Marcellin)	Margaux	Third	No longer exists
35	4.8	Duluc aîné	Saint-Julien	Fourth	Branaire-Ducru
36	4.9	Ferrière	Margaux	Third	Ferrière
37	4.10	Lafon Rochet, Camarsac	Saint-Estèphe	Fourth	Lafon-Rochet
38	4.11	La Lagune, Mme veuve Joffray	Ludon	Third	La Lagune
39	4.12	Lesparre-Duroc, Milon Mandavy	Pauillac	Fourth	Duhart-Milon-Rothschild
40	4.13	Mac-Daniel (formerly Solberg)	Margaux	Fourth	Marquis de Terme
41	4.14	Pagès (formerly Durand, at Prieuré)	Cantenac	Fourth	Prieuré-Lichine
42	4.15	Palmer (property of the administ[on] of the Caisse Hypothécaire)	Margaux	Third	Palmer
43	4.16	St-Pierre divided among Bontemps du Barry, Roullet and Galoupeau	Saint-Julien *Id.* *Id.*	Fourth	Saint-Pierre
44	5.1	Batalley, Guestier père	Pauillac	Fifth	Batailley/Haut-Batailley
45	5.2	Bedout (de) formerly Duboscq	Saint-Julien		
46	5.3	Bourran (de) formerly Mlle Lynch	Cantenac	Not classed	Pontac-Lynch
47	5.4	Canet Pontet	Pauillac	Fifth	Pontet-Canet
48	5.5	Cantemerle (baron de Villeneuve)	Macau	Fifth	Cantemerle
49	5.6	Chaullet (formerly Duclerq at Bages)	Pauillac	Not classed	Cordeillan-Bages
50	5.7	Constant (Vve.) at Bages	*Id.*		
51	5.8	Cos Labory	Saint-Estèphe	Fifth	Cos-Labory
52	5.9	Coutanceau Devez	Saint-Laurent	Fifth	Belgrave
53	5.10	Croizet at Bages	Pauillac	Fifth	Croizet-Bages
54	5.11	Ducasse (veuve)	*Id.*	Fifth	Grand-Puy-Ducasse
55	5.12	Grand Puy, Lacoste (formerly St-Guirons)	*Id.*	Fifth	Grand-Puy-Lacoste
56	5.13	Jurine at Bages	*Id.*	Fifth	Lynch-Bages
57	5.14	Libéral at Bages	*Id.*	Fifth	Haut-Bages-Libéral
58	5.15	Liversan d'Anglade	Saint-Sauveur	Not classed	Liversan
59	5.16	Lynch Moussas	Pauillac	Fifth	Lynch-Moussas

60	5.17	Mission (la) near Haut-Brion (Chiapella)	Pessac	Not classed	La Mission-Haut-Brion
61	5.18	Mouton, d'Armailhacq	Pauillac	Fifth	Mouton-d'Armailhac
62	5.19	Monpelou, formerly Castéja, now divided between MM. Badimon and Constant	Pauillac	Not classed	Haut-Bages-Monpelou
63	5.20	Popp	Saint-Laurent	Fifth	Camensac
64	5.21	Seguineau Deyries	Margaux	Not classed	Marsac-Séguineau
65	BB.1	Marquis d'Aligre (Château de Bel-Air)	Soussans	Not classed	Bel Air-Marquis d'Aligre
66	BB.2	Le Boscq, Camiran aîné	Saint-Estèphe	Not classed	Le Boscq
67	BB.3	Crû de Morin, Camiran père	St-Corbian, St-Estèphe	Not classed	Morin
68	BB.4	Lanessan, Louis Delbos	Cussac	Not classed	Lanessan
69	BB.5	Merman (veuve) (au Crock)	Saint-Estèphe	Not classed	Le Crock
70	BB.6	Le Paveil Bretonneau	Soussans	Not classed	Paveil de Luze
71	BB.7	Pedesclaux	Pauillac	Fifth	Pédesclaux
72	BB.8	Tronquoy-Lalande	Saint-Estèphe	Not classed	Tronquoy-Lalande

BB—Bon Bourgeois

No. 12C: Classification According to Franck, Third Edition (1853)

		Property	Commune	1855 Position	Name Today
1	1.1	Château-Margaux	Margaux	First	Margaux
2	1.2	Château Lafite	Pauillac	First	Lafite-Rothschild
3	1.3	Latour	Idem.	First	Latour
4	1.4	Haut-Brion, Larrieu	Pessac	First	Haut-Brion
5	2.1	De Brannes, formerly Gorsse	Cantenac	Second	Brane-Cantenac
6	2.2	Cos-Destournel, today Martyns	St-Estèphe	Second	Cos-d'Estournel
7	2.3	Durefort, de Vivens	Margaux	Second	Durfort-Vivens
8	2.4	Gruaud-Laroze, divided among Mrs Bethmann, Boisgérard and the heirs of Bon Sarget	St-Julien	Second	Gruaud-Larose
9	2.5	Lascombe (L.A. Hue), formerly Fabre	Margaux	Second	Lascombes
10	2.6	Léoville, divided in three Marquis de Lascases Bon Poyféré de Cères Barton	 St-Julien Idem. Idem.	 Second	 Léoville-Las-Cases/ Léoville-Poyferré/ Léoville-Barton
11	2.7	Mouton-Thuret	Pauillac	Second	Mouton-Rothschild
12	2.8	Pichon de Longueville	St-Lambert	Second	Pichon-Longueville (Baron and Comtesse de Lalande)
13	2.9	Rauzan-Rauzan (baronne de Sigla), and Rauzan-Gassies (Chabrier)	Margaux	Second	Rausan-Ségla/Rauzan-Gassies
14	3.1	Blanchy, Chât.-d'Issan	Cantenac	Third	d'Issan
15	3.2	Desmirail	Margaux	Third	Desmirail
16	3.3	Dubignon (Philippe), formerly Talbot	Idem.	Third	No longer exists
17	3.4	Ducru, at Maucaillou, formerly Bergeron	St-Julien	Second	Ducru-Beaucaillou
18	3.5	Fruitier, formerly Brown	Cantenac	Third	Boyd-Cantenac/ Cantenac Brown
19	3.6	Ganet (vicomte de Lasalle)	Idem.	Fourth	Became part of Kirwan
20	3.7	Giscours, Pescatore	Labarde	Third	Giscours
21	3.8	Kirwan (de Scryver junior)	Cantenac	Third	Kirwan
22	3.9	Lagrange, Duchâtel, formerly Brown	St-Julien	Third	Lagrange
23	3.10	Langoa, Barton, formerly Pontet	Idem.	Third	Langoa-Barton
24	3.11	Lanoire	Margaux	Not classed	La Gurgue
25	3.12	Montrose, Dumoulin	St-Estèphe	Second	Montrose
26	3.13	Pougets, de Chavaille	Cantenac	Fourth	Pouget

27	3.14	Comtesse de St-Exupéry, formerly Malescot	Margaux	Third	Malescot-Saint-Exupéry
28	4.1	Marquis d'Aux	St-Julien, at Talbot, growth of Delage	Fourth	Talbot
29	4.2	Beychevelle (Guestier junior)	St-Julien	Fourth	Beychevelle
30	4.3	Calon-Lestapis (was Ségur)	St-Estèphe	Third	Calon-Ségur
31	4.4	Carnet (heirs of Luetkens)	St-Laurent	Fourth	La Tour-Carnet
32	4.5	Castéja, formerly veuve Duhard, Milon	Pauillac	Fourth	Duhart-Milon-Rothschild
33	4.6	Dubignon (M.)	Margaux	Third	No longer exists
34	4.7	Duluc aîné	St-Julien	Fourth	Branaire-Ducru
35	4.8	Ferrière	Margaux	Third	Ferrière
36	4.9	Lafon-Rochet, Camarsac	St-Estèphe	Fourth	Lafon-Rochet
37	4.10	La Lagune, Mme veuve Joffray	Ludon	Third	La Lagune
38	4.11	Lesparre-Duroc, Milon-Mandavy	Pauillac	Fourth	Duhart-Milon-Rothschild
39	4.12	Solberg	Margaux	Fourth	Marquis de Terme
40	4.13	Pagès, formerly Durand, at Prieuré	Cantenac	Fourth	Prieuré-Lichine
41	4.14	Palmer (property of the administ^{on} of the Caisse hypothécaire)	Idem.	Third	Palmer
42	4.15	St-Pierre divided among Bontemps du Barry, Roullet and Galoupeau	St-Julien Idem.	Fourth	Saint-Pierre
43	5.1	Batalley, Lawton	Pauillac	Fifth	Batailley/Haut-Batailley
44	5.2	De Bedout, formerly Duboscq	St-Julien		
45	5.3	Canet-Pontet	Pauillac	Fifth	Pontet-Canet
46	5.4	Cantemerle (baron de Villeneuve)	Macau	Fifth	Cantemerle
47	5.5	Chollet, formerly Duclerq, at Bages	Pauillac	Not classed	Cordeillan-Bages
48	5.6	Ve Constant, at Bages	Idem.		
49	5.7	Cos-Labory	St-Estèphe	Fifth	Cos-Labory
50	5.8	Coutanceau-Devez	St-Laurent	Fifth	Belgrave
51	5.9	Croizet, à Bages	Pauillac	Fifth	Croizet-Bages
52	5.10	Veuve Ducasse	Idem.	Fifth	Grand-Puy-Ducasse
53	5.11	Grand Puy, Lacoste, formerly St-Guirons	Idem.	Fifth	Grand-Puy-Lacoste
54	5.12	Jurine, at Bages	Idem.	Fifth	Lynch-Bages
55	5.13	Libéral, at Bages	Idem.	Fifth	Haut-Bages-Libéral
56	5.14	Liversan-d'Anglade	St-Sauveur	Not classed	Liversan
57	5.15	Lynch-Moussas	Pauillac	Fifth	Lynch-Moussas

58	5.16	Mission (la) near Haut-Brion (Chiapella)	Pessac	Not classed	La Mission-Haut-Brion
59	5.17	Mouton, Tharet*	Pauillac	Fifth	Mouton-d'Armailhac
60	5.18	Monpelou, formerly Castéja, now divided between MM. Badimon and Constant	Pauillac	Not classed	Haut-Bages-Monpelou
61	5.19	Popp	St-Laurent	Fifth	Camensac
62	5.20	Perganson, E. Lahens	Idem.	Not classed	Larose-Trintaudon
63	BB.1	Mme de Pomereu (Château de Bel-Air)	Soussans	Not classed	Bel Air-Marquis d'Aligre
64	BB.2	Minvielle (Château-Paveuil)	Idem.	Not classed	Paveil de Luze
65	BB.3	Le Boscq, Camiran aîné	St-Estèphe	Not classed	Le Boscq
66	BB.4	Crû de Morin, Camiran père	St-Corbian, St-Estèphe	Not classed	Morin
67	BB.5	Lanessan, Louis Delbos	Cussac	Not classed	Lanessan
68	BB.6	Pedesclaux	Pauillac	Fifth	Pédesclaux
69	BB.7	Tronquoy-Lalande	St-Estèphe	Not classed	Tronquoy-Lalande

* This is a confusion with Mouton Thuret, the second growth; the property "Mouton, d'Armailhacq" was classed just after La Mission in the 1845 edition of the Franck classification.

BB—Bon Bourgeois

No. 12D: Classification According to Franck, Fourth Edition (1860)

		Property	Commune	1855 Position	Name Today
1	1.1	Château-Margaux	Margaux	First	Margaux
2	1.2	Château Lafite	Pauillac	First	Lafite-Rothschild
3	1.3	Latour	Idem.	First	Latour
4	1.4	Haut-Brion, Larrieu	Pessac	First	Haut-Brion
5	2.1	De Brannes, formerly Gorsse	Cantenac	Second	Brane-Cantenac
6	2.2	Cos-Destournel, now Martyns	St-Estèphe	Second	Cos-d'Estournel
7	2.3	Durefort, de Vivens	Margaux	Second	Durfort-Vivens
8	2.4	Gruaud-Laroze, divided among Mrs Bethmann, Boisgérard, and the heirs of Bon Sarget	St-Julien	Second	Gruaud-Larose
9	2.5	Lascombe (L.A. Hue), formerly Fabre	Margaux	Second	Lascombes
10	2.6	Léoville, divided in three Marquis de Lascases Bon Poyféré de Cères Barton	 St-Julien Idem. Idem.	Second	Léoville-Las-Cases/ Léoville-Poyferré/ Léoville-Barton
11	2.7	Mouton-Thuret	Pauillac	Second	Mouton-Rothschild
12	2.8	Pichon de Longueville	St-Lambert	Second	Pichon-Longueville (Baron and Comtesse de Lalande)
13	2.9	Rauzan-Rauzan (baronne de Sigla), and Rauzan-Gassies (Chabrier)	Margaux	Second	Rausan-Ségla/Rauzan-Gassies
14	3.1	Blanchy, Chât.-d'Issan	Cantenac	Third	d'Issan
15	3.2	Desmirail	Margaux	Third	Desmirail
16	3.3	Dubignon (Philippe), formerly Talbot	Idem.	Third	No longer exists
17	3.4	Ducru, à Maucaillou, formerly Bergeron	St-Julien	Second	Ducru-Beaucaillou
18	3.5	Fruitier, formerly Brown	Cantenac	Third	Boyd-Cantenac/Cantenac Brown
19	3.6	Ganet (vicomte de Lasalle)	Idem.	Fourth	Became part of Kirwan
20	3.7	Giscours, Pescatore	Labarde	Third	Giscours
21	3.8	Kirwan (de Scryver junior)	Cantenac	Third	Kirwan
22	3.9	Lagrange, Duchâtel, formerly Brown	St-Julien	Third	Lagrange
23	3.10	Langoa, Barton, formerly Pontet	Idem.	Third	Langoa-Barton
24	3.11	Lanoire	Margaux	Not classed	La Gurgue
25	3.12	Montrose, Dumoulin	St-Estèphe	Second	Montrose

26	3.13	Pougets, de Chavaille	Cantenac	Fourth	Pouget
27	3.14	Comtesse de St-Exupéry, formerly Malescot	Margaux	Third	Malescot-Saint-Exupéry
28	4.1	Marquis d'Aux	St-Julien, at Talbot, growth of Delage	Fourth	Talbot
29	4.2	Beychevelle (Guestier junior)	St-Julien	Fourth	Beychevelle
30	4.3	Calon-Lestapis (was Ségur)	St-Estèphe	Third	Calon-Ségur
31	4.4	Carnet (heirs of Luetkens)	St-Laurent	Fourth	La Tour-Carnet
32	4.5	Castéja, formerly veuve Duhard, Milon	Pauillac	Fourth	Duhart-Milon-Rothschild
33	4.6	Dubignon (M.)	Margaux	Third	No longer exists
34	4.7	Duluc aîné	St-Julien	Fourth	Branaire-Ducru
35	4.8	Ferrière	Margaux	Third	Ferrière
36	4.9	Lafon-Rochet, Camarsac	St-Estèphe	Fourth	Lafon-Rochet
37	4.10	La Lagune, Mme veuve Joffray	Ludon	Third	La Lagune
38	4.11	Lesparre-Duroc, Milon-Mandavy	Pauillac	Fourth	Duhart-Milon-Rothschild
39	4.12	Solberg	Margaux	Fourth	Marquis de Terme
40	4.13	Pagès, formerly Durand, at Prieuré	Cantenac	Fourth	Prieuré-Lichine
41	4.14	Palmer (property of the administ^{on} of the Caisse hypothécaire)	Idem.	Third	Palmer
42	4.15	St-Pierre divided among Bontemps du Barry, Roullet and Galoupeau	St-Julien Idem.	Fourth	Saint-Pierre
43	5.1	Batalley, Lawton	Pauillac	Fifth	Batailley/Haut-Batailley
44	5.2	De Bedout, formerly Duboscq	St-Julien		
45	5.3	Canet-Pontet	Pauillac	Fifth	Pontet-Canet
46	5.4	Cantemerle (baron de Villeneuve)	Macau	Fifth	Cantemerle
47	5.5	Chollet, formerly Duclerq, at Bages	Pauillac	Not classed	Cordeillan-Bages
48	5.6	Ve Constant, at Bages	Idem.		
49	5.7	Cos-Labory	St-Estèphe	Fifth	Cos-Labory
50	5.8	Coutanceau-Devez	St-Laurent	Fifth	Belgrave
51	5.9	Croizet, at Bages	Pauillac	Fifth	Croizet-Bages
52	5.10	Veuve Ducasse	Idem.	Fifth	Grand-Puy-Ducasse
53	5.11	Grand Puy, Lacoste, formerly St-Guirons	Idem.	Fifth	Grand-Puy-Lacoste
54	5.12	Jurine, at Bages	Idem.	Fifth	Lynch-Bages
55	5.13	Libéral, at Bages	Idem.	Fifth	Haut-Bages-Libéral
56	5.14	Liversan-d'Anglade	St-Sauveur	Not classed	Liversan
57	5.15	Lynch-Moussas	Pauillac	Fifth	Lynch-Moussas

58	5.16	Mission (la) near Haut-Brion (Chiapella)	Pessac	Not classed	La Mission-Haut-Brion
59	5.17	Mouton, Tharet*	Pauillac	Fifth	Mouton-d'Armailhac
60	5.18	Monpelou, formerly Castéja, now divided between MM. Badimont and Constant	Pauillac	Not classed	Haut-Bages-Monpelou
61	5.19	Popp	St-Laurent	Fifth	Camensac
62	5.20	Perganson, E. Lahens	Idem.	Not classed	Larose-Trintaudon
63	BB.1	Mme de Pomereu (Château de Bel-Air)	Soussans	Not classed	Bel Air-Marquis d'Aligre
64	BB.2	Minvielle (Château-Paveuil)	Idem.	Not classed	Paveil de Luze
65	BB.3	Le Boscq, Camiran aîné	St-Estèphe	Not classed	Le Boscq
66	BB.4	Crû de Morin, Camiran père	St-Corbian, St-Estèphe	Not classed	Morin
67	BB.5	Lanessan, Louis Delbos	Cussac	Not classed	Lanessan
68	BB.6	Pedesclaux	Pauillac	Fifth	Pédesclaux
69	BB.7	Tronquoy-Lalande	St-Estèphe	Not classed	Tronquoy-Lalande

* This is a confusion with Mouton Thuret, the second growth; the property "Mouton, d'Armailhacq" was classed just after La Mission in the 1845 edition of the Franck classification.

BB—Bon Bourgeois

No. 13A: Classification According to Le Guide de l'Etranger—*Fillastre (1825)*

		Property	Commune	1855 Position	Name Today
1	1.1	Château-Margaux	Margaux	First	Margaux
2	1.2	Château-Lafitte	Pauillac	First	Lafite-Rothschild
3	1.3	Latour	St-Lambert	First	Latour
4	1.4	Haut-Brion	Pessac	First	Haut-Brion
5	2.1	Brane-Mouton	Pauillac	Second	Mouton-Rothschild
6	2.2	Rauzan	Margaux	Second	Rausan-Ségla/Rauzan-Gassies
7	2.3	Léovile	St-Julien	Second	Léoville-Las-Cases/Léoville-Poyferré/ Léoville-Barton
8	2.4	Gruau	St-Julien	Second	Gruaud-Larose
9	3.1	Gorse	Cantenac	Second	Brane-Cantenac
10	3.2	Pichon-Longueville	St-Lambert	Second	Pichon-Longueville (Baron and Comtesse de Lalande)
11	3.3	Cos-Destournel	St-Estèphe	Second	Cos-d'Estournel
12	3.4	Lascombes	Margaux	Second	Lascombes
13	3.5	Bergeron (Ducru)	St-Julien	Second	Ducru-Beaucaillou
14	3.6	Branes-Arbouet (Cabarrus)	St-Julien	Third	Lagrange
15	3.7	Pontet-Langlois (Bartero)	St-Julien	Third	Langoa-Barton
16	4.1	Kirwan	Cantenac	Third	Kirwan
17	4.2	Le chât. de Candale (Mad^e. de Castelnau)	Cantenac	Third	d'Issan
18	4.3	Giscours	Labarde	Third	Giscours
19	4.4	St-Pierre	St-Julien	Fourth	Saint-Pierre
20	4.5	Duluc	St-Julien	Fourth	Branaire-Ducru
21	4.6	Durefort (de Viviens)	Margaux	Second	Durfort-Vivens
22	4.7	Malescot (Dunoguès)	Margaux	Third	Malescot-Saint-Exupéry
23	4.8	Loyac	Margaux	Third as part of	Malescot-Saint-Exupéry
24	4.9	Mandavit (Milon)	Pauillac	Fourth	Duhart-Milon-Rothschild
25	4.10	Canet (Pontet)	Pauillac	Fifth	Pontet-Canet
26	4.11	Dinac, St-Guirons	Pauillac	Fifth	Grand-Puy-Ducasse
27	4.12	Lacolonie	Margaux	Third as part of	Malescot-Saint-Exupéry
28	4.13	Ferrière	Margaux	Third	Ferrière
29	4.14	Tronquoy	St-Estèphe	Not classed	Tronquoy-Lalande
30	4.15	Ducasse	Pauillac	Fifth	Grand-Puy-Ducasse
31	4.16	Poujet	Cantenac	Fourth	Pouget
32	4.17	Determe	Cantenac	Fourth	Marquis de Terme
33	4.18	Boyd (Brown)	Cantenac	Third	Boyd-Cantenac

No 13B: Classification According to Le Guide de l'Etranger— *Fillastre, Second Edition (1827)*

		Property	Commune	1855 Position	Name Today
1	1.1	Château-Margaux	Margaux	First	Margaux
2	1.2	Château-Lafitte	Pauillac	First	Lafite-Rothschild
3	1.3	Latour	St-Lambert	First	Latour
4	2.1	Brane-Mouton	Pauillac	Second	Mouton-Rothschild
5	2.2	Rauzan	Margaux	Second	Rausan-Ségla/Rauzan-Gassies
6	2.3	Lascombes	Margaux	Second	Lascombes
7	2.4	Durfort (de Viviens)	Margaux	Second	Durfort-Vivens
8	2.5	Gorse	Cantenac	Second	Brane-Cantenac
9	2.6	Léoville	St-Julien	Second	Léoville-Las-Cases/Léoville-Poyferré/Léoville-Barton
10	2.7	Gruau, or la Rose	St-Julien	Second	Gruaud-Larose
11	3.1	Pichon-Longueville	St-Lambert	Second	Pichon-Longueville (Baron and Comtesse de Lalande)
12	3.2	Cos-Destournel	St-Estèphe	Second	Cos-d'Estournel
13	3.3	Bergeron (Ducru)	St-Julien	Second	Ducru-Beaucaillou
14	3.4	Branes-Arbouet (Cabarrus)	St-Julien	Third	Lagrange
15	3.5	Pontet-Langlois (Bartero)	St-Julien	Third	Langoa-Barton
16	3.6	Kirwan	Cantenac	Third	Kirwan
17	3.7	Le château de Candale (Duluc)	Cantenac	Third	d'Issan
18	3.8	Malescot (Pierlot)	Margaux	Third	Malescot-Saint-Exupéry
19	3.9	De Loyac	Margaux	Third as part of	Malescot-Saint-Exupéry
20	3.10	M. Brown	Margaux	Third	Cantenac Brown
21	3.11	Ferrière	Margaux	Third	Ferrière
22	4.1	Giscours	Labarde	Third	Giscours
23	4.2	St-Pierre	St-Julien	Fourth	Saint-Pierre
24	4.3	Duluc	St-Julien	Fourth	Branaire-Ducru
25	4.4	Mandavit (Milon)	Pauillac	Fourth	Duhart-Milon-Rothschild
26	4.5	Canet (Pontet)	Pauillac	Fifth	Pontet-Canet
27	4.6	Dinac, St-Guirons	Pauillac	Fifth	Grand-Puy-Ducasse
28	4.7	Lacolonie	Margaux	Third as part of	Malescot-Saint-Exupéry
29	4.8	Ferrière*	Margaux	Third	Ferrière
30	4.9	Tronquoy	St-Estèphe	Not classed	Tronquoy-Lalande
31	4.10	Ducasse	Pauillac	Fifth	Grand-Puy-Ducasse
32	4.11	Poujet	Cantenac	Fourth	Pouget
33	4.12	Determe	Cantenac	Fourth	Marquis de Terme
34	4.13	Boyd (Brown)	Cantenac	Third	Boyd-Cantenac

* This property appears twice, here and as a third growth.

No. 13C: Classification According to Le Guide de l'Etranger—*Fillastre, Third Edition (1834)*

		Property	Commune	1855 Position	Name Today
1	1.1	Château-Margaux	Margaux	First	Margaux
2	1.2	Château-Lafitte	Pauillac	First	Lafite-Rothschild
3	1.3	Latour	Pauillac	First	Latour
4	1.4	Haut-Brion Beyerman	Pessac	First	Haut-Brion
5	2.1	Rauzan	Margaux	Second	Rausan-Ségla/Rauzan-Gassies
6	2.2	Mouton-Branne	Pauillac	Second	Mouton-Rothschild
7	2.3	Léoville	St-Julien	Second	Léoville-Las-Cases/Léoville-Poyferré/Léoville-Barton
8	2.4	Gruau, Larose or Fonbedeau	St-Julien	Second	Gruaud-Larose
9	2.5	Pichon de Longueville	St-Lambert	Second	Pichon-Longueville (Baron and Comtesse de Lalande)
10	2.6	Durfort de Vivens	Margaux	Second	Durfort-Vivens
11	2.7	De Gorse of M. Brannes	Margaux	Second	Brane-Cantenac
12	2.8	Lascombe of M. Loriague	Margaux	Second	Lascombes
13	2.9	Cos-d'Estournelle	St-Estèphe	Second	Cos-d'Estournel
14	3.1	Le chât. d'Issan of M. Duluc	Cantenac	Third	d'Issan
15	3.2	Pougets, of M. Ganets	Cantenac	Fourth	Became part of Kirwan
16	3.3	Pougets, of M. de Chavaille	Cantenac	Fourth	Pouget
17	3.4	Kirwan	Cantenac	Third	Kirwan
18	3.5	M. Beker	Margaux	Third	Marquis d'Alesme-Becker
19	3.6	M. Brown	Margaux	Third	Cantenac Brown
20	3.7	M. Desmirail	Margaux	Third	Desmirail
21	3.8	Malescot, M. le Comte de St-Exupéry	Margaux	Third	Malescot-Saint-Exupéry
22	3.9	The heirs of Lacolonie	Margaux	Third as part of	Malescot-Saint-Exupéry
23	3.10	Ferrière	Margaux	Third	Ferrière
24	3.11	Giscours, of M. Promis	Labarde	Third	Giscours
25	3.12	Langoa, of M. Barton	St-Julien	Third	Langoa-Barton
26	3.13	Bergeron, of the heirs Ducru	St-Julien	Second	Ducru-Beaucaillou
27	3.14	Cabarus, of M. Brown	St-Julien	Third	Lagrange
28	3.15	Calon Ségur, of M. Lestapis	St-Estèphe	Third	Calon-Ségur
29	3.16	Monrose, of M. Dumoulin	St-Estèphe	Second	Montrose
30	3.17	Lanoir	Margaux	Not classed	La Gurgue
31	4^1.1	M. le Mis Délux	St-Julien		
32	4^1.2	M. Duluc aîné	St-Julien	Fourth	Branaire-Ducru
33	4^1.3	St-Pierre (M. Roullet and Galoupeau)	St-Julien	Fourth	Saint-Pierre

34	$4^1.4$	St-Pierre (M. Bontemps du Barry)	St-Julien	Fourth	Saint-Pierre
35	$4^1.5$	Le chât. de Bechev[lle], M. Guestier fils	St-Julien	Fourth	Beychevelle
36	$4^1.6$	Le chât. de Carnot, the heirs Luetkens	St-Laurent	Fourth	La Tour-Carnet
37	$4^1.7$	Ve Duhard, Milon	Pauillac	Fourth	Duhart-Milon-Rothschild
38	$4^1.8$	La Lagune, the heirs Piston	Ludon	Third	La Lagune
39	$4^1.9$	Dubignon	Margaux	Third	No longer exists
40	$4^1.10$	Solbery	Margaux	Fourth	Marquis de Terme
41	$4^1.11$	De Therme	Cantenac	Fourth	Marquis de Terme
42	$4^1.12$	Durand	Margaux	Fourth	Prieuré-Lichine
43	$4^2.1$	Milon Mandavy	Pauillac	Fourth	Duhart-Milon-Rothschild
44	$4^2.2$	Duboscq, of M. de Bedout	St-Julien		
45	$4^2.3$	Canet, of M. Pontet	Pauillac	Fifth	Pontet-Canet
46	$4^2.4$	Le grand Puy, of M. Lacoste	Pauillac	Fifth	Grand-Puy-Ducasse
47	$4^2.5$	Bages Juvine	Pauillac	Fifth	Lynch-Bages
48	$4^2.6$	Lynch, of Moussan	Pauillac	Fifth	Lynch-Moussas
49	$4^2.7$	Ve Ducasse	Pauillac	Fifth	Grand-Puy-Lacoste
50	$4^2.8$	Mouton d'Armailhacq	Pauillac	Fifth	Mouton-d'Armailhac
51	$4^2.9$	Batailley, M. Guestier père	Pauillac	Fifth	Batailley/Haut-Batailley
52	$4^2.10$	Croisit, of Bages	Pauillac	Fifth	Croizet-Bages
53	$4^2.11$	Cos Labory	St-Estèphe	Fifth	Cos-Labory
54	$4^2.12$	Laf[on] Roch[et], M. Camarsac	St-Estèphe	Fourth	Lafon-Rochet
55	$4^2.13$	Tronquoy Lalande	St-Estèphe	Not classed	Tronquoy-Lalande
56	$4^2.14$	Mompeloup Castéja	Pauillac	Not classed	Haut-Bages-Monpelou
57	$4^2.15$	Libéral	Pauillac	Fifth	Haut-Bages-Libéral
58	$4^2.16$	Liversan d'Anglade	St-Sauveur	Not classed	Liversan
59	$4^2.17$	Pergauson Delarose	St-Laurent	Not classed	Larose-Trintaudon
60	$4^2.18$	Coutanceau, of M. Devez	St-Laurent	Fifth	Belgrave
61	$4^2.19$	Pappe	St-Laurent	Fifth	Camensac
62	$4^2.20$	Le Boscq, le C[t] de Carle	St-Estèphe	Not classed	Le Boscq
63	$4^2.21$	The heirs of Morin	St-Courbian	Not classed	Morin
64	$4^2.22$	Le comte Lynch	Labarde	Fifth	Dauzac
65	$4^2.23$	Mlle Leguch	Cantenac		
66	$4^2.24$	Le marquis d'Alligre	Soussans	Not classed	Bel Air-Marquis d'Aligre
67	$4^2.25$	Le Paveil Bretonneau, Mynvielle	Soussans	Not classed	Paveil de Luze
68	$4^2.26$	Lannessan, of M. Delbos	Cussac	Not classed	Lanessan
69	$4^2.27$	Cantemerle, of M. le baron de Villeneuve	Macau	Fifth	Cantemerle
70	$4^2.28$	La Mission, near le Haut-Brion, closely following in price	Pessac	Not classed	La Mission-Haut-Brion

No. 14: Classification According to Table in Paguierre (1828 English Edition and 1829 French Edition)

		Property	1855 Position	Name Today
1	1.1	Château-Margaux	First	Margaux
2	1.2	Château-Lafitte	First	Lafite-Rothschild
3	1.3	Château-Latour	First	Latour
4	1.4	Château Haut-Brion*	First	Haut-Brion
5	2.1	Brane-Mouton	Second	Mouton-Rothschild
6	2.2	Rauzan	Second	Rausan-Ségla/Rauzan-Gassies
7	2.3	Léoville	Second	Léoville-Las-Cases/Léoville-Poyferré/Léoville-Barton
8	2.4	Gruau or Larose	Second	Gruaud-Larose
9	2.5	Clos Brane-Mouton	Second	Mouton-Rothschild
		Pichon-Longueville [according to text]	Second	Pichon-Longueville (Baron and Comtesse de Lalande)
10	3.1	Gorse	Second	Brane-Cantenac
11	3.2	Pichon-Longueville [according to table]	Second	Pichon-Longueville (Baron and Comtesse de Lalande)
12	3.3	Cas-Destournel	Second	Cos-d'Estournel
13	3.4	Lascombes	Second	Lascombes
14	3.5	Ducru	Second	Ducru-Beaucaillou
15	3.6	Branes-Arbouet or Cabarrus	Third	Lagrange
16	3.7	Pontet-Langlois	Third	Langoa-Barton
		Calon [according to text]	Third	Calon-Ségur
		Carnet [according to text]	Third	La Tour-Carnet
		Giscours [according to text]	Third	Giscours
		La Lagune [according to text]	Third	La Lagune
17	4.1	Kirwan	Third	Kirwan
18	4.2	Château de Candale	Third	d'Issan
19	4.3	Giscours [according to table]	Third	Giscours
20	4.4	St.-Pierre	Fourth	Saint-Pierre
21	4.5	Duluc	Fourth	Brainaire-Ducru
22	4.6	Durefort	Second	Durfort-Vivens

* There is a note at the end of the table which states: "We can here add the wine of Haut-Brion, because it is similar and equal in quality to the best growths of the Médoc."

23	4.7	Malescot	Third	Malescot-Saint-Exupéry
24	4.8	Loyac	Third as part of	Malescot-Saint-Exupéry
25	4.9	Mandavit	Fourth	Duhart-Milon-Rothschild
26	4.10	Canet	Fifth	Pontet-Canet
27	4.11	Dinac	Fifth	Grand-Puy-Lacoste
28	4.12	La Colonie	Third as part of	Malescot-Saint-Exupéry
29	4.13	Ferrière	Third	Ferrière
30	4.14	Tronquay	not classed	Tronquoy-Lalande
31	4.15	Ducasse	Fifth	Grand-Puy-Ducasse
32	4.16	Poujet	Fourth	Pouget
33	4.17	Déterme	Fourth	Marquis de Terme
34	4.18	Boyd	Third	Boyd-Cantenac

Note: This table is a virtual reproduction of the classification in Franck (1824).

No. 15: Classification According to Redding (1833)

		Property	1855 Position	Name Today
1	1.1	Lafitte	First	Lafite-Rothschild
2	1.2	Latour	First	Latour
3	1.3	Château Margaux	First	Margaux
4	1.4	Haut-Brion	First	Haut-Brion
5	1.5	St. Brix		
6	1.6	Carbonnieux	Not classed	Carbonnieux
7	1.7	Pontac		
	1.8	Sauterne		
	1.9	Barsac		
	1.10	Preignac and Beaumes		
8	2.1	Rozan	Second	Rausan-Ségla/Rauzan-Gassies
9	2.2	Gorze	Second	Brane-Cantenac
10	2.3	Léoville	Second	Léoville-Las-Cases/Léoville-Poyferré/Léoville-Barton
11	2.4	Larose	Second	Gruaud-Larose
12	2.5	Brane-Mouton	Second	Mouton-Rothschild
13	2.6	Pichon-Longueville	Second	Pichon-Longueville (Baron and Comtesse de Lalande)
14	2.7	Calon	Third	Calon-Ségur
	2.8	Langon		
	2.9	Cerons		
	2.10	Podensac		

For the third class, Redding does not name specific properties, but instead lists parishes and communes:
Pauillac, Margaux, Pessac, Saint Estèphe, Saint-Julien,
Castelnau de Médoc, Cantenac, Talence, Mérignac, Canon,
Pujols, Ilats, Landiras, Virelade, St. Croix du Mont, Loupiac

No. 16: Classification According to Statistique Œnologique *(1834)*

		Property	Commune	Owner	1855 Position	Name Today
			RED WINES OF THE MÉDOC			
1	1.1	Latour	Pauillac	Beaumont	First	Latour
2	1.2	Château-Margaux	Margaux	De la Conilla	First	Margaux
3	1.3	Lafitte	Pauillac	Sir Scott	First	Lafite-Rothschild
4	2.1	Mouton	Pauillac	Thouret	Second	Mouton-Rothschild
5	2.2	Rauzan	Margaux	Rauzan (heirs)	Second	Rausan-Ségla/Rauzan-Gassies
6	2.3	Léoville	St.-Julien	Barton (Hughes)	Second	Léoville-Barton
7	2.4	Léoville	St.-Julien	Poiféré	Second	Léoville-Poyferré
8	2.5	Léoville	St.-Julien	De Lascases	Second	Léoville-Las-Cases
9	2.6	Durefort	Blanquefort*	Lafont*	Second	Durfort-Vivens
10	2.7	Larose	St.-Julien	Balguerie and C°	Second	Gruaud-Larose
11	2.8	Pichon	Pauillac	Pichon de Longueville	Second	Pichon-Longueville (Baron and Comtesse de Lalande)
12	2.9	Gorsse	Margaux	Gorsse or Gorce	Second	Brane-Cantenac
13	3.1	Ducru	St.-Julien	Ducru	Second	Ducru-Beaucaillou
14	3.2	Kirwan	Cantenac	Kirwan	Third	Kirwan
15	3.3	Calon	St.-Estèphe	Lestapie	Third	Calon-Ségur
16	3.4	Giscour	Labarde	Promis	Third	Giscours
17	3.5	Cabarrus	St.-Julien	Cabarrus	Third	Lagrange
18	3.6	Destournel	St.-Estèphe	Destournel	Second	Cos-d'Estournel
19	3.7	Daux	St.-Julien	Daux (Cte)	Third	Talbot
20	3.8	Desmirail	Margaux	Desmirail	Fourth	Desmirail
21	3.9	Mercier	Margaux	Talbot Dubignon	Third	No longer exists
22	3.10	St.-Pierre	St.-Julien	Roulet and others	Fourth	Saint-Pierre
23	4.1	Pontet	Pauillac	Pontet	Fifth	Pontet-Canet
24	4.2	Bechevelle	St.-Julien	Duluc	Fourth	Beychevelle
25	4.3	Grand-Puy	Pauillac	Lacoste St.-Guirons	Fifth	Grand-Puy-Lacoste
26	4.4	Cos	St.-Estèphe	Gaston (V[e])	Fifth	Cos-Labory
27	4.5	Becker	Margaux	Becker	Third	Marquis d'Alesme-Becker
28	4.6	Lalande	St.-Estèphe	Tronquoy	Not classed	Tronquoy-Lalande
29	4.7	Ferrière	Margaux	Ferrière	Third	Ferrière
30	4.8	Ratalley	St.-Julien	Guestier Daniel	Fifth	Batailley/Haut-Batailley
		Commune de S[t].-Julien		Various		
		Commune de S[t].-Estèphe		Various		

*This is evidently incorrect, perhaps resulting from a confusion with a similarly named property in Blanquefort.

		RED WINES OF THE GRAVES				
31	1.1	Haut Brion	Pessac	Beyermann and Company	First	Haut-Brion
32	1.2	La Mission	Talence		Not classed	La Mission-Haut-Brion
33	2.1	Domaine du Pape-Clément	Pessac	Jarrige	Not classed	Pape-Clément
34	2.2	Domaine du Pape-Clément	Pessac	Castera	Not classed	Pape-Clément
35	2.3	Domaine du Pape-Clément	Pessac	Magonty	Not classed	Pape-Clément
36	2.4	Domaine du Pape-Clément	Pessac	Lurine	Not classed	Pape-Clément
37	2.5	Catelan	Pessac	Catelan		
38	3.1	Château de Talence	Talence	Declerc and Tarteyron		
39	3.2	Latour	Talence	Lacoste		
40	3.3	Villesurane	Talence	Villesurane (veuve)		
41	3.4	Vieille	Talence	Vieille		
		RED WINES OF THE CÔTES				
42	1.1	Canole	St.-Emilion	Canole		
43	1.2	Pavie	St.-Emilion	Talmon	Not classed	Pavie/Pavie-Oecesse
44	1.3	Mondot	St.-Emilion	Fourcaud		
45	1.4	Mondot	St.-Emilion	Izambert		
		Canon	Fronsac	Ruleau, duc de Cazes, Lavaud and Solmignac, Fontémoing, Chaperon, St.-Julien		
	2	Pomerol, Certan, petit village	Pomerol	Demai Certan, Chaperon	Not classed	Certain de May-de-Certain/ Petit-Village
46	3.1	Barbe-Blanche	Lussac	Jay Laussac	Not classed	Barbe-Blanche
47	3.2	Grenet	Lussac	Favereau de Terrien Lavignerie		
		Commune of St.-Emilion		Various		
		SWEET WHITE WINES				
		Iquem	Sauternes	De Saluces, Guiraud, Brun, etc.		
		Duroy or Suduiraut and de Male	Preignac	Guillot, Apiau, de Saluces, etc.		
		Contet	Barsac	De Saluces, Binaud, Delone, Cotineau, Cave, etc.		

		Bommes	Lafaurie, Deyme, Lacoste, etc.		
		Fargues	Various, premier crus		
			DRY WHITE WINES		
48	S^{t}.-Bris	Villnave d'Ornon	Lelamendi, Silvela or Sibeland		
49	Carbonnieux	Leognan	Bouchereau	Not classed	Carbonnieux
50	Dulamont or Pontac	Blanquefort	Dariste		

No. 17: Classification According to the Report by J. Exshaw (dated 1833)in Commercial Relations *(1835)*

Classification of the Wines of the Gironde Department, with Average Prices at Which, since the Peace, They Have Been Sold by the Growers When New

		Property	1855 Position	Name Today	Price (in francs)		
					Good Year	Middling	Bad
				MÉDOC			
1	1.1	Laffitte	First	Lafite-Rothschild	3000	1750	400
2	1.2	Latour	First	Latour			
3	1.3	Château Margaux	First	Margaux			
4	2.1	Rausan	Second	Rausan-Ségla/Rauzan-Gassies	2700	1400	350
5	2.2	Durfort	Second	Durfort-Vivens			
6	2.3	Lascombe	Second	Lascombes			
7	2.4	Leoville	Second	Léoville-Las-Cases/Léoville-Poyferré/Léoville-Barton			
8	2.5	Branne Mouton	Second	Mouton-Rothschild			
9	2.6	Larose	Second	Gruaud-Larose			
10	3.1	Gorce	Second	Brane-Cantenac	2400	1200	325
11	3.2	Kirwan	Third	Kirwan			
12	3.3	Château d'Isson	Third	d'Issan			
13	3.4	Malescot	Third	Malescot-Saint-Exupéry			
14	3.5	Brown	Third	Boyd-Cantenac/Cantenac Brown			
15	3.6	Ducru	Second	Ducru-Beaucaillou			
16	3.7	Tichon	Second	Pichon-Longueville (Baron and Comtesse de Lalande)			
17	3.8	Cabarrus	Third	Lagrange			
18	3.9	Cosse	Second	Cos-d'Estournel			
19	4.1	Calon	Third	Calon-Ségur	1800	1000	300
20	4.2	Giscours	Third	Giscours			
21	4.3	Toujet	Fourth	Pouget			
22	4.4	Loyac	Third as part of	Malescot-Saint-Exupéry			
23	4.5	Lacolonie	Third as part of	Malescot-Saint-Exupéry			
24	4.6	Lorlagune	Third	La Lagune			
25	4.7	Daleure	Third	Marquis d'Alesme-Becker			

26	4.8	Dubignon	Third	No longer exists			
27	4.9	Ferriere	Third	Ferrière			
28	4.10	Durand	Fourth	Prieuré-Lichine			
29	4.11	Palmer	Third	Palmer			
30	4.12	Desmirail	Third	Desmirail			
31	4.13	St. Pierre	Fourth	Saint-Pierre			
32	4.14	Duluc	Fourth	Branaire-Ducru			
33	4.15	Bechevelle	Fourth	Beychevelle			
34	4.16	Mandari	Fourth	Duhart-Milon-Rothschild			
35	4.17	Montrose	Second	Montrose			
36	4.18	Daux	Fourth	Talbot			
37	5.1	Pontet Canet	Fifth	Pontet-Canet	1500	900	300
38	5.2	Bedout					
39	5.3	Ducasse	Fifth	Grand-Puy-Ducasse			
40	5.4	Grand Pui	Fifth	Grand-Puy-Lacoste			
41	5.5	Turine	Fifth	Lynch-Bages			
42	5.6	Darmaillac	Fifth	Mouton-d'Armailhac			
43	5.7	Montpelou	Not classed	Haut-Bages-Monpelou			
44	5.8	Batailly	Fifth	Batailley/Haut-Batailley			
45	5.9	Duliard					
46	5.10	Croiset	Fifth	Croizet-Bages			
47	5.11	Carnet	Fourth	La Tour-Carnet			
48	5.12	Coutanceau	Fifth	Belgrave			
49	5.13	Pop	Fifth	Camensac			
50	5.14	Perganson	Not classed	Larose-Trintaudon			
51	5.15	Tronquoy	Not classed	Tronquoy-Lalande			
52	5.16	Morin	Not classed	Morin			
53	5.17	Lebose	Not classed	Le Boscq			
				RED GRAVES			
54		Hautbrion	First	Haut-Brion	2700	1600	350
		Second class			1500	700	300
		Third class			800	500	280
		Common			500	300	250
				ST. EMILION			
		First class			700	400	225
		Second class			450	280	200

Since the peace, none but the best wines of the best years are exported to England.							
WHITE WINES							
1	1.1	Yguem	First-superior	Yquem	1100	700	300
2	1.2	Coulet	First	Coutet			
3	1.3	Durvi					
4	1.4	La faurie	First	Lafaurie-Peyraguey			
5	1.5	Binaud					
6	1.6	Dayme	Second	Doisy-Daëne			
7	2.1	Perot			950	600	300
8	2.2	Dert					
9	2.3	Guiroux	First	Guiraud			
10	2.4	Baptiste	Second	Lamothe/Lamothe-Guignard			
11	2.5	Carle					
12	2.6	Pernaud					
13	2.7	Cave					
14	2.8	Latoure blanche	First	La Tour-Blanche			
15	2.9	Duboscq					
16	2.10	Riousec	First	Rieussec			
17	2.11	Bouchraud	Not classed	Carbonnieux			
18	2.12	St. Brice					
19	3.1	Filhau	Second	Filhot	600	400	240
20	3.2	Hersoc					
21	3.3	Fiton					
22	3.4	Emérigon	Not classed	Mauras			
23	3.5	Darche	Second	d'Arche			
24	3.6	Mareilhac					
25	3.7	Laffont					
26	3.8	Laborde					
27	3.9	Monfaillis					
28	3.10	Dlles. Duboscq					
29	3.11	Brun					

Bordeaux, March 27, 1833, J. Exshaw.

No. 18A: Classification According to the Price Quotations in Le Producteur *(January 1838)*

		Name of the Vineyard	Commune	Names of the Owners	The tun, 1837	1855 Position	Name Today
				RED WINES OF THE MÉDOC			
1	1.1	Latour	Pauillac	De Beaumont	**2400–3000**	First	Latour
2	1.2	Château Margaux	Margaux	Aguado		First	Margaux
3	1.3	Lafitte	Pauillac	Sir Scott		First	Lafite-Rothschild
4	2.1	Mouton, 1er.-2e. crus	Pauillac	Thuret	**1800–2000**	Second	Mouton-Rothschild
5	2.2	Pichon, 1er.-2e. crus	Pauillac	Pichon de Longueville		Second	Pichon-Longueville (Baron and Comtesse de Lalande)
6	2.3	Cos-Destournel	Saint-Estèphe	Destournel		Second	Cos-d'Estournel
7	2.4	Rozan	Margaux	De Segla and others		Second	Rausan-Ségla/ Rauzan-Gassies
8	2.5	Léoville ou Labadie	Saint-Julien	De Lascazes and others		Second	Léoville-Las-Cases Léoville-Poyferré Léoville-Barton
9	2.6	Gruau-Larose	Saint-Julien	Balguerie		Second	Gruaud-Larose
10	2.7	Gorse-Guy	Cantenac and Margaux	Brannes		Second	Brane-Cantenac
11	2.8	Lascombes	Margaux	None listed		Second	Lascombes
12	2.9	Durefort de Vivens	Margaux	De Vivens		Second	Durfort-Vivens
13	2.10	Monrose	Saint-Estèphe	Dumoulin		Second	Montrose
14	3.1	Pontet-Canet	Pauillac	De Pontet	**1400–1600**	Fifth	Pontet-Canet
15	3.2	Kirwan	Cantenac	Kirwan		Third	Kirwan
16	3.3	Cabarus (Brand-Arbouet)	Saint-Julien	Cabarus		Third	Lagrange
17	3.4	Giscours	Labarde	Promis		Third	Giscours
18	3.5	Daux	Saint-Julien	Daux (Comte)		Fourth	Talbot
19	3.6	Bergeron	Saint-Julien	Ducru		Second	Ducru-Beaucaillou
20	3.7	Pontet-Langlois	Saint-Julien	Barton		Third	Barton-Langoa
21	3.8	Calon-Ségur	Saint-Estèphe	Lestapy		Third	Calon-Ségur
22	3.9	Desmirail	Margaux	Desmirail		Third	Desmirail
23	3.10	Château de Candal (Duluc)	Saint-Julien	Duluc		Fourth	Branaire-Ducru
24	3.11	Milon	Pauillac	Veuve Duhar		Fourth	Duhart-Milon-Rothschild
25	3.12	Mouton d'Armaillac	Pauillac	D'Armaillac		Fifth	Mouton-d'Armailhac

26	3.13	Lynch, à Moussas	Pauillac	De Lynch (comte)		Fifth	Lynch-Moussas
27	3.14	Bages, Jurine	Pauillac	Jurine		Fifth	Lynch-Bages
28	3.15	Saint-Pierre-Roulet	Saint-Julien	Poulet et veuve Galoupeau		Fourth	Saint-Pierre
29	3.16	Saint-Pierre-Dubarry	Saint-Julien	Bontemps-Dubarry		Fourth	Saint-Pierre
30	3.17	Delage	Saint-Julien	De Bedou			
31	3.18	Malescot et Loyac	Margaux	De St.-Exupery		Third	Malescot-Saint-Exupéry
32	3.19	Lafon-Rochet	Saint-Estèphe	Lafon Camarsac		Fourth	Lafon-Rochet
33	3.20	Cos-Labory	Saint-Estèphe	Mme. Gaston Labory		Fifth	Cos-Labory
34	3.21	Mercier	Margaux	Talbot-Dubignon		Third	No longer exists
35	3.22	Juste	Margaux	J.B. Lanoire		Not classed	La Gurgue
36	3.23	Seguineau-Piston Lalagune	Ludon	Pitton		Third	La Lagune
37	3.24	Palmer	Cantenac and Margaux	Palmer		Third	Palmer
38	3.25	Ferrière	Margaux	Ferrière		Third	Ferrière
39	3.26	D'Alème d'Arche Beker	Margaux	Beker		Third	Marquis d'Alesme-Becker
40	3.27	Ganet-Chavaille	Cantenac	Chavaille		Fourth	Pouget
41	3.28	Pontet-Perganson, Larose	Saint-Laurent	De Larose		Not classed	Larose-Trintaudon
42	3.29	Luëtkens	Saint-Laurent	Luëtkens		Fourth	La Tour-Carnet
43	3.30	Lynch	Cantenac	M. de Lynch		Not classed	Pontac-Lynch
44	4.1	Malescot	Pauillac	Weltener	900–1000		
45	4.2	Château Beychevelle	Saint-Julien	Guestier, Junion		Fourth	Beychevelle
46	4.3	Brown	Cantenac	Brown		Third	Boyd-Cantenac/ Cantenac Brown
47	4.4	De Gères	Pauillac	De Gères			
48	4.5	Desse	Pauillac	Desse		Not classed	Colombier-Monpelou
49	4.6	Batailley	Pauillac	Guestier père		Fifth	Batailley/ Haut-Batailley
50	4.7	Ducasse	Pauillac	Veuve Ducasse		Fifth	Grand-Puy-Ducasse
51	4.8	Constant Martial	Pauillac	Constant Martial			
52	4.9	Mompeloup, Casteja	Pauillac	Casteja		Not classed	Haut-Bages-Monpelou
53	4.10	Lalande	Saint-Estèphe	Tronquoy		Not classed	Tronquoy-Lalande
54	4.11	Libéral	Pauillac	Libéral		Fifth	Haut-Bages-Libéral
55	4.12	Morin-Camiran	Saint-Estèphe	De Camiran		Not classed	Morin
56	4.13	Mercier Terrefort	Saint-Estèphe	Mme. de Carles			

57	4.14	Defumel	Saint-Estèphe	Tarteyron	Not classed	Pez
58	4.15	Luëtkens (les Feuillants)	Saint-Estèphe	Soutard	Not classed	Meyney
59	4.16	Pomis	Saint-Estèphe	Destournel	Not classed	Pomys
60	4.17	Merman	Saint-Estèphe	Merman	Not classed	Le Crock
61	4.18	Phelan	Saint-Estèphe	Phelan	Not classed	Phélan-Ségur
62	4.19	Fatin-Maccarthy	Saint-Estèphe	Maccoarthy	Not classed	Mac Carthy
63	4.20	Eyquem-Pantoche	Margaux	Eyquem	Third as part of	Malescot-Saint-Exupéry
64	4.21	Château Dubreuil	Cissac	Baron Dubreuil		
65	4.22	Château Larriveaux	Cissac	Parroi	Not classed	Larrivaux
66	4.23	Martiny	Cissac	Martiny	Not classed	Cissac
67	4.24	Pedesclaux	Pauillac	Pedesclaux	Fifth	Pédesclaux
68	4.25	Bergeron	Cussac	Bergeron	Not classed	Lamothe-Bergeron
69	4.26	Guy (le tertre)	Arsac	Brezet	Fifth	du Tertre
70	4.27	Desmirail	Arsac	Desmirail	Third	Desmirail
71	4.28	Bretonneau	Soussans	Minvielle	Third as part of	Malescot Saint-Exupéry
72	4.29	Mercier-Belair	Soussans	Marq^s. d'Alligres	Not classed	Bel Air-Marquis d'Aligre
73	4.30	De Secondat	Soussans	Demont de Dune		
74	4.31	Deyrem	Soussans	Larigaudière	Not classed	Deyrem-Valentin
75	4.32	Champés aîné	Soussans	Champés aîné		
76	4.33	Garat	Arcins	Pressac		
77	4.34	Subercaseaux	Arcins	Subercaseaux	Not classed	Arcins
78	4.35	Duroc-Lesparre	Pauillac	Duroc Lesparre		
79	4.36	Lacoste-Grand-Puy	Pauillac	Lacoste	Fifth	Grand-Puy-Lacoste
80	4.37	Lemoine	Ludon	Brincou	Not classed	Lemoine-Lafon-Rochet
81	4.38	Pommier	Ludon	Castera	Not classed	Agassac
82	4.39	D'Arche	Ludon	Barthelots (veuve)	Not classed	Arche
83	4.40	Couleau	Ludon	Daudebar		
84	4.41	Coudot	Saint-Estèphe	Bernard		
85	4.42	Cambon	Macau	Cambon	Not classed	Cambon la Pelouse
86	4.43	Cantemerle	Macau	Le Bon de Villeneuve	Fifth	Cantemerle
87	4.44	Lassus	Macau	Duranteau		
88	4.45	Roborel	Macau	Roborel		
89	4.46	Burke	Macau	Burke	Not classed	La Houringue
90	4.47	Lalanne-Dudevant	Macau	Dudevant		

91	4.48	Feloneau-Boutet	Macau	Boutet		Not classed	Guittot-Fellonneau
92	4.49	Luëtkens	Saint-Laurent	Van Dahren			
93	4.50	Carteau	Saint-Sauveur	De Lynch		Not classed	Haut-Madrac
94	4.51	Cazeau	Saint-Estèphe	Cazeau			
95	5.1	Bages-Croizet	Pauillac	Croizet (veuve)	550–650	Fifth	Croizet-Bages
96	5.2	Beaumont	Saint-Sauveur	Danglade		Not classed	Liversan
97	5.3	Bages-Martin	Pauillac	Martin			
98	5.4	Lacaussade	Pauillac	Laucassade			
99	5.5	Mariot	Saint-Estèphe	Bernard			
100	5.6	Capbern	Saint-Estèphe	Capbern		Not classed	Capbern-Gasqueton
101	5.7	Penicaud	Saint-Estèphe	Lattaderose			
102	5.8	Superville	Saint-Estèphe	Bonie			
103	5.9	L'abbé Fournier	Saint-Estèphe	Lafitte			
104	5.10	Pinet	Saint-Estèphe	Casteja (veuve)			
105	5.11	Comes	Saint-Estèphe	D^{lles}. Comes		Not classed	Côme
106	5.12	Ademar et Saujein	St-Seurin de Cadourne	Bacon			
107	5.13	Brochon	St-Seurin de Cadourne	Andron fils		Not classed	Sociando-Mallet
108	5.14	Brannes	St-Seurin de Cadourne	Cabarrus		Not classed	Pontoise-Cabarrus
109	5.15	Verthamon	St-Seurin de Cadourne	Andron père		Not classed	Coufran
110	5.16	Le P. Basterot	St-Seurin de Cadourne	Boué père			
111	5.17	Bonnet-Degrange	St-Seurin de Cadourne	Daux			
112	5.18	Gérome Figeron	St-Seurin de Cadourne	Gérome			
113	5.19	Molinié	Saint-Laurent	Pik			
114	5.20	Popp	Saint-Laurent	Popp		Fifth	Camensac
115	5.21	Le Galant	Saint-Laurent	Siau			
116	5.22	Hosten	Saint-Laurent	Hosten			
117	5.23	Maurin	Saint-Laurent	Lahens			
118	5.24	Madéran	Saint-Laurent	Madéran (the h^{eirs}.)			
119	5.25	Duchileau	Cissac	Garrigoux		Not classed	Hanteillan
120	5.26	Dumouzeau	Cissac	Dumousseau			
121	5.27	Camiran (de)	Vertheuil	Camiran (de)			
122	5.28	Labbaye	Vertheuil	Skiner			
123	5.29	Luëtkins	Vertheuil	Bon fils			

124	5.30	Gorrand	Vertheuil	Plaignard		
125	5.31	Lasalle	Vertheuil	Mme. Lafon		
126	5.32	Clemenceau	Vertheuil	Bernard		
127	5.33	Blanchard	Vertheuil	Blanchard		
128	5.34	Baron de Larsan	Saint-Germain	Baron de Larsan	Not classed	Hautrive
129	5.35	N	Saint-Germain	Mme. Verthamon	Not classed	Hautrive
130	5.36	Carteau, à Madras	Saint-Sauveur	Le conte de Lynche	Not classed	Haut-Madrac
131	5.37	Varé	Saint-Sauveur	Le B^{on}. de Cavaignac	Not classed	Peyrabon
132	5.38	Masperier	Saint-Estèphe	Moulinier		
133	5.39	Barre	Saint-Estèphe	Barre		
134	5.40	Solberg	Cantenac	Marq^{s}. de Therme	Fourth	Marquis de Terme
135	5.41	Lacolonie	Margaux	Lacolonie	Third as part of	Malescot-Saint-Exupéry
136	5.42	Lapeyruche	Margaux	Solberg		
137	5.43	Le Pt. Barbot	Soussans	Benoit		
138	5.44	Séguineau	Soussans	Jh. Dayries	Not classed	Marsac-Séguineau
139	5.45	Dubedat	Arcins	Arnauld	Not classed	Arnauld
140	5.46	Cru de Bareyre	Arcins	Dupérier		
141	5.47	Bracier ou Budos	Lamarque	Sauvage	Not classed	Lamarque
142	5.48	Pigneguy	Lamarque	Pineguy		
143	5.49	Bergeron	Lamarque	Mme. Bergeron		
144	5.50	Van der Kun	Lamarque	Von Hemert		
145	5.51	Blanchard	Lamarque	Perrins		
146	5.52	Labarthe	Cussac	Dufour fils		
147	5.53	Bernones	Cussac	Bouet	Not classed	Bernones
148	5.54	Pénicaut	Cussac	Martin		
149	5.55	Camarsac	Cussac	Camarsac		
150	5.56	Lanessan	Cussac	Mme. Delbos	Not classed	Lanessan
151	5.57	Delarose	Le Taillan	Fornerod		
152	5.58	Michau	Le Taillan	Michau		
153	5.59	Delavie	Le Taillan	Marq. de Brias	Not classed	Taillan
154	5.60	Duroussel	Le Taillan	By. curé		
155	5.61	Cursol	Le Taillan	H^{ers}. Pierre Pierre		
156	5.62	Chalard	Le Pian	Baour	Not classed	Sénéjac
157	5.63	Basterot	Le Pian	Barthez		
158	5.64	Laporte	Le Pian	Mussinot		

159	5.65	Rejaumont	Castelnau	Lameletie		
160	5.66	St.-Guiron	Castelnau	St.-Guiron		
161	5.67	Château Citran	Avensan	Laroche-Jacquelin	Not classed	Citran
162	5.68	Gressier	Moulis	Veuve Gressier	Not classed	Gressier Grand Poujeaux
163	5.69	Brassier	Moulis	Castaing	Not classed	Poujeaux
164	5.70	Momand	Listrac	S^{t}.-Guirons		
165	5.71	Ducluseau	Listrac	Ducluseau	Not classed	Ducluzeau
166	5.72	Hosten	Listrac	Hosten	Not classed	Fourcas Hosten
167	5.73	Duranteau	Listrac	Von Hemert		
168	5.74	Labeurthe	Listrac	Le Ch. Bernard		
169	5.75	Clarke	Listrac	St.-Guirons	Not classed	Clarke
170	5.76	Deroly	St-Seurin de Cadourne	Darboucare		
171	5.77	Lamothe	St-Seurin de Cadourne	Alaret		
172	5.78	Grandis	St-Seurin de Cadourne	Grandis	Not classed	Grandis
173	5.79	Boudey et Ducasse	St-Seurin de Cadourne	Chomel		
174	5.80	Laumoneir	St-Seurin de Cadourne	Laumonier		
175	5.81	Laumoneir	St-Seurin de Cadourne	Fiston		
176	5.82	Ferrusac-Josset de Pomies	St-Seurin de Cadourne	B^{on}. Dubreuil		
177	5.83	Pepin d'Escurac	Civrac	Pepin d'Escurac		
178	5.84	N	Civrac	Comte de Ségur		
179	5.85	Ch. Romefort et Cardoze	Blaignan	Guilhory		
180	5.86	Costant et Cardanno	Blaignan	Constant		
181	5.87	Desvernines	Potensac	Galet		
182	5.88	N	Saint-Yzan	Subrecaseau		
183	5.89	Cop-Martin	St-Christoly et Couqueques	Cop-Martin		
184	5.90	De Maignol	St-Christoly et Couqueques	De Maignol		
185	5.91	Seguin	St-Christoly et Couqueques	Seguin		
186	5.92	Desse	St-Christoly et Couqueques	Desse		

Omissions and Rectifications to the Above Classification as Listed in* Le Producteur, *February 1838

		Name of the Vineyard	Commune	Names of the Owners	The Tun 1837	1855 Position	Name Today
Deuxièmes crus							
1	2.1	Gorse	Cantenac	Baron de Brane	1800–2000	Second	Brane-Cantenac
Troisièmes crus							
2	3.1	Milon-Duroc, was Mandavy	Pauillac	Lesparre Duroc	1400–1600	Fourth	Duhart-Milon-Rothschild
3	3.2	Weltener	Margaux	Capelle		Not classed	Labegorce
Quatrièmes crus							
4	4.1	Duroc	Pauillac	Lesparre-Duroc	900–1000	Not classed	
Cinquièmes crus, dits bourgeois supérieurs							
5	5.1	Bethman	Lamarque	Bethman	550–650	Not classed	Cartillon
6	5.2	Mme. Castelnau	Cussac	Phelan, à Ste.-Gem.			
7	5.3	Roudey and Ducasse	St-Seurin de Cadourne	Tronquoy		Not classed	Bel Orme Tronquoy de Lalande
8	5.4	Arbouet	Saint-Estèphe	Luco and Asmus			
9	5.5	N.	Saint-Yzans	De Marcellus (the B^on^)		Not classed	Loudenne

Omissions and Rectifications to the Above Classification as Listed in* Le Producteur, *March 1838

		Name of the Vineyard	Commune	Names of the Owners	The Tun 1837	1855 Position	Name Today
Deuxièmes crus							
1	2.1	Brane-Cantenac (Gorse)	Cantenac	Baron de Brane	1800–2000	Second	Brane-Cantenac
2	2.2	Lascombe	Margaux	Loriague		Second	Lascombes
Troisièmes crus							
3	3.1	Cabarrus	Saint-Julien	Brown, at Lagrange	1400–1600	Third	Lagrange
4	3.2	Pouget	Cantenac	Chavaille		Fourth	Pouget
5	3.3	Ganet	Cantenac	De Lassale		Fourth	Became part of Kirwan
6	3.4	Le Prieuré	Cantenac	Pagès		Fourth	Prieuré-Lichine
Quatrièmes crus							
7	4.1	Marq. de Therme (Solbert)	Cantenac	Mac-Daniel	900–1000	Fourth	Marquis de Terme
8	4.2	Lacolonie	Margaux	Lehoult		Not classed	Became part of Malescot-Saint-Exupèry
9	4.3	Faget	Labarde	Geneste			

10	4.4	Angludet-Legras	Cantenac	D'Anglade Legras Angludet Roborel Lamorère Legras aîné Legras Lagrave		Not classed	Angludet
11	4.5	Le château d'Arsac	Arsac	Rubichon		Not classed	Arsac
12	4.6	Copmartin	Arsac	De Montbrison		Not classed	Monbrison
13	4.7	Monpontet	Arsac	Chappaz			
14	4.8	Château-Citran	Avensan	Borie		Not classed	Citran
15	4.9	Paveil	Soussans	Minvielle		Not classed	Paveil de Luze
16	4.10	Ducasse	St-Seurin de Cadourne	Chomel			
17	4.11	Roudey	St-Seurin de Cadourne	Tronquoy de Lalande		Not classed	Bel Orme Tronquoy de Lalande
Cinquièmes crus							
18	5.1	Gérôme Figeroux	St-Seurin de Cadourne	Gérôme Figeroux	550–650		
19	5.2	Labarthe	Cussac	Marquis d'Aligre			
20	5.3	Laporte	Le Pian	Lemonier			
21	5.4	Cursol	Le Taillan	Petit-Delfau			
22	5.5	Grandis	St-Seurin de Cadourne	Andron		Not classed	Grandis
23	5.6	Desvernines	Potensac	Galais			
24	5.7	Seguignac	Saint-Yzans	Subercaseau		Not classed	Sigognac

Omissions and Rectifications to the Above Classification as Listed in* Le Producteur, *April 1838

		Name of the Vineyard	Commune	Names of the Owners	The Tun 1837	1855 Position	Name Today
Deuxièmes crus							
1	2.1	Larose	Saint-Laurent	De Larose	1800–2000	Not classed	Larose Trintaudon
Troisièmes crus							
2	3.1	Tour de Carnet	Saint-Laurent	Luëtkins	1400–1600	Fourth	La Tour-Carnet
Quatrièmes crus							
3	4.1	Balac	Saint-Laurent	Vondohren	900–1000	Not classed	Balac
Cinquièmes crus dits bourgeois supérieurs							
4	5.1	N	Bégadan	Cabarrus Adrien	550–650		
5	5.2	Château Carcanieux	Carcanieux	Veuve Montouroy			
6	5.3	Gourmeron	Pauillac	Gourmeron, chanoine archiprêtre de Saint-André			

Omissions and Rectifications to the Above Classification as Listed in* Le Producteur, *June 1838

		Name of the Vineyard	Commune	Names of the Owners	The Tun 1837	1855 Position	Name Today
Cinquièmes crus dits bourgeois supérieurs							
1	5.1	Charmail	St-Seurin de Cadourne	M. Louvet	550–650	Not classed	Charmail

Omissions and Rectifications to the Above Classification as Listed in* Le Producteur, *August 1838

		Name of the Vineyard	Commune	Names of the Owners	The Tun Futures	1855 Position	Name Today
Quatrièmes crus							
1	4.1	Dubosc (Château Siran)	Labarde	Mme la comtesse de Lautrec	700–1200	Not classed	Siran

Omissions and Rectifications to the Above Classification as Listed in* Le Producteur, *September 1838

		Name of the Vineyard	Commune	Names of the Owners	The Tun Futures	1855 Position	Name Today
Cinquièmes crus dits bourgeois supérieurs							
1	5.1	Dureton Maucailloux	Lamarque	Pigneguy-Rosset	550–600	Not classed	Maucaillou

Omissions and Rectifications to the Above Classification as Listed in* Le Producteur, *December 1838

		Name of the vineyard	Commune	Names of the Owners	The Tun Futures	1855 Position	Name Today
Quatrièmes crus							
1	4.1	Danglade (Village de Doumens)	Margaux	Danglade	700–1000		
Cinquièmes crus							
2	5.1	N.	Lamarque	Bergeron aîné	500–700		
3	5.2	Cru Pérès (formerly Deyrem)	Soussans	Jean Pérès	550, 700, and 800		

Omissions and Rectifications to the Above Classification as Listed in* Le Producteur, *February 1839

		Name of the Vineyard	Commune	Names of the Owners	The Tun Futures	1855 Position	Name Today
Quatrièmes crus							
1	4.1	La Gravette-Trois-Moulins	Soussans	Rambaud aîné	700–1000	Not classed	Rambaud

Omissions and Rectifications to the Above Classification as Listed in* Le Producteur, *July 1839

		Name of the Vineyard	Commune	Names of the Owners	The Tun Futures	1855 Position	Name Today
Quatrièmes crus							
1	5.1	Belair	Blanquefort	Davin de Boismarin	500–600		

No. 18B: Classification of White Wines According to the Price Quotations in Le Producteur *(June 1838)*

		Names of the Vineyards	Names of the Owners	The Tun, Futures	Name Today
		WHITE WINES OF THE GRAVES			
Commune of Villenave-d'Ornon					
1	1.1	Château-Carbonnieux	Bouchereau brothers	300–800 and 1200	Carbonnieux
2	1.2	St. Bris	Oxéda		
3	1.3	Cave	Roux		
4	2.1	La Fabrique	Leclerc (brothers)	200–600	
5	2.2	Pontac	Echevairia		
6	2.3		De Pradine		
7	2.4		Heirs of Larché		
8	2.5	Former property of M. Bousquet	M. Bousquet		
9	3.1	Désert	Dufour Debarte	180–400	
10	3.2	Barret	Fauchey		
11	3.3		De Basquiat (Alexis)		
12	3.4		De Basquiat (Ray)		
13	3.5	Pont de Langon	Duprat		
14	3.6		Rougier		
15	3.7		Mme. Rondeau		
16	3.8		Latransaa		
17	3.9		Witfooth		
18	3.10		Heirs of Pensan		
19	3.11		Baraste		
20	3.12		Albo		
21	3.13		Escrivan		
22	3.14		Lapointe		
23	3.15		Pereyra		
24	3.16		Various small owners		
First Growths of the Commune, 2nd growths according to the general classification					
25			Dubosq	200–600	
26		Château Louvière	Mareilhac brothers		La Louvière
Second Growths of the Commune, 3rd growths according to the classification					
27			Depiot	180–400	
28			Renaud		
29			Dauriol		
30			Comagères		
Third Growths of the Commune, 4th growths according to the classification					
31			Peasants of Méchires	120–300	

No. 19: Classification According to Leclerc (1842)

		Property	1855 Position	Name Today
1	1.1	Château-Margaux	First	Margaux
2	1.2	Château-Lafitte [also in separate text]	First	Lafite-Rothschild
3	1.3	Château-Latour [also in separate text]	First	Latour
4	1.4	Château Haut-Brion	First	Haut-Brion
5	2.1	Rauzan	Second	Rausan-Ségla/Rauzan-Gassies
6	2.2	Brane-Mouton [also in separate text]	Second	Mouton-Rothschild
7	2.3	Léoville	Second	Léoville-Las-Cases/Léoville-Poyferré/Léoville-Barton
8	2.4	Gruau, Larose	Second	Gruaud-Larose
9	2.5	Pichon-Longueville [also in separate text]	Second	Pichon-Longueville (Baron and Comtesse de Lalande)
10	2.6	Durfort	Second	Durfort-Vivens
11	2.7	Degorse	Second	Brane-Cantenac
12	2.8	Lascombe	Second	Lascombes
13	2.9	Cos-Destournelle [also in separate text]	Second	Cos-d'Estournel
14	3.1	Château-d'Issan	Third	d'Issan
15	3.2	Pougets	Fourth	Pouget
		Several clos of Cantenac and Margaux		
16	3.3	Malescot	Third	Malescot-Saint-Exupéry
17	3.4	Ferrière	Third	Ferrière
18	3.5	Giscours [also in separate text]	Third	Giscours
19	3.6	Langoa	Third	Langoa-Barton
20	3.7	Bergeron	Second	Ducru-Beaucaillou
21	3.8	Cabarus	Third	Lagrange
22	3.9	Calon-Ségur [also in separate text]	Third	Calon-Ségur
23	3.10	Montrose [also in separate text]	Second	Montrose
24	3.11	Lanoir	Not classed	La Gurgue
		Saint-Julien		
25	4^1.1	Béchevelle-Saint-Pierre	Fourth	Saint-Pierre
26	4^1.2	Château-de-Béchevelle	Fourth	Beychevelle
27	4^1.3	Château-Carnot	Fourth	La Tour-Carnet
		Several Margaux and Cantenac		
28	4^1.4	La Lagune [in separate text]	Third	La Lagune
	4^2	The large proprietors of Pauillac and Saint-Estèphe		
	4^2	Several others of Labarde and Margaux		
	5	Many wines still worthy of esteem of Pauillac, Saint-Estèphe, Saint-Julien, Soussans, Labarde, Ludon, Macau, Cantenac		

Note: This table is extracted from a classification presented in paragraph form. The text referred to for several properties is part of a section several pages later titled "Particularities of the Great Wines of Bordeaux (Topographic Details)."

No. 20A: Classification According to Le Nouveau Conducteur de l'Etranger—Chaumas, *New Edition (1843)*

		MÉDOC					
		Property	**Proprietor**	**Commune**	**Price**	**1855 Position**	**Name Today**
1	1.1	Château-Margaux	Héritiers-Aguado	Margaux	2000–3000	First	Margaux
2	1.2	Château-Lafitte	Sir Scott	Pauillac		First	Lafite-Rothschild
3	1.3	Latour	Various	Pauillac		First	Latour
4	2.1	Rauzan	Mme de Ségla.Pellier	Margaux	1000–2000	Second	Rausan-Ségla/ Rauzan-Gassies
5	2.2	Mouton	Thuret	Pauillac		Second	Mouton-Rothschild
6	2.3	Léoville	De Lascazes	St-Julien		Second	Léoville-Las-Cases/ Léoville-Poyferré/ Léoville-Barton
7	2.4	Durfort de Vivens	De Vivens	Margaux		Second	Durfort-Vivens
8	2.5	Brannes	Brannes	Cantenac		Second	Brane-Cantenac
9	2.6	Gruau-Laroze	Bethmann and Sarget	St-Julien		Second	Gruaud-Larose
10	2.7	Pichon-Longueville	Pichon Longueville	St-Lambert		Second	Pichon-Longueville (Baron and Comtesse de Lalande)
11	2.8	Lascombe	Fabre	Margaux		Second	Lascombes
12	2.9	Cos-Destournel	Destournel	St-Estèphe		Second	Cos-d'Estournel
13	3.1	Château d'Issan	Duluc	Cantenac	800–1000	Third	d'Issan
14	3.2	Kirwan	Deschryver	Cantenac		Third	Kirwan
15	3.3	Château Pouget	Chavaille	Cantenac		Fourth	Pouget
16	3.4	Desmirail	Desmirail	Margaux		Third	Desmirail
17	3.5	Malescot	St-Exupéry	Margaux		Third	Malescot-Saint-Exupéry
18	3.6	Palmer	Palmer (General)	Margaux		Third	Palmer
19	3.7	Bekker	Divers	Margaux		Third	Marquis d'Alesme-Becker
20	3.8	Giscours	Promis	Labarde		Third	Giscours
21	3.9	Langua	Barton	St-Julien		Third	Langoa-Barton
22	3.10	Bergeron	Ducru	St-Julien		Second	Ducru-Beaucaillou
23	3.11	Cabarus	Duchâtel	St-Julien		Third	Lagrange
24	3.12	Calon-Ségur	Lestapis	St-Estèphe		Third	Calon-Ségur
25	3.13	Montrose	Dumoulin	St-Estèphe		Second	Montrose

26	3.14	Lanoir	Lanoir	Margaux		Not classed	La Gurgue
27	3.15	Ferrières	Ferrières	Margaux		Third	Ferrière
28	3.16	Lalagune	Joffray	Ludon		Third	La Lagune
29	4.1	Duluc, aîné	Duluc, aîné	St-Julien	600–800	Fourth	Branaire-Ducru
30	4.2	St-Pierre	Bontems and Roullet	St-Julien		Fourth	Saint-Pierre
31	4.3	Chât. Beychevelle	Guestier	St-Julien		Fourth	Beychevelle
32	4.4	Château Carnot	De Classun	St-Julien		Fourth	La Tour-Carnet
33	4.5	Duhard-Milon	Castéja	Pauillac		Fourth	Duhart-Milon-Rothschild
34	4.6	Solberg	Solberg	Margaux		Fourth	Marquis de Terme
35	4.7	Dubignon	Dubignon	Margaux		Third	No longer exists
36	4.8	Durand	Pages	Margaux		Fourth	Prieuré-Lichine

RED WINES OF THE GRAVES

		Property	Commune	Price
37	1.1	Haut-Brion	Pessac	1200–1600
38	1.2	La Mission	Talence	900–1000
39	2.1	Pape-Clément	Pessac	800–900
40	3.1	Château-Talence	Talence	400–500
	3.2	Bons-Bourgeois	Merignac	250–300
	3.3	Bonnes-Graves	Léognan	240–270
	3.4	Graves-Ordinaires	Gradignan, Martillac	220–240
	3.5	Petits-Graves	La Brède, Eysines	200–220

RED WINES OF THE CÔTES DE BORDEAUX

1.1	Canon	St-Emilion, Fronsac	700–800
2.1	Saint-Emilion	Pomerol	350–500
3.1	Pomerol	Lussac	250–300
3.2	Bonnes-Côtes	Latresne, Floirac, Cenon, St-Loubès, Lormont, etc.	220–250
	Côtes-de-Bourg	Various	200–220
	Côtes-Ordinaires	Various	100–120
	Petites-Côtes	Blaye, Saint-Macaire	80–100

PALUS WINES

1.1	Queyries	Opposite the Chartrons	280–300
2,3,4 & 5		Monferrand	150–190
		Bassens	220–250

FINE WHITE WINES			
1.1	Lur-Saluces, Tauzin	Sauternes, Barsac	2000–2500
1.2	Cabarus, Deloste	Preignac, Bommes	2000–2500
2.1		Cerons, Podensac, Langon, etc.	300–400
WHITE WINES OF THE GRAVES			
1.1	Saint-Bris-Carbonnieux	Villenave-d'Ornon	300–400
1.2	Dulamon	Blanquefort	300–400
2.1	Graves-Ordinaires	Various	230–250
3.1	Petits-Graves	Various	190–200
WHITE WINES OF THE CÔTES DE BORDEAUX			
1st quality	Sainte-Croix-du-Mont	Sainte-Croix-du-Mont	150–200
1st quality	Loupiac	Loupiac	120–150

No. 20B: Classification According to Le Nouveau Conducteur de l'Etranger—*Chaumas, Fourth Edition (1851)*

MÉDOC							
		Property	**Proprietor**	**Commune**	**Price**	**1855 Position**	**Name Today**
1	1.1	Château-Margaux	Héritiers Aguado	Margaux	4000–6000	First	Margaux
2	1.2	Château-Lafitte	Sir Scott	Pauillac		First	Lafite-Rothschild
3	1.3	Château-Latour	Various	Pauillac		First	Latour
4	1.4	Haut-Brion	Larrieu	Pessac		First	Haut-Brion
5	2.1	Rauzan	Castelpers, Gassies, and Puilboreau	Margaux	2000–3000	Second	Rausan-Ségla/ Rauzan-Gassies
6	2.2	Mouton	Thuret	Pauillac		Second	Mouton-Rothschild
7	2.3	Léoville	De Lascazes and others	St-Julien		Second	Léoville-Las-Cases/ Léoville-Poyferré/ Léoville-Barton
8	2.4	Durfort de Vivens	De Vivens	Margaux		Second	Durfort-Vivens
9	2.5	Brannes	Brannes	Cantenac		Second	Brane-Cantenac
10	2.6	Gruaud-Laroze	Bethmann and Sarget	St-Julien		Second	Gruaud-Larose
11	2.7	Pichon Longueville	Pichon de Longueville	St-Lambert		Second	Pichon-Longueville (Baron and Comtesse de Lalande)
12	2.8	Lascombe	L.A. Hue	Margaux		Second	Lascombes
13	2.9	Cos Destournel	Destournel	St-Estèphe		Second	Cos-d'Estournel
14	3.1	Château d'Issan	Duluc	Cantenac	800–2000	Third	d'Issan
15	3.2	Kirwan	Deschryver junior	Cantenac		Third	Kirwan
16	3.3	Pouget	Chevaille (de)	Cantenac		Fourth	Pouget
17	3.4	Desmirail	Desmirail	Margaux		Third	Desmirail
18	3.5	Malescot	Mme St-Exupéry	Margaux		Third	Malescot-Saint-Exupéry
19	3.6	Bekker	Various	Margaux		Third	Marquis d'Alesme Becker
20	3.7	Ganet (Ve) de Lasalle	None listed	Cantenac		Fourth	Became part of Kirwan
21	3.8	Giscours	Pescator	Labarde		Third	Giscours
22	3.9	Langoa	Barton	St-Julien		Third	Langoa-Barton
23	3.10	Bergeron	Ducru	St-Julien		Second	Ducru-Beaucaillou
24	3.11	Cabarrus	Duchâtel	St-Julien		Third	Lagrange
25	3.12	Calon-Ségur	Lestapis	St-Estèphe		Third	Calon-Ségur
26	3.13	Montrose	Dumoulin	St-Estèphe		Second	Montrose
27	3.14	Lanoire	Lanoire	Margaux		Not classed	La Gurgue

28	3.15	Ferrières	Ferrières	Margaux		Third	Ferrière
29	3.16	La Lagune	Joffray (veuve)	Ludon		Third	La Lagune
30	4.1	Palmer	In receivership	Margaux	600–800	Third	Palmer
31	4.2	Duluc, aîné	Duluc, aîné	St-Julien		Fourth	Branaire-Ducru
32	4.3	St-Pierre	Bontemps and Roullet	St-Julien		Fourth	Saint-Pierre
33	4.4	Cht. Beychevelle	Guestier junior	St-Julien		Fourth	Beychevelle
34	4.5	Carnet	Luetkens	St-Laurent		Fourth	La Tour-Carnet
35	4.6	Duhard-Milon	Castéja	Pauillac		Fourth	Duhart-Milon-Rothschild
36	4.7	Solberg	Solberg	Margaux		Fourth	Marquis de Terme
37	4.8	Dubignon (Marcellin)	Dubignon	Margaux		Third	No longer exists
38	4.9	Durand	Pagès	Margaux		Fourth	Prieuré-Lichine

RED WINES OF THE GRAVES

		Property	**Commune**	Price
39	1.1	Haut-Brion	Pessac	1200–1600
40	1.2	La Mission	Talence	900–1000
41	2.1	Pape-Clément	Pessac	800–900
42	3.1	Château-Talence	Talence	400–500
	3.2	Bons-Bourgeois	Merignac	250–300
	3.3	Bonnes-Graves	Léognan	240–270
	3.4	Graves-Ordinaires	Gradignan, Martillac	220–240
	3.5	Petits-Graves	La Bréde, Eysines	200–220

RED WINES OF THE CÔTES DE BORDEAUX

1.1	Canon	St-Emilion, Fronsac	700–800
2.1	Saint-Emilion	Pomerol	350–500
3.1	Bonnes-Côtes	Pomerol	250–300
		Latresne, Floirac, Cenon, St-Loubès, Lormont, etc.	220–250
	Côtes-de-Bourg	Various	200–220
	Côtes-Ordinaires	Various	100–120
	Petites-Côtes	Blaye, Saint-Macaire	80–100

PALUS WINES

1.1	Queyries	Opposite the Chartrons	280–300
2,3,4 & 5		Monferrand	150–190
		Bassens	220–250

FINE WHITE WINES			
1.1	Lur-Saluces, Tauzin	Sauternes, Barsac	2000–2500
1.2	Cabarus, Deloste	Preignac	2000–2500
2.1		Cerons, Podensac, Langon, etc.	300–400
WHITE WINES OF THE GRAVES			
1.1	Saint-Bris-Carbonnieux	Villenave-d'Ornon	300–400
1.2	Dulamon	Blanquefort	300–400
2.1	Graves-Ordinaires	Various	230–250
3.1	Petits-Graves	Various	190–200
WHITE WINES OF THE CÔTES DE BORDEAUX			
1st quality	Sainte-Croix-du-Mont	Sainte-Croix-du-Mont	150–200
1st quality	Loupiac	Loupiac	120–150

No. 20C: Classification According to Le Nouveau Guide de l'Etranger—*Chaumas (1856)*

		Property	Proprietor	Commune	Price	1855 Position	Name Today
				MÉDOC			
1	1.1	Château-Margaux	Heirs of Aguado	Margaux	4000–6000	First	Margaux
2	1.2	Château-Lafitte	Sir Samuel Scott	Pauillac		First	Lafite-Rothschild
3	1.3	Château-Latour	Various	Pauillac		First	Latour
4	1.4	Haut-Brion	Larieu	Pessac		First	Haut-Brion
5	2.1	Rauzan	Comte de Castelpert	Margaux	2000–3000	Second	Rausan-Ségla/ Rauzan-Gassies
6	2.2	Mouton	N. de Rothschild	Pauillac		Second	Mouton-Rothschild
7	2.3	Léoville	De Lascazes and others	St-Julien		Second	Léoville-Las-Cases/ Léoville-Poyferré/ Léoville-Barton
8	2.4	Durfort de Vivens	De Vivens	Margaux		Second	Durfort-Vivens
9	2.5	Brannes	Baron de Brane	Cantenac		Second	Brane-Cantenac
10	2.6	Gruaud-Laroze	Bethmann, Boisgérard and Sarget	St-Julien		Second	Gruaud-Larose
11	2.7	Pichon Longueville	Pichon de Longueville	Pauillac		Second	Pichon-Longueville (Baron and Comtesse de Lalande)
12	2.8	Lascombe	Mlle Hue	Margaux		Second	Lascombes
13	2.9	Cos Destournel	C.-C. Martyns	St-Estèphe		Second	Cos-d'Estournel
14	2.10	Montrose	Dumoulin	St-Estèphe		Second	Montrose
15	3.1	Château d'Issan	Blanchy	Cantenac	800–2000	Third	d'Issan
16	3.2	Kirwan	Deschryver junior	Cantenac		Third	Kirwan
17	3.3	Desmirail	Sipière	Margaux		Third	Desmirail
18	3.4	Boyd	Several owners	Cantenac		Third	Boyd-Cantenac/ Cantenac Brown
19	3.5	Dubignon	P.-M. Dubignon	Margaux		Third	No longer exists
20	3.6	Malescot	R. Fourcade	Margaux		Third	Malescot-Saint-Exupéry
21	3.7	Becker	Szjardinski and Rolland	Margaux		Third	Marquis d'Alesme-Becker
22	3.8	Giscours	Pescatore	Labarde		Third	Giscours
23	3.9	Langoa	Barton	St-Julien		Third	Langoa-Barton
24	3.10	Bergeron	Ducru	St-Julien		Second	Ducru-Beaucaillou

25	3.11	Lagrange	Duchâtel	St-Julien		Third	Lagrange
26	3.12	Calon	Lestapis	St-Estèphe		Third	Calon-Ségur
27	3.13	Ferrière	Ferrière	Margaux		Third	Ferrière
28	3.14	La Lagune	Ve Jouffroy-Piston	Ludon		Third	La Lagune
29	3.15	Palmer	Émile Pereyre	Cantenac		Third	Palmer
30	4.1	Duluc, aîné	Duluc aîné	St-Julien	600–800	Fourth	Branaire-Ducru
31	4.2	St-Pierre	Bontemps and Ve Roullet	St-Julien		Fourth	Saint-Pierre
32	4.3	Château-Beychevelle	Guestier junior	St-Julien		Fourth	Beychevelle
33	4.4	Carnet	Luetkens	St-Laurent		Fourth	La Tour-Carnet
34	4.5	Duhar-Milon	Castéja	Pauillac		Fourth	Duhart-Milon-Rothschild
35	4.6	De Thermes	Solberg	Margaux		Fourth	Marquis de Terme
36	4.7	Le Prieuré	Ve Pagès	Cantenac		Fourth	Prieuré-Lichine
37	4.8	Poujet-Lassalle	Izan	Cantenac		Fourth	Became part of Kirwan
38	4.9	Poujet	De Chavaille	Cantenac		Fourth	Pouget
39	4.10	Rochet	Ve Lafon de Camarsac	St-Estèphe		Fourth	Lafon-Rochet
40	4.11	Talbot	Marquis d'Aux	St-Julien		Fourth	Talbot

RED WINES OF THE GRAVES

		Property	**Commune**	**Price**
41	1.1	Haut-Brion	Pessac	1200–1600
42	1.2	La Mission	Talence	900–1000
43	2.1	Pape-Clément	Pessac	800–900
44	3.1	Château-Talence	Talence	400–500
	3.2	Bons-Bourgeois	Merignac	250–300
	3.3	Bonnes-Graves	Léognan	240–270
	3.4	Graves-Ordinaires	Gradignan, Martillac	220–240
	3.5	Petits-Graves	La Brède, Eysines	200–240

RED WINES OF THE CÔTES DE BORDEAUX

1.1	Canon	St-Emilion, Fronsac	700–800
2.1	Saint-Emilion	Pomerol	350–500
3.1	Bonnes-Côtes	Pomerol	250–300
		Lussac La Tresne, Floirac, Cenon, St-Loubès	220–250

No. 21A: Classification According to Cocks, English Edition (1846)

		Property	Commune	Proprietor	1855 Position	Name Today
				RED WINES		
1	1.1	Lafite	Pauillac	Sir Samuel Scott	First	Lafite-Rothschild
2	1.2	Château Margaux	Margaux	Heirs of Agauado, Marquis de las Masrismas	First	Margaux
3	1.3	Latour	Pauillac	Marquis de Beaumont	First	Latour
4	1.4	Haut-Brion	Pessac	Larrieu	First	Haut-Brion
5	2.1	Mouton	Pauillac	Thuret	Second	Mouton-Rothschild
6	2.2	Léoville	Saint-Julien	Baron Poyféré de Cerès Barton Marquis de Lascazes	Second	Léoville-Las-Cases Léoville-Poyferré Léoville-Barton
7	2.3	Rauzan	Margaux	Castelpert and Gassies	Second	Rausan-Ségla/Rauzan-Gassies
8	2.4	Durfort	Margaux	De Vivens	Second	Durfort-Vivens
9	2.5	Gruand-Larose	Saint-Julien	Baron Sarget and the heirs of Balguerie Stuttenberg	Second	Gruaud-Larose
10	2.6	Lascombes	Margaux	L.A. Hue	Second	Lascombes
11	2.7	Gorse	Cantenac	De Brannes	Second	Brane-Cantenac
12	3/4/5.1	Ducru	Saint-Julien	Ducru	Second	Ducru-Beaucaillou
13	3/4/5.2	Pichon de Longueville	Saint-Lambert	Pichon de Longueville	Second	Pichon-Longueville (Baron and Comtesse de Lalande)
14	3/4/5.3	Cos. Destournel	Saint-Estèphe	Destournel	Second	Cos-d'Estournel
15	3/4/5.4	Lagrange	Saint-Julien	Duchâtel	Third	Lagrange
16	3/4/5.5	Langoa	Saint-Julien	Barton	Third	Langoa-Barton
17	3/4/5.6	Kirwan	Cantenac	De Scryver	Third	Kirwan
18	3/4/5.7	Château d'Issan	Cantenac	Duluc	Third	d'Issan
19	3/4/5.8	Boyd, Brown, or Fruitier	Cantenac	None listed	Third	Boyd-Cantenac/ Cantenac Brown
20	3/4/5.9	Malescot	Margaux	Saint-Exupéry	Third	Malescot-Saint-Exupéry
21	3/4/5.10	Montrose	Saint-Estèphe	Dumoulin	Second	Montrose
22	3/4/5.11	Saint-Pierre	Saint-Julien	Bontemps duBarry Roullet and Galoupeau	Fourth	Saint-Pierre
23	3/4/5.12	Duluc	Saint-Julien	Duluc	Fourth	Branaire-Ducru
24	3/4/5.13	Talbot	Saint-Julien	Marquis D'Aux	Fourth	Talbot

25	3/4/5.14	Lesparre-Duroc	Pauillac	Milon Mandavy	Fourth	Duhart-Milon-Rothschild
26	3/4/5.15	Bekker	Margaux	Bekker	Third	Marquis d'Alesme-Becker
27	3/4/5.16	Dubignon	Margaux	Marcellin and Talbot	Third	No longer exists
28	3/4/5.17	Desmirail	Margaux	Desmirail	Third	Desmirail
29	3/4/5.18	Calon	Saint-Estèphe	Lestapis	Third	Calon-Ségur
30	3/4/5.19	Carnet	Saint-Laurent	(Luctkins)	Fourth	La Tour-Carnet
31	3/4/5.20	La Lagune	Ludon	Joffray	Third	La Lagune
32	3/4/5.21	Beychevelle	Saint-Julien	P.F. Guestier	Fourth	Beychevelle
33	3/4/5.22	Giscours	Labarde	Promis	Third	Giscours
34	3/4/5.23	Ferrière	Margaux	Ferrière	Third	Ferrière
35	3/4/5.24	Pougets	Cantenac	De Chavaille	Fourth	Pouget
36	3/4/5.25	Lafon-Rochet	Saint-Estèphe	Camarsac	Fourth	Lafon-Rochet
37	3/4/5.26	Casteja (formerly Duhard)	Pauillac	Casteja	Fourth	Duhart-Milon-Rothschild
38	3/4/5.27	Canet Pontet	Pauillac	Pontet	Fifth	Pontet-Canet
39	3/4/5.28	Jurine, at Bages	Pauillac	Jurine	Fifth	Lynch-Bages
40	3/4/5.29	D'Armailhacq	Pauillac	d'Armailhacq	Fifth	Mouton-d'Armailhac
41	3/4/5.30	Ducasse	Pauillac	Ducasse	Fifth	Grand-Puy-Ducasse
42	3/4/5.31	Batalley	Pauillac	D. Guestier	Fifth	Batailley/Haut-Batailley
43	3/4/5.32	Grand Puy	Pauillac	Lacoste (St. Girons)	Fifth	Grand-Puy-Lacoste
44	3/4/5.33	De Bourran (formerly Lynch)	Cantenac	De Bourran	Not classed	Pontac-Lynch
45	3/4/5.34	La Mission	Pessac	Chiapella	Not classed	La Mission-Haut-Brion
46	3/4/5.35	Seguireau Deyries	Margaux	Seguireau Deyries	Not classed	Marsac-Séguineau
47	3/4/5.36	Lanoire	Margaux	Lanoire	Not classed	La Gurgue

WHITE WINES

		Property	Proprietor	1855 Position	Name Today
			SAUTERNES		
1	1.1	Yquem	Madame la Marquise de Lur Saluces	First-superior	Yquem
2	1.2	Yquem*	Guiraud	First	Guiraud
3	2.1	Filhiol	Marquis de Lur Saluces	Second	Filhot
4	2.2	Baptiste	Baptiste	Second	Lamothe-Despujols/ Lamothe-Guignard
5	3.1	Château d'Arche	Lafaurie	Second	d'Arche

*This Second listing of Yquem is clearly in error; it should read "Guiraud."

6	3.2	Rabat	Rabat		
7	3.3	Lafon	Lafon	Not classed	Lafon
			BOMMES		
8	1.1	Vigneau	Madame la Baronne de Rayne	First	Rayne-Vigneau
9	1.2	La Tour Blanche	Focke	First	La Tour-Blanche
10	1.3	Peyruguey	Lafaurie (Sr.)	First	Lafaurie-Peyraguey/ Clos Haut-Peyraguey
11	1.4	Rabant	Deyme	First	Rabaud-Promis/ Sigalas-Rabaud
12	2.1	Lasalle	Emerigon		
13	2.2	Pechotte	Lacoste	Second	Became part of Rabaud-Promis
			PREIGNAC		
14	1.1	Soudiraut	Duroy, Guilhot	First	Suduiraut
15	2.1	Lamontagne	Larrieu	Not classed	Bastor-Lamontagne
16	2.2	Montalier	Le Comte de la Myre Mory	Second	Romer du Hayot
17	2.3	Château de Malle	Le Comte Alexandre de Lur Saluces	Second	de Malle
18	2.4	Les Ormes	Appiau	Not classed	D'Armajan-des-Ormes
			FARGUES		
19	1.1	Mareillac	Mareillac	First	Rieussec
20	2.1	Amé	Amé		
21	2.2	Charon	Brustis		
			BARSAC		
22	1.1	Coutet	Marquis de Lur Saluces	First	Coutet
23	1.2	Climenz	Lacoste	First	Climens
24	1.3	Myrat	Perrot	Second	de Myrat
25	1.4	Daune	Daune	Second	Doisy-Daëne
26	2.1	Vedrine	Madame Dubocq	Second	Doisy-Védrines
27	2.2	Chemizard	Chemizard		
28	2.3	Pernaud	Comtesse de Lur Saluces	Not classed	Pernaud
29	2.4	Suhaute	Marion	Second	Suau
30	2.5	Nérac	Capdeville	Second	Nairac
31	2.6	Guitte-Ronde	A. Journu	Not classed	Guiteronde du Hayot

No. 21B: Classification According to Cocks, French Edition (1850)

		Property	Commune	Proprietor	1855 Position	Name Today
1	1.1	Lafite	Pauillac	Sir S. Scott	First	Lafite-Rothschild
2	1.2	Château Margaux	Margaux	Agauado	First	Margaux
3	1.3	Latour	Pauillac	De Beaumont and others	First	Latour
4	1.4	Haut-Brion	Pessac	Larrieu	First	Haut-Brion
5	2.1	Mouton	Pauillac	Thuret	Second	Mouton-Rothschild
6	2.2	Léoville	Saint-Julien	De Lascazes, Poyféré de Cérès, H. Barton	Second	Léoville-Las-Cases Léoville-Poyferré Léoville-Barton
7	2.3	Rauzan	Margaux	De Castelpers Chabrier du Gol	Second	Rausan-Ségla Rauzan-Gassies
8	2.4	Durfort	Margaux	De Vivens	Second	Durfort-Vivens
9	2.5	Gruaud-Larose	Saint-Julien	Sarget, Bethmann, and Boisgerard	Second	Gruaud-Larose
10	2.6	Lascombes	Margaux	L.-A. Hue	Second	Lascombes
11	2.7	Gorse	Cantenac	De Brane	Second	Brane-Cantenac
12	2.8	Pichon de Longueville	Saint-Lambert	Pichon de Longueville	Second	Pichon-Longueville (Baron and Comtesse de Lalande)
13	3.1	Cos-Destournel	Saint-Estèphe	Destournel	Second	Cos-d'Estournel
14	3.2	Ducru	Saint-Julien	Ducru	Second	Ducru-Beaucaillou
15	3.3	Montrose	Saint-Estèphe	Dumoulin	Second	Montrose
16	3.4	Kirwan	Cantenac	De Scryver	Third	Kirwan
17	3.5	Malescot	Margaux	Madame de Saint-Exupéry	Third	Malescot-Saint-Exupéry
18	3.6	Château d'Issan	Cantenac	Duluc	Third	d'Issan
19	3.7	Lagrange	Saint-Julien	Duchâtel	Third	Lagrange
20	3.8	Langoa	Saint-Julien	Barton	Third	Langoa-Barton
21	3.9	Brown	Fruitier	Cantenac	Third	Boyd-Cantenac/ Cantenac Brown
22	3.1 0	La Lagune	Ludon	Joffray	Third	La Lagune
23	4.1	Desmirail	Margaux	Desmirail	Third	Desmirail
24	4.2	Saint-Pierre	Saint-Julien	Bontemps-Dubarry, Roullet, Galoupeau	Fourth	Saint-Pierre
25	4.3	Dubignon	Margaux	Philippe	Third	No longer exists
26	4.4	Palmer	Cantenac	None listed	Third	Palmer
27	4.5	Duluc	Saint-Julien	Duluc	Fourth	Branaire-Ducru
28	4.6	Bekker	Margaux	Bekker	Third	Marquis d'Alesme-Becker

29	4.7	Dubignon	Margaux	Marcelin	Third	No longer exists
30	4.8	Talbot	Saint-Julien	D'Aux	Fourth	Talbot
31	4.9	Giscours	Labarde	Piscatore	Third	Giscours
32	4.10	Marquis de Thermes	Cantenac	Mac-Daniel	Fourth	Marquis de Terme
33	4.11	Lafon-Rochet	Saint-Estèphe	Camarsac	Fourth	Lafon-Rochet
34	4.12	Castéja	Pauillac	Castéja	Not classed	Haut-Bages-Monpelou
35	4.13	Lesparre-Duroc	Pauillac	None listed	Fourth	Duhart-Milon-Rothschild
36	4.14	Calon	Saint-Estèphe	Lestapis	Third	Calon-Ségur
37	4.15	Carnet	Saint-Laurent	Luetkens	Fourth	La Tour-Carnet
38	4.16	Beychevelle	Saint-Julien	Guestier	Fourth	Beychevelle
39	4.17	Poujet	Cantenac	De Chavaille Lasalle	Fourth	Pouget
40	4.18	Ferrière	Margaux	Ferrière	Third	Ferrière
41	4.19	Pagès	Cantenac	Pagès	Fourth	Prieuré-Lichine
42	5.1	Canet-Pontet	Pauillac	Pontet	Fifth	Pontet-Canet
43	5.2	Chauvet	Pauillac	Chauvet	Fifth	Grand-Puy-Ducasse
44	5.3	Batailley	Pauillac	Lawton	Fifth	Batailley/Haut-Batailley
45	5.4	Jurine, at Bages	Pauillac	Jurine	Fifth	Lynch-Bages
46	5.5	Grand-Moussas	Pauillac	Vasquez	Fifth	Lynch-Moussas
47	5.6	D'Armailhac	Pauillac	D'Armailhac	Fifth	Mouton-Baronne-Philippe
48	5.7	Grand-Puy	Pauillac	Lacoste	Fifth	Grand-Puy-Lacoste
49	5.8	Seguineau-Deyries	Margaux	Seguineau-Deyries	Not classed	Marsac-Séguineau
50	5.9	Lynch	Cantenac	Lynch	Not classed	Pontac-Lynch
51	5.10	Croizet, at Bages	Pauillac	Croizet	Fifth	Croizet-Bages
52	5.11	Danglade	Saint-Sauveur	Danglade	Not classed	Liversan
53	5.12	Popp	Saint-Laurent	Popp	Fifth	Camensac
54	5.13	Bruno-Devez	Saint-Laurent	Bruno-Devez	Fifth	Belgrave
55	5.14	Monpelou	Pauillac	Badimon and Constant	Not classed	Haut-Bages-Monpelou
56	5.15	Constant, at Bages	Pauillac	Constant		
57	5.16	Chollet, at Bages	Pauillac	Chollet	Not classed	Cordeillan Bages
58	5.17	Solberg	Margaux	Mac-Daniel	Fourth	Marquis de Terme
59	5.18	Labégorce	Margaux	Vastapani	Not classed	Labegorce
60	5.19	Veuve de Gorce	Margaux	Veuve de Gorce	Not classed	
61	5.20	Cantemerle	Macau	None listed	Fifth	Cantemerle
62	5.21	La Mission	Pessac	Chapella	Not classed	La-Mission-Haut-Brion
63	5.22	Pape-Clément Sainte-Marie	Pessac	Clouzet	Not classed	Pape-Clément

		WHITE WINES				
		Property	**Commune**	**Proprietor**	**1855 Position**	**Name Today**
1	1.1	Yquem	Sauternes	Madame de Lur-Saluces	First-superior	Yquem
2	1.2	La Tour-Blanche	Bommes	Focke	First	La Tour-Blanche
3	1.3	Coutet	Barsac	De Lur-Saluces	First	Coutet
4	1.4	Climenz	Barsac	Lacoste	First	Climens
5	1.5	Vigneau	Bommes	Madame de Rayne	First	Rayne-Vigneau
6	1.6	Guiraud	Sauternes	Cautériau	First	Guiraud
7	1.7	Rambaut	Bommes	Deyme	First	Rabaud-Promis/ Sigalas-Rabaud
8	1.8	Peyraguey	Bommes	Lafaurie	First	Lafaurie-Peyraguey/ Clos Haut-Peyraguey
9	1.9	Sudiraut	Preignac	Guilhot	First	Suduiraut
10	1.10	Daëne	Barsac	Daëne	Second	Doisy-Daëne
11	1.11	Faux	Barsac	Faux		
12	2.1	Rieussec	Fargues	Maillé	First	Rieussec
13	2.2	Myrat	Barsac	Perrot	Second	de Myrat
14	2.3	Vedrine	Barsac	Madame Dubosq	Second	Doisy-Védrines
15	2.4	Chemizard	Barsac	Chemizard		
16	2.5	Filhiot	Sauternes	De Lur-Saluces	Second	Filhot
17	2.6	Château-d'Arche	Sauternes	Lafaurie	Second	d'Arche
18	2.7	Lamotte	Sauternes	Baptiste	Second	Lamothe
19	2.8	Lafon	Sauternes	Lafon	Not classed	Lafon
20	2.9	Lassalle	Bommes	In receivership		
21	2.10	Pexotto	Bommes	Lacoste	Second	Became part of Rabaud-Promis
22	2.11	Montalier	Preignac	De la Myre-Mory	Second	Romer du Hayot
23	2.12	Pernaud	Barsac	De Lur-Saluces	Not classed	Pernaud
24	2.13	Suau	Barsac	Marion	Second	Suau
25	3.1	Château de Malle	Preignac	De Lur-Saluces	Second	de Malle
26	3.2	La Montagne	Preignac	Larrieu	Not classed	Bastor-Lamontagne
27	3.3	Raba	Sauternes	Raba		
28	3.4	Nérac	Barsac	Capdeville	Second	Nairac
29	3.5	Les Ormes	Preignac	Appiau	Not classed	d'Armajan-des-Ormes
30	3.6	Guitte-Ronde	Barsac	A. Journu	Not classed	Guiteronde du Hayot
31	3.7	Charron	Fargues	Brustis		
32	3.8	Amé	Fargues	Amé		
33	3.9	Château de Cérons	Cérons	De Calvimont	Not classed	de Cérons
34	3.1 0	Anice	Cérons	Biarnès		

No. 22: Classification According to Prefect's Survey (Lesparre, 1849)

		Property	Commune	1855 Position	Name Today
1	1	Château Lafitte	Pauillac	First	Lafite-Rothschild
2	1	Château Latour	Pauillac	First	Latour
3	2	Brane-Mouton	Pauillac	Second	Mouton-Rothschild
4	2	Pichon Longueville	Pauillac	Second	Pichon-Longueville (Baron and Comtesse de Lalande)
5	4	Castera et Lesparre	Pauillac	Fourth	Duhart-Milon-Rothschild
6	4	Duroc amillou	Pauillac	Fourth	Duhart-Milon-Rothschild
7	4	Guetier, Weltner à Batailley	Pauillac	Fifth	Batailley/Haut Batailley
8	4	Vasques à Moussat	Pauillac	Fifth	Lynch-Moussas
9	5	de Ponet à Canet	Pauillac	Fifth	Pontet-Canet
10	5	Darmailhacq à Mouton	Pauillac	Fifth	Mouton-d'Armailhac
11	5	de Chauvet à Pauillac	Pauillac	Fifth	Grand-Puy-Ducasse
12	5	Lacoste au Grand Puy	Pauillac	Fifth	Grand-Puy-Lacoste
13	5	Jurine et Croiste à bages	Pauillac	Fifth	Lynch-Bages
14	5	Jurine et Croiste à bages	Pauillac	Fifth	Croizet-Bages
15	5	Ferchaud et St. Lambert	Pauillac		
16	6	Weltener à Tastin	Pauillac		
17	6	de Gerès à Foubadet	Pauillac	Not classed	Fonbadet
18	6	Ste. Colombe et Vve Couttan à Pauillac	Pauillac		
19	2	Leoville (de Las Caze et Poyfere de Cèse)	Saint-Julien	Second	Léoville-Las-Cases/ Léoville-Poyféré
20	2	Barton Leoville	Saint-Julien	Second	Léoville-Barton
21	2	Gruau Laroze à MM. Sarget et Bethmann	Saint-Julien	Second	Gruaud-Larose
22	2	Pichon Longueville already mentioned in Pauillac where the residence is located	Saint Julien	Second	Part of Pichon-Longueville (Comtesse de Lalande)
23	3	Château de Lagrange à M. Duchatel	Saint-Julien	Third	Lagrange
24	3	Ducru	Saint-Julien	Second	Ducru-Beaucaillou
25	4	Duluc	Saint-Julien	Fourth	Branaire-Ducru
26	4	Bontemps-Dubarry, St. Pierre, MM. Roultet et Galoupeau	Saint-Julien	Fourth	Saint-Pierre
27	4	de Bedout	Saint-Julien		
28	4	Talbot à M. d'Aux	Saint-Julien	Fourth	Talbot

29	4	Barton Langoa	Saint-Julien	Third	Langoa-Barton
30	4	Chateau de Beychevelle à Mr Guestier	Saint-Julien	Fourth	Beychevelle
31	5	Mr Weltener who has his residence in Pauillac where he is also classed among the Fourth growths	Saint-Julien		
32	1	Caillavo, attached to Chateau Lafitte	Saint-Estèphe	First	Part of Lafite-Rothschild
33	2	Cos, M. Destournel	Saint-Estèphe	Second	Cos-d'Estournel
34	2	Calon M. Lestapis	Saint-Estèphe	Third	Calon-Ségur
35	2	Montrose à M. Dumoulin	Saint-Estèphe	Second	Montrose
36	3	Lalande à Mme Vve Tronquoy	Saint-Estèphe	Not classed	Tronquoy-Lalande
37	3	Le haut vignoble a M. de Canivau	Saint-Estèphe		
38	3	Le bosc au même de Pouehet à M. de Luetkens	Saint-Estèphe		
39	3	Château Lafaye	Saint-Estèphe	Not classed	La Haye
40	3	Cos Laborie à M. Destournel	Saint-Estèphe	Fifth	Cos-Labory
41	3	Pomys à M. Destournel	Saint-Estèphe	Not classed	Pomys
42	3	Cru de croc	Saint-Estèphe	Not classed	Le Crock
43	3	de Ségur a M. Phélan	Saint-Estèphe	Not classed	Phélan-Ségur
44	4	Meyney	Saint-Estèphe	Not classed	Meyney
45	4	Chateau de Pez	Saint-Estèphe	Not classed	de Pez
46	4	Romineau de Leyssac à M. Vve Bernard	Saint-Estèphe		
47	4	Marbuset a Mme Vve Cauyret, et à M. Plaignard	Saint-Estèphe		
48	4	Canteloup à M. de Lilla	Saint-Estèphe	Not classed	Canteloup
49	4	Parramey	Saint-Estèphe		
50	4	Fonpetit	Saint-Estèphe	Not classed	Fonpetit
51	4	Cru de bourg à M. Faget	Saint-Estèphe		
52	5	Malerne	Saint-Estèphe		
53	5	Casteja des demoiselles Cômes	Saint-Estèphe	Not classed	Côme
54	5	Dauteillan	Saint-Estèphe		
55	5	Ladoys	Saint-Estèphe	Not classed	Lilian Ladouys
56	5	Camave au bourg	Saint-Estèphe		
57	5	Moudan a Leyssac	Saint-Estèphe		
58	5	Lauzac à Mr Lille	Saint-Estèphe		

59	6	Vilain Marbuzet Cantetout à la veuve Bernard	Saint-Estèphe		
60	3	Trentaudau à M. de Laroze	Saint-Laurent	Not classed	Larose-Trentaudon
61	4	Carnet à M. de Luetkens	Saint-Laurent	Fourth	La Tour-Carnet
62	4	Several vines belonging to M. Duluc, attached to the domain located in St Julien	Saint-Laurent	Fourth	Part of Branaire-Ducru
63	5	Camarsac à M. Popp	Saint-Laurent	Fifth	Camarsac
64	5	Darmouth à M. Devès	Saint-Laurent	Fifth	Belgrave
65	5	Pergauson à M. de Laroze	Saint-Laurent	Not classed	Larose-Perganson
66	1	Château	Margaux	First	Margaux
67	2	Rauzan	Margaux	Second	Rausan-Ségla/Rauzan-Gassies
68	2	Durfort	Margaux	Second	Durfort-Vivens
69	2	Lascombe	Margaux	Second	Lascombes

Note: The spelling of property names in the third column has been retained as it appears on the original document.

No. 23: Classification According to Biarnez (1849)

		Property	Comment	1855 Position	Name Today
1	1.1	Château-Margaux	"Here's one of the three kings, the trio celestial! . . . Although compared to it, the two others turn pale. Of the three its the one about which gourmets sing: It's alone on its throne, it's the king among kings."	First	Margaux
2	1.2	Laffitte	"In Pauillac another royal scepter is found here. . ."	First	Lafite-Rothschild
3	1.3	Latour	"These walls unimposing, roof and rafters so plain House a glorious king, lord of this great domain."	First	Latour
4	2.1	Château-Rauzan	". . . Venerable Rauzan, a great dignitary, A prince, a true blue blood, to kings almost equal...."	Second	Rausan-Ségla/ Rauzan-Gassies
5	2.2	Cos-Destournel	"A second growth vineyard it could be considered, As long as in bottles, not bulk, it's delivered"	Second	Cos-d'Estournel
6	2.3	Durfort	"Durfort also does claim, in a manner most bold, the crown of a second and all that it holds. I contest not its rank, nor its class, nor degree, It's rock-solid terrain's proof of its dignity: But, the greater the name, all the more we expect, Vesta's flame can't stay lit when it suffers neglect. . . . Thus it is with Durfort whose brillance has been dimmed, And though second growth rank its not had to rescind It has only the glow of an empty prestige. . . ."	Second	Durfort-Vivens
7	2.4	Gruau-Larose	"Even with so much land some would say too fecund, One can not take away its rank as a second. . . . If revolts in July with their wild anarchy Had not deprived the French of their old monarchy, A decree would have passed under royal signature Making Larose a first, of this we can be sure."	Second	Gruaud-Larose
8 **9** **10**	2.5 2.6 2.7	Léoville Barton Léoville Lascase Léoville Poiféré	"Léoville is the peer of the firsts all will say Be it Barton by name, Lascase or Poiféré, . . . I cannot understand by what test ill-defined Experts rank Léoville as a second class wine; How the grandest of all, the divine Poiféré, Could have been so misjudged by our elders this way!"	Second	Léoville-Las-Cases/ Léoville-Poyferré/ Léoville-Barton
11	2.8	Mouton	"Who'd believe that Mouton, wine both modest and great Can come after Lafite, and is but second rate?"	Second	Mouton- Rothschild
12	2.9	Pichon de Longueville	"It is not quite Rauzan, nor is it Léoville, But it's true to itself, it's Pichon de Longueville."	Second	Pichon-Longueville (Baron and Comtesse de Lalande)
13	3.1	Château-Kirwan	"Let us stop for awhile; here is Château Kirwan: It's the first of the thirds; of the thirds the most grand."	Third	Kirwan

14	3.2	Château d'Issan	". . . Here is Château d'Issan; once again, a third growth."	Third	d'Issan
15	3.3	Ducru-Bergeron	"Ducru-Bergeron in a manner most bold, Among second growth wines covets a place to hold."	Second	Ducru-Beaucaillou
16	3.4	Langoa	"A third growth that enjoys the love and protection Lavished by an owner in search of perfection;"	Third	Langoa-Barton
17	3.5	Montrose	"And Montrose today, with its delicate flavor, Almost like a second in finesse and savor; If '34s standard were met every year It could challenge those higher with nothing to fear."	Second	Montrose
18	4.1	Bêchevelle	"With soil the reflection of this château's treasure, The wine is a fourth growth in splendour and measure."	Fourth	Beychevelle
19	4.2	Becker	"And Becker, whose surface has been so diminished, . . . Nobly classed among fourths, on occasion it's heard That their aroma makes them the rival of thirds."	Third	Marquis d'Alesme-Becker
20	4.3	Calon-Ségur	"When Calon-Ségur once belonged to another, Its wine was proclaimed to be worthy of honor; Hardly had it passed from its master's possession, Then went it from third down to fourth in concession."	Third	Calon-Ségur
21	4.4	La Lagune	". . . But it is unctuous, it is rich, it is frank, Vermillion in color, it shines in the fourth rank."	Third	La Lagune
22	4.5	de Terme/ Mac-Daniel	"Elegant Desmirail, whose vines closely planted Make wine touched with fire, like amber decanted,	Fourth	Marquis de Terme
23	4.6	Desmirail	De Terme or Mac-Daniel and Dubignon-Talbot, The other Dubignon, Ferrière and Malescot,	Third	Desmirail
24	4.7	Dubignon	Nobly classed among fourths, on occasion it's heard	Third	No longer exists
25	4.8	Dubignon-Talbot	That their aroma makes them the rival of thirds."	Third	No longer exists
26	4.9	Duhart	"Within Pauillac's boundaries is the quarter Milon, Where Duroc and Duhart, both fourth growths	Fourth	Duhart-Milon-Rothschild
27	4.10		located, Draw richness and flavor from land highly rated."	Fourth	Duhart-Milon-Rothschild
28	4.11	Duluc	"Bechevelle's close neighbor, Duluc's a heavy wine; Though with the same ranking, its nose does not linger.	Fourth	Branaire-Ducru
29	4.12	Ferrière	"Nobly classed among fourths, on occasion it's heard That their aroma makes them the rival of thirds."	Third	Ferrière
30	4.13	Giscours	". . . Giscours, whose production has seen augmentation, Had formerly rested among the fourth station. Will the recent change made in its land and its vines, Result in production of greatly improved wine?"	Third	Giscours
31	4.14	Lagrange	"A fourth growth at first sight, to raise its condition, A wealthy new owner has changed its tradition."	Third	Lagrange

32	4.15	La Tour Carnet	"The owner also claims with conviction extreme That wine drinkers all hold an opinion absurd, Classifying his wine in the fourth class, not third."	Fourth	La Tour-Carnet
33	4.16	Malescot	"Nobly classed among fourths, on occasion it's heard That their aroma makes them the rival of thirds."	Third	Malescot-Saint-Exupéry
34	4.17	Poujet	". . . And your wine, always pure, so warm and so tender, Is almost the equal of third growths in splendor."	Fourth	Pouget
35	4.18	Prieuré	"In a merited rise to the Fourth rank reclassed Its wine glimmers today thanks to its brilliant past."	Fourth	Prieuré-Lichine
36	4.19	Saint-Pierre	"The two wines of Saint-Pierre are both fourths in the trade; Although many gourmets would promote them a grade."	Fourth	Talbot
37	4.20	Talbot	"All the charm and the grace that a fourth growth can claim Does the wine d'Aux-Talbot well attach to its name."	Fourth	Saint-Pierre
38	5.1	Batailley	"Here shines Pauillac's terrain, from which fine vineyards spring, Fifth growths benefiting from all that such soils bring. . . . Batailley, elegant, replete with *œnantine*."	Fifth	Batailley/Haut-Batailley
39	5.2	Camensac	"Devèze-Camensac was, we quite recently find, But a premier bourgeois, just a simply made wine; But a gentleman blessed with an innate virtue, Full of clever ideas and intelligence too, Will soon see his star rise to the heights of the sky, And success recompense his efforts by and by. Thus it is Camensac claims its place in the sun"	Fifth	Camensac
40	5.3	Darmaillac	"Here shines Pauillac's terrain, from which fine vineyards spring, Fifth growths benefiting from all that such soils bring. . . . Darmaillac, Linch-Moussas and the vineyard Jurine;"	Fifth	Mouton-d'Armailhac
41	5.4	Deveze	"Deveze is a fifth growth whose quality shines bright, and might rise further still which well would be its right."	Fifth	Belgrave
42	5.5	Grand-Puy-Lacoste	"Here shines Pauillac's terrain, from which fine vineyards spring,	Fifth	Grand-Puy-Lacoste
43	5.6	Grand-Puy-Ducase	Fifth growths benefiting from all that such soils bring. . . . Here are the two grand Puys, both Lacoste and Ducasse:"	Fifth	Grand-Puy-Ducasse
44	5.7	Jurine	"Here shines Pauillac's terrain, from which fine vineyards spring,	Fifth	Lynch-Bages
45	5.8	Linch-Moussas	Fifth growths benefiting from all that such soils bring. . . . Darmaillac, Linch-Moussas and the vineyard Jurine;"	Fifth	Lynch-Moussas

46	5.9	Pontet	"Here shines Pauillac's terrain, from which fine vineyards spring, Fifth growths benefiting from all that such soils bring. Up there look at Pontet, the best wine of its class;"	Fifth	Pontet-Canet
47	artisan	Palmer	"In Margaux there's a growth among those which aspire To the rank of a prince in this golden empire; In the not distant past this was almost achieved: But for quite a long time it saw these hopes deceived . . . Palmer, in the grip of a hand that was unlearned, Began to lose all that noble vines had once earned; The effect of poor work and bad practice combined Relegated this growth to that of homemede wine; But delivered from this ownership ill-advised, We will see once again how its fortunes will rise;"	Third	Palmer
1		Iquem	"Venerable Iquem's at the head of the list;"	First superior	Yquem
2		Clémens	"Then comes Rayne, or Vigneau, and Coutet of Barsac, And Clémems, and Mirat, and Duroy of Preignac, And the full-bodied wine oh so sweet and so sound, That's produced by Tour-Blanche from the best land around"	First	Climens
3		Coutet		First	Coutet
4		Duroy		First	Suduiraut
5		La Tour-Blanche		First	La Tour Blanche
6		Mirat		Second	Myrat
7		De Rayne ou de Vigneau		First	Rayne-Vigneau

Note: Classifications in the above chart are based on where Biarnez says the various properties are generally rated, not on where he thinks they should be. Since, with few exceptions, he does not position properties within classes, the above listings are presented alphabetically.

No. 24: Classification According to Royer (1852)

		Property	Commune	Proprietor	1855 Position	Name Today
1	1.1	Latour	Pauillac	De Beaumont and consorts	First	Latour
2	1.2	Château Margaux	Margaux	Agauado family	First	Margaux
3	1.3	Lafitte	Pauillac	Sir Samuel Scott	First	Lafite-Rothschild
4	2.1	Mouton	Pauillac	Tharet	Second	Mouton-Rothschild
5	2.2	Pichon	Saint-Lambert	de Longueville	Second	Pichon-Longueville (Baron and Comtesse de Lalande)
6	2.3	La Rose	Saint-Julien	Sarget, Bethmann, and Boisregard	Second	Gruaud-Larose
7	2.4	Léoville	Saint-Julien	De Lascazes Poyféré de Cérès and Barton	Second	Léoville-Las-Cases Léoville-Poyferré Léoville-Barton
8	2.5	De Gorse	Cantenac	Brane	Second	Brane-Cantenac
9	2.6	Rauzan	Margaux	Chabrier de Castelper	Second	Rausan-Ségla/ Rauzan-Gassies
10 **11**	2.7 2.8	Lascombes and Durfort	Margaux ensemble		Second	Lascombes and Durfort-Vivens
12	3.1	Lagrange (Cabarus)	Saint-Julien	Duchâtel	Third	Lagrange
13	3.2	Château de Langoa	Saint-Julien	Barton	Third	Langoa-Barton
14	3.3	Montrose	Saint-Estèphe	Dumoulin	Second	Montrose
15	3.4	Cos-Destournel	Saint-Estèphe	Destournel	Second	Cos-d'Estournel
16	3.5	Ducru	Saint-Julien		Second	Ducru-Beaucaillou
17	3.6	Calon	Saint-Estèphe	Lestapis	Third	Calon-Ségur
18	3.7	Château d'Issan	Cantenac		Third	d'Issan
19	3.8	Malescot	Margaux	These properties are cited as third growths in a separate paragraph following the table	Third	Malescot-Saint-Exupéry
20	3.9	Kirwan	Cantenac		Third	Kirwan
21	3.10	Brown			Third	Boyd-Cantenac/ Cantenac Brown
22	3.11	La Lagune	Ludon		Third	La Lagune
23	4.1	Palmer	Cantenac	Palmer	Third	Palmer
24	4.2	Duluc	Saint-Julien	Duluc	Fourth	Branaire-Ducru
25	4.3	Giscours	Labarde	Piscatore	Third	Giscours
26	4.4	Château de Beychevelle	Saint-Julien	Guestier	Fourth	Beychevelle

27	4.5	Talbot	Saint-Julien	D'Aux	Fourth	Talbot
28	4.6	Carnet	Saint-Laurent	Luetkens	Fourth	La Tour-Carnet
29	4.7	Jurine	Pauillac	Bages	Fifth	Lynch-Bages
30	4.8	Pontet-Canet	Pauillac		Fifth	Pontet-Canet
31	4.9	Mouton d'Armaillac	Pauillac		Fifth	Mouton-d'Armailhac
32	4.10	Cantemerle	Macau		Fifth	Cantemerle
33	4.11	Batailley	Pauillac	Guestier	Fifth	Batailley/Haut-Batailley
34	4.12	Saint-Pierre	Saint-Julien	Various	Fourth	Saint-Pierre

No. 25: Classification According to Armailhacq (1855)

		Property	Proprietor	Comments	1855 Position	Name Today
1	1.1	Lafite	Samuel Scott		First	Lafite-Rothschild
2	1.2	Latour	de Beaumont de Coutivron de Flers		First	Latour
3	1.3	Château-Margaux	Aguado		First	Margaux
4	2.1	Cos-Destournel	Martyns	The trade had long contested it as a second	Second	Cos-d'Estournel
5	2.2	Brane-Mouton	Rothschild	Some feel that it is the equal of Lafite	Second	Mouton-Rothschild
6	2.3	Pichon-Longueville	Pichon-Longueville		Second	Pichon-Longueville (Baron and Comtesse de Lalande)
7	2.4	Léoville	Lascases Poiferé Barton		Second	Léoville-Las-Cases Léoville-Poyferré Léoville-Barton
8	2.5	Beau-Caillou	Ducru	Should be placed among the seconds, although it doesn't quite attain the price of the seconds; Franck wrongly classes it as a third	Second	Ducru-Beaucaillou
9	2.6	Gruau-Larose	Sarget Balguerie Bethmann Bois-Gérard		Second	Gruaud-Larose
10	2.7	Durfort de Vivens	Puységur		Second	Durfort-Vivens
11	2.8	Rausan	Castelpers Chabrier		Second	Rausan-Ségla Rauzan-Gassies
12	2.9	Lascombe	Hue		Second	Lascombes
13	2.10	Brane-Cantenac	Brane		Second	Brane-Cantenac
14	3.1	Monrose	Dumoulin	It had debuted as a second, but the trade refused to keep it there	Second	Montrose
15	3.2	Lagrange	Du Chatel		Third	Lagrange
16	3.3	Trentaudon	Larose	Several merchants rate it no more than a fourth; its class has not yet been exactly determined	Not classed	Larose-Trintaudon
17	3.4	La Tour de Carnet	Luetkens	Used to be placed among the thirds, and is likely to remain so, although Franck places it among the fourths	Fourth	La Tour-Carnet

18	3.5	Lacolonie and Malescot	Saint-Exuperi		Third	Malescot-Saint-Exupéry
19	3.6	Desmirail	Desmirail		Third	Desmirail
20	3.7	Dubignon	Dubignon		Third	No longer exists
21	3.8	Palmer	Pereyre		Third	Palmer
22	3.9	Issan	Blanchy		Third	d'Issan
23	3.10	Kirwan	Deschryver		Third	Kirwan
24	3.11	Brown	Fruitier and C°		Third	Boyd-Cantenac/ Cantenac Brown
25	3.12	Prieuré	Pagès		Fourth	Prieuré-Lichine
26	3.13	Ganet	Lassalle		Fourth	Became part of Kirwan
27	3.14	Pouget	de Chaville		Fourth	Pouget
28	3.15	Giscours	Pescatore		Third	Giscours
29	3.16	La Lagune	Piston	Was classed among the thirds; nevertheless, Franck places it among the fourths	Third	La Lagune
30	4.1	Calon-Ségur		It had been at the head of the thirds; it will make a comeback	Third	Calon-Ségur
31	4.2	Cos-Labory	Martyns	A second-fourth	Fifth	Cos-Labory
32	4.3	Rochet	Lafon de Camarsac		Fourth	Lafon-Rochet
33	4.4	Mouton-d'Armailhacq	d'Armailhacq	A second-fourth	Fifth	Mouton-d'Armailhac
34	4.5	Pontet-Canet	de Pontet	Among the head of the second-fourths	Fifth	Pontet-Canet
35	4.6	Castéja	Castéja	A fourth according to Franck; others think it a third	Fourth	Duhart-Milon-Rothschild
36	4.7	Batailley	Lawton	A second-fourth	Fifth	Batailley/Haut-Batailley
37	4.8	Langoa	Barton	A third according to Franck; others in the trade think it a fourth; "[Talbot] like Langoa, is classed among the fourth growths."	Third	Langoa-Barton
38	4.9	Talbot	d'Aux		Fourth	Talbot
39	4.10	Château de Beychevelle	Guestier		Fourth	Beychevelle
40	4.11	Duluc	Duluc	Classed among the fourths, it sometimes sells for almost as much as the thirds	Fourth	Branaire-Ducru

41	4.12	Saint-Pierre	Bontemps du Barri veuve Roulet Galoupeau	Sometimes sells like the thirds	Fourth	Saint-Pierre
42	4.13	Ferrière	Ferrière	Franck places it among the fourths, but several times it has sold like the thirds	Third	Ferrière
43	4.14	Solberg	Solberg		Fourth	Marquis de Terme
44	4.15	Becker	Szjasderski Rolland		Third	Marquis d'Alesme-Becker
45	4.16	Verrière and Arquié	Verrière	Purchased vines from M. Brown (third growth), and should have kept that class, but it is only classed as a fourth		
46	4.17	Château du Tertre	Henry	Used to be a fifth, and has since found great favor; is now classed among the fourths	Fifth	du Tertre
47	5.1	Libéral	Libéral		Fifth	Haut-Bages-Libéral
48	5.2	Pedesclaux	Pedesclaux		Fifth	Pédesclaux
49	5.3	Jurine	Jurine		Fifth	Lynch-Bages
50	5.4	Bages	Calvé		Fifth	Croizet-Bages
51	5.5	Grand-Puy	Lacoste	Advantageously placed among the fifths	Fifth	Grand-Puy-Lacoste
52	5.6	Mompeloup	Castéja	Priced like the preceding wines (fifths)	Not classed	Haut-Bages-Monpelou
53	5.7	De Bedout	De Bedout			
54	5.8	Liversan	Danglade		Not classed	Liversan
55	5.9	Perganson	Lahens	Often sells as a fifth, but this ranking is contested	Not classed	Larose-Trintaudon
56	5.10	Popp	Popp		Fifth	Camensac
57	5.11	Bruneau-Devez	Bruneau-Devez	A fifth, or second-fourth	Fifth	Belgrave
58	5.12	Labegorce	Vastapani		Not classed	Labegorce
59	5.13	Gorse	Gorse			
60	5.14	Angludet	Fleuri d'Anglade Legras		Not classed	Angludet
61	5.15	Dauzac	Viebrock		Fifth	Dauzac
62	5.16	Cantemerle	Villeneuve	A fifth or second-fourth	Fifth	Cantemerle
63		Ducasse*	Duroi		Fifth	Grand-Puy-Ducasse
64		Moussas*	Vasquez		Fifth	Lynch-Moussas

*These two properties are mentioned in the text which is dedicated to a discussion of classed-growth properties, but no clear ranking is assigned to them.

No. 26: Classification According to Saint-Amant (1855)

		Property	Commune	Comments	1855 Position	Name Today
1	1.1	Lafite	Pauillac		First	Lafite-Rothschild
2	1.2	Latour	Pauillac		First	Latour
3	1.3	Château-Margaux	Margaux		First	Margaux
4	1.4	Haut-Brion	Pessac (Graves)	Although acknowledged as a first, it is felt that given its current quality, it would be lucky to be a second	First	Haut-Brion
5	2.1	Cos-Destournel	Saint-Estèphe	In a difficult year, the wine has so little body that it is inferior to wines below it in the classification	Second	Cos-d'Estournel
6	2.2	Branne-Mouton	Pauillac	It should definitely be raised to a first	Second	Mouton-Rothschild
7	2.3	Pichon-Longueville	Pauillac		Second	Pichon-Longueville (Baron and Comtesse de Lalande)
8	2.4	Léoville	Saint-Julien		Second	Léoville-Las-Cases/ Léoville-Poyferré/ Léoville-Barton
9	2.5	Monrose	Saint-Estèphe	Although alternatively placed as a third, it is well and truly a second	Second	Montrose
10	2.6	Gruau-Larose (Fonbedeau)	Saint-Julien		Second	Gruaud-Larose
11	2.7	Durfort-Puységur	Margaux		Second	Durfort-Vivens
12	2.8	Rausan	Margaux	Mentions "the two Rausans" as being equal to the Château (Margaux)	Second	Rausan-Ségla/ Rauzan-Gassies
13	2.9	Rausan	Margaux		Second	Rausan-Ségla/ Rauzan-Gassies
14	2.10	Lascombe	Margaux		Second	Lascombes
15	2.11	Gorce	Cantenac		Second	Brane-Cantenac
16	3.1	Beau-Caillou	Saint-Julien	Owing to its fine exposure, this property is in the process of pushing from the third toward the second rank	Second	Ducru-Beaucaillou
17	3.2	Lagrange	Saint-Julien	Once a fourth, it has risen to a third. Will this be its peak?	Third	Lagrange
18	3.3	Calon-Ségur	Saint-Estèphe	It can be a third or a fourth depending on the year	Third	Calon-Ségur
19	3.4	Malescot	Margaux		Third	Malescot-Saint-Exupéry
20	3.5	Desmirail	Margaux		Third	Desmirail

21	3.6	Dubignon	Margaux		Third	No longer exists
22	3.7	Issan	Cantenac		Third	d'Issan
23	3.8	Brown-Fruitier	Cantenac		Third	Boyd-Cantenac/ Cantenac Brown
24	3.9	Prieuré	Cantenac		Fourth	Prieuré-Lichine
25	3.10	Chavaille	Cantenac		Fourth	Pouget
26	3.11	Giscours	Labarde		Third	Giscours
27	4.1	La Lagune	Ludon		Third	La Lagune
28	4.2	La Tour de Carnet	Saint-Laurent	Used to be a third, it has fallen a notch	Fourth	La Tour-Carnet
29	4.3	Palmer	Cantenac	We soon expect it to be a third	Third	Palmer
30	4.4	Rochet	Cantenac	The proprietors feel that they are better than a fourth	Fourth	Lafon-Rochet
31	4.5	Langoa	Saint-Julien		Third	Langoa-Barton
32	4.6	Talbot	Saint-Julien	Like its neighbor Langoa, Talbot is a fourth	Fourth	Talbot
33	4.7	Château de Beychevelle	Saint-Julien	More than one wine classed as a third is not as distinctive as this	Fourth	Beychevelle
34	4.8	Duluc aîné	Saint-Julien	Classed as a fourth, many thirds are not as good; it depends on the year	Fourth	Branaire-Ducru
35	4.9	Saint-Pierre	Saint-Julien	Classed as a fourth, many thirds are not as good; it depends on the year	Fourth	Saint-Pierre
36	4.10	Detherme	Margaux		Fourth	Marquis de Terme
37	4.11	du Tertre	Arsac		Fifth	du Tertre
38	5.1	Libéral	Pauillac		Fifth	Haut-Bages-Libéral
39	5.2	Mouton-d'Armailhacq	Pauillac	Given the innovations of the owner, M. d'Armailhacq, this will soon be a fourth	Fifth	Mouton-d'Armailhac
40	5.3	Cos-Labory	Saint-Estèphe		Fifth	Cos-Labory
41	5.4	Batailley	Pauillac		Fifth	Batailley/Haut-Batailley
42	5.5	Castéja	Pauillac		Fourth	Duhart-Milon-Rothschild
43	5.6	Jurine	Pauillac		Fifth	Lynch-Bages
44	5.7	Lacoste	Pauillac		Fifth	Grand-Puy-Lacoste
45	5.8	Pontet-Canet	Pauillac		Fifth	Pontet-Canet
46	5.9	Liversan	Saint-Sauveur	Advantageously placed among the fifths	Not classed	Liversan
47	5.10	Moussas	Pauillac		Fifth	Lynch-Moussas
48	5.11	Ducasse	Pauillac		Fifth	Grand-Puy-Ducasse
49	5.12	Sauves-Cantemerle	Macau		Fifth	Cantemerle

No. 27: Classification According to Lamothe (1856)

		Property	Commune	1855 Position	Name Today
			MÉDOC		
1	1.1	Château Margaux	Margaux	First	Margaux
2	1.2	Château-Lafitte	Pauillac	First	Lafite-Rothschild
3	1.3	Château-Latour	Pauillac	First	Latour
4	1.4	Haut-Brion	Pessac	First	Haut-Brion
5	2.1	Rauzan	Margaux	Second	Rausan-Ségla/Rauzan-Gassies
6	2.2	Mouton	Pauillac	Second	Mouton-Rothschild
7	2.3	Léoville	Saint-Julien	Second	Léoville-Las-Cases/Léoville-Poyferré/ Léoville-Barton
8	2.4	Durfort de Vivens	Margaux	Second	Durfort-Vivens
9	2.5	Brane	Cantenac	Second	Brane-Cantenac
10	2.6	Gruaud-Laroze	Saint-Julien	Second	Gruaud-Larose
11	2.7	Pichon-Longueville	Pauillac	Second	Pichon-Longueville (Baron and Comtesse de Lalande)
12	2.8	Lascombe	Margaux	Second	Lascombes
13	2.9	Cos-Destournel	Saint-Estèphe	Second	Cos-d'Estournel
14	2.10	Montrose	Saint-Estèphe	Second	Montrose
15	3.1	Château-d'Issan	Cantenac	Third	d'Issan
16	3.2	Kirwan	Cantenac	Third	Kirwan
17	3.3	Desmirail	Margaux	Third	Desmirail
18	3.4	Boyd	Cantenac	Third	Boyd-Cantenac/Cantenac Brown
19	3.5	Dubignon	Margaux	Third	No longer exists
20	3.6	Malescot	Margaux	Third	Malescot-Saint-Exupéry
21	3.7	Becker	Margaux	Third	Marquis d'Alesme-Becker
22	3.8	Giscours	Labarde	Third	Giscours
23	3.9	Langoa	Saint-Julien	Third	Langoa-Barton
24	3.10	Bergeron	Saint-Julien	Second	Ducru-Beaucaillou
25	3.11	Lagrange	Saint-Julien	Third	Lagrange
26	3.12	Calon	Saint-Estèphe	Third	Calon-Ségur
27	3.13	Ferrière	Margaux	Third	Ferrière
28	3.14	La Lagune	Ludon	Third	La Lagune
29	3.15	Palmer	Cantenac	Third	Palmer
30	4.1	Duluc aîné	Saint-Julien	Fourth	Brainare-Ducru
31	4.2	Saint-Pierre	Saint-Julien	Fourth	Saint-Pierre

32	4.3	Château-Beychevelle	Saint-Julien	Fourth	Beychevelle
33	4.4	Carnet	Saint-Laurent	Fourth	La Tour-Carnet
34	4.5	Duhar-Milon	Pauillac	Fourth	Duhart-Milon-Rothschild
35	4.6	De Thermes	Margaux	Fourth	Marquis de Terme
36	4.7	Le Prieuré	Cantenac	Fourth	Prieuré-Lichine
37	4.8	Poujet-Lassalle	Cantenac	Fourth	Became part of Kirwan
38	4.9	Poujet	Cantenac	Fourth	Pouget
39	4.10	Rochet	Saint-Estèphe	Fourth	Lafon-Rochet
40	4.11	Talbot	Saint-Julien	Fourth	Talbot
			GRAVES		
41	1.1	Haut-Brion	Pessac	First	Haut-Brion
42	1.2	La Mission	Talence	Not classed	La Mission-Haut-Brion
43	2.1	Pape Clément	Pessac	Not classed	Pape Clément
44	3.1	Château-Talence	Talence		
		Bons Bourgeois	Mérignac		
		Bonnes Graves	Léognan		
		Graves ordinaires	Gradignan, Martillac		
		Petites Graves	La Brède, Eyzines		
			CÔTES		
		Canon	Saint-Émilion		
		Saint-Émilion	Pomerol		
		Bonnes Côtes	Pomerol Lussac La Tresne, Floirac Cenon, Saint-Loubès		

No. 28: Classification According to Lamorillière (1857)

		Property	Commune	1855 Position	Name Today
1	1.1	Château Margaux	Margaux	First	Margaux
2	1.2	Château-Lafitte	Pauillac	First	Lafite-Rothschild
3	1.3	Château-Latour	Pauillac	First	Latour
4	1.4	Haut-Brion	Pessac	First	Haut-Brion
5	1.5	La Mission	Talence	Not classed	La Mission-Haut-Brion
6	2.1	Rauzan	Margaux	Second	Rausan-Ségla/Rauzan-Gassies
7	2.2	Mouton	Pauillac	Second	Mouton-Rothschild
8	2.3	Léoville	Saint-Julien	Second	Léoville-Las-Cases/Léoville-Poyferré/ Léoville-Barton
9	2.4	Durfort de Vivens	Margaux	Second	Durfort-Vivens
10	2.5	Brane	Cantenac	Second	Brane-Cantenac
11	2.6	Gruaud-Laroze	Saint-Julien	Second	Gruaud-Larose
12	2.7	Pichon-Longueville	Pauillac	Second	Pichon-Longueville (Baron and Comtesse de Lalande)
13	2.8	Lascombe	Margaux	Second	Lascombes
14	2.9	Cos-Destournel	Saint-Estèphe	Second	Cos-d'Estournel
15	2.10	Montrose	Saint-Estèphe	Second	Montrose
16	2.11	Pape Clément	Pessac	Not classed	Pape-Clément
17	3.1	Château-d'Issan	Cantenac	Third	d'Issan
18	3.2	Kirwan	Cantenac	Third	Kirwan
19	3.3	Desmirail	Margaux	Third	Desmirail
20	3.4	Boyd	Cantenac	Third	Boyd-Cantenac/Cantenac Brown
21	3.5	Dubignon	Margaux	Third	No longer exists
22	3.6	Malescot	Margaux	Third	Malescot-Saint-Exupéry
23	3.7	Becker	Margaux	Third	Marquis d'Alesme-Becker
24	3.8	Giscours	Labarde	Third	Giscours
25	3.9	Langoa	Saint-Julien	Third	Langoa-Barton
26	3.10	Bergeron	Saint-Julien	Second	Ducru-Beaucaillou
27	3.11	Lagrange	Saint-Julien	Third	Lagrange
28	3.12	Calon	Saint-Estèphe	Third	Calon-Ségur
29	3.13	Ferrière	Margaux	Third	Ferrière
30	3.14	Château-Talence	Talence		
31	3.15	La Lagune	Ludon	Third	La Lagune
32	3.16	Palmer	Cantenac	Third	Palmer
33	4.1	Duluc aîné	Saint-Julien	Fourth	Brainare-Ducru

34	4.2	Saint-Pierre	Saint-Julien	Fourth	Saint-Pierre
35	4.3	Château-Beychevelle	Saint-Julien	Fourth	Beychevelle
36	4.4	Carnet	Saint-Laurent	Fourth	La Tour-Carnet
37	4.5	Duhar-Milon	Pauillac	Fourth	Duhart-Milon-Rothschild
38	4.6	De Thermes	Margaux	Fourth	Marquis de Terme
39	4.7	Le Prieuré	Cantenac	Fourth	Prieuré-Lichine
40	4.8	Poujet-Lassalle	Cantenac	Fourth	Became part of Kirwan
41	4.9	Poujet	Cantenac	Fourth	Pouget
42	4.10	Rochet	Saint-Estèphe	Fourth	Lafon-Rochet
43	4.11	Talbot	Saint-Julien	Fourth	Talbot

No. 29: Classification According to Redding (1860)

		Proprietor	Commune	1855 Position	Name Today
1	1.1	Château Margaux	Margaux	First	Margaux
2	1.2	Château Lafitte	Pauillac	First	Lafite-Rothschild
3	1.3	Latour	Pauillac	First	Latour
4	1.4	Haut-Brion	Pessac	First	Haut-Brion
5	2.1	De Brannes, formerly Gorse	Cantenac	Second	Brane-Cantenac
6	2.2	Cos-Destournel, now Martyns	Saint-Estèphe	Second	Cos-d'Estournel
7	2.3	Durefort, de Vivens	Margaux	Second	Durfort-Vivens
8	2.4	Gruaud-Larose, several proprietors	Saint-Julien	Second	Gruaud-Larose
9	2.5	Lascombe, formerly Fabre	Margaux	Second	Lascombes
10	2.6	Léoville, three proprietors	Saint-Julien	Second	Léoville-Las-Cases/ Léoville-Poyferré/ Léoville-Barton
11	2.7	Mouton-Thuret	Pauillac	Second	Mouton-Rothschild
12	2.8	Pichon de Longueville	Pauillac	Second	Pichon-Longueville (Baron and Comtesse de Lalande)
13	2.9	Rauzan-Rauzan	Margaux	Second	Rausan-Ségla/Rauzan-Gassies
14	3.1	Blanchy, Château d'Issan	Cantenac	Third	d'Issan
15	3.2	Desmirail	Margaux	Third	Desmirail
16	3.3	Dubignon, formerly Talbot	Margaux	Third	No longer exists
17	3.4	Duan, formerly Bergeron, often sells as second class	Saint-Julien	Second	Ducru-Beaucaillou
18	3.5	Fruitier, formerly Brown	Cantenac	Third	Boyd-Cantenac/Cantenac Brown
19	3.6	Viscount de Lasalle, Ganet	Cantenac	Fourth	Pouget
20	3.7	Giscours, Pescatore	Labarde	Third	Giscours
21	3.8	Kirwan, De Scryver, junior	Cantenac	Third	Kirwan
22	3.9	Lagrange Duchâtel, formerly Brown	Saint-Julien	Third	Lagrange
23	3.10	Langoa, B., formerly Pontet	Saint-Julien	Third	Langoa-Barton
24	3.11	Lanoire	Margaux	Not classed	La Gurgue
25	3.12	Montrose, Dumoulin, often sells as second-class wine	Saint-Estèphe	Second	Montrose
26	3.13	Pougets, de Chavaille	Cantenac	Fourth	Pouget
27	3.14	Countess de Exupéry, formerly Malescot	Margaux	Third	Malescot-Saint-Exupéry
28	4.1	Marquis d'Aux	Saint-Julien	Fourth	Talbot
29	4.2	Beychevelle, Guestier, junior	Saint-Julien	Fourth	Beychevelle
30	4.3	Calon Lestapis, formerly Segur, sometimes sold as third class	Saint-Estèphe	Third	Calon-Ségur

31	4.4	Carnet	Saint-Laurent	Fourth	La Tour-Carnet
32	4.5	Castéja, formerly Widow Duhard, Milon	Pauillac	Fourth	Duhart-Milon-Rothschild
33	4.6	Dubignon, M.	Margaux	Third	No longer exists
34	4.7	Duluc, the elder	Saint-Julien	Fourth	Branaire-Ducru
35	4.8	Ferrière	Margaux	Third	Ferrière
36	4.9	Lafon Rochet, Camarsac	Saint-Estèphe	Fourth	Lafon-Rochet
37	4.10	La Lagune, Widow Jeffray	Ludon	Third	La Lagune
38	4.11	Lesparre-Duroc, Milon-Mandavy	Pauillac	Fourth	Duhart-Milon-Rothschild
39	4.12	Solberg	Margaux	Fourth	Marquis de Terme
40	4.13	Pagès, formerly Durand, the Priory	Cantenac	Fourth	Prieuré-Lichine
41	4.14	Palmer, the property of the administration of the Caisse hypothecaire	Cantenac	Third	Palmer
42	4.15	Saint-Pierre, three proprietors	Saint-Julien	Fourth	Saint-Pierre
43	5.1	Batailley, Lawton	Pauillac	Fifth	Batailley/Haut-Batailley
44	5.2	De Bedout, formerly Duboscq	Saint-Julien		
45	5.3	Canet-Pontet	Pauillac	Fifth	Pontet-Canet
46	5.4	Cantemerle, Baron de Villeneuve	Macau	Fifth	Cantemerle
47	5.5	Chollet, formerly Duclerq at Bages	Pauillac	Not classed	Cordeillan-Bages
48	5.6	V. Constant, at Bages	Pauillac		
49	5.7	Cos-Labory	Saint-Estèphe	Fifth	Cos-Labory
50	5.8	Coutanceau-Devez	Saint-Laurent	Fifth	Belgrave
51	5.9	Croizet at Bages	Pauillac	Fifth	Croizet-Bages
52	5.10	Widow Ducasse	Pauillac	Fifth	Grand-Puy-Ducasse
53	5.11	Grand Puy, Lacoste, formerly St. Guirons	Pauillac	Fifth	Grand-Puy-Lacoste
54	5.12	Jurine at Bages	Pauillac	Fifth	Lynch-Bages
55	5.13	Libéral at Bages	Pauillac	Fifth	Haut-Bages-Libéral
56	5.14	Liversan-d'Anglade	Saint-Sauveur	Not classed	Liversan
57	5.15	Lynch Moussas	Pauillac	Fifth	Lynch-Moussas
58	5.16	Mission, The, near Haut-Brien, Chiapella	Pessac	Not classed	La Mission-Haut-Brion
59	5.17	Mouton, Tharet*	Pauillac	Fifth	Mouton-d'Armailhac
60	5.18	Monpelou, formerly Castéja	Pauillac	Not classed	Haut-Bages-Monpelou
61	5.19	Popp	Saint-Laurent	Fifth	Camensac
62	5.20	Perganson, E. Lahens	Saint-Laurent	Not classed	Larose-Trintaudon

*This is clearly a confusion with Mouton-d'Armailhac; "Mouton-Thuret" is listed previously as a second growth.

No. 30: Classification According to Cocks (1865)

		Property	Commune	Proprietor	1855 Position	Name Today
				RED WINES		
1	1.1	Lafite	Pauillac	Sir S. Scott	First	Lafite-Rothschild
2	1.2	Château Margaux	Margaux	Agauado	First	Margaux
3	1.3	Latour	Pauillac	De Beaumont De Courtivron De Flers	First	Latour
4	1.4	Haut-Brion	Pessac	Larrieu	First	Haut-Brion
5	2.1	Mouton	Pauillac	Bon N. de Rothschild	Second	Mouton-Rothschild
6	2.2	Léoville	Saint-Julien	De Lascazes De Poyféré H. Barton	Second	Léoville-Las-Cases Léoville-Poyferré Léoville-Barton
7	2.3	Rauzan-Segala	Margaux	De Castelpers	Second	Rausan-Ségla
8	2.4	Rauzan-Gassies	Margaux	Viguerie	Second	Rauzan-Gassies
9	2.5	Durfort-Vivens	Margaux	Various	Second	Durfort-Vivens
10	2.6	Gruau-Larose	Saint-Julien	None listed	Second	Gruaud-Larose
11	2.7	Lascombes	Margaux	Mlle Hue	Second	Lascombes
12	2.8	De Brane	Cantenac	Baron de Brane	Second	Brane-Cantenac
13	2.9	Pichon-Longueville	Pauillac	Baron de Pichon	Second	Pichon-Longueville (Baron and Comtesse de Lalande)
14	2.10	Cos-Destournel	Saint-Estèphe	Martyns	Second	Cos-d'Estournel
				WHITE WINES*		
1	1.1	Yquem	Sauternes	Madame de Lur-Saluces	First-superior	Yquem
2	1.2	Pichard-Lafaurie	Bommes	Saint-Rieul-Dupouy	First	Lafaurie-Peyraguey/ Clos-Haut-Peyraguey
3	1.3	La Tour-Blanche	Bommes	Various	First	La Tour-Blanche
4	1.4	Le Vigneau	Bommes	De Pontac	First	Rayne-Vigneau
5	1.5	Guiraud	Sauternes	Bernard	First	Guiraud
6	1.6	Sudiraut	Preignac	Guilhot	First	Suduiraut

*This table is titled "Premiers Crus de Vins Blancs."

No. 31: Classification of White Wines According to Daney (March 27, 1867)

		Property	Commune	1855 Position	Name Today
1	1.1	Yquem	Sauternes	First-superior	Yquem
2	1.2	Vigneau	Bommes	First	Rayne-Vigneau
3	1.3	Peyraguey	Barsac	First	Lafaurie-Peyraguey/ Clos-Haut-Peyraguey
4	1.4	Guiraud	Sauternes	First	Guiraud
5	1.5	La-Tour-Blanche	Bommes	First	La Tour-Blanche
6	1.6	Rieussec	Fargues	First	Rieussec
7	1.7	Suduiraut	Preignac	First	Suduiraut
8	1.8	Coutet	Barsac	First	Coutet
9	1.9	Climens	Barsac	First	Climens
10	1.10	Rabaut	Bommes	First	Rabaud-Promis/ Sigalas-Rabaud
11	2.1	Peyxotto	Bommes	Second	Became part of Rabaud-Promis
12	2.2	Doisy-Védrines-Boireau	Barsac	Second	Doisy-Védrines
13	2.3	Myrat	Barsac	Second	de Myrat
14	2.4	Doisy-Daëne	Barsac	Second	Doisy-Daëne
15	2.5	Filhot	Sauternes	Second	Filhot
16	2.6	Château-d'Arche	Sauternes	Second	d'Arche
17	2.7	Caillou	Barsac	Second	Caillou
18	2.8	Dudon	Barsac	Not classed	Dudon
19	2.9	Daney (crû Sahuc)	Preignac		
20	2.10	Lamothe	Sauternes	Second	Lamothe-Despujols/ Lamothe-Guignard
21	2.11	Crû Carles-Destrac	Barsac	Not classed	de Carles
22	2.12	Crû Lafond (Raymond)	Sauternes	Not classed	Raymond-Lafon
23	2.13	Crû Lafon et Bertin	Preignac		
24	2.14	Crû Latapy	Preignac	Not classed	Cru d'Arche-Pugneau
25	2.15	Crû Lafon (François)	Sauternes		
26	2.16	Crû Lafon (Désir)	Sauternes	Not classed	Lafon
27	2.17	Crû Bertin-Chevalier	Preignac		
28	2.18	Crû Magey frères	Preignac		
29	2.19	Crû Fabre	Preignac		
30	2.20	Crû Pinsan Pieda	Barsac		

31	2.21	Doisy-Debans	Barsac		
32	2.22	Crû Dubroca	Barsac	Second	Doisy-Dubroca
33	2.23	Crû Destanque Publicain	Barsac		
34	2.24	Crû Dubourg-Ricard	Barsac		
35	2.25	Crû Lacoste-Lapatate	Barsac		
36	2.26	Montalier-Romer	Preignac	Second	Romer du Hayot
37	2.27	Malle	Preignac	Second	de Malle
38	2.28	des-Rochers	Preignac		
39	2.29	Crû Godart	Preignac		
40	2.30	La-Montagne	Preignac	Not classed	Bastor-Lamontagne
41	2.31	Veyres	Preignac	Not classed	Veyres
42	2.32	Crû Ducaule	Barsac		
43	2.33	Crû Dubedat	Sauternes		
44	2.34	Crû Lahens	Preignac		
45	2.35	Crû Laborde	Barsac	Not classed	Ménota

No. 32: Classification of White Wines According to Armailhacq, Second Edition (1867)

		Property	Commune	Proprietor	1855 Position	Name Today
1	1.1	Yquem	Sauternes	M. le marquis de Lur-Saluces	First-superior	Yquem
2	1.2	Vigneau	Bommes	M. le vicomte de Pontac	First	Rayne-Vigneau
3	1.3	Peyraguey	Barsac	M. le comte Duchâtel	First	Lafaurie-Peyraguey/ Clos-Haut-Peyraguey
4	1.4	Guiraud	Sauternes	M. Bernard	First	Guiraud
5	1.5	La-Tour-Blanche	Bommes	MM. Maître and Merman	First	La Tour-Blanche
6	1.6	Suduiraut	Preignac	M. Guillot	First	Suduiraut
7	1.7	Coutet	Barsac	M. le marquis de Lur-Saluces	First	Coutet
8	1.8	Climens	Barsac	M. Lacoste (Eloi)	First	Climens
9	1.9	Rieussec	Fargues	M. Mayé	First	Rieussec
10	1.10	Rabeau	Bommes	M. Drouillet de Sigalas	First	Rabaud-Promis/ Sigalas-Rabaud
11	2.1	Peyxotto-Ninseq	Bommes	M. Ribet	Second	Became part of Rabaud-Promis
12	2.2	Doisy-Védrines	Barsac	M. Boireau	Second	Doisy-Védrines
13	2.3	Mirat	Barsac	Mme veuve Moller	Second	de Myrat
14	2.4	Doisy	Barsac	M. Deane	Second	Doisy-Daëne
15	2.5	Filhot	Sauternes	M. le marquis de Lur-Saluces	Second	Filhot
16	2.6	Château-d'Arche	Sauternes	Various	Second	d'Arche
17	2.7	Caillou	Barsac	M. Sarraute	Second	Caillou
18	2.8	Dudon	Barsac	M. Pichard	Not classed	Dudon
19	2.9	Daney (crû Sahuc)	Preignac			
20	2.10	Lamothe	Sauternes	MM. Massieu and Diets	Second	Lamothe-Despujols/ Lamothe-Guignard
21	2.11	Crû Carles	Barsac	M. Destrac	Not classed	de Carles
22	2.12	Crû Lafond (Raymond)	Sauternes	M. Lafon	Not classed	Raymond-Lafon
23	2.13	Crû Lafon et Bertin	Preignac	M. Lafon and Bertin		
24	2.14	Crû Latapy	Preignac	M. Latapy	Not classed	Cru d'Arche-Pugneau
25	2.15	Crû Lafon (François)	Sauternes	M. Lafon aîné		
26	2.16	Crû Lafon (Désir)	Sauternes	M. Désir Lafon	Not classed	Lafon
27	2.17	Crû Bertin-Chevalier	Preignac	M. Bertin Chevalier		

28	2.18	Crû Magey frères	Preignac	MM. Magey frères		
29	2.19	Crû Fabre	Preignac	M. Fabre		
30	2.20	Crû Pinsan Pieda	Barsac	M. Pinsan Piéda		
31	3.1	Doisy	Barsac	M. Debans		
32	3.2	Crû Dubroca	Barsac	M. Dubroca	Second	Doisy-Dubroca
33	3.3	Crû Destanque Publicain	Barsac	M. Destanque Publicain		
34	3.4	Crû Dubourg-Ricard	Barsac	MM. Dubourg, Ricaud and Roumieu		
35	3.5	Crû Lacoste-Lapatate	Barsac	M. Lacoste-Lapatate		
36	3.6	Montalier-Roumerc	Preignac	M. le comte de Lamyre-Mory	Second	Romer du Hayot
37	3.7	Malle	Preignac	M. le comte Henry de Lur-Saluces	Second	de Malle
38	3.8	Crû Godart	Preignac	M. Godart		
39	3.9	Lamontagne	Preignac	M. Larrieu	Not classed	Bastor-Lamontagne
40	3.10	Veyres	Preignac	Mme veuve Delbos	Not classed	Veyres
41	3.11	des-Rochers	Preignac	M. le marquis de Rolland		
42	3.12	Crû Ducole	Barsac	M. Ducole		
43	3.13	Crû Dubedat	Sauternes	M. Dubedat, dit Coco		
44	3.14	Crû Lahens	Preignac	M. Lahens		
45	3.15	Crû Boireau	Preignac	M. Boireau		
46	3.16	Crû Laborde	Barsac	M. Laborde	Not classed	Ménota

No. 33A Classification of White Wines According to **Bordeaux et ses Vins,** *Second Edition (1868)*

		Property	Proprietor	1855 Position	Name Today
			SAUTERNES		
1	1.1	Yquem	Heirs of Marquis B. de Lur Saluces	First-superior	Yquem
2	1.2	Guiraud	Bernard	First	Guiraud
3	2.1	Crû d'Arche	Camille Lafaurie	Second	d'Arche
4	2.2	Château d'Arche	Méric	Second	d'Arche
5	2.3	D'Arche Vimeney	Comet	Not classed	Now part of Lafaurie-Peyraguey
6	2.4	Château d'Arche	Dupeyron	Second	d'Arche
7	2.5	Filhot	Heirs of Marquis B. de Lur Saluces	Second	Filhot
8	2.6	Crû de Lamothe	Massieux	Second	Lamothe-Despujols
9	2.7	Crû de Lamothe	Dietz	Second	Lamothe-Guignard
10	2.8	A Chaoure	Désir Lafon	Not classed	Lafon
11	2.9	Au Puits	Raymond Lafon	Not classed	Raymond-Lafon
12	2.10	Au Puits	André Lafon		
			BOMMES		
13	1.1	Vigneau	Gabriel de Pontac	First	Rayne-Vigneau
14	1.2	Peyraguey	Comtesse Duchâtel	First	Lafaurie-Peyraguey/ Clos-Haut-Peyraguey
15	1.3	La-Tour-Blanche	MM. Maître and G. Merman	First	La Tour-Blanche
16	1.4	Rabaut	Drouillet de Sigalas	First	Sigalas-Rabaud
17	2.1	Peixotto	Alfred Ribet	Second	Now part of Rabaud-Promis
			PREIGNAC		
18	1.1	Suduiraut	Guillot de Suduiraut frères	First	Suduiraut
19	2.1	Malle	Comte Henri de Lur Saluces	Second	de Malle
20	2.2	Romer	Comte de La Mire-Mory	Second	Romer du Hayot
			FARGUES		
21	1.1	Rieussec	Ch. Crépin-Mayé	First	Rieussec
22	2.1	Romer	de La Myre Mory	Second	Romer du Hayot
			BARSAC		
23	1.1	Coutet	Heirs of Marquis Bertrand de Lur-Saluces	First	Coutet
24	1.2	Climens	Éloi Lacoste	First	Climens
25	2.1	Myrat	veuve H. Moller	Second	de Myrat

26	2.2	Broustet	veuve H. Moller	Second	Broustet
27	2.3	Caillou	Louis Sarraute	Second	Caillou
28	2.4	Nairac	Brunet-Capdeville	Second	Nairac
29	2.5	Doisy	Daenne	Second	Doisy-Daëne
30	2.6	Doisy-Védrines	Boireau fils frères	Second	Doisy-Védrines
31	2.7	Suau	Jean Marion	Second	Suau

No. 33B: Classification of White Wines According to **Bordeaux et ses Vins,** *Third Edition (1874)*

		Property	Proprietor	1855 Position	Name Today
			SAUTERNES		
1	1.1	Yquem	Heirs of Marquis B. de Lur-Saluces	First-superior	Yquem
2	1.2	Guiraud	Bernard	First	Guiraud
3	2.1	Raymond-Lafon	Raymond Lafon	Not classed	Raymond-Lafon
4	2.2	Crû d'Arche	C. Lafaurie	Second	d'Arche
5	2.3	Château d'Arche	Méricq	Second	d'Arche
6	2.4	Château d'Arche	Dupeyron	Second	d'Arche
7	2.5	Château D'Arche Vimeney	Comet	Not classed	Now part of Lafaurie-Peyraguey
8	2.6	Lafon	Désir Lafon		
9	2.7	Au Pouit	François Lafon		
10	2.8	Filhot	Heirs of Marquis B. de Lur-Saluces	Second	Filhot
11	2.9	Crû Lamothe	Conseil	Second	Lamothe-Despujols
12	2.10	Crû Lamothe	Dietz	Second	Lamothe-Guignard
			BOMMES		
13	1.1	Vigneau	Gabriel de Pontac	First	Rayne-Vigneau
14	1.2	Peyraguey	Comtesse Duchâtel	First	Lafaurie-Peyraguey/ Clos-Haut-Peyraguey
15	1.3	La-Tour-Blanche	MM. Paul Maître and G. Merman	First	La Tour-Blanche
16	1.4	Rabaut	Drouilhet de Sigalas	First	Sigalas-Rabaud
17	2.1	Peyxotto	Alfred Ribet	Second	Now part of Rabaud-Promis
			PREIGNAC		
18	1.1	Suduiraut	Guillot de Suduiraut frères	First	Suduiraut
19	2.1	Montalier-Romer	Comte de la Myre Mory	Second	Romer du Hayot
20	2.2	Crû de Malle	Comte H. de Lur-Saluces	Second	de Malle
21	2.3	des-Rochers	Marquis de Rolland		
			FARGUES		
22	1.1	Rieussec	Ch. Crépin	First	Rieussec
23	2.1	Romer	de la Myre Mory	Second	Romer du Hayot
24	2.2	Claveries	Vve Becquet		
25	2.3	Au Peyron	Champetié		

BARSAC					
26	1.1	Coutet	Heirs of Mis B. de Lur-Saluces	First	Coutet
27	1.2	Climens	Alfred Ribet	First	Climens
28	2.1	Myrat-Broustet	Vve H. Moller	Second	de Myrat and Broustet
29	2.2	Caillou	L. Sarraute	Second	Caillou
30	2.3	Pernaud	Tenré fils	Not classed	Pernaud
31	2.4	Crû Carle	René Destrac	Not classed	de Carles
32	2.5	Cantegril	Ballande	Not classed	Cantegril
33	2.6	Clos Bonneau	Dufour		
34	2.7	Doisy-Védrines	Boireau fils frères	Second	Doisy-Védrines
35	2.8	Doisy Gravas	Dubroca frères	Second	Doisy-Dubroca
36	2.9	Doisy	Daëne	Second	Doisy-Daëne
37	2.10	Nairac	Brunet-Capdeville	Second	Nairac
38	2.11	Roumieux	Dubourg		
39	2.12	A Lapinesse	Th. Lacoste		
40	2.13	A Piéda	Pinsan		
41	2.14	Dudon	Pichard	Not classed	Dudon
42	2.15	Suau	Vve Paris	Second	Suau
43	2.16	de Rolland	Froidefond	Not classed	de Roland
44	2.17	Prost-Jeanlève	Boireau frères	Not classed	Prost
45	2.18	Quitteronde	R. Sarraute	Not classed	Guiteronde-du-Hayot
46	2.19	Grillon, ancien Lacombe	Labarthe	Not classed	Grillon
47	2.20	Ménota	Laborde Pascal	Not classed	Ménota
48	2.21	Mercier	Publicain Destanque		
49	2.22	Hallet	Ducaule Laguerre	Not classed	Hallet
50	2.23	Piot	Glaëne	Not classed	Piot-David
51	2.24	A Lapinesse	Pontalier	Not classed	Farluret
52	2.25	A Lapinesse	Pascaud Mamou		
53	2.26	A Lapinesse	Boireau Latrésotte		
54	2.27	Beaulac	Barbe frères		
55	2.28	Bouillot	Roustaing		
56	2.29	A Mathalin	Lussac		
57	2.30	A Labouade	Ferrand		
58	2.31	A Pléguemate	Dugoua		
59	2.32	A Plantey	Dubroca		

No. 33C: Classification of White Wines According to **Bordeaux et ses Vins**, *Fourth Edition (1881)*

		Property	Proprietor	1855 Position	Name Today
			SAUTERNES		
1	1.1	Yquem	Heirs of Marquis B. de Lur-Saluces	First-superior	Yquem
2	1.2	Guiraud	P. Bernard	First	Guiraud
3	2.1	Raymond-Lafon	R. Lafon	Not classed	Raymond-Lafon
4	2.2	Lafon	Désir Lafon	Not classed	Lafon
5	2.3	Crû d'Arche	C. Lafaurie	Second	d'Arche
6	2.4	Château d'Arche	Méricq	Second	d'Arche
7	2.5	Château D'Arche Vimeney	Comet	Not classed	Now part of Lafaurie-Peyraguey
8	2.6	Au Pouit	François Lafon		
9	2.7	Filhot	Marquis B. de Lur-Saluces	Second	Filhot
10	2.8	Crû Lamothe	Conseil	Second	Lamothe-Depujols
11	2.9	Crû Lamothe	Dietz	Second	Lamothe-Guignard
			BOMMES		
12	1.1	Vigneau	Gabriel de Pontac	First	Rayne-Vigneau
13	1.2	Peyraguey	Farinel and Grédy	First	Lafaurie-Peyraguey
14	1.3	Haut-Peyraguey	E. Grillon	First	Clos-Haut-Peyraguey
15	1.4	A Barrail-Dulle-Peyraguey	Bertin		
16	1.5	La-Tour-Blanche	Osiris	First	La Tour-Blanche
17	1.6	Rabaut	Drouilhet de Sigalas	First	Sigalas-Rabaud
18	2.1	Peyxotto	Alfred Ribet	Second	Now part of Rabaud-Promis
			PREIGNAC		
19	1.1	Suduiraut	Emile Petit	First	Suduiraut
20	2.1	Montalier-Romer	Comte de la Myre Mory	Second	Romer du Hayot
21	2.2	Crû de Malle	Comte H. de Lur-Saluces	Second	de Malle
22	2.3	des-Rochers	Marquis de Rolland		
23	2.[1]	La Montagne	Heirs of Amédée Larrieu	Not classed	Bastor-Lamontagne
24	2.[2]	Au Mayne	Mme. de Chalup		
25	2.[3]	Sahuc	Darosney-Daney		
26	2.[4]	Veyres	E. Grillon	Not classed	Veyres

27	$2.^{5}$	Saint-Amant	Vve. Godard	Not classed	Saint-Amand
28	$2.^{6}$	Laville	Larroumet		
29	$2.^{7}$	Aux Arrieux	Lapougnanne		
30	$2.^{8}$	A Lamothe	Bursio		
31	$2.^{9}$	A Lamothe	Vve. Guichard		
32	$2.^{10}$	Bordesoule	Despiet		
33	$2.^{11}$	A Jonka	Ladonne		
34	$2.^{12}$	A Monteil	Paris-Desjardons		
35	$2.^{13}$	Solon	Férodé		
36	$2.^{14}$	Solon	Beguey dit Caquet		
37	$2.^{15}$	des Ormes	Delbourg		
38	$2.^{16}$	A Arrançon	A. Lafon-Bertin		
39	$2.^{17}$	A Boutoc	Fabre		
40	$2.^{18}$	A Boutoc	Latapy, ship's lieutenant	Not classed	d'Arche-Pugneau
41	$2.^{19}$	A Boutoc	Lassauvaju-Magey		
42	$2.^{20}$	A Boutoc	Boyreau-Bouyrelot		
43	$2.^{21}$	A Boutoc	Lados		
44	$2.^{22}$	A Boutoc	Comet		
45	$2.^{23}$	A Boutoc	Pierre Bertin		
46	$2.^{24}$	A Boutoc	Lafon frères		
47	$2.^{25}$	A Boutoc	Bertin cadet		
48	$2.^{26}$	A Boutoc	Capdeville		
49	$2.^{27}$	A Arrançon	Lahiteau		
50	$2.^{28}$	A Arrançon	Marquette fils		
51	$2.^{29}$	A Arrançon	Marquette cadet		
			FARGUES		
52	1.1	Rieussec	Ch. Crépin	First	Rieussec
53	2.1	Romer	de la Myre Mory	Second	Romer du Hayot
54	2.2	Claveries	Champetié		
55	2.3	Au Peyron	J.L. Lignières		
			BARSAC		
56	1.1	Coutet	Heirs of Mis B. de Lur-Saluces	First	Coutet
57	1.2	Climens	Alfred Ribet	First	Climens
58	2.1	Caillou	L. Sarraute	Second	Caillou

59	2.2	Myrat-Broustet	Vve H. Moller	Second	de Myrat and Broustet
60	2.3	Doisy	Juhel Bilot	Second	Doisy-Daëne
61	2.4	Doisy-Védrines	Boireau fils frères	Second	Doisy-Védrines
62	2.5	Doisy Gravas	Dubroca frères	Second	Doisy-Dubroca
63	2.6	Suau	Mme. Chaine	Second	Suau
64	2.7	Pernaud	Alphonse Chaumette and C°	Not classed	Pernaud
65	2.8	Cantegril	Bérard	Not classed	Cantegril
66	2.9	Clos Bonneau-Clouiscot	Dufour		
67	2.10	A Piéda	Pinsan		
68	2.11	Crû de Carle	René Destrac	Not classed	de Carles
69	2.12	Quitteronde	Vve. R. Sarraute	Not classed	Guiteronde-du-Hayot
70	2.13	Prost-Jeanlève	Boireau fils frères	Not classed	Prost
71	2.14	Nairac	Brunet-Capdeville	Second	Nairac
72	2.15	Roumieux	Dubourg	Not classed	Roumieu
73	2.16	Crû Lapinesse	Dugoua		
74	2.17	Crû Lapinesse	Th. Lacoste		
75	2.18	de Rolland	Froidefond	Not classed	de Roland
76	2.19	Dudon	Pichard	Not classed	Dudon
77	2.20	A Plantey	Dubroca	Not classed	
78	2.21	Grillon, ancien Lacombe	Ramond and Marchand		Grillon
79	2.22	Mercier	Publicain Destanque		
80	2.23	Hallet	Pauly	Not classed	Hallet
81	2.24	A Ménota	Teyssonneau	Not classed	Ménota
82	2.25	Piot	Boudin	Not classed	Piot-David
83	2.26	A Lapinesse	Pontalier	Not classed	Farluret
84	2.27	A Lapinesse	Pascaud-Mamou		
85	2.28	A Lapinesse	Boireau Latrésotte		
86	2.29	A Beaulac	Barbe frères		
87	2.30	A Mathalin	Lussac		
88	2.31	A Liot	Cadillon Léon		
89	2.32	A Bouyot	Vve. Roustaing		
90	2.33	A Labouade	Ferrand		
91	2.34	Au Grand-Carretey	Dugoua		
92	2.35	A Blanquine	Lalanne		

No. 33D: Classification of White Wines According to Bordeaux et ses Vins, *Fifth Edition (1886)*

		Property	Proprietor	1855 Position	Name Today
			SAUTERNES		
1	1.1	Yquem	Madame la Marquise de Lur Saluces	First-superior	Yquem
2	1.2	Guiraud	P. Bernard	First	Guiraud
3	2.1	Raymond-Lafon	Raymond Lafon	Not classed	Raymond-Lafon
4	2.2	Lafon	Désir Lafon	Not classed	Lafon
5	2.3	Cru d'Arche	C. Lafaurie	Second	d'Arche
6	2.4	Château d'Arche	Méricq	Second	d'Arche
7	2.5	Château D'Arche Vimeney	P. Lacoste	Not classed	Now part of Lafaurie-Peyraguey
8	2.6	Au pouit	François Lafon		
9	2.7	Filhot	Marquis de Lur Saluces	Second	Filhot
10	2.8	Cru Lamothe	J. Dubédat Biou	Second	Lamothe-Despujols
11	2.9	Cru Lamothe	Numa Espagnet	Second	Lamothe-Guignard
			BOMMES		
12	1.1	Vigneau	Gab. de Pontac	First	Rayne-Vigneau
13	1.2	Peyraguey	Farinel and Grédy	First	Lafaurie-Peyraguey
14	1.3	Haut-Peyraguey	E. Grillon	First	Clos-Haut-Peyraguey
15	1.4	A Barrail-Dulle-Peyraguey	Bertin		
16	1.5	Barrail Peyraguey	Lassauvajue		
17	1.6	La-Tour-Blanche	Osiris	First	La Tour-Blanche
18	1.7	Rabaut	Drouilhet de Sigalas	First	Sigalas-Rabaud
19	2.1	Peyxotto	Drouilhet de Sigalas	Second	Now part of Rabaud-Promis
			PREIGNAC		
20	1.1	de Suduiraut	Emile Petit	First	Suduiraut
21	2.1	Montalier-Romer	Comte de la Myre Mory	Second	Romer du Hayot
22	2.2	Romer	de Beaurepaire	Second	Romer du Hayot
23	2.3	Cru de Malle	Comte H. de Lur Saluces	Second	de Malle
24	2.4	des-Rochers	Marquise de Rolland		
			FARGUES		
25	1.1	Rieussec	Defolie	First	Rieussec
26	2.1	Romer	de la Myre Mory	Second	Romer du Hayot
27	2.2	Romer	de Beaurepaire	Second	Romer du Hayot

28	2.3	Claveries	Champetié		
29	2.4	Au Peyron	J.L. Lignières		
			BARSAC		
30	1.1	Coutet	Heirs of Mis B. de Lur Saluces	First	Coutet
31	1.2	Climens	Henri Gounouilhou	First	Climens
32	2.1	Mirat	Flaugergues and C^o	Second	de Myrat
33	2.2	Caillou	L. Sarraute	Second	Caillou
34	2.3	Doisy	Dubroca frères	Second	Doisy-Dubroca
35	2.4	Doisy-Daëne	Juhel Bilot	Second	Doisy-Daëne
36	2.5	Doisy-Védrines	Boireau fils frères	Second	Doisy-Védrines
37	2.6	Suau	Mme Chaine	Second	Suau
38	2.7	Cantegril	Ballande	Not classed	Cantegril
39	2.8	Pernaud	Vve Lyon-Allemand and fils	Not classed	Pernaud
40	2.9	A Sarançon	Henri Lacoste and Mauriac		
41	2.10	Clos Bonneau-Clouiscot	Dufour		
42	2.11	A Piéda	Pinsan		
43	2.12	Cru de Carle	René Destrac	Not classed	de Carles
44	2.13	A Ménauta	J. Teyssonneau	Not classed	Ménota
45	2.14	Guiteronde	Vve R. Sarraute	Not classed	Guiteronde-du-Hayot
46	2.15	Prost-Jeanlève	Boireau Louis	Not classed	Prost
47	2.16	Nairac	Brunet-Capdeville	Second	Nairac
48	2.17	Cru Lapinesse	Dugoua		
49	2.18	Cru Lapinesse	Th. Lacoste		
50	2.19	A Roumieux	Dubourg	Not classed	Roumieu
51	2.20	Bagas	Loyet		
52	2.21	de Rolland	Froidefond	Not classed	de Roland
53	2.22	Dudon	Balayet	Not classed	Dudon
54	2.23	A Plantey	Dubroca		
55	2.24	Grillon, ancien Lacombe	Vianne Lazare	Not classed	Grillon
56	2.25	Mercier	Publicain Destanque		
57	2.26	Hallet	Pauly	Not classed	Hallet
58	2.27	A Piot	Boudin	Not classed	Piot-David
59	2.28	A Lapinesse	Pontalier	Not classed	Farluret
60	2.29	A Lapinesse	Pascaud-Mamou		
61	2.30	A Lapinesse	Boireau-Latrésotte		

62	2.31	A Beaulac	Barbe frères
63	2.32	A Mathalin	Lussac
64	2.33	A Liot	Cadillon Léon
65	2.34	A Bouyot	Dupeyron
66	2.35	A Labouade	Ferrand
67	2.36	Au Grand-Carretey	Dugoua
68	2.37	A Blanquine	Lalande
69	2.38	Camperos	Loyet
70	2.39	Dom du Basque	Loyet

No. 33E: Classification of White Wines According to **Bordeaux et ses Vins,** *Sixth Edition (1893)*

		Property	Proprietor	1855 Position	Name Today
			SAUTERNES		
1	1.1	Yquem	Heirs of Marquis B. de Lur Saluces	First-superior	Yquem
2	1.2	Guiraud	Heirs of P. Bernard	First	Guiraud
3	2.1	Château D'Arche Vimeney	P. Lacoste	Not classed	Now part of Lafaurie-Peyraguey
4	2.2	Château d'Arche	J. Lafaurie	Second	d'Arche
5	2.3	Château d'Arche	Méricq	Second	d'Arche
6	2.4	Raymond-Lafon	R. Lafon	Not classed	Raymond-Lafon
7	2.5	Lafon	Désir Lafon	Not classed	Lafon
8	2.6	Filhot	Heirs of Marquis B. de Lur Saluces	Second	Filhot
9	2.7	Au pouit	François Lafon		
10	2.8	Cru Lamothe	J. Dubédat Biou	Second	Lamothe-Despujols
11	2.9	Cru Lamothe	Numa Espagnet	Second	Lamothe-Guignard
			BOMMES		
12	1.1	Vigneau	Vte Albert de Pontac	First	Rayne-Vigneau
13	1.2	Haut-Peyraguey	E. Grillon	First	Clos-Haut-Peyraguey
14	1.3	La-Tour-Blanche	Osiris	First	La Tour-Blanche
15	1.4	Lafaurie-Peyraguey	Fr. Grédy	First	Lafaurie-Peyraguey
16	1.5	Rabaut	Drouilhet de Sigalas	First	Sigalas-Rabaud
			PREIGNAC		
17	1.1	de Suduiraut	Emile Petit de Forest	First	Suduiraut
18	2.1	Cru de Malle	Comte Pierre de Lur Saluces	Second	de Malle
19	2.2	des-Rochers	Marquise de Rolland		
20	2.3	Cru de Romer	Comte de Beaurepaire-Louvagny	Second	Romer du Hayot
			FARGUES		
21	1.1	Rieussec	Paul Defolie	First	Rieussec
			BARSAC		
22	1.1	Coutet	Heirs of Marquis B. de Lur Saluces	First	Coutet
23	1.2	Climens	Henri Gounouilhou	First	Climens
24	2.1	Caillou	L. Sarraute	Second	Caillou
25	2.2	Cantegril	Ch. Rodberg, Belgian consul	Not classed	Cantegril
26	2.3	Doisy-Daene	Debans frères	Second	Doisy-Daëne

27	2.4	Doisy-Gravas	Dubroca frères	Second	Doisy-Dubroca
28	2.5	Doisy-Védrines	Boireau-Teysonneau	Second	Doisy-Védrines
29	2.6	Mirat	P. Flaujergues and C°	Second	de Myrat
30	2.7	Piada	E. Brunet	Not classed	Piada
31	2.8	Clos Bonneau-Clouiscot	Dufour		
32	2.9	Pernaud	Comptoir Lyon, Alemand and son	Not classed	Pernaud
33	2.10	Clos Mathalin	J. Ferbos		
34	2.11	Masserau-Lapachère	Paul Pinsan		
35	2.12	A Roumieux	Goyaud	Not classed	Roumieu
36	2.13	A Carle	Lacoste	Not classed	de Carles
37	2.14	A Hallet	Ducale-Pauly	Not classed	Hallet
38	2.15	Menauta	J. Teyssonneau	Not classed	Ménota
39	2.16	Dudon	Balayet	Not classed	Dudon
40	2.17	Camperos	Loyet		
41	2.18	Quitteronde	P. Sarraute	Not classed	Guiteronde-du-Hayot
42	2.19	Barreyre *or* Cru Grand-Jagua	Barreyre		
43	2.20	A Piot	Boudin	Not classed	Piot-David
44	2.21	Prost-Jeanlève	V. Boireau	Not classed	Prost
45	2.22	Suau	V. Chaine	Second	Suau
46	2.23	de Rolland	Ve Froidefond and son	Not classed	de Rolland
47	2.24	Liot	L. Cadillon	Not classed	Liot
48	2.25	Nairac	Brunet-Capdeville	Second	Nairac
49	2.26	de Rocard	L.-E. Pinsan		

No. 33F: Classification of White Wines According to Bordeaux et ses Vins, *Seventh Edition (1898)*

		Property	Proprietor	1855 Position	Name Today
			SAUTERNES		
1	1.1	Yquem	Heirs of Marquis B. de Lur Saluces	First-superior	Yquem
2	1.2	Guiraud	Heirs of P. Bernard	First	Guiraud
3	2.1	Château d'Arche	J. Lafaurie	Second	d'Arche
4	2.2	Raymond-Lafon	R. Lafon	Not classed	Raymond-Lafon
5	2.3	Lafon	Désir Lafon	Not classed	Lafon
6	2.4	Château D'Arche Vimeney	P. Lacoste	Not classed	Now part of Lafaurie-Peyraguey
7	2.5	Château d'Arche	Grégoire Dubédat	Second	d'Arche
8	2.6	Filhot	Heirs of Marquis B. de Lur Saluces	Second	Filhot
9	2.7	Au pouit	Ve François Lafon		
10	2.8	Cru Lamothe	Heirs of Chéri Dubédat-Biou	Second	Lamothe-Despujols
11	2.9	Cru Lamothe	Numa Espagnet	Second	Lamothe-Guignard
			BOMMES		
12	1.1	de Rayne-Vigneau	Vicomte A. de Pontac	First	Rayne-Vigneau
13	1.2	La-Tour-Blanche	Osiris	First	La Tour-Blanche
14	1.3	Rabaud	Drouilhet de Sigalas and Promis	First	Sigalas-Rabaud
15	1.4	Haut-Peyraguey	E. Grillon	First	Clos-Haut-Peyraguey
16	1.5	Lafaurie-Peyraguey	Fr. Grédy	First	Lafaurie-Peyraguey
			PREIGNAC		
17	1.1	de Suduiraut	Emile Petit de Forest	First	Suduiraut
18	2.1	Cru de Malle	Comte Pierre de Lur Saluces	Second	de Malle
19	2.2	des-Rochers	Marquise de Rolland		
20	2.3	Cru de Romer	Comte de Beaurepaire-Louvagny	Second	Romer du Hayot
21	2.4	Pleytegeat	Heirs of E. Larrieu	Not classed	Pleytegeat
			FARGUES		
22	1.1	Rieussec	Paul Defolie	First	Rieussec
			BARSAC		
23	1.1	Coutet	Heirs of Marquis B. de Lur Saluces	First	Coutet
24	1.2	Climens	Henri Gounouilhou	First	Climens
25	2.1	Mirat	P. Flaujergues and P. Martineau	Second	de Myrat
26	2.2	Caillou	L. Sarraute	Second	Caillou

27	2.3	Cantegril	Ch. Rodberg, Belgian consul	Not classed	Cantegril
28	2.4	Doisy-Daene	Jules Debans	Second	Doisy-Daëne
29	2.5	Doisy-Gravas	M. Dubroca	Second	Doisy-Dubroca
30	2.6	Doisy-Védrines	Boireau-Teysonneau	Second	Doisy-Védrines
31	2.7	Piada	E. Brunet	Not classed	Piada
32	2.8	Suau	Emile Garros	Second	Suau
33	2.9	du Closiot			
34	2.10	Pernaud		Not classed	Pernaud
35	2.11	Clos Mathalin			
36	2.12	Masserau-Lapachère			
37	2.13	Guiteronde		Not classed	Guiteronde-du-Hayot
38	2.14	Ducasse			
39	2.15	Dudon	Balayet	Not classed	Dudon
40	2.16	Camperos	Loyet		
41	2.17	Roumieux	Goyaud	Not classed	Roumieu
42	2.18	Roumieux	Bernadet	Not classed	Roumieu (Bernadet)
43	2.19	Roumieux	Léon Lacoste	Not classed	Roûmieu-Lacoste
44	2.20	Cru Hallet	Ducale-Pauly	Not classed	Hallet
45	2.21	Menauta	J. Teyssonneau	Not classed	Ménota
46	2.22	Broustet	Mme Moller, M. G. Supau, tenant	Second	Broustet
47	2.23	Barreyre *or* Cru Grand-Jagua	Arthur Barreyre		
48	2.24	Piot	Dubourg	Not classed	Piot-David
49	2.25	de Rolland	Ve Froidefond	Not classed	de Rolland
50	2.26	Grillon	Vianne-Lazare	Not classed	Grillon
51	2.27	Padouen	Henri Clissey	Not classed	Padouën
52	2.28	Liot	L. Cadillon	Not classed	Liot
53	2.29	Mayne-Bert	Bert		
54	2.30	Cru Carle	Lacoste	Not classed	de Carles
55	2.31	Nairac	Brunet-Capdeville	Second	Nairac

No. 33G: Classification of White Wines According to **Bordeaux et ses Vins,** *Eighth Edition (1908)*

		Property	Proprietor	1855 Position	Name Today
		SAUTERNES			
1	1.1	Yquem	Heirs of Mis B. de Lur Saluces	First-superior	Yquem
2	1.2	Guiraud	Heirs of P. Bernard	First	Guiraud
3	2.1	Château d'Arche	J. Lafaurie	Second	d'Arche
4	2.2	Raymond-Lafon	Louis Pontallier	Not classed	Raymond-Lafon
5	2.3	Lafon	Edmond-Désir Lafon	Not classed	Lafon
6	2.4	Château D'Arche Vimeney	Pierre Sarraute	Not classed	Now part of Lafaurie-Peyraguey
7	2.5	Château d'Arche	Grégoire Dubédat	Second	d'Arche
8	2.6	Filhot	Heirs of Mis B. de Lur Saluces	Second	Filhot
9	2.7	Lamothe	Jos. Bergey	Second	Lamothe-Despujols
10	2.8	Lamothe	Numa Espagnet	Second	Lamothe-Guignard
		BOMMES			
11	1.1	de Rayne-Vigneau	Vicomte de Pontac	First	Rayne-Vigneau
12	1.2	La-Tour-Blanche	The state, owner	First	La Tour-Blanche
13	1.3	Rabaud-Promis	Adrien Promis	First	Rabaud-Promis
14	1.4	Sigalas-Rabaud	Drouilhet de Sigalas	First	Sigalas-Rabaud
15	1.5	Haut-Peyraguey	Ve E. Grillon	First	Clos-Haut-Peyraguey
16	1.6	Lafaurie-Peyraguey	Fr. Grédy	First	Lafaurie-Peyraguey
		PREIGNAC			
17	1.1	de Suduiraut	Vve Emile Petit de Forest	First	Suduiraut
18	2.1	de Malle	Comte Pierre de Lur Saluces	Second	de Malle
19	2.2	de Romer	Vte de Beaurepaire	Second	Romer du Hayot
20	2.3	Cru de Romer-Cadeau-Ramey	Vve Cadeau-Ramey	Second	Romer du Hayot
21	2.4	des-Rochers	Marquise de Rolland		
22	2.5	Bastor-la-Montagne	Commandant René Milleret	Not classed	Bastor-Lamontagne
23	2.6	Cru d'Arche-Pugneau	Roger Duthil	Not classed	Cru d'Arche-Pugneau
24	2.7	Cru Fontebride	Heirs of Fontebride		
25	2.8	Dom. du Mayne	Cte de Chalup		
26	2.9	Dom. de Lamothe	Vve Bursio		
27	2.10	A Boutoc	Lafon frères		
28	2.11	A Boutoc *cru Peyraguey-Le Rousset*	Paul Destanque	Not classed	Cru Rousset-Peyraguey

29	2.12	A Boutoc	Comet-Magey	Not classed	Comet-Magey
30	2.13	A Boutoc *cru de Miselle*	Raoul Comet		
31	2.14	A Boutoc *cru de Miselle*	Albert Comet		
32	2.15	A Boutoc	Capdeville frères		
33	2.16	A Boutoc	Marcelin Dufau		
34	2.17	A Boutoc	Boireau aîné		
35	2.18	A Boutoc	Léopold Boireau		
36	2.19	A Boutoc	Vve Martin Fernand		
37	2.20	A Boutoc	Eug. Capdeville		
38	2.21	Au Haire	Pinsan		
39	2.22	Au Haire	Antoine Pinsan		
40	2.23	Au Haire	Cartier	Not classed	du Haire
41	2.24	Au Haire	Louis Boireau		
42	2.25	Au Haire	Lamothe Sélerin		
43	2.26	Au Haire	Clavier		
44	2.27	A Laville	Larroumet fils	Not classed	Laville
45	2.28	Cru Saint-Amand	Delol, maire	Not classed	Saint-Amand
46	2.29	A Arrançon	Victor Lahiteau		
47	2.30	Sahuc-la-Tour	P.-J. Dubois	Not classed	Sahuc-La-Tour
48	2.31	Dom. de La Forêt	Guischard and Mathieu		
49	2.32	Au bourg	Louis Pinsan		
50	2.33	A Bordessoulles	Justin Lacoste		
51	2.34	A Jonka	Jules Latapy		
52	2.35	A Jonka	C. Fazembat		
53	2.36	A Monteil	Patachon frères		
			FARGUES		
54	1.1	Rieussec	Edgar and Marc Bannel	First	Rieussec
			BARSAC		
55	1.1	Coutet	Heirs of Marquis B. de Lur Saluces	First	Coutet
56	1.2	Climens	Henri Gounouilhou	First	Climens
57	2.1	Myrat	P. Martineau	Second	de Myrat
58	2.2	Doisy-Dubroca	Marcel Dubroca	Second	Doisy-Dubroca
59	2.3	Védrines	Vve J. Teysonneau	Second	Doisy-Védrines
60	2.4	Doisy-Daene	Déjean, of Maison Cazalet and son	Second	Doisy-Daëne
61	2.5	Cantegril	Emile Raymond	Not classed	Cantegril
62	2.6	Suau	Emile Garros	Second	Suau

63	2.7	Broustet	G. Supau	Second	Broustet
64	2.8	Caillou	L. Sarraute	Second	Caillou
65	2.9	Piada	E. Brunet	Not classed	Piada
66	2.10	Roumieux	Goyaud	Not classed	Roumieu
67	2.11	Roumieux	Bernadet	Not classed	Roumieu (Bernadet)
68	2.12	Roumieux	Léon Lacoste	Not classed	Roûmieu-Lacoste
69	2.13	Cru de Carles	René Destrac, F. Barbe, veterinarian, at Podensac	Not classed	de Carles
70	2.14	Mathalin	Vve J. Ferbos		
71	2.15	Guiteronde	P. Sarraute	Not classed	Guiteronde-du-Hayot
72	2.16	Ducasse	Paul Simon		
73	2.17	du Cloziot, former cru Bonneau	Edmond Saint-Jean		
74	2.18	Masserau-Lapachère	Paul Pinsan		
75	2.19	Rolland	R. Froidefond	Not classed	de Rolland
76	2.20	Dudon	Balayé	Not classed	Dudon
77	2.21	Pernaud	Comptoir Lyon-Alemand	Not classed	Pernaud
78	2.22	Piot	Dubourg	Not classed	Piot-David
79	2.23	Prost-Jeanlève	V. Boireau	Not classed	Prost
80	2.24	Grillon	E. Plomby	Not classed	Grillon
81	2.25	Cru Hallet	Pauly	Not classed	Hallet
82	2.26	de Bastard	Vve Baudère et ses fils		
83	2.27	Liot	L. Cadillon	Not classed	Liot
84	2.28	Camperos	Louis Loyet		
85	2.29	Mayne-Bert	Louis Bert		
86	2.30	Cru Laclotte and Cazalis	G. Lacoste		
87	2.31	Cru Haut-Bouyet	J. Larré	Not classed	Bouyot
88	2.32	Menauta	Vve J. Teyssonneau	Not classed	Ménota
89	2.33	Cru du Mayne	Maurice Janin	Not classed	du Mayne

No. 33H: Classification of White Wines According to Bordeaux et ses Vins, *Ninth Edition (1922)*

		Property	Proprietor	1855 Position	Name Today
			SAUTERNES		
1	1.1	Yquem	Comte Eugène de Lur Saluces	First-superior	Yquem
2	1.2	Guiraud	Heirs of P. Bernard	First	Guiraud
3	2.1	Château d'Arche	J. Lafaurie	Second	d'Arche
4	2.2	Château d'Arche	G. Dubédat	Second	d'Arche
5	2.3	Raymond-Lafon	Louis Pontallier	Not classed	Raymond-Lafon
6	2.4	Lafon	Edm.-Désir Lafon, mayor	Not classed	Lafon
7	2.5	Château D'Arche Vimeney	Lucien Lafon	Not classed	Now part of Lafaurie-Peyraguey
8	2.6	Filhot	Comte Eugène de Lur Saluces	Second	Filhot
9	2.7	Lamothe	J. Bergey	Second	Lamothe-Despujols
10	2.8	Lamothe	Louis Espagnet	Second	Lamothe-Guignard
			BOMMES		
11	1.1	de Rayne-Vigneau	Vicomte de Pontac	First	Rayne-Vigneau
12	1.2	La-Tour-Blanche	The state, owner	First	La Tour-Blanche
13	1.3	Rabaud-Promis	Vve Adrien Promis	First	Rabaud-Promis
14	1.4	Sigalas-Rabaud	Drouilhet de Sigalas	First	Sigalas-Rabaud
15	1.5	Haut-Peyraguey	E. Garbay and F. Ginestet	First	Clos-Haut-Peyraguey
16	1.6	Lafaurie-Peyraguey	D. Cordier	First	Lafaurie-Peyraguey
			PREIGNAC		
17	1.1	de Suduiraut	Vve E. Petit de Forest	First	Suduiraut
18	2.1	de Malle	Comte Pierre de Lur Saluces	Second	de Malle
19	2.2	des-Rochers	Marquise de Rolland		
20	2.3	Bastor-la-Montagne	Colonel René Milleret	Not classed	Bastor-Lamontagne
21	2.4	Cru d'Arche-Pugneau	Vve Duthil	Not classed	Cru d'Arche-Pugneau
22	2.5	d'Armajan-des-Ormes	A. Gallice	Not classed	d'Armajan des Ormes
23	2.6	Cru Fontebride	E. Plantey		
24	2.7	Dom. du Mayne	Cte de Chalup	Not classed	du Mayne
25	2.8	Veyres	L. Dequeker	Not classed	Veyres
26	2.9	Dom. de Lamothe	Vigneau		
27	2.10	A Boutoc	Joseph Lafon		
28	2.11	A Boutoc *cru Peyraguey-Le Rousset*	Paul Destanque	Not classed	Cru Rousset-Peyraguey
29	2.12	A Boutoc	Magey-Vigouroux	Not classed	Comet-Magey
30	2.13	A Boutoc *cru de Miselle*	R. Commet		

31	2.13	A Boutoc *cru de Miselle*	A. Commet		
32	2.14	A Boutoc	Capdeville brothers		
33	2.15	A Boutoc	Marcelin Dufau		
34	2.16	A Boutoc	Julien Brice		
35	2.17	A Boutoc	Louis Landau		
36	2.18	A Boutoc	Lesquerre		
37	2.19	A Boutoc	The sons of Eug. Capdeville		
38	2.20	A Boutoc	A. Capdeville		
39	2.21	Au Haire	R. Despujols		
40	2.22	Au Haire	P. Pinsan		
41	2.23	Au Haire	Cartier	Not classed	du Haire
42	2.24	Au Haire	A. Ricaud		
43	2.25	Au Haire	Lamothe Sélerin		
44	2.26	Au Haire	Clavier		
45	2.27	Au Haire	Dubrey		
46	2.28	A Laville	Larroumet fils	Not classed	Laville
47	2.29	Guimbalet	E. Huillet		
48	2.30	Cru Saint-Amand	Ricard	Not classed	Saint-Amand
49	2.31	Bouyreau	E. Huillet		
50	2.32	A Arrançon	V. Lahiteau		
51	2.33	A Arrançon	Ed. Lahiteau		
52	2.34	Sahuc-La-Tour	L. Dequeker		
53	2.35	Sahuc-La-Tour	Dryvers		
54	2.36	Dom. de La Forêt	Guichard and Mathieu		
55	2.37	Au bourg	Louis Pinsan		
56	2.38	A Jonka	Jules Latapy		
57	2.39	A Jonka	C. Fazembat		
58	2.40	A Bordessoulles	Merle		
59	2.41	A Bordessoulles	Louis Lacoste		
60	2.42	A Bordessoulles	Léon Lacoste		
61	2.43	A Monteil	M. Patachon		
62	2.44	Monteil	Gaussens		
			FARGUES		
63	1.1	Rieussec	Vve Lassèverie and Henri Gasqueton	First	Rieussec
64	2.1	Romer-de la Mire-Mory	Arth. P. Lafon	Second	Romer du Hayot
			BARSAC		
65	1.1	Coutet	Société Immoblière des Grands Crus de France	First	Coutet

66	1.2	Climens	Heirs of Henri Gounouilhou	First	Climens
67	2.1	Myrat	Vve Martineau	Second	de Myrat
68	2.2	Doisy-Dubroca	Marcel Dubroca	Second	Doisy-Dubroca
69	2.3	Védrines	Vve J. Teysonneau	Second	Doisy-Védrines
70	2.4	Doisy-Daene	Déjean, of Maison Cazalet fils	Second	Doisy-Daëne
71	2.5	Cantegril	E. Raymond	Not classed	Cantegril
72	2.6	Suau	Em. Garros	Second	Suau
73	2.7	Broustet	G. Supau	Second	Broustet
74	2.8	Caillou	Jos. Ballan	Second	Caillou
75	2.9	Piada	E. Brunet	Not classed	Piada
76	2.10	Roumieux	Goyaud	Not classed	Roumieu
77	2.11	de Carles	F. Barbe	Not classed	de Carles
78	2.12	Nairac	Ch. Perpezat	Second	Nairac
79	2.13	Roumieux	Cl. Bernadet	Not classed	Roumieu (Bernadet)
80	2.14	Roumieux	L. Lacoste	Not classed	Roûmieu-Lacoste
81	2.15	Mathalin	Vve J. Ferbos		
82	2.16	Guiteronde	N. Lagueyte	Not classed	Guiteronde-du-Hayot
83	2.17	Ducasse	Azémar		
84	2.18	du Closiot	R. Héricourt		
85	2.19	Massereau-Lapachère	P. Pinsan		
86	2.20	du Roc	F. Plazaneix		
87	2.21	Rolland	R. Froidefond	Not classed	de Rolland
88	2.22	Dudon	Balayé	Not classed	Dudon
89	2.23	Pernaud	Frank Chassaigne	Not classed	Pernaud
90	2.24	Prost-Jeanlève	V. Boireau	Not classed	Prost
91	2.25	de Bastard	Vve Baudère and Sons		
92	2.26	Liot	Léon Cadillon	Not classed	Liot
93	2.27	Camperos	Louis Bert		
94	2.28	Mayne-Bert	L. Bert		
95	2.29	Cru Laclotte-Cazalis	Jean Lacoste		
96	2.30	Grillon	E. Plomby	Not classed	Grillon
97	2.31	Piot	Mme O. Dubourg		
98	2.32	Piot	Mme Boireau-Dubourg		
99	2.33	Bouyot	Vve J. Larré	Not classed	Bouyot
100	2.34	Cru Hallet	J. Ballan	Not classed	Hallet
101	2.35	Menauta	Vve J. Teyssonneau	Not classed	Ménota

No. 331: Classification of White Wines According to **Bordeaux et ses Vins,** *Tenth Edition (1929)*

		Property	Proprietor	1855 Position	Name Today
			SAUTERNES		
1	1.1	Yquem	Marquis de Lur-Saluces	First-superior	Yquem
2	1.2	Guiraud	Heirs of P. Bernard	First	Guiraud
3	2.1	Raymond-Lafon	A. Pontalier	Not classed	Raymond-Lafon
4	2.2	Château d'Arche-Lafaurie	Pellequer	Second	d'Arche
5	2.3	Château d'Arche	Bastit-Saint-Martin	Second	d'Arche
6	2.4	Château Lafon	André Lafon	Not classed	Lafon
7	2.5	Château D'Arche Vimeney	Lucien Lafon	Not classed	Now part of Lafaurie-Peyraguey
8	2.6	Château Filhot	Marquis de Lur-Saluces	Second	Filhot
9	2.7	Château Lamothe	J. Bergey	Second	Lamothe-Despujols
10	2.8	Château Lamothe	Louis Espagnet	Second	Lamothe-Guignard
			BOMMES		
11	1.1	La-Tour-Blanche	The state, owner; Société civile D. Cordier, grower	First	La Tour-Blanche
12	1.2	Château Lafaurie-Peyraguey	Société civile des propriétés de famille D. Cordier	First	Lafaurie-Peyraguey
13	1.3	Château de Rayne-Vigneau	Heirs of M. le Vicomte de Pontac	First	Rayne-Vigneau
14	1.4	Château Rabaud-Promis	Vve Adrien Promis	First	Rabaud-Promis
15	1.5	Château Sigalas-Rabaud	G. Drouilhet de Sigalas	First	Sigalas-Rabaud
16	1.6	Château Haut-Peyraguey	Société du clos Haut-Peyraguey	First	Clos-Haut-Peyraguey
			PREIGNAC		
17	1.1	Château de Suduiraut	Vve E. Petit de Forest	First	Suduiraut
18	2.1	Château de Malle	Comte Pierre de Lur-Saluces	Second	de Malle
			FARGUES		
19	1.1	Château Rieussec	Vicomte du Bouzet	First	Rieussec
20	2.1	Château Romer-Lafon	Arthur-P. Lafon	Second	Romer du Hayot
21	2.2	Château Romer de la Mire-Mory	R. Obissier (in process of reconstitution)	Second	Romer du Hayot
22	2.3	Château Romer	Farges	Second	Romer du Hayot
			BARSAC		
23	1.1	Château Coutet	Heirs of L. Guy	First	Coutet
24	1.2	Château Climens	Heirs of Henri Gounouilhou	First	Climens
25	2.1	Château Myrat	Vve P. Martineau	Second	de Myrat
26	2.2	Château Doisy-Dubroca	Marcel Dubroca	Second	Doisy-Dubroca

27	2.3	Château Doisy-Védrines	Vve J. Teyssonneau	Second	Doisy-Védrines
28	2.4	Château Doisy-Daëne	J.-G. Dubourdieu	Second	Doisy-Daëne
29	2.5	Château Cantegril	Lhermite	Not classed	Cantegril
30	2.6	Château Suau	Michel Garros	Second	Suau
31	2.7	Château Broustet	Vve G. Supau	Second	Broustet
32	2.8	Château Caillou	Joseph Ballan	Second	Caillou
33	2.9	Château Piada	Vve E. Brunet	Not classed	Piada
34	2.10	Château Roumieux	Vve Goyaud	Not classed	Roumieu
35	2.11	Château de Carles	Vve F. Barbe	Not classed	de Carles
36	2.12	Château Nairac	Ch. Perpezat	Second	Nairac
37	2.13	Château Roumieux	Cl. Bernadet	Not classed	Roumieu (Bernadet)
38	2.14	Château Roumieux	L. Lacoste	Not classed	Roûmieu-Lacoste
39	2.15	Château Mathalin	M. Chaumel		
40	2.16	Château Guiteronde	N. Lagueyte	Not classed	Guiteronde-du-Hayot
41	2.17	Château Brassens-Guiteronde	A. Fouillet and A. Mathieu		
42	2.18	Château Ducasse	Azemar		
43	2.19	Château du Closiot	R. Héricourt		
44	2.20	Château Massereau-Lapachère	P. Pinsan		
45	2.21	Château du Roc	Plazaneix		
46	2.22	Château de Rolland	F. Froidefond	Not classed	de Rolland
47	2.23	Château de Bastard	MM. Baudère		
48	2.24	Château Dudon	Vve Balayé	Not classed	Dudon
49	2.25	Château Pernaud	Vve F. Chassaigne	Not classed	Pernaud
50	2.26	Château Prost-Jeanlève	V. Boireau	Not classed	Prost
51	2.27	Clos de Luziès	G. Perromat		
52	2.28	Château Liot	G. Béguey	Not classed	Liot
53	2.29	Château Hallet	Vve J. Ballan	Not classed	Hallet
54	2.30	Château Camperos	Louis Bert (with Château Magne Bert)		
55	2.31	Château Mayne-Bert	Louis Bert		
56	2.32	Clos de Montalivet	Louis Bert		
57	2.33	Cru Laclotte-Cazalis	Jean Lacoste		
58	2.34	Château Grillon	Henri Cameleyre	Not classed	Grillon
59	2.35	Château Piot	Mme O. Dubourg		
60	2.36	Château Piot	Mme Boireau-Dubourg		
61	2.37	Château du Bouyot	Lucien Dubourg	Not classed	Bouyot
62	2.38	Château Menauta	Vve J. Teyssonneau	Not classed	Ménota
63	2.39	Château Jacques-le-Haut	Dr R. Despujols		
64	2.40	Château Mont-Joye	Dr R. Despujols	Not classed	Mont-Joye

No. 33J: Classification of White Wines According to **Bordeaux et ses Vins,** *Eleventh Edition (1949)*

		Property	Proprietor	1855 Position	Name Today
			SAUTERNES		
1	1.1	Yquem	Marquis de Lur-Saluces	First-superior	Yquem
2	1.2	Guiraud	Paul Rival	First	Guiraud
3	2.1	Filhot	Comtesse Durieu de Lacarelle, née Lur-Saluces	Second	Filhot
4	2.2	Château d'Arche	A. Bastit-Saint-Martin	Second	d'Arche
5	2.3	Lamotte	A. Bastit-Saint-Martin	Second	Lamothe-Despujols
6	2.4	Raymond-Lafon	A. Pontallier	Not classed	Raymond-Lafon
7	2.5	Château d'Arche-Lafaurie	Pellequer	Second	d'Arche
8	2.6	Château D'Arche Vimeney	L. Lafon	Not classed	Now part of Lafaurie-Peyraguey
9	2.7	Lamothe-Bergey	Mme Tissot	Second	Lamothe-Guignard
			BOMMES		
10	1.1	La-Tour-Blanche	The state, owner; Société civile D. Cordier, grower	First	La Tour-Blanche
11	1.2	Lafaurie-Peyraguey	Société civile des propriétés de famille D. Cordier	First	Lafaurie-Peyraguey
12	1.3	de Rayne-Vigneau	Heirs of M. le Vicomte de Pontac	First	Rayne-Vigneau
13	1.4	Rabaud	Société civile du Château Rabaud	First	Rabaud-Promis/Sigalas-Rabaud
14	1.5	Haut-Peyraguey	Société du Clos Haut-Peyraguey	First	Clos-Haut-Peyraguey
			PREIGNAC		
15	1.1	de Suduiraut	L. Fonquernie	First	Suduiraut
16	2.1	de Malle	Heirs of Comte Pierre de Lur-Saluces	Second	de Malle
			FARGUES		
17	1.1	Rieussec	P.-F. Berry	First	Rieussec
18	2.1	Romer	E. Farges	Second	Romer du Hayot
			BARSAC		
19	1.1	Coutet	M. and Mme Rolland-Guy	First	Coutet
20	1.2	Climens	Heirs of Henri Gounouilhou	First	Climens
21	2.1	Doisy-Védrines	Vve J. Teyssonneau	Second	Doisy-Védrines
22	2.2	Doisy-Daëne	Jean Dubourdieu	Second	Doisy-Daëne

23	2.3	Myrat	Comte Max de Pontac	Second	de Myrat
24	2.4	Doisy-Dubroca	Marcel Dubroca	Second	Doisy-Dubroca
25	2.5	Broustet	Société civile de Château Broustet	Second	Broustet
26	2.6	Caillou	J. Bravo	Second	Caillou
27	2.7	Suau	Michel Garros	Second	Suau
28	2.8	Nairac	Ch. Perpezat	Second	Nairac

No. 34: Homologation of the Wines of the Gironde According to the 1943 Legislation des Prix

		RED WINES	
		Property	**Price per Tun (francs)**
		CLASSED GROWTHS	
1	1.1	Lafite	100,000
2	1.2	Latour	100,000
3	1.3	Margaux	100,000
4	2.1	Mouton-Rothschild	100,000
5	2.2	Brane-Cantenac	80,000
6	2.3	Cos d'Estournel	80,000
7	2.4	Ducru-Beaucaillou	80,000
8	2.5	Durfort-Vivens	80,000
9	2.6	Gruaud-Larose	80,000
10	2.7	Lascombes	80,000
11	2.8	Léoville-Barton	80,000
12	2.9	Léoville-Lascases	80,000
13	2.10	Léoville-Poyferré	80,000
14	2.11	Montrose	80,000
15	2.12	Pichon-Longueville-Baron	80,000
16	2.13	Pichon-Longueville-Lalande	80,000
17	2.14	Rauzan-Gassies	80,000
18	2.15	Rausan-Ségla	80,000
19	3.1	Giscours	75,000
20	3.2	La Lagune	75,000
21	3.3	Palmer	75,000
22	3.4	Boyd-Cantenac	70,000
23	3.5	Calon-Ségur	70,000
24	3.6	Cantenac-Brown	70,000
25	3.7	Desmirail	70,000
26	3.8	Ferrière	70,000
27	3.9	Issan	70,000
28	3.10	Kirwan	70,000
29	3.11	Lagrange	70,000
30	3.12	Langoa-Barton	70,000
31	3.13	Malescot-Saint-Exupéry	70,000
32	3.14	Marquis d'Alesme-Becker	70,000

33	4.1	Beychevelle	75,000
34	4.2	Branaire-Ducru	75,000
35	4.3	Talbot	70,000
36	4.4	Duhart-Milon	65,000
37	4.5	Lafon-Rochet	65,000
38	4.6	La Tour Carnet	65,000
39	4.7	Le Prieuré	65,000
40	4.8	Marquis de Termes	65,000
41	4.9	Pouget de Chavailles	65,000
42	4.10	Saint-Pierre	65,000
43	5.1	Cantemerle	75,000
44	5.2	Mouton d'Armailhacq	75,000
45	5.3	Pontet-Canet	75,000
46	5.4	Batailley	65,000
47	5.5	Lynch-Bages	65,000
48	5.6	Belgrave	60,000
49	5.7	Camensac	60,000
50	5.8	Clerc-Milon	60,000
51	5.9	Cos-Labory	60,000
52	5.10	Croizet-Bages	60,000
53	5.11	Dauzac	60,000
54	5.12	Grand-Puy-Ducasse	60,000
55	5.13	Grand-Puy-Lacoste	60,000
56	5.14	Haut-Bages-Libéral	60,000
57	5.15	Le Tertre	60,000
58	5.16	Lynch-Moussas	60,000
59	5.17	Pédesclaux	60,000
		SAINT-EMILION	
60	1	Ausone	100,000
61	2	Cheval Blanc	100,000
62	3	Beauséjour (Fagouet)	75,000
63	4	Beauséjour (Lagarosse)	75,000
64	5	Canon	75,000
65	6	Clos Fourtet	75,000
66	7	La Gaffelière	75,000
67	8	Magdeleine	75,000
68	9	Belair	70,000
69	10	Chapelle Madeleine	70,000

70	11	Cure Bon la Madeleine	70,000
71	12	Figeac	70,000
72	13	Trotevieille	70,000
73	14	L'Arrosée	65,000
74	15	Bellevue	65,000
75	16	Canon La Gaffelière	65,000
76	17	Cadet Bon	60,000
77	18	Cadet Piola	65,000
78	19	Coutet	60,000
79	20	La Dominique	65,000
80	21	Pavie	65,000
81	22	Soutard	65,000
82	23	Clos Saint-Martin	65,000
83	24	Tertre Daugay	65,000
84	25	Villemaurine	65,000
85	26	Balestard la Tonnelle	60,000
86	27	Berliquet	60,000
87	28	Cadet Pavillon	60,000
88	29	Lecouvent	60,000
89	30	Cap de Mourlin	60,000
90	31	Fonplegade	60,000
91	32	Clos des Grandes Murailles	60,000
92	33	Jean Faure	60,000
93	34	Larcis Ducasse	60,000
94	35	Moulin du Cadet	60,000
95	36	Pavie Macquin	60,000
96	37	Ripeau	60,000
97	38	Saint-Georges Côtes Pavie	60,000
98	39	Troplong Mondot	60,000
99	40	Croque Michotte	60,000
		POMEROL	
100	1	Petrus	80,000
101	2	Certan	75,000
102	3	La Conseillante	75,000
103	4	L'Evangile	75,000
104	5	Petit Village	75,000
105	6	Trotanoy	75,000
106	7	Vieux Château Certan	75,000

107	8		Gazin	70,000
108	9		La Croix de Gay	60,000
109	10		La Fleur Petrus	65,000
110	11		Domaine de l'Eglise	65,000
111	12		La Graves Trigant	65,000
112	13		Clos l'Eglise	65,000
113	14		Latour	65,000
114	15		Lafleur	70,000
115	16		Beauregard	60,000
116	17		Certan Mazelle	60,000
117	18		Clinet	60,000
118	19		Gombaude Guillot	60,000
119	20		Guillot	60,000
120	21		L'Eglise Clinet	60,000
121	22		Le Gay	65,000
122	23		Lagrande	60,000
123	24		Nenin	60,000
124	25		La Pointe	60,000
125	26		La Vraye Croix de Gay	60,000
			CANON-FRONSAC	
126	1		Vrai Canon Boyer	65,000
127	2		Canon	60,000
128	3		Canon de Laage	60,000
129	4		Vrai Canon Bouche	60,000
130	5		Vrai Canon Bodet	60,000
		Commune	**Property**	**Price per Tun (francs)**
			GRAVES (Including White Wines as Indicated)	
131	1	**Arbanats**	Tourteau-Chollet	60,000
132	2	**Cadaujac**	Bouscaut	60,000
133	3	**Léognan**	Haut-Bailly	80,000
134	4		Domaine de Chevalier	80,000
135	5		Carbonnieux	70,000 (red)/60,000 (white)
136	6		de Fieuzal	70,000
137	7		Lagravière-Malarctic	65,000
138	8		Olivier	60,000 (red and white)
139	9		La Louvière	60,000 (white)
140	10	**Martillac**	Smith Haut-Lafitte	60,000
141	11	**Pessac**	Haut-Brion	100,000

142	12		La Mission Haut-Brion	88,000
143	13		Les Carmes Haut-Brion	65,000
144	14		Laville Haut-Brion	60,000
145	15		La Tour Haut-Brion	60,000
146	16	**Villenave d'Ornon**	Couhins Cantebeau	60,000

WHITE WINES

		Property	Price per Tun (francs)
		CLASSED GROWTHS	
1	Exceptional growth	Yquem	130,000
2	First growth	Climens	90,000
3	1.2	Coutet	90,000
4	1.3	Guiraud	90,000
5	1.4	Haut-Peyraguey	90,000
6	1.5	La Tour Blanche	90,000
7	1.6	Rabaud	90,000
8	1.7	Rieussec	90,000
9	1.8	Suduiraut	90,000
10	1.9	Rayne Vignau	90,000
11	1.10	Lafaurie Peyraguey	90,000
12	Second growth	Arche-Dubedat	77,000
13	2.2	Doisy-Daëne	77,000
14	Second growth—1st class	Doisy-Vedrines	77,000
15	2^1.2	Filhot	77,000
16	Second growth—2nd class	Broustet	73,000
17	2^2.2	Caillou	73,000
18	2^2.3	Arche-Lafaurie	73,000
19	2^2.4	Myrat	73,000
20	2^2.5	Malle	73,000
21	2^2.6	Doisy-Dubroca	73,000
22	Second growth—3rd class	Lamothe Bergey	70,000
23	2^3.2	Lamothe-Bastit	70,000
24	2^3.3	Nairac	70,000
25	2^3.4	Romer	70,000
26	2^3.5	Suau	70,000
27	2^3.6	Peixotto	70,000

		Commune	Property	Price per Tun (francs)
			APPELLATION SAUTERNES-BARSAC	
28	1	**Barsac**	Piada	70,000
29	2		Roumieu (Goyaud)	70,000
30	3		Roumieu (Dubourdieu)	70,000
31	4		Roumieu (Bernadet)	70,000
32	5	**Preignac**	Arche-Pugneau	73,000
33	6		Armajean-les-Ormes	70,000
34	7		Bastor-la-Montagne	70,000
35	8		Carles	70,000
36	9		Fontebride	70,000
37	10		Peyraguey-le-Rousset	70,000
38	11		Pleytegeat	70,000
39	12		Pic	70,000
40	13	**Sauternes**	Raymond-Lafon	73,000
41	14		Arche-Vimeney	70,000

Note: The complete homologation dated June 29, 1943 was a 32-page document which listed hundreds of properties, not only from the Gironde but from Monbazillac and Burgundy as well. The above chart includes only those properties from the Bordeaux appellations whose price per tun was equal to or higher than the classed-growth minimums (60,000 francs for red and dry white wines, 70,000 francs for sweet white wines).

Appendix II

PRICE TABLES

The following table is a selection of prices published over forty-six years in the Prix-Courant Général, the public record of transactions in wines and other goods, which were traded on the Bordeaux marketplace. These lists, at first printed as simple broadsheets, and later growing from two pages to four, appeared several times per week to keep the city's merchants apprised of the changing state of the market. As such, they were akin to the stock market quotations in the financial pages of modern newspapers. Naturally enough, the Bordeaux Chamber of Commerce was a subscriber to the Prix-Courant Général, compiling these lists into a series comprising nineteen bound volumes, and it is from this collection that the following information was drawn.

Ranging over almost half a century, the original lists provide rich testimony about the evolving state of the Bordeaux wine trade: its varying fortunes as reflected by the rate at which prices changed in the wake of greater or lesser demand, the ever-growing number of vintages available in the marketplace, and the state of development at which wines were sold (on the lees—"sur lie" —or ready for bottling—"tiré au fin") to cite but three examples. More pertinent to the question of the classification of Bordeaux wines and how it evolved, the price lists offer evidence of the gradual expansion of the number of levels in the hierarchy as fourth and fifth growths shook off the label "bourgeois supérieurs" and assumed full classed-growth status; there is the appearance of Château d'Yquem in a class by itself in the 1840s; and one can see the stirrings of a nascent hierarchy among red Graves wines with the emergence of a second-growth level beginning in 1852.

Perhaps the most significant information that a study of these price lists yields, however, is the answer to one of the most commonly asked questions about the brokers' list of classed growths: why were the wines of Saint-Emilion and the Graves (or any other area of the Gironde region for that matter) not included in the 1855 classification? A glance at the Prix-Courant during any period clearly shows that these wines were simply not selling at prices high enough to earn inclusion among even the lowest level of the classed growths—indeed, their prices were habitually well below those of the Médoc's bourgeois growths. It would be several decades before these wines would begin attaining prices which would bring them to parity with the long-established classed growths.

Year:	1808	1809	1810	1811	1812
Month:	**16 January**	**3 May**	**6 January**	**1 January**	**4 January**
Red Wines of:	**1807**	**1808**	**1808**	**1808**	**1808**
First growth Médoc (Lafite, Latour, Château-Margaux, Haut-Brion)	2400–2500	1100–1200	900–1000	900–1000	900–1000
Médoc 2nd growths	1800–2100	700–900	600–800	600–800	600–800
3rd growths	1500–1600	550–600	500–600	500–600	500–600
First quality	1100–1200	400–450	400–500	400–500	400–500
2nd quality	700–800	330–350	350–400	350–400	350–400
3rd quality	500–600	280–300	300–350	320–350	300–350
4th quality	300–400	200–220	250–300	280–320	280–320
First quality Graves	750–900	300–350	400–500	400–500	400–500
St Emilion	250–300	170–200	240–300	260–300	260–300
White Wines of:	**1807**	**1808**	**1808**	**1808**	**1808**
Haut-Barsac, Haut-Preignac, Sauternes, Bommes	350–400	280–300	280–300	280–300	280–300
First quality Graves	350–400	280–300	280–300	280–300	280–300

Year:	1812		1812		1813	
Month:	**8 February**		**3 October**		**6 March**	
Red Wines of:	**1810**	**1811**	**1811**		**1812**	
First growth Médoc (Lafite, Latour, Château-Margaux, Haut-Brion)	700	800	1500–1600		900–1000	
2nd growth Médoc	400	500	1000–1200		600–700	
3rd growth	350	400	600–800		500–600	
First quality	300	350	500–550		400–500	
2nd quality	250	250	400–450		350–400	
3rd quality	220	210	300–350		300–330	
4th quality	180	180	230–250		250–300	
First quality Graves	300	300	500–550		400–450	
St Emilion	300	260	280–330		220–270	
White Wines of:	**1810**	**1811**	**1810**	**1811**	**1810**	**1811**
Haut-Barsac, Haut-Preignac, Sauternes, Bommes	180	170	180	170	180	170
First quality Graves	180	160	180	160	180	160

Year:	1814
Month:	4 May
Red Wines of:	**1813**
First growth Médoc (Lafite, Latour, Château-Margaux, Haut-Brion)	1000–1100
2nd growth Médoc	700–800
3rd growth	550–650
First quality	450–500
2nd quality	400–450
3rd quality	370–400
4th quality	340–360
First quality Graves	450–500
St Emilion	300–340
White Wines of:	**1813**
Haut-Barsac, Haut-Preignac, Sauternes, Bommes	400–420
First quality Graves	380–400

Year:	1815		1816		1817	
Month:	2 January		1 March		2 May	
Red Wines of:	**1813**	**1814**	**1814**	**1815**	**1814 & 1815**	**1816**
Four first growths: Haut-Brion, Château Margaux, Latour, and Lafite	1200–1400	Sold	No price	3000–3100	4200–4600	"
Second growth Médoc—Rauzan, Léoville, Gorsse, etc.	900–1000	2300–2500	2400–2600	2300–2500	3600–3800	300–400
Third growths	700–800	1600–1900	2000–2200	2000–2200	2700–3000	300–400
Fourth growths	600–700	1400–1600	1500–1800	1600–1850	1800–2000	350–375
Bourgeois supérieurs from good parishes of Cantenac, Margaux, Saint-Julien, Pauillac, and Saint-Estèphe	500–650	1100–1300	1200–1400	1200–1550	1500–1600	340–350
Peasant wines from good parishes	400–450	500–600	600–700	650–800	900–1000	300–310
First quality Graves	550–600	1000–1200	1100–1300	1300–1600	1250–1550	350–360
Canon and St-Emilion	425–460	500–600	600–700	600–700	800–950	340–360
White Wines of:	**1813**	**1814**	**1814**	**1815**	**1815**	**1816**
Ht-Barsac, Ch. Suduiraut, Preignac, Bommes, Sauternes	600–650	850–950	800–1000	800–900	1500–1700	400–500
St-Bris, Carbonnieux, Pontac or Dulamon	400–500	800–900	850–1000	Uncertain	1500–1700	300–320

Year:	**1818**		**1819**		**1820**	
Month:	**3 April**		**1 January**		**11 August**	
Red Wines of:	**1814 and 1815**	**1817**	**1814 and 1815**	**1818**	**1814, 1815, etc.**	**1819**
Four first growths: Haut-Brion, Château Margaux, Latour and Lafite	No price	No prices established at present for these wines.	No price	3400–3500	No price	3000
Second growth Médoc—Rauzan, Léoville, Gorsse, etc.	3400–4600		3500–4800	3000–3200	3500–4800	1500–2000
Third growths	2800–4000		2800–4200	2200–2500	2800–4200	1000–1200
Fourth growths	2000–3200		2000–3600	1500–1700	2000–3600	800–900
Bourgeois supérieurs from good parishes of Cantenac, Margaux, Saint-Julien, Pauillac, and Saint-Estèphe	1600–2800	900–1000	1500–2800	1000–1400	1500–2800	650–700
Peasant wines from good parishes	1000–1500	700–750	1000–1500	500–550	1000–1500	450–500
First quality Graves	1600–2400	"	1600–2500	1000–1200	1600–2500	900–1000
Canon and St-Emilion	900–1200	600–650	1000–1200	500–650	1000–1200	450–550
White Wines of:	**1815**	**1817**	**1815**	**1818**	**1815**	
Ht-Barsac, Ch. Suduiraut, Preignac, Bommes, Sauternes	1650–2000	900–960	1650–2000	800–860	1650–2000	1000–1500
St-Bris, Carbonnieux, Pontac or Dulamon	No price	920–950	No price	750–800	No price	800–900

Year:	**1821**		**1822**		**1823**	
Month:	**13 April**		**17 May**		**3 January**	
Red Wines of:	**1819**	**1820**	**1820**	**1821**	**1821**	**1822**
Four first growths: Haut-Brion, Château Margaux, Latour and Lafite	3000		"		900–1000	2500–3000
Second growth Médoc—Rauzan, Léoville, Durefort, Loriague, Larose, Mouton, Gorsse, etc.	2400–2600	2100	2200–2400	"	900–1000	2100–2200
Third growths	1800–2000	1300	1600–1800	800–900	500–600	1700–1800
Fourth and fifth growths or bourgeois supérieurs	1200–1600	1050	1200–1400	700–750	450–500	1000–1400
Bons bourgeois	900–1000	750–1000	900–1000	600–650	380–420	700–900
Peasant wines from good parishes	650–700	450–550	550–600	350–375	270–280	450–600
First quality Graves	1200–1500	900–1000	1000–1100	500–600	300–400	600–700
St-Emilion and first quality Canon	650–700	600–700	600–650	400–450	300–400	400–500
White Wines of:	**1819**		**1820**	**1821**	**1821**	**1822**
Haut-Barsac, Preignac, Bommes, Sauternes	1000–1500	700–800	700–825	450–550	500–520	800–900
St-Bris, Carbonnieux, Pontac or Dulamon	900–1000	700–750	550–600	"	"	"

Year:	1824		1825		1826	
Month:	2 April		2 May		2 January	
Red Wines of:	**1822**	**1823**	**1823**	**1824**	**1824**	***Sur lie* 1825**
Four first growths: Haut-Brion, Château Margaux, Latour and Lafite	3500–3600	1500	2400–2500	"	"	3600–3700
Second growth Médoc—Rauzan, Léoville, Durefort, Loriague, Larose, Mouton, Gorsse, etc.	2800–3000	1200–1300	1800–2100	"	1100–1200	3200–3400
Third growths	2400–2500	800–900	1600–1700	850–950	900–1000	2500–2900
Fourth and fifth growths or bourgeois supérieurs	1800–2000	560–700	1000–1500	600–760	800–900	1600–2300
Bons bourgeois	1200–1500	450–550	700–900	500–560	650–700	1400–1550
Peasant wines from good parishes	400–450	300–325	400–460	360–435	400–450	"
First quality Graves	1000–1200	500–600	600–660	350–420	500–600	1500–1800
St-Emilion and first quality Canon	600–650	280–320	400–430	320–370	500–550	850–1000
White Wines of:	**1822**	**1823**	**1823**	**1824**	**1824**	***Sur lie* 1825**
Haut-Barsac, Preignac, Bommes, Sauternes	950–1200	250–320	440–515	360–420	320–400	1200–1700
St-Bris, Carbonnieux, Pontac or Dulamon	700–800	225–250	360–390	300–350	300–320	1100–1200

Year:	1827	
Month:	4 May	
Red Wines of:	**1825**	**1826**
First growths—Château Margaux, Latour and Lafite	"	1600
Second growth Médoc—Rauzan, Léoville, Durefort, Loriague, Larose, Mouton, Gorsse, etc.	"	"
Third growths	"	900–1000
Fourth and fifth growths or bourgeois supérieurs	1700–1800	600–800
Bons bourgeois	1400–1600	500–600
Peasant wines from good parishes	"	250–360
First quality Graves	1500–1700	500–700
St-Emilion and first quality Canon	750–900	300–350
White Wines of:	**1825**	***Tiré au fin* 1826**
Haut-Preignac, Haut-Barsac	850–1450	200–260
Haut-Bommes, Haut-Sauternes		250–350
First quality Graves	950–1050	200–220

Year:	1828	
Month:	4 April	
Red Wines of:	**1826**	**1827**
First growths—Château Margaux, Latour and Lafite	1600–1700	1600–1700
Second growth Médoc—Rauzan, Léoville, Durefort, Loriague, Larose, Mouton, Gorsse, etc.	1300–1400	1300–1400
Third growths	900–1000	1000–1100
Fourth and fifth growths or bourgeois supérieurs	600–700	600–850
Bons bourgeois	450–550	450–500
Peasant wines from good parishes	250–350	250–325
First quality Graves	500–650	600–800
St-Emilion and first quality Canon	280–310	280–325
White Wines of:	**1826**	***Tiré au fin* 1827**
Haut-Preignac, Barsac, Bommes, Sauternes	250–350	370–500
First quality Graves	220–240	285–300

Year:	1829		1830		1831	
Month:	2 March		3 August		2 December	
Red Wines of:	**1827**	**1828**	**1828**	**1829**	**1829**	**1830**
First growth—Château Margaux, Latour and Lafite	2400–2500	1700–1800	2600–2800	"	Impossible to estimate price	2500–2600
Second growth Médoc—Rauzan, Léoville, Durefort, Loriague, Larose, Mouton, Gorsse, etc.	2000–2200	1300–1400	2300–2400	"	600–700	2100–2200
Third growths	1600–1800	1000–1100	1800–2000	"	450–500	1700–1900
Fourth growths or bourgeois supérieur	1000–1200	750–900	1400–1500	"	400–450	1200–1500
Fifth growths or bourgeois supérieur	700–800	550–650	1100–1200	"	350–380	900–1000
Bons bourgeois	550–600	400–450	800–900	"	300–320	600–750
Peasant wines from good parishes	380–420	250–350	450–500	360–400	270–280	350–400
First quality Graves	300–350	550–650	900–1000	500–600	400–500	1000–1200
St-Emilion and first quality Canon	280–300	300–350	550–600	"	330–360	450–500
White Wines of:	**1827**	**Estimated price *tirés au fin* 1828**	**1828**	**1829**	**1829**	**1830**
Haut-Preignac, Barsac, Bommes, Sauternes	360–800	260–400	500–700	230–280	210–280	300–400
First quality Graves	270–300	200–240	500–530	190–200	220–230	300–350

Year:	**1832**	
Month:	**2 March**	
Red Wines of:	**1830**	**1831**
First growths—Château Margaux, Latour and Lafite	2500–2600	2500–2600
Second growth Médoc—Rauzan, Léoville, Durefort, Loriague, Larose, Mouton, Gorsse, etc.	2100–2200	2200–2400
Third growths	1700–1900	1900–2100
Fourth growths or bourgeois supérieur	1200–1500	1400–1700
Fifth growths or bourgeois supérieur	800–1000	1000–1200
Bons bourgeois	550–750	750–900
Peasant wines from good parishes	360–480	450–550
First quality Graves	800–1000	800–1000
St-Emilion and first quality Canon	400–450	350–400
White Wines of:	**1830**	**1831**
Haut-Preignac, Barsac, Bommes, Sauternes	300–400	360–600
First quality Graves	300–350	400–420

Year:	**1833**	
Month:	**5 July**	
Red Wines of:	**1831**	**1832**
First growths—Château Margaux, Latour and Lafite	3000–3200	2100–2200
Second growth Médoc—Rauzan, Léoville, Durefort, Loriague, Larose, Mouton, Gorsse, etc.	2700–2800	1800–1900
Third growths	2300–2500	1500–1600
Fourth growths	1500–2000	1100–1300
Fifth growths or bourgeois supérieur	1000–1200	800–1000
Bons bourgeois	750–900	600–700
Peasant wines from good parishes	550–650	400–480
First quality Graves	800–1000	650–700
St-Emilion and first quality Canon	400–450	250–350
White Wines of:	**1831**	***Tiré au fin* 1832**
Haut-Preignac, Haut-Barsac	400–1400	350–650
Haut-Bommes, Haut-Sauternes	400–1400	350–550
First quality Graves	480–550	430–450

Year:	1834	
Month:	7 March	
Red Wines of:	1832	1833
First growths—Château Margaux, Latour and Lafite	2400–2500	1400–1500
Second growth Médoc—Rauzan, Léoville, Durefort, Loriague, Larose, Mouton, Gorsse, etc.	1800–2000	1100–1200
Third growths	1500–1600	900–950
Fourth growths	1100–1300	700–800
Fifth growths or bourgeois supérieur	800–1000	550–650
Bons bourgeois	600–700	450–500
Peasant wines from good parishes	400–500	300–400
First quality Graves	650–700	400–450
St-Emilion and first quality Canon	300–450	300–320
White Wines of:	**1832**	***Tiré au fin* 1833**
Haut-Preignac, Barsac, Bommes, Sauternes	360–660	210–350
First quality Graves	440–460	240–270

Year:	1835	
Month:	6 February	
Red Wines of:	1833	1834
First growths—Château Margaux, Latour and Lafite	2100–2300	3200–3400
Second growth Médoc—Rauzan, Léoville, Durefort, Loriague, Larose, Mouton, Gorsse, etc.	1800–2000	2400–2600
Third growths	1500–1600	1800–2000
Fourth growths	1200–1300	1500–1600
Fifth growths or bourgeois supérieur	1000–1100	1300–1400
Bons bourgeois	750–900	850–1000
Peasant wines from good parishes	450–600	450–600
First quality Graves	700–800	700–800
St-Emilion and first quality Canon	450–500	425–550
White Wines of:	***Tiré au fin* 1833**	**1834**
Haut-Preignac, Haut-Barsac	250–500	550–1250
Haut-Bommes, Haut-Sauternes	250–500	550–1200
First quality Graves	230–280	430–480

Year:	1836	
Month:	8 March	
Red Wines of:	1834	1835
First growths—Château Margaux, Latour and Lafite	3000–3600	1700–1800
Second growth Médoc—Rauzan, Léoville, Durefort, Loriague, Larose, Mouton, Gorsse, etc.	2200–2900	1000–1200
Third growths	1900–2100	860–900
Fourth growths	*	*
Fifth growths or bourgeois supérieur	*	*
Bons bourgeois	700–900	440–550
Peasant wines from good parishes	380–450	210–250
First quality Graves	900–1000	550–600
St-Emilion and first quality Canon	450–500	340–360
White Wines of:	**1834**	**1835**
Haut-Preignac, Haut-Barsac	600–1800	200–280
Haut-Bommes, Haut-Sauternes	600–1800	200–280
First quality Graves	900–1000	200–220

* In lieu of prices for fourth and fifth growths, there are only communal listings for Margaux, Saint-Julien, Pauillac, and Saint-Estèphe in the price lists for 1836.

Year:	1837	
Month:	1 April	
Red Wines of:	1835	1836
First growths—Château Margaux, Latour, Lafite and Haut-Brion	1700–2000	1800–2000
Second growth Médoc—Rauzan, Mouton, Larose, Léoville, Lascombes	1600–1700	1500–1700
Third growths—Kirwan, Pichon-Longueville, Destournel-Cos, Bergeron, etc.	1200–1300	1200–1400
Fourth and fifth growths	900–1000	750–1000
Médoc bourgeois supérfins	750–800	600–700
First peasant wines	450–500	360–400
first quality Graves	350–450	300–350
St-Emilion and Canon	280–350	260–320
White Wines of:	**1834**	**1835**
Haut-Preignac, Barsac, Bommes, Sauternes	850–3000	250–350
First quality Graves	700–1000	250–280

Year:	1838	
Month:	3 January	
Red Wines of:	**1836**	**1837**
First growths—Château Margaux, Latour, Lafite and Haut-Brion	1800–2000	2100–2400
Second growth Médoc—Rauzan, Mouton, Larose, Léoville, Lascombes	1400–1500	1700–1800
Third growths—Kirwan, Pichon-Longueville, Destournel-Cos, Bergeron, etc.	1100–1200	1400–1500
Fourth and fifth growths	800–1000	900–1200
Médoc bourgeois supérfins	600–700	750–800
First peasant wines	250–300	380–450
First quality Graves	300–400	450–500
St-Emilion and Canon	250–300	300–350
White Wines of:	**1836**	**1837**
Haut-Preignac, Haut-Barsac	280–650	330–700
Haut-Bommes, Haut-Sauternes	280–650	300–350
First quality Graves	260–400	300–450

Year:	1839	
Month:	1 January	
Red Wines of:	**1836**	**1837**
First growths—Château Margaux, Latour, Lafite and Haut-Brion	1800–2000	2400–2500
Second growth Médoc—Rauzan, Mouton, Larose, Léoville, Lascombes	1400–1500	1700–1800
Third growths—Kirwan, Pichon-Longueville, Destournel-Cos, Bergeron, etc.	1100–1200	1400–1500
Fourth and fifth growths	800–1000	900–1200
Médoc bourgeois supérfins	600–700	650–800
First peasant wines	300–350	360–420
First quality Graves	350–450	480–550
St-Emilion and Canon	250–300	280–400
White Wines of:	**1836**	**1837**
Haut-Preignac, Barsac, Bommes, Sauternes	280–650	380–800
First quality Graves	260–400	300–450

Year:	1840			1841		
Month:	19 May			9 March		
Red Wines of:	**1837**	**1838**	**1839**	**1837**	**1839**	**1840**
First growths—Château Margaux, Latour, Lafite and Haut-Brion	2800–3000	2200–2400	2600–2800	2800–3000	2700–2900	1500–1600
Second growth Médoc—Rauzan, Mouton, Larose, Léoville, Lascombes	2500–2600	1500–1800	1800–2200	2500–2600	1800–2200	1200–1390
Third growths—Kirwan, Pichon-Longueville, Destournel-Cos, Bergeron, etc.	1800–2200	1400–1600	1400–1600	1500–1800	1400–1500	800–900
Fourth growths	1400–1600	900–1000	1100–1200	1200–1500	1100–1200	700–800
Fifth growths	1000–1200	600–700	700–825	900–1000	700–800	600–670
Bons bourgeois	700–825	525–550	550–580	600–700	500–600	450–550
Peasant wines from good parishes	450–500	360–400	400–450	400–450	360–380	350–400
First quality Graves	650–750	500–650	200–700	650–750	600–700	500–600
St-Emilion and Canon	400–450	260–380	250–340	500–550	360–450	240–290
White Wines of:	**1837**	**1838**	**1839**	**1837**	**1839**	**1840**
First growth Ht-Barsac, Preignac, Bommes, Sauternes	530–1110	400–600	500–850	700–1240	600–1410	400–600
Second growth Ht-Barsac, Preignac, Bommes, Sauternes	440–460	350–370	280–350	440–560	380–500	"
First quality Graves	450–500	350–400	420–440	450–500	420–440	300–350

Year:	1842		
Month:	1 February		
Red Wines of:	**1839**	**1840**	**1841**
First growths— Château Margaux, Latour, Lafite	3000–3500	1800–2000	1500–1800
Second growth Médoc	2200–2400	1400–1700	1200–1300
Third growths	1600–1800	1000–1100	900–1000
Fourth growths	1300–1400	800–900	700–800
Fifth growths	1000–1100	600–700	600–625
Bons bourgeois	700–800	500–550	500–550
Peasant wines from good parishes	500–530	360–440	330–400
First quality Graves	600–700	500–550	450–500
St-Emilion and Canon	350–500	250–450	180–400
White Wines of:	**1839**	**1840**	**1841**
First growth Ht-Barsac, Preignac, Bommes, Sauternes	700–1400	550–1100	350–370
Second growth Ht-Barsac, Preignac, Bommes, Sauternes	450–625	400–500	220–250
First quality Graves	460–550	420–425	240–260

Year:	1843		
Month:	**2 August**		
Red Wines of:	**1840**	**1841**	**1842**
First growths—Château Margaux, Latour, Lafite	3000–3200	2600–3200	1200–1300
Second growth Médoc	2800–2600	1600–2300	950–1000
Third growths	1600–1700	1200–1500	750–800
Fourth growths	1800–1300	900–1000	600–650
Fifth growths	700–1000	700–800	450–500
Bons bourgeois	600–700	500–600	350–400
Peasant wines from good parishes	350–450	300–400	260–300
First quality Graves	600–700	450–550	350–400
St-Emilion and Canon	300–550	220–400	200–300
White Wines of:	**1840**	**1841**	**1842**
Haut-Barsac, Preignac, Bommes, Sauternes	380–1000	250–400	170–220
Château d'Yquem	1900–2100	600–625	280–300
First quality Graves	320–400	210–230	150–170

Year:	1844			1845		
Month:	**7 February**			**4 January**		
Red Wines of:	**1840, 1841**	**1842**	**1843**	**1840, 1841**	**1842**	**1844**
First growths—Château Margaux, Latour, Lafite	3500–4000	1500–1600	1300–1400	4500–6000	2500–2800	4000–4500
Second growth Médoc	2700–3000	1000–1200	900–1000	3500–4000	1600–1800	3000–3500
Third growths	1700–2000	800–900	700–750	2400–2700	1100–1400	2500–2700
Fourth growths	1400–1600	700–750	600–650	1600–2000	850–1000	1900–2300
Fifth growths	900–1000	600–650	500–525	1200–1500	750–800	1400–1700
Bons bourgeois	700–800	500–550	440–470	800–1000	550–650	1000–1100
Peasant wines from good parishes	450–550	350–450	300–400	450–600	350–440	500–700
First quality Graves	800–900	500–600	380–460	1000–1500	600–700	1200–1600
St-Emilion and Canon	430–700	340–550	300–400	430–700	340–500	450–500
White Wines of:	**1840, 1841**	**1842**	**1843**	**1840, 1841**	**1842**	**1844**
First growth Ht-Barsac, Preignac, Bommes, Sauternes	1200–1500	700–800	500–600	1200–2000	700–900	1000–1200
Second growth Ht-Barsac, Preignac, Bommes, Sauternes	900–1000	450–500	375–440	700–900	450–550	400–525
First quality Graves	500–600	360–580	270–310	500–600	400–440	360–380

Year:	1846		
Month:	**4 September**		
Red Wines of:	**1841**	**1844**	**1845**
First growths—Château Margaux, Latour, Lafite	5500–6000	5000–6000	800
First growth—Haut-Brion, Graves	4000–4700	4000–4500	"
Second growths—Rauzan, Léoville, Durfort, Brane, Cantenac, Mouton, Larose, Pichon	3500–4000	3500–4000	450
Third growths—Chât. d'Issan, Kirwan, Ducru, etc.	2800–3000	2700–3000	400
Fourth growths—St. Exupery, Desmirail, St. Pierre, Dubignon, LaGrange, Duluc, etc., etc.	2200–2600	2300–2500	350
Fifth growths—Pontet Canet, Lacoste-Grand-Puy, Chauvet, Jurine, Pontac, Cantenac, Dauzac-Labarde	1600–2000	1500–1800	300
Bourgeois supérieurs from Margaux, St. Julien, Pauillac, Labarde, and St. Estèphe	1000–1200	900–1000	250–275
Bons bourgeois from Pauillac, St. Estèphe, Soussans, and Listrac	650–800	600–750	200–240
Peasant supérieurs from Margaux, Cantenac, St. Julien and Pauillac	600–700	550–650	270–280
First quality Graves	800–900	800–900	"
St-Emilion and first quality Canon	700–800	550–700	"
White Wines of:		**1844**	**1845**
Château d'Yquem		2200–2400	375–400
Bourgeois from Haut-Barsac, Preignac, Bommes, Sauternes		500–600	250–260
First quality Graves		350–450	220–240

Year:	1847			
Month:	2 April			
Red Wines of:	**1841**	**1844**	**1845**	**1846**
First growths—Château Margaux, Latour, Lafite	5500–6500	5000–6000	800	"
First growth—Haut-Brion, Graves	4000–4700	4000–4500	"	"
Second growths—Rauzan, Léoville, Durfort, Brane, Cantenac, Mouton, Larose, Pichon	3500–4000	3500–4000	450–575	2000–2100
Third growths—Chât. d'Issan, Kirwan, Ducru, etc.	2800–3000	2700–3000	420–430	1700–1800
Fourth growths—St. Exupery, Desmirail, St. Pierre, Dubignon, LaGrange, Duluc, etc.	2200–2600	2300–2500	380–400	1400–1500
Fifth growths—Pontet Canet, Lacoste-Grand-Puy, Chauvet, Jurine, Pontac, Cantenac, Dauzac-Labarde	1600–2000	1500–1800	350–380	1100–1200
Bourgeois supérieurs from Margaux, St. Julien, Pauillac, Labarde, and St. Estèphe	1000–1200	900–1000	300–325	800–850
Bons bourgeois from Pauillac, St. Estèphe, Soussans, and Listrac	650–800	600–750	280–300	550–700
Peasant supérieurs from Margaux, Cantenac, St. Julien and Pauillac	600–700	550–650	270–280	500–550
First quality Graves	800–900	800–900	"	"
St-Emilion and first quality Canon	700–800	550–700	"	500–550
White Wines of:		**1844**	**1845**	**1846**
Château d'Yquem		2200–2400	375–400	1100–1200
Bourgeois from Haut-Barsac, Preignac, Bommes, Sauternes		500–600	300–325	450–750
First quality Graves		350–450	250–275	340–500

Year:	1848			
Month:	8 January			
Red Wines of:	**1841–1844**	**1845**	**1846**	**1847**
First growths—Château Margaux, Latour, Lafite	5500–6500	800	"	"
First growth—Haut-Brion, Graves	4400–4500	"	"	"
Second growths—Rauzan, Léoville, Durfort, Brane, Cantenac, Mouton, Larose, Pichon	3500–4000	600–625	2000–2100	"
Third growths—Chât. d'Issan, Kirwan, Ducru, etc.	2700–3000	450–460	1700–1800	"
Fourth growths—St. Exupery, Desmirail, St. Pierre, Dubignon, LaGrange, Duluc, etc.	2300–2500	450–480	1400–1500	"
Fifth growths—Pontet Canet, Lacoste-Grand-Puy, Chauvet, Jurine, Pontac, Cantenac, Dauzac-Labarde	1800–2000	400–410	1100–1200	525–550
Bourgeois supérieurs from Margaux, St. Julien, Pauillac, Labarde, and St. Estèphe	1000–1200	350–360	800–850	350–400
Bons bourgeois from Pauillac, St. Estèphe, Soussans, and Listrac	750–800	300–350	550–700	320–350
Peasant supérieurs from Margaux, Cantenac, St. Julien, and Pauillac	650–700	270–300	500–550	310–320
First quality Graves	800–900	"	"	"
St-Emilion and first quality Canon	650–700	"	500–550	"
White Wines of:		**1845**	**1846**	**1847**
Château d'Yquem		375–400	1400–1600	700–800
Bourgeois from Haut-Barsac, Preignac, Bommes, Sauternes		300–350	650–1000	400–500
First quality Graves		250–275	340–500	250–350

Year:	1849			
Month:	2 June			
Red Wines of:	**1844**	**1846**	**1847**	**1848**
First growths—Château Margaux, Latour, Lafite	5500–6500	3500–4000	2500	"
First growth—Haut-Brion, Graves	4400–4500	2400–3000	1800–2000	"
Second growths—Rauzan, Léoville, Durfort, Brane, Cantenac, Mouton, Larose, Pichon	3500–4000	2000–2100	1500–1800	"
Third growths—Chât. d'Issan, Kirwan, Ducru, etc.	2700–3000	1700–1800	1000–1200	650–700
Fourth growths—St. Exupery, Desmirail, St. Pierre, Dubignon, LaGrange, Duluc, etc.	2300–2500	1400–1500	800–950	550–750
Fifth growths—Pontet Canet, Lacoste-Grand-Puy, Chauvet, Jurine, Pontac, Cantenac, Dauzac-Labarde	1800–2000	1100–1200	425–450	400–450
Bourgeois supérieurs from Margaux, St. Julien, Pauillac, Labarde, and St. Estèphe	1000–1200	800–850	350–370	360–370
Bons bourgeois from Pauillac, St. Estèphe, Soussans and Listrac	750–800	550–700	310–320	280–350
Peasant supérieurs from Margaux, Cantenac, St. Julien, and Pauillac	650–700	500–550	310–320	250–280
First quality Graves	800–900	"	"	"
St-Emilion and first quality Canon	650–700	500–550	260–320	200–250
White Wines of:		**1846**	**1847**	**1848**
Château d'Yquem		1800–2000	1200–1300	450–500
Bourgeois from Haut-Barsac, Preignac, Bommes, Sauternes		650–1000	400–650	300–325
First quality Graves		340–500	250–350	180–250

Year:	1850			
Month:	7 September			
Red Wines of:	**1844**	**1846**	**1847–1848**	**1849**
First growths—Château Margaux, Latour, Lafite	5500–6500	3500–4000	2800–3000	"
First growth—Haut-Brion, Graves	4400–4500	2400–3000	1800–2000	"
Second growths—Rauzan, Léoville, Durfort, Brane, Cantenac, Mouton, Larose, Pichon	3500–4000	2000–2100	1100–1800	"
Third growths—Chât. d'Issan, Kirwan, Ducru, etc.	2700–3000	1700–1800	800–1200	"
Fourth growths—St. Exupery, Desmirail, St. Pierre, Dubignon, LaGrange, Duluc, etc.	2300–2500	1400–1500	750–1000	500–550
Fifth growths—Pontet Canet, Lacoste-Grand-Puy, Chauvet, Jurine, Pontac, Cantenac, Dauzac-Labarde	1800–2000	1200–1300	650–800	450–500
Bourgeois supérieurs from Margaux, St. Julien, Pauillac, Labarde, and St. Estèphe	1000–1200	900–1000	600–700	450–450
Bons bourgeois from Pauillac, St. Estèphe, Soussans, and Listrac	750–800	650–800	450–550	350–400
Peasant supérieurs from Margaux, Cantenac, St. Julien, and Pauillac	650–700	500–550	350–400	300–400
First quality Graves	800–900	"	"	260–350
St-Emilion and first quality Canon	650–700	500–550	400–500	350–400
White Wines of:		**1847**	**1848**	**1849**
Château d'Yquem		1800–2000	550–600	450–500
Bourgeois from Haut-Barsac, Preignac, Bommes, Sauternes		500–900	350–450	350–400
First quality Graves		350–400	250–280	250–300

Year:	1851				
Month:	**4 April**				
Red Wines of:	**1844**	**1846**	**1848**	**1849**	**1850**
First growths—Château Margaux, Latour, Lafite	5500–6500	3500–4000	3000	"	"
First growth—Haut-Brion, Graves	4400–4500	2400–3000	2000	"	"
Second growths—Rauzan, Léoville, Durfort, Brane, Cantenac, Mouton, Larose, Pichon	3500–4000	2000–2100	1800	700–800	600–650
Third growths—Chât. d'Issan, Kirwan, Ducru, etc.	2700–3000	1100–1200	1200	500–600	450–500
Fourth growths—St. Exupery, Desmirail, St. Pierre, Dubignon, LaGrange, Duluc, etc.	2300–2500	1400–1500	1000	500–560	400–450
Fifth growths—Pontet Canet, Lacoste-Grand-Puy, Chauvet, Jurine, Pontac, Cantenac, Dauzac-Labarde	1800–2000	1000–1100	800–900	450–500	360–400
Bourgeois supérieurs de Margaux, St. Julien, Pauillac, Labarde, and St. Estèphe	1000–1200	900–1000	600–700	450–500	280–340
Bons bourgeois from Pauillac, St. Estèphe, Soussans, and Listrac	750–800	650–800	550	350–400	250–280
Peasant supérieurs from Margaux, Cantenac, St. Julien, and Pauillac	650–700	500–650	400	300–400	260–300
First quality Graves	800–900	600–650	400–450	260–350	250–260
St-Emilion and first quality Canon	650–700	500–550	500	350–400	"
White Wines of:		**1847**	**1848**	**1849**	**1850**
Château d'Yquem		1800–2000	650–700	650–700	"
Bourgeois from Haut-Barsac, Preignac, Bommes, Sauternes		500–900	400–450	370–420	"
First quality Graves		440–500	270–280	250–310	130–145

Year:	1852				
Month:	7 May				
Red Wines of:	**1846**	**1847–1848**	**1849**	**1850**	**1851**
First growths—Lafite, Latour, Château Margaux	4000–4200	3800–4000	1200–1500	800–1000	1900–2000
Second growths—Larose, Léoville, Brannes-Mouton, etc.	2400–2500	2200–2400	900–1000	650–700	1000–1200
Third growths—Kirwan, Chât. d'Issan, etc.	1500–1800	1500–1800	700–800	550–575	800–850
Fourth growths—Duluc, St. Pierre, Desmirail	1100–1200	1100–1200	600–700	500–550	750–800
Fifth growths—Lacoste-Grand-Puy, Pontet, Jurine, etc.	1000–1100	900–1010	550–600	480–500	580–625
Bourgeois supérieurs	900–1000	900–1000	500–550	400–450	450–500
Peasant wines from superior parishes	"	"	300–450	260–320	350–400
First growth—Graves, Haut-Brion	2400–3000	2200–2400	"	"	1400–1500
Second growths—Graves	600–650	600–650	500–600	300–320	400–425
St-Emilion and first growth Canon	500–550	500–600	350–450	240–300	350–450
White Wines of:		**1848**	**1849**	**1850**	**1851**
Château d'Yquem		850–900	950–1000	300–325	900–1000
Bourgeois from Haut-Barsac, Preignac, Bommes, Sauternes		510–550	470–520	250–270	550–600
First quality Graves		350–400	340–375	210–225	350–420

Year:	1853			
Month:	4 March			
Red Wines of:	**1849**	**1850**	**1851**	**1852**
First growths—Lafite, Latour, Château Margaux	2000	1000–1100	3300–3600	1500–1600
Second growths—Larose, Léoville, Brannes-Mouton, etc.	1200–1500	800–900	2200–2500	1000–1300
Third growths—Kirwan, Chât. d'Issan, etc.	900–1000	700–750	1700–1800	700–800
Fourth growths—Duluc, St. Pierre, Desmirail	800–850	600–650	1400–1500	700
Fifth growths—Lacoste-Grand-Puy, Pontet, Jurine, etc.	750–800	500–550	1200–1300	525–550
Bourgeois supérieurs	600–670	425–475	800–1000	425–450
Peasant wines from superior parishes	500–550	350–400	500–550	350–400
First growth—Graves, Haut-Brion	"	"	1800–2000	750–850
Second growths—Graves	650–700	350–400	700–800	450–500
St-Emilion and first growth Canon	500–600	"	550–600	300–350
White Wines of:	**1849**	**1850**	**1851**	**1852**
Château d'Yquem	1500	"	1600	900–1000
Bourgeois from Haut-Barsac, Preignac, Bommes, Sauternes	690–800	"	950–1000	500–600
First quality Graves	"	"	450–720	300–400

Year:	1854			
Month:	**6 October**			
Red Wines of:	**1849**	**1851**	**1852**	**1853**
First growths—Château Lafite, Château Latour, Château Margaux	2600	5000	1800–2000	"
Second growths—Larose, Léoville, Rauzan, Mouton, etc.	1600–1800	3500–3800	1600–1700	"
Third growths	1400–1500	2600–2800	1300–1400	"
Fourth growths	1350–1400	2200–2400	1100–1200	900
Fifth growths	1000–1100	1900–2000	1000–1050	"
Bourgeois supérieurs	900	1400–1500	750–850	"
Peasant wines from superior parishes	750–800	1000–1100	650–700	550–600
First growth—Graves, Château Haut-Brion	"	4000–4500	1800–2000	"
Second growths—Graves	850–900	1200–1400	700–800	"
St-Emilion and first growth Canon	800–900	1000–1110	700–750	"
White Wines of:	**1849**	**1850**	**1851**	**1852**
Château d'Yquem	3600–4000		3000	2500–3000
Bourgeois from Haut-Barsac, Preignac, Bommes, Sauternes	2000–2800		2000–2500	1500–1800
First quality Graves	"		1000–1200	740–775

Year:	1854				
Month:	**29 December**				
Red Wines of:	**1849**	**1851**	**1852**	**1853**	**1854**
First growths—Château Lafite, Château Latour, Château Margaux	2800	5000	2000–2200	1100	5000–5500
Second growths—Larose, Léoville, Rauzan, Mouton, etc.	1800	3500–3800	1700–1800	"	4500–5000
Third growths	1500	2600–2800	1400–1500	"	2800–3000
Fourth growths	1400	2200–2400	1200–1300	900	2400
Fifth growths	1200	1900–2000	1000–1100	"	2100
Bourgeois supérieurs	1000	1400–1500	800–850	"	1500–1600
Peasant wines from superior parishes	775	1000–1100	700–750	600–650	1000–1200
First growth—Graves, Château Haut-Brion	"	4000–4500	1800–2000	"	"
Second growths—Graves	875	1200–1400	700–800	"	1000
St-Emilion and first growth Canon	875	1000–1110	700–750	"	"
White Wines of:	**1849**	**1851**	**1852**		**1854**
Château d'Yquem	3600–4000	3200–3600	3500–4000		3500–4000
Bourgeois from Haut-Barsac, Preignac, Bommes, Sauternes	2400–2800	2200–2600	1800–2000		1800–2000
First quality Graves	"	1200–1500	800–900		800–900

Appendix III

SELECTED PRICE QUOTATIONS FOR THE BORDEAUX CLASSED GROWTHS

The charts on the following pages are based on a synthesis of information from two complementary sources: the sales prices for the individual classed growths as recorded in the archives of the Tastet & Lawton brokerage firm, and the overall prices for the various classes of wines as published in the nineteen volumes of the Prix-Courant Général formerly in the library of the Bordeaux Chamber of Commerce.

The Tastet & Lawton data come from two sources in its archives: for the years 1854 through 1831, prices and comments were extracted from the series of notebooks in which notable occurrences in Bordeaux's vineyards and marketplace were registered; information prior to 1831 comes from a register in which details concerning these wines' prices and yields were gathered from various records throughout the firm's offices.

Although the prices of these wines were recorded clearly and faithfully, for the modern observer looking at them from a distance of over 150 years, these sales figures have become free-floating numbers. Property X, a fourth growth, may well have sold its wine from a particular vintage at a particular price, whereas another fourth growth, Property Y, may have sold its wine for much less. Does this mean that X was a better wine than Y? Not necessarily. Property Y may have sold its wine right after trading for that vintage began, whereas X chose not to sell its wine until several months or years later when the vintage had become more scarce, and thus more expensive. Such factors must be taken into account when looking at these charts: it is important to consider not only the prices that the wines brought, but also the date of the sale and any associated terms in the column "Other Notes" to get a full picture of the transaction.

Even more subtle is the question of where the sales price of a wine ranked a property in the classification. For many proprietors, this was often the prime consideration in determining when they would sell their wine: if they were unable to get a price that would maintain their property at its rank in the hierarchy, they might keep their wine off the market until finally able to obtain a more appropriate amount. In order to determine where a wine's sales price placed it in relation to the overall state of the classification at the moment of the sale, the charts which follow compare the price obtained by the wine with the prices that were current in the Bordeaux marketplace according to the Prix-Courant Général for the month in which the transaction occurred. It should be stressed that only when there was an exact correspondence between the date of a wine's sale and the availability of published prices for a vintage was it possible to include an entry in the charts. Occasionally, according to the Tastet & Lawton records, a wine would enter the marketplace long after most of that vintage had been traded, and so that year would no longer be listed in the Prix-Courant Général In such cases, no accurate comparison was possible and thus there is no entry on the chart for that vintage. In addition, although the register for the classed growths prior to 1831 provides sales prices for the wines, no mention is made of when the transactions occurred, making it impossible to establish any correspondence with the Prix-Courant. For this reason, there are no entries on the charts for these years.

These charts offer a twofold interest. First, they indicate not only how well proprietors were able to maintain their wines' sales price at their rank in the classification, but also how successful the wines were within the growth itself. Prices for each class of wine usually covered a certain range, and by overlaying the Tastet & Lawton figures onto those of the Prix-Courant it can be seen how a wine's price positioned it within its class in a given year.

Second, it becomes evident that a property's inclusion in the classification was not due to a sudden run of good vintages in the years just preceding 1855, but rather that its prices were established at classed-growth levels well before the brokers drew up their list. Indeed, for a property such as Ducru-Beaucaillou, it is possible to trace its progression from a third growth—where classifications like the Statistique Œnologique *and* Le Producteur *placed it in the 1830s—to its position among the seconds in 1855.*

However, some charts appear to belie the idea that a property's standing was based on the price of its wine—Cos d'Estournel and Calon-Ségur are perhaps the most prominent examples, their prices regularly falling well below their classification ranking. Because it was not in the nature of either brokers or merchants to make a gift of a property's classification, it is necessary to try and understand the circumstances that would allow a property to maintain its ranking—or even to improve it—while the price of its wine was consistently below that of its peers. In the case of Cos-d'Estournel, the precarious state of Louis-Joseph-Gaspard d'Estournel's finances brought on by his insatiable speculation in vineyard land was well known on the Bordeaux marketplace, making it impossible for him to pursue the hard line in negotiations with the merchants that other proprietors could employ. The prices offered in Bordeaux were indeed well below what the wines' quality merited, and it was to achieve a more equitable return that Estournel resorted to exporting his production directly to markets as far away as India where he was able to obtain prices that justified his property's position as a second growth. (It is important to remember that the prices in the Tastet & Lawton records reflect the prices in the Bordeaux marketplace, not what Estournel would have earned abroad.) For Calon-Ségur, evidence of the circumstances that led to its run of abnormally low prices can be found in contemporary accounts such as the poetic commentary of Pierre Biarnez (see Classification 23 in Appendix I). The property was passing through one of those periods that has beset every one of the classed growths at some period in their history, and although it may have resulted in a downward shift of Calon's position within the ranks of the third growths, the conservative nature of the Bordeaux marketplace maintained the property at its traditional rank, confident that the conditions at Calon were of a temporary nature and that it would once again be capable of producing wine worthy of a third growth when circumstances at the property improved—which has subsequently been proved true.

Because Tastet & Lawton specialized in wines from the Médoc, its archives contain no records for the classed growths from the Sauternes region, and thus no charts could be produced for these properties.

Château Lafite-Rothschild

Year	Price	Current Name	Other Notes
1854	5000	Ch. Lafite	23 tuns/with ⅔ of 1853 @ 1100/December 1854
1853	1100	Ch. Lafite	45 tuns/with the 1854/December 1854
1852	1100	Lafite	100 tuns/December 1852
1851	3000	Lafite	95 tuns/December 1852
1850	1500	Lafitte	110 tuns/August 1856
1849	2000	Lafite	100 tuns/April 1852
1848	2800	Lafite	100 tuns/December 1849
1847	1025	Lafite	150 tuns/September 1848
1846	4000	Lafite	70 tuns/partial sale/March 1850
1845	800	Lafite	100 tuns/April 1846
1844	4500	Lafite	80 tuns/1844–1845
1843	800	Lafite	70 tuns/April 1846
1842	2500	Lafite	80 tuns/with the 1841/April 1844
1841	5500	Lafite	105 tuns/with the 1842/April 1844
1840	1800	Lafite	150 tuns/good/March 1842
1839	2600	Chateau Lafite	64 tuns/good/1840
1838	—	Chateau Lafitte	100 tuns/good
1837	2400	Chateau Lafitte	115 tuns/good/January 1838
1836	—	Chateau Lafitte	92 tuns
1835	1800	Chateau Lafitte	100 tuns/very good/March 1837
1834	2800	Chateau Lafitte	85 tuns/good/November 1834
1833	1400	Ch. Lafitte	170 tuns/February 1834
1832	2100	Ch. Lafitte	80 tuns/February 1833
1831	2400	Ch. Lafitte	24 tuns

Year	Price	Current Name	Other Notes
1830	—	Ch. Lafitte	22 tuns
1829	550	Ch. Lafitte	120 tuns
1828	1600	Ch. Lafitte	120 tuns
1827	1680	Ch. Lafitte	120 tuns
1826	1600	Ch. Lafitte	100 tuns
1825	3500	Ch. Lafitte	No other notes
1824	—	Ch. Lafitte	55 tuns
1823	1650	Ch. Lafitte	120 tuns
1822	2600	Ch. Lafitte	135 tuns
1821			No listings for 1821
1820			No listings for 1820
1819	3000	Ch. Lafitte	130 tuns
1818	3350	Ch. Lafitte	50 tuns
1817			No listings for 1817
1816			No listings for 1816
1815	3100	Ch. Lafitte	50 tuns
1775	1200–1300	Ch. Lafitte	No other notes

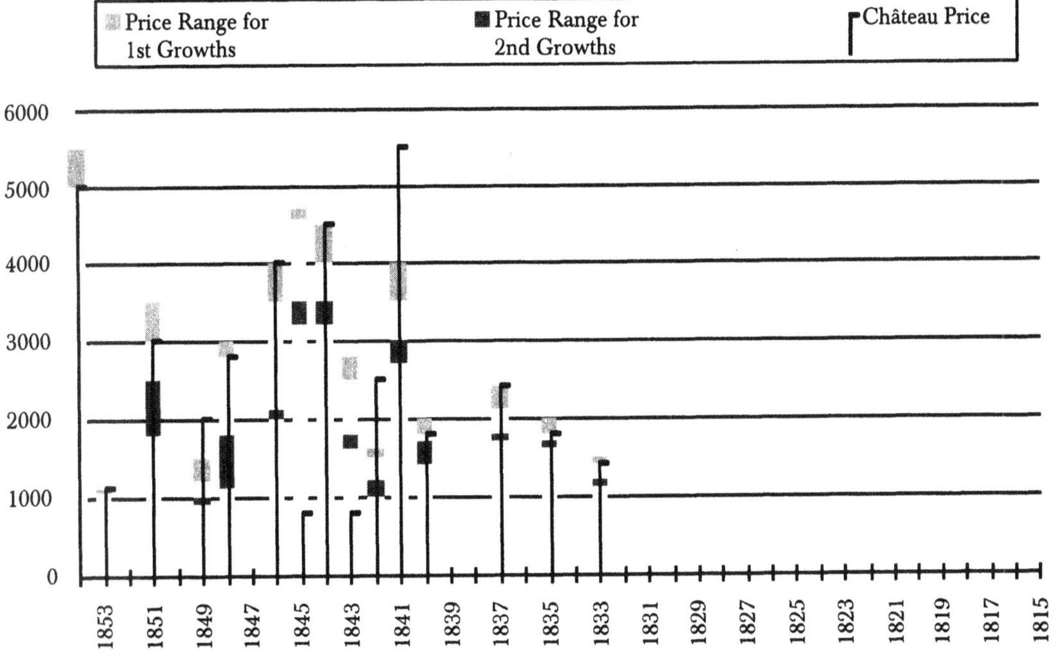

Château Latour

Year	Price	Current Name	Other Notes
1854	5000	Ch. Latour	14½ tuns/1855
1853	1750	Ch. Latour	40 tuns/subscription
1852	1750	Ch. Latour	86½ tuns/subscribed
1851	1750	Ch Latour	78 tuns
1850	1750	Ch. Latour	83 tuns/subscribed
1849	1750	Latour	55 tuns/subscribed
1848	1750	Latour	77 tuns/subscribed
1847	1750	Latour	73 tuns/subscribed/resold 1000/1848
1846	1750	Latour	55 tuns/subscribed
1845	1750	Lambert Latour	36 tuns/subscribed/resold 800/March 1847
1844	1750	Latour	61 tuns/subscribed
1843	—	Latour	20 tuns
1842	1700	Latour	63 tuns/partial sale
1841	1800	Latour	90 tuns/August 1842
1840	1800	Latour	106 tuns/good/March 1842
1839	—	Latour	45 tuns/full
1838	2400	Chateau Latour	50 tuns/better/partial sale
1837	2100	Chateau Latour	71 tuns/good/December 1837
1836	1800	Chateau Latour	72 tuns/February 1837
1835	1700	Chateau Latour	85 tuns/good/January 1837
1834	2400	Chateau Latour	63 tuns/good/November 1834
1833	1550	Latour	82 tuns/ordinary/August 1834
1832	2100	Ch. Latour	51 tuns/very good/February 1833
1831	2600	Latour	27 tuns/fine delightful

Year	Price	Current Name	Other Notes
1830	1600	Latour	12 tuns
1829	600	Latour	80 tuns
1828	1300	Latour	No other notes
1827	1680	Latour	100 tuns
1826	1600	Latour	85 tuns
1825	3500	Latour	No other notes
1824	—	Latour	No trades reported
1823	1500	Latour	65 tuns
1822	2600	Latour	78 tuns
1821			No listings for 1821
1820			No listings for 1820
1819	2400	Latour	104 tuns
1818	3350	Latour	60 tuns
1817			No listings for 1817
1816			No listings for 1816
1815	3100	Latour	45 tuns
1775	1200–1300	Latour	No other notes

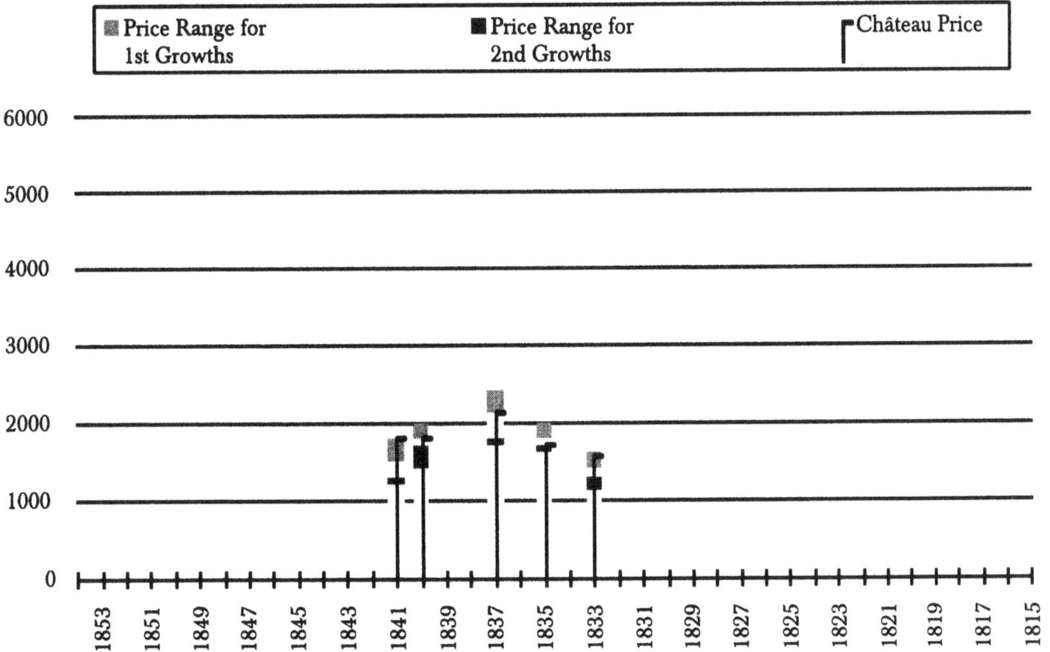

Château Margaux

Year	Price	Current Name	Other Notes
1854	5500	le Château	16 tuns/December 1855
1853	1000	le Château	42 tuns
1852	2100	Le Château	72½ tuns/subscribed
1851	2100	Le Château	85 tuns/subscribed
1850	2100	Le Château	108 tuns/subscribed
1849	2100	Château	110 tuns/subscribed
1848	2100	Château	105 tuns/subscribed
1847	2100	Château	150 tuns/subscribed/resold 1000/August 1848
1846	2100	Château	80 tuns/subscribed
1845	2100	Château	66 tuns/subscribed
1844	2100	Château	72 tuns/subscribed
1843	1000	Château	36 tuns/September 1846
1842	1700	Château	70 tuns/February 1845
1841	2500	Château	135 tuns
1840	2300	Château	95 tuns/very good/March 1842
1839	—	Château Margaux	60 tuns
1838	—	Château	60 tuns
1837	2100	Château	62 tuns/June 1839/with second wine
1836	1800	Château	72 tuns/June 1839/with second wine
1835	1700	Chat. Margaux	60 tuns/small, fine/June 1839/with second wine
1834	4000	Ch. Margaux	40 tuns/good/May 1836
1833	—	Château	57 tuns/subscribed
1832	—	Le Château	33 tuns/sold by subscription
1831	—	Château	30 tuns/leased

Year	Price	Current Name	Other Notes
1830	—	Château (Lacolonila)	10 tuns
1829	—	Château (Lacolonila)	Leased
1828	—	Château (Lacolonila)	Leased
1827	—	Château (Lacolonila)	Leased
1826	—	Château (Lacolonila)	Leased
1825	3500	Château (Lacolonila)	No other notes
1824	—	Château (Lacolonila)	40 tuns
1823	1500	Château (Lacolonila)	60 tuns
1822	—	Château (Lacolonila)	Touched by hail
1821			No listings for 1821
1820			No listings for 1820
1819	2400	Château (Lacolonila)	60 tuns
1818	3350	Château (Lacolonila)	No other notes
1817			No listings for 1817
1816			No listings for 1816
1815	3100	Château (Lacolonila)	60 tuns
1775	1200–1300	Château (Lacolonila)	No other notes

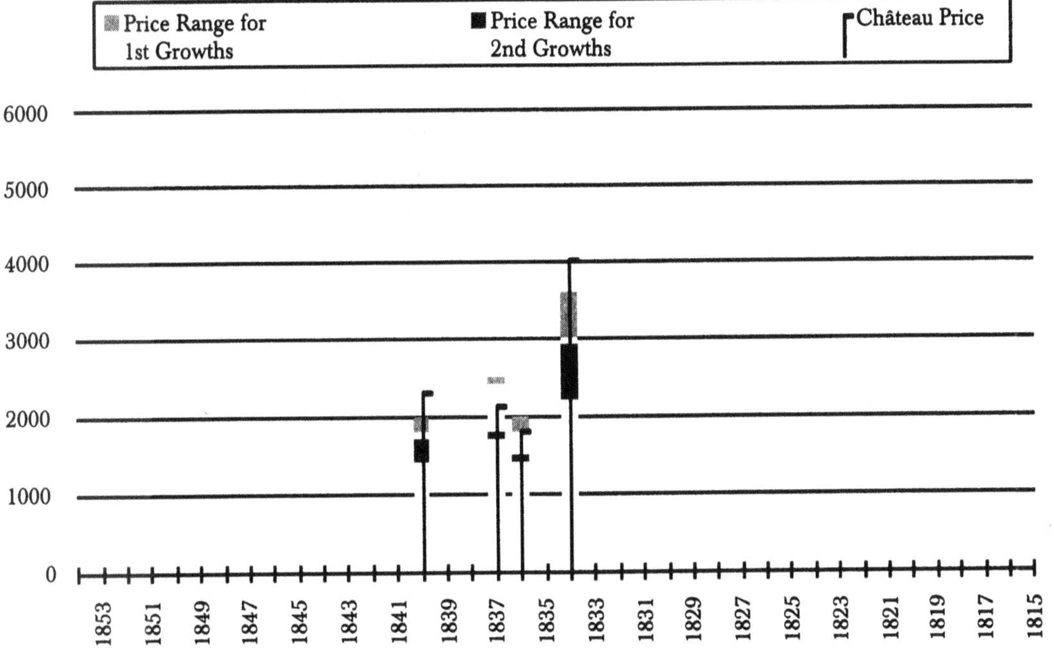

Château Mouton-Rothschild

Year	Price	Current Name	Other Notes
1854	5000	Mouton	10 tuns/December 1854
1853	1100	Mouton	36 tuns
1852	1300	Mouton	71 tuns/January 1853 for 20 tuns
1851	1500	Mouton	65 tuns/June 1852/last 20 tuns @ 3800
1850	700	Mouton	77 tuns/June 1851
1849	1000	Mouton	68 tuns/January 1852
1848	1200	Mouton	63 tuns/partial sale/July 1852/altered
1847	800	Mouton	98 tuns/November 1848
1846	2000	Mouton	65 tuns/February 1849
1845	575	Mouton	95 tuns/October 1846
1844	2100	Mouton	68 tuns/October 1844/with reserve*
1843	600	Mouton	37 tuns/October 1843
1842	1200	Mouton	80 tuns/March 1845
1841	1400	Mouton	95 tuns/August 1842
1840	1400	Mouton	124 tuns/v. good/February 1842
1839	1200	Mouton	67 tuns/v.g./January 1840
1838	1700	Mouton	100 tuns/full/September 1839
1837	1800	Mouton	119 tuns/good/December 1837
1836	1600	Mouton	89 tuns/February 1837
1835	1200	Mouton	85 tuns/very good/February 1836
1834	2100	Mouton	83 tuns/fresh taste/November 1834
1833	1000	Mouton	105 tuns/very green/to Paris/1838
1832	1800	Mouton	70 tuns/perfect/April 1833
1831	2000	Mouton	13 tuns/hard bad

Year	Price	Current Name	Other Notes
1830	2100	Mouton	14½ tuns
1829	550	Mouton	90 tuns
1828	825	Mouton	100 tuns
1827	1350	Mouton	100 tuns
1826	—	Mouton	No trades reported
1825	3350	Mouton	No other notes
1824	—	Mouton	No trades reported
1823	1360	Mouton	105 tuns
1822	2100	Mouton	No other notes
1821			No listings for 1821
1820			No listings for 1820
1819	1600	Mouton	120 tuns
1818	2650	Mouton	160 tuns
1817			No listings for 1817
1816			No listings for 1816
1815	2350	Mouton	62 tuns
1775	800	Mouton	No other notes

* A note in the 1844 listing indicates that the wine was sold at 2100 francs with the reserve that its price would automatically rise higher than any of the other second growths.

Mouton-Rothschild

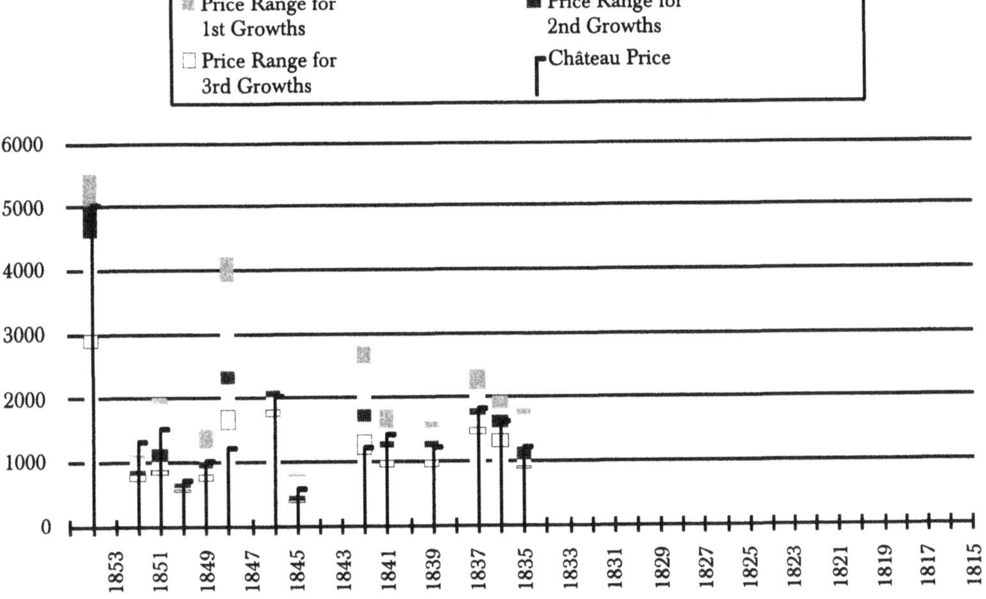

Château Rausan-Ségla

Year	Price	Current Name	Other Notes
1854	1200	Ségla	8½ tuns/subscribed to the English
1853	1200	Ségla	14 tuns/subscribed to the English
1852	1000	Ségla	35 tuns/January 1853
1851	1200	Ségla	48 tuns/April 1852
1850	600	Rauzan Ségla	35 tuns/April 1851
1849	1200	Rausan Ségla	40 tuns/July 1853
1848	800	Rausan Ségla	46 tuns/September 1849
1847	525	Rausan Ségla	57 tuns/July 1848
1846	2000	Rausan Ségla	33 tuns/partial sale
1845	450	Rausan	July 1846
1844	2500	Rausan Segla	36 tuns/October 1844
1843	—	Rausan Segla	16 tuns
1842	1000	Segla	34 tuns/April 1846
1841	1400	Segla	50 tuns/August 1842
1840	1200	Segla	50 tuns/good/March 1841
1839	1200	Rauzan Segla	22 tuns/very good/February 1840
1838	800	Segla	21 tuns/good/July 1842
1837	—	de Segla	24 tuns
1836	—	de Segla	40 tuns
1835	1200	de Segla	28 tuns/very good/1836
1834	2100	Rauzan	9 tuns/November 1835
1833	1400	Segla	22 tuns/thin/December 1834
1832	1800	Segla	14 tuns/good/August 1833
1831	2400	de Segla	9 tuns/good

Year	Price	Current Name	Other Notes
1830	—	Rauzan	6 tuns
1829			No listings for 1829
1828	—	Rauzan	36 tuns
1827	1350	Rauzan	55 tuns
1826	1300	Rauzan	No other notes
1825	3000	Rauzan	No other notes
1824	500	Rauzan	15 tuns
1823	1200	Rauzan	No other notes
1822	—	Rauzan	No trades reported
1821			No listings for 1821
1820			No listings for 1820
1819	1500	Rauzan	49 tuns
1818	2500	Rauzan	No other notes
1817			No listings for 1817
1816			No listings for 1816
1815	2500	Rauzan	45 tuns
1775	1000	Rauzan	No other notes

Rausan-Ségla

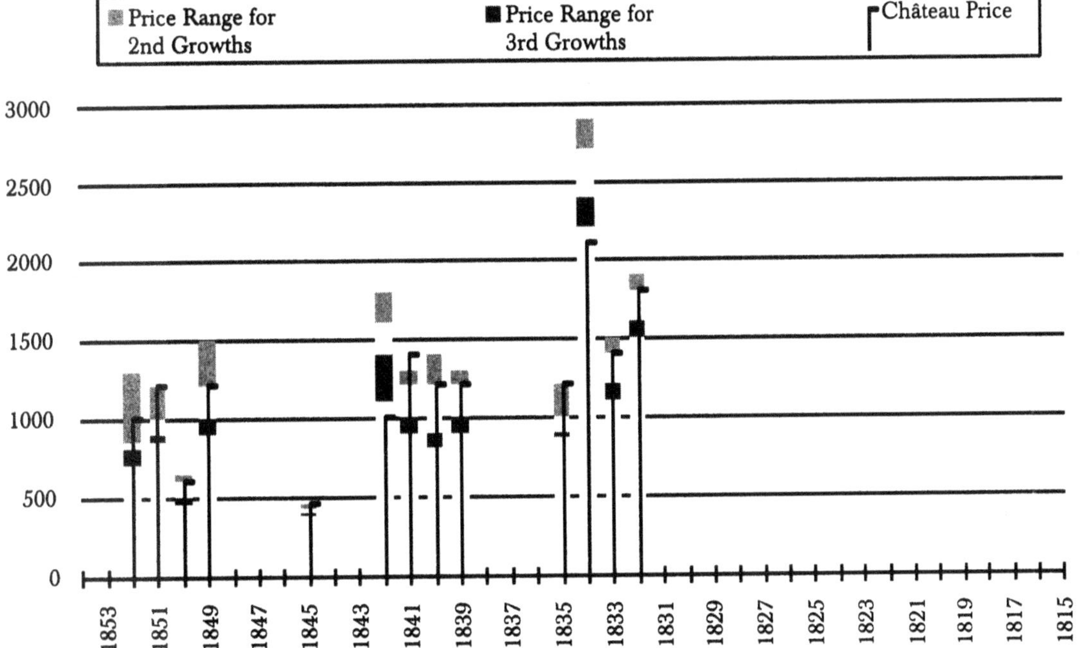

Château Rauzan-Gassies

Year	Price	Current Name	Other Notes
1854	4000	Pélier	6½ tuns/December 1855
1853	—	Pélier	11 tuns
1852	1000	Pélier	23 tuns/January 1853
1851	1200	Rauzan Gassies	34 tuns/April 1852
1850	600	Rauzan Gassies	23 tuns/April 1851
1849	—	Rausan Chabrier	19 tuns
1848	900	Rausan Chabrier	27 tuns/October 1849
1847	710	Chabrier	38 tuns/October 1848
1846	2000	Chabrier	16 tuns/1849
1845	500	Rausan Pellier	12 tuns/March 1847
1844	2500	Rausan Gassies	27 tuns/October 1844
1843	550	Rausan Gassies	13 tuns/October 1845
1842	1000	Gassies	23 tuns/April 1846
1841	1400	Gassies	32 tuns/1843
1840	1200	Pellier	32 tuns/very good/February 1841
1839	1200	Rauzan Gassies	19 tuns/good/February 1840
1838	500	Gassies	14 tuns/good/July 1844
1837	—	Pellier	21 tuns
1836	1500	Pellier	12 tuns/1837
1835	—	Gassies	20 tuns/ordinary
1834	—	Pellier	4 tuns
1833	1050	Puilboreau	9 tuns/good/January 1834
1832	1800	Pelier	11½ tuns/better/December 1833
1831	2400	Chevalier	5 tuns

Year	Price	Current Name	Other Notes
1830	—	Pellier	No trades reported
1829			No listings for 1829
1828	—	Pellier	14 tuns
1827	1400	Pellier	20 tuns
1826	—	Pellier	20 tuns
1825	3000	Pellier	No other notes
1824	500	Pellier	No other notes
1823	1200	Pellier	No other notes
1822	—	Pellier	No trades reported
1821			No listings for 1821
1820			No listings for 1820
1819	1500	Pellier	17 tuns
1818	2000	Pellier	18 tuns
1817			No listings for 1817
1816			No listings for 1816
1815	2150	Pellier	15 tuns
1775	800–900	Pellier	No other notes

Rauzan-Gassies

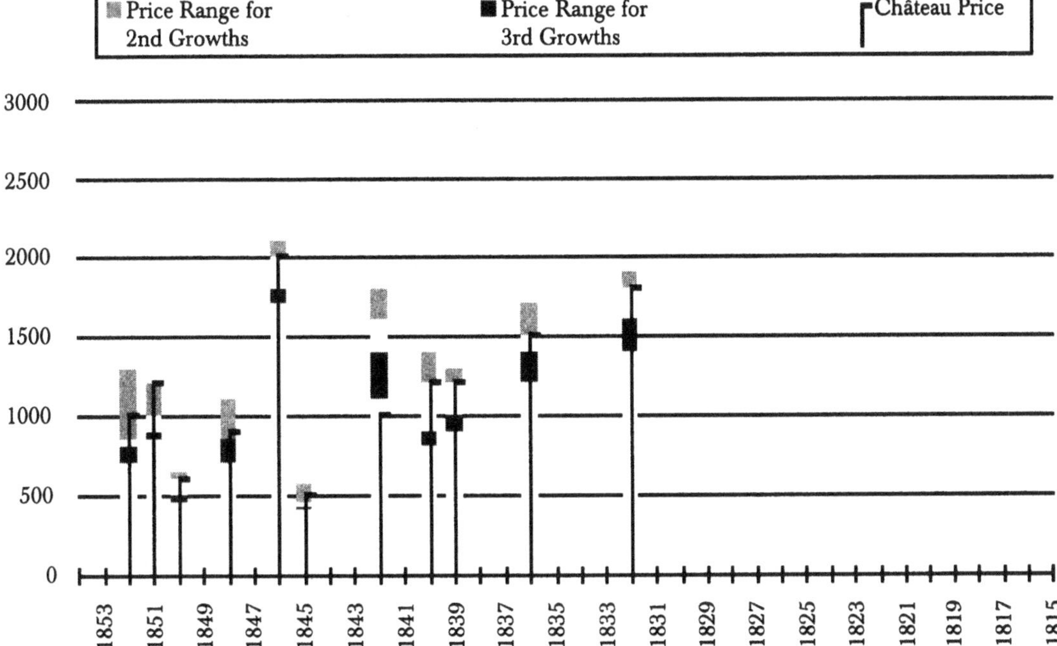

Château Léoville-Las-Cases

Year	Price	Current Name	Other Notes
1854	4000	de Las Cases	2¾ tuns
1853	—	de Las Cases	20 tuns
1852	1000	de Las Cases	95 tuns/January 1853
1851	1000	Las Cases	104 tuns/50 tuns/March 1852
1850	625	Las Cases	122 tuns/April 1851
1849	900	Lascases	84 tuns/April 1851
1848	800	Lascases	113 tuns/September 1849
1847	525	Lascases	155 tuns/July 1848
1846	2000	Lascases	98 tuns/October 1848
1845	450	de Lascases	84 tuns/December 1846
1844	2500	de Lascase	95 tuns/November 1844
1843	—	de Lascase	30 tuns
1842	—	Lascaze	82 tuns
1841	1400	Lascaze	107 tuns/January 1843
1840	1400	de Lascaze	125 tuns/elegant
1839	1200	de Lascazes	50 tuns/thin/February 1840
1838	1700	De Lascaze	58 tuns/fine/September 1839
1837	1800	Lascaze	110 tuns/good/1840
1836	1000	de Lascaze	104 tuns
1835	1200	de Lascazes	120 tuns/elegant/February 1836
1834	2100	De Lascazes	80 tuns/good/November 1834
1833	1000	de Lascaze	130 tuns/fine, elegant/December 1833
1832	1800	de Lascazes	80 tuns/perfect, flowing/several tuns @ 1800
1831	2100	de Lascaze	43 tuns/full-bodied

Year	Price	Current Name	Other Notes
1830	—	Lascaze	21 tuns
1829	350	Lascaze	No other notes
1828	—	Lascaze	No trades reported
1827	1350	Lascaze	110 tuns
1826	1300	Lascaze	No other notes
1825	3150–3300	Lascaze	No other notes
1824	500	Lascaze	36 tuns
1823	1200	Lascaze	60 tuns
1822	2100	Lascaze	No other notes
1821			No listings for 1821
1820			No listings for 1820
1819	650	Lascaze	36 tuns
1818	2500–3100	Lascaze	No other notes
1817			No listings for 1817
1816			No listings for 1816
1815	2250	Lascaze	No other notes
1775	1000	Lascaze	No other notes

Léoville-Las-Cases

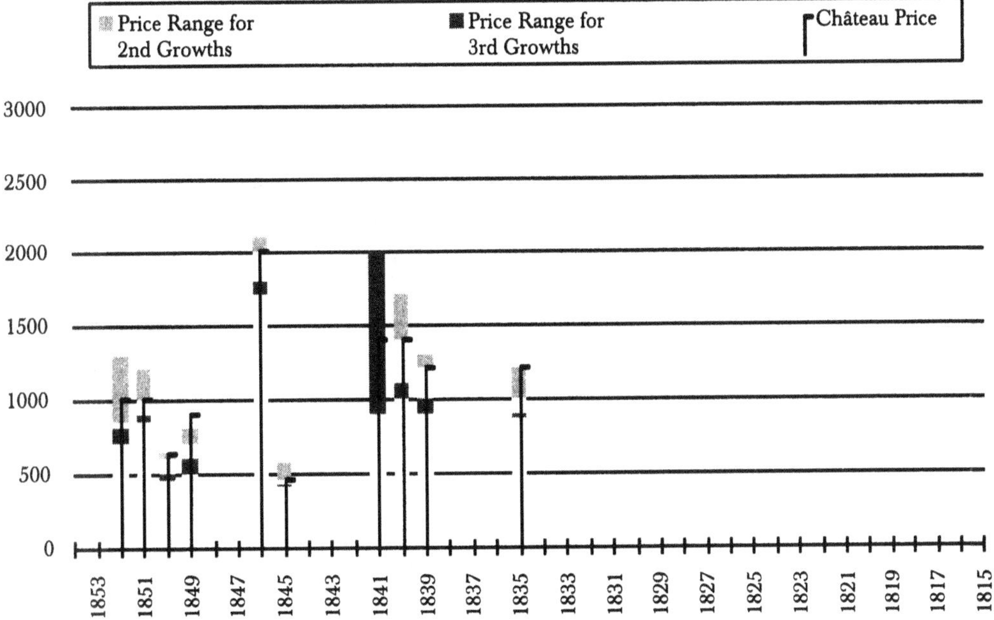

Note: In January 1843, prices for second growths from 1841 were 1400–1600.

Château Léoville-Poyferré

Year	Price	Current Name	Other Notes
1854	4000	de Poyféré	4½ tuns/July 1856
1853	900	de Poyféré	18 tuns/September 1856
1852	800	de Poyféré	48 tuns/November 1852
1851	1000	de Poyféré	65 tuns/30 tuns/March 1852
1850	600	de Poyferré	56 tuns/January 1851
1849	1300	Poyféré	43 tuns/October 1853
1848	800	Poyféré	80 tuns/September 1849
1847	525	Poyféré	95 tuns/July 1848
1846	2000	Poyféré	60 tuns/1849
1845	450	Poyféré	50 tuns/July 1846
1844	2100	Poyféré	60 tuns/August 1844
1843	600	Poyféré	18 tuns/October 1845
1842	1000	Poyféré	57 tuns/September 1843
1841	1400	Poyféré	60 tuns/August 1842
1840	1200	Poyféré	50 tuns/good/January 1841
1839	1200	de Poyféré	23 tuns/good/January 1840
1838	—	de Poyféré	29 tuns/very good/1841
1837	1800	Poyféré	46 tuns/good/December 1837
1836	1500	Poyféré	43 tuns/January 1837
1835	900	Leoville Dab.	52 tuns/mellow/January 1836
1834	2100	Dabadie	25 tuns/fine/November 1834
1833	1000	Dabadie	60 tuns/good–mell./December 1833
1832	2100	Dabadie	38 tuns/mellow, perfect/1838
1831	2100	Dabadie	23 tuns/very good

Year	Price	Current Name	Other Notes
1830	—	Dabadie	9 tuns
1829	350	Dabadie	No other notes
1828	—	Dabadie	No trades reported
1827	1350	Dabadie	50 tuns
1826	1300	Dabadie	No other notes
1825	3300	Dabadie	No other notes
1824	500	Dabadie	13 tuns
1823	1200	Dabadie	47 tuns
1822	2100	Dabadie	No other notes
1821			No listings for 1821
1820			No listings for 1820
1819	1600	Dabadie	27 tuns
1818	2500	Dabadie	No other notes
1817			No listings for 1817
1816			No listings for 1816
1815	2250	Dabadie	No other notes
1775	—	Dabadie	No other notes

Léoville-Poyferré

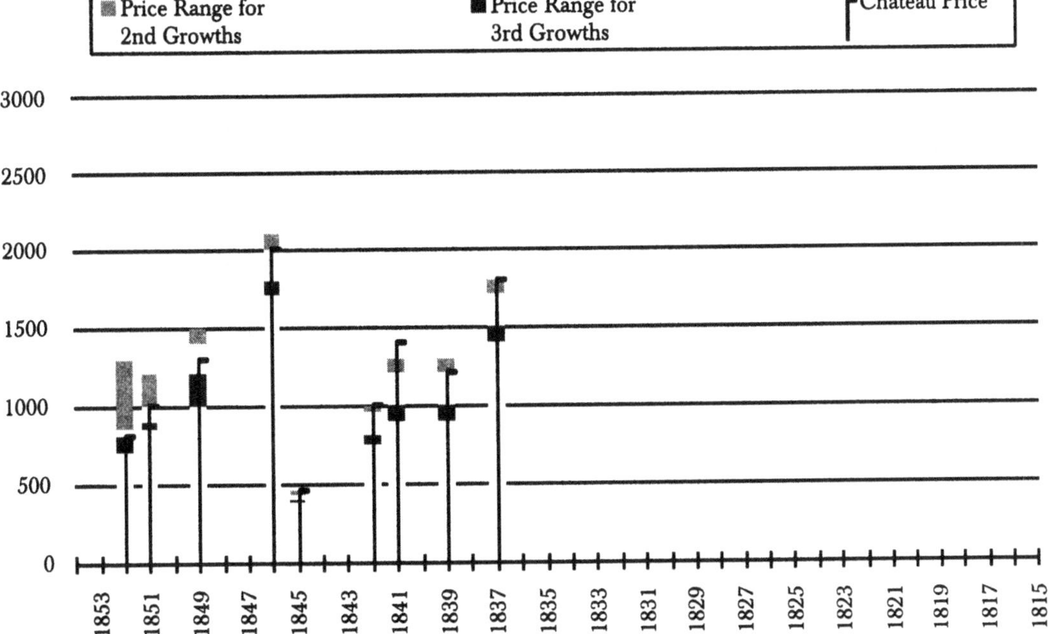

Château Léoville-Barton

Year	Price	Current Name	Other Notes
1854	—	Barton	6½ tuns/December 1854/Barton & Guestier
1853	—	Barton	19 tuns
1852	1000	Barton	42 tuns/January 1853
1851	—	Barton	50 tuns/Barton & Guestier
1850	625	Barton	40 tuns/October 1851
1849	1200	Barton	32 tuns/October 1852
1848	850	Barton	62 tuns/October 1849
1847	525	Barton	68 tuns/July 1848
1846	2000	Barton	50 tuns/partial sale
1845	450	Barton Léoville	40 tuns/September 1846
1844	—	Barton Léoville	50 tuns/Barton & Guestier/1844
1843	600	Barton Léoville	16 tuns/October 1845
1842	1050	Barton	42 tuns/December 1843
1841	—	Barton	50 tuns/In house [Barton & Guestier]
1840	1200	Barton Léoville	60 tuns/good
1839	1200	Barton Léoville	50 tuns/v. good/February 1840
1838	700	Barton Léoville	33 tuns/very good/January 1843
1837	1800	Barton	45 tuns/good/December 1837
1836	600	Barton	45 tuns
1835	900	Barton	63 tuns/good/February 1836
1834	—	Barton	48 tuns/kept by the house [Barton & Guestier]
1833	1400	Barton	130 tuns/elegant/July 1834
1832	1800	Barton	Thin finished/February 1833
1831	—	Barton	31 tuns/very good/Barton & Guestier

Year	Price	Current Name	Other Notes
1830	—	Barton	No trades reported
1829	350	Barton	No other notes
1828	—	Barton	No trades reported
1827	—	Barton	No trades reported
1826	—	Barton	No trades reported
1825	3300	Chevalier	No other notes
	—	Barton	No other notes
1824	—	Chevalier	3 tuns
	—	Monbalon	No other notes
1823	1200	Chevalier	15 tuns
	1200	Monbalon	No other notes
1822	1500	Chevalier	No other notes
	2100	Monbalon	No other notes
1821			No listings for 1821
1820			No listings for 1820
1819	1600	Chevalier	10 tuns
	1600	Monbalon	No other notes
1818	2500	Chevalier	No other notes
	2500	Monbalon	No other notes
1817			No listings for 1817
1816			No listings for 1816
1815	2250	Chevalier	No other notes
	2250	Monbalon	No other notes
1775	—	Chevalier	No other notes
	—	Monbalon	No other notes

Note: Chevalier and Monbalon were the owners of two propeties that comprised one-quarter of the Léoville vineyard; they were bought by Hugh Barton in 1826.

Léoville-Barton

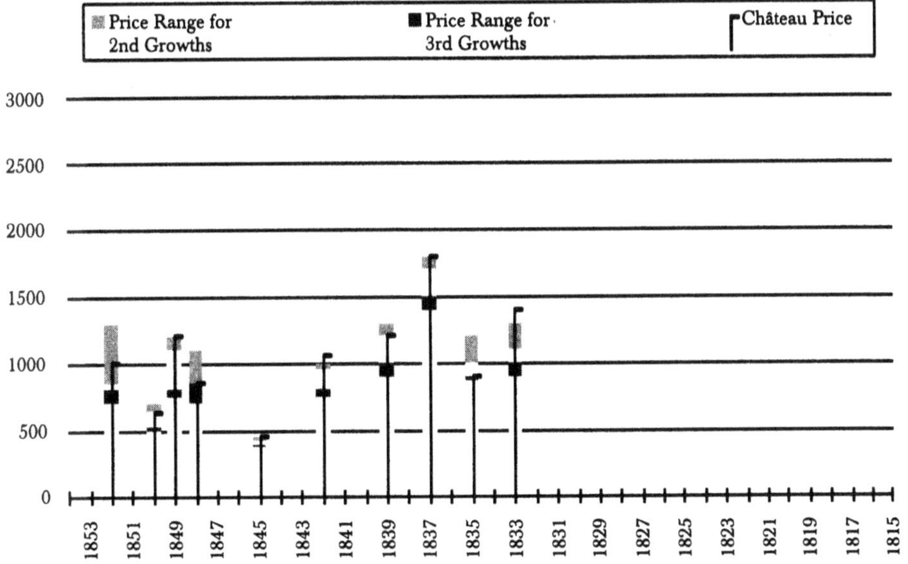

Château Durfort-Vivens

Year	Price	Current Name	Other Notes
1854	4000	de Vivens	7 tuns/December 1855
1853	600	de Vivens	16 tuns/February 1856
1852	1000	de Vivens	37 tuns/January 1853
1851	1000	de Vivens	45 tuns/half/March 1852
1850	600	Durfort	34 tuns/April 1851
1849	1600	Durfort	40 tuns/January 1856
1848	1100	Durfort	50 tuns/October 1849
1847	525	Durfort	56 tuns/July 1848
1846	—	Durfort	26 tuns
1845	450	Durfort	27 tuns/November 1846
1844	2500	de Vivens	36 tuns/September 1844
1843	600	de Vivens	18 tuns/March 1847
1842	1000	Durfors	36 tuns/December 1843
1841	1400	Durfors	44 tuns/January 1843
1840	1200	Vivens	35 tuns/very good/April 1841
1839	1400	Vivens	23 tuns/very good/February 1840
1838	—	Durfort	21 tuns/good
1837	—	de Vivens	31 tuns
1836	1600	Vivens	25 tuns/February 1837
1835	1200	Durfort	25 tuns/good/September 1836
1834	2100	de Vivens	8 tuns/May 1838
1833	1200	de Vivens	12 tuns/very good/February 1834
1832	2400	Vivens	10½ tuns/very good/March 1833
1831	2400	de Vivens	8 tuns

Year	Price	Current Name	Other Notes
1830	—	Vivens	4½ tuns
1829			No listings for 1829
1828	—	Vivens	18 tuns
1827	1400	Vivens	18 tuns
1826	1200	Vivens	10 tuns
1825	3000	Vivens	No other notes
1824	500	Vivens	No other notes
1823	1200	Vivens	No other notes
1822	—	Vivens	No trades reported
1821			No listings for 1821
1820			No listings for 1820
1819	1500	Monbrison	15 tuns
	1500	Vivens	16 tuns
1818	2550	Monbrison	17 tuns/10 tuns [two transactions]
	1650	Vivens	No other notes
1817			No listings for 1817
1816			No listings for 1816
1815	2150	Monbrison	No other notes
	—	Vivens	No trades reported
1775	900	Monbrison	No other notes
	900	Vivens	No other notes

Durfort-Vivens

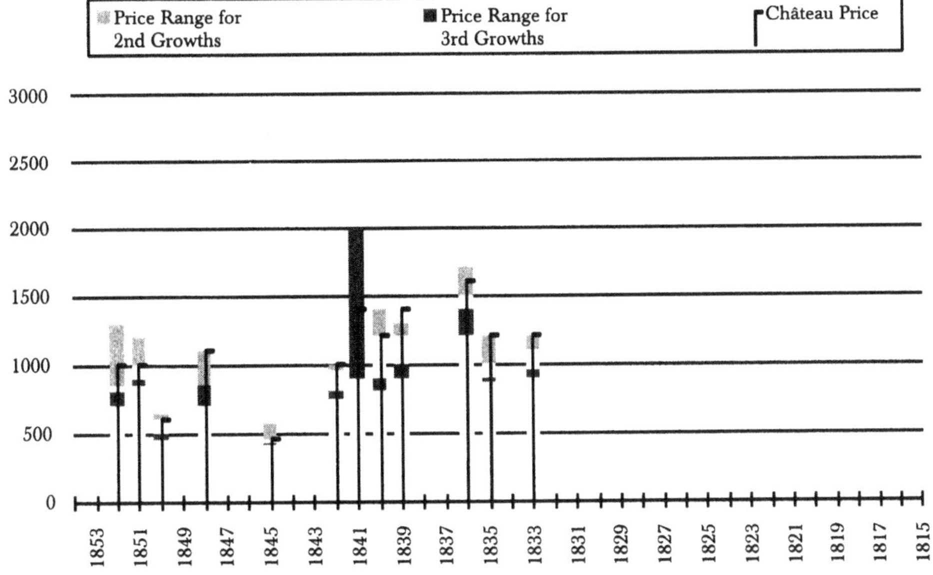

Note: In January 1843, prices for second growths from 1841 were 1400–1600.

Château Gruaud-Larose

Year	Price	Current Name	Other Notes
1854	4000	Gruau	20 tuns/December 1855
1853	—	Gruau	50 tuns
1852	1000	Gruau	114 tuns/January 1853
1851	1000	Gruau	50 tuns/March 1852
1850	650	Gruaud	140 tuns/November 1851
1849	1100	Gruaud	72 tuns/April 1852
1848	1000	Gruaud	160 tuns/December 1849
1847	525	Gruau	160 tuns/July 1848
1846	2000	Gruau	68 tuns/partial sale
1845	500	Larose Gruau	95 tuns/March 1847
1844	2100	Gruau	132 tuns/August 1844
1843	525	Gruau	50 tuns/April 1845
1842	1050	Gruau	92 tuns/December 1843
1841	1400	Gruau	144 tuns/March 1843
1840	1200	Gruau	140 tuns/perf.
1839	1200	Laroze	76 tuns/good/December 1840
1838	600	Gruau	70 tuns/very good/June 1842
1837	1200	Gruau	145 tuns/good/May 1838/all
1836	1500	Gruau	103 tuns/December 1836
1835	850	Larose	130 tuns/hard finish/January 1836
1834	2100	Larose	42 tuns/
1833	1000	Balguerie	160 tuns/good/December 1833
1832	—	Gruau	51 tuns/full, g.
1831	2100	Larose	50 tuns/good, full-bodied

Year	Price	Current Name	Other Notes
1830	2100	Laroze	18 tuns
1829	300	Laroze	150 tuns
1828	—	Laroze	140 tuns
1827	1350	Laroze	150 tuns
1826	1300	Laroze	100 tuns
1825	3100	Laroze	No other notes
1824	—	Laroze	No trades reported
1823	1200	Laroze	140 tuns
1822	2100	Laroze	95 tuns
1821			No listings for 1821
1820			No listings for 1820
1819	1500	Laroze	104 tuns
1818	2600	Laroze	85 tuns
1817			No listings for 1817
1816			No listings for 1816
1815	2250	Laroze	No other notes
1775	1000	Laroze	No other notes

Gruaud-Larose

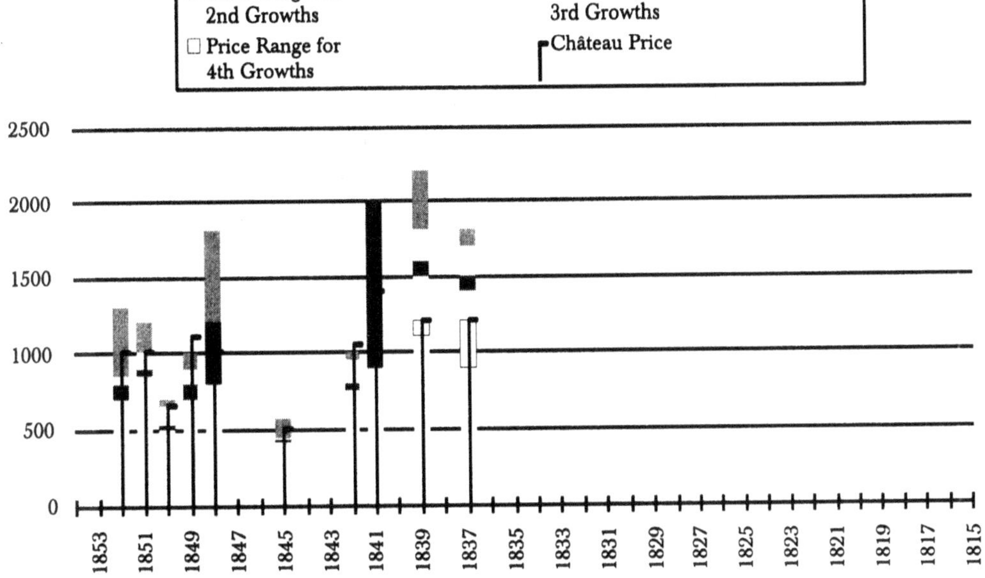

Note: In March 1843, prices for second growths from 1841 were 1400–1600.

Château Lascombes

Year	Price	Current Name	Other Notes
1854	—	Hue	1½ tuns
1853	—	Hue	7 tuns
1852	1000	Hue	9 tuns
1851	—	Hue	18 tuns
1850	600	Lascombes	5 tuns/January 1851
1849	—	Lascombes	No trades reported
1848	—	Lascombes	Employed
1847	—	Lascombes	Employed
1846	—	Lascombes	No trades reported
1845	—	Hue	No trades reported
1844	2500	Hue	10 tuns/September 1844
1843	—	Hue	No trades reported
1842	1050	Lascombes	9 tuns/May 1845
1841	1400	Lascombes	14 tuns/March 1843
1840	1200	Lascombes	11 tuns
1839	1200	Lascombes	10 tuns/fine/February 1840
1838	—	Lascombes	7 tuns
1837	—	Lascombe	15 tuns
1836	1500	Lascombes	9 tuns/January 1837
1835	1200	Lascombes	8 tuns/September 1836
1834	—	Loriaque	1¾ tuns
1833	1000	Loriaque	8 tuns/dry/August 1834
1832	1800	Loriaque	5½ tuns/full-bodied/March 1833
1831	2100	Loriaque	Does not appear in 1831

Year	Price	Current Name	Other Notes
1830	—	Loriaque	No trades reported
1829			No listings for 1829
1828	—	Loriaque	6 tuns
1827	1250	Loriaque	No other notes
1826	—	Loriaque	No trades reported
1825	—	Loriaque	No trades reported
1824	—	Loriaque	No trades reported
1823	—	Loriaque	No trades reported
1822	—	Loriaque	No trades reported
1821			No listings for 1821
1820			No listings for 1820
1819	—	Loriaque	No trades reported
1818	—	Loriaque	No trades reported
1817			No listings for 1817
1816			No listings for 1816
1815	2300	Loriaque	No other notes
1775	800–900	Loriaque	No other notes

Lascombes

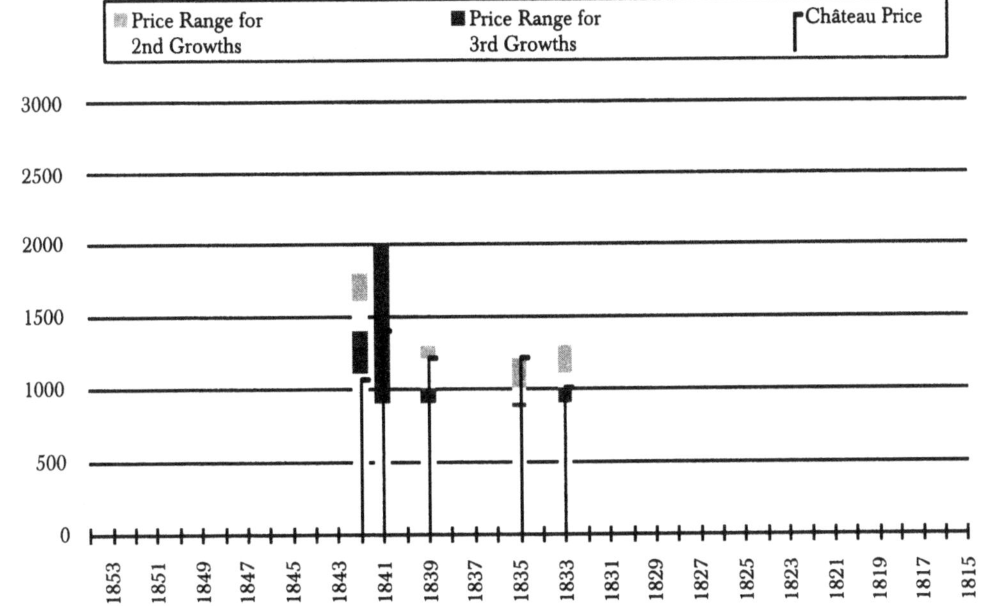

Note: In March 1843, prices for second growths from 1841 were 1400–1600.

Château Brane-Cantenac

Year	Price	Current Name	Other Notes
1854	1200	Brane	11 tuns/by subscription to the English
1853	1200	Bon de Branne	35 tuns/subscription
1852	800	Bon de Brane	62 tuns/December 1852
1851	1100	Bon de Brane	79 tuns/April 1852/small portion with the 1849 & 1846
1850	650	de Brane	62 tuns/April 1852
1849	1100	de Brane	72 tuns/May 1852/several tuns with the 1846 & 1851
1848	1100	de Brane	80 tuns/June 1850
1847	800	Brane	75 tuns/December 1848
1846	2000	Brane	51 tuns
1845	500	Bon Brane	52 tuns/March 1847
1844	2500	Branne	42 tuns/August 1844
1843	500	Branne	21 tuns/1848
1842	1300	Branne	55 tuns/in part 1846
1841	1400	Branne	60 tuns/May 1843
1840	—	de Branne	47 tuns/lovely
1839	1200	Branne Gorce	28 tuns/rich/February 1840
1838	—	Branne	21 tuns/sold to an Englishman with 1837 & 1840
1837	—	de Branne	13 tuns/to an Englishman with 1838 & 1840
1836	—	de Branne	18 tuns/put in bottles
1835	1200	Gorce	12 tuns/very good/August 1836
1834	—	Branne	2½ tuns
1833	750	Gorce	36 tuns/check again/1836
1832	1500	Guy	15 tuns/thin/April 1833
1831	2100	Guy	2¼ tuns/ordinary

Year	Price	Current Name	Other Notes
1830	—	Guy (Gorce)	1 tun
1829			No listings for 1829
1828	—	Guy (Gorce)	No trades reported
1827	1300	Guy (Gorce)	30 tuns
1826	1250	Guy (Gorce)	No other notes
1825	2450	Guy (Gorce)	No other notes
1824	—	Guy (Gorce)	16 tuns
1823	1100	Guy (Gorce)	60 tuns
1822	—	Guy (Gorce)	Touched by hail
1821			No listings for 1821
1820			No listings for 1820
1819	1400	Guy (Gorce)	28 tuns
1818	2400	Guy (Gorce)	16 tuns
1817			No listings for 1817
1816			No listings for 1816
1815	2250	Guy (Gorce)	23 tuns
1775	850–900	Guy (Gorce)	No other notes

Brane-Cantenac

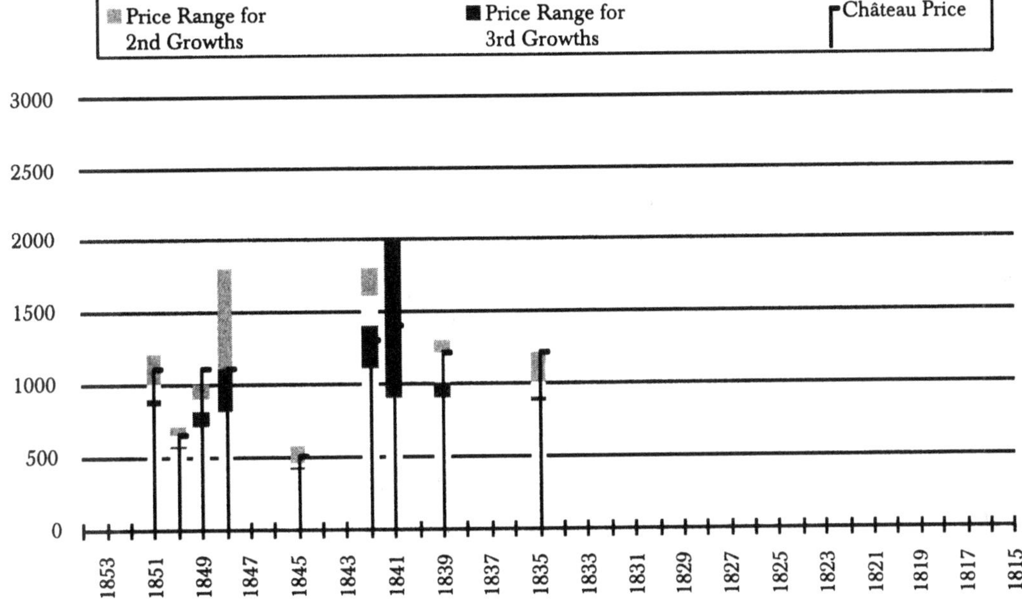

Note: In May 1843, prices for second growths from 1841 were 1400–1600.

Château Pichon-Longueville (Baron)

Year	Price	Current Name	Other Notes
1854	5300	de Pichon	6½ tuns/April 1857
1853	—	de Pichon	27 tuns/combined with de Lalande
1852	1000	de Pichon	94 tuns/with de Lalande/January 1853
1851	1050	de Pichon	87 tuns/April 1852
1850	600	de Pichon	20 tuns/April 1851
1849	—	Pichon Longueville	88 tuns
1848	1100	Pichon Longueville	100 tuns/partial sale/November 1849
1847	525	de Pichon	120 tuns/July 1848
1846	2000	de Pichon	80 tuns/partial sale
1845	450	Pichon	100 tuns/November 1846
1844	2100	Pichon Longueville	84 tuns/October 1844
1843	550	Pichon Longueville	34 tuns/partial sale/October 1845
1842	1200	de Pichon	84 tuns/March 1847
1841	3000	de Pichon	120 tuns/partial sale
1840	1400	Pichon	120 tuns/fine
1839	1300	Pichon Longueville	60 tuns/fine/March 1840
1838	700	Pichon Longueville	78 tuns/elegant/1844
1837	1700	Pichon Longueville	115 tuns/v. good/December 1837
1836	500	Pichon Longueville	110 tuns/September 1844
1835	—	Pichon Longueville	115 tuns/fine
1834	2000	Pichon Longueville	58 tuns/good/November 1834
1833	1000	Pichon	150 tuns/elegant/December 1833
1832	2200	Pichon Longueville	80 tuns/fine full-bodied
1831	2100	Pichon Longueville	50 tuns/elegant
1830	1400	Pichon	16 tuns
1829	425	Pichon	120 tuns
1828	825	Pichon	90 tuns
1827	1250	Pichon	130 tuns
1826	—	Pichon	100 tuns
1825	2700	Pichon	No other notes
1824	600	Pichon	No other notes
1823	1100	Pichon	118 tuns
1822	2000	Pichon	60 tuns

Year	Price	Current Name	Other Notes
1821			No listings for 1821
1820			No listings for 1820
1819	1400	Pichon	90 tuns
1818	1200	Pichon	70 tuns
1817			No listings for 1817
1816			No listings for 1816
1815	2350	Pichon	50 tuns
1775	650–750	Pichon	No other notes

Château Pichon-Longueville-Comtesse de Lalande

Year	Price	Current Name	Other Notes
1854	5300	de Lalande	6½ tuns/April 1857
1853	—	de Lalande	27 tuns
1852	1000	de Lalande	94 tuns/January 1853
1851	1050	de Lalande	87 tuns/April 1852
1850	600	de Lalande	40 tuns/April 1851
1849	***From this year down, the property is undivided and appears only as Pichon Longueville***		

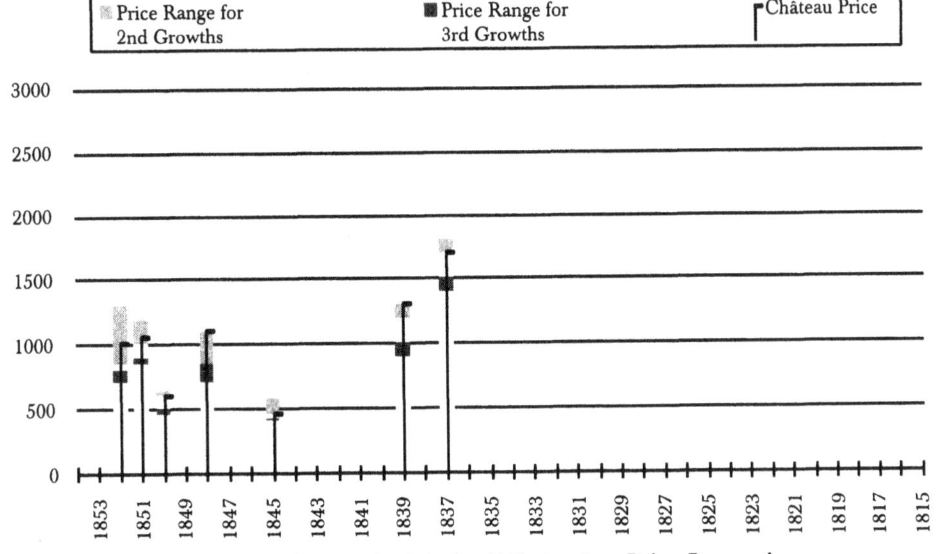

Note: Before 1849, Pichon-Longueville was undivided; after 1849 wines from Pichon-Baron and Comtesse de Lalande continued to be sold at the same price and under the same conditions of sale, hence one graph for both properties.

Château Ducru-Beaucaillou

Year	Price	Current Name	Other Notes
1854	4000	Ducrû	7½ tuns/April 1856
1853	—	Ducrû	27 tuns
1852	500	Ducrû	70 tuns/October 1852
1851	2200	Ducrû	100 tuns/July 1853
1850	600	Ducrû	126 tuns/partial sale/October 1852
1849	1300	Ducru	80 tuns/several tuns/July 1853
1848	1100	Ducru	124 tuns/July 1850
1847	600	Ducru	140 tuns/August 1848
1846	—	Ducru	95 tuns
1845	400	Ducru	80 tuns/November 1846
1844	2500	Ducru	92 tuns/November 1844
1843	—	Ducru	40 tuns/October 1846
1842	950	Ducru	82 tuns/March 1847
1841	1400	Ducru	90 tuns/August 1843
1840	1200	Ducru	90 tuns/beautiful/December 1842
1839	1100	Ducru	40 tuns/good/February 1840
1838	—	Ducru	50 tuns/good
1837	1300	Ducru	96 tuns/February 1839
1836	—	Ducru	80 tuns
1835	1000	Ducru	85 tuns/September 1838
1834	2200	Ducru	45 tuns/good/September 1838
1833	975	Ducru	80 tuns/ordinary/January 1834
1832	950	Ducru	52 tuns/good
1831	2000	Ducru	40 tuns/good

Year	Price	Current Name	Other Notes
1830	—	Ducru	No trades reported
1829	350	Ducru	No other notes
1828	—	Ducru	No trades reported
1827	—	Ducru	60 tuns
1826	—	Ducru	50 tuns
1825	3350	Ducru	No other notes
1824	—	Ducru	No trades reported
1823	—	Ducru	80 tuns
1822	2200	Ducru	No other notes
1821			No listings for 1821
1820			No listings for 1820
1819	1600	Ducru	40 tuns
1818	2200	Ducru	No other notes
1817			No listings for 1817
1816			No listings for 1816
1815	2200	Ducru	No other notes
1775	500	Ducru	No other notes

Ducru-Beaucaillou

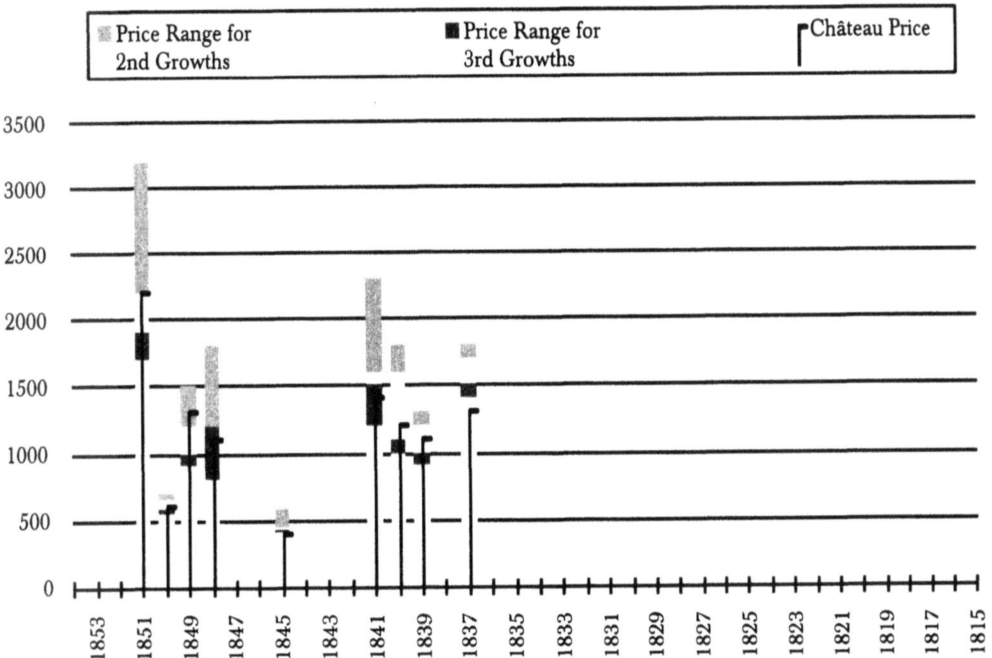

Château Cos-d'Estournel

Year	Price	Current Name	Other Notes
1854	3700	Cos d'Estournel	26¾ tuns/December 1855
1853	850	Cos d'Estournel	76 tuns/August 1856
1852	1000	Cos d'Estournel	80 tuns/November 1853
1851	2000	Cos d'Estournel	90 tuns/public auction/September 1853
1850	660	Cos	140 tuns/September 1853
1849	1000	Cos	150 tuns/September 1853
1848	1780	Cos	123 tuns/public auction
1847	360	Cos	June 1848
1846	1000	Cos	Public auction/September 1849
1845	412	Cos	75 tuns/November 1846
1844	3000	Destournel Cos	80 tuns/partial sale/August 1846
1843	500	Destournel Cos	40 tuns/January 1847
1842	360	Destournel Cos	August 1848
1841	500	Destournel Cos	100 tuns/public auction/1848
1840	—	Destournel Cos	100 tuns/very good
1839		Destournel	No trades reported
1838		Destournel	No trades reported
1837	—	Destournel Cos	India
1836	—	Destournel Cos	No trades reported
1835	—	Destournel Cos	50 tuns/good
1834	—	Destournel	50 tuns/excellent/sent to India
1833	1400	Destournel Cos	100 tuns/pretty successful/July 1834
1832	—	Cos	60 tuns/elegant full-bodied
1831	—	Destournel Cos	40 tuns/very good/sent to Calcutta

Year	Price	Current Name	Other Notes
1830	—	Destournelle Cos	25 tuns
1829	—	Destournelle Cos	90 tuns/exported
1828	—	Destournelle Cos	35 tuns
1827	—	Destournelle Cos	60 tuns
1826	—	Destournelle Cos	No trades reported
1825	2700	Destournelle Cos	No other notes
1824	—	Destournelle Cos	No trades reported
1823	900	Destournelle Cos	No other notes
1822	1600	Destournelle Cos	No other notes
1821			No listings for 1821
1820			No listings for 1820
1819	1800	Destournelle Cos	No other notes
1818	2200	Destournelle Cos	No other notes
1817			No listings for 1817
1816			No listings for 1816
1815	2200	Destournelle Cos	28 tuns

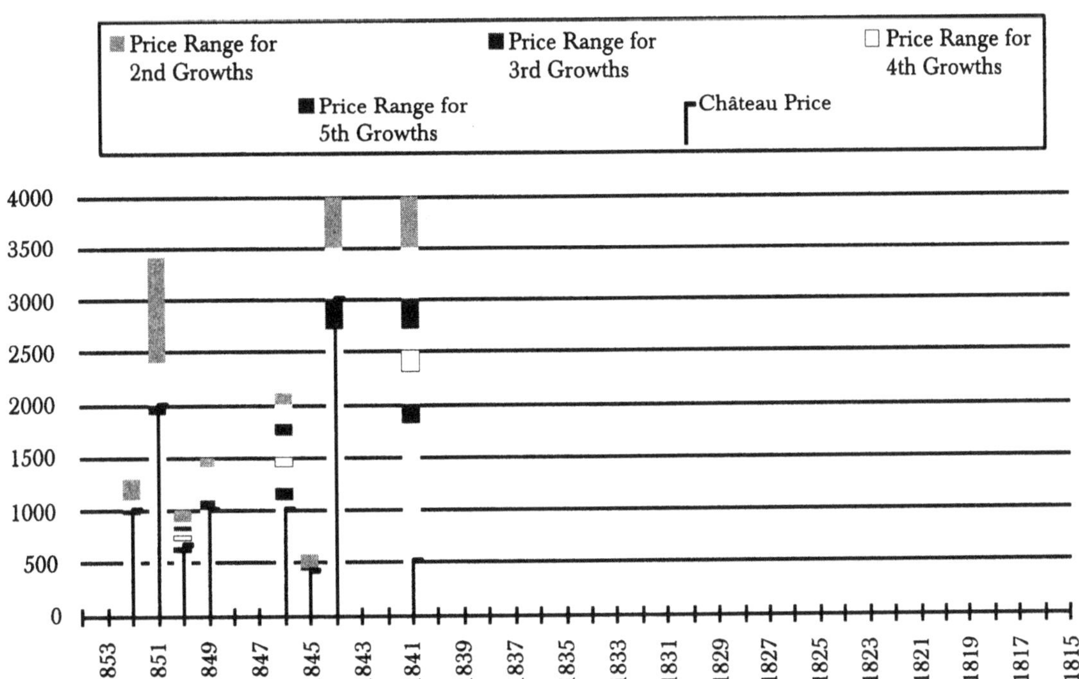

Château Montrose

Year	Price	Current Name	Other Notes
1854	4000	Monrose	22 tuns/September 1856
1853	775	Monrose	40 tuns/September 1856
1852	600	Monrose	123 tuns/December 1852
1851	1200	Monrose	130 tuns/November 1852
1850	650	Monrose	133 tuns
1849	950	Monrose	110 tuns/April 1852
1848	850	Monrose	134 tuns/April 1849
1847	500	Monrose	135 tuns/October 1848
1846	1400	Monrose	65 tuns/partial sale
1845	220	Monrose	118 tuns/October 1848
1844	2600	Monrose	120 tuns/1847
1843	—	Monrose	20 tuns/August 1848
1842	—	Monrose	84 tuns
1841	—	Monrose	120 tuns/sold at low price (bad)
1840	1400	Monrose	117 tuns/quite good/May 1843
1839	1200	Monrose	30 tuns/rich/1840
1838	1000	Monrose	83 tuns/good/partial sale/July 1842
1837	1200	Monrose	96 tuns/rich/May 1838
1836	1000	Monrose	66 tuns/July 1841
1835	500	Monrose	50 tuns/bad/April 1838
1834	2200	Monrose	63 tuns/mellow/September 1835
1833	1000	Monrose	70 tuns/good full-bodied/May 1834
1832	1350	Dumoulin	24 tuns/elegant/March 1833
1831	2000	Monrose	11 tuns/ordinary

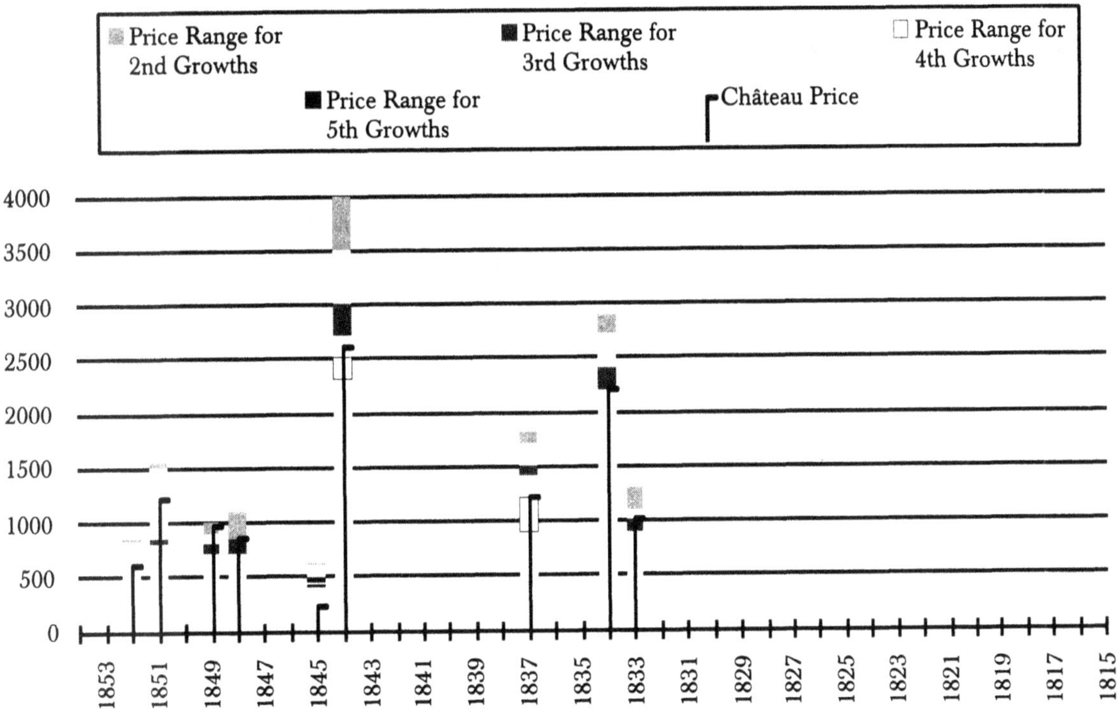
Montrose
Price Range for 2nd Growths
Price Range for 3rd Growths
Price Range for 4th Growths
Price Range for 5th Growths
Château Price
4000
3500
3000
2500
2000
1500
1000
500
0
1853
1851
1849
1847
1845
1843
1841
1839
1837
1835
1833
1831
1829
1827
1825
1823
1821
1819
1817
1815

Château Kirwan

Year	Price	Current Name	Other Notes
1854	2400	Kirwan	16 tuns/November 1854
1853	—	Kirwan	18 tuns
1852	800	Kirwan	30 tuns/January 1853
1851	800	Kirwan	45 tuns/20 tuns/March 1852
1850	425	Kirwan	38 tuns/December 1850
1849	700	Kirwan	72 tuns/several tuns/May 1852
1848	700	Kirwan	48 tuns/partial sale/October 1849
1847	500	Kirwan	42 tuns/November 1848
1846	—	Kirwan	17 tuns
1845	450	Kirwan	25 tuns/March 1847
1844	1850	Kirwan	33 tuns/August 1844
1843	—	Kirwan	15 tuns
1842	750	Lanoire	30 tuns/November 1843
1841	1000	Lanoire	43 tuns/August 1842
1840	825	Kirwan	44 tuns/fine/1841
1839	900	de Lanoy	27 tuns/good/February 1840
1838	—	Lanoy	24 tuns
1837	—	Kirwan	23 tuns/good
1836	675	Kirwan	35 tuns/February 1840
1835	700	Kirwan	30 tuns/good/June 1838
1834	1500	Lanoy	6 tuns/October 1836
1833	1000	Lanoy	30 tuns/rough/February 1834
1832	2100	Lanoy	6 tuns/perfect/February 1834
1831	2100	Kirwan	3¼ tuns/good

Year	Price	Current Name	Other Notes
1830	—	Kirwan	No trades reported
1829			No listings for 1829
1828	—	Kirwan	30 tuns
1827	—	Kirwan	50 tuns
1826	900	Kirwan	32 tuns
1825	2150	Kirwan	No other notes
1824	—	Kirwan	11 tuns
1823	1000	Kirwan	48 tuns
1822	1200	Kirwan	11 tuns
1821			No listings for 1821
1820			No listings for 1820
1819	1000	Kirwan	30 tuns
1818	1850	Kirwan	No other notes
1817			No listings for 1817
1816			No listings for 1816
1815	1850	Kirwan	20 tuns
1775	650–700		No other notes

Kirwan

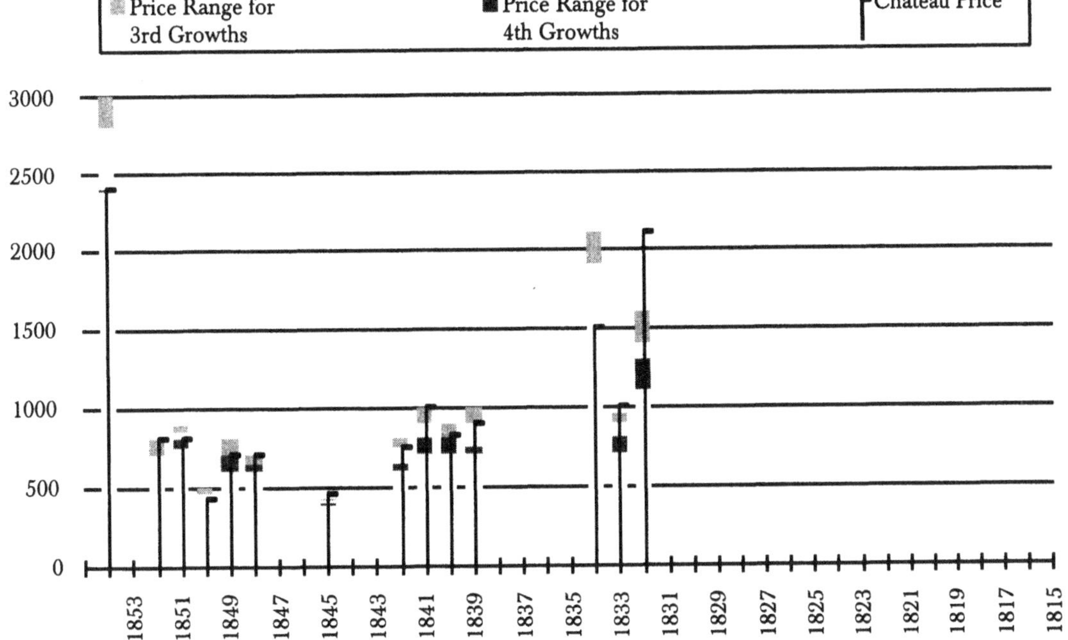

Château d'Issan

Year	Price	Current Name	Other Notes
1854	3300	Blanchy	11 tuns/December 1854
1853	700	Blanchy	30 tuns/August 1856
1852	800	Blanchy	43 tuns/January 1853
1851	800	Du Luc	70 tuns/April 1852
1850	450	Du Luc	70 tuns/February 1851
1849	700	Ch. d'Issan	85 tuns/1852
1848	650	Ch. d'Issan	98 tuns/March 1849
1847	400	Duluc	90 tuns/1848
1846	Various	Duluc	30 tuns
1845	400	Duluc	55 tuns/September 1846
1844	1800	Duluc	60 tuns/August 1844
1843	500	Duluc	25 tuns/1847
1842	—	Duluc	55 tuns
1841	1000	Duluc	70 tuns/March 1843
1840	850	Duluc	70 tuns/ord./March 1842
1839	900	Duluc	38 tuns/good/February 1840
1838	800	Duluc	30 tuns/partial sale
1837	900	Issan	39 tuns/good/September 1839
1836	900	Duluc	50 tuns/January 1839
1835	850	Duluc	42 tuns/very good/1836
1834	2300	Duluc	12 tuns/June 1836
1833	1100	Duluc	32 tuns/mediocre/February 1835
1832	1500	Duluc	18 tuns/ordinary/September 1833
1831	2100	Duluc	7 tuns/good
1830	— —	Candalle (Ch. Issan)/ Castelnau	1 tun No other notes
1829			No listings for 1829
1828	600 id.	Candalle (Ch. Issan)/ Castelnau	35 tuns
1827	1025 id.	Candalle (Ch. Issan)/ Castelnau	45 tuns
1826	1000 id.	Candalle (Ch. Issan)/ Castelnau	No other notes
1825	2100 2100	Candalle (Ch. Issan)/ Castelnau	No other notes

Year	Price	Current Name	Other Notes
1824	380 id.	Candalle (Ch. Issan)/ Castelnau	11 tuns
1823	600 450	Candalle (Ch. Issan)/ Castelnau	32 tuns 23 tuns
1822	750 —	Candalle (Ch. Issan)/ Castelnau	No other notes No trades reported
1821			No listings for 1821
1820			No listings for 1820
1819	850 1050	Candalle (Ch. Issan)/ Castelnau	25 tuns 17 tuns
1818	1200 —	Candalle (Ch. Issan)/ Castelnau	25 tuns No trades reported
1817			No listings for 1817
1816			No listings for 1816
1815	1625 —	Candalle (Ch. Issan)/ Castelnau	No other notes No trades reported
1775	850–900 850–900	Candalle (Ch. Issan)/ Castelnau	No other notes No other notes

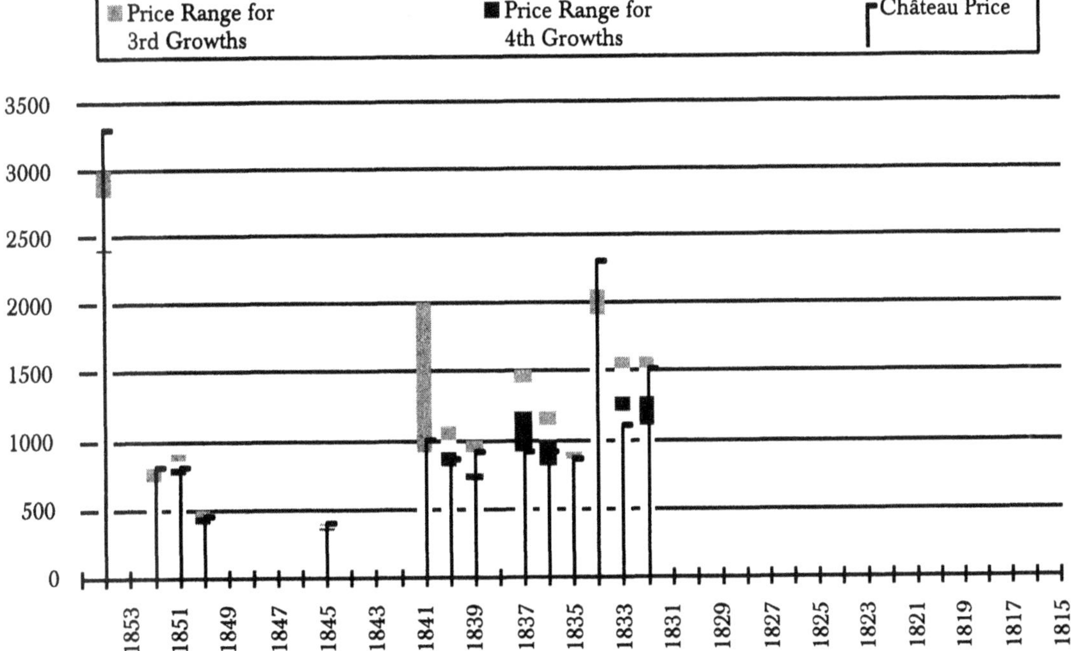

Château Lagrange

Year	Price	Current Name	Other Notes
1854	3000	Lagrange	40 tuns/December 1855
1853	800	Lagrange	80 tuns/December 1856
1852	850	Lagrange	164 tuns/January 1853
1851	1300	Lagrange	209 tuns/November 1852
1850	525	Lagrange	220 tuns/April 1851
1849	900	Lagrange	128 tuns/August 1852
1848	650	Lagrange	265 tuns/October 1849
1847	550	Lagrange	264 tuns/April 1848
1846	—	Lagrange	180 tuns
1845	380	Duchatel	145 tuns/August 1846
1844	1900	La Grange	180 tuns/November 1844
1843	400	La Grange	60 tuns/June 1845
1842	750	Lagrange	160 tuns/September 1843
1841	1600	Lagrange	190 tuns/April 1844
1840	850	Lagrange	203 tuns/successful
1839	900	Cabarrus	118 tuns/good/February 1840
1838	—	Brown	85 tuns/ordinary
1837	1400	Brown	192 tuns/good/February 1838
1836	1200	Brown	130 tuns/December 1836
1835	800	Cabarrus	150 tuns/very good/January 1836
1834	1800	Cabarrus	46 tuns/good/November 1836
1833	900	Cabarrus	150 tuns/good/December 1833
1832	—	Cabarrus	50 tuns/thin
1831	1800	Cabarrus	58 tuns/a little hard

Year	Price	Current Name	Other Notes
1830	1800	Cabarrus	18 tuns
1829	350	Cabarrus	150 tuns
1828	—	Cabarrus	103 tuns
1827	1100	Cabarrus	No other notes
1826	1150	Cabarrus	No other notes
1825	2916	Cabarrus	No other notes
1824	450	Cabarrus	70 tuns
1823	1000	Cabarrus	100 tuns
1822	1800	Cabarrus	No other notes
1821			No listings for 1821
1820			No listings for 1820
1819	1350	Cabarrus	90 tuns
1818	2300	Cabarrus	85 tuns
1817			No listings for 1817
1816			No listings for 1816
1815	1900	Cabarrus	No other notes
1775	600	Cabarrus	No other notes

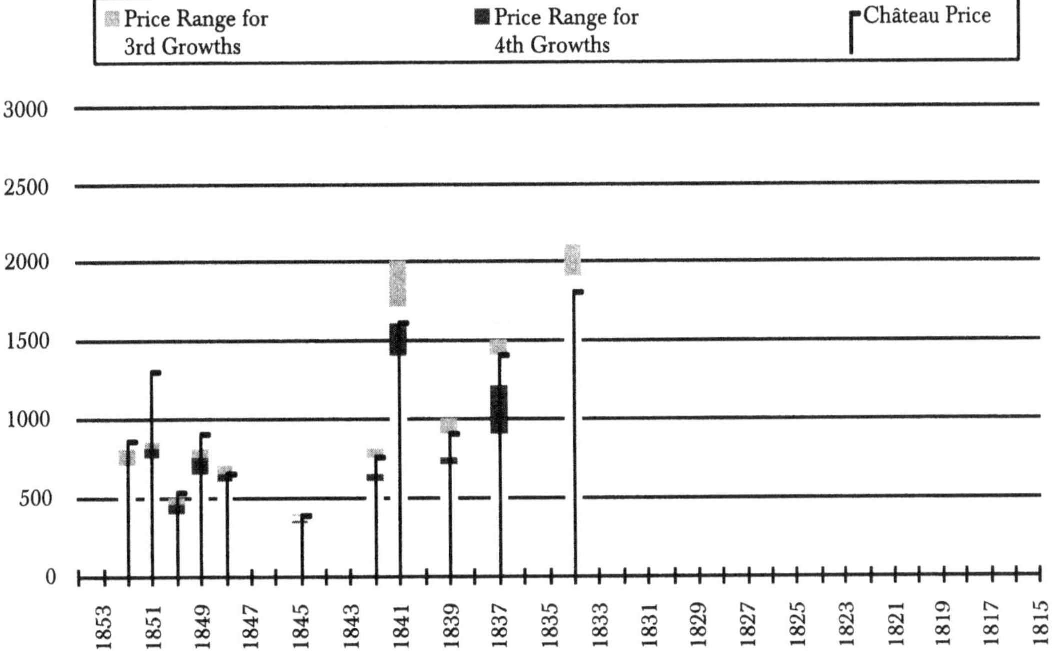

Château Langoa-Barton

Year	Price	Current Name	Other Notes
1854	—	Langoa	11 tuns/Barton & Guestier/December 1854
1853	—	Langoa	39 tuns
1852	800	Langoa	84 tuns/January 1853
1851	900	Langoa	115 tuns/partial sale/April 1852
1850	525	Langoa	80 tuns/October 1851
1849	1000	Langoa	57 tuns/several tuns/Barton & Guestier/June 1853
1848	750	Langoa	125 tuns/November 1849
1847	375	Langoa	150 tuns/July 1848
1846	1600	Langoa	80 tuns/1849
1845	400	Langoa	100 tuns/September 1846
1844	—	Barton Langoa	132 tuns/Barton & Guestier/1844
1843	450	Barton Langoa	30 tuns/October 1846
1842	750	Langoa	90 tuns/December 1843
1841	—	Langoa	128 tuns/In-house [Barton & Guestier]
1840	900	Barton Langoa	120 tuns/good
1839	900	Barton Langoa	50 tuns/v. good/February 1840
1838	500	Langoa	48 tuns/good/January 1843
1837	1400	Langoa	105 tuns/December 1837
1836	400	Langoa	70 tuns/returned [from India?]/January 1837
1835	750	Langoa	73 tuns/good/February 1836
1834			Does not appear in 1834
1833			Does not appear in 1833
1832			Does not appear in 1832
1831			Does not appear in 1831

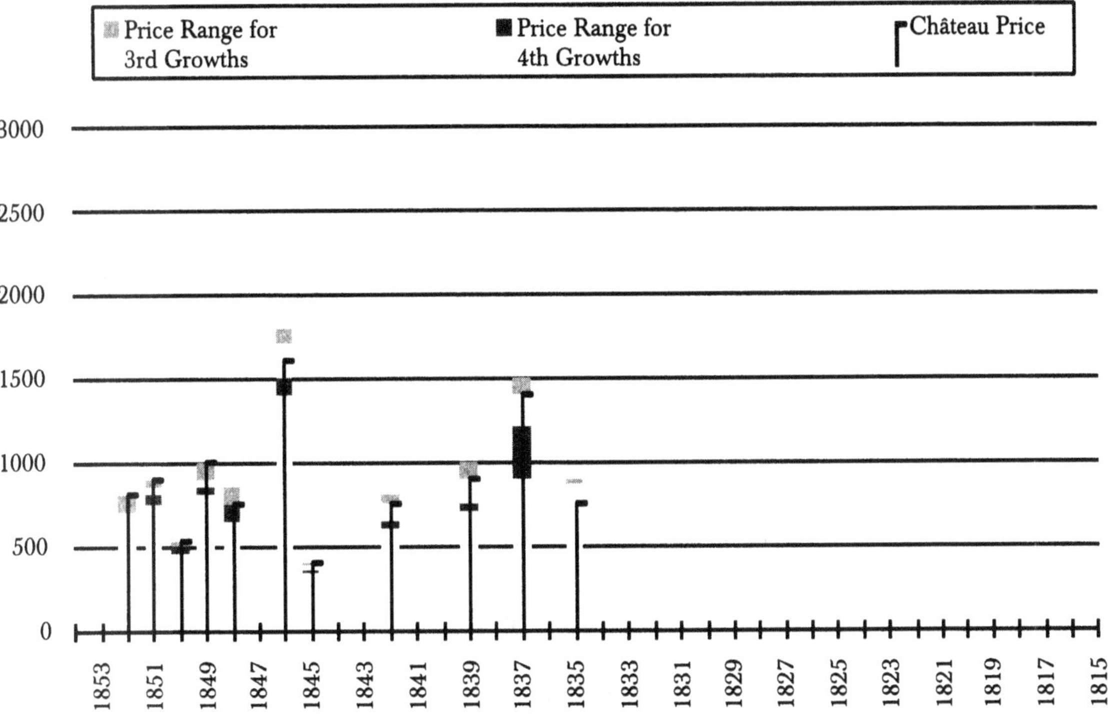
Langoa-Barton
Price Range for 3rd Growths
Price Range for 4th Growths
Château Price
3000
2500
2000
1500
1000
500
0
1853
1851
1849
1847
1845
1843
1841
1839
1837
1835
1833
1831
1829
1827
1825
1823
1821
1819
1817
1815

Château Giscours

Year	Price	Current Name	Other Notes
1854	3000	Giscours	9 tuns/April 1856
1853	800	Giscours	28 tuns/December 1856
1852	1200	Giscours	41 tuns/July 1856
1851	2500	Giscours	56 tuns/March 1857
1850	600	Giscours	50 tuns/December 1851
1849	1000	Giscours	60 tuns/several tuns/July 1853
1848	1000	Giscours	90 tuns/September 1850
1847	750	Giscours	90 tuns/November 1849
1846	—	Giscours	30 tuns
1845	400	Giscours	60 tuns/October 1846
1844	1800	Giscours	62 tuns/September 1844
1843	500	Giscours	35 tuns/March 1846
1842	700	Giscours	72 tuns/March 1846
1841	1600	Giscours	120 tuns/partial sale/1845
1840	825	Giscours	90 tuns/ord./March 1842
1839	900	Giscours	50 tuns/good/February 1840
1838	—	Giscours	70 tuns/ordinary
1837	—	Giscours	102 tuns
1836	—	Giscours	75 tuns
1835	850	Giscours	70 tuns/good
1834	2000	Giscours	35 tuns/hard exchange/July 1838
1833	1000	Giscours	90 tuns/thin/November 1834
1832	1400	Giscours	50 tuns/good/March 1833
1831	2100	Giscours	20 tuns/perfect

Year	Price	Current Name	Other Notes
1830	800	Jacob	12 tuns
1829	450	Jacob	No other notes
1828	—	Jacob	37 tuns
1827	1100	Jacob	No other notes
1826	—	Jacob	No trades reported
1825	2500	Jacob	60 tuns
1824	—	Jacob	No trades reported
1823	—	Jacob	36 tuns
1822	850	Jacob	6 tuns
1821			No listings for 1821
1820			No listings for 1820
1819	650	Jacob	No other notes
1818	1500	Jacob	No other notes
1817			No listings for 1817
1816			No listings for 1816
1815	1450	Jacob	16 tuns
1775	600–650	Jacob	No other notes

Giscours

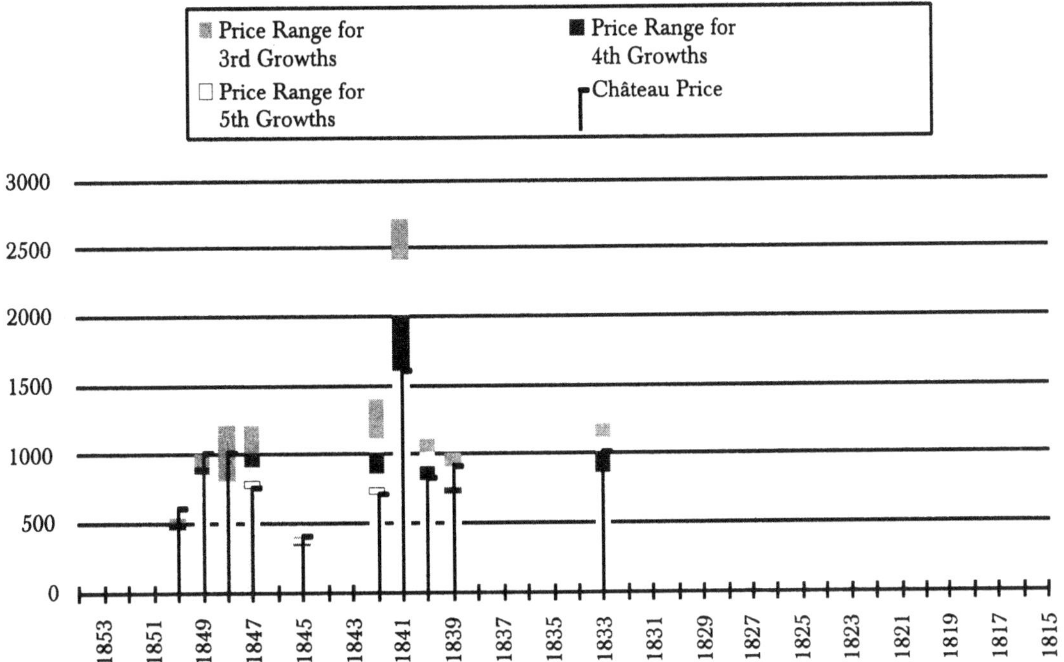

Château Malescot-Saint-Exupéry

Year	Price	Current Name	Other Notes
1854	2800	Fourcade	8 tuns/December 1854
1853	800	Fourcade	19 tuns/December 1856
1852	650	St Exupéry	47 tuns/December 1852
1851	1550	St Exupéry	49 tuns/September 1853
1850	450	St Exupéry	45 tuns/March 1851
1849	850	St Exupéry	38 tuns/1853
1848	750	St Exupéry	60 tuns/November 1849
1847	410	St Exupéry	76 tuns/August 1848
1846	—	St Exupéry	35 tuns
1845	400	St Exupéry	40 tuns/1848
1844	2000	Saint Exupéry	38 tuns/October 1844
1843	450	Saint Exupéry	22 tuns/April 1847
1842	750	St Exupéry	35 tuns/January 1844
1841	1600	St Exupéry	60 tuns/May 1844
1840	800	St Exupéry	50 tuns
1839	900	St Exupéry	30 tuns/good/February 1840
1838	550	St Exupéry	32 tuns/very good/July 1842
1837	—	St Exupéry	54 tuns/August 1841
1836	—	St Exupéry	22 tuns
1835	800	St Exupéry	13 tuns/March 1837
1834	2000	St Exupéry	6 tuns/1836
1833	900	St Exupéry	38 tuns/thin/December 1833
1832	1400	Exupéry	8 tuns/excellent/August 1833
1831	2100	St Exupéry	4 tuns/good

Year	Price	Current Name	Other Notes
1830	—	Lacolonie	3 tuns
1829			No listings for 1829
1828	—	Lacolonie	12 tuns
1827	950	Lacolonie	16 tuns
1826	—	Lacolonie	13 tuns
1825	—	Lacolonie	No trades reported
1824	—	Lacolonie	5½ tuns
1823	750	Lacolonie	25 tuns
1822	900	Lacolonie	6 tuns
1821			No listings for 1821
1820			No listings for 1820
1819	750	Lacolonie	19 tuns
1818	1550	Lacolonie	No other notes
1817			No listings for 1817
1816			No listings for 1816
1815	1550	Lacolonie	15 tuns
1775	600–700	Lacolonie	No other notes

Malescot-Saint-Exupéry

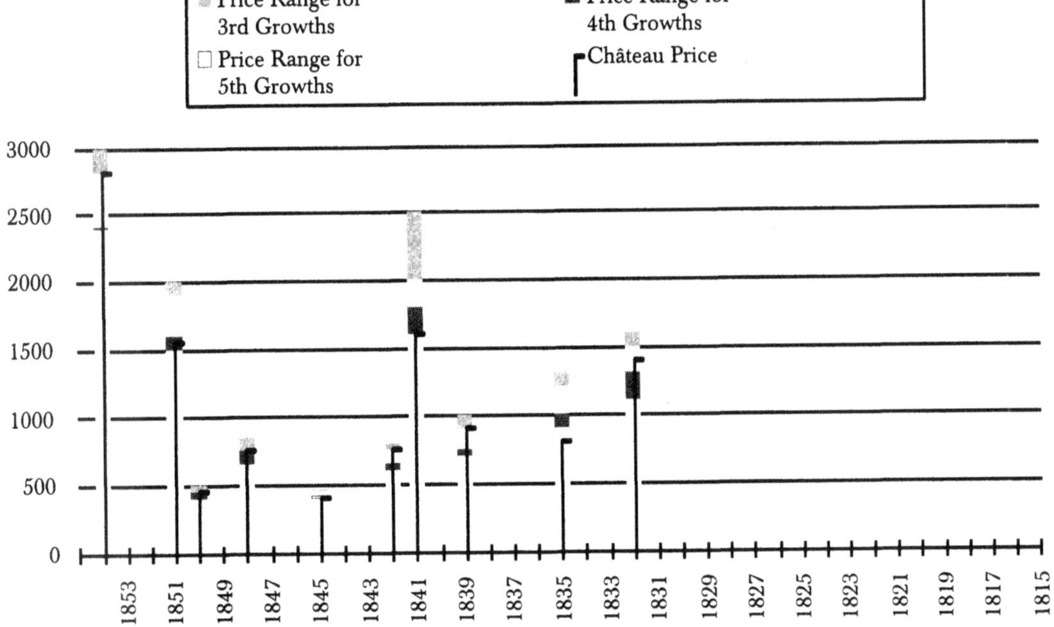

Château Boyd-Cantenac/Cantenac Brown

Year	Price	Current Name	Other Notes
1854	2800	Boyd	15 tuns/December 1854
1853	750	Boyd	33 tuns/December 1856
1852	650	Boyd	56 tuns/December 1852
1851	850	Boyd	83 tuns/partial sale/August 1852
1850	450	Boyd	78 tuns/March 1851
1849	1000	Boyd	88 tuns/December 1852
1848	750	Boyd	83 tuns/March 1850
1847	410	Boyd	80 tuns/October 1848
1846	—	Boyd	40 tuns
1845			Does not appear in 1845
1844	—	Boyd	60 tuns
1843	375	Boyd	25 tuns/March 1842
1842	700	Brown	78 tuns/1846
1841	800	Brown	100 tuns/March 1843
1840	850	Brown	123 tuns/v good/1841
1839	850	Brown	80 tuns/very good/February 1840
1838	—	Brown	60 tuns
1837	700	Brown	70 tuns/public auction/1840
1836	1200	Brown	56 tuns/November 1836
1835	800	Brown	58 tuns/fine/September 1836
1834	—	Brown	17 tuns
1833	1000	Brown	55 tuns/very good/March 1834
1832	1500	Brown	37 tuns/good
1831	2100	Brown	12 tuns

Year	Price	Current Name	Other Notes
1830	—	Brown (Massac)	3¾ tuns
1829			No listings for 1829
1828	—	Brown (Massac)	No trades reported
1827	—	Brown (Massac)	No trades reported
1826	—	Brown (Massac)	No trades reported
1825	1300	Brown (Massac)	Holland
1824	—	Brown (Massac)	No trades reported
1823	—	Brown (Massac)	70 tuns/shipped
1822	—	Brown (Massac)	No trades reported
1821			No listings for 1821
1820			No listings for 1820
1819	1100	Brown (Massac)	14 tuns
1818	—	Brown (Massac)	Shipped
1817			No listings for 1817
1816			No listings for 1816
1815	—	Brown (Massac)	No trades reported
1775	450–500	Brown (Massac)	No other notes

Boyd-Cantenac/Cantenac Brown

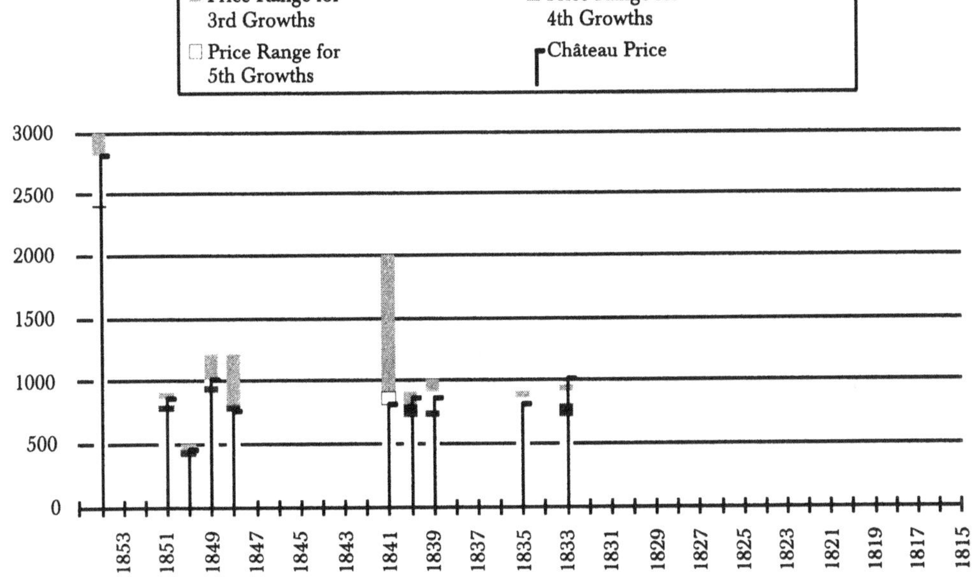

Note: In March 1850, prices for fourth growths from 1848 were 750–1000; the March 1843 price for fourth growths from 1841 was 1700 and fifth growths were 800–1200.

Château Palmer

Year	Price	Current Name	Other Notes
1854	4000	Palmer	14 tuns/April 1854
1853	—	Palmer	30 tuns
1852	—	Palmer	62 tuns
1851	1300	Palmer	80 tuns/April 1853
1850	450	Palmer	66 tuns/April 1851
1849	—	Palmer	68 tuns
1848	750	Palmer	76 tuns/November 1849
1847	400	Palmer	90 tuns/August 1848
1846	—	Palmer	40 tuns
1845	310	Palmer	November 1846
1844	1500	Palmer	60 tuns/1849
1843	450	Palmer	20 tuns/April 1847
1842	650	Palmer	80 tuns
1841	1650	Palmer	120 tuns/August 1842
1840	700	Palmer	110 tuns/good/March 1841
1839	750	Palmer	60 tuns/good/February 1840
1838	600	Palmer	65 tuns
1837	750	Palmer	98 tuns/March 1839
1836	Various	Palmer	110 tuns
1835	700	Palmer	60 tuns/ordinary/June 1837
1834	1450	Palmer	12 tuns/good/1836
1833	800	Palmer	50 tuns/delicious/January 1834
1832	1300	Palmer	33 tuns
1831	1480	Palmer	14 tuns/hard

There are two listings for Palmer in Cantenac from 1830 to 1775; no prices are given except for 1775: one property is listed as 600–625 and the other as 450–500.

Palmer

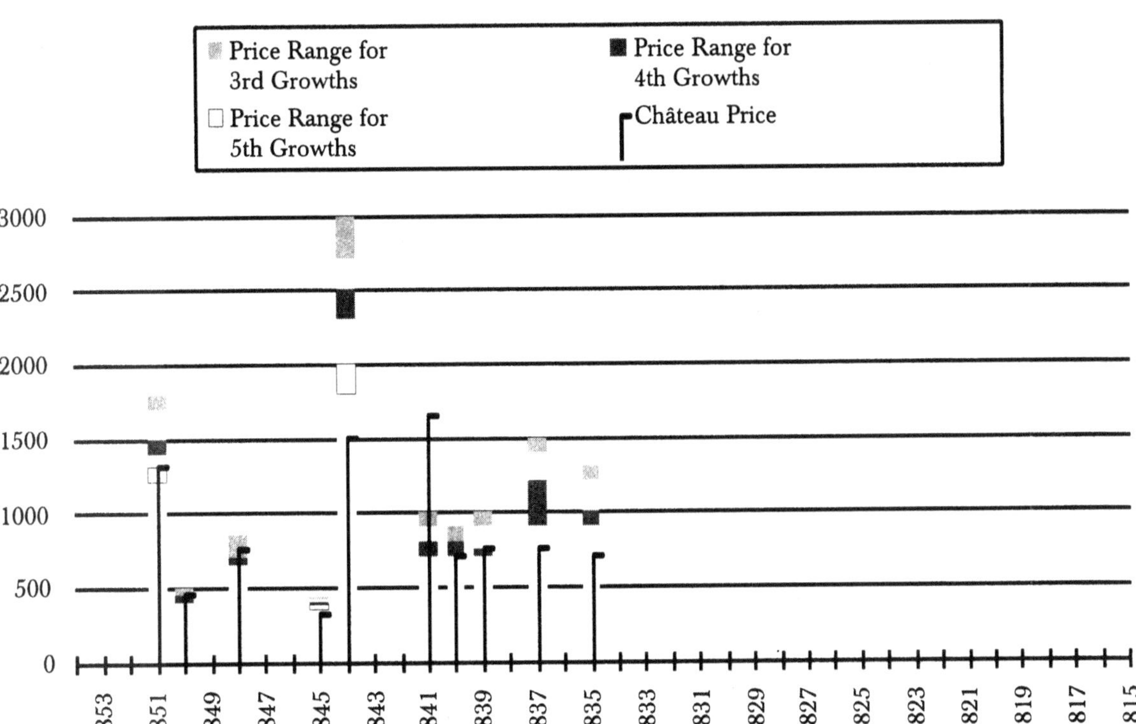
Price Range for 3rd Growths
Price Range for 4th Growths
Price Range for 5th Growths
Château Price
3000
2500
2000
1500
1000
500
0
1853
1851
1849
1847
1845
1843
1841
1839
1837
1835
1833
1831
1829
1827
1825
1823
1821
1819
1817
1815

Château La Lagune

Year	Price	Current Name	Other Notes
1854	2450	Geoffrey	4¾ tuns/November 1854
1853	900	Geoffroy	16 tuns/1855
1852	650	Geoffroy	23 tuns/December 1852
1851	2400	Lagune	23 tuns/December 1855
1850	500	Lagune	15 tuns/September 1852
1849	900	Lagune	29 tuns/April 1853
1848	850	Lagune	36 tuns/partial sale
1847	750	Lagune	32 tuns/October 1849
1846	—	Lagune	18 tuns
1845	—	Lagune	30 tuns
1844	1800	Geoffroy	27 tuns/August 1844
1843	400	Geoffroy	14 tuns/August 1845
1842	850	Lagune	30 tuns/March 1846
1841	1500	Lagune	57 tuns/April 1844
1840	1000	Lagune	40 tuns/good/February 1842
1839	1000	Lalagune	29 tuns/good/February 1840
1838	—	Lagune	29 tuns/good
1837	700	Lagune	47 tuns/1841
1836	1000	Lagune	36 tuns/1841
1835	850	Lalagune	24 tuns/August 1836
1834	2000	Lalagune	10 tuns/May 1837
1833	900	Lalagune	47 tuns/May 1834
1832	1600	Geoffroi	18 tuns/round wine/May 1835
1831	1800	Piston	12 tuns/fine/December 1831

Year	Price	Current Name	Other Notes
1830	—	Lalagune (Dumas/Biston)	No trades reported
1829	—	Lalagune (Dumas/Biston)	No trades reported
1828	2000	Lalagune (Dumas/Biston)	35 tuns
1827	—	Lalagune (Dumas/Biston)	No trades reported
1826	—	Lalagune (Dumas/Biston)	30 tuns
1825	2100	Lalagune (Dumas/Biston)	No other notes
1824	—	Lalagune (Dumas/Biston)	No trades reported
1823	950	Lalagune (Dumas/Biston)	40 tuns
1822	1300	Lalagune (Dumas/Biston)	No other notes
1821			No listings for 1821
1820			No listings for 1820
1819	1200	Lalagune (Dumas/Biston)	16 tuns
1818	1300	Lalagune (Dumas/Biston)	13 tuns
1817			No listings for 1817
1816			No listings for 1816
1815	1200	Lalagune (Dumas/Biston)	13 tuns
1775	550–600	Lalagune (Dumas/Biston)	No other notes

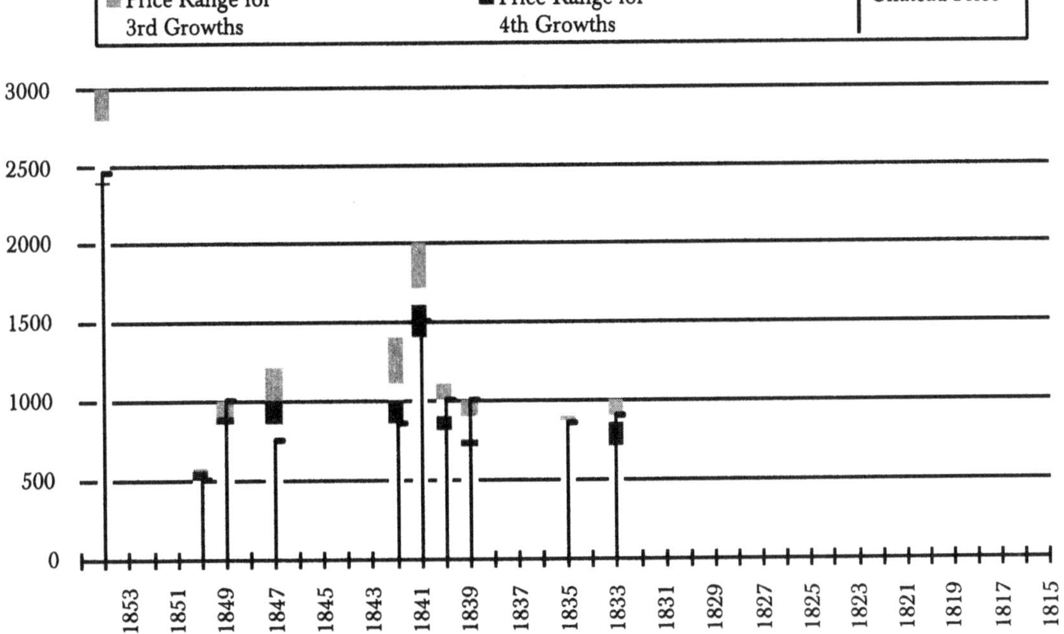

Château Desmirail

Year	Price	Current Name	Other Notes
1854	—	Desmirail	8 tuns/March 1855
1853	—	Desmirail	19 tuns
1852	600	Desmirail	31 tuns/November 1852
1851	800	Desmirail	42 tuns/June 1852
1850	450	Desmirail	38 tuns/partial sale/August 1851
1849	—	Desmirail	45 tuns
1848	650	Desmirail	45 tuns/October 1849
1847	410	Desmirail	46 tuns/August 1848
1846	1500	Desmirail	28 tuns/August 1851
1845	400	Desmirail	September 1846
1844	1800	Desmirail	27 tuns/October 1844
1843	500	Desmirail	15 tuns/April 1847
1842	750	Desmirail	31 tuns/January 1844
1841	950	Desmirail	34 tuns/August 1842
1840	850	Desmirail	32 tuns/fine
1839	850	Desmirail	20 tuns/very good/February 1840
1838	700	Desmirail	21 tuns/very good
1837	900	Desmirail	20 tuns/September 1839
1836	900	Desmirail	22 tuns/September 1839
1835	750	Desmirail	20 tuns/fine/June 1837
1834	2300	Desmirail	6 tuns/weak/July 1836
1833	900	Desmirail	10 tuns/fine/January 1834
1832	1400	Desmirail	7 tuns/excellent/August 1833
1831	2000	Desmirail	4½ tuns/good

Year	Price	Current Name	Other Notes
1830	—	Desmirail	1½ tuns
1829			No listings for 1829
1828	—	Desmirail	12 tuns
1827	1025	Desmirail	No other notes
1826	1000	Desmirail	No other notes
1825	2100	Desmirail	No other notes
1824	—	Desmirail	No trades reported
1823	700	Desmirail	18 tuns
1822	—	Desmirail	No trades reported
1821			No listings for 1821
1820			No listings for 1820
1819	—	Desmirail	16 tuns
1818	2000	Desmirail	No other notes
1817			No listings for 1817
1816			No listings for 1816
1815	2000	Desmirail	15 tuns
1775	600–625	Desmirail	No other notes

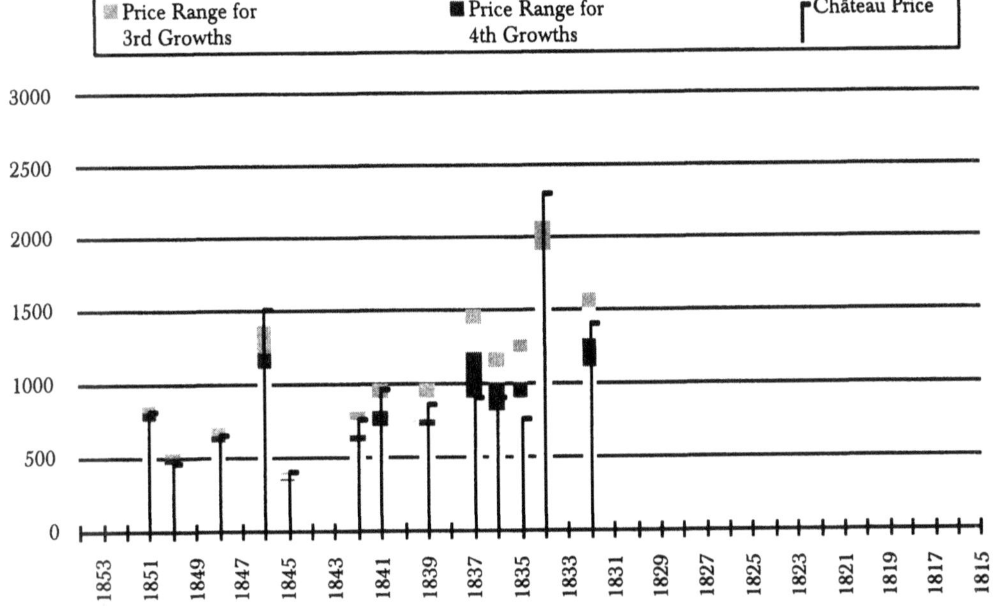

Note: In October 1849, prices for fourth growths from 1848 were 600–750.

Château Dubignon (P)

Year	Price	Current Name	Other Notes
1854	—	Dubignon-P	1¾ tuns
1853	—	Dubignon-P	8 tuns
1852	—	Dubignon-P	18 tuns
1851			No listings for 1851
1850	450	Dubignon (Ph)	18 tuns/April 1852
1849	—	Ph. Dubignon	15 tuns
1848	500	Ph. Dubignon	24 tuns/April 1849
1847	400	Dubignon	23 tuns/June 1848
1846	—	Dubignon	14 tuns
1845	—	Dubignon	10 tuns
1844	2200	Dubignon-T	15 tuns/October 1844
1843	—	Dubignon-T	7 tuns
1842	600	Dubignon	14 tuns/January 1847
1841	—	Dubignon	17 tuns
1840	800	Dubignon	18 tuns/elegant
1839	900	Dubignon	10 tuns/fine/March 1840
1838	—	Dubignon	9 tuns
1837	—	Dubignon	13 tuns
1836	—	Dubignon	13 tuns
1835	650	Dubignon	12 tuns/thin/1837
1834	—	Dubignon	4½ tuns
1833	900	Dubignon	18 tuns/thin/January 1834
1832	800	Dubignon	9¼ tuns/very good
1831	2100	Dubignon	4½ tuns/fine

Year	Price	Current Name	Other Notes
1830	—	Dubignon	1 tun
1829			No listings for 1829
1828	—	Dubignon	9 tuns
1827	920	Dubignon	10 tuns
1826	1000	Dubignon	8 tuns
1825	—	Dubignon	No trades reported
1824	—	Dubignon	No trades reported
1823	700	Dubignon	10 tuns
1822	700	Dubignon	No other notes
1821			No listings for 1821
1820			No listings for 1820
1819	800	Dubignon	18 tuns
1818	1750	Dubignon	16 tuns
1817			No listings for 1817
1816			No listings for 1816
1815	1400	Dubignon	11 tuns
1775	600–700	Dubignon	No other notes

Dubignon (P)

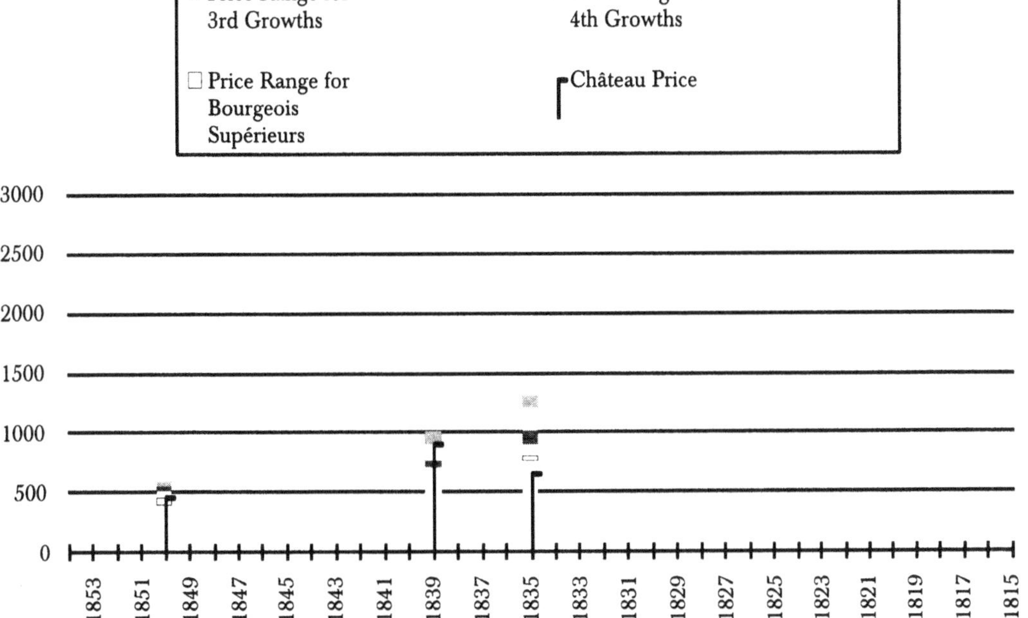

Château Dubignon (M)

Year	Price	Current Name	Other Notes
1854	—	Dubignon-M	No trades reported
1853	—	Dubignon-M	No trades reported
1852	—	Dubignon-M	5 tuns
1851			No listings for 1851
1850	—	Dubignon	7 tuns
1849	—	Dubignon	No trades reported
1848	700	Dubignon	8 tuns/February 1850
1847	400	Dubignon	14 tuns
1846	—	Dubignon	No trades reported
1845	—	Dubignon	10 tuns
1844	2000	Dubignon	5½ tuns/October 1844
1843	—	Dubignon	3 tuns
1842	600	Dubignon	5½ tuns/January 1847
1841	—	Dubignon	14 tuns
1840	—	Dubignon	11 tuns/full-bodied
1839	900	Dubignon Bernard	8 tuns/good/February 1840
1838	***From this year down, the property is undivided and appears only as Dubignon***		

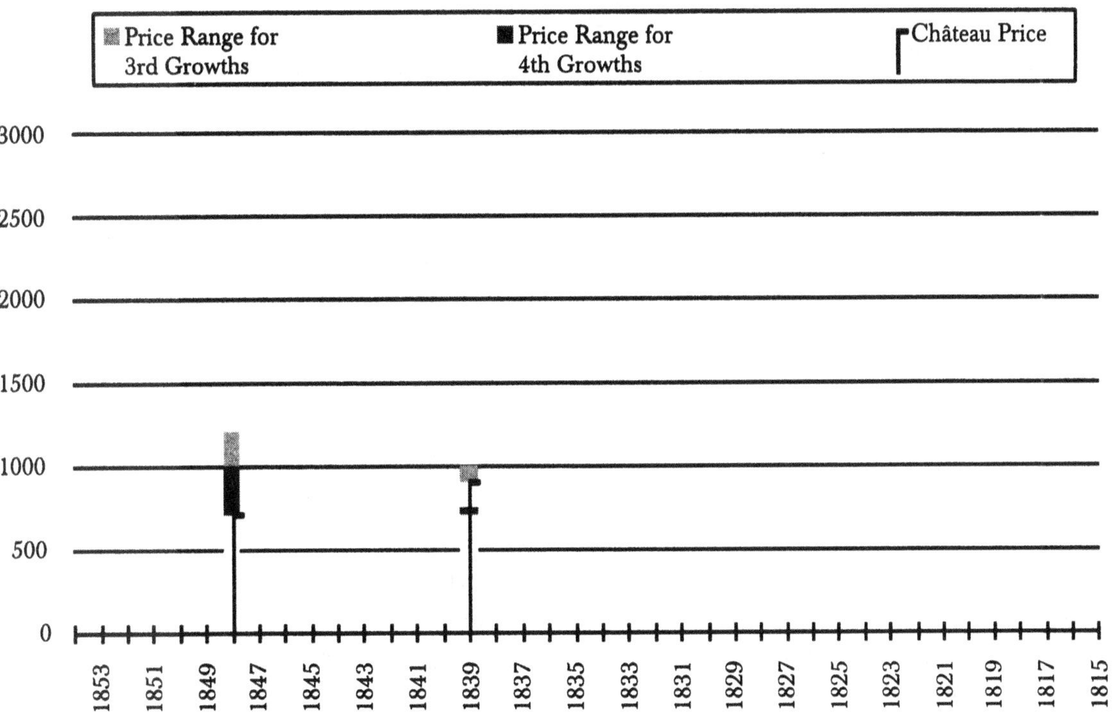
Dubignon (M)
Price Range for 3rd Growths
Price Range for 4th Growths
Château Price
3000
2500
2000
1500
1000
500
0
1853
1851
1849
1847
1845
1843
1841
1839
1837
1835
1833
1831
1829
1827
1825
1823
1821
1819
1817
1815

Château Calon-Ségur

Year	Price	Current Name	Other Notes
1854	2000	Calon	19 tuns/May 1857
1853	600	Calon	62 tuns/September 1856
1852	600	Calon	77 tuns/January 1853
1851	1200	Calon	80 tuns/40 tuns/July 1853
1850	500	Calon	90 tuns/September 1852
1849	1000	Calon	70 tuns/several tuns/April 1856
1848	500	Calon	130 tuns/December 1849
1847	400	Calon	110 tuns/December 1848
1846	650	Calon	54 tuns/February 1850
1845	400	Calon	109 tuns/November 1846
1844	1800	Calon	84 tuns/partial sale/February 1850
1843	400	Calon	45 tuns/January 1846
1842	500	Calon	90 tuns/July 1843
1841	750	Calon	143 tuns/September 1843
1840	700	Calon	106 tuns/rich/March 1842
1839	900	Calon	45 tuns/closed/April 1840
1838	500	Calon	106 tuns/full-bodied/November 1841
1837	700	Calon	119 tuns/good/May 1839
1836	500	Calon	104 tuns/July 1840
1835	780	Calon	105 tuns/good/December 1836
1834	1550	Calon	80 tuns/good/November 1834
1833	700	Calon	107 tuns/a little hard/January 1834
1832	800	Lestapis	75 tuns/full-bodied/May 1838
1831	1800	Calon	50 tuns/good

Year	Price	Current Name	Other Notes
1830	660	Calon (Dumoulin)	26 tuns
1829	300	Calon (Dumoulin)	80 tuns
1828	—	Calon (Dumoulin)	90 tuns
1827	—	Calon (Dumoulin)	No trades reported
1826	—	Calon (Dumoulin)	No trades reported
1825	2500	Calon (Dumoulin)	No other notes
1824	—	Calon (Dumoulin)	No trades reported
1823	750	Calon (Dumoulin)	150 tuns
1822	1350	Calon (Dumoulin)	100 tuns
1821			No listings for 1821
1820			No listings for 1820
1819	950	Calon (Dumoulin)	130 tuns
1818	1900	Calon (Dumoulin)	No other notes
1817			No listings for 1817
1816			No listings for 1816
1815	1500	Calon (Dumoulin)	No other notes
1775	500–600	Calon (Dumoulin)	No other notes

Calon-Ségur

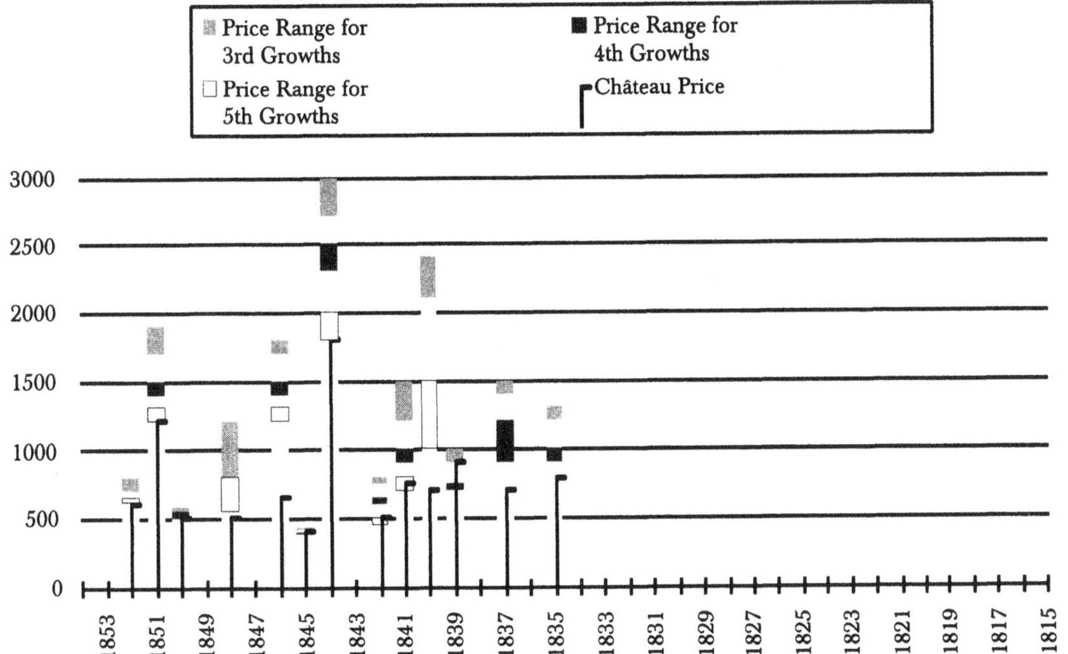

Château Ferrière

Year	Price	Current Name	Other Notes
1854	2400	Ferrière	1¾ tuns/December 1854
1853	—	Ferrière	5 tuns
1852	—	Ferrière	10 tuns
1851		Ferrière	12 tuns
1850	450	Ferrière	9½ tuns/June 1852
1849	—	Ferrière	9½ tuns
1848	—	Ferrière	12 tuns/December 1849
1847	—	Ferrière	14 tuns/August 1848
1846	—	Ferrière	7 tuns
1845	—	Ferrière	10 tuns/1846
1844	1800	Ferrière	10 tuns/October 1844
1843	—	Ferrière	No trades reported
1842	700	Ferrière	9 tuns/March 1844
1841	800	Ferrière	15 tuns/retail/1847
1840	750	Ferrière	16 tuns/good
1839	850	Ferrière	10 tuns/very good/February 1840
1838	—	Ferrière	7 tuns
1837	—	Ferrière	12 tuns
1836	950	Ferrière	8 tuns/February 1837
1835	700	Ferrière	7 tuns/ordinary/June 1837
1834	—	Ferrière	3 tuns
1833	900	Ferrière	8 tuns/good/January 1834
1832	1500	Ferrière	5 tuns/elegant/December 1833
1831	1700	Ferrière	4 tuns/good

Year	Price	Current Name	Other Notes
1830	—	Ferrières (à Segonnes)	1½ tuns
1829			No listings for 1829
1828	—	Ferrières (à Segonnes)	9¾ tuns
1827	900	Ferrières (à Segonnes)	No other notes
1826	—	Ferrières (à Segonnes)	No trades reported
1825	2100	Ferrières (à Segonnes)	No other notes
1824	—	Ferrières (à Segonnes)	No trades reported
1823	—	Ferrières (à Segonnes)	No trades reported
1822	—	Ferrières (à Segonnes)	No trades reported
1821			No listings for 1821
1820			No listings for 1820
1819	1700	Ferrières (à Segonnes)	5 tuns/6 tuns
1818	1800	Ferrières (à Segonnes)	No other notes
1817			No listings for 1817
1816			No listings for 1816
1815		Ferrières (à Segonnes)	No trades reported
1775		Ferrières (à Segonnes)	No trades reported

Ferrière

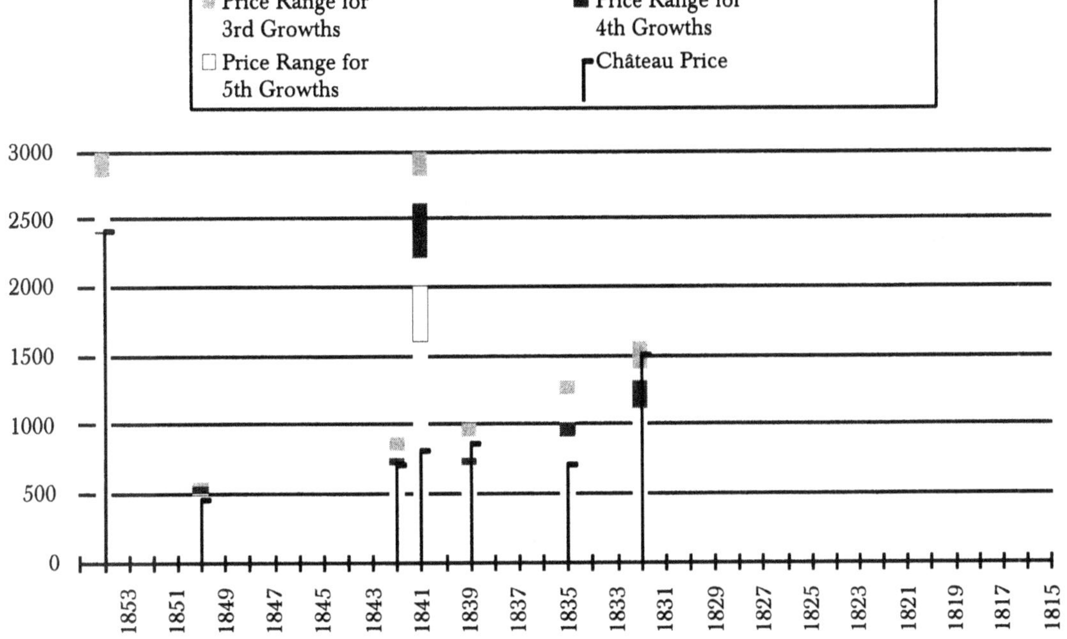

Château Marquis d'Alesme-Becker

Year	Price	Current Name	Other Notes
1854	—	Becker	Nothing
1853	—	Becker	No trades reported
1852	—	Becker	No trades reported
1851			No listings for 1851
1850	—	Becker	5 tuns
1849	—	Becker	6 tuns
1848	500	Becker	6 tuns/December 1849
1847	400	Becker	8 tuns/August 1848
1846	—	Becker	No trades reported
1845	—	Becker	No trades reported
1844	2200	Becker	4 tuns/September 1844
1843	—	Becker	No trades reported
1842	—	Becker	3½ tuns
1841	750	Becker	No other notes
1840	750	Rolland	No other notes
1839	850	Becker	4 tuns/ordinary/March 1840
1838	—	Becker	4 tuns
1837	—	Roland	8 tuns
1836	950	Roland	8 tuns/February 1837
1835	Commune	Becker	4 tuns/ordinary/1836
1834	—	Becker	3 tuns
1833	875	Becker	good/January 1834
1832	—	Becker	6 tuns/elegant, mellow/May 1833
1831	2100	Becker	2½ tuns/fine

Year	Price	Current Name	Other Notes
1830	—	Becker	No trades listed
1829			No listings for 1829
1828	—	Becker	12 tuns
1827	850	Becker	No other notes
1826	900	Becker	17 tuns
1825	2000	Becker	No other notes
1824	400	Becker	No other notes
1823	700	Becker	25 tuns
1822	—	Becker	No trades reported
1821			No listings for 1821
1820			No listings for 1820
1819	200	Becker	No other notes
1818	1500	Becker	No other notes
1817			No listings for 1817
1816			No listings for 1816
1815	1500	Becker	No other notes
1775	600–700	Becker	No other notes

Marquis d'Alesme-Becker

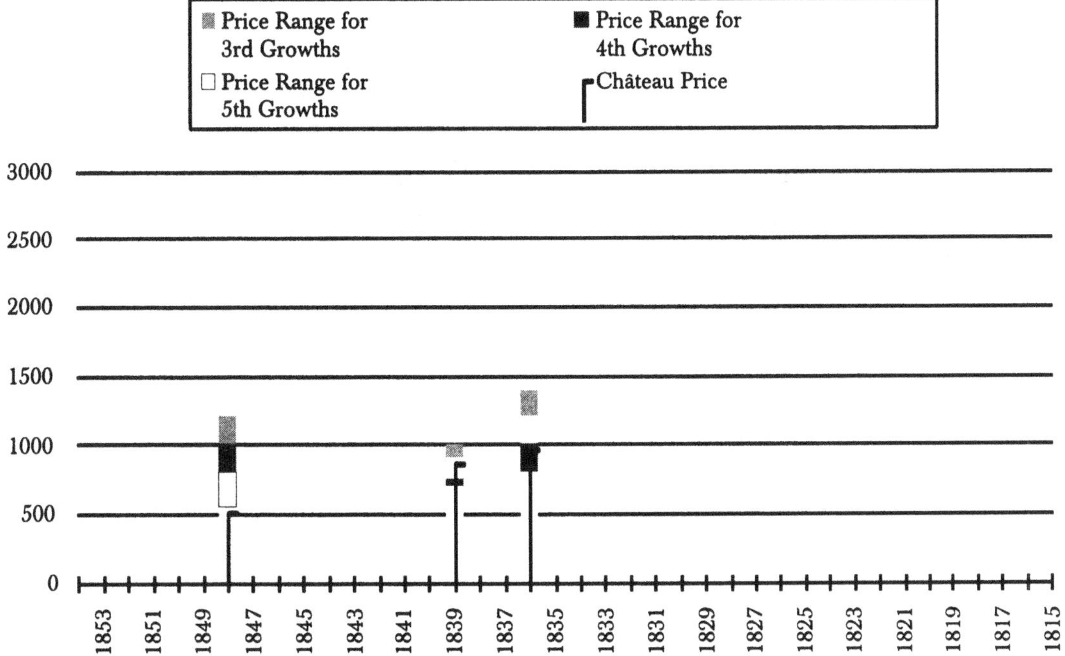

Château Saint-Pierre (Bontemps)

Year	Price	Current Name	Other Notes
1854	3000	Bontemps	3 tuns/April 1856
1853	—	Bontemps	19 tuns
1852	700	Bontemps	38 tuns/January 1853
1851	1200	Bontemps	43 tuns/November 1852
1850	500	Bontems	50 tuns/25 tuns/April 1851
1849	—	Bontemps	25 tuns
1848	800	Bontemps	52 tuns/partial sale/April 1850
1847	440	Bontemps	59 tuns/August 1848
1846	—	Bontemps	36 tuns
1845	425	Bontemps	40 tuns/partial sale/1846
1844	1800	Bontemps	42 tuns/November 1844
1843	—	Bontemps	10 tuns
1842	800	Bontemps	35 tuns
1841	1050	Bontemps	50 tuns/March 1843
1840	900	Bontemps	35 tuns/good/February 1841
1839	900	Bontemps	20 tuns/very good/February 1840
1838	—	Bontemps	24 tuns/less [good, compared with Roullet]
1837	950	Bontemps	33 tuns/good/May 1838
1836	—	Bontemps	30 tuns
1835	725	Bontemps	30 tuns/good/January 1836
1834	1550	Bontemps	12 tuns/bad/August 1834
1833	750	Bontemps	40 tuns/ordinary/January 1834
1832	—	Bontemps	shipped retail
1831	1500	Bontemps	9 tuns/elegant

Year	Price	Current Name	Other Notes
1830	—	Bontems	4½ tuns
1829	300	Bontems	20 tuns
1828	—	Bontems	20 tuns
1827	900	Bontems	30 tuns
1826	—	Bontems	No trades reported
1825	1800	Bontems	No other notes
1824	—	Bontems	No trades reported
1823	825	Bontems	15 tuns
1822	1300	Bontems	No other notes
1821			No listings for 1821
1820			No listings for 1820
1819	825	Bontems	No other notes
1818	1550	Bontems	No other notes
1817			No listings for 1817
1816			No listings for 1816
1815	1500	Bontems	No other notes
1775	—	Bontems	No other notes

Saint-Pierre-Bontemps

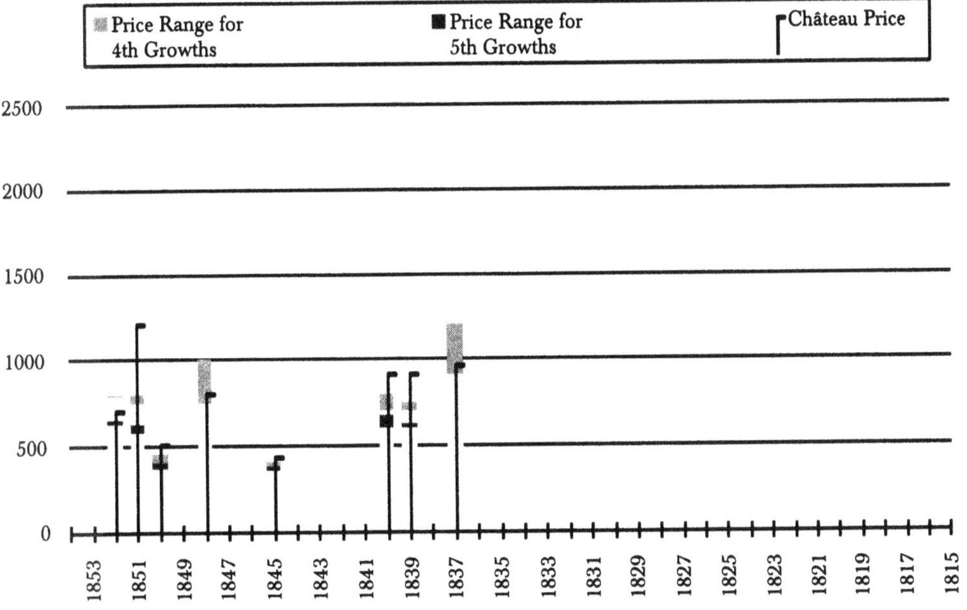

Note: When the 1837 vintage was sold there was just one price category for fourth and fifth growths combined.

Château Saint-Pierre (Roulet)

Year	Price	Current Name	Other Notes
1854	—	Roulet	1 tun
1853	—	Roulet	10 tuns
1852	700	Roulet	20 tuns/January 1853
1851	750	Roulet	36 tuns/May 1852
1850	475	Roulet	46 tuns/April 1851
1849	—	Roulez	25 tuns
1848	700	Roulez	50 tuns/December 1849
1847	425	Roullez	58 tuns/August 1848
1846	—	Roullez	40 tuns
1845	—	Roullez	35 tuns
1844	1600	Roullez	40 tuns/August 1844
1843	—	Roullez	10 tuns
1842	700	Roulez	32 tuns/September 1843
1841	1600	Roulez	50 tuns
1840	900	Roulet	38 tuns/ordinary/September 1841
1839	900	Roulez	21 tuns/good/February 1840
1838	—	Roullet	20 tuns/also good
1837	1200	Roullet	37 tuns/good/December 1837
1836	—	Roullet	29 tuns
1835	700	Roullet	30 tuns/good/January 1836
1834	1550	Roullet	12 tuns/bad/January 1835
1833	750	Roullet	38 tuns/January 1834
1832	1400	Roulez	38 tuns/check again
1831	1600	Roulez	9 tuns/elegant

Year	Price	Current Name	Other Notes
1830	800	Roulet	4½ tuns
1829	300	Roulet	20 tuns
1828	—	Roulet	20 tuns
1827	1600	Roulet	30 tuns
1826	—	Roulet	No trades reported
1825	1800	Roulet	No other notes
1824	—	Roulet	20 tuns
1823	825	Roulet	60 tuns
1822	1300	Roulet	No other notes
1821			No listings for 1821
1820			No listings for 1820
1819	825	Roulet	50 tuns
1818	1550	Roulet	No other notes
1817			No listings for 1817
1816			No listings for 1816
1815	1500	Roulet	No other notes
1775	400	Roulet	No other notes

Saint-Pierre-Roulet

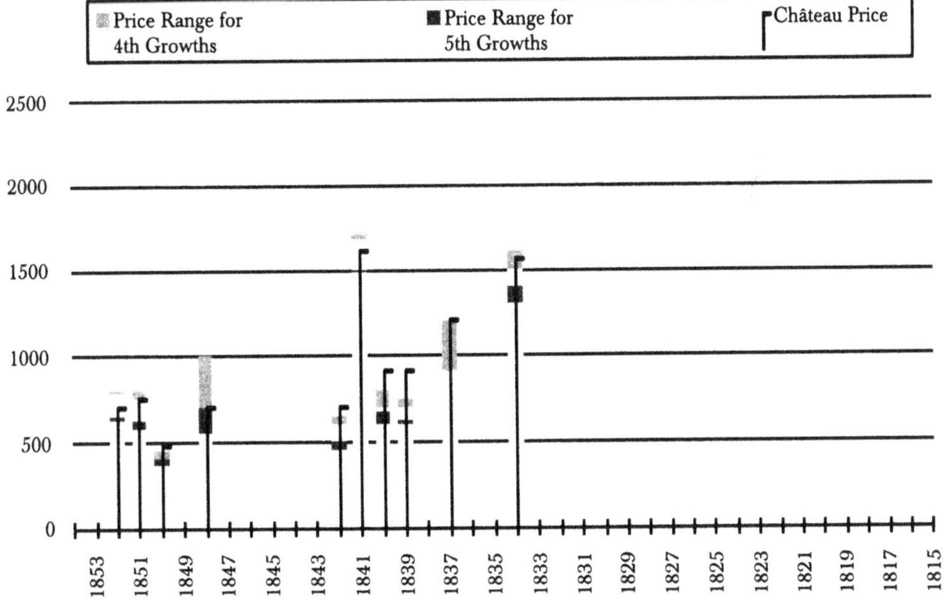

Note: When the 1837 vintage was sold there was just one price category for fourth and fifth growths combined.

Château Saint-Pierre (Galoupeau)

Year	Price	Current Name	Other Notes
1854	3000	Galoupeau	2 tuns
1853	1200	Galoupeau	10 tuns
1852	700	Galoupeau	20 tuns/January 1853
1851			No listings for 1851
1850	***From 1834 to 1850, this property does not appear***		
1833	750	Galoupeau	40 tuns/fine good/January 1834
1832	1400	Galoupeau	38 tuns/check again
1831	1650	Galoupeau	9 tuns/elegant
1830	—	Galoupeau	4½ tuns
1829	300	Galoupeau	20 tuns
1828	—	Galoupeau	20 tuns
1827	900	Galoupeau	30 tuns
1826	900	Galoupeau	No other notes
1825	1800	Galoupeau	No other notes
1824	—	Galoupeau	No trades reported
1823	825	Galoupeau	No other notes
1822	1300	Galoupeau	No other notes
1821			No listings for 1821
1820			No listings for 1820
1819	825	Galoupeau	104 tuns
1818	1550	Galoupeau	No other notes
1817			No listings for 1817
1816			No listings for 1816
1815	1550	Galoupeau	No other notes
1775	—	Galoupeau	No other notes

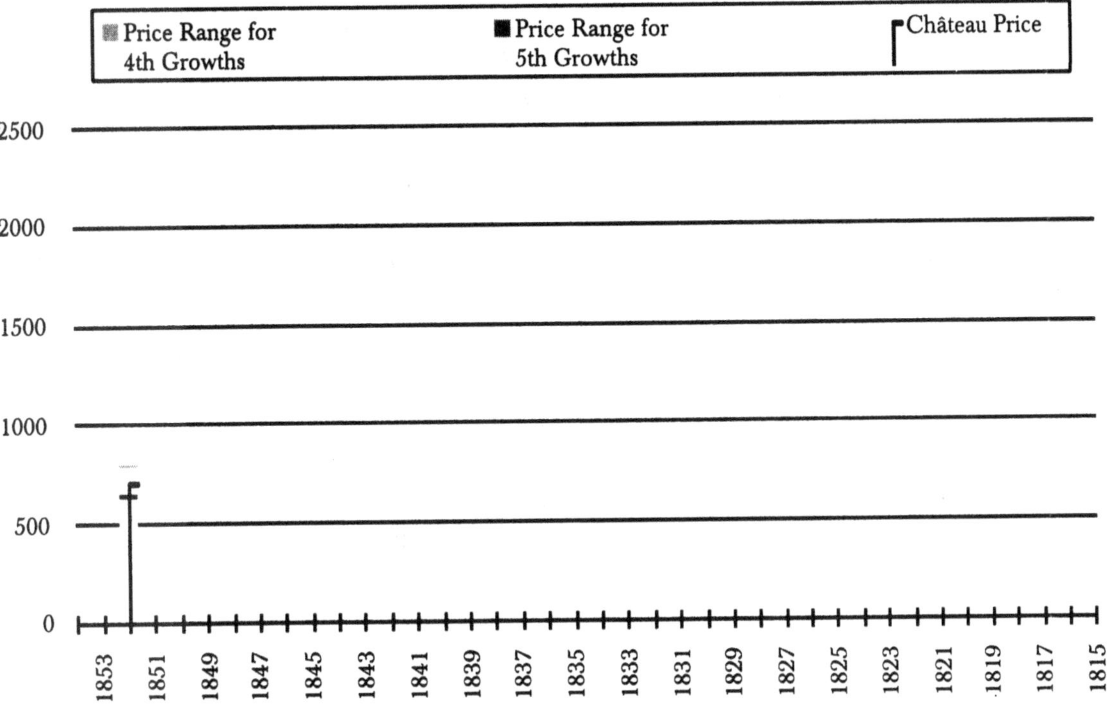
Saint-Pierre (Galoupeau)
Price Range for 4th Growths
Price Range for 5th Growths
Château Price
2500
2000
1500
1000
500
0
1853
1851
1849
1847
1845
1843
1841
1839
1837
1835
1833
1831
1829
1827
1825
1823
1821
1819
1817
1815

Château Talbot

Year	Price	Current Name	Other Notes
1854	—	d'Aux	28 tuns
1853	750	d'Aux	60 tuns/November 1856
1852	700	d'Aux	145 tuns/January 1853
1851	1550	d'Aux	150 tuns/August 1858
1850	475	d'Aux	135 tuns/April 1851
1849	1000	D'Aux	100 tuns/several tuns/April 1853
1848	900	D'Aux	120 tuns/December 1850
1847	400	D'Aux	160 tuns/August 1848
1846	—	D'Aux	120 tuns
1845	360	D'Aux	97 tuns/September 1846
1844	1800	Daux	105 tuns/September 1844
1843	425	Daux	45 tuns/October 1845
1842	700	Daux	106 tuns/February 1844
1841	—	Daux	135 tuns
1840	900	Daux	130 tuns/fine
1839	900	Daux	80 tuns/good/February 1840
1838	—	Daux	72 tuns/ordinary
1837	1000	Daux	105 tuns/good/June 1839
1836	500	Daux	95 tuns
1835	725	D'aux	110 tuns/very fine/January 1836
1834	—	Daux	24 tuns/elegant
1833	760	Daux	110 tuns/good/January 1834
1832	—	Daux	52 tuns/ordinary
1831	1800	Daux	34 tuns/fine full-bodied

Year	Price	Current Name	Other Notes
1830	—	Daux	12 tuns
1829	—	Daux	92 tuns
1828	—	Daux	64 tuns
1827	—	Daux	100 tuns
1826	800	Daux	70 tuns
1825	1800	Daux	No other notes
1824	500	Daux	30 tuns
1823	700	Daux	80 tuns
1822	1300	Daux	70 tuns
1821			No listings for 1821
1820			No listings for 1820
1819	900	Daux	50 tuns
1818	1530	Daux	50 tuns
1817			No listings for 1817
1816			No listings for 1816
1815	1350	Daux	No other notes
1775	400	Daux	No other notes

Talbot

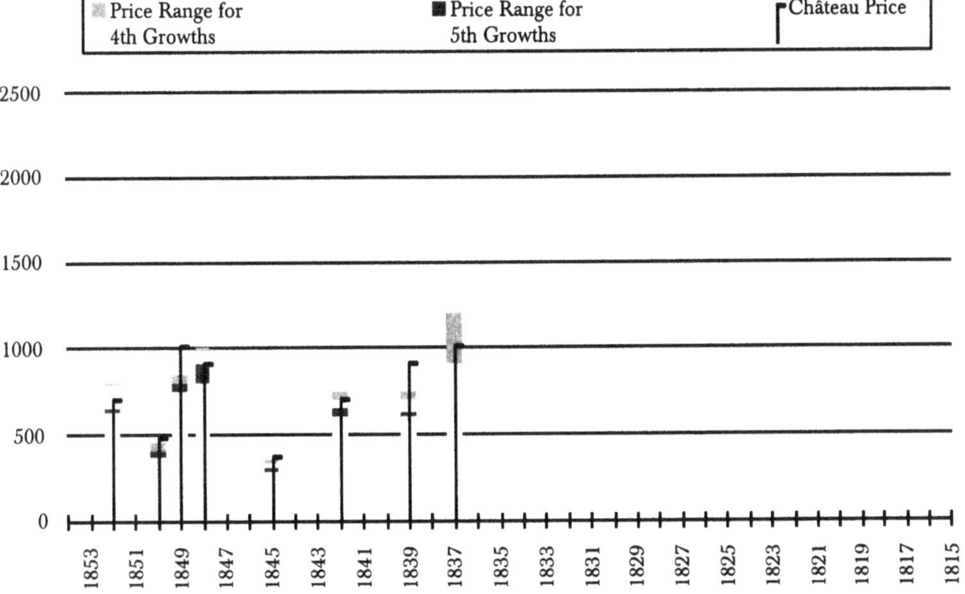

Note: When the 1837 vintage was sold there was just one price category for fourth and fifth growths combined.

Château Branaire-Ducru

Year	Price	Current Name	Other Notes
1854	—	Du Luc	19 tuns
1853	700	Du Luc	36 tuns/September 1856
1852	650	Du Luc	125 tuns/January 1853
1851	1000	Du Luc	130 tuns
1850	475	Du Luc	125 tuns/April 1851
1849	1150	Duluc	80 tuns
1848	750	Duluc	150 tuns/December 1949
1847	400	Duluc	155 tuns/August 1848
1846	—	Duluc	100 tuns
1845	350	Duluc	95 tuns/September 1846
1844	1800	Duluc	110 tuns/September 1844
1843	425	Duluc	30 tuns/October 1845
1842	600	Duluc	62 tuns/September 1847
1841	1600	Duluc	107 tuns/March 1844
1840	900	Duluc	100 tuns/good
1839	900	Duluc	72 tuns/good/February 1840
1838	—	Duluc	56 tuns/good
1837	900	Duluc	120 tuns/good/November 1838
1836	500	Duluc	100 tuns/March 1846
1835	725	Duluc	100 tuns/good/January 1836
1834	2300	Duluc	36 tuns/ordinary/December 1838
1833	750	Duluc	140 tuns/good/January 1834
1832	1500	Duluc	50 tuns/very good
1831	1650	Duluc	50 tuns/very good

Year	Price	Current Name	Other Notes
1830	—	Duluc	18 tuns
1829	375	Duluc	120 tuns
1828	—	Duluc	80 tuns
1827	2400	Duluc	120 tuns
1826	900	Duluc	100 tuns
1825	1800	Duluc	No other notes
1824	—	Duluc	No trades reported
1823	700	Duluc	63 tuns
1822	1300	Duluc	45 tuns
1821			No listings for 1821
1820			No listings for 1820
1819	865	Duluc	80 tuns
1818	1550	Duluc	No other notes
1817			No listings for 1817
1816			No listings for 1816
1815	1500	Duluc	50 tuns
1775	500	Duluc	No other notes

Branaire-Ducru

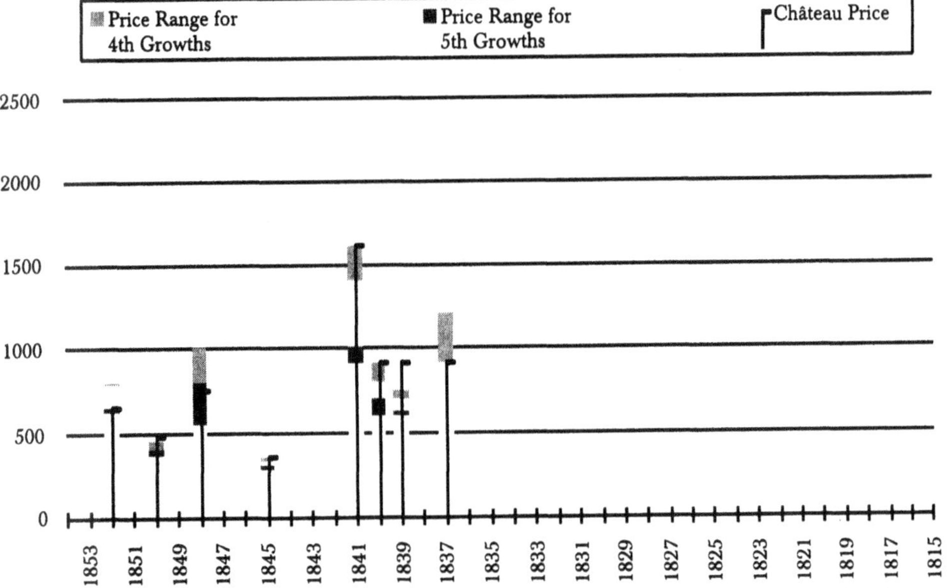

Note: When the 1837 vintage was sold there was just one price category for fourth and fifth growths combined.

Château Duhart-Milon-Rothschild

Year	Price	Current Name	Other Notes
1854	2400	Castéja	10 tuns/December 1854
1853	—	Castéja	20 tuns/November 1856
1852	700	Duhart	42 tuns/January 1853
1851	1200	Duhart	40 tuns/December 1852
1850	—	Duhart	45 tuns
1849	—	Duhart	68 tuns
1848	750	Duhart	43 tuns/December 1849
1847	425	Castéja	60 tuns/August 1848
1846	1200	Castéja	36 tuns
1845	400	Duhart	40 tuns/partial sale/November 1846
1844	1500	Castéja Milon	40 tuns/October 1844
1843	500	Castéja Milon	16 tuns/September 1846
1842	700	Duhar	30 tuns/January 1844
1841	800	Duhar	35 tuns/December 1842
1840	800	Duhart	45 tuns/good
1839	800	Duhart	22 tuns/elegant/March 1840
1838	—	Duhart	No trades reported
1837	850	Duhart	53 tuns/fine/March 1841
1836	—	Duhart	35 tuns
1835	750	Duhart	32 tuns/very good/August 1836
1834	1550	Duhart	15 tuns/good/March 1835
1833	700	Duhart	40 tuns/fine/March 1834
1832	850	Duhart	25 tuns/thin/August 1833
1831	—	Duhart	8 tuns

Year	Price	Current Name	Other Notes
1830	—	Mendavy Milon	8 tuns
1829	300	Mendavy Milon	32 tuns
1828	—	Mendavy Milon	25 tuns
1827	600	Mendavy Milon	27 tuns
1826	—	Mendavy Milon	No trades reported
1825	1900	Mendavy Milon	No other notes
1824	—	Mendavy Milon	13 tuns
1823	900	Mendavy Milon	60 tuns
1822	—	Mendavy Milon	No trades reported
1821			No listings for 1821
1820			No listings for 1820
1819	1400	Mendavy Milon	30 tuns
1818	1400	Mendavy Milon	18 tuns
1817			No listings for 1817
1816			No listings for 1816
1815	1400	Mendavy Milon	16 tuns
1775	—	Mendavy Milon	No other notes

Duhart-Milon-Rothschild

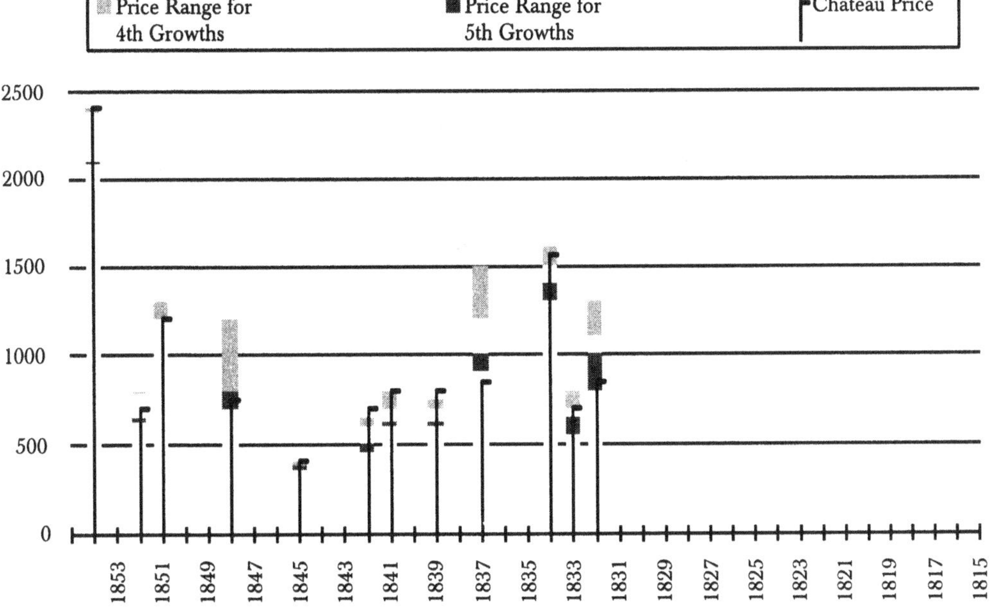

Note: In December 1852, prices for fifth growths from 1851 were 1200–1500.

Château Pouget

Year	Price	Current Name	Other Notes
1854	2200	Chavaille	2 tuns/December 1854
1853	—	Chavaille	No trades reported
1852	700	Chavaille	11 tuns/March 1853
1851	750	Chavaille	January 1852
1850	375	Chavaille	April 1851
1849	400	Chavaille	15 tuns/June 1850
1848	500	Chavaille	16 tuns
1847	400	Chavaille	15 tuns/with 1846/June 1848
1846	400	Chavaille	8 tuns/with 1847/June 1848
1845	400	Chavaille	November 1846
1844	1850	Chavaille	August 1844
1843	—	Chavaille	4 tuns
1842	550	Chavaille	12 tuns/December 1844
1841	800	Chavaille	15 tuns/March 1843
1840	800	Chavaille	17 tuns/ord/March 1841
1839	850	Chavaille	11 tuns/bad/February 1840
1838	—	Chavaille	9 tuns
1837	650	Chavaille	12 tuns/1840
1836	—	Chavaille	18 tuns
1835	800	Chavaille	15 tuns/ordinary/July 1836
1834	—	Chavaille	2 tuns
1833	775	Chavaille	12 tuns/fine, very good/January 1834
1832	1400	Chavaille	6½ tuns/good/September 1833
1831	2000	Chavaille	2½ tuns/fine

Year	Price	Current Name	Other Notes
1830	—	Chavaille	No trades reported
1829			No listings for 1829
1828	—	Chavaille	14 tuns
1827	750	Chavaille	15 tuns
1826	700	Chavaille	8 tuns
1825	1600	Chavaille	No other notes
1824	450	Chavaille	No other notes
1823	750	Chavaille	No other notes
1822	—	Chavaille	8 tuns
1821			No listings for 1821
1820			No listings for 1820
1819	800	Chavaille	30 tuns
1818	1200	Chavaille	8½ tuns
1817			No listings for 1817
1816			No listings for 1816
1815	1300–1400	Chavaille	No other notes
1775	650–700	Chavaille	No other notes

Pouget

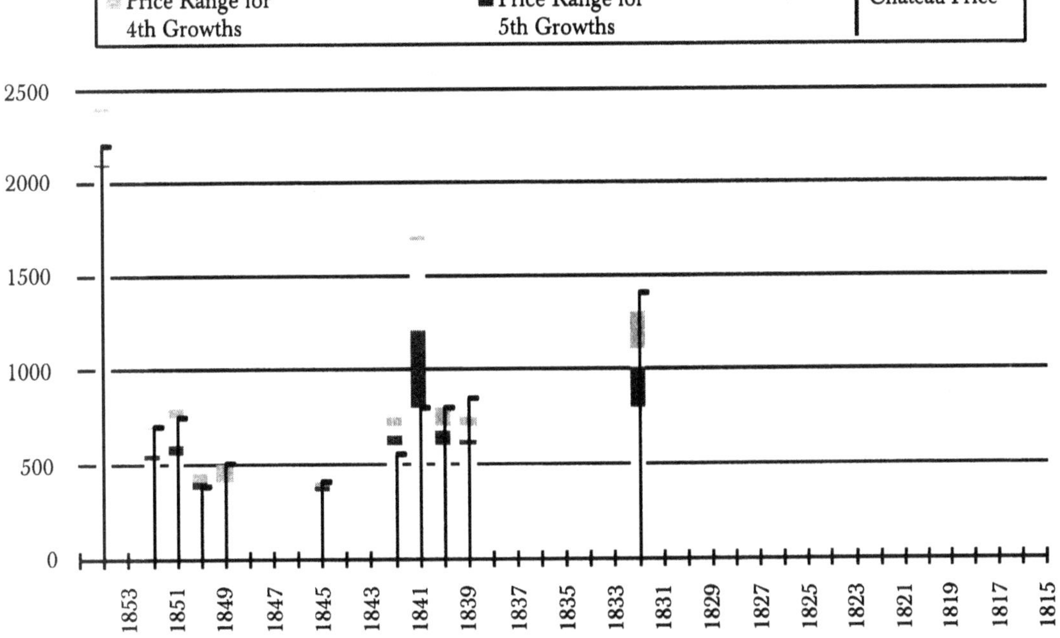

Château Pouget-Lassalle

Year	Price	Current Name	Other Notes
1854	—	Lassalle	No trades reported
1853	—	Lassalle	6 tuns
1852	700	Lassalle	12 tuns/March 1853
1851	625	Lassalle	22 tuns/April 1852
1850	—	Lassalle	15 tuns/August 1851
1849	—	Lassalle	15 tuns
1848	—	Lassalle	16 tuns
1847	375	Delassalle	15 tuns/August 1848
1846	—	Delassalle	7 tuns
1845	—	Lassalle	10 tuns
1844	1850	Delassalle	August 1844
1843	—	Delassalle	3½ tuns
1842	600	Delassalle	10 tuns/February 1845
1841	—	Delassalle	14 tuns
1840	700	Delassalle	13 tuns/fine/March 1841
1839	650	Lassalle	8 tuns/good/January 1840
1838	—	Delassalle	7 tuns
1837	—	Lassalle	10 tuns
1836	700	Lassalle	12 tuns/March 1837
1835	650	Ganet	8 tuns/good/July 1836
1834	—	Delassalle	1 tun
1833	900	Delassalle	9 tuns/mediocre/April 1834
1832	1050	Ganet	4 tuns/good/August 1833
1831	1500	Ganet	1¼ tuns

Year	Price	Current Name	Other Notes
1830	—	Ganet	No trades reported
1829		Ganet	No listings for 1829
1828	—	Ganet	11 tuns
1827	650	Ganet	No other notes
1826	—	Ganet	No trades reported
1825	1600	Ganet	No other notes
1824	—	Ganet	No trades reported
1823	650	Ganet	15 tuns
1822	—	Ganet	No trades reported
1821			No listings for 1821
1820			No listings for 1820
1819	—	Ganet	14 tuns
1818	1200	Ganet	10 tuns
1817			No listings for 1817
1816			No listings for 1816
1815	—	Ganet	No trades reported
1775	—	Ganet	No trades reported

Pouget-Lassalle

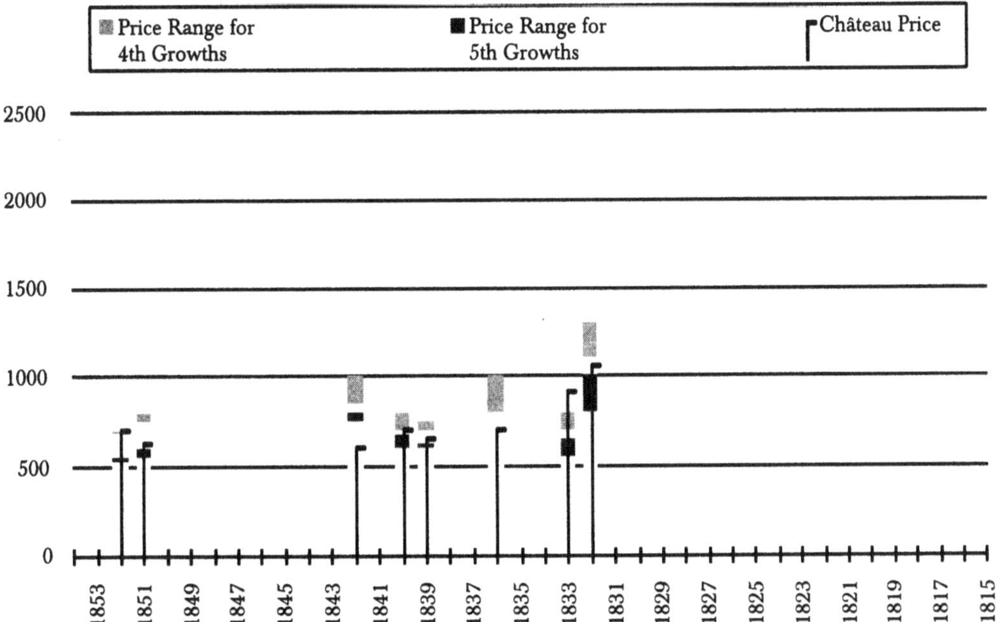

Note: When the 1836 vintage was sold there was just one price category for fourth and fifth growths combined.

Château La Tour-Carnet

Year	Price	Current Name	Other Notes
1854	2800	Carnet	14 tuns/April 1856
1853	775	Carnet	35 tuns/December 1856
1852	1050	Carnet	60 tuns/July 1854
1851	—	Carnet	70 tuns
1850	800	Carnet	90 tuns/September 1853
1849	—	Carnet	78 tuns
1848	650	Carnet	98 tuns/December 1849
1847	400	Carnet	140 tuns/November 1848
1846	—	Carnet	60 tuns
1845	400	Carnet	1846
1844	1700	Carnet	97 tuns/October 1845
1843	500	Carnet	45 tuns/1846
1842	700	Carnet	March 1844
1841	1500	Carnet	100 tuns/April 1844
1840	750	Carnet	103 tuns/thin/July 1843
1839	800	Carnet	49 tuns/ordinary/March 1840
1838	600	Carnet	60 tuns/July 1842
1837	900	Carnet	96 tuns/1840
1836	500	Carnet	75 tuns/1840
1835	750	Carnet	70 tuns/ordinary/June 1838
1834	1500	Carnet	33 tuns/June 1836
1833	650	Carnet	70 tuns/good/January 1834
1832	—	Carnet	55 tuns
1831	1500	Luetkens	17 tuns/full-bodied, rich

Year	Price	Current Name	Other Notes
1830	—	Carnet (Luetkens)	No trades reported
1829	375	Carnet (Luetkens)	75 tuns
1828	—	Carnet (Luetkens)	55 tuns
1827	—	Carnet (Luetkens)	80 tuns
1826	—	Carnet (Luetkens)	No trades reported
1825	2000	Carnet (Luetkens)	No other notes
1824	—	Carnet (Luetkens)	No trades reported
1823	575	Carnet (Luetkens)	90 tuns
1822	900	Carnet (Luetkens)	35 tuns
1821			No listings for 1821
1820			No listings for 1820
1819	700	Carnet (Luetkens)	65 tuns
1818	664	Carnet (Luetkens)	15 tuns
1817			No listings for 1817
1816			No listings for 1816
1815	1200	Carnet (Luetkens)	60 tuns
1775	500	Carnet (Luetkens)	No other notes

La Tour Carnet

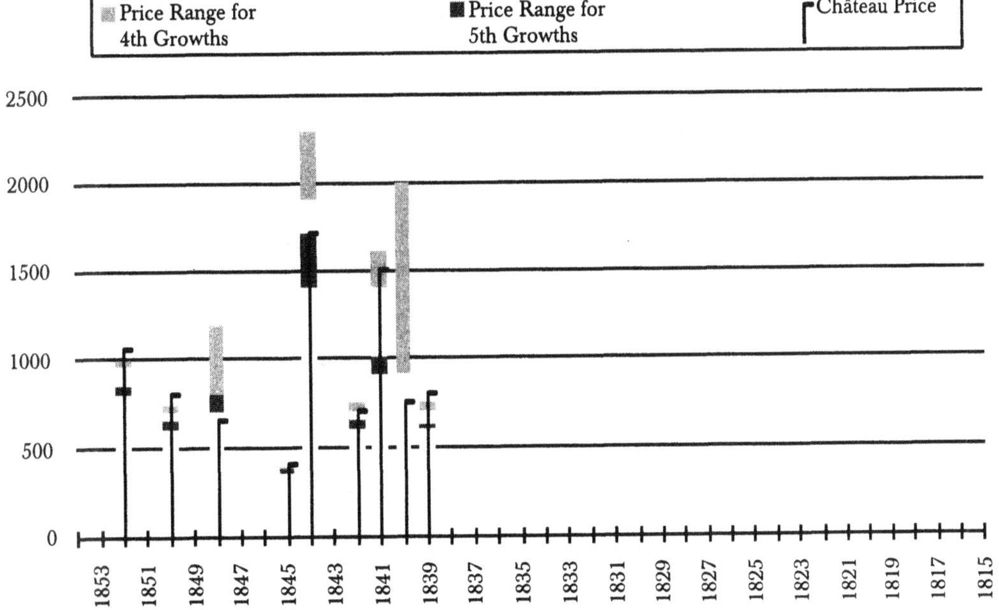

Note: In July 1843, prices for fifth growths from 1840 were 1000–1500.

Château Lafon-Rochet

Year	Price	Current Name	Other Notes
1854	1700	Rochet	7 tuns/November 1854
1853	—	Rochet	17 tuns
1852	—	Rochet	37 tuns
1851	1800	Rochet	35 tuns/June 1856
1850	375	Lafon Rochet	35 tuns/November 1851
1849	—	Lafon Rochet	40 tuns
1848	—	Lafon Rochet	40 tuns/partial sale/1849
1847	300	Rochet	48 tuns/July 1848
1846	—	Rochet	No trades reported
1845	—	Rochez	15 tuns/at Libourne/August 1846
1844	1800	Rochet	40 tuns/November 1844
1843	—	Rochet	10 tuns
1842	600	Rochet	37 tuns/March 1847
1841	1650	Rochet	40 tuns/April 1845
1840	900	Rochet	40 tuns/v. good/March 1842
1839	1100	Rochet	5 tuns/rich/April 1840
1838	1000	Rochet	30 tuns/good
1837	900	Rochette	50 tuns/1840
1836	1000	Rochet	34 tuns/January 1839
1835	400	Rochet	22 tuns/thin/July 1837
1834	1550	Lafon Rochet	21 tuns/perf./December 1834
1833	800	Camarchac	42 tuns/good/August 1834
1832	950	Rochet	25 tuns/very good/March 1833
1831	1400	Rochet	7 tuns/full-bodied, rich

Year	Price	Current Name	Other Notes
1830	—	Rochet (Lafon)	3 tuns
1829	350	Rochet (Lafon)	20 tuns
1828	—	Rochet (Lafon)	12 tuns
1827	—	Rochet (Lafon)	No trades reported
1826	—	Rochet (Lafon)	No trades reported
1825	1500	Rochet (Lafon)	No other notes
1824	—	Rochet (Lafon)	No trades reported
1823	500	Rochet (Lafon)	23 tuns
1822	—	Rochet (Lafon)	No trades reported
1821			No listings for 1821
1820			No listings for 1820
1819	600	Rochet (Lafon)	63 tuns
1818	1000	Rochet (Lafon)	50 tuns
1817			No listings for 1817
1816			No listings for 1816
1815	850–950	Rochet (Lafon)	29 tuns
1775	300–320	Rochet (Lafon)	No other notes

Lafon-Rochet

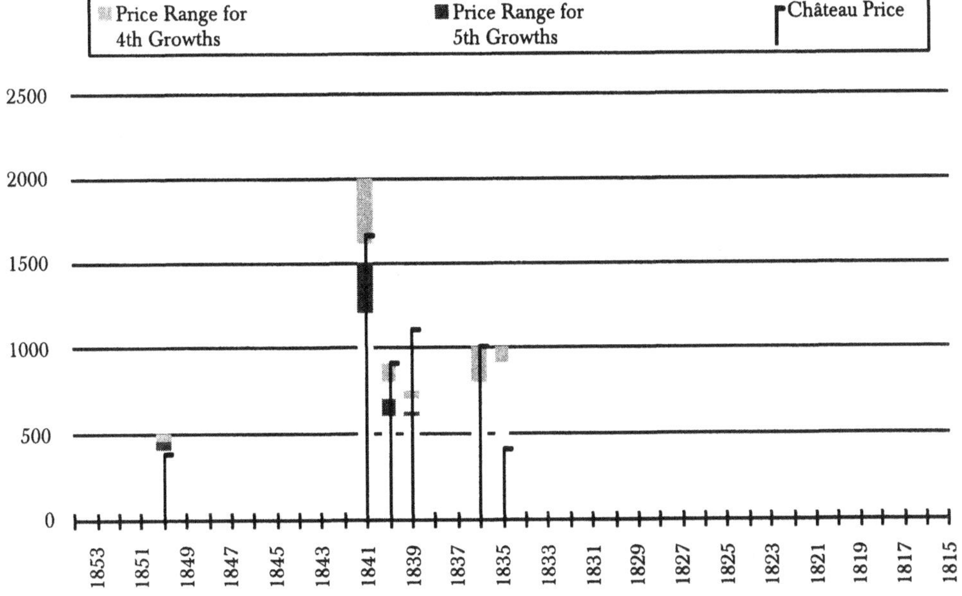

Note: When the 1835 and 1836 vintages were sold there was just one price category for fourth and fifth growths combined.

Château Beychevelle

Year	Price	Current Name	Other Notes
1854	—	Beychevelle	8¾ tuns/December 1854
1853	—	Beychevelle	40 tuns/employed
1852	650	Beychevelle	105 tuns/January 1853
1851	1000	Beychevelle	114 tuns/November 1852
1850	450	Beychevelle	136 tuns/November 1851
1849	550	Beychevelle	90 tuns/September 1851
1848	480	Beychevelle	160 tuns/September 1849
1847	360	Beychevelle	149 tuns/September 1848
1846	—	Beychevelle	108 tuns
1845	—	Beychevelle	100 tuns/employed
1844	1600	Guestier	140 tuns/40 tuns/September 1844
1843	425	Guestier	55 tuns/October 1845
1842	575	Beychevelle	110 tuns/June 1845
1841	800	Beychevelle	182 tuns/50 tuns/March 1843
1840	800	Beychevelle	128 tuns/good/partial sale
1839	750	Beychevelle	70 tuns/February 1840
1838	500	Guestier	70 tuns/thin
1837	1200	Guestier	130 tuns/fine/December 1837
1836	—	Guestier	119 tuns
1835	700	Bechevelle	125 tuns/thin/March 1836
1834	1550	Guestier	70 tuns/elegant/kept by Barton & Guestier
1833	700	Bechevelle	95 tuns/thin/December 1833
1832	1300	Bechevelle	72 tuns/delicious/March 1833
1831	1500	Bechevelle	50 tuns/unp. thin/employed

Year	Price	Current Name	Other Notes
1830	—	Bechevelle	17 tuns
1829	310	Bechevelle	96 tuns
1828	—	Bechevelle	69 tuns
1827	—	Bechevelle	150 tuns
1826	—	Bechevelle	94 tuns
1825	—	Bechevelle	English
1824	—	Bechevelle	22 tuns
1823	575	Bechevelle	100 tuns
1822	1200	Bechevelle	80 tuns
1821			No listings for 1821
1820			No listings for 1820
1819	750	Bechevelle	75 tuns/16 tuns
1818	1300	Bechevelle	No other notes
1817			No listings for 1817
1816			No listings for 1816
1815	—	Bechevelle	No trades reported
1775	500	Bechevelle	No other notes

Beychevelle

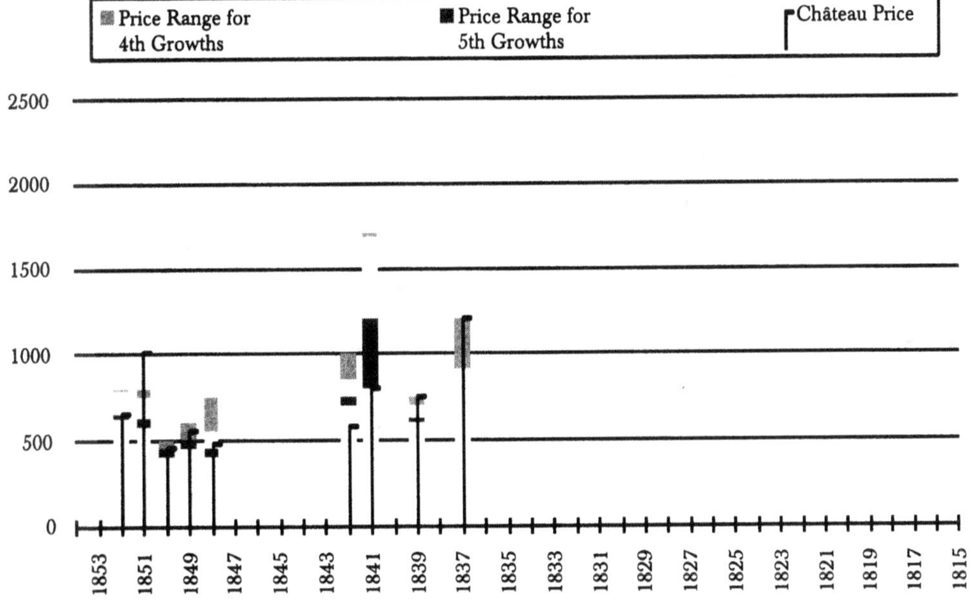

Note: When the 1837 vintage was sold there was just one price category for fourth and fifth growths combined.

Château Prieuré-Lichine

Year	Price	Current Name	Other Notes
1854	—	Pagès	7 tuns
1853	—	Pagès	14 tuns
1852	—	Pagès	12 tuns/January 1853
1851	1600	Pagès	26 tuns/January 1854
1850	400	Pagès	20 tuns/September 1852
1849	—	Pagès	20 tuns
1848	400	Pagès	10 tuns
1847	300	Pagès	12 tuns/August 1848
1846	—	Pagès	7 tuns
1845	—	Pagès	No trades reported
1844	1600	Pagès	15 tuns/August 1844
1843	—	Pagès	4 tuns
1842	550	Pagès	16 tuns/1844
1841	—	Pagès	No trades reported
1840	700	Pagès	23 tuns/March 1842
1839	800	Pagès	10 tuns/fine/February 1840
1838	—	Pagès	6 tuns
1837	—	Pagès	No trades reported
1836	—	Pagès	22 tuns
1835	650	Pagès	15 tuns/fine/July 1839
1834	—	Pagès	3 tuns
1833	1050	Pagès	11 tuns/thin finish/February 1835
1832	1300	Pagès	8 tuns/October 1833
1831	1600	Pagès	4 tuns

Prieuré-Lichine

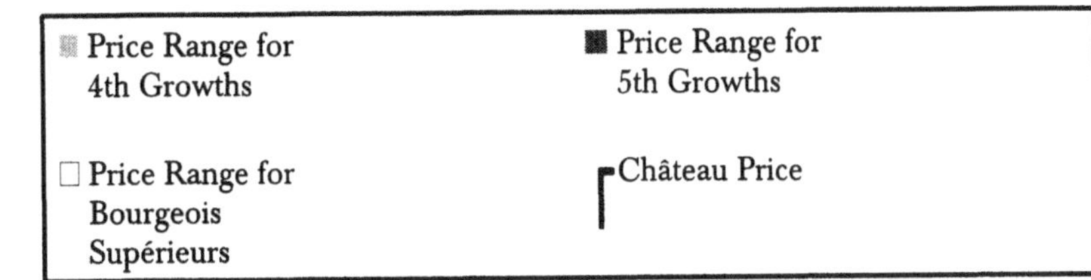

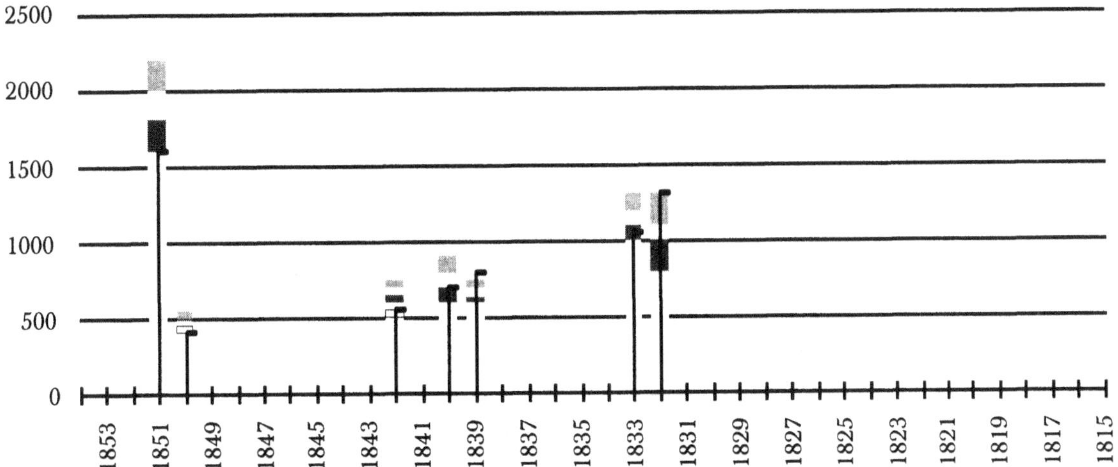

Château Marquis de Terme

Year	Price	Current Name	Other Notes
1854	2000	Solberg	8¾ tuns/December 1854
1853	—	Solberg	20 tuns
1852	500	Solberg	45 tuns/October 1852
1851	—	Solberg	50 tuns
1850	400	Thermes	48 tuns/December 1851
1849	600	Thermes	46 tuns/November 1851
1848	475	Thermes	50 tuns/March 1849
1847	500	Solberg	60 tuns/February 1848
1846	900	Solberg	28 tuns/partial sale
1845	—	Solberg	20 tuns
1844	1400	Thermes	25 tuns/August 1844
1843	—	Thermes	9 tuns
1842	625	Solberg	25 tuns/January 1844
1841	750	Solberg	34 tuns/August 1842
1840	700	Mac Daniel	20 tuns/good
1839	750	Mac Daniel	20 tuns
1838	—	M. Daniel	No trades reported
1837	600	Solberg	4 tuns/June 1840
1836	600	Solberg	5 tuns
1835	650	Mac-Daniel	14 tuns/good/July 1836
1834	1400	Solberg	3 tuns/good/August 1836
1833	775	Solberg	May 1834
1832	850	Solberg	8 tuns/February 1833
1831	—	Solberg	4 tuns

Year	Price	Current Name	Other Notes
1830	—	Solberg (de Therme)	No trades reported
1829			No listings for 1829
1828	600	Solberg (de Therme)	6 tuns
1827	700	Solberg (de Therme)	10 tuns
1826	—	Solberg (de Therme)	10 tuns
1825	1850	Solberg (de Therme)	No other notes
1824	—	Solberg (de Therme)	No trades reported
1823	—	Solberg (de Therme)	No trades reported
1822	—	Solberg (de Therme)	No trades reported
1821			No listings for 1821
1820			No listings for 1820
1819	—	Solberg (de Therme)	No trades reported
1818	—	Solberg (de Therme)	20 tuns
1817			No listings for 1817
1816			No listings for 1816
1815	1000	Solberg (de Therme)	No other notes
1775	650–700	Solberg (de Therme)	No other notes

Marquis de Terme

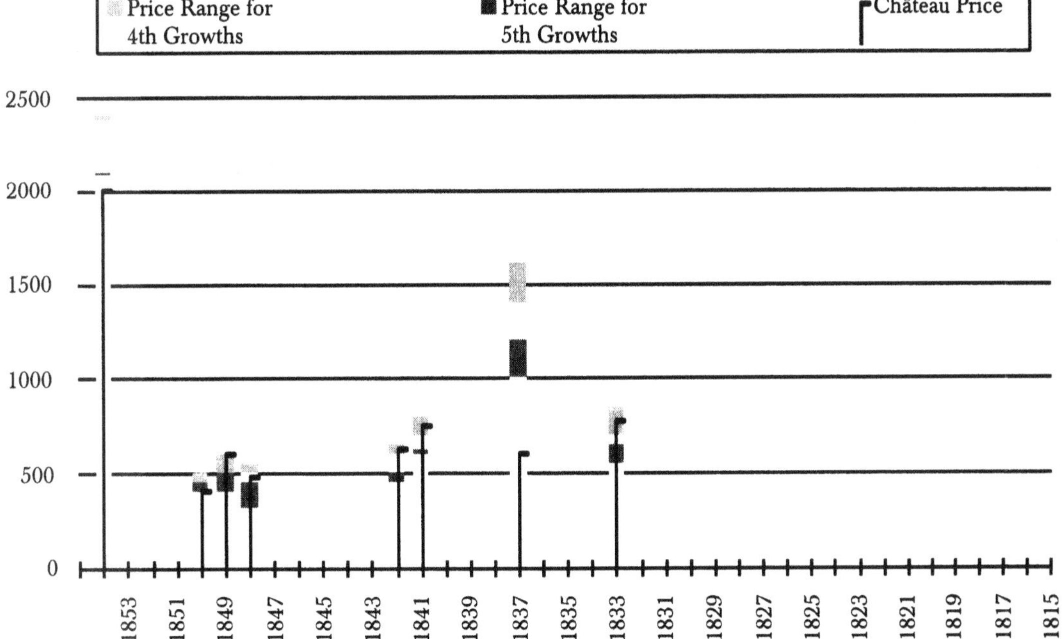

Château Pontet-Canet

Year	Price	Current Name	Other Notes
1854	2100	de Pontet	30 tuns/December 1854
1853	700	de Pontet	80 tuns/September 1853
1852	525	de Pontet	130 tuns/November 1852
1851	1000	de Pontet	130 tuns/December 1852
1850	400	de Pontet	145 tuns/April 1851
1849	600	Pontet	90 tuns/August 1852
1848	600	Pontet	123 tuns/November 1849
1847	300	Pontet	172 tuns/June 1848
1846	1000	Pontet	108 tuns/partial sale/December 1850
1845	350	de Pontet	112 tuns/April 1846
1844	1300	Pontet	110 tuns/October 1844
1843	425	Pontet	65 tuns/March 1846
1842	450	Pontet	122 tuns/June 1843
1841	1000	Pontet	126 tuns/1843
1840	600	Canet	165 tuns/good
1839	600	Pontet Canet	86 tuns/rich/January 1840
1838	500	Pontet	130 tuns/cond. wine/partial sale/June 1842
1837	675	Pontet	145 tuns/good/April 1838
1836	500	Pontet	118 tuns/April 1839
1835	650	Pontet Cannet	140 tuns/very good/February 1836
1834	1200	Pontet	100 tuns/full-bodied, good/November 1834
1833	600	Pontet	130 tuns/good, elegant/December 1833
1832	750	Pontet	112 tuns/good, thin at finish/January 1833
1831	1200	Pontet	27 tuns

Year	Price	Current Name	Other Notes
1830	—	Pontet Cannet	48 tuns
1829	325	Pontet Cannet	150 tuns
1828	600	Pontet Cannet	140 tuns
1827	700	Pontet Cannet	130 tuns
1826	720	Pontet Cannet	No other notes
1825	1500	Pontet Cannet	No other notes
1824	600	Pontet Cannet	45 tuns
1823	560	Pontet Cannet	150 tuns
1822	1400	Pontet Cannet	80 tuns
1821			No listings for 1821
1820			No listings for 1820
1819	800	Pontet Cannet	130 tuns
1818	1400	Pontet Cannet	98 tuns
1817			No listings for 1817
1816			No listings for 1816
1815	1400	Pontet Cannet	100 tuns
1775	500–550	Pontet Cannet	No other notes

Pontet-Canet

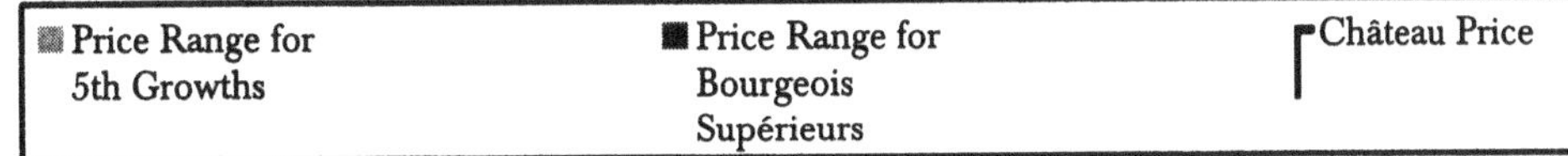

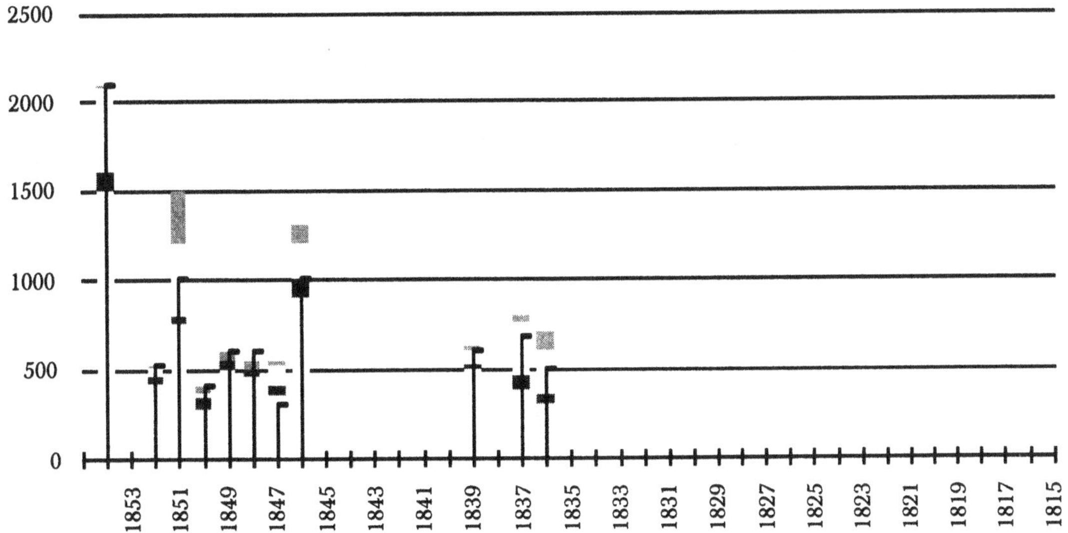

Château Batailley/Haut-Batailley

Year	Price	Current Name	Other Notes
1854	—	Batailley	9½ tuns/kept for the house [Barton & Guestier]
1853	—	Batailley	33 tuns/Barton & Guestier
1852	525	Batailley	75½ tuns/November 1852
1851	600	Batailley	79 tuns/December 1851
1850	—	Batailley	67 tuns/April 1851
1849	500	Batailley	60 tuns/September 1850
1848	450	Batailley	70 tuns/March 1849
1847	525	Batailley	75 tuns/January 1848
1846	1100	Batailley	60 tuns/December 1846
1845	—	Batailley	45 tuns
1844	—	Batailley	72 tuns/Barton & Guestier/1844
1843	—	Batailley	20 tuns
1842	500	Batailley	47 tuns/March 1843
1841	700	Batailley	60 tuns/November 1842
1840	700	Batailley	100 tuns/fine
1839	725	Batailley	50 tuns/March 1840
1838	700	Batailley	135 tuns/good/1845
1837	1000	Guestier	83 tuns/fine/In-house [Barton & Guestier]/1837
1836	750	Guestier	64 tuns/January 1837
1835	550	Batailley	85 tuns/fine/January 1836
1834	1200	Guestier	32 tuns/good/kept by the house [Barton & Guestier]
1833	600	Guestier	84 tuns/good/December 1833
1832	750	Guestier	52 tuns/ordinary/February 1833
1831	—	Guestier	20 tuns/quite good/employed

Year	Price	Current Name	Other Notes
1830	—	Batailley (Bedou)	4 tuns
1829	425	Batailley (Bedou)	40 tuns
1828	600	Batailley (Bedou)	70 tuns
1827	—	Batailley (Bedou)	English
1826	—	Batailley (Bedou)	English
1825	—	Batailley (Bedou)	English
1824	—	Batailley (Bedou)	No trades reported
1823	560	Batailley (Bedou)	80 tuns
1822	950	Batailley (Bedou)	45 tuns
1821			No listings for 1821
1820			No listings for 1820
1819	700	Batailley (Bedou)	60 tuns
1818	1000	Batailley (Bedou)	No other notes
1817			No listings for 1817
1816			No listings for 1816
1815	800	Batailley (Bedou)	No other notes
1775	270–300	Batailley (Bedou)	No other notes

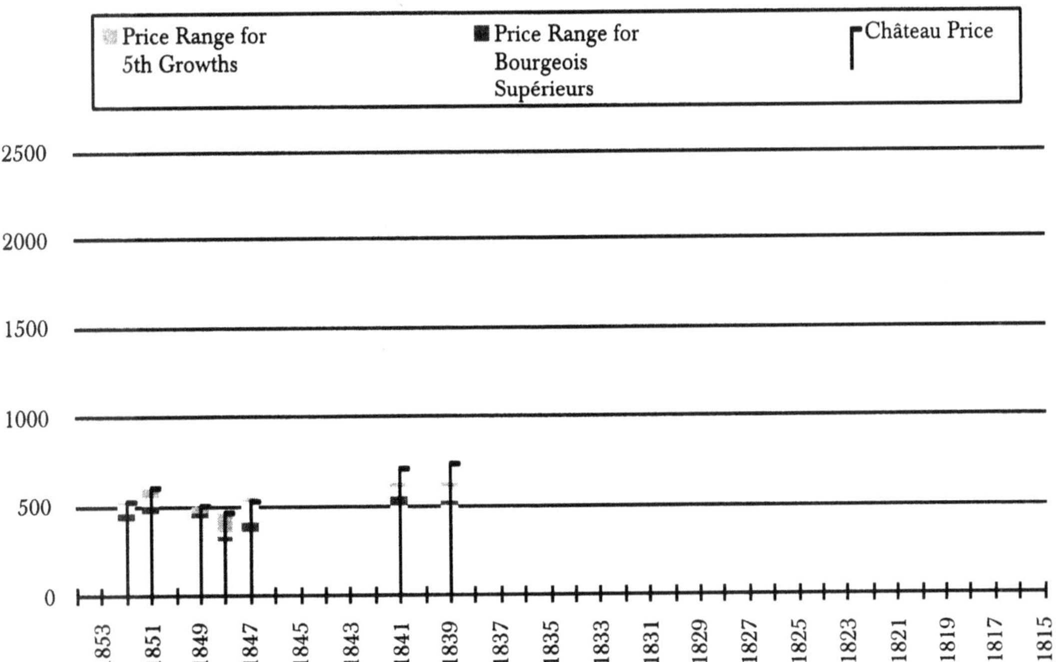

Château Grand-Puy-Lacoste

Year	Price	Current Name	Other Notes
1854	2100	Lacoste	12 tuns/December 1854
1853	—	Lacoste	53 tuns/November 1856
1852	525	Lacoste	95 tuns/January 1853
1851	575	Lacoste	100 tuns/50 tuns/December 1851
1850	375	Lacoste	100 tuns/April 1851
1849	1000	Lacoste	77 tuns
1848	600	Lacoste	100 tuns/December 1849
1847	475	Lacoste	125 tuns/February 1848
1846	1000	Lacoste	66 tuns
1845	350	Lacoste	80 tuns/April 1847
1844	1300	Lacoste	100 tuns/October 1844
1843	425	Lacoste	42 tuns/March 1846
1842	400	Lacoste	75 tuns/March 1843
1841	1000	Lacoste	100 tuns/December 1843
1840	500	Lacoste	125 tuns
1839	625	Lacoste	70 tuns/good/February 1840
1838	325	Lacoste	100 tuns/supple/October 1842
1837	—	Lacoste	116 tuns/elegant
1836	500	Lacoste	90 tuns/1841
1835	650	Lacoste	100 tuns/light/February 1836
1834	1225	Lacoste	50 tuns/rich/November 1834
1833	630	Lacoste	130 tuns/January 1834
1832	800	Lacoste	85 tuns/perfect/with the 1830/January 1833
1831	1200	Lacoste	33 tuns/very good

Year	Price	Current Name	Other Notes
1830	800	S[t] Guirons au G. Puy	12 tuns
1829	350	St Guirons au G. Puy	100 tuns
1828	600	St Guirons au G. Puy	50 tuns
1827	700	St Guirons au G. Puy	80 tuns
1826	700	St Guirons au G. Puy	No other notes
1825	1500	St Guirons au G. Puy	No other notes
1824	—	St Guirons au G. Puy	No trades reported
1823	560	St Guirons au G. Puy	80 tuns
1822	1000	St Guirons au G. Puy	No other notes
1821			No listings for 1821
1820			No listings for 1820
1819	800	St Guirons au G. Puy	80 tuns
1818	1300	St Guirons au G. Puy	No other notes
1817			No listings for 1817
1816			No listings for 1816
1815	1200	St Guirons au G. Puy	55 tuns
1775	370–400	St Guirons au G. Puy	No other notes

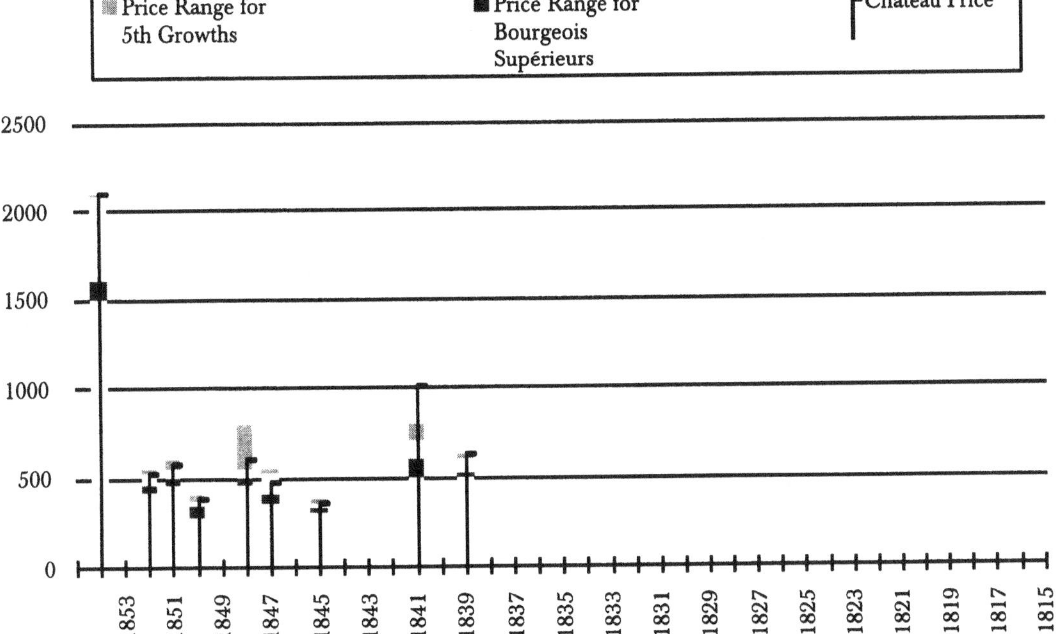

Château Grand-Puy-Ducasse

Year	Price	Current Name	Other Notes
1854	2100	Ducasse	26 tuns/June 1856
1853	900	Ducasse	53 tuns
1852	800	Ducasse	90 tuns/December 1853
1851	1000	Ducasse	95 tuns/several tuns
1850	850	Ducasse	110 tuns/partial sale/October 1855
1849	500	Chauvet	96 tuns/1851–1852
1848	450	Chauvet	110 tuns/September 1849
1847	300	de Chauvet	120 tuns/July 1848
1846	825	de Chauvet	94 tuns/partial sale
1845	350	Ducasse	100 tuns/September 1846
1844	1200	Chauvet	100 tuns/October 1844
1843	375	Chauvet	55 tuns/October 1845
1842	450	Chauvez	90 tuns/August 1843
1841	1000	Chauvez	110 tuns/March 1844
1840	600	Ducasse	130 tuns/beautiful
1839	600	Chauvet	90 tuns/good/February 1840
1838	400	Chauvet	120 tuns/August 1842
1837	675	Ducasse	118 tuns/good/April 1838
1836	475	Chauvet	85 tuns/good/September 1837
1835	650	Ducasse	90 tuns/good/February 1836
1834	1250	Ducasse	35 tuns/v. successful/November 1834
1833	600	Ducasse	116 tuns/quite good finish/December 1833
1832	750	Ducasse	80 tuns/very good/January 1833
1831	1100	Ducasse	24 tuns/elegant

Year	Price	Current Name	Other Notes
1830	550	Ducasse au G. Puy	18½ tuns
1829	300	Ducasse au G. Puy	92 tuns
1828	600	Ducasse au G. Puy	80 tuns
1827	625	Ducasse au G. Puy	110 tuns
1826	600	Ducasse au G. Puy	No other notes
1825	1500	Ducasse au G. Puy	No other notes
1824	—	Ducasse au G. Puy	No trades reported
1823	560	Ducasse au G. Puy	90 tuns
1822	1100	Ducasse au G. Puy	No other notes
1821			No listings for 1821
1820			No listings for 1820
1819	—	Ducasse au G. Puy	50 tuns
1818	1300	Ducasse au G. Puy	No other notes
1817			No listings for 1817
1816			No listings for 1816
1815	1200	Ducasse au G. Puy	50 tuns
1775	370–400	Ducasse au G. Puy	No other notes

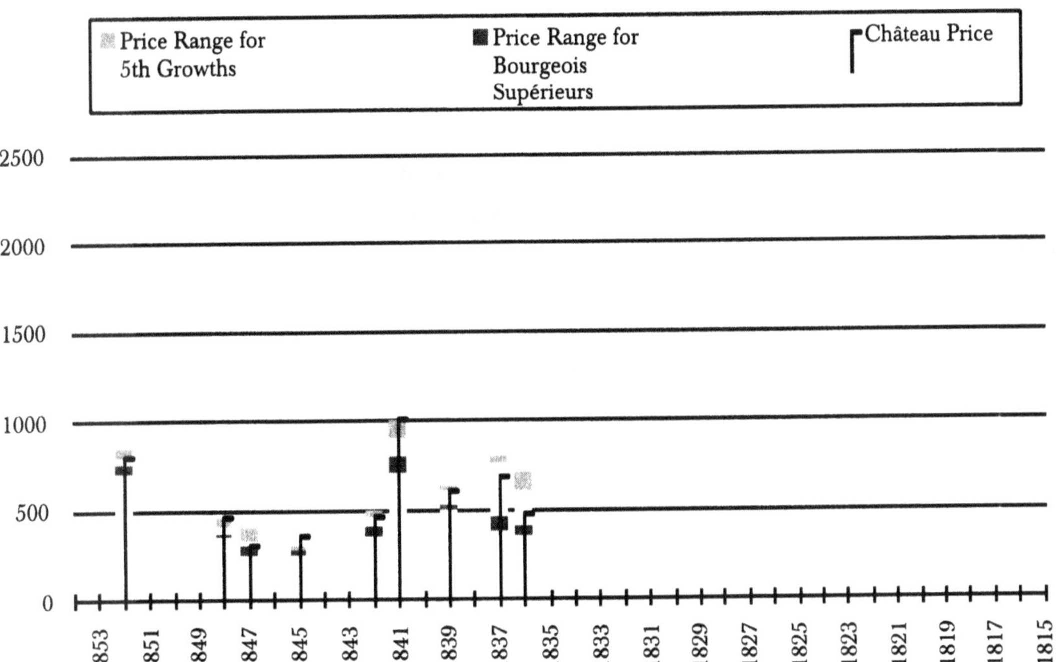

Château Lynch-Bages

Year	Price	Current Name	Other Notes
1854	2000	Jurine	12 tuns/January 1856
1853	700	Jurine	35 tuns/November 1856
1852	525	Jurine	90 tuns/December 1852
1851	750	Jurine	67 tuns/September 1852
1850	—	Jurine	82 tuns
1849	—	Jurine	40 tuns
1848	400	Jurine	67 tuns/September 1849
1847	300	Jurine	115 tuns/August 1848
1846	825	Jurine	54 tuns/partial sale
1845	325	Jurine	70 tuns
1844	1400	Jurine	62 tuns/1849
1843	375	Jurine	46 tuns/October 1845
1842	625	Jurine	60 tuns/1846
1841	750	Jurine	79 tuns/March 1843
1840	700	Jurine	95 tuns/good/March 1842
1839	650	Jurine	52 tuns/good/February 1840
1838	750	Jurine	80 tuns/v. good/September 1839
1837	675	Jurine	84 tuns/good/January 1838
1836	600	Jurine	73 tuns/1840
1835	650	Jurine	80 tuns/good/February 1836
1834	1225	Jurine	46 tuns/good/November 1834
1833	615	Jurine	100 tuns/good wine/January 1834
1832	750	Lynch	60 tuns/good/January 1833
1831	1225	Jurine	21 tuns

Year	Price	Current Name	Other Notes
1830	500	Lynch Batges	24 tuns
1829	310	Lynch Batges	60 tuns
1828	600	Lynch Batges	60 tuns
1827	—	Lynch Batges	98 tuns
1826	900	Lynch Batges	No other notes
1825	1800	Lynch Batges	No other notes
1824	—	Lynch Batges	30 tuns
1823	560	Lynch Batges	No other notes
1822	1000	Lynch Batges	No other notes
1821			No listings for 1821
1820			No listings for 1820
1819	700	Lynch Batges	85 tuns
1818	1200	Lynch Batges	45 tuns
1817			No listings for 1817
1816			No listings for 1816
1815	1200	Lynch Batges	62 tuns
1775	370–400	Lynch Batges	No other notes

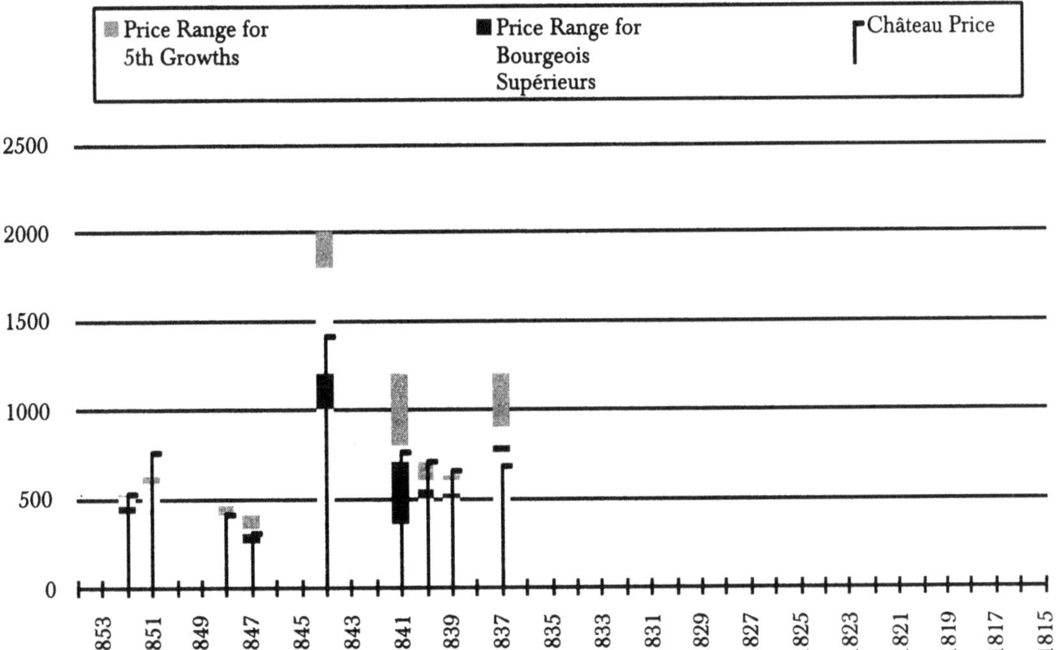

Château Lynch-Moussas

Year	Price	Current Name	Other Notes
1854	2100	Moussas	10 tuns/December 1854
1853	800	Moussas	36 tuns/February 1857
1852	525	Moussas	90 tuns/December 1852
1851	575	Moussas	88 tuns/November 1851
1850	900	Moussas	95 tuns/April 1853
1849	600	Moussas	January 1852
1848	525	Moussas	80 tuns/December 1849
1847	395	Moussas	66 tuns/partial sale/December 1848
1846	—	Moussas	40 tuns
1845	—	Moussas	No trades reported
1844	1200	Moussas	50 tuns/August 1844
1843	375	Moussas	15 tuns/August 1845
1842	425	Moussas	36 tuns/March 1843
1841	550	Moussas	41 tuns/September 1842
1840	550	Lynch Moussas	59 tuns
1839	550	Lynch Moussas	32 tuns/good/December 1839
1838	—	Moussas	No trades reported
1837	600	Lynch Moussas	50 tuns/good/1838
1836	750	Lynch Moussas	56 tuns/January 1837
1835	575	Lynch Moussas	40 tuns/good/February 1836
1834	800	Peyrounier	16 tuns/May 1835
1833	500	Peyrounier	40 tuns/July 1834
1832			Does not appear in 1832
1831	850	Peyrounier	10 tuns/very good

Year	Price	Current Name	Other Notes
1830	500	Peyrońet	6¾ tuns
1829	—	Peyrońet	14 tuns
1828	450	Peyrońet	19 tuns
1827	—	Peyrońet	22 tuns
1826	450	Peyrońet	No other notes
1825	1200	Peyrońet	No other notes
1824	—	Peyrońet	18 tuns
1823	320	Peyrońet	18 tuns
1822	500	Peyrońet	No other notes
1821			No listings for 1821
1820			No listings for 1820
1819	600	Peyrońet	42 tuns
1818	900–1000	Peyrońet	No other notes
1817			No listings for 1817
1816			No listings for 1816
1815	650	Peyrońet	12 tuns
1775	—	Peyrońet	No other notes

Lynch-Moussas

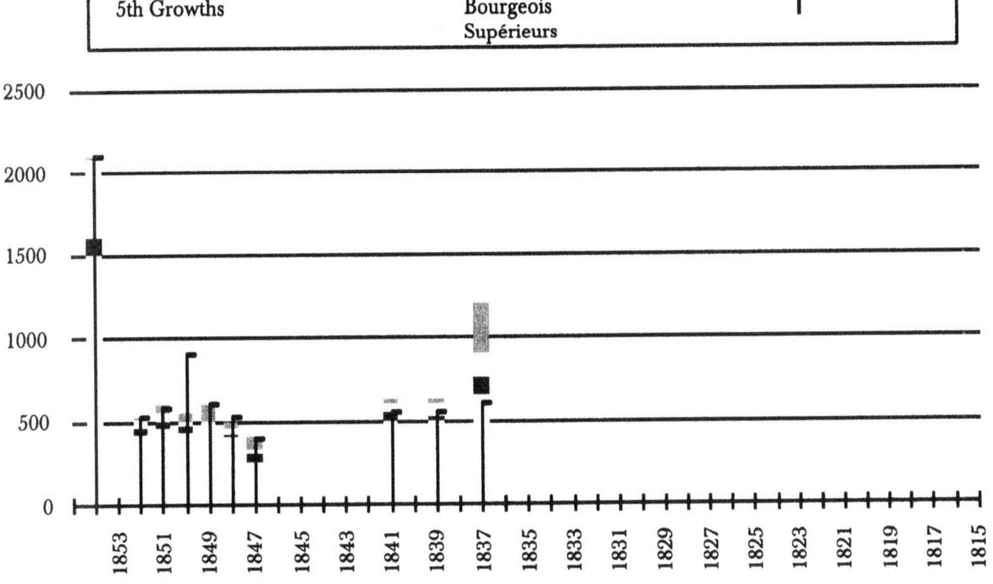

Note: In January 1852, prices for bourgeois superiéurs from 1849 were 500–550.

Château Dauzac

Year	Price	Current Name	Other Notes
1854	2000	Lynch	19 tuns/December 1854
1853	575	Lynch	September 1856
1852	500	Lynch	57 tuns/November 1852
1851	600	Lynch	60 tuns/November 1851
1850	450	Lynch	41 tuns/November 1851
1849	525	Lynch	39 tuns/January 1851
1848	425	Lynch	80 tuns/March 1849
1847	400	Lynch	75 tuns/January 1849
1846	650	Lynch	17 tuns/May 1851
1845	315	Lynch	60 tuns/1846
1844	1300	Lynch	60 tuns/September 1844
1843	425	Lynch	35 tuns/with the 1842
1842	425	Lynch	48 tuns/together with the 1843
1841	600	Lynch	80 tuns/March 1843
1840	550	Lynch	70 tuns/fine/March 1842
1839	550	Lynch	50 tuns/good/January 1840
1838	400	Lynch	58 tuns/good
1837	550	Lynch	84 tuns/May 1839
1836	500	Lynch	50 tuns/good/October 1838
1835	625	Lynch	50 tuns/very good/1836
1834	1200	Lynch	10 tuns/good/March 1836
1833	800	Lynch	40 tuns/ripe/October 1834
1832	800	Lynch	37 tuns/January 1833
1831	1200	Lynch	15 tuns/good

Year	Price	Current Name	Other Notes
1830	—	Lynch	No trades reported
1829	—	Lynch	No trades reported
1828	—	Lynch	40 tuns
1827	—	Lynch	No trades reported
1826	—	Lynch	No trades reported
1825	1400	Lynch	No other notes
1824	—	Lynch	No trades reported
1823	500	Lynch	65 tuns
1822	900	Lynch	No other notes
1821			No listings for 1821
1820			No listings for 1820
1819	700	Lynch	60 tuns
1818	900	Lynch	No other notes
1817			No listings for 1817
1816			No listings for 1816
1815	900	Lynch	24 tuns
1775	320–350	Lynch	No other notes

Dauzac

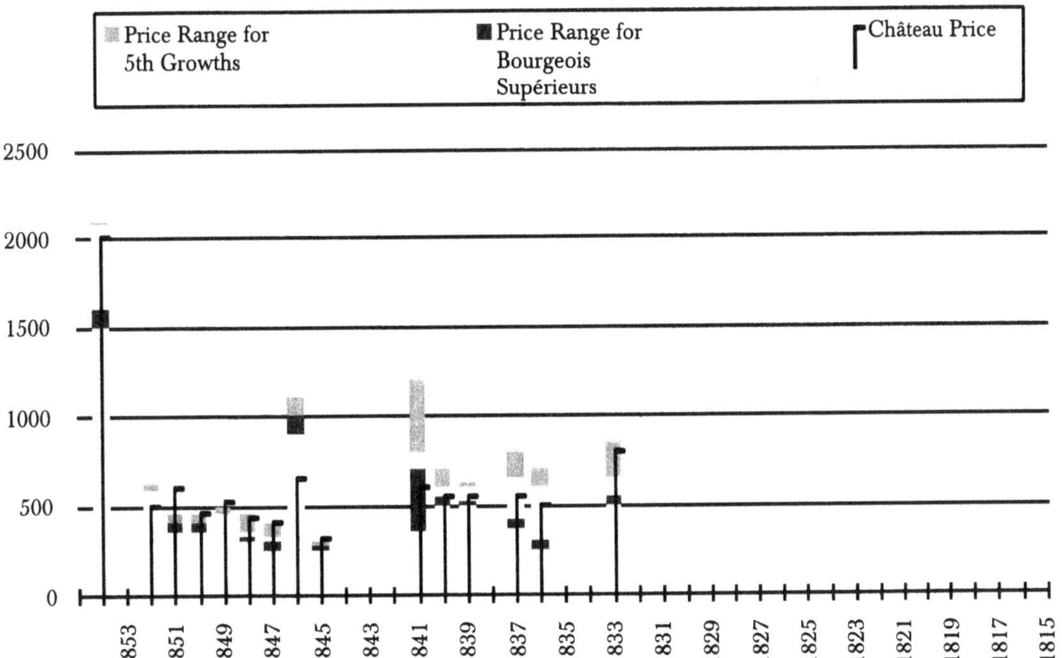

Château Mouton-d'Armailhac

Year	Price	Current Name	Other Notes
1854	2050	d'Armailhacq	23 tuns/December 1854
1853	650	d'Armailhac	50 tuns/August 1856
1852	525	d'Armailhacq	105 tuns/December 1852
1851	1800	d'Armailhacq	81 tuns/March 1857
1850	400	d'Armailhac	92 tuns/partial sale/March 1852
1849	—	D'Armailhac	94 tuns
1848	400	D'Armailhac	110 tuns/September 1849
1847	300	D'Armailhac	160 tuns/June 1848
1846	—	D'Armailhac	110 tuns
1845	325	D'Armaillacq	130 tuns/September 1846
1844	1300	D'Armailhacq	100 tuns/October 1844
1843	—	D'Armailhacq	50 tuns
1842	400	Darmaillacq	106 tuns/March 1843
1841	400	Darmaillacq	130 tuns/June 1843
1840	550	Darmaillac	174 tuns/good
1839	650	Darmaillacq	86 tuns/fine/February 1840
1838	480	D'Armaillacq	135 tuns/to see/July 1842
1837	600	Darmaillacq	148 tuns/good/August 1838
1836	500	Darmaillacq	120 tuns/several sales throughout 1840
1835	650	Darmaillacq	140 tuns/good/February 1836
1834	1200	Darmaillac	70 tuns/mellow/November 1834
1833	600	Darmaillacq	180 tuns/supple/January 1834
1832	700	Darmaillac	120 tuns/very good/January 1833
1831	1400	Darmaillac	45 tuns/ordinary

Year	Price	Current Name	Other Notes
1830	600	Darmailhac	40 tuns
1829	325	Darmailhac	180 tuns
1828	600	Darmailhac	145 tuns
1827	1200	Darmailhac	No other notes
1826	820	Darmailhac	No other notes
1825	1500	Darmailhac	No other notes
1824	—	Darmailhac	No trades reported
1823	540	Darmailhac	180 tuns
1822	1000	Darmailhac	70 tuns
1821			No listings for 1821
1820			No listings for 1820
1819	650	Darmailhac	176 tuns
1818	1200	Darmailhac	No other notes
1817			No listings for 1817
1816			No listings for 1816
1815	1000	Darmailhac	110 tuns
1775	370–400	Darmailhac	No other notes

Mouton-d'Armailhac

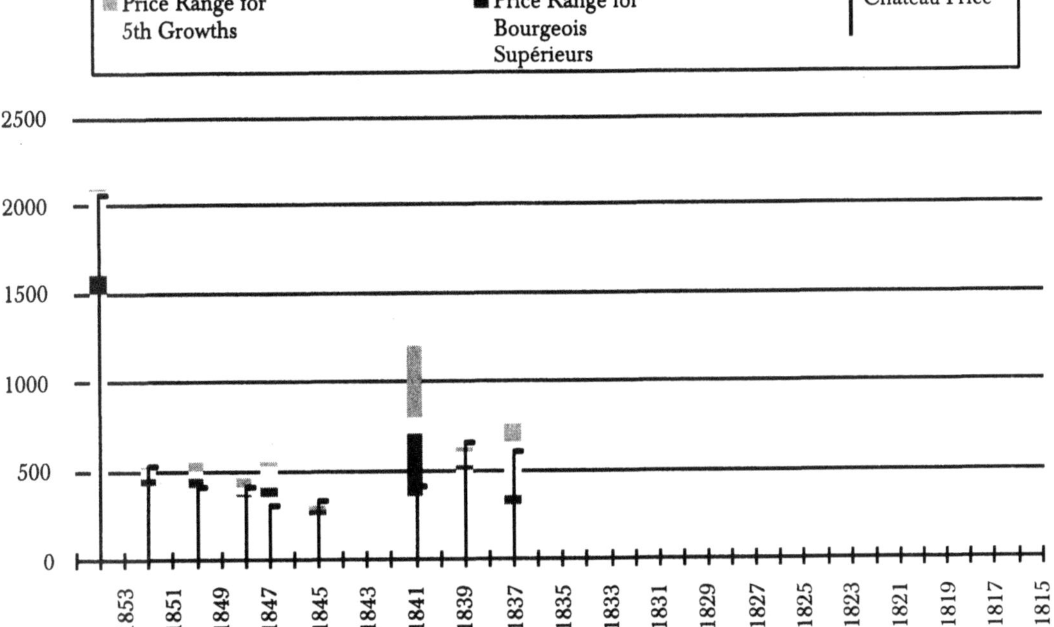

Château du Tertre

Year	Price	Current Name	Other Notes
1854	2000	Henry	8 tuns/July 1856
1853	600	Henry	No other notes
1852	700	Henry	40 tuns/January 1853
1851	1600	Tertre	60 tuns
1850	400	Tertre	42 tuns/July 1852
1849	630	Tertre	42 tuns/April 1852
1848	725	Tertre	50 tuns/September 1850
1847	475	Tertre	40 tuns/March 1849
1846	—	Tertre	No trades recorded
1845	300	Tertre	20 tuns
1844	1200	Tertre	12 tuns/January 1846
1843	—	Tertre	No trades reported
1842	450	Tertre	18 tuns/September 1843
1841	400	Tertre	30 tuns/March 1843
1840	425	Bresetz	20 tuns/good
1839	500	Tertre	25 tuns/thin/March 1840
1838	425	Tertre	35 tuns/March 1839
1837	400	Tertre	52 tuns/good/December 1837
1836	425	Tertre	40 tuns/February 1837
1835	450	Tertre	30 tuns/good/January 1836
1834	1000	Tertre	17 tuns/April 1835
1833	450	Le Tertre	45 tuns/thin/January 1834
1832	650	Le Tertre	16 tuns/thin/December 1832
1831	1100	Bresetz	8 tuns

Year	Price	Current Name	Other Notes
1830		Tertre (Ducluseau)	No listings for 1830
1829			No listings for 1829
1828			No listings for 1828
1827			No listings for 1827
1826			No listings for 1826
1825	1350	Tertre (Ducluseau)	No other notes
1824	—	Tertre (Ducluseau)	12 tuns
1823	325	Tertre (Ducluseau)	30 tuns
1822	—	Tertre (Ducluseau)	No trades reported
1821			No listings for 1821
1820			No listings for 1820
1819	660	Tertre (Ducluseau)	17 tuns
1818	900	Tertre (Ducluseau)	15 tuns
1817			No listings for 1817
1816			No listings for 1816
1815	900	Tertre (Ducluseau)	27 tuns
1775	350–400	Tertre (Ducluseau)	No other notes

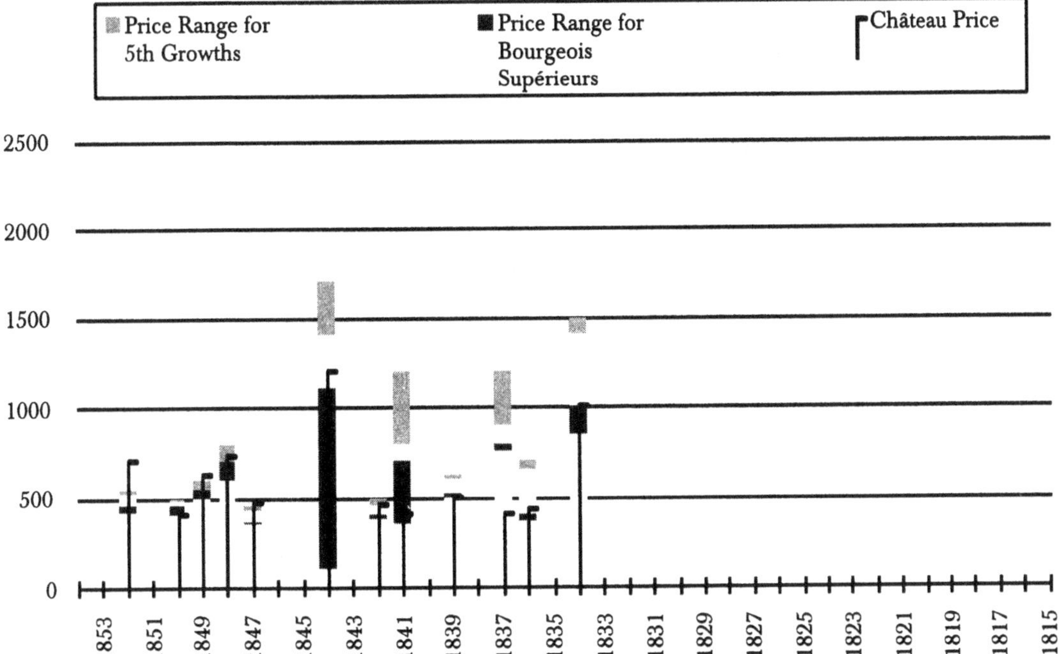

Château Haut-Bages-Libéral

Year	Price	Current Name	Other Notes
1854	2000	Libéral	2½ tuns/October 1855
1853	600	Liberal	8 tuns/Easter 1856
1852	—	Libéral	20 tuns
1851			No listings for 1851
1850		Libéral	No trades reported
1849	—	Libéral	No trades reported
1848	—	Libéral	No trades reported
1847	500	Libéral	January 1848
1846	—	Libéral	December 1846
1845	300	Libéral	July 1846
1844	1200	Libéral	1844
1843	—	Libéral	15 tuns/1845
1842	500	Libéral	18 tuns/February 1844
1841	—	Libéral	26 tuns as futures
1840	—	Libéral	38 tuns/good/to Paris
1839	—	Libéral	20 tuns/good
1838	—	Libéral	30 tuns/very good
1837	—	Libéral	32 tuns/1837
1836	800	Libéral	29 tuns/December 1836
1835	—	Libéral	good/sent to Holland
1834	1000	Libéral	good/November 1834
1833	—	Darribaux	Holland
1832	750	Darribaux (now Libéral)	No other notes
1831	—	Darribaux	No other notes

Year	Price	Current Name	Other Notes
1830	—	Libéral	9 tuns
1829	—	Libéral	No trades reported
1828	—	Libéral	11 tuns
1827	650	Libéral	14 tuns
1826	—	Libéral	No trades reported
1825	1400	Libéral	No other notes
1824	—	Libéral	No trades reported
1823	500	Libéral	No other notes
1822	—	Libéral	No trades reported
1821			No listings for 1821
1820			No listings for 1820
1819	500	Libéral	14 tuns
1818	575	Libéral	No other notes
1817			No listings for 1817
1816			No listings for 1816
1815	650	Libéral	8 tuns
1775	—	Libéral	No other notes

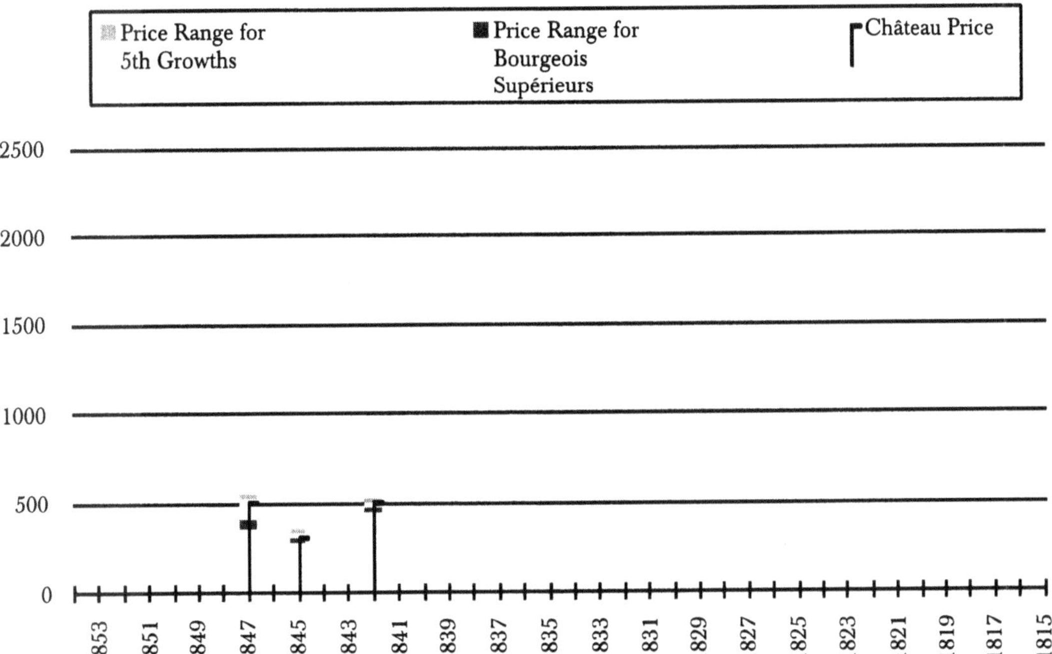

Château Pédesclaux

Year	Price	Current Name	Other Notes
1854	2100	Pédesclaux	4 tuns/December 1854
1853	700	Pédesclaux	11 tuns/August 1855
1852	525	Pédesclaux	25 tuns/December 1852
1851			No listings for 1851
1850	425	Pédesclaux	24 tuns/June 1852
1849	—	Pédesclaux	10 tuns
1848	600	Pédesclaux	23 tuns/November 1850
1847	300	Pédesclaux	30 tuns/October 1848
1846	—	Pédesclaux	15 tuns
1845	—	Pédesclaux	1846
1844	1200	Pédesclaux	20 tuns/October 1844
1843	—	Pédesclaux	16 tuns/1845
1842	—	Pédesclaux	22 tuns
1841	1000	Pédesclaux	23 tuns/August 1844
1840	600	Pédesclaux	32 tuns/good
1839	600	Pédesclaux	20 tuns/good/February 1840
1838	—	Pédesclaux	33 tuns/fine
1837	525	Pédesclaux	30 tuns/fine/1837
1836	450	Pédesclaux	27 tuns/September 1840
1835	525	Pédesclaux	32 tuns/thin/February 1836
1834	1100	Pédesclaux	26 tuns/very good/November 1834
1833	525	Pédesclaux	36 tuns/quite nice/December 1833
1832	700	Pédesclaux	28 tuns/very good/January 1833
1831	1000	Pédesclaux	9 tuns/very good

Year	Price	Current Name	Other Notes
1830	—	Pédesclaux	9 tuns
1829	—	Pédesclaux	No trades reported
1828	450	Pédesclaux	25 tuns
1827	500	Pédesclaux	25 tuns
1826	500	Pédesclaux	18 tuns
1825	1400	Pédesclaux	No other notes
1824	—	Pédesclaux	No trades reported
1823	500	Pédesclaux	30 tuns
1822	550–600	Pédesclaux	No other notes
1821			No listings for 1821
1820			No listings for 1820
1819	—	Pédesclaux	No trades reported
1818	1000	Pédesclaux	No other notes
1817			No listings for 1817
1816			No listings for 1816
1815	1000	Pédesclaux	No other notes
1775	250–260	Pédesclaux	No other notes

Pédesclaux

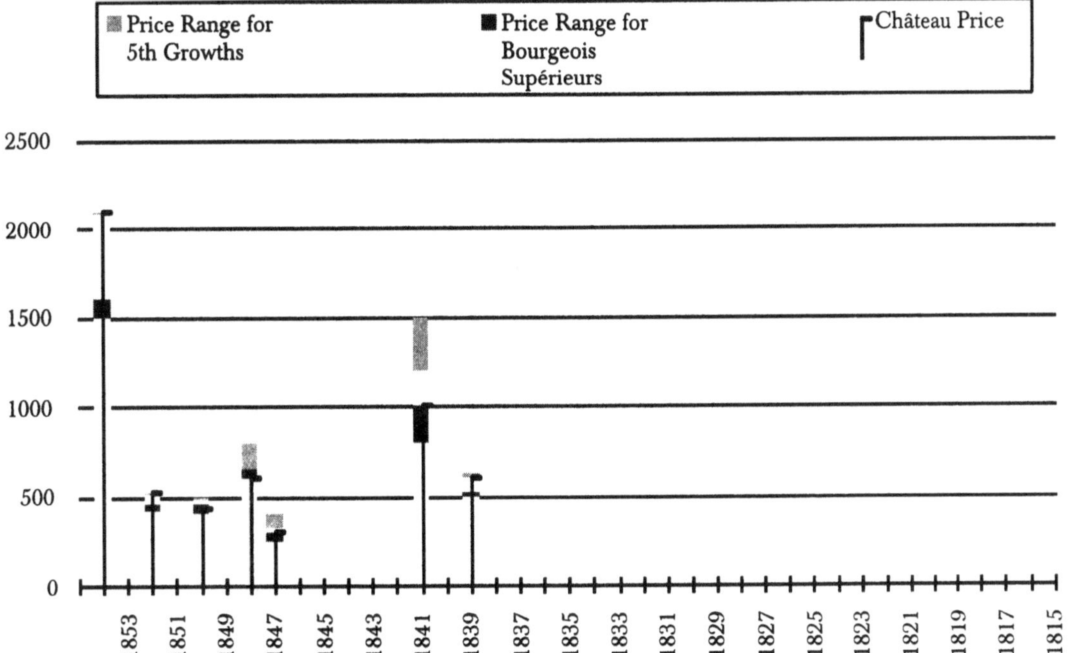

Château Belgrave

Year	Price	Current Name	Other Notes
1854	1800	Devez	14½ tuns/November 1855
1853	—	Devez	21 tuns
1852	1050	Devez	49 tuns/March 1857
1851	1000	Devez	42 tuns/December 1852
1850	—	Devez	50 tuns
1849	500	Devez	partial sale/March 1852
1848	600	Devez	70 tuns
1847	300	Devez	70 tuns/August 1848
1846	—	Devez	55 tuns
1845	325	Devez	1846
1844	700	Devez	55 tuns/March 1849
1843	380	Devez	20 tuns/August 1845
1842	450	Devez	47 tuns/August 1845
1841	1300	Devez	May 1844
1840	600	Devez	68 tuns/good
1839	625	Boisé	36 tuns/good/March 1840
1838	500	Devez	40 tuns
1837	650	Devez	52 tuns/March 1838
1836	500	Devez	45 tuns/1841
1835	625	Roué	35 tuns/ordinary/February 1836
1834	1225	Devez	12 tuns/November 1834
1833	600	Coutanceau	19 tuns/very good/January 1833
1832	775	Dubos	18 tuns/good/May 1833
1831	1200	Coutanceau	13 tuns

Year	Price	Current Name	Other Notes
1830	—	Coutanceau	No trades reported
1829	230	Coutanceau	28 tuns
1828	—	Coutanceau	30 tuns
1827	—	Coutanceau	45 tuns
1826	—	Coutanceau	No trades reported
1825	1200	Coutanceau	No other notes
1824	—	Coutanceau	No trades reported
1823	560	Coutanceau	No other notes
1822	—	Coutanceau	No trades reported
1821			No listings for 1821
1820			No listings for 1820
1819	650	Coutanceau	18 tuns
1818	1000	Coutanceau	15 tuns
1817			No listings for 1817
1816			No listings for 1816
1815	1000	Coutanceau	15 tuns
1775	—	Coutanceau	No other notes

Belgrave

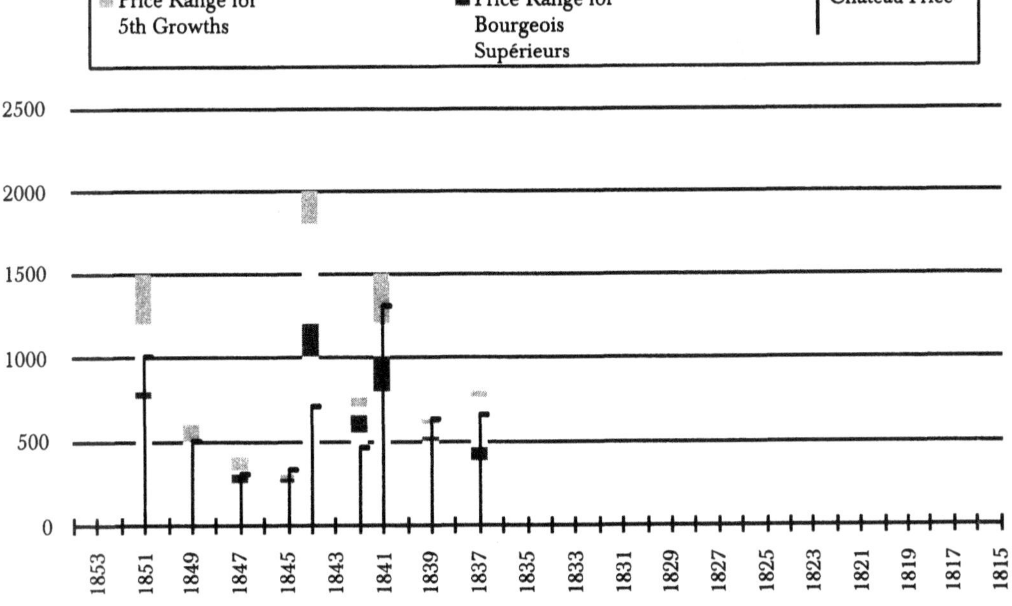

Note: In March 1852, prices for bourgeois superiéurs from 1849 were 500–550.

Château Camensac

Year	Price	Current Name	Other Notes
1854	1800	Popp	7½ tuns/December 1855
1853	—	Popp	18 tuns
1852	550	Popp	50 tuns/March 1853
1851	1000	Popp	60 tuns/December 1852
1850	425	Popp	45 tuns/with the 1849/September 1851
1849	425	Popp	35 tuns/with the 1850/September 1851
1848	400	Popp	80 tuns/September 1849
1847	300	Popp	80 tuns/August 1848
1846	—	Popp	52 tuns
1845	300	Popp	August 1846
1844	1200	Popp	45 tuns/February 1846
1843	380	Popp	15 tuns/September 1845
1842	400	Popp	48 tuns/April 1843
1841	1000	Popp	68 tuns/1846
1840	600	Popp	40 tuns/good
1839	—	Popp	27 tuns/elegant/February 1840
1838	500	Popp	30 tuns
1837	650	Popp	45 tuns/March 1838
1836	—	Popp	30 tuns
1835	550	Popp	20 tuns/fine/February 1836
1834	1250	Popp	10 tuns/December 1834
1833	600	Popp	19 tuns/very good/February 1834
1832	800	Poppe	15 tuns/excellent/February 1834
1831	1200	Popp	8 tuns/elegant

Year	Price	Current Name	Other Notes
1830	—	Camensac (Pope)	No trades reported
1829	300	Camensac (Pope)	18 tuns
1828	—	Camensac (Pope)	17 tuns
1827	—	Camensac (Pope)	28 tuns
1826	—	Camensac (Pope)	No trades reported
1825	1200	Camensac (Pope)	No other notes
1824	—	Camensac (Pope)	No trades reported
1823	560	Camensac (Pope)	No other notes
1822	850	Camensac (Pope)	No other notes
1821			No listings for 1821
1820			No listings for 1820
1819	625	Camensac (Pope)	20 tuns
1818	1000	Camensac (Pope)	18 tuns
1817			No listings for 1817
1816			No listings for 1816
1815	1000	Camensac (Pope)	25 tuns
1775	—	Camensac (Pope)	No other notes

Camensac

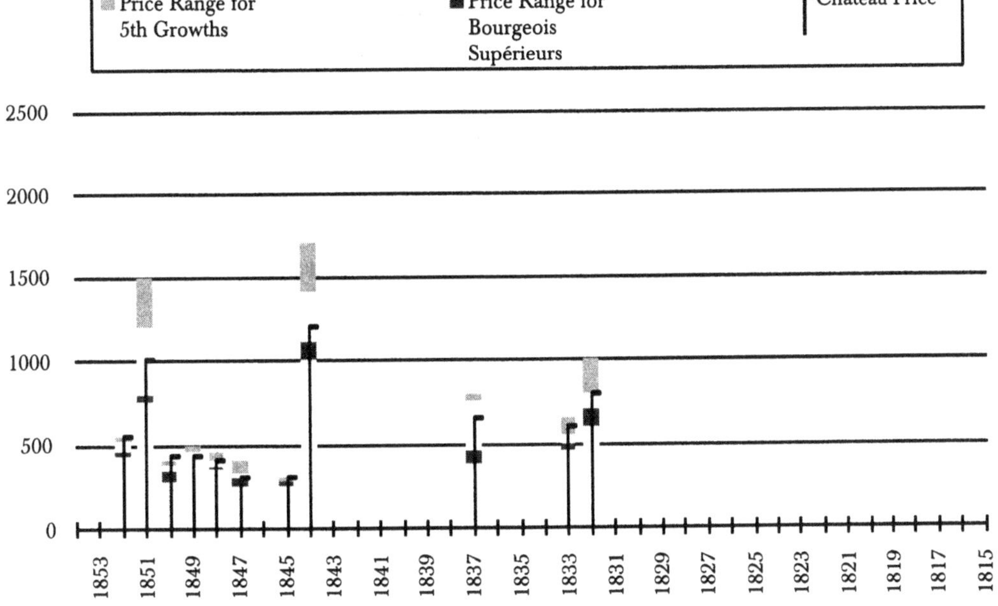

Note: In July 1852, prices for bourgeois superiéurs from 1849 were 450–500.

Château Cos-Labory

Year	Price	Current Name	Other Notes
1854	1800	Labory	15 tuns/December 1855
1853	—	Labory	No trades reported
1852	600	Labory	55 tuns/July 1853
1851	—	Labory	With Cos-d'Estournel/public auction
1850	—	Labory	With Cos-d'Estournel
1849		Labory	Does not appear
1848	—	Labory	With Cos-d'Estournel
1847	—	Labory	80 tuns/December 1848
1846	—	Labory	No trades reported
1845	250	Labory	May 1846
1844	1300	Labory	50 tuns/November 1844
1843	—	Labory	50 tuns/1844
1842	—	Labory	60 tuns/1843
1841	650	Labory	72 tuns/February 1843
1840	560	Labory	60 tuns/elegant
1839	575	Labory	10 tuns/January 1840
1838	—	Labory	63 tuns/elegant
1837	675	Labory Cos	75 tuns/fine/1838
1836	—	Labory	55 tuns
1835	350	Labory	26 tuns/spoiled/January 1837
1834	1200	Labory	37 tuns/supple/November 1834
1833	500	Labory	90 tuns/elegant finish/December 1833
1832	750	Labory	60 tuns/good/January 1833
1831	1100	Labory	14 tuns/thin at finish

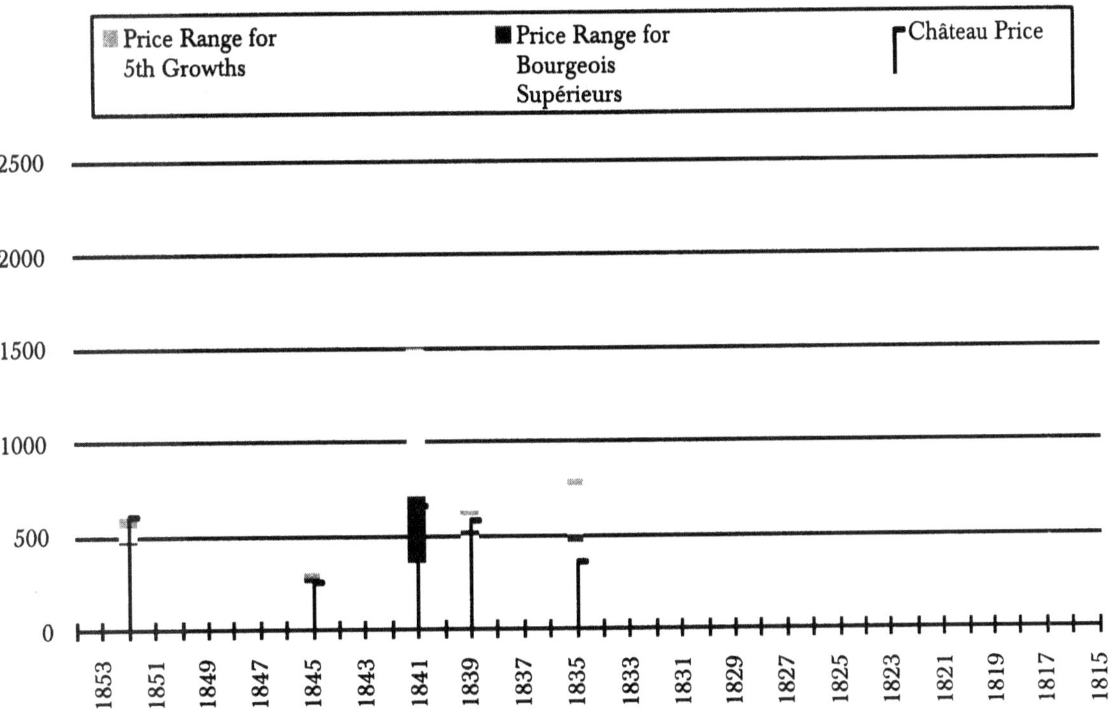
Cos Labory
Price Range for 5th Growths
Price Range for Bourgeois Supérieurs
Château Price
2500
2000
1500
1000
500
0
1853
1851
1849
1847
1845
1843
1841
1839
1837
1835
1833
1831
1829
1827
1825
1823
1821
1819
1817
1815

Château Clerc-Milon

Year	Price	Current Name	Other Notes
1854	1200	Clerc Milon	9½ tuns/November 1854
1853	550	Clerc Milon	28 tuns/July 1856
1852	500	Clerc	55 tuns/February 1853
1851			No listings for 1851
1850	—	Clerc Milon	80 tuns
1849		Clerc Milon	No trades recorded
1848	500	Clerc Milon	57 tuns/November 1849
1847	300	Clerc Milon	45 tuns/October 1848
1846	—	Clerc Milon	32 tuns
1845	—	Clerc Milon	30 tuns
1844	—	Clerc Milon	40 tuns
1843	—	Clerc Milon	16 tuns
1842	425	Clerc Milon	30 tuns/June 1845
1841	—	Clerc Milon	40 tuns
1840	—	Clerc	30 tuns/common
1839	—	Clerc	20 tuns/common
1838			Does not appear in 1838
1837	—	Clerc	32 tuns
1836	—	Clerc	No trades recorded
1835	550	Clerc	23 tuns/supple/April 1837
1834	—	Clerc Milon	14 tuns/good
1833		Clerc	Does not appear in 1833
1832	650	Clerc	23 tuns/thin/July 1833
1831			Does not appear in 1831

Year	Price	Current Name	Other Notes
1830	—	Clerc	5 tuns
1829	—	Clerc	No trades reported
1828	600	Clerc	No other notes
1827	—	Clerc	No trades reported
1826	470	Clerc	No other notes
1825	—	Clerc	No trades reported
1824	—	Clerc	No trades reported
1823	—	Clerc	No trades reported
1822	—	Clerc	No trades reported
1821			No listings for 1821
1820			No listings for 1820
1819	—	Clerc	No trades reported
1818	—	Clerc	No trades reported
1817			No listings for 1817
1816			No listings for 1816
1815	—	Clerc	No trades reported
1775	—	Clerc	No other notes

Clerc Milon

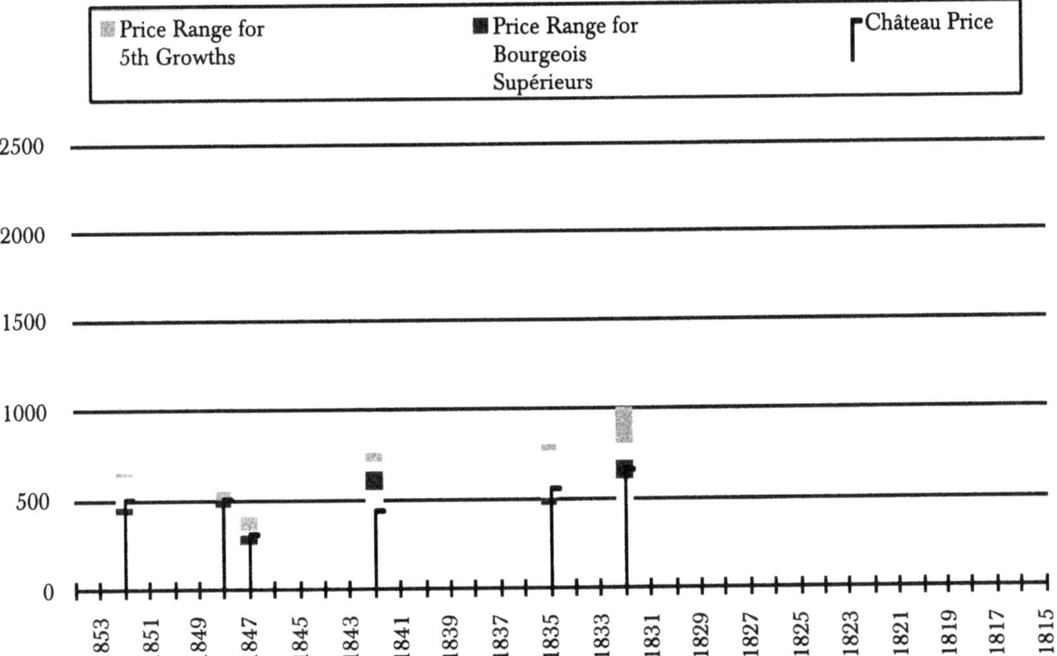

Château Croizet-Bages

Year	Price	Current Name	Other Notes
1854	2000	Croizet Bages	5 tuns
1853	—	Croizet Bages	January 1855
1852	700	Croizet Bages	51 tuns/November 1853
1851		Croizet Bages	47 tuns
1850	300	Croizet Bages	April 1851
1849	—	Croizet Bages	No trades recorded
1848	—	Croizet Bages	No trades recorded
1847	250	Croizet Bages	65 tuns/September 1848
1846	—	Croizet Bages	44 tuns
1845	250	Croizet Bages	50 tuns/June 1846
1844	1000	Croizet Bages	52 tuns/May & June 1845
1843	315	Croizet Bages	30 tuns/October 1845
1842	325	Croizet Bages	40 tuns/July 1843
1841	1000	Croizet Bages	75 tuns/1844
1840	—	Croizet Bages	90 tuns
1839	575	Croizet Bages	45 tuns/fine/February 1840
1838	400	Croizet Bages	70 tuns/good/July 1843
1837	550	Croizet Bages	70 tuns/fine/July 1838
1836	750	Croizet Bages	49 tuns
1835	650	Croizet Batges	62 tuns/December 1836
1834	1225	Croiset	34 tuns/good/November 1834
1833	600	Croiset Batges	72 tuns/January 1834
1832	750	Croiset Batges	49 tuns/thin at finish/February 1833
1831	1200	Croiset Batges	16 tuns/very good

Year	Price	Current Name	Other Notes
1830	—	Croiset Ve Batges	14 tuns
1829	350	Croiset Ve Batges	45 tuns
1828	600	Croiset Ve Batges	42 tuns
1827	750	Croiset Ve Batges	53 tuns
1826	550	Croiset Ve Batges	45 tuns
1825	1500	Croiset Ve Batges	No other notes
1824	—	Croiset Ve Batges	No trades reported
1823	500	Croiset Ve Batges	55 tuns
1822	1000	Croiset Ve Batges	40 tuns
1821			No listings for 1821
1820			No listings for 1820
1819	750	Croiset Ve Batges	53 tuns
1818	1000	Croiset Ve Batges	19 tuns
1817			No listings for 1817
1816			No listings for 1816
1815	900	Croiset Ve Batges	20 tuns
1775	270–300	Croiset Ve Batges	No other notes

Croizet-Bages

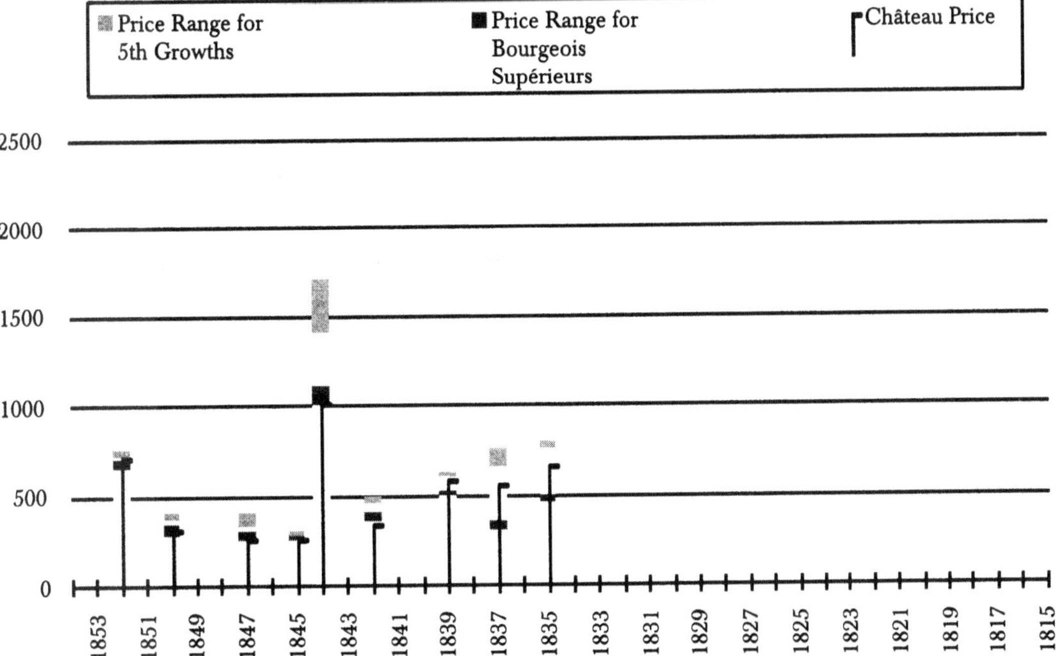

Château Cantemerle

Year	Price	Current Name	Other Notes
1854	2100	de Villeneuve	35 tuns/January 1855
1853	—	de Villeneuve	70 tuns/Holland
1852	—	de Villeneuve	170 tuns/Holland
1851	—	de Villeneuve	Shipped to Holland
1850	—	de Villeneuve	Holland
1849	—	Villeneuve	47 tuns/Holland
1848	—	Villeneuve	Holland
1847	—	Villeneuve	Holland
1846	—	Villeneuve	60 tuns/Holland
1845	—	Villeneuve	Holland
1844	—	Villeneuve	86 tuns/Holland
1843	—	Villeneuve	90 tuns/Holland
1842	—	Villeneuve	125 tuns/Holland
1841	—	Villeneuve	220 tuns/Holland
1840	—	de Villeneuve	200 tuns/Holland
1839	—	de Villeneuve	146 tuns/Holland/June 1840
1838	—	de Villeneuve	60 hogsheads/Holland/May 1839
1837	—	de Villeneuve	160 tuns/Holland
1836	—	de Villeneuve	124 tuns/Holland/June 1837
1835	—	de Villeneuve	125 tuns/48 hogsheads/June 1836
1834	—	Villeneuve	50 tuns/91 hogsheads/Holland
1833	—	Villeneuve	150 tuns/67–68 hogsheads/Holland
1832	—	Villeneuve	30 tuns/fine/shipped
1831	—	Villeneuve	42 tuns/good/shipped/wholesale

Year	Price	Current Name	Other Notes
1830	—	Villeneuve	25 tuns
1829	—	Villeneuve	No trades reported
1828	—	Villeneuve	No trades reported
1827	—	Villeneuve	No trades reported
1826	—	Villeneuve	No trades reported
1825	1500	Villeneuve	No other notes
1824	—	Villeneuve	No trades reported
1823	—	Villeneuve	63 wholesale/Holland
1822	—	Villeneuve	80 wholesale/Holland
1821			No listings for 1821
1820			No listings for 1820
1819	850	Villeneuve	Holland
1818	710	Villeneuve	Holland
1817			No listings for 1817
1816			No listings for 1816
1815	850	Villeneuve	60 tuns/Holland
1775	300–330	Villeneuve	No other notes

Cantemerle

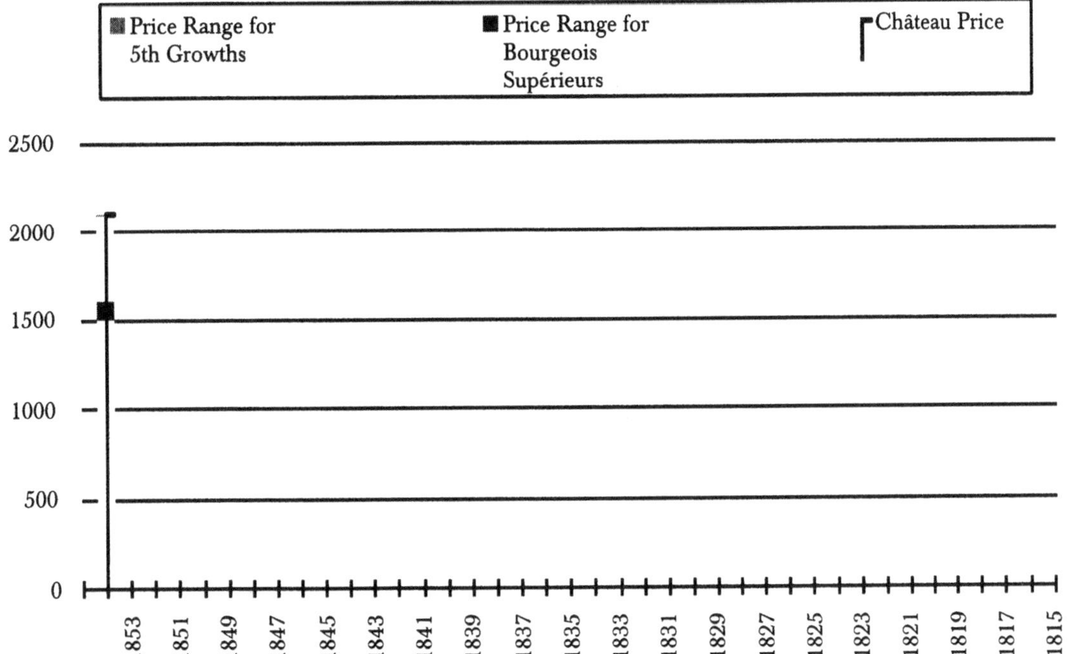

Appendix IV

DOCUMENTS FROM THE ARCHIVES OF THE BORDEAUX CHAMBER OF COMMERCE

One of the more common misconceptions about the 1855 brokers' classification is that only properties that sent their wines to the Universal Exposition in Paris became classed growths. In fact, the brokers' list was drawn up completely apart from the collection of samples by the Chamber of Commerce, and these were sent off to Paris before the brokers ever started work on their classification. As the following document in the Bordeaux Chamber of Commerce archives shows, there was less than complete representation among the classed-growth properties, while many non-classed growths were included in the display at the Universal Exposition. A property's presence or absence in the Chamber of Commerce's display had nothing to do with the brokers declaring it a classified growth or not.

This same list was reprinted in December 1855 on the front page of the Bordeaux daily newspaper La Gironde, *incorporating relatively minor changes. Most of the changes concerned the communal wines, but there was also the addition of Giscours and Lynch (Bages) among the classed growths responding to the Chamber of Commerce's request. Apparently their samples arrived too late to be included on this list or to be indicated by the markings on the broker's classification (both properties are marked "point"); nonetheless, wines from both properties appeared as part of the Chamber of Commerce's display at the Universal Exposition.*

List of Classed Growths [Sent to the Universal Exposition] According to the Labels Prepared [for the Bottles]

Mouton	Pauillac	M^{r} le Bon N. de Rothschild
Desmirail	Margaux	Mr Sipierre
Cos Destournel	St. Estèphe	Mr Martyns
Léoville 1847	St. Julien	M^{rs} le Marquis de las Cases
		le Baron de Poyféré
		Barton
Carnet	Pauillac	Mr de Pontet
Palmer	Canenac	Mr Emile Pereire
Château Margaux	Margaux	Mr Aguado
		Mis de las Marismas
Château Latour	Pauillac	Mrs de Beaumont
		de Courtivron
		de Flers
Château de Beychevelle	St. Julien	Mr P.F. Gustier Junior
Calon	St. Estèphe	Mr Sévère Lestapis de Paris
Château Lafitte 1846	Pauillac	Sir Samuel Scott, Baronnet
Château Lafite 1848	Pauillac	Sir Samuel Scott, Baronnet
Batailley 1844	Pauillac	Mr P.F. Guestier Junior
Carnet	St Laurent	Mr de Luetkens
St Pierre	St Julien	Mr Bontemps Dubary
		Mme Vve Roullet
		Mme Vve Galloupeau
Langoa 1846	St. Julien	Mr Barton
Grand Puy	Pauillac	Mr F. Lacoste aîné
Talbot	St Julien	M^{r} le Marquis d'aux
Haut Pessac		Mr Pomez
Haut Talence		Mr Pomez
Ducru	St Julien	Mrs Gevers & Stehelin
Grand vin Dubosc	St Julien	Mr Bertou
La Grange	St Julien	M^{r} le comte Duchatel
Vivens Durfort	Margaux	Mr de Puységur

List of Classed Growth White Wines

Suduiraut	Preignac	Mrs Guillot frères
Malle	Preignac	Mr Henry de Lur-Saluces
Romer	Preignac	M[r] le Comte de Lamyre Mory
Château Carbonnieux 2 cases	Graves	Mr Bouchereau
Crû de St Aman	Preignac	Mr Godard
Haut Sauternes	Guiraud	Mr Caubet Jeune
Commune de Bommes*		Lafaurie aîné
Commune de Cérons		Mr de Calvimont
Bergerac		Mr Raoul Balguerie
Haut Sauternes Guiraud		Mr Caubet Jeune

* In the version of this list which appeared in *La Gironde* on December 13, 1855, this property appears as "Peyraguey."

List of Communes and Cantons [Whose Wine Was Sent to the Universal Exposition] According to the Labels Prepared [for the Bottles]

Communes	Cantons
St Quentin	Branne
Floriac	Carbon-Blanc
Castillon	Castillon
Bayron	Bourg
St Ciers Lalande	St Ciers Lalande
Salles	Castillon
St Morillon	Labrède
Quinsac	Créon
St Michel de la Rivière	Fronsac
Bassens	Carbon-Blanc
Margueron	Ste Foy la Grande
St Médard Deyrans	Labrède
Pauillac	Pauillac Mr Darmailhac
Langoiran	Cadillac
St Avit de Soulège	Ste Foy
Prignac & Cazelle	Bourg
St Paul	Blaye
Plassac	Blaye
Cars	Blaye
Verdelais	St Macaire
St Christophe-de-Doubens	Coutras
Dardenac	Branne
Campugnan	Blaye
St Denis	Guitres
St Romain-la-Rivière	Fronsac
Villenave d'Ornon	Pessac
St Estèphe (2 cases)	Mr Lafon de Camarsac
St Trojean	Bourg
Fieux	Coutras
Ste Croix du Mont	Cadillac
Fronsac	Fronsac
Samonac	Bourg
Fargues	Créon
St Estèphe	Mr Luetkens Meyney
d'Eyrans	Bourg
du Pian	Blanquefort

Communes	**Cantons**
Mazion	Blaye
Ste André du Bois	St Macaire
Ste Médard de Guizière	Coutras
Virelade	Podensac
St Caprais	Créon
Pauillac	Pauillac
	Mr de Pichon de Longueville
Pessac	Pessac
Carbon-Blanc	Carbon-Blanc
Montferrand	Carbon-Blanc
d'Espiet	Branne
d'Arbanats	Podensac
Mérignac	Pessac
St Ciers d'Abzac	Guitres
Branne	Branne
Labarde	Castelneau
Comps	Bourg
Lugoud de l'Ile	Fronsac
La Bastide	Carbon-Blanc
Pauillac	de Pauillac
	Mr Jurine.
Margaux	Mme Vve Ferrière
Talence	Bordeaux
St Paul	Blaye
St Seurin de Cursac	Lesparre
Lansac	Bourg
Margaux	Mr Dubignon
Lamarque	Castelneau
Blaignan	Lesparre
Castelneau	Castelneau
Soussans	Castelneau
Margaux	Mr Lanoire
Dardenac	Branne
d'Avensan	Castelneau
Campugnan	Blaye
Moulis	Castelneau
St Ysans	Lesparre
Margaux (2 cases)	Castelneau
Ludon	Blanquefort

NOTES

Abbreviations used in notes:

ADG Archives Départementales de la Gironde.

CCLET *Copies de lettres de la chambre de commerce de Bordeaux.* Ledgers. January 19, 1853–February 9, 1855; February 9, 1855–September 24, 1856. Bordeaux Chamber of Commerce Archives

CCPV *Extraits des procès-verbaux, lettres et mémoires de la chambre de commerce de Bordeaux.* 2d ser. 5 (1854); 6 (1855); 7 (1856); 11 (1861); 12 (1862).

CLA Château Lafite Archives.

REU *Rapport sur l'exposition universelle de 1855: présenté à l'empereur par S.A.I. le prince Napoléon.* Paris: Imprimerie Impériale, 1857.

TLA Tastet & Lawton Archives.

Introduction

1. had learned nothing and forgot nothing: Napoléon Bonaparte, Proclamation of March 1, 1815.

2. "I will strive without end": Hauterive, 54.

2. "The working class has nothing": Bonaparte, *Extinction du paupérisme*, 11–12.

3. "We have immense uncultivated territories to clear": Séguin, 190.

6. a Bordeaux resident named Quinton: *La Guienne*, December 3, 1855.

7. "The progress of the human race": *Official Catalogue*, 2.

8. "If France had been able": *Moniteur Universel*, June 4, 1850.

8. "apparatus for aerating and clarifying Champagne": *Official Catalogue*, 241.

8. According to French explanations, wine itself was not admitted: *Moniteur Universel*, June 4, 1850.

8. "The whole range of alcohols": *Illustrated London News*, July 19, 1851.

8. "six bottles of champagne wine": ibid.

9. "I insist on claiming for France": REU, 2–3.

9. "The French exhibition of 1854": *Illustrated London News*, May 17, 1851.

Chapter 1

11. "The emperor, in his great concern": Minister of the Interior, Circular 20, April 8, 1853.

12. "For a long time": Princess Mathilde, *Revue des Deux Mondes*, 730.

13. "I believe that it is impossible": Strombeck, *Revue des Etudes Napoléoniennes*, 182.

13. "the same Roman-medal profile": Flammarion, 26.
13. "he had a 'hot finger'": La Rüe, 307.
14. "The Emperor": Girard, 193.
15. "I have learned with great sorrow": Hauterive, 75.
15. "From the day following my election": Ollivier, 177–178.
16. "the services rendered to industry": REU, 27.
18. "The Chamber": ADG, 8M-94.
19. "As to the ongoing question": CCPV, VI, 184.
21. Burgundy and Champagne were planning to send: ADG, 8M-94, Departmental Committee minutes.
21. "The Committee responsible": *L'Indicateur*, November 9, 1854; also *Memorial Bordelais*, November 9, 1854; *Courrier de la Gironde*, November 10, 1854.
22. "a great number": ADG, 8M-94, Departmental Committee minutes.
23. "Before giving a definitive answer": Bordeaux Chamber of Commerce Archives, carton 81, A, 308.

Chapter 2

26. "Sirs": Bordeaux Chamber of Commerce Archives, carton 81, A, 308.
27. "I'm impatient": Henri Courteault, 64.
27. "Engage yourself": ibid.
27. "My problem": ibid., 69.
28. "he was right": Gautier, 1st Year, 391.
29. "My ambition": Butel, 173.
29. "We face no danger here": Biarnez, 8.
29. "A distinguished new growth": *Le Producteur*, June 1838.
30. "For me, the touchstone of civilization": Butel, 190.
30. In 1838, the vineyard of Gorce: *Le Producteur*, March 1838.
30. the property of Rausan-Gassies was variously known: see the listing in Appendix III.
30. the case of Nicolas-Edme Guillot: Suduiraut, 379.
31. "This method of proceeding": *Historique du Château Suduiraut*, 7.
31. "The proprietors' pretensions": TLA, *Livre de raisonnements*, December 11, 1833.
31. "profited from my distress": Lamothe, director of Château Latour, letter dated March 30, 1812. Quoted in Pijassou, *Le Médoc*, 606.
32. "Leave it to the proprietors": Saint-Amant, 39.
32–34. "Sirs": ADG, 8M-94.
34. Then the floor was opened for discussion: ADG, 8M-94, Departmental Committee minutes.
36–37. "Please take into account": CCPV, V, 9.
37. "among drunkards and gourmets": Saint-Amant, 135.
37. "allies itself completely": CCPV, V, 9.
37. "A new and very important question": *Feuille du Dimanche*, April 22, 1855.

Chapter 3

39. "destroying a classification": ADG, 8M-94.
40. a series of lucrative privileges granted to Bordeaux's own vineyard owners: Kehrig, *Le privilège des vins*, 2–6.
40. the Médoc was prohibited from shipping wines directly to the sea: Dion, 388–389.

40. the development of Libourne as a secondary commercial center: Renouard, 245.

42. Dutch merchants used their considerable influence: Enjalbert, *La naissance des grands vins*, 65.

42. "For cargo or for ocean shipping": Document dated February 22, 1813, Nathaniel Johnston et Fils Archives.

43. "the scarcity of wine was general": Vins de la Sénéchaussée, 21 8bre 1647, Archives Municipales de Bordeaux, ii–29.

43. "a prodigious quantity": ibid.

44. "first jurat very eloquently explained": ibid.

44. a decree establishing minimum and maximum prices: Registre de la Jurade 1647–1648 (16 septembre 1647 au 31 juillet 1648), Archives Municipales de Bordeaux, BB45.

45. "No nation in the universe": "Angleterre: Observation sur le retablissement du Commerce avec ce Royaume." Report of the French Conseil de Commerce, June 26, 1711, Archives Nationales, microfilm F1256.

45. "A tun of the best wine": Locke, 142.

45. "the English love to raise the market on themselves": ibid., 143.

46. Graves wines did not decrease in quality: Baurein, I, 364.

46. "The Médoc is a canton in favor": Bidet, II, 269.

47. "St. Emilion has several growths": TLA, *Observations Générales*, 1815.

47. "State of the parishes": ADG, C-1613.

48. "The peasant's wine must be bought pretty early": "Directions about Wines copied from a Note of My Grandfather's Dated April 1765," Nathaniel Johnston et Fils Archives.

48. "Price of wines in good Years from 1745 and after": TLA, *Livre des Raisonnements*, 69.

49. a 1795 list for Cantenac: Lebègue, 17–19.

49. "First known classification": copy made available by Bruno Prats at Château Cos-d'Estournel.

50. an unsigned document: Public Record Office, FO-27–27–19.

51. his notes of those visits: Jefferson, reel 7, series 1; March 8–September 6, 1787.

52. "Today I have begun harvesting at Latour": CLA, letter from Pierre Lamothe to J. Eyméric dated September 30, 1820.

52. "Starting with a price of 2400 francs": Document dated February 22, 1813, Nathaniel Johnston et Fils Archives; see also: Franck (1845), 170; Armailhacq (1855), 475; *Notice sur la carte vinicole*, 4.

52. "detestable": Tastet & Lawton, *Tableau*.

52. first growths sold for 500 francs: TLA, "Prix courant des vins 1782–1822".

52. "telling me that it was the proportion": CLA, letter from Monplaisir Goudal to Samuel Scott dated November 26, 1852.

53. "As for Cos": TLA, *Observations Générales*, 1815.

55. An analysis of contemporary sale prices: Pijassou, *Le Médoc*, 539–541.

56. "The quantity harvested is so considerable": Jullien (1832), 175.

58. "the knowledge acquired": Franck (1824), 12–13.

58. "inexorable": Higounet, *Latour*, 308.

58. "to make the sun rise and set": ibid.

58–59. "In each parish are numerous proprietors": TLA *Observations Générales*, 1815.

59. "Our Property": ibid.

60. a memorandum dated February 22, 1813: Nathaniel Johnston et Fils Archives.

60. "a competent and respected magistrature": Arthaud, 239.

61. "I have considered the wines in general": Jullien (1816), xvii–xviii.

62. "The English, who are great lovers of them": Paguierre (1828), 79; see also: Chaptal, 79–80; Pijassou, *Le Médoc*, 408.

62. "all which sells in Paris": Jullien, 203.

62. "Lafitte..offers wines that are light": ibid., 209.

62. "[Lafite] is the most choice and delicate": Henderson, 184.

63. "It is not without mistrust": Franck (1824), 7.

63. "in a manner best designed": ibid.

63. "We now arrive at the most delicate part of our work": Franck (1845), 169.

63. "Mr. Franck, who is in Germany": ibid., i.

63–64. "Perhaps the attempt": ibid., ii–iii.

64. "These classes have been established by the brokers": Cavoleau, 127.

65. "many details": ibid., 110.

65. several extended passages of text appear to have been lifted verbatim from the same source as well: Compare the section titled "Introduction" in Franck (1824) with the "Introduction Générale" in Paguierre (1829).

65. "There is also in this parish": Paguierre (1828), 79–80.

65. "a friend of the Editor": ibid., 8.

65. "an Appendix has been added": ibid., 9.

66. "According to the statement": Bowring, 99.

66–67. "They could not be classified by communes": ibid., 131.

67. "who would believe it": *Le Producteur*, January 1840.

67. this was the method Jullien adopted: See also the Thomas Jefferson classification.

68. "bought only little-quality white wines": ADG, 8M-62, Bordeaux Chamber of Commerce memorandum, 25, Prairial an 12.

70. "Except for the small number": Saint-Amant, 39.

70. "the wines rival the best thirds": Cocks, *Bordeaux et ses vins* (1922), 127.

70. "will defend the interests of the Gironde's vineyards": *Le Producteur*, January 1838.

70. "From where comes this evil?": ibid.

70–71. "The wine classifications": *Le Producteur*, November 1840.

71. the elevation of Mouton: *Le Producteur*, January 1838.

71. Pichon-Longueville was the equivalent in quality of Latour: ibid.

71. "The trade will doubtless appreciate our candor": ibid.

71. "The established classification": *Le Producteur*, February 1838.

72. "price varies even more than the quality": Bowring, 131.

73. "several *clos* of Cantenac and Margaux": Joubert, 51.

73. "the large properties": ibid.

73. "in which are ordered many wines": ibid., 52.

74. "more advantageously situated than many others": Batilliat, 9–10.

74. "a new path": ibid., 11.

74. "their classification by order of merit": ibid., 12.

74. "Translator of 'Priests, Women, and Families,'": Cocks, *Bordeaux: Its Wines and the Claret Country*, title page.

74. "to consult all the most authentic documents": ibid., ix.

74. "little volume": ibid.

75. "In forming, therefore, the following lists": ibid., 194.
75. "As I have already stated": ibid., 195.
75. "to give this part": Cocks, *Bordeaux, ses environs et ses vins*, ii.
76. "one would fall into the greatest mistake": Franck (1845), 170.
76. "a journal titled *Le Producteur*": Cocks, ibid., ii.
78. "several vines belonging to Mr. Duluc": ADG, 7M-173, "Culture de la vigne, evaluation des produits en 1847 et 1848".
78. "As for the mere mayors of communes": Balzac, 202.
79. "I can not understand by what test ill-defined": Biarnez, 36–37.
79. "Who'd believe that Mouton": ibid., 45.
79. "A fourth growth at first sight": ibid., 33.
79. "In a merited rise to the fourth rank reclassed": ibid., 16.
79. "And Montrose, today, with its delicate flavor": ibid., 47.
79. "Although this wine is not classed": ibid., 6.
80. wine from 1838, 1839, 1842, and 1843 that remained in their cellars: Higounet, 341.
80. "harvests piled up in his cellars": Saint-Amant, 94.
81. "The result of all this": Armailhacq, 475.
81. "Mouton, being the first of the second growths": Letter from Lestapis to Issac Thuret dated March 24, 1851. Quoted in Pijassou, *Le Médoc*, 675.
81. "to maintain an absolute silence": Letter from Theodore Galos dated May 27, 1852. ibid.
81. "Now that experience has taught us": ibid., 676.
82. "a white powder first appears": Armailhacq, 557.
83. "among the fifth great growths": Saint-Amant, 99.
84. "the two Rausans": ibid., 61.
84. "we have been present": ibid., 133, 134.

Chapter 4

86. "The aim we have set for ourselves": CCLET, January 11, 1855, 235 verso–236 recto.
86. "they are from 60 to 70 in number": ibid. 157–158.
86. "We have reason to believe": ibid.
86. "I have had the honor": CCPV, VI, 33.
87. "Dear Sir": CCLET, March 9, 1855, 11 recto.
87. "the principal winemaking regions": CCPV, VI, 10.
87. "We ask that you send us": ibid.
90. "Enemies he never had": *Courrier de la Gironde*, July 7, 1873.
92. "We were asked": CCLET, March 30, 1855, 20 recto.
92. "a member announced": CCPV, VI, 54.
92. "The Chamber of Commerce informs the proprietors": *Courrier de la Gironde*, March 1, 1855; see also *Memorial Bordelais*, March 2, 1855.
93. This did not prevent Count Duchatel: see "List of Classed Growths" in Appendix IV.
93. "Despite the repeated request": CCPV, VI, 59.
93. "a large enough number of proprietors": CCLET, January 25, 1855, 241 recto.
93. "a large enough number of cases of wine samples": CCLET, February 16, 1855, 4 verso.

93. it was an incomplete representation that was eventually put on display in Paris: *La Gironde*, December 13, 1855.

93. only twenty-three red- and ten white-wine samples were submitted: see "List of Classed Growths" in Appendix IV.

94. "from good years": CCPV, VI, 10.

94. "ordinary": Tastet & Lawton, *Tableau*.

94. "full-bodied, good": ibid.

94. "exquisite, not very full-bodied": ibid.

95. "What could they see, what could they appreciate": Saint-Amant, 134.

95. "This large-scale map": CCPV, VI, 59.

96. "the part of our exhibit": CCLET, May 11, 1855, 35 verso.

96. "No one is unaware": *Notice sur la carte vinicole*, 1.

98. "Sirs": CCLET, April 5, 1855, 22 verso–23 recto.

98. "Brokers will gather together": ADG, 8M-63, "Table of Commercial Brokers, 1821".

98. In 1855 this board of directors was presided over by: *Memorial Bordelais*, December 23, 1854.

99. "a list as exact and complete as possible": CCLET, April 5, 1855, 22 verso.

106. "Sirs": Bordeaux Chamber of Commerce Archives, 69A.VI.313.821.

106. these were not necessarily the classification's authors—their names would be: ADG, 8M-63, "Table of Commercial Brokers, 1857".

107. "Note presented by the Union for the *shipment of wines to the Exposition*": TLA, *Observations Générales*, 1855.

Chapter 5

110. the 1798 Lafite white was particularly well esteemed in Amsterdam: CLA, Letter from Goll & Co. to Joseph Goudal dated March 17, 1803.

110. "Never had the highest price": CLA, letter from Joseph Goudal to Claude E. Scott dated November 9, 1828.

110–111. In the winter of 1827: the history of this fraud is recounted in CLA, letters from Claude E. Scott dated October 31 and November 20, 1828.

111. He had already established the practice: CLA, letter from Monplaisir Goudal to Samuel Scott dated December 10, 1854.

111. "vicious": CLA, letter from Monplaisir Goudal to Samuel Scott dated October 29, 1852.

111. "I must tell you": CLA, letter from Monplaisir Goudal to Pierre Mondon dated May 28, 1845.

112. "Commercially, Lafite [is] placed": Saint-Amant, 87.

113. "at the top of the tree": CLA, letter from Monplaisir Goudal to Samuel Scott dated June 18, 1852.

113. as attested to by the property's letterhead: CLA, letter from Eugène Giresse to Pierre Mondon dated September 20, 1847.

113. "asking if you would be interested": CLA, letter from Monplaisir Goudal to Samuel Scott dated December 10, 1854.

113. sending two cases containing fifty bottles each to India: CLA, letter from Monplaisir Goudal to Samuel Scott dated April 11, 1853.

114. "Sir": CCLET, March 10, 1855, 13 recto.

115. "The Chamber of Commerce": CLA, letter from Monplaisir Goudal to Samuel Scott dated May 9, 1855.

115. "One thing that must not be lost sight of": Barton Family Archives, letter from Nathaniel Barton to his son, Bertram, dated May 2, 1853.

116. "He found the regulations": *Illustrated London News*, September 1, 1855.

116. "wild spirit of thoughtless activity": ibid.

116. "the plans of the Commissioners were reconsidered": ibid.

116. a property that the Emperor himself had been rumored especially desirous of seeing: CLA, letter from Monplasir Goudal to Samuel Scott dated August 11, 1852.

116. "This audience was accorded me right away": letter from Monplaisir Goudal to Samuel Scott dated May 9, 1855.

117. "By an innovation based, I believe, on justice": REU, 92.

117. "in industry a new status, that of *collaborator*": ibid., 101.

117. "he was a born dialectician": Benoist, 233–234.

117. "In doubtful circumstances": REU, 38.

118. "As for the collective display": CCPV, VI, 93.

118. "You know very well": CCLET, April 20, 1855, 27 verso.

119–120. "Your Highness": CCPV, VI, 94–95.

120. "As for our classed growths": ADG, 8M-94.

121. "I hope": CCLET, May 2, 1855, 32 verso.

121. "We won't answer this letter": ibid.

122. "I explained your position": CCPV, VI, 105.

122. "we have obtained in large part what we have wanted": ibid., 107.

122. "*that we have sent*": ibid.

Chapter 6

123. "Never has our Spring been so slow in arriving": *L'Illustration*, May 26, 1855.

123. "Despite the frigid temperatures": ibid., May 5, 1855.

124. "a temple of peace": Napoleon III inauguration speech, REU, 403.

124. "Ideas very different": *Notice historique sur l'exposition universelle de 1855*, 7.

124. "This question of buildings": REU, 47.

126. "It is only in the aggregate": Tresca, 9.

126–127. "The installation of glass panels": *Notice historique sur l'exposition universelle de 1855*, 48.

127. "It cost us ten francs": *L'Illustration*, May 26, 1855.

127. "To see the activity which prevails": *L'Illustration*, April 21, 1855.

127. "We ask that you get in touch": CCLET, March 30, 1855, 20 recto.

128. "whom I have known for a long time": CCPV, VI, 105.

128–129. "After reflecting on the matter": CCLET, May 11, 1855, 35 recto.

129. "the wine map of the Gironde": ibid., 35 recto–35 verso.

129. "We do not think": CCLET, May 18, 1855, 37 recto–37 verso.

129–130. "This last object": ibid.

130. "We do not think": CCLET, June 9, 1855, 45 verso.

131. "The idea of substituting red-colored water": ibid., 45 recto.

131. "This excavation": ibid., 45 verso.

132. "very unpleasant": CCPV, VI, 138.

132. "Mr. Henri Galos": ibid., 139.

133. "... [T]he Commission whose work": ibid.

133. "From 10 till 12 o'clock": *The Times*, May 16, 1855.

133–134. "the outfits of the ladies": *L'Indicateur*, May 17, 1855.

134. "There is America": *Illustrated London News*, April 28, 1855.

135. "What can the imperial Commissioners do": ibid.

135. "In light of exhibitors' continued persistence": *Moniteur Universel*, June 28, 1855.

135. "No product will be admitted": REU, 177.

135–136. "I have received word from Paris": CLA, letter from Monplaisir Goudal to Samuel Scott dated July 12, 1855.

136. "It is less a matter of preventing Mr. Goudal": CCLET, July 12, 1855, 54 verso.

136. "It goes without saying": ibid.

Chapter 7

137. "You must come": Gaubert, 407.

138. "left something to be desired": ibid., 455.

138. "very good for": ibid.

138. "terrible": ibid., 457.

138. "exquisite": ibid., 455.

139. "tiresome work": *Rapports du Jury Mixte International*, 629.

140. "the fabrication of wine": ibid.

140. "The wines of: Bordeaux": ibid.

141. "We think, like you": CCLET, July 19, 1855, 57 verso.

141. "We will thus avoid": ibid.

142. "that all takes place": ibid.

142–143. "The morning occupations of our jury": Owen, II, 8–10.

143. "Sir, we are answering your letter": CCPV, VI, 152–153.

144–145. "*Neither must Mouton*": ibid.

145. "Mr. Larrieu, the owner of this growth": CCLET, August 2, 1855, 63 recto.

145–146. "We continue to insist": ibid.

146. "We are really sorry": ibid.

146. "we thank you": CCLET, August 9, 1885, 64 recto.

146. "His request is illegal": CLA, letter from Monplaisir Goudal to Samuel Scott dated August 30, 1855.

147. "Finally, after a good many difficulties": CCPV, VI, 182.

147. "This success has somewhat surprised the Chamber": CCLET, August 24, 1855, 69 recto.

147. "for its precious collection of wines": CCPV, VI, 183.

147. "I took care to note": ibid.

147. "a completely accidental occurrence": ibid.

147. "Mouton returns to its place": ibid.

147. "These are, Sirs": ibid.

148. "The success was very important": ibid., 184.

148. "Is it not to be feared": ibid.

148. "As they cannot give two awards": CLA, letter from Monplaisir Goudal to Samuel Scott dated August 30, 1855.

149. "objects whose low price and good quality": REU, 390.

149. "Whatever a wine's price": *Rapports du jury mixte international*, 1417.

149. "The jury dismissed": ibid.

150. "Please look into what has to be done": CCLET, October 27, 1855, 87 verso.

151. "After our meeting": CCLET, November 3, 1855, 88 verso.

153. it was the collection of anonymous communal wines: *La Gironde*, December 12, 1855.

Chapter 8

155. "Before proceeding further": *La Gironde*, December 13, 1855.

156. "Sirs": Letter from M.Bernet and F. Ducasse Jeune dated January 3, 1856, Chamber of Commerce Archives, VI 313–829 Divers.

156. "all the parcels of my vineyard": Letter from Louis de Chavaille dated December 28, 1855, Chamber of Commerce Archives, VI 313–829 Divers.

156. "I therefore demand": ibid.

157. "You will easily understand": CCLET, January 1, 1856, 116 verso.

157. "We attach to this correspondence": CCLET, January 12, 1856, 119 verso.

157. "In the event of any demands and complaints": CCPV, VI, 153.

158. "The Union of brokers has written": Minutes for Bordeaux Chamber of Commerce meeting of September 19, 1855, manuscript copy, Chamber of Commerce Archives.

158. "The Wines of Macau": TLA, *Observations Générales*, 1815.

158. owned by the Villeneuve family since 1579: Lorbac, 150–151.

158. born in 1758: ADG, 3M-473, "Liste de Présentation par le Maire de la Ville de Bordeaux de trois candidates pour la place laissée vacante dans le Conseil Municipal de la dite ville par M. Dufourg (Philippe-Joachim) demissionnaire (2eme moitié)".

158. serving as the mayor of Macau: ADG, 2M-8.

159. "[Villeneuve is in the] 1st rank of this commune": TLA, *Observations Générales*, 1815.

159. On December 13, 1834, Jean de Villeneuve-Durfort died: ADG, 3Q-9139.

159. Born Caroline Joséphine Françoise Josephe de Lalande: ibid.

159. her sister had wed one of the Médoc's other noble proprietors, the Baron Joseph de Pichon Longueville: ADG, Procuration dated December 19, 1834, Maurice Grangeneuve, notary.

159. in August 1844, Pierre Jules de Villeneuve-Durfort unexpectedly died: ADG, 3Q-9143.

160. Such a defense led the widow Villeneuve-Durfort to embark upon legal proceedings in 1845: ADG, Jugements d'Audience, July 19, 1845, 76–77.

160. "a trial which has remained famous in the Gironde": Lorbac, 151–152.

161. "by far the most magnificent in France": Young, 46.

161–162. "the state of ruin": *La Gironde*, January 8, 1856.

162. "Bordeaux's wines": ibid.

162. "The day before yesterday": CLA, letter number 156 dated January 9, 1855, in register "Copie des lettres," 137.

164. "class is numerous": Redding, *French Wines and Vineyards*, 101.

164. "These [fifth growths] are composed": ibid.

164. "The *sixth growths* or *Bourgeois Supérieurs":* Guillon, 302.

164. "1st, 2nd, and 3rd growths": Document dated February 22, 1813. Nathaniel Johnston et Fils Archives.

165. "finally, the most remarkable of the bourgeois growths": Laumond, 10.

165 "the most delicate part of our work": Franck (1845), 169.

165. "To bring some clarity": Franck (1860), 200.

166. "A proprietor at Saint-Sauveur": Franck (1868), 127.

167. "Given the observation": ADG, Jugements d'Audience—Premier Chambre du Tribunal de Première Instance de Bordeaux, January13, 1869, 64 recto and 65 recto.

167. "Perhaps it will come to pass": Guillon, 213.

167. "the current classification is only transitory": Bigeat, 54–56.

167. "*one* tun of Latour": ibid., 5.

167–168. "an official base which shelters me": ibid., 8.

168. "In touching on the holy ark": Lorbach, 35.

168. Charles Cocks having died: Crossley, 378.

168. "Mr. Edouard Féret neglected no information": Cocks (1868), ii.

169. "we have followed the text": ibid., 89–90.

170. "in this circumstance": CCPV, XI, 270.

171. "115,000 francs necessary to underwrite": CCPV, XII, 113.

171. "state of abandon": CCPV, ibid., 391.

171. "Mr. Prefect": ibid., 394.

172. "the text of the last official document": Cocks (1868), 89–90.

173. "This classification serves as the basis": ibid., 90.

173. "we will visit each individual commune": ibid., 92.

173. "the practical science of the brokers": ibid., ii.

173. "This work": Cocks (1874), 265.

173. "the Lawton of white wines": Barton Family Archives, letter from P.F. Guestier to Bertram Barton dated December 3, 1857.

174. "450 up to 1,200 fr.": Franck (1845), 150.

174. "first growths occasionally sell": ibid., 170.

174. "Seconds sell at 2,100 to 2,050 fr.": ibid., 171.

175. "important modifications": Cocks (1874), 263.

176. "a crowd of well-situated smaller proprietors": ibid., 264.

176. "For several years": ibid., 273.

180. "We should remember": *Le Vignoble Girondin*, May 15, 1947.

180. a 1946 survey: *La Feuille Vinicole*, February 5, 1946.

180. "The American is": ibid., March 5, 1946.

180. "Americans have become more 'wine-conscious'": ibid., February 5, 1946.

181. "The classification is: An Instrument of Notoriety": *Commentaires sur la mise a jour du classement de 1855*, 5.

181. "an instrument": ibid.

Chapter 9

183. "Like all human institutions": Cocks (1865), 90.

188. "situated in the commune of Margaux": Château Malescot-Saint-Exupéry Archives, extract from the minutes of the Clerk of the Bordeaux County Court: Sale by court order of St. Exupéry, June 21, 1853.

188. "so-called bourgeois or peasant wines": Arthaud, 177.

189. "What is the cause of these differences": ibid., 177–178.

189. "the broker is right": Aussel, 138.

190. "a patch of land four meters large": Château Cos-d'Estournel Archives, *Titres de Cos d'Estournel, Cos Labory, Pomis, L'abbaye, et Bedilloux; acquisitions de M.M. d'Estournel et Merman,* notarial act for the sale of Cos-d'Estournel and the other properties of M. Estournel to M. Martyns dated August 14, 1852.

190. by the 1760s: Château Rausan-Ségla Archives, memoir dated 1770 concerning Marie-Anne de Briet v. Philippe-Simon de Rauzan.

192. "has equally bought vines from Mr. Brown": Armailhacq (1855), 503.

194. "an experience which goes back over a century": CCPV, VI, 94.

195. "By general opinion": Peynaud, 194.

195. "the team of workers was the same": ibid.

195. "the fortune of Latour's proprietors": Château Latour Archives, "Rapport sur les exercises 1866–1867."

196. "*Durfort-Puységur* cedes nothing to its two neighbors *Rauzan*": Saint-Amant, 61.

197. "[S]ince the period": Ferrier, 144.

197–198. "A congress to taste the red and white wines": ibid., 145–148.

BIBLIOGRAPHY

Un Agronome. *Statistique œnologique du département de la Gironde, contenant les procédés de culture de la vigne: la quantité d'hectares consacrés à cette culture; le nom des cépages; le prix, année moyenne, des vins, par tonneau et par classe, des crus les plus renommés; les quantités récoltées, année moyenne, les frais de culture, etc.* Bordeaux: n.p., 1834.

Allwood, John. *The Great Exhibitions.* London: Studio Vista, 1977.

Andrieu, Pierre. *Petite histoire de Bordeaux et de son vignoble.* Montpellier: La Journée Vinicole, 1955.

Annales de chimie, ou recueil de mémoires concernant la chimie et les arts qui en dépendent, 30 (1800).

Aperçu historique sur les vins de Graves. Bordeaux: Imprimerie A. Barthélemy, n.d.

Armailhacq, Armand d'. *La culture des vignes, la vinification et les vins dans le Médoc: avec un état des vignobles d'après leur réputation.* Bordeaux: P. Chaumas, 1855.

———. 2nd ed. Bordeaux: P. Chaumas, 1858.

———. 3rd ed. Bordeaux: P. Chaumas, 1867.

Arthaud, Docteur. *De la vigne et de ses produits.* Paris: Mme Ve Bouchard-Huzard, 1858.

Aussel, Docteur. *La Gironde à vol d'oiseau.* Bordeaux: Féret, 1865.

Balzac, Honoré de. *Les Paysans.* Paris: Gallimard, 1975.

Bargeton, René, et al. *Les préfets du 11 ventôse an VIII au 4 septembre 1870: répertoires nominatif et territorial.* Paris: Archives Nationales, 1981.

Barry, Sir Edward. *Observations Historical, Critical, and Medical, on the Wines of the Ancients, and the Analogy between Them and Modern Wines: With General Observations on the Principles and Qualities of Water, and in Particular on Those of Bath.* London: T. Cadell, 1775.

Barton, Anthony, and Claude Petit-Castelli. *La saga des Barton.* Levallois (Hauts-de-Seine): Manya, 1991.

Batilliat, P. *Traité sur les vins de la France, des phénomènes qui se passent dans les vins, et des moyens d'en accélérer ou d'en retarder la marche: des moyens de vieillir ou de rajeunir les vins, d'en prévenir ou d'en corriger les altérations; des produits qui dérivent des vins: eaux-de-vie, esprits, vinaigre, tartre et vinasses.* Paris: Chez Mathias, 1846.

Baurein, Abbé. *Variétés bordeloises ou essai historique et critique sur la topographie ancienne et moderne du diocèse de Bordeaux.* Rev. ed., 4 vols. Bordeaux: Féret et Fils, 1876.

Benoist, Charles. *Souverains, hommes d'état, hommes d'église.* Paris: Lecene, Oudin et Cie., 1893.

Bertall [Charles Albert d'Arnould]. *La Vigne: voyage autour des vins de France.* Paris: Plon, 1878.

Biarnez, Pierre. *Les grands vins de Bordeaux.* Paris: Plon frères, 1849.

Bidet, Nicolas. *Traité sur la nature et sur la culture de la vigne: sur le vin, la façon de le faire, et la manière de le bien gouverner; à l'usage des différens vignobles du roïaume de France.* 2nd ed., 2 vols. Paris: Savoie, 1759.

Bigeat, C. *Notice sur le Médoc.* Bordeaux: P. Chaumas, 1866.

Bloch, Jean-Jacques and Mariane Delort. *Quand Paris allait "à l'expo."* Paris: Fayard, 1980.

Bonaparte, Louis-Napoléon. *L'Extinction du paupérisme.* 4th ed. Paris: Ch. Ed. Temblaire, 1848.

Bonaparte, Napoléon-Joseph-Charles-Paul. *Rapport sur l'exposition universelle de 1855 présenté à l'empereur.* Paris: Imprimerie Impériale, 1857.

Boutruche, Robert, ed. *Bordeaux de 1453 à 1715.* Histoire de Bordeaux. Charles Higounet, ed. Bordeaux: Fédération historique du Sud-Ouest, 1966.

Bowring, John. *Second Report on the Commercial Relations between France and Great Britain: Silks & Wine.* London: William Clowes and Sons, 1835.

Boyd, Julian P., ed. *The Papers of Thomas Jefferson.* Vol. 11. Princeton: Princeton University Press, 1955.

Briggs, Asa. *Haut-Brion: An Illustrious Lineage.* London: Faber and Faber, 1994.

Brisse, Baron L., et al. *Album de l'exposition universelle: dédié à S.A.I. le prince Napoléon.* Vol. 2. Paris: Bureaux de l'Abeille Impériale, 1857.

Brook, Stephen. *Sauternes and Other Sweet Wines of Bordeaux.* London: Faber and Faber, 1995.

Buisson, F., ed. *Dictionnaire universel de commerce, banque, manufactures, douanes, pêche, navigation marchande; des lois et administration du commerce.* 2 vols. Paris: F. Buisson, 1805.

Bury, J. P. T. *France, 1814–1940.* 5th ed. London: Routledge, 1985.

Bussy, Pascal. *Château de Malle: un grand cru du Sauternais.* Panayrac (Haute-Garonne): Editions Daniel Briand, n.d.

Butel, Paul, ed. *Histoire de la chambre de commerce et d'industrie de Bordeaux des origines à nos jours, 1705–1985.* Bordeaux: Chambre de Commerce et d'Industrie, 1988.

Campagne, Maurice. *Des Mesures de Rauzan: une famille bordelaise, dix-septième & dix-huitième siècles.* Bergerac: Imprimerie Générale du Sud-Ouest, 1904.

Cavignac, Jean. *Les vingt cinq familles: les négociants à Bordeaux sous Louis Philippe.* Bordeaux: Les Cahiers de l'I.A.E.S., 1985.

Cavoleau, Jean-Alexandre. Œnologie française, ou statistique de tous les vignobles et de toutes les boissons vineuses et spiritueuses de la France, suivie de considerations générales sur la culture de la vigne. Paris: Madame Huzard, 1827.

Chambre de Commerce et d'Industrie de Bordeaux Archives. *Copies de lettres de la chambre de commerce de Bordeaux.* Ledgers. January 19, 1851–February 9, 1855; February 9–September 24, 1856. Bordeaux Chamber of Commerce Archives.

———. *Extraits des procès-verbaux, lettres et mémoires de la Chambre de commerce de Bordeaux.* 2d ser. 5 (1854); 6 (1855); 7 (1856); 11 (1861); 12 (1862).

———. *Le palais de la bourse: les œuvres d'intérêt historique ou artistique qui s'y trouvent.* Bordeaux: Imprimerie Castera, 1977.

———. *Séances de la chambre de commerce de Bordeaux.* Manuscript. Vol. 19: July 12, 1854–January 21, 1857.

Chaptal, Jean-Antoine-Claude, et al. *Traité théorique et pratique sur la culture de la vigne, avec l'art de faire le vin, les eaux-de-vie, esprit-de-vin, vinaigres simples et composés.* 2 vols. Paris: chez Delalain, fils, 1801.

Charles, A. "La viticulture en gironde et le commerce des vins de Bordeaux sous le second empire." *Revue historique de Bordeaux et du département de la Gironde,* n.s., 11 (1962): 193–220.

Charmolüe, Jean-Louis. *Château Montrose.* Bordeaux: n.p., 1984.

Chassagnac, Pierre. *La vente des vins de Bordeaux.* Bordeaux: Editions Universitaires TEX, 1957.

Clément, Pierre. *Lettres, instructions et mémoires de Colbert, publiés d'après les ordres de l'Empereur, sur la proposition de son excellence M. Magne, ministre secrétaire d'état des finances.* Vol. 6. Paris: Imprimerie Impériale, 1869.

Cocks, Charles. *Bordeaux: Its Wines and the Claret Country.* London: Longman, Brown, Green, and Longmans, 1846.

———. *Bordeaux, ses environs et ses vins classés par ordre de mérite: guide de l'étranger à Bordeaux.* Bordeaux: Féret et Fils, 1850.

———. 2nd ed. Edouard Féret, ed. 1865.

———. *Bordeaux et ses vins classés par ordre de mérite.* 2nd ed. Bordeaux: Féret et Fils., 1868.

———. 3rd ed. Bordeaux: Féret et Fils, 1874.

———. 4th ed. Bordeaux: Féret et Fils, 1881.

———. 5th ed. Bordeaux: Féret et Fils, 1886.

———. 6th ed. Bordeaux: Féret et Fils, 1893.

———. 7th ed. Bordeaux: Féret et Fils, 1898.

———. 8th ed. Bordeaux: Féret et Fils, 1908.

———. 9th ed. Bordeaux: Féret et Fils, 1922.

Cocks, Charles and Edouard Féret. 10th ed. Bordeaux: Féret et Fils. 1929.

———. 11th ed. Bordeaux: Féret et Fils. 1949.

———. Claude Féret, ed. 12th ed. Bordeaux: Féret et Fils. 1969.

Commentaires sur la mise à jour du classement de 1855: étude à l'intention de monsieur le président et messieurs les membres de l'Institut National des Appellations d'Origine. N.p., 1959.

Conquet, André. *Napoleon III et les chambres de commerce.* Paris: A.C.F.C.I. [Assemblée des Chambres Françaises de Commerce et d'Industrie], 1990.

Courteault, Henri. "La formation commerciale d'un jeune bordelais il y a cent ans." *Revue philomathique de Bordeaux et du Sud-Ouest* (1923): 62–70.

Courteault, Paul. "Les origines des foires franches de Bordeaux." *Revue historique de Bordeaux et du département de la Gironde* 34 (1941): 49–69; 35 (1942): 37–49.

———. "A propos du cours du XXX Juillet." *Revue philomathique de Bordeaux et du Sud-Ouest* (1926): 178–188.

Crossley, Ceri. "Charles Cocks: un intermédiaire oublié entre la France et la Grande-Bretagne." *Revue de littérature comparée.* 3 (1988): 377–390.

Danflou, Alfred. *Les grandes crus bordelais.* Bordeaux: Librarie Goudin, 1867.

Démy, Adolphe. *Essai historique sur les expositions universelles de Paris.* Paris: Libraire Alphonse Picard et Fils, 1907.

Dictionnaire de biographie française. 17 vols. to date. Paris: Librarie Letouzey et Ané, 1933–.

Dion, Roger. *Histoire de la vigne et du vin en France des origines au dix-neuvième siècle.* Paris: Flammarion, 1977.

Les douze expositions de l'industrie en France de 1798 à 1855. Paris: Martinon, 1855.

Drouin, Jean-Claude. "Remarques sur le vignoble girondin au milieu du dix-neuvième siècle." In *Vignobles et Vins d'Aquitaine.* Bordeaux: Biscaye Frères, 1970.

Duffour-Dubergier, Lodi-Martin. *Chroniques du Château de Gironville: extraits de la chronique latine de Turpin, de la chronique arabe de Ben-Thamar, et d'un poème norvégien du neuvième siècle.* Paris: Plon frères, 1854.

———. *Discours prononcé par M. Dufour-Dubergier, maire de la ville de Bordeaux.* Bordeaux: Imprimerie Gazay, 1842.

Dupont-Ferrier, Gustave. *Les officiers royaux des bailliages et sénéchaussées et les institutions monarchiques locales en France à la fin du moyen age.* Paris: Librairie Émile Bouillon, 1902.

E.-A., C. d'. *Dictionnaire des familles françaises: anciennes ou notables à la fin du dix-neuvième siècle.* Evreux (Eure): Imprimerie Charles Hérissey, 1915.

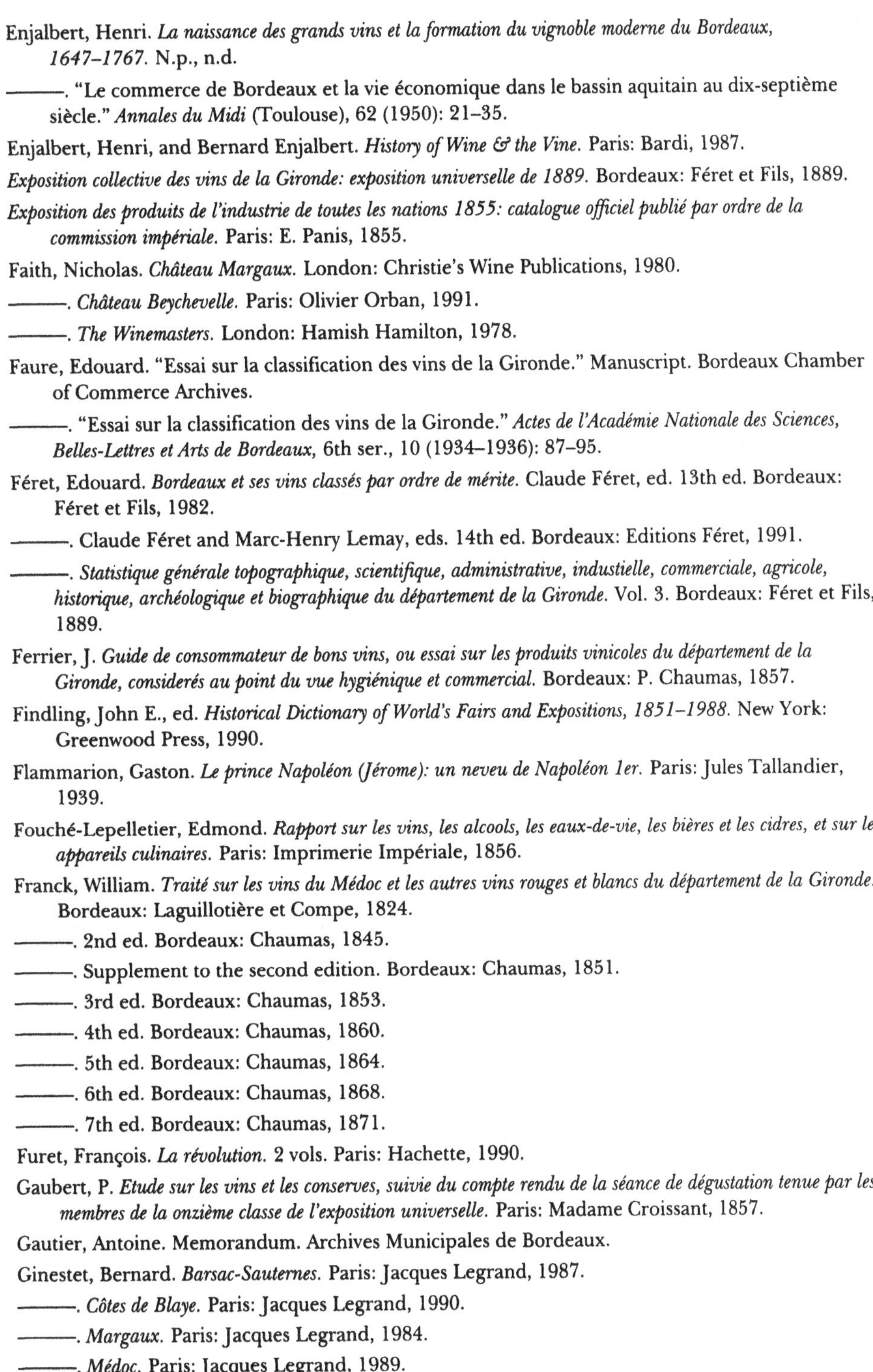

Enjalbert, Henri. *La naissance des grands vins et la formation du vignoble moderne du Bordeaux, 1647–1767.* N.p., n.d.

———. "Le commerce de Bordeaux et la vie économique dans le bassin aquitain au dix-septième siècle." *Annales du Midi* (Toulouse), 62 (1950): 21–35.

Enjalbert, Henri, and Bernard Enjalbert. *History of Wine & the Vine.* Paris: Bardi, 1987.

Exposition collective des vins de la Gironde: exposition universelle de 1889. Bordeaux: Féret et Fils, 1889.

Exposition des produits de l'industrie de toutes les nations 1855: catalogue officiel publié par ordre de la commission impériale. Paris: E. Panis, 1855.

Faith, Nicholas. *Château Margaux.* London: Christie's Wine Publications, 1980.

———. *Château Beychevelle.* Paris: Olivier Orban, 1991.

———. *The Winemasters.* London: Hamish Hamilton, 1978.

Faure, Edouard. "Essai sur la classification des vins de la Gironde." Manuscript. Bordeaux Chamber of Commerce Archives.

———. "Essai sur la classification des vins de la Gironde." *Actes de l'Académie Nationale des Sciences, Belles-Lettres et Arts de Bordeaux,* 6th ser., 10 (1934–1936): 87–95.

Féret, Edouard. *Bordeaux et ses vins classés par ordre de mérite.* Claude Féret, ed. 13th ed. Bordeaux: Féret et Fils, 1982.

———. Claude Féret and Marc-Henry Lemay, eds. 14th ed. Bordeaux: Editions Féret, 1991.

———. *Statistique générale topographique, scientifique, administrative, industielle, commerciale, agricole, historique, archéologique et biographique du département de la Gironde.* Vol. 3. Bordeaux: Féret et Fils, 1889.

Ferrier, J. *Guide de consommateur de bons vins, ou essai sur les produits vinicoles du département de la Gironde, considerés au point du vue hygiénique et commercial.* Bordeaux: P. Chaumas, 1857.

Findling, John E., ed. *Historical Dictionary of World's Fairs and Expositions, 1851–1988.* New York: Greenwood Press, 1990.

Flammarion, Gaston. *Le prince Napoléon (Jérome): un neveu de Napoléon 1er.* Paris: Jules Tallandier, 1939.

Fouché-Lepelletier, Edmond. *Rapport sur les vins, les alcools, les eaux-de-vie, les bières et les cidres, et sur les appareils culinaires.* Paris: Imprimerie Impériale, 1856.

Franck, William. *Traité sur les vins du Médoc et les autres vins rouges et blancs du département de la Gironde.* Bordeaux: Laguillotière et Compe, 1824.

———. 2nd ed. Bordeaux: Chaumas, 1845.

———. Supplement to the second edition. Bordeaux: Chaumas, 1851.

———. 3rd ed. Bordeaux: Chaumas, 1853.

———. 4th ed. Bordeaux: Chaumas, 1860.

———. 5th ed. Bordeaux: Chaumas, 1864.

———. 6th ed. Bordeaux: Chaumas, 1868.

———. 7th ed. Bordeaux: Chaumas, 1871.

Furet, François. *La révolution.* 2 vols. Paris: Hachette, 1990.

Gaubert, P. *Etude sur les vins et les conserves, suivie du compte rendu de la séance de dégustation tenue par les membres de la onzième classe de l'exposition universelle.* Paris: Madame Croissant, 1857.

Gautier, Antoine. Memorandum. Archives Municipales de Bordeaux.

Ginestet, Bernard. *Barsac-Sauternes.* Paris: Jacques Legrand, 1987.

———. *Côtes de Blaye.* Paris: Jacques Legrand, 1990.

———. *Margaux.* Paris: Jacques Legrand, 1984.

———. *Médoc.* Paris: Jacques Legrand, 1989.

———. *Pauillac.* Paris: Jacques Legrand, 1985.

———. *Saint-Estèphe.* Boulogne (Haut-de-Seine): Jacques Legrand, 1985.

———. *Saint-Julien.* Boulogne (Haut-de-Seine): Jacques Legrand, 1984.

Girard, Louis. *Napoléon III.* Paris: Hachette, 1993.

Goubert, Pierre. *The Course of French History.* London: Routledge, 1988.

La grande encyclopédie: inventaire randonné des sciences des lettres et des arts. Paris: Société anonyme de la Grande Encyclopédie, n.d.

Grands crus classés du Médoc, classement officiel de 1855: étude pour la mise à jour du classement à l'intention de messieurs les propriétaires des grands crus classés du Médoc. 2nd ed. N.p., 1960.

Les grands vins de Bordeaux. Bordeaux: Editions Dussaut, 1984.

Guide dans l'exposition universelle des produits de l'industrie et des beaux-arts de toutes les nations, 1855. Paris: Paulin et Le Chevalier, 1855.

Le guide ou conducteur de l'étranger à Bordeaux: département de la Gironde. Bordeaux: Fillastre et neveu, 1825.

———. 2nd ed. Bordeaux: Fillastre et neveu, 1827.

———. 3rd ed. Bordeaux: Fillastre père, fils et neveu, 1834.

———. 4th ed. Bordeaux: Fillastre frères, 1839.

Guillier, Henry. *Les vins de la Gironde illustrés.* Liborune: n.d.

Guillon, Édouard. *Les châteaux historiques et vinicoles de la Gironde: avec la description des communes, la nature de leurs vins et la désignation des principaux crus.* 4 vols. Bordeaux: Coderc, Degréteau & Poujol, 1866–1869.

Hauterive, Ernest d'. *Napoléon III et le prince Napoléon: Correspondance inédite.* Paris: Calmann-Lévy, 1925.

Henderson, Alexander. *The History of Ancient and Modern Wines.* London: Baldwin, Cradock, and Joy, 1824.

Higounet, Charles, ed. *La seigneurie et le vignoble de Château Latour.* 2 vols. Bordeaux: Fédération historique du Sud-Ouest, 1974.

Historique du Château Suduiraut. N.p., n.d. Château Suduiraut Archives .

Hoefer, Ferdinand. *Nouvelle biographie générale depuis les temps les plus reculés jusqu'à nos jours.* Paris: Firmin Didot frères, fils et Cie, 1857.

Holt, Edgar. *Plon-Plon: The Life of Prince Napoléon, 1822–1891.* London: Michael Joseph, 1973.

Isay, Raymond. "Panorama des expositions universelles: l'exposition de 1855." *Revue des deux mondes* (1936): 344–365.

Jeannin, Pierre. *L'Europe du nord-ouest et du nord aux dix-septième et dix-huitième siècles.* 2nd ed. Paris: Presses Universitaires de France, 1987.

Jefferson, Thomas. *The Thomas Jefferson Papers.* Presidential Papers Microfilm. Washington, D.C.: Library of Congress, 1974.

Joanne, Paul, ed. *Dictionnaire géographique et administratif de la France et de ses colonies.* 7 vols. Paris: Librairie Hachette et Cie., 1896.

Joubert, Alexis-François. *Les vins: manière de les soigner et de les servir.* Paris: Paul Renouard, 1842.

Jullien, André. *Topographie de tous les vignobles connus, contenant leur position géographique, l'indication du genre et de la qualité des produits de chaque crû, les lieux où se font les chargemens et le principal commerce de vin, le nom et la capacité des tonneaux et des mesures en usage, les moyens de transport ordinairement employés, etc., etc.: précédée d'une notice sur les vins des anciens, et suivie d'une classification générale des vins.* Rev. and enl. Paris: Madame Huzard, 1816.

———. 2nd ed. Paris: Madame Huzard, 1822.

———. 3rd ed. Paris: Madame Huzard, 1832.

———. *The Topography of All the Known Vineyards: Containing a Description of the Kind and Quality of Their Products, and a Classification: Translated from the French* [1822 edition] *and Abridged So as to Form a Manual and Guide to All Importers and Purchasers in the Choice of Wines.* London: G and W. B. Whittaker, 1824.

Kehrig, Henri. *Les origins du prestige des vins de Bordeaux: maintien de ce prestige au vingtième siècle.* Bordeaux: Féret et Fils, 1904.

———. *Le privilège des vins à Bordeaux jusqu'en 1789.* Paris: G. Masson, 1886.

La Rüe, A. de. *Les chasses du second empire, 1852–1870.* Paris: Firmin-Didot, 1882.

Lamorillière, Raoul L. de. *Guide-poche de l'étranger à Bordeaux et sur les lignes du Midi.* Bordeaux: Imprimerie générale de Mme. Crugy, 1857.

Lamothe, Léonce. *Nouveau guide de l'étranger à Bordeaux et dans le département de la Gironde.* Bordeaux: Chaumas, 1856.

Laumond, Auguste. *Notice sur les vignobles et les vins du département de la Gironde.* Bordeaux: Imprimerie Miocque-Balarac, 1869.

Lavertujon, André. *Monographie des produits de la Gironde au palais de l'industrie.* Bordeaux: Typographie G. Guun, 1856.

Lebègue, René. *Une commune viticole du Médoc sous l'ancien régime et pendant l'époque révolutionnaire (Cantenac).* Bordeaux: La Feuille Vinicole, 1920.

Lee, Nathanial Armitage. *Origines et descendance des Johnston de Bordeaux.* Blanquefort (Gironde): n.p., 1984.

Lemay, Marc-Henry. *Bordeaux et ses vins classés par ordre de mérite.* 15th ed. Bordeaux: Editions Féret, 1994.

Léon, Alexandre. *Rapport sur la huitième exposition des produits des arts et de l'industrie présenté à la société philomathique de Bordeaux.* Bordeaux: Chaumas-Gayet, 1850.

Liste générale par ordre alphabétique des exposants inscrits au catalogue officiel. Paris: Imprimerie Impériale, 1855.

Le livre des expositions universelles, 1851–1989. Paris: Union Centrale des Arts Décoratifs, 1983.

Locke, John. *Locke's Travels in France, 1675–1679: As Related in His Journals, Correspondence and Other Papers.* John Lough, ed. Cambridge: University Press, 1953.

Lorbac, Charles de [Charles Cabrol]. *Les richesses gastronomiques de la France: les vins de Bordeaux.* Paris: Hetzel, 1868.

Luckhurst, Kenneth W. *The Story of Exhibitions.* London: Studio Publications, 1951.

Malvezin, Frantz. *Bordeaux: histoire de la vigne et du vin en Aquitaine depuis les origines jusqu'à nos jours.* Bordeaux: Delmas, 1919.

Malvezin, Théophile. *Les grands vins de Bordeaux: de la science de les acheter et de l'art de les boire.* Caudéran (Gironde): l' «Œnophile», n.d.

Martin, Georges. "Les limites historiques de la région des Graves." *Revue historique de Bordeaux et du département de la Gironde,* 7 (1914): 81–97.

Mathilde, Princess. "Souvenirs des années d'exil." *Revue des deux mondes.* 42 (1927): 721–752.

Merman, Georges, and Gustave Brunet. *Notice sur les vins de Bordeaux.* Paris: Imprimerie Jouaust, 1867.

Miquel, Pierre. *Le second empire.* Paris: Plon, 1992.

Moquet, André Marie. *Tableau analytique & synoptique des prix des vins rouges et blancs, et des spiriteux dans le département de la Gironde, depuis 1808 jusqu'au mois d'Avril 1850.* Bordeaux: J. Lafon, n.d.

Morris, Helen. *Portrait of a Chef: The Life of Alexis Soyer, Sometime Chef to the Reform Club.* Cambridge: Cambridge University Press, 1938.

Mothe, Florence. *Graves de Bordeaux.* Paris: Jacques Legrand, 1985.

Notice historique sur l'exposition universelle de 1855. Paris: Ch. Lahure, 1855.

Notice sur la carte vinicole du département de la Gironde. Bordeaux: P. Chaumas, 1856.

Nouveau conducteur de l'étranger à Bordeaux. Rev. ed. Bordeaux: Chaumas, 1843.

———. 4th ed. Bordeaux: Chaumas, 1851.

Official Catalogue of the Great Exhibition of the Works of Industry of All Nations, 1851. Corrected Edition. London: Spicer Brothers, 1851.

Ollivier, Emile. *L'Empire libéral.* Vol. 6. Paris: Garnier Frères, 1902.

Ory, Pascal. *Les expositions universelles de Paris: panorama raisonné, avec des aperçus nouveaux et des illustrations par les meilleurs auteurs.* Paris: Ramsay, 1982.

Owen, Richard (Startin). *The Life of Richard Owen.* 2 vols. London: John Murray, 1894.

Paguierre, M. *Classification and Description of the Wines of Bordeaux: To Which Are Prefixed, Notices of the History and Culture of the Vine, Process of Making Wine, &c.* Edinburgh: William Blackwood, 1828.

———. *Classification et description des vins de Bordeaux et des cépages particuliers au département de la Gironde: mode de culture, préparation des vins, selon les marchés auxquels ils sont destinés.* Paris: Audot, 1829.

———. Reprint, with a preface by Alain Huetz de Lemps, Bordeaux: Société des Bibliophiles de Guyenne, 1977.

Pariset, François-Georges, ed. *Bordeaux au dix-huitième siècle.* Histoire de Bordeaux. Charles Higounet, ed. Bordeaux: Fédération Historique du Sud-Ouest, 1968.

Penning-Rowsell, Edmund. *The Wines of Bordeaux.* 6th ed. London: Penguin Books, 1989.

Petit-Lafitte, Auguste. *Le vignoble bordelais en 1858.* Bordeaux: Imprimerie de B. Coudert, 1858.

Peynaud, Emile. *Œnologue dans le siècle: entretiens avec Michel Guillard.* Paris: La Table Ronde, 1995.

Pijassou, René. "Un château du Médoc: Palmer." *Revue historique de Bordeaux et du département de la Gironde,* n.s., 13 (1964): 183–203.

———. *Le Médoc: un grand vignoble de qualité.* Paris: Librairie Jules Tallandier, 1980.

———. "Le vignoble Bordelais: la naissance des grands crus."

Plaidoyer pour M. Julien Calvé, appelant contre M. et Mme. de Lambert-Desgrangs, intimés. Bordeaux: Imprimerie de Durand, 1858.

Rapports du jury mixte international: publiés sous la direction de S.A.I. le prince Napoléon. Paris: Imprimerie Impériale, 1856.

Ray, Cyril. *Lafite.* 3rd rev. ed. London: Christie's Wine Publications, 1985.

———. *Mouton-Rothschild.* Rev. ed. London: Christie's Wine Publications, 1980.

Reach, Angus B. *Claret and Olives, from the Garonne to the Rhone: Or Notes, Social, Picturesque, and Legendary, by the Way.* London: David Bogue, 1852.

Redding, Cyrus. *A History and Description of Modern Wines.* London: Whittaker, Treacher, & Arnot, 1833.

———. 2nd ed. London: Whittaker & Co., 1836.

———. 3rd ed. London: Henry G. Bohn, 1851.

———. *French Wines and Vineyards: And the Way to Find Them.* London: Houlston and Wright, 1860.

Renouard, Yves, ed. *Bordeaux sous les rois d'Angleterre.* Histoire de Bordeaux. Charles Higounet, ed. Bordeaux: Fédération historique du Sud-Ouest, 1965.

Répertoire numérique détaillé de la serie M.: administration générale et economie du département, 1800–1940. Bordeaux: Archives Départementales, 1979.

Richards, Thomas. *The Commodity Culture of Victorian England: Advertising and Spectacle, 1851–1914.* Stanford: Stanford University Press, 1990.

Robert, Adolphe, Edgar Bourloton, and Gaston Cougny, eds. *Dictionnaire des parlementaires français.* Paris: Bourloton, 1891.

Robin, Charles. *Histoire illustrée de l'exposition universelle par catégories d'industries avec notices sur les exposants.* Paris: Furne, 1855.

Rothschild, Baron Philippe de. *Vivre la vigne: du ghetto de Francfort à Mouton Rothschild, 1744–1981.* Paris: Presses de la Cité, 1981.

Roudié, Philippe. *Vignobles et Vignerons du Bordelais, 1850–1980.* 2nd ed. Talence (Gironde): Presses Universitaires de Bordeaux, 1994.

Rouget de Lisle, Amedée. *Extraits de la description jointe au brevet d'invention de 15 ans pris le 11 février 1853, pour des appareils et des procédés propres à préparer et à conserver les substances alimentaires, les boissons, les liquides volatiles et gazeux, la levure de bière, les engrais stercoraux et azotés, etc.* Paris: Maulde et Renou, n.d.

———. *Nouveau manuel complet du fabricant d'eaux et boissons gazeuses.* Paris: Roret, 1863.

———. *La vérité sur la paternité de la Marseillaise: faits et documents authentiques.* Paris: n.p., 1865.

Rousseau, Corine. "Etude viticole en Sauternais: le Château d'Arche, le Château Nairac, le Château Guiraud." Master's thesis, Université Michel de Montaigne, Bordeaux III, 1994.

Roux, Jeanne. *Le Médoc: essai d'économie régionale.* Bordeaux: Delmas, 1938.

Roy, Gustave-Emmanuel. *Souvenirs, 1823–1906.* Nancy: Imprimerie Berger-Levrault & Cie, 1906.

Rules and Regulations for the Government of the Reform Club: With an Alphabetical List of the Members. London: T. Brettell, 1840.

Saint-Amant, Charles Pierre de. *Le vin de Bordeaux: promenade en Médoc, 1855.* Paris: Mme Ve Huzard, 1855.

Seeley, James. *Great Bordeaux Wines.* London: Secker & Warburg, 1986.

Séguin, Philippe. *Louis Napoléon le grand.* Paris: Grasset, 1990.

Shaw, Thomas George. *Wine, the Vine, and the Cellar.* 2nd ed. London: Longman, Green, Longman, Roberts, & Green, 1864.

Sire, Pierre, Henri Bertrand, and Roger Alléguède. *Mission d'etude et d'information sur le marché des vins de Bordeaux: rapport au ministère de l'agriculture.* N.p., 1970.

Strombeck, Baron Frédéric-Charles de. "Les Bonaparte à Florence et à Rome." *Revue des études Napoléoniennes,* 21 (1923): 180–189.

Suduiraut, Bertrand Guillot de. *Tableaux de famille: chroniques et généalogies.* Ciboure près Saint-Jean-de-Luz: chez l'auteur, 1993.

Syndicat des Grands Crus Classés du Médoc. *Album des grands crus classés du Médoc.* Bordeaux: Delmas, 1926.

Tastet & Lawton. *Tableau relatif aux récoltes des vins rouges de la Gironde depuis 1795.* N.p., n.d.

Ters, Didier. *Haut-Médoc.* Paris: Jacques Legrand, 1987.

———. *Moulis Listrac.* Paris: Jacques Legrand, 1987.

Toussaint-Samat, Maguelonne, and Mathias Lair. *Grande et petite histoire des cuisiniers de l'antiquité à nos jours.* Paris: Robert Laffont, 1989.

Tresca, ed. *Visite à l'exposition universelle de Paris, en 1855: contenant 1° l'énumération des objets sur lesquels doit se porter principalement l'attention des visiteurs, 2° l'indication des places où se trouvent ces objets, 3° tous les renseignements nécessaires relatifs à leur mécanisme, à leur emploi, à leur fabrication, à leur prix, etc.* Rev. ed. Paris: L. Hachette et Cie., 1855.

Unal-Serres, Jean-Maurille. *Carte vinicole du département de la Gironde, dressée sur les données de M. Duffour Dubergier, président de la chambre de commerce de Bordeaux.* Bordeaux: P. Chaumas, 1856.

Union Syndicale des Négociants en Vins-de-Bordeaux, eds. *Les Grands Vins de Bordeaux.* Bordeaux: Delmas, 1910.

Vandyke Price, Pamela. *Wines of the Graves.* London: Sotheby's Publications, 1988.

Vecherre. *Tableau général des qualités et du prix des vins qui se font aux environs de Bordeaux.* Bordeaux: Fernel, 1816.

Victoria, Queen. *The Letters of Queen Victoria: A Selection from Her Majesty's Correspondence between the Years 1837 and 1861.* Arthur Christopher Benson and Viscount Reginald Esher, eds. Vol. 3. London: John Murray, 1907.

Villepigue, Robert, and André Villepigue. *L'aire de production des vins de Saint-Emilion: avec un essai de classement scientific de ses crus.* Manuscript. Bordeaux Chamber of Commerce Archives, 1931.

———. *L'aire de production des vins de Saint-Emilion: avec un essai de classement scientific de ses crus.* Paris: Revue de Viticulture, 1934.

Les vins de Bordeaux à l'exposition universelle de Londres en 1862. Bordeaux: Charles Noblet, 1862.

Vizetelly, Henry. *The Wines of the World Characterized & Classed: With Some Particulars Respecting the Beers of Europe.* London: Ward, Lock, & Tyler, Warwick House, 1875.

A Walk Through the Universal Exhibition of 1855. Paris: A. and W. Galignani and Co., 1855.

Young, Arthur. *Travels, During the Years 1787, 1788, and 1789: Undertaken More Particularly with a View of Ascertaining the Cultivation, Wealth, Resources, and National Prosperity of the Kingdom of France.* London: W. Richardson, Royal-Exchange, London, 1792.

Newspapers and Journals

Courrier de Bordeaux. August 21, 1839.

Courrier de la Gironde (Bordeaux). November 1851–March 1852; November 1854–January 1856; July–August 1873.

Feuille du Dimanche (Bordeaux). April 22, 1855.

La Feuille Vinicole. February 5–March 5, 1946.

La Gironde.(Bordeaux). June 1853; January 1855–January 1856.

La Guienne (Bordeaux). January–December 1855.

Illustrated London News. April 28, 1855.

L'Illustration (Paris). April 21–May 26, 1855.

L'Indicateur (Bordeaux). November 1854–June 1855.

Le Journal des Debats (Paris). August 21, 1855.

Memorial Bordelaise. August 2, 1830; November 1854–January 1856.

Le Moniteur Universel (Paris). June 4, 1850; March–December 1855.

Le Producteur (Bordeaux). 1838–1841.

The Times (London). May 16, 1855.

Le Vignoble Girondin (Bordeaux). May 15, 1947; January 15, 1948.

INDEX

The text of 1855 is set in ITC New Baskerville, a revised version of a typeface created in the mid-eighteenth century by John Baskerville, an English type designer best known among his contemporaries for his innovative work as a printer. The character of the typeface places it in the typographic category known as "transitional," in part because of the letters' increased vertical stress which contrasts with the rounder, "old style" of earlier alphabets and the more pronounced verticality of later "modern" designs. Since its creation Baskerville's typeface has enjoyed continued popularity because of its elegant design; its recent reworking by the Mergenthaler Linotype Company and International Typeface Corporation emphasizes the letterforms' traditional, graceful aspect while subtly altering their original proportions to promote an enhanced legibility.

The chapter numbers are set in Englische Schreibschrift, a modern rendition of English copperplate script (as its name in German suggests), designed in the early 1970s by the Berthold Corporation.

CPSIA information can be obtained
at www.ICGtesting.com
Printed in the USA
FSHW012324230122
87863FS

9 780471 194217